# EXTRADITION AND MUTUAL LEGAL ASSISTANCE HANDBOOK

# EXTRADITION AND MUTUAL LEGAL ASSISTANCE HANDBOOK

## SECOND EDITION

*General Editor*

### JOHN R W D JONES

*Barrister, Doughty Street Chambers*

*Assistant Editor*

### ROSEMARY DAVIDSON

*Barrister, 6 King's Bench Walk*

*Contributors*

### ARVINDER SAMBEI

*Barrister & Director, Amicus Legal Consultants Ltd*

### BRIAN GIBBINS

*Barrister, Middle Temple and the Inn of Court of Northern Ireland*

### VICTORIA AILES

*Barrister, 6 King's Bench Walk*

## OXFORD
UNIVERSITY PRESS

*This book has been printed digitally and produced in a standard specification
in order to ensure its continuing availability*

# OXFORD
UNIVERSITY PRESS

Great Clarendon Street, Oxford OX2 6DP
United Kingdom

Oxford University Press is a department of the University of Oxford.
It furthers the University's objective of excellence in research, scholarship,
and education by publishing worldwide. Oxford is a registered trade mark of
Oxford University Press in the UK and in certain other countries

© John Jones, Rosemary Davidson, and the various contributors 2010

The moral rights of the author have been asserted

Reprinted 2013

British Library Cataloguing in Publication Data
Data available

Library of Congress Cataloging in Publication Data
Data available

ISBN 978-0-19-957404-9

# FOREWORD

This is an important book. The law of extradition used to be regarded as an arcane subject, a little-known speciality. The force of many factors has transformed it. The law of the European Union has given us the European Arrest Warrant: a challenging instance of harmonization. The law of the European Convention on Human Rights has given a new edge to extradition: a challenge to extradition's legal limits. Much crime is international, and knows no boundaries: fuelled by the internet, email, and other technologies, it exerts a further challenge, demanding that extradition procedures be swift and efficient. The law of extradition is no longer an arcane subject, and certainly ought not any longer to be a little-known speciality.

That is why this is an important book. It spans the history of the subject. So it should. Any area of law which touches the relations between sovereign states is likely to be in close contact with its own history, and its practitioners need to understand as much. History aside, this book is a comprehensive *vade mecum* through the modern British law of extradition, principally contained in the Extradition Act 2003. It explains the procedural and substantive law in great detail and does so clearly in no-nonsense language. It is especially helpful that the procedures are properly described, not least since extradition remains an area of the law where the relationship between judiciary and executive is unusual and perhaps unique. I think the book is particularly good on the bars to extradition and the impact of human rights law. The section on the relationship between extradition law and asylum law is also very useful—these are closely related territories, and lawyers practising in the area will be better informed as to the relation between them.

The book also ventures into broader, more strategic territory, with sections on International Criminal Courts and Tribunals and extradition law and practice in other jurisdictions. This is excellent. Specialist areas of our law become more and more isolationist. These comparisons are something of an antidote.

My impression is that the number of extradition cases coming before the Divisional Court is increasing. There are certainly many of them, and the arguments deployed are increasingly refined. This is a thoroughly modern, high quality textbook which will equip the profession as it needs to be equipped. I wish this second edition every success.

Lord Justice Laws
August 2010

# FOREWORD TO THE FIRST EDITION

The Law of Extradition has become a highly specialized subject which can have significant international repercussions. The Law and Practice are changing rapidly and I am delighted to welcome this work written by two very experienced practitioners. It will prove a valuable and readable resource.

Tim Workman
Senior District Judge
Bow Street Magistrates' Court
London

# ACKNOWLEDGEMENTS

We are very grateful to all the people who made this book possible. Our thanks go to Fadi Daoud for his guide for duty solicitors (Appendix 1), to David West (Trinidad & Tobago), Jason E Carter (United States), Arun Gupta (India), Anton Katz SC and Martin Polaine for their contributions to Chapter 13 ('Extradition Law and Practice in Other Jurisdictions'), and to Katrina Orme and Marie Lewiecki, both pupils at 6 King's Bench Walk, for proof-reading and citation checking. We are particularly indebted to Faye Judges of Oxford University Press, without whose professional guidance and enthusiastic support this book would not have been possible.

The texts of the Commonwealth Scheme for the Rendition of Fugitive Offenders and of the Harare Scheme relating to Mutual Assistance in Criminal Matters 2000 are reproduced with the kind permission of the Commonwealth Secretariat.

The texts of the European Convention on Extradition (ETS No 024), the European Convention on Mutual Assistance in Criminal Matters (ETS No 030), and the European Convention on Mutual Assistance 2000 are reproduced with the kind permission of the Council of Europe.

Finally, we would like to thank all of our family members for their love, support, and patience.

July 2010

# CONTENTS—SUMMARY

# CONTENTS

Contents

## APPENDICES

# TABLE OF CASES

# TABLE OF LEGISLATION

*Page numbers in italics refer to pages in the Appendices*

### GERMANY

### GRENADA

# STATUTORY INSTRUMENTS

## UNITED STATES OF AMERICA

# LIST OF ABBREVIATIONS

| | |
|---|---|
| ADX Florence | United States's federal 'Supermax' facility in Florence, Colorado |
| AFRC | Armed Forces Revolutionary Council |
| ATP | Authority to Proceed |
| CAWT | Caricom Arrest Warrant Treaty |
| CDF | Civil Defence Forces |
| CG | Country Guidance |
| CICA | Crime (International Co-operation) Act 2003 |
| CLA | Caprivi Liberation Army |
| COPFS | Crown Office and Procurator Fiscal Service |
| CPS | Crown Prosecution Service |
| CSONI | Crown Solicitor's Office Northern Ireland |
| CWMC | City of Westminster Magistrates' Court |
| DOJ | Department of Justice |
| EAW | European Arrest Warrant |
| ECCC | Extraordinary Chambers in the Courts of Cambodia |
| ECHR | European Convention on Human Rights |
| ECtHR | European Court of Human Rights |
| ELR | exceptional leave to remain |
| ETSP | East Timor Special Panel |
| FARC | Revolutionary Armed Forces of Columbia |
| HRA 1998 | Human Rights Act 1998 |
| ICC | International Criminal Court |
| ICTR | United Nations International Criminal Tribunal for Rwanda |
| ICTY | United Nations International Criminal Tribunal for the former Yugoslavia |
| IJA | issuing judicial authority |
| ILR | indefinite leave to remain |
| MLA Guidelines | Mutual Assistance Guidelines for the United Kingdom |
| MLATs | mutual legal assistance treaties |
| MPA | Metropolitan Police Authority |
| MPS | Metropolitan Police Service |
| OIA | Office of International Affairs |
| POCA | Proceeds of Crime Act 2002 |
| RUF | Revolutionary United Front |
| SAMs | Special Administrative Measures |
| SCSL | Special Court for Sierra Leone |
| SIS | Schengen Information System |
| SOCA | Serious Organised Crime Agency |
| STL | Special Tribunal for Lebanon |
| the 1989 Act | Extradition Act 1989 |
| the 2003 Act | Extradition Act 2003 |
| the European Convention | European Convention on Extradition 1957 |

| | |
|---|---|
| the Framework Decision | The European Union Council Framework Decision on the European arrest warrant and surrender procedures between Member States 2002 |
| the London Scheme | the Commonwealth Scheme |
| UNTAET | United Nations Transitional Administration in East Timor |
| USAO | US Attorney's Office |

# LIST OF CONTRIBUTORS

## Editors

**John Jones** is a barrister at Doughty Street Chambers specializing in extradition, war crimes, and counter-terrorism. He has appeared in many reported extradition cases and is consistently recommended by the directories in the field of extradition. He also publishes the *Extradition Law Reports*. He has appeared as counsel before a number of international courts and tribunals, including the International Criminal Tribunal for the former Yugoslavia, the Special Court for Sierra Leone and the European Court of Justice. He is also admitted to practise law in the District of Columbia, USA and the Kingdom of Cambodia.

**Rosemary Davidson** is a barrister at 6 King's Bench Walk. She is an extradition specialist, with extensive experience of advising and representing clients at all stages of contested extradition proceedings. Her appellate experience includes a number of reported extradition cases and she recently published an article on the principle of triviality in European Arrest Warrant cases. Rosemary is appointed to the Attorney General's civil panel as well as the Attorney General's unified list of prosecutors. Her wider practice includes criminal law, public law, and immigration. She also has international experience, having spent four months as an intern at the United Nations International Criminal Tribunal for Rwanda.

## Contributors

**Arvinder Sambei** is a barrister and director of Amicus Legal Consultants Ltd. She was, formerly, the Head of the Criminal Law Section, Legal & Constitutional Affairs Division at the Commonwealth Secretariat and was responsible for the day-to-day running of the Section and ensuring design and delivery of programmes of assistance and training for member states to enhance criminal law systems and international co-operation. As a senior Crown Prosecutor within the Crown Prosecution Service, Arvinder specialized in extradition law and international co-operation, international human rights and international humanitarian law, and counter-terrorism. In that role, she had conduct of many of the United Kingdom's high profile extradition, counter-terrorism, transnational, and war crimes cases. Prior to joining the Commonwealth Secretariat in 2005, Arvinder was employed by the Ministry of Defence as the Legal Adviser to the Permanent Joint Headquarters (PJHQ). She is the co-author of the *Extradition Law Handbook* (Oxford University Press, 2005), and, along with Martin Polaine and Anton du Plessis, *Counter-Terrorism Law & Practice: An International Handbook* (Oxford University Press, 2009).

**Brian Gibbins** is a barrister. He is currently employed as Crown Advocate at the Extradition Unit of Crown Prosecution Service Special Casework Division. He has previously worked at the International Policy and Advisory Division of the Revenue and Customs Prosecutions Office and in the European and International Division of Crown Prosecution Service

Policy Directorate. In 2006-07 he was a member of a team which carried out the evaluation of Ireland's implementation of the European Arrest Warrant scheme for the EU.

**Victoria Ailes** is a barrister at 6 King's Bench Walk, undertaking the full range of criminal work, both prosecution and defence. During her time at the Chambers, she has been involved in work across a wide range of areas, including extradition, human rights, judicial review, appellate work, and confiscation. She has also been involved with preparation for appeals to the European Court of Human Rights.

## Appendix Contributor

**Fadi Daoud** is a partner and practising solicitor advocate at Lawrence & Co Solicitors. He heads a dedicated extradition department at the firm and appears regularly at the City of Westminster Magistrates' Court dealing with extradition hearings. He has been involved in a number of leading reported extradition cases that are cited regularly. He has varied experience running, and overseeing serious high profile cases within the firm and sits as an adviser on the Dedicated Drugs Court Steering Group.

# PART I

# EXTRADITION

# 1

# INTRODUCTION

## A.  Definition

The term 'extradition' is frequently misused. It is therefore essential at the outset to define clearly its scope.  **1.01**

Extradition is the formal, legal process for returning persons located in one country to another for one of the following purposes:  **1.02**

- criminal prosecution;
- sentencing (if they have already been tried and convicted); or
- the carrying out of a sentence already imposed.

The transfer of persons for any other purpose cannot be termed extradition. Thus, for example, extradition does not lie where the purpose of return is to investigate an offence.  **1.03**

**1.04**  As its name suggests, 'extraordinary rendition'—the forcible transfer by state agents from one state to another without recourse to formal legal process—also falls outside the concept of extradition.

# B.  Origins

### Early history

**1.05**  A detailed analysis of the history of extradition law is outside the scope of this work.[1] However, a number of key events and themes are instructive in understanding the present system.

**1.06**  Examples of what may loosely be termed extradition can be found as long ago as the twelfth century. Such transactions were rare, reflecting the jealousy with which states guarded their own sovereignty. Although from time to time there was debate on the issue, it would seem that they did not require a platform of domestic procedure or legislation.

### Extradition Act 1870

**1.07**  By the nineteenth century, however, an increasing number of international extradition treaties targeting general crime required a coherent legislative basis in domestic law and led to the Extradition Act 1870 ('the 1870 Act'), the first comprehensive domestic legislation in this field.

### Characteristics

**1.08**  One characteristic of the earliest extradition arrangements has shaped the United Kingdom's domestic procedural machinery for determining extradition cases from the 1870 Act through to the Extradition Act 1989 ('the 1989 Act'): because extradition was considered to impinge upon state sovereignty, requests were naturally made on a state-to-state basis through diplomatic channels.[2]

**1.09**  It was, therefore, for the executive to first authorize the initiation of extradition proceedings before the courts, for the judiciary to then determine whether the subject was, as a matter of law, liable to extradition, and for the executive finally to decide whether a person deemed to be so liable should in fact be extradited.

**1.10**  As a further reflection of the seriousness with which interference with state sovereignty was regarded, most extradition treaties required a request for extradition to be supported by prima facie evidence in admissible format.

**1.11**  Older extradition treaties tended to contain lists of crimes, generically described, for which extradition would lie. At the domestic level there was an additional requirement to show dual criminality, namely that the conduct relied upon in the request amounted to an offence in both the requesting and the requested jurisdictions.

**1.12**  Small wonder then that a disproportionate number of leading decisions on evidence and offence definitions arise from extradition cases.

---

[1] For a detailed review of the history of extradition, see Alun Jones and Anand Doobay, *Extradition and Mutual Assistance* (3rd edn, Sweet and Maxwell, 2004).

[2] For a helpful summary of the bases upon which a state may assert criminal jurisdiction, see the previous edition of this work at 1.03–1.21.

### European Convention on Extradition 1957

The first major inroad into these weighty requirements came in the form of the European **1.13**
Convention on Extradition 1957 ('the European Convention'), to which the United
Kingdom acceded somewhat late in the day in 1990. As between participating states it
removed the requirement to provide a prima facie case. Instead, a description of the offend-
ing conduct sufficient to satisfy the dual criminality test was all that was required.

### Commonwealth Scheme

In this regard, the European Convention was significantly in advance of the other main **1.14**
multilateral scheme, the Commonwealth Scheme ('the London Scheme'). Although, having
the status of an agreement rather than a multilateral treaty, the London Scheme sought to
provide a consistent overarching scheme to be reflected in the domestic extradition laws of
Commonwealth states.

The emergence at international level of increasingly different schemes of extradition **1.15**
has inevitably meant that domestic legislation has become lengthy and consolidatory in
nature.

### Extradition Act 1989

The Extradition Act 1989—which provided the framework for extradition law for more **1.16**
than a decade until the beginning of 2003—was such an act. It encompassed essentially five
extradition schemes:

- the European Convention on Extradition;
- the London Scheme;
- treaty countries—primarily the United States (governed by Schedule 1 to the 1989 Act);
- United Nations conventions—section 22 of, and paragraph 15 of Schedule 1 to, the 1989
  Act; and
- 'ad hoc' treaties.

Although now largely superseded by the Extradition Act 2003 ('the 2003 Act'), the 1989 **1.17**
Act retains some relevance. Firstly, all requests that were being considered by the courts
and/or the Home Office before 1 January 2004 will still be governed by the 1989 Act.
Secondly, the 2003 Act replicates some of the terminology used in the 1989 Act, such
as 'unjust and oppressive',[3] and adopts parts of the 1989 Act (for example, section 6 of
the 1989 Act is now contained within the 'bars to extradition' in sections 11 and 79 of the
2003 Act).

Against the backdrop of split judicial and executive functions, the emergence of judicial **1.18**
review effectively opened up a second means of challenge to extradition proceedings, thereby
adding considerably to the delay and expense of the process. During the main period of
operation of the 1989 Act, a fugitive could at the outset seek judicial review of the Home
Secretary's authorization of the commencement of proceedings. He could then appeal those
proceedings by way of an application for a Writ of *habeas corpus ad subjiciendum* before

---

[3] See ss 11(3) and 12(2) of the 1989 Act and ss 14, 25, 82, and 91(2) of the 2003 Act.

finally resorting to judicial review to challenge the Home Secretary's decision to order his extradition.

**Extradition Act 2003**

1.19   The means of reducing the potential for delay, it was believed, lay in part in what has been described as the 'judicialization' of extradition—that is, taking it out of the state-to-state arena and turning it into a transaction between judicial authorities. It is this step change which lies at the heart of the Framework Decision scheme and which is provided for by Parts 1 and 3 of the 2003 Act.

1.20   Like its predecessor, the 2003 Act seeks to consolidate a number of schemes (as well as codifying police powers in relation to search and seizure in extradition cases):

- Part 1: Extradition to category 1 territories (gives effect to the European Arrest Warrant (EAW) in export cases);
- Part 2: Extradition to category 2 territories (covers all bilateral and multilateral treaties);
- Part 3: Extradition to the United Kingdom from category 1 territories (and limited provisions relating to extradition from category 2 territories);
- Part 4: Police powers in extradition cases;
- Part 5: Miscellaneous, including international conventions and ad hoc arrangements.

It entered into force on 1 January 2004.

1.21   In addition to implementing the EAW scheme, the 2003 Act seeks to expedite and simplify proceedings under the other schemes by:

- limiting the role of the Home Secretary in Part 2 cases (and thereby reducing the prospect of judicial review proceedings); and
- removing the prima facie case requirement with respect to requests from countries such as the United States and some Commonwealth and other countries.

1.22   There is no doubt that overall processing times for extradition cases and numbers of judicial review applications have been significantly reduced under the 2003 Act. However, the huge numbers of EAW cases now being processed have placed great strain on all stages of what is still a relatively complex and cumbersome procedure. It seems likely that further change will be required.

## C. Types of extradition arrangement

1.23   Extradition arrangements made between states fall into one of four broad categories.

**Bilateral extradition treaties**

1.24   As the term implies, bilateral extradition treaties regulate extradition between two states only. Many of the United Kingdom's bilateral treaties are now extremely old and, in some cases, moribund. Notwithstanding the trend towards multilateral arrangements, bilateral treaties continue to be used to regulate key parts of the United Kingdom's extradition traffic, the most recent examples being the UK–USA Treaty of 2003 and the UK–UAE Treaty of 2006.

**Multilateral arrangements**

The term 'multilateral arrangement' may refer to a scheme targeted specifically at extradition[4] **1.25** or one targeted at a particular type of criminality and which provides for extradition as part of a range of measures to combat that criminality.[5]

**Framework schemes**

Framework schemes set out at an international level an overall framework for extradition **1.26** transactions between participating states but leave the detail of implementation to national legislation. Two 'framework' schemes are of particular relevance to UK practitioners.

The Commonwealth (or 'London') Scheme, originally established in 1966, regulates extra- **1.27** dition between Commonwealth member states.

The European Union Council Framework Decision on the European arrest warrant and sur- **1.28** render procedures between Member States 2002 ('the Framework Decision') was originally conceived as a simple 'backing of warrants' system.

The initial proposal having stalled somewhat, the initiative derived renewed impetus in the **1.29** aftermath of the World Trade Center attacks and was eventually concluded on 7 June 2002.

It sets out a framework for expedited return between judicial authorities of member states. It **1.30** is based on the high level of mutual trust ('mutual recognition') presumed to exist between member states. It is this which allows EAWs to be transmitted and dealt with as between judicial authorities of the states concerned, rather than on the conventional state-to-state basis.

The Framework Decision prescribes such matters as the format of the EAW, time limits for **1.31** conclusion of processes, and a limited number of bars to surrender, but leaves implementation to member states. In some, domestic enabling legislation simply adopts the Framework Decision in its entirety. In others, notably the United Kingdom and Ireland, the domestic legislation itself creates a scheme intended to reflect and implement the Framework Decision at national level.

**Ad hoc/special arrangements**

'Ad hoc' extradition arrangements effectively entail a treaty specifically negotiated to secure **1.32** the return of an individual or group of individuals. As such, they are the modern incarnation of the very earliest extradition arrangements. Unsurprisingly, they are rare. Circumstances warranting their use might include the need to extradite a particularly high-profile criminal or as a precursor to the conclusion of a bilateral treaty.

# D. Terminology

Like most specialisms, extradition law has generated its own terminology. It may be helpful **1.33** at this stage to provide a brief explanation of the most frequently encountered terms.

---

[4] For example, the European Convention on Extradition 1957.
[5] For example, the United Nations Convention against Illicit Traffic in Narcotic Drugs and Psychotropic Substances 1988 ('the Vienna Convention').

**Export extradition**

**1.34** Export extradition is the term used by some practitioners to describe extradition *from* the United Kingdom. Confusingly, such requests are sometimes referred to as *incoming* requests.

**Import extradition**

**1.35** Import extradition is the term used by some practitioners to describe extradition *to* the United Kingdom. Such requests are sometimes described as *outgoing* requests.

**Provisional arrest**

**1.36** Provisional arrest refers to the facility in most extradition schemes to secure the emergency arrest and detention of a person pending submission of the full extradition request. Arrest and detention is 'provisional' upon the submission of the full request within a given period specified under the relevant scheme. It will be considered in detail later.

**Full order request**

**1.37** The term full order request is a throwback to the earlier Extradition Acts under which the Secretary of State had to authorize formal commencement of extradition proceedings with an Authority or Order to Proceed. It continues to be used in the context of proceedings under Part 2 of the 2003 Act to distinguish proceedings initiated following the submission of a formal request for extradition and the issue of the Secretary of State's certificate from those initiated by provisional arrest.

**Speciality/specialty**

**1.38** Speciality/specialty is the protection afforded to persons surrendered or extradited. In essence it concerns the principle that, upon return, the surrendered person may only be dealt with for prior offences in respect of which his or her return was ordered. Those matters will hopefully have been the subject of the EAW or extradition request. However, the scope of the order for extradition may be narrower than the EAW or request. The exceptions to the general rule will be considered in detail later.

**Veiled extradition**

**1.39** Veiled extradition describes the circumvention of lawful extradition procedures. In this jurisdiction it may be held to amount to an abuse of the court's process resulting in a stay of the criminal proceedings if the person is extradited.

**The person**

**1.40** The person is the term introduced by the 2003 Act to describe the subject of extradition proceedings. He or she is also sometimes referred to as 'the requested person'.

**Issuing judicial authority (IJA)**

**1.41** Issuing judicial authority (IJA) is the term used by the Framework Decision to describe whichever authority is empowered under a member state's domestic law to issue an EAW. In the United Kingdom, warrants must be issued by a court, but that is not necessarily the case elsewhere.[6]

---

[6] See for example *Johannes Enander v The Governor of Her Majesty's Prison, Brixton and The Swedish National Police Board* [2005] EWHC 3036 (Admin), where the Administrative Court rejected a challenge to an EAW issued in a conviction case by a Swedish police inspector in accordance with Swedish law.

### Central authority

Central authority is the term used by the Framework Decision to describe whichever auth-  **1.42**
ority is designated under domestic law as the central point for receiving/transmitting EAWs.
The designated central authority for England, Wales, and Northern Ireland is the Serious
Organised Crime Agency. For Scotland it is the Crown Agent.

Executing judicial authority is the term used by the Framework Decision to describe which-  **1.43**
ever authority is designated under domestic law to order surrender on an EAW. In England
and Wales this is a District Judge sitting at the City of Westminster Magistrates' Court in
London, in Scotland, the Sheriff of Borders and Lothian, and in Northern Ireland, the
Recorder of Belfast.

### The Schengen Information System (SIS)

The Schengen Information System (SIS) is an EU-wide secure database for the collection and  **1.44**
exchange of information relating to immigration, policing, and criminal law, for the purposes
of law enforcement and immigration control. It supports the practical operation of the
Schengen Convention for the abolition of border controls which entered into force in 1995.

Currently operated by fifteen EU member states, SIS uses a 'star architecture', with national  **1.45**
systems updating a central system based in Strasbourg and vice versa in real time. Types of alert
which may be placed on SIS include alerts for persons wanted on EAWs. The placing of such
alerts obviates the need for an IJA to direct an EAW to a particular member state and should
result in the initiation of extradition proceedings as soon as the person comes to notice.

In 2000 agreement was reached on the United Kingdom's partial participation in Schengen:  **1.46**
the police and judicial cooperation aspects ('third pillar') but not the immigration and border
control aspects ('first pillar'). The United Kingdom's partial participation commenced on 1
January 2005. Technical difficulties have meant however that the United Kingdom does not
yet operate SIS. This means that EAWs for persons in the United Kingdom have to be sent
here once it has been established that the person is within this jurisdiction. Similarly, all the
United Kingdom's outgoing EAWs have to be sent to a particular country rather than lodged
by way of a pan-European alert.

### Rendition

Rendition describes the extradition process between Commonwealth states. It simply means  **1.47**
extradition. It is used where there is no formal treaty in existence but participating states have
made an 'arrangement' the terms of which are then incorporated into domestic legislation.

### Surrender

Surrender has been used to describe three distinct processes. Firstly, it was used in the context  **1.48**
of extraditions between the United Kingdom and Ireland, prior to the entry into force of
the EAW scheme. Until then, all Irish cases ran on the 'backing of warrants' system.
Underlying this system was the notion that, as neighbouring states with close ties, it was
convenient and appropriate for the United Kingdom and Ireland to adopt an expedited
procedure in which the issues to be considered were limited. Thus an Irish request to the
United Kingdom would simply involve sending a warrant to the United Kingdom where a
police officer would place it before a magistrate for 'backing' (endorsement). The fugitive
would then be arrested on the backed warrant and taken before a magistrate who would

order his surrender to Ireland subject to the safeguards under section 2 of the Backing of Warrants (Republic of Ireland) Act 1965.

**1.49** The second type of surrender relates to international criminal courts and tribunals: the United Nations International Criminal Tribunal for the former Yugoslavia (ICTY), the United Nations International Criminal Tribunal for Rwanda (ICTR), the International Criminal Court (ICC) and the East Timor Special Panel for Serious Crimes (the list has grown and may continue to do so).[7] Here the legal basis for transferring an individual from the United Kingdom to the jurisdiction of the international court or tribunal is very different from ordinary extradition procedures.

**1.50** The ICTY and ICTR were established by the United Nations following the atrocities committed in the former Yugoslavia and Rwanda, respectively. As these bodies were created under Chapter VII of the United Nations Charter,[8] all member states have an obligation to surrender persons indicted by these tribunals and these proceedings take precedence over any other domestic or extradition request from any other country. The obligations and procedures for surrender to these tribunals are contained in the relevant statutory instrument or Order in Council and no reference is made to these bodies in either of the two Extradition Acts. In the event that a request for surrender is received from any United Nations-established tribunal, the relevant Order in Council or statutory instrument will set out the necessary procedure and the crimes. In the case of surrender to the ICTY and ICTR, the UK court may only look at one issue—identity.

**1.51** The East Timor Special Panel (ETSP) was created by regulations adopted by the United Nations Transitional Administration in East Timor (UNTAET). There is, therefore, no binding obligation on member states to cooperate with it or to comply with its orders and requests. The fact that the ETSP was not created under Chapter VII of the UN Charter does not, however, mean that states will not surrender persons indicted by it. Given the nature of the crimes over which the ETSP exercises jurisdiction, it would be unusual for a state not to comply with a request for a person's surrender, provided that a legal procedure is available.

**1.52** The ICC was established by treaty at the United Nations Diplomatic Conference of Plenipotentiaries on the Establishment of an International Criminal Court in Rome on 17 July 1998. It has jurisdiction over the 'core crimes' under international law: genocide, crimes against humanity, and war crimes. The Rome Statute received the requisite sixty ratifications on 11 April 2002 and it entered into force on 1 July 2002. The ICC therefore only has jurisdiction over crimes committed after that date. Requests from the ICC will be given effect by the International Criminal Court Act 2001.

**1.53** The third type of surrender is return under the EAW system. Interestingly, in its domestic enabling legislation—Parts 1 and 3 of the 2003 Act—the United Kingdom has chosen to avoid the term 'surrender' and to continue to use the term 'extradition'.

---

[7] For details as to the practice and procedure of international criminal courts and tribunals, see John RWD Jones and Steven Powles, *International Criminal Practice* (3rd edn, Oxford University Press/Transnational Publishers, 2003).

[8] The ICTY was created by United Nations Security Council Resolution 827 (1993) and given effect in the UK by SI 1996/716. The ICTR was created by United Nations Security Council Resolution 955 (1994) and given effect in the UK by SI 1996/1296.

## E.  The key players

The multiplicity of agencies fulfilling different functions in the United Kingdom's extradition processes is the product of three separate jurisdictions, the introduction of the EAW, and the retention of more formal arrangements with countries outside the EU. The functions of the main agencies are summarized below.    **1.54**

### Serious Organised Crime Agency (SOCA)

SOCA's Fugitives Unit has five principal functions in relation to EAWs:    **1.55**

- Certification. Under section 2 of the 2003 Act, it certifies incoming EAWs in respect of persons in England, Wales, or Northern Ireland. Certification means that the person may, without more, be arrested on the basis of the EAW.
- Coordination of EAW arrests.
- Transmission of requests for further information in respect of extradition proceedings in court and receipt of responses thereto.
- Coordination of surrender arrangements in respect of persons whose extradition has been ordered.
- Transmission of EAWs issued in England, Wales, and Northern Ireland to other EU member states.

In due course it will operate the Schengen Information System.

### Interpol

Interpol is responsible for the transmission and reception of requests for provisional arrest to countries outside the EU. Its UK office is co-located with SOCA's Fugitives Unit.    **1.56**

### Home Office

Notwithstanding the 'judicialization' of extradition in cases involving the EAW, the Home Office retains a key role in extradition. In addition to an overall policy and legislative remit in relation to extradition, the Judicial Cooperation Unit has the following responsibilities:    **1.57**

- Certification of incoming extradition requests from non-EU countries in respect of persons located in England and Wales. Certification permits the initiation of extradition proceedings.
- Transmission of requests for further information and receipt of responses thereto.
- In Part 2 cases briefing ministers in respect of whether or not to order extradition.

### The Metropolitan Police Service (MPS)

The MPS' Extradition and International Assistance Unit ('the Extradition Squad') is responsible for:    **1.58**

- The arrest of all persons wanted on EAWs who are located in the Metropolitan Police Authority (MPA) area. EAW arrests outside the MPA area are the responsibility of the relevant local force.
- The arrest of all persons whose extradition is sought under Part 2 of the 2003 Act who are located anywhere in England or Wales.

- Effecting the handover of persons whose extradition has been ordered from England, Wales, or Northern Ireland, whether or not they were originally arrested in the MPA area.

- Escorting back to the United Kingdom persons whose extradition has been ordered from non-EU countries.

### Crown Prosecution Service (CPS)

**1.59** The Extradition Unit of the Special Crime Division of CPS HQ represents the issuing judicial authority or requesting state in extradition proceedings before the English courts. Its role is considered in greater detail at F (below).

### Crown Office and Procurator Fiscal Service (COPFS)

**1.60** COPFS performs a similar function to CPS in providing representation for issuing judicial authorities/requesting states in extradition proceedings before the Scottish courts. The important distinction is that COPFS also performs the certification function in relation to EAWs carried out by SOCA in respect of cases in England, Wales, and Northern Ireland.

### Crown Solicitor's Office Northern Ireland (CSONI)

**1.61** The CSONI provides representation for issuing judicial authorities/requesting states in extradition proceedings before the Northern Ireland courts.

### City of Westminster Magistrates' Court (CWMC)

**1.62** All first instance extradition hearings in respect of persons arrested in England and Wales are conducted before one of a number of specially authorized District Judges sitting at CWMC.

### Belfast Recorder's Court

**1.63** All first instance extradition hearings in respect of persons arrested in Northern Ireland are conducted in Belfast before the Recorder of Belfast.

### Court of the Sheriff of Borders and Lothian

**1.64** All first instance extradition hearings in respect of persons arrested in Scotland are conducted in Edinburgh before a Sheriff of Borders and Lothian.

### Administrative Court

**1.65** All statutory extradition appeals from first instance decisions of the City of Westminster Magistrates' Court and/or the Home Secretary are heard by the Administrative Court sitting in London. The Administrative Court also deals with extradition-related judicial review applications. Most appeals are determined by a Divisional Court, comprising a Lord Justice of Appeal and a High Court Judge. However against a backdrop of a relentlessly increasing caseload a number of matters deemed to be suitable are being now heard by a single High Court Judge. Appeals in Northern Ireland are heard by the Queen's Bench Division of the Northern Ireland High Court and in Scotland by the High Court of Justiciary.

## F. The role of the Crown Prosecution Service

**1.66** Originally, requesting states were represented in extradition proceedings before the English courts by the Attorney General, reflecting the state-to-state nature of extradition requests.

By the 1930s however, much of the day-to-day conduct of the work had been informally **1.67** devolved from the Attorney to the Director of Public Prosecutions, although there are recorded instances of the Attorney personally conducting advocacy in such cases even as late as the 1950s.[9] However, no formal transfer of extradition functions from the Attorney to the Director took place until 1996.

The role was finally put on a statutory footing by section 190 of the 2003 Act which amended **1.68** the list of the Director's functions in section 3(2) of the Prosecution of Offences Act 1985 to include:

• The conduct of any extradition proceedings.
• The provision of such advice as he considers appropriate in relation to actual or proposed extradition proceedings.

Similar provision is made in respect of the Lord Advocate in Scotland and the Crown Solicitor **1.69** and Director of Public Prosecutions in Northern Ireland by sections 191 and 192 of the 2003 Act, respectively.

Although the Director is obliged to act in extradition proceedings and will do so automati- **1.70** cally, the issuing judicial authority or requesting state may elect to instruct its own representation at its own cost.

The CPS' export extradition caseload is allocated to specialist extradition lawyers in the **1.71** Extradition Unit of its Special Crime Division in London.

From time to time the nature of the role has been considered by the courts and it is now pos- **1.72** sible to discern a number of principles.

First and foremost, when conducting extradition proceedings, the CPS is not acting in its **1.73** ordinary capacity of domestic prosecutor. Accordingly, it has no power of its own motion to discontinue those proceedings because they are not a prosecution within the meaning of the Prosecution of Offences Act 1985.[10]

Rather, the relationship between the CPS and the requesting authority or state is akin to that **1.74** of a solicitor and client.[11] As a result, the CPS regards all its advices to the 'client' authority or state as covered by legal professional privilege.

In the context of such a relationship it is hardly surprising that the Administrative Court **1.75** appears to have concluded that CPS lawyers (or counsel instructed by them) may on occasion draft extradition papers for use in English proceedings.[12] Whether it would be proper for them to draft the whole EAW or extradition request is less certain and to draft papers

---

[9] *R v Governor of Brixton Prison ex p Kolczynski* [1955] 1 QB 540.
[10] *R v Director of Public Prosecutions ex p Thom* [1996] Crim LR 116, followed in the context of the 2003 Act in *Government of Germany v Kleinschmidt* [2005] EWHC 1373 (Admin).
[11] *Ibid.*
[12] *R (on the application of the Government of the USA and the Senior District Judge, Bow Street Magistrates' Court) v Stanley and Beatrice Tollman; R (on the application of the Central Examining Court, Madrid and the District Judge, Bow Street Magistrates' Court) v Sander and ors* [2006] EWHC 2256 (Admin) per Phillips LCJ at para 126.

without the prior or subsequent knowledge and approval of the requesting authority or state inevitably risks an abuse of process challenge.[13]

**1.76** In the event that a domestic prosecution on the basis of the requested conduct is also being considered, the CPS will ensure that 'Chinese walls' are put in place to separate its domestic prosecutors from its extradition lawyers, thereby avoiding any potential for conflict.[14]

**1.77** Although the CPS will usually follow the instructions of the requesting authority or state, circumstances might exceptionally arise where a conflict between those instructions and its public role require the CPS to consider whether to withdraw from the case.[15]

**1.78** When carrying out its export extradition functions, the CPS remains a public authority for the purposes of section 6 of the Human Rights Act 1988. As a result, serious default by a CPS official in doing so can warrant the Home Secretary making an order for compensation under his ex gratia compensation scheme.[16]

---

[13] *Central Examining Court of the National Court of Madrid v City of Westminster Magistrates' Court* [2007] EWHC 2059 (Admin).
[14] *R (on the application of Syed Talha Ahsan) v The DPP and the Government of the United States of America* [2008] EWHC 666 (Admin).
[15] *R (on the application of Lotfi Raissi) v Secretary of State for the Home Department* [2007] EWCA Civ 243 per Auld LJ at para 48.
[16] *Ibid.*

# 2

## OVERVIEW

## A. Export extradition—procedure for dealing with category 1 requests (European Arrest Warrants)

Extradition proceedings in relation to a European Arrest Warrant (EAW) are regulated by **2.01** Part 1 of the Extradition Act 2003 ('the 2003 Act'). They are initiated in one of two ways:

- provisional arrest; or
- arrest pursuant to a certified EAW.

### Provisional arrest

Under section 5 of the 2003 Act, a person may be arrested without a warrant by a constable, **2.02** customs officer, or service policeman who has reasonable grounds for believing that an EAW has been or will be issued in respect of that person.

Following arrest, section 6 provides that the person must be given a copy of the EAW as soon **2.03** as practicable after arrest and produced before the 'appropriate judge' within a *forty-eight hour* period running from the moment of arrest. Failure to serve the person with a copy of the warrant confers on the judge a discretion to order his or her discharge on application. Failure to produce the person within this period obliges the judge on application to order his or her discharge.

The person must be produced before the appropriate judge along with copies of the EAW **2.04** and the Serious Organised Crime Agency (SOCA) certificate. If it is not possible to produce these documents within the initial forty-eight hour period, then the judge may, on application on notice by the issuing judicial authority (IJA), grant a further forty-eight hour extension if he or she is satisfied on a balance of probabilities that it was not reasonably practicable to do so within the initial forty-eight hour period. In calculating the forty-eight hour periods for these purposes, no account is taken of weekends, Christmas Day, Good Friday, or bank holidays.

**Arrest on certified EAW**

**2.05**  The procedure for arrests under a Part 1 warrant is governed by sections 2 to 4 of the 2003 Act. It depends upon two preliminary steps.

**2.06**  Firstly, the IJA issues and transmits the EAW to SOCA.

**2.07**  Secondly, SOCA considers whether the EAW complies with the following requirements set out in section 2:

- The EAW must have been issued by a judicial authority of a category 1 territory.
- In an accusation case, it must contain a statement that the person is accused of an offence specified and is issued with a view to his arrest and extradition.
- In a conviction case, it must contain a statement that the person is alleged to be unlawfully at large after conviction in respect of an offence specified and the warrant is issued with a view to his arrest and extradition for the purpose of being sentenced or serving a sentence or other form of detention already imposed.
- The EAW must also contain other information, including:
  - particulars of identity;
  - particulars of any other warrant issued;
  - particulars of the circumstances in which the person is alleged to have committed the offence, the conduct, the date, time, and place of the offence and the law; and
  - the relevant sentence if one was imposed.

**2.08**  If the EAW complies with these requirements and SOCA believes that the authority which issued the Part 1 warrant has the function of issuing warrants in that territory, SOCA may issue its certificate.

**2.09**  Once the certificate is issued, section 3 permits the person to be arrested on the basis of the EAW by a constable or customs officer in any part of the United Kingdom.

**2.10**  Under section 4, the person must be given a copy of the EAW and produced before the 'appropriate judge' *as soon as practicable* after arrest.

**2.11**  Failure to serve the person with a copy of the warrant confers on the judge a discretion on application to order his discharge. Failure to produce the person within this period obliges the judge on application to order his discharge.

**Initial hearing**

**2.12**  At the initial hearing the judge must decide, on a balance of probabilities, whether the person before him is the person referred to in the warrant. If he is so satisfied, then the matter is remanded for the extradition hearing within the permitted period (twenty-one days starting from the date of arrest) and the person is:

- informed of the contents of the Part 1 warrant;

- provided with an explanation of the effect of and procedure for consenting to extradition. The consent must be given in writing and, once given, is irrevocable; and
- remanded in custody or on bail.

Section 8(5) of the 2003 Act permits applications for an extension of the permitted period **2.13** by either party. Such an application is only granted if the judge 'believes that it is in the interests of justice to do so'.

The 2003 Act provides for the person to be discharged, whether or not he applies for his **2.14** discharge, if the extradition hearing does not commence on or before the date fixed for the hearing (this must be read subject to any application for an extension under section 8(5)), unless reasonable cause is shown for the delay.

### Extradition hearing

At the extradition hearing, the appropriate judge must first consider whether the conduct set **2.15** out in the EAW constitutes an extradition offence as defined in sections 64 or 65 of the 2003 Act. If the conduct does not constitute an extradition offence as defined then the person must be discharged.

If an extradition offence is disclosed, the judge moves on to consider whether any of the bars **2.16** to extradition or other matters set out in sections 11 to 25 of the 2003 Act apply. These include:

- the rule against double jeopardy;
- oppression or injustice resulting from the passage of time;
- extraneous considerations (underlying prejudicial motive behind the issuance of the EAW/risk of prejudice on return);
- whether extradition would be compatible with the person's human rights; and
- whether the person's mental or physical condition requires deferment or refusal of extradition.

If any of these matters are established to the necessary standard, the person must be discharged. If not, the judge is obliged to order extradition. **2.17**

### Appeals

Whichever party is unsuccessful at the extradition hearing may, as of right, appeal the decision of the appropriate judge. The appeal must be filed and served within seven days of the order for extradition/discharge. **2.18**

Appeals in England and Wales are heard by the Administrative Court, in Scotland by the **2.19** High Court of Justiciary, and in Northern Ireland by the Northern Ireland High Court.

The appeal hearing must commence within forty days of the decision complained of, although **2.20** this may be extended if the High Court considers it in the interests of justice to do so.

The appeal entails a reconsideration of the issues considered by the appropriate judge at the **2.21** extradition hearing, although the court will normally rely on the appropriate judge's findings of fact. The appeal court may either allow or dismiss the appeal.

**2.22** Thereafter, an appeal may lie to the Supreme Court but only if the High Court certifies that it entails a point of law of general public importance *and* either the High Court or the Supreme Court grants leave.

## B. Export extradition—procedure for dealing with category 2 requests (from non-EU countries)

**2.23** Extradition proceedings in relation to requests from countries outside the EU are regulated by Part 2 of the 2003 Act. Although the procedures are similar to those involved for EAWs, they are not identical. They may be initiated in one of two ways:

- provisional arrest, or
- arrest following the receipt and certification of a full extradition request.

**Provisional arrest**

**2.24** Section 73 of the 2003 Act governs the procedure for provisional arrest. A justice of the peace may issue a warrant if he has reasonable grounds to believe that the person sought is accused or convicted of an extradition offence and there is written evidence or information that the person sought is accused of the commission of an offence in a category 2 territory or is unlawfully at large after conviction.

**2.25** Following the issue of the provisional warrant, the person may be arrested by any person to whom it is directed or any constable or customs officer in any part of the United Kingdom. The warrant may be executed whether or not the person authorized to execute it has possession of the warrant or simply a copy of it. However, a copy of the warrant must be served on the person as soon as practicable after arrest: failure to do so may (but not must) lead to discharge upon an application by the person arrested. The person must be brought before an appropriate judge as soon as practicable after arrest; failure to do so obliges the judge upon application by the person to order discharge.

**2.26** At the first appearance, the judge must:

- inform the arrested person that he is accused or unlawfully at large after conviction in a category 2 territory,
- provide him with the required information about consent and explain the effect and procedure of the consent (the consent must be given in writing and is irrevocable); and
- remand him in custody or on bail (the general right to bail now applies to extradition proceedings).

**2.27** The matter is then adjourned for receipt by the court of the extradition request and the Secretary of State's certificate within a forty-five day period, starting with the day of arrest or such longer period as allowed for in an order made by the Secretary of State.

**2.28** Upon receipt of:

- the request; and
- the certificate,

the judge must fix a date for the commencement of the extradition hearing. This must be within the 'required period'—that is, two months starting on the day on which the above documents are received by the court. The required period can be extended on the application of either party provided the judge believes that it is in the interests of justice to do so.

**Arrest following receipt and certification of full extradition request**

The procedure for arrest following receipt and certification of a full extradition request is governed by sections 70 to 72 of the 2003 Act.  **2.29**

Under section 70, upon receipt of a 'valid request' the Secretary of State *must* issue a certificate unless:  **2.30**

- there is a competing extradition request and he decides to order deferment of the proceedings on the present request under section 126 of the Act; or
- he has granted the person refugee status or asylum from the requesting country.

For these purposes a request will be considered to be valid if it:  **2.31**

- contains a statement that the person:
  - is accused in the requesting territory of committing the offence specified in the request and that the request is made in order to secure his arrest and extradition to the requesting country for the purpose of prosecuting him for it; or
  - has been convicted of the offence specified in the request and the request is made in order to secure his arrest and extradition to the requesting country so that he can be sentenced for it or, if already sentenced to imprisonment, so that the sentence can be enforced,

and

- it is made in the 'approved way', that is, either:
  - by a person whom the Secretary of State believes to have the function of making extradition requests in the requesting state, or
  - by a recognized diplomatic/consular representative of the requesting state.

Once the certificate is issued, the Secretary of State sends the request and certificate to the appropriate judge.  **2.32**

Under section 71, upon receipt of the above documents, the appropriate judge may issue a warrant of arrest if he has reasonable grounds to believe that the offence is an extradition offence and that there is sufficient evidence/information to justify the issue of a warrant.  **2.33**

The warrant may be executed in any part of the United Kingdom by any person to whom it is directed or by any constable or customs officer.  **2.34**

Following his arrest, section 72 provides that the person must be served with a copy of the warrant as soon as practicable. Failure to do so allows him to apply for discharge, and the judge *may* order his discharge. In practice, this rarely happens because, provided the documents are given to the defence at the first hearing, it will be almost impossible to establish that any meaningful prejudice has been suffered.  **2.35**

Section 72 also provides that the person must be brought before an appropriate judge as soon as practicable, unless he has been granted bail by the constable or the Secretary of State has received a competing extradition request under section 126 and decides that this request is not to be proceeded with. Failure to bring the person arrested before an appropriate judge as soon as practicable allows the person to apply for discharge, which the judge *must* grant.  **2.36**

**2.37** At the first hearing following arrest, the appropriate judge must inform the person of the contents of the request and explain to him about the possibility of consenting to extradition and its effects. If consent is not forthcoming, the judge will then remand the requested person in custody or on bail and fix a date for the commencement of the extradition hearing. This must be no later than two months starting on the date of the person's first appearance before the appropriate judge.

**Extradition hearing**

**2.38** Once the extradition hearing commences, the appropriate judge must first be satisfied that the documentation provided comprises:

- the extradition request;
- the Secretary of State's certificate;
- particulars of the requested person;
- particulars of the offence for which extradition is sought; and
- a warrant for his arrest issued in the requesting country (accusation cases) or a memorandum of conviction and (if sentence) details of the sentence imposed (conviction cases).

Failure to provide any of these will oblige the appropriate judge to order the person's discharge.

**2.39** If satisfied that the documentation is in order, the judge moves on to consider whether:

- the person before him is the person whose extradition has been requested;
- the offence for which extradition is requested constitutes an extradition offence as defined in sections 137 or 138 of the 2003 Act; and
- copies of the request and the Secretary of State's certificate have been served on the requested person.

If the judge is not satisfied in relation to any of these matters, he is obliged to order the person's discharge.

**2.40** If satisfied that the documentation is in order, the judge then considers whether any of the bars to extradition set out in sections 79 to 83 are established. These include:

- the rule against double jeopardy;
- extraneous considerations; and
- passage of time.

**2.41** In a case where the person has not been convicted, section 84 then requires the judge to consider whether the request contains evidence establishing a prima facie case in respect of the offence for which extradition is sought. However, this requirement is disapplied for many of the United Kingdom's main extradition partners outside the EU, including the United States, Australia, Canada, and New Zealand. For those countries where the requirement is retained, its effect is softened by subsections (3) and (4), which allow the requesting state to rely on hearsay evidence rather than statements from each and every prima facie witness (as was the case under the 1989 Act).

**2.42** In conviction cases, section 85 requires the appropriate judge to consider whether the conviction was entered in the person's presence or absence. If the conviction was obtained in absentia but the person was not deliberately absent from his trial, the judge must order discharge unless satisfied that he would, upon return, be entitled to a retrial.

Finally, section 87 requires the appropriate judge to decide whether extradition would **2.43** be compatible with the person's human rights. If he concludes that it would, he must send the case to the Secretary of State to decide whether or not to order extradition. If not, then he must order the person's discharge.

### Consideration by Secretary of State

Section 93 specifies only four matters which the Secretary of State must consider in deciding **2.44** whether or not to order extradition namely:

- whether the person has been, will or might be sentenced to death for the offence concerned;
- whether speciality arrangements exist between the United Kingdom and the requesting country;
- whether the person has previously been extradited to the United Kingdom from another country and the consent of that other country to the onward extradition is required but has not been obtained; and
- whether the person has previously been transferred to the United Kingdom from the International Criminal Court (ICC) and the consent of the ICC presidency to the onward extradition is required but has not been obtained.

If any of these apply, then the Secretary of State cannot order extradition. If not, then he is **2.45** obliged to do so, within a period of two months starting on the 'appropriate day' as defined in section 102 and which will usually be the day on which the appropriate judge sends the case to the Secretary of State.

### Appeals

The appeal provisions applicable to Part 2 cases are set out in sections 103 to 116 of the 2003 **2.46** Act. They are rather more complex than their counterparts under Part 1 because they have to take account of the two decision-makers involved—the appropriate judge and the Secretary of State. The unsuccessful party may appeal the decision of either or both, as of right, to the Administrative Court.

Appeals by the person against the appropriate judge's decision to send the case to the Secretary **2.47** of State are regulated by sections 103 and 104. Appeals by the requesting state against the District Judge's decision to discharge the requested person are regulated by sections 105 and 106. Appeals against the decision of the Secretary of State to order extradition are dealt with by sections 108 and 109, and against his decision to discharge the requested person by section 110 and 111.

The aim is to avoid time being wasted on hearing unnecessary appeals. Thus for example, **2.48** there is no point in hearing an appeal against the District Judge's order for extradition in isolation, if the Secretary of State subsequently declines to order extradition. The appeal will only be heard once the Secretary of State has ordered the person's extradition and will be dealt with at the same time as any appeal against the Secretary of State's decision.

**2.49**    Unlike appeals under Part 1 (where the Administrative Court can only allow or refuse the appeal and then discharge or affirm the order for extradition), on appeals against the order of the appropriate judge under Part 2, the Administrative Court may additionally remit the matter to him for reconsideration.

**2.50**    As with Part 1 cases, appeal lies from the Administrative Court to the Supreme Court provided that the Administrative Court certifies that the matter involves a point of law of general public importance and either the Administrative Court or the Supreme Court grants leave for the appeal to be brought.

## C.  Import extradition—requests to EU member states

**2.51**    Part 3 of the 2003 Act regulates the issue of EAWs by UK courts.

**2.52**    Section 142 provides that an EAW may be issued upon the application of a constable or 'appropriate person'[1] provided that there are reasonable grounds for believing that the person has committed an extradition offence as defined by section 148 and that a domestic warrant has been issued for the person's arrest in an accusation case or the person is unlawfully at large following conviction. The section goes on to prescribe what the EAW must contain.

**2.53**    In England and Wales arrangements between the CPS and the police mean that all EAWs will be drafted by a Crown Prosecutor and then applied for either by the prosecutor or a police officer as deemed appropriate in the circumstances of the case. Once issued, the EAW is passed to SOCA for transmission.

**2.54**    Speciality protection for a person returned to the United Kingdom pursuant to an EAW is provided by section 146.

## D.  Import extradition—requests to non-EU states

**2.55**    Extradition requests to countries outside the EU are made pursuant to the Royal Prerogative.

**2.56**    Other than limited provisions relating chiefly to speciality protection upon return, requests to non-EU countries are not regulated by statute. The relevant requirements are determined by the scheme governing extradition between the United Kingdom and the country concerned. Older treaties require the provision of prima facie evidence, others (usually more modern ones) simply an account of the prima facie evidence or of the facts.

**2.57**    The usual practice is for the prosecutor to prepare the supporting documentation required by the relevant extradition arrangement and then pass it to the Home Office which makes the request by diplomatic note.

**2.58**    Most schemes make provision for provisional arrest pending submission of the formal request and supporting documentation within a specified period. Arrangements exist for prosecutors to submit provisional arrest requests through Interpol. Before such a request is

---

[1]  Defined to include any Crown Prosecutor and any designated member of the Serious Fraud Office: para 2(2) of the Extradition Act 2003 (Part 3 Designation) Order 2003, SI 2003/3335.

made, the prosecutor will have to be satisfied that the full request can be finalized (including any translation) and transmitted to the requested state before the applicable time limit. If the deadline is not met the person will inevitably be discharged.

In making requests to foreign states, although the ordinary rules of disclosure do not apply,   **2.59**
the prosecutor is nonetheless bound by the duty of candour and good faith. In pursuance of that duty, he should disclose evidence which destroys or very severely undermines the evidence on which his case relies, in particular previous inconsistent statements.[2]

It is important to bear in mind that subsequent criminal proceedings may be stayed as an   **2.60**
abuse of process if it can be shown that the proper extradition process was either manipulated or circumvented altogether ('veiled extradition'). The leading authorities in this area include:

- *R v Horseferry Road Magistrates' Court, ex p Bennett* [1994] 1 AC 42; *R v Horseferry Road Magistrates' Court, ex p Bennett (No 3)* [1995] 1 Cr App R 147;
- *R v Staines Magistrates' Court, ex p Westfallen* [1998] 1 WLR 652;
- *R v Mullen* [1999] 2 Cr App R 143; and
- *R v Daniel Burns* (CA, 31 May 2002).

---

[2] *Ahmad and Aswat v The Government of the USA* [2006] EWHC 2927 (Admin).

# 3

# MUTUAL TRUST AND ABUSE OF PROCESS

## A. Introduction

If a practitioner were to base him- or herself solely on the 'black-letter' law of the Extradition Act 2003 ('the 2003 Act'), he or she would be unaware of certain core principles of extradition law which are not set out in the Act. **3.01**

Foremost among these, particularly in respect of Part 1 of the 2003 Act and the European Arrest Warrant (EAW) scheme is the notion that extradition is built on mutual trust among extradition partners, and the presumption, albeit a rebuttable one, that the requesting state or judicial authority is acting in good faith. Allied to this is the feature that Part 1 of the 2003 Act only applies to states which are EU member states, and thus parties to the ECHR (as are all Council of Europe states), and with limited exceptions, the courts consider that those states are to be presumed capable of ensuring a fair trial under Article 6 of the ECHR and of eliminating any injustice which might result from the passage of time.[1] **3.02**

At the other end of the spectrum is a concept which is also not enunciated in the 2003 Act but which may successfully be invoked to oppose extradition, namely abuse of process. **3.03**

In this short chapter, these two concepts will be briefly explored. **3.04**

## B. Mutual trust

**Mutual trust in general**

It is a fundamental principle of extradition that extradition is only available between friendly states. There is, accordingly, a fundamental presumption that the requesting state is acting in **3.05**

---

[1] See, eg, *Arnas Baranauskas v Ministry of Justice of the Republic of Lithuania (Lithuanian Judicial Authority)* [2009] EWHC 1859 (Admin) at para 11: '*We consider that ... those countries that are signatories to the Convention would be assumed to be capable of protecting the rights of people in their country.*'

good faith in seeking the return of a requested person, which 'is a premise of effective relations between sovereign States'.[2]

**3.06**  The courts have thus consistently interpreted the 2003 Act so as to facilitate, rather than to frustrate extradition. In *Caldarelli*,[3] Laws LJ spoke, at paragraph 41, of 'the need to apply to the 2003 Act "a broad and generous construction so far as the text permits it in order to facilitate extradition"'.

**3.07**  The House of Lords recently reiterated these core principles in *Gomes and Goodyear v Government of the Republic of Trinidad and Tobago*,[4] at paragraph 36:

> The extradition process, it must be remembered, is only available for returning suspects to friendly foreign states with whom this country has entered into multi-lateral or bilateral treaty obligations involving mutually agreed and reciprocal commitments. The arrangements are founded on mutual trust and respect. There is a strong public interest in respecting such treaty obligations. As has repeatedly been stated, international cooperation in this field is ever more important to bring to justice those accused of serious cross-border crimes and to ensure that fugitives cannot find safe havens abroad.

**3.08**  These principles have important implications for any argument that a person's extradition is incompatible with their human rights or will be unjust due to the passage of time.[5]

### Mutual trust and category 1 territories

**3.09**  As set out in more detail elsewhere in this book,[6] Part 1 of the 2003 Act was enacted in order to give effect to the Framework Decision on the EAW ('the Framework Decision'). As Lord Bingham said in *Dabas*,[7] at paragraph 4:

> The important underlying assumption of the Framework Decision is that member states, sharing common values and recognising common rights, can and should trust the integrity and fairness of each other's judicial institutions.

**3.10**  Moreover, all states which are part of the EAW scheme are signatories to the ECHR and are therefore presumed to be capable of protecting an individual's rights under the ECHR.

**3.11**  In *Hilali*,[8] Scott Baker LJ stated at paragraph 77:

> It seems to us that the courts should give great weight to the fact that Spain is a western democracy, subject to the rule of law, a signatory of the European Convention of Human Rights and a party to the Framework Decision; it is a country which has and which applies the same human rights standards and is subject to the same international obligations as the United Kingdom. These surely are highly relevant matters which strongly militate against refusing extradition on the grounds of the risk of violating those standards and obligations.

---

[2] *Serbeh v Governor of HMP Brixton* [2002] EWHC 2356 (Admin) per Kennedy LJ at para 40.
[3] *Caldarelli v Court of Naples* [2007] EWHC 1624 (Admin).
[4] [2009] UKHL 21.
[5] See Chapter 10 ('Extradition and Human Rights') and paras 6.19–6.28 (passage of time), where these issues are explored in more detail.
[6] See 1.19–1.22 above.
[7] *Dabas v High Court of Justice in Madrid, Spain* [2007] UKHL 6, [2007] 2 AC 31.
[8] *Farid Hilali v The Central Court of Criminal Proceedings Number 5 of the National Court, Madrid* [2006] EWHC 1239 (Admin).

The same applies to EU member states' ratification of other human rights conventions. **3.12**

These considerations are regularly relied on by the courts and explain the overwhelming **3.13** inclination, evident since the 2003 Act came into force, in favour of extradition, in particular in relation to category 1 territories.

## C. Abuse of process

Abuse of process is another important subject in extradition law which does not find expres- **3.14** sion anywhere in the 2003 Act.

In *Bermingham and Others*,[9] the Administrative Court held that, under the 2003 Act, the **3.15** magistrates' court has jurisdiction to ensure that 'the regime's integrity' is not usurped by abuse of process, although the question whether abuse is demonstrated has to be 'asked and answered in light of the specifics of the statutory scheme'.

In *Tollman*,[10] the Administrative Court, at paragraph 82, endorsed the conclusion that the **3.16** judge conducting extradition proceedings has jurisdiction to consider an allegation of abuse of process. Rose LJ went on to apply to extradition proceedings the statement made by Bingham LJ, in relation to conventional criminal proceedings in *R v Liverpool Stipendiary Magistrate, ex p Ellison*:[11]

> If any criminal court at any time has cause to suspect that a prosecutor may be manipulating or using the procedures of the court in order to oppress or unfairly to prejudice a defendant before the court, I have no doubt that it is the duty of the court to inquire into the situation and ensure that its procedure is not being abused. Usually no doubt such inquiry will be prompted by a complaint on the part of the defendant. But the duty of the court in my view exists even in the absence of a complaint.

In *Tollman*, the court, at paragraph 84, set out the proper procedure for dealing with an **3.17** allegation of abuse of process:

> Where an allegation of abuse of process is made, the first step must be to insist on the conduct alleged to constitute the abuse being identified with particularity. The judge must then con- sider whether the conduct, if established, is capable of amounting to an abuse of process. If it is, he must next consider whether there are reasonable grounds for believing that such conduct may have occurred. If there are, then the judge should not accede to the request for extradition unless he has satisfied himself that such abuse has not occurred.

Accordingly, the approach taken by the courts where abuse of process is raised in extradition **3.18** proceedings is to follow the three-step *Tollman* process.[12] *Dytlow and Dytlow*[13] is a relatively recent example where the proceedings were found to amount to an abuse of process. In that case, the Administrative Court held that it would amount to an abuse of process to order the extradition of a person enjoying the status of a refugee in the United Kingdom to the country

---

[9] *Bermingham and Others* [2006] EWHC 200 (Admin).
[10] *Tollman* [2006] EWHC 2256 (Admin).
[11] *R v Liverpool Stipendiary Magistrate, ex p Ellison* [1990] RTR 220.
[12] See, eg, *Lopetas v Minister of Justice for Lithuania* [2007] EWHC 2407(Admin) and *Central Examining Court of the National Court of Madrid v City of Westminster Magistrates' Court & Malkit Singh* [2007] EWHC 2059 (Admin).
[13] *District Court in Ostroleka v (1) Dytlow and (2) Dytlow* [2009] EWHC 1009 (Admin).

from which he had sought asylum. An even more recent example is *Republic of Serbia v Ganic* (27 July 2010), in which Senior District Judge Workman, sitting at City of Westminster Magistrates' Court, found that the extradition request brought by Serbia against a former President of Bosnia and Herzegovina on allegations of war crimes was an abuse of process for a host of reasons, including on the basis of being politically motivated.

# 4

# EXTRADITION OFFENCES

## A. Introduction

Extradition under the Extradition Act 2003 ('the 2003 Act') is based on the notion of the **4.01** 'extradition offence'. In the case of *Cando Armas* Lord Hope stated:

> The definitions of what constitute an extradition offence … are based on the principle, recognised in international law, that States claim criminal jurisdiction over conduct which takes place within their territory. The judge need not concern himself with the criminal law of the requesting state when he is addressing the question whether the offence specified in the Part 1 warrant is an extradition offence. But he does have to consider where the conduct which is alleged to constitute the offence took place.[1]

There are two requirements common to all extradition offences: firstly, the conduct must **4.02** either meet the dual criminality test or, in respect of Part 1 cases the issuing judicial authority must certify that the offence is included on the European Framework list. Secondly, the penalty must meet the minimum sentence thresholds set out in the 2003 Act.

The dual criminality test requires the conduct for which extradition is sought to constitute a **4.03** crime under the law of both the requesting state and the requested state.[2] In order to determine whether the conduct contained in the extradition request or warrant meets the dual criminality test, the conduct in the requesting state is transposed to the United Kingdom and

---

[1] *King's Prosecutor, Brussels v Cando Armas and anor* [2006] 2 AC 1 (HL) at para 30.
[2] *R v Bow Street Metropolitan Stipendiary Magistrate ex p Pinochet Ugarte (No 3)* [2000] 1 AC 147 at 189.

a determination is then made as to whether or not the conduct would amount to an offence under English law.

**4.04**  The key cases are as follows:

- *Cando Armas*;[3]
- *Dabas*;[4] and
- *Norris*.[5]

## B.  Category 1 territories (EAW)

**4.05**  As explained previously, the 2003 Act is divided into category 1 territories (EAW) and category 2 territories. The definition of an extradition offence differs depending on which part of the 2003 Act is being applied. Not all Part 1 extradition offences require dual criminality to be established.

**4.06**  The EAW has two distinct categories of extradition offence:

1.  Offences punishable with imprisonment for twelve months or more;
2.  Offences contained in the Framework list punishable with imprisonment for three years or more.

### The Framework list

**4.07**  The Council Framework Decision of 13 June 2002[6] identifies a list of offences agreed by all member states to be sufficiently serious to warrant extradition. Where the issuing judicial authority certifies that the offence contained in the warrant is a Framework list offence, then it does not need to meet the double criminality requirement in respect of that offence.

**4.08**  The Framework list offences are set out in paragraph 2 of Article 2 of the Framework Decision and are contained in the body of the text of the pro forma EAW.[7] The underlying rationale for the dispensation of the requirement of double criminality in the Framework list is the unstated assumption that the offences contained on it are of a universal nature and will feature in some form in the criminal law of all member states.[8]

**4.09**  The introduction of the Framework list and the consequent removal of the requirement of dual criminality has been extremely controversial, as recognized by Lord Scott in *Dabas* when he acknowledged that 'the possibility of surrender for prosecution in relation to conduct that would not be criminal in the requested state is a very live one'.[9]

**4.10**  The wording of the relevant sections of the 2003 Act suggest that all that is required of the requesting authority is to issue a certificate showing that the conduct falls within the European framework list. However, in *Haynes* the court accepted the argument that the ticking of the

---

[3] [2006] 2 AC 1 (HL).
[4] [2007] 2 AC 31 (HL).
[5] [2008] 1 AC 920 (HL).
[6] *Official Journal of the European Communities*, Volume 45, L190/1.
[7] Appendix 6.
[8] See *King's Prosecutor, Brussels v Cando Armas and anor* [2006] 2 AC 1(HL) at para 5.
[9] *Dabas v High Court of Justice, Madrid* [2007] 2 AC 31 (HL) per Lord Scott at para 59.

Framework list on the warrant was insufficient. The court also had to look at the conduct in order to see whether it could amount to a framework offence.[10]

### Accused persons and persons convicted and sentenced

Section 10 of the 2003 Act requires the judge to decide whether the offence specified in the Part 1 warrant is an extradition offence. The Act draws a distinction between so-called 'accusation cases' (section 64) and 'conviction cases' (section 65). **4.11**

Section 64 applies where the person is accused or convicted but not sentenced. Section 64(2) to (7) sets out the conditions to be met in order for the conduct to constitute an extradition offence, as set out below. **4.12**

Section 65 applies to persons convicted *and* sentenced. It provides for identical conditions to those set out under section 64 except that, for offences outside the European Framework list, the person must have been sentenced to imprisonment for four months or more. Persons convicted of Framework list offences must have been sentenced to imprisonment of twelve months or more. **4.13**

Although there is no express statutory power for a judge conducting an extradition hearing to request further information from the issuing judicial authority, such a power is inferred under the principle of judicial cooperation embodied in the Framework Decision.[11] **4.14**

### Territorial offences

The 2003 Act divides offences into territorial and extra-territorial offences. Section 64(2) and (3)[12] are territorial offences requiring the conduct to occur within the territory of the requesting judicial authority. The conditions in section 64(2) are as follows: **4.15**

(a) the conduct must occur in the territory of the requesting judicial authority with no part of it occurring in the United Kingdom;
(b) a certificate must have been issued to confirm that the conduct falls within the Framework list; and
(c) the certificate must confirm that the penalty for the offence under the law of the territory is imprisonment or other form of detention for a term of three years or more.[13]

Section 64(3) covers offences, other than those in the Framework list, which meet the following conditions: **4.16**

(a) the conduct must occur in the territory of the requesting judicial authority;
(b) the conduct would constitute an offence if it occurred in the United Kingdom; and
(c) the conduct is punishable under the law of the territory with imprisonment for twelve months or more.

---

[10] *Haynes v Court of Magistrates, Malta* [2007] EWHC 2651 (Admin) (DC).
[11] *Dabas v High Court of Justice, Madrid* [2007] 2 AC 31 (HL) at para 49.
[12] Paragraphs 4.15 to 4.20 refer to s 64 but apply equally to s 65.
[13] Extradition Act 2003, s 64(2).

**Extra-territorial offences**

**4.17** Section 64(4) to (6) of the 2003 Act allows for extra-territorial offences and further splits those into three types of conduct. One type of conduct is set out in section 64(4), and comprises three conditions:

(a) the conduct occurs outside the territory of the requesting judicial authority;
(b) the conduct is punishable with imprisonment for twelve months or more under the law of that territory; and
(c) in corresponding circumstances, the conduct would amount to an extra-territorial offence under United Kingdom law.

**4.18** A second type of conduct is set out in section 64(5). Again, three conditions must be met:

(a) the conduct occurs outside the territory of the requesting judicial authority and no part of it occurs in the United Kingdom;
(b) the conduct would constitute an offence attracting imprisonment for twelve months or more if it occurred in the United Kingdom; and
(c) the conduct is so punishable under the law of the territory of the requesting judicial authority.

**4.19** The third type of conduct is set out in section 64(6). The following conditions must be met:

(a) the conduct occurs outside the territory of the requesting judicial authority and no part of it occurs in the United Kingdom;
(b) the conduct is punishable with imprisonment for twelve months or more under the law of that territory; and
(c) the conduct constitutes, or if committed in the United Kingdom would constitute, an offence under section 64(7).

**4.20** Section 64(7) deals with crimes under the Statute of the International Criminal Court (ICC), namely, the crimes of genocide, crimes against humanity, and war crimes.

**4.21** The subsections of sections 64 and 65 are not mutually exclusive but constitute a cumulative and overlapping list. Conduct will constitute an extradition offence if any one of the subsections applies to it.[14]

## C. Category 2 territories

**4.22** The extradition 'schemes' covered are:

• European Convention on Extradition;
• Commonwealth and overseas territories;
• treaty countries; and
• ad hoc and UN conventions.

---

[14] *King's Prosecutor, Brussels v Armas and anor* [2005] 1 WLR 1389 (DC) at para 26; *King's Prosecutor, Brussels v Armas and anor* [2006] 2 AC 1 (HL) at paras 11, 17; *Osunta v The Public Prosecutor's Office In Dusseldorf* [2008] QB 785 (DC) at para 18.

---

As under Part 1 above, the appropriate judge must be satisfied that the 'offence specified in **4.23** the request is an extradition offence'.[15]

### Accused persons

Section 137 of the 2003 Act defines an 'extradition offence' in respect of requests from **4.24** category 2 territories for the extradition of persons accused or convicted but not sentenced (accusation cases). As under Part 1, the 2003 Act distinguishes between territorial offences (section 137(2)) and extra-territorial offences (section 137(3)–(5)). The four types of extradition offences contained in section 137 are as follows:

- The conduct occurs *in* the requesting state and the conduct when transposed would amount to an offence under United Kingdom law. The offence is punishable with imprisonment of twelve months or more in the United Kingdom and the requesting state.[16]
- The conduct occurs *outside* the requesting state and in corresponding circumstances it would amount to an extra-territorial offence under United Kingdom law. The offence is punishable with imprisonment of twelve months or more in the United Kingdom and the requesting state.[17]
- The conduct occurs *outside* the requesting state, no part of it occurs in the United Kingdom and when transposed it would amount to an offence under United Kingdom law. The offence is punishable with imprisonment of twelve months or more in the United Kingdom and the requesting state.[18]
- The conduct occurs *outside* the requesting state, no part of it occurs in the United Kingdom and it constitutes, or would when transposed constitute, an offence under the International Criminal Court Act 2001.[19] The offence is punishable with imprisonment of twelve months or more in the requesting state. There is no requirement that the offence should meet the penalty threshold under United Kingdom law. However, given the nature of the offences under the International Criminal Court Act 2001, it is unlikely that they would be punishable with less than twelve months' imprisonment.[20]

### Military offences

Section 137(7) states that if an offence in the request is an offence under military law, then it **4.25** must also be an offence under the general criminal law of the requesting state, in order to constitute an extradition offence.

### Persons convicted and sentenced

Section 138 of the 2003 Act defines extradition offences in respect of requests from category **4.26** 2 territories for persons who have been convicted and sentenced. The requirements of section 138 are identical to those in section 137 set out above, save that the person must have received a sentence of imprisonment or any other form of detention of four months or more.

---

[15] Extradition Act 2003, s 78(4) ('Initial stages of extradition hearing').
[16] Extradition Act 2003, s 137(2).
[17] Extradition Act 2003, s 137(3).
[18] Extradition Act 2003, s 137(4).
[19] Namely, genocide, crimes against humanity and war crimes.
[20] Extradition Act 2003, s 137(5).

## D. The meaning of 'conduct' in the 2003 Act

**4.27**   The 'conduct' referred to in the 2003 Act is the conduct complained of or relied on in the warrant or extradition request.[21] Although the description of the conduct may include relevant and admissible events in order to set the scene, what is relevant is the conduct itself and not the background narrative.[22] It is not necessary to expressly aver all of the elements of an offence in the EAW or request so long as they can be properly inferred from the description of the conduct.[23]

**4.28**   The date at which dual criminality is to be assessed is the date on which the offence occurred rather than the date of the extradition hearing. In cases in which the relevant provision of United Kingdom law came into force after the conduct began, the judge may ask that the scope of the warrant or request be limited. In effect the part of the conduct that occurred at a time when it would not amount to criminal conduct in the United Kingdom is removed (so-called 'temporal excision'). If this is not practicable, the judge can order extradition only in respect of the conduct that meets the dual criminality requirement.[24]

**4.29**   Where sections 64(2), (5), or (6) apply,[25] and part of the conduct occurs in the United Kingdom, that part of the conduct may be excised and the remaining conduct relied upon so long as it comprises the necessary offences (so-called 'geographical excision').[26]

**4.30**   Where the 2003 Act requires the conduct to have occurred in a particular territory, it is sufficient if any part of the conduct occurred there even if the majority of the conduct took place in another jurisdiction. Once it is proved that any part of the conduct occurred in the requesting state, it is not necessary to establish that the conduct was 'targeted' at the category 2 territory in that its harmful effects were felt there.[27]

**4.31**   Express reference to 'an extra-territorial offence'[28] engages 'true extraterritoriality' in the sense that, when conducting the transposition exercise, the court must ask whether in corresponding circumstances equivalent conduct would constitute an offence in the relevant part of the United Kingdom. For these types of extradition offence, the court need only consider whether the conduct would constitute an offence in the United Kingdom if it occurred there, even if it did in fact occur there.[29] The test of whether conduct occurred in a particular territory is satisfied so long as its effects were intentionally felt there, irrespective of where the person was when he did the acts.[30]

---

[21]   *King's Prosecutor, Brussels v Cando Armas and anor* [2006] 2 AC 1 (HL) at paras 16 and 30.

[22]   *Dabas v High Court of Justice, Madrid* [2007] 2 AC 31 (HL) at para 48.

[23]   *Zak v Regional Court of Bydgoszcz Poland* [2008] EWHC 470 (Admin) (DC) at para 16.

[24]   *Dabas v High Court of Justice, Madrid* [2007] 2 AC 31 (HL) at paras 46 and 51, applying *R v Metropolitan Stipendiary Magistrate ex p Pinochet (No 3)* [2000] AC 147 (HL).

[25]   Or Extradition Act 2003, s 137(4) and (5).

[26]   *Osunta v The Public Prosecutor's Office in Dusseldorf* [2008] QB 785 (DC) at paras 21–22 and 24.

[27]   *King's Prosecutor, Brussels v Cando Armas and anor* [2006] 2 AC 1 (HL) at paras 36, 40; *Bermingham and ors v Director of the Serious Fraud Office & Anor* [2007] QB 727 (DC) at paras 83–84.

[28]   Extradition Act 2003, ss 64(4), 65(4), 137(3) and 138(3).

[29]   *Hosseini and ors v Courts of Higher Instance, Paris, France* [2006] EWHC 1333 (Admin) (DC) at para 32.

[30]   *King's Prosecutor, Brussels v Cando Armas and anor* [2006] 2 AC 1 (HL) at para 40.

## Dual criminality

Each offence in an EAW or extradition request must be considered separately.[31] In accusation **4.32**
cases the words 'would constitute an offence' in sections 64 and 137 mean 'would, if proved,
constitute' the English offence, and the words 'if it occurred' mean 'if it is proved to have
occurred'.[32]

 In considering whether the dual criminality test is met the court does not need to be satisfied **4.33**
that the elements of the offence in the warrant or request correspond to the elements of the
equivalent English offence (the offence test). Instead, the court must consider whether the
conduct, if it occurred in the United Kingdom, would amount to an offence (the conduct
test). If it would then the dual criminality test is satisfied. In *Norris* the House of Lords held
that:

> the conduct test should be applied consistently throughout the 2003 Act, the conduct relevant
> under Part 2 of the Act being that described in the documents constituting the request (the
> equivalent of the arrest warrant under Part 1), ignoring in both cases mere narrative back-
> ground but taking account of such allegations as are relevant to the description of the corre-
> sponding United Kingdom offence. [33]

Where the conduct alleged includes an offence specific to the requesting state, such as an **4.34**
allegation of perverting the course of justice in that state, the court in transposing the conduct to the United Kingdom must look not only at the acts of the accused, but also at the
criminality alleged. In the example given, the conduct when transposed should be seen as a
person in the United Kingdom perverting the course of justice in the United Kingdom.[34]

## Aggregate sentences

In some jurisdictions one sentence can be imposed in respect of a number of offences **4.35**
(an 'aggregate sentence'). Where extradition is sought in respect of an aggregate sentence the
court does not need to consider whether the sentence passed for each offence meets the minimum sentence threshold set out in the relevant subsection of the 2003 Act, only whether the
sentence for the conduct taken as a whole meets that threshold.[35] Even where one of the
offences in the warrant or request fails the double criminality requirement the court should
not look behind the aggregate sentence but must continue to apply it to the remaining
conduct.[36]

## Ad hoc arrangements

Ad hoc arrangements are provided for under section 194 of the 2003 Act. As they follow **4.36**
identical procedures to those existing for category 2 territories the definition of an 'extradition offence' in sections 137 and 138 of the 2003 Act applies.

---

[31] *Boudhiba v Central Examining Court No 5 of the National Court of Justice Madrid Spain* [2007] 1 WLR
124 (DC) at para 34.
[32] *Mauro v Government of the United States of America* [2009] EWHC 150 (Admin) (DC) at para 9; *Hilali v
The National Court, Madrid and anor* [2006] EWHC 1239 (Admin) (DC) at para 42.
[33] [2008] 1 AC 920 (HL) at para 91.
[34] *Norris v United States of America and ors* [2008] 1 AC 920 (HL) at paras 96–97 and 99.
[35] *Pilecki v Circuit Court of Legnica, Poland* [2008] 1 WLR 325 (HL) at para 34.
[36] *Kucera v The District Court of Karvina, Czech Republic* [2009] 1 WLR 806 (DC) at paras 55–57.

**United Nations conventions**

**4.37**   Section 193 of the 2003 Act gives effect to the various UN conventions, where the relevant UN convention acts as the basis for the extradition request. The conduct that amounts to an 'extradition offence' is governed by the UN convention itself and the relevant United Kingdom statute. In the case of an extradition request based on a UN convention it is necessary to consider the convention itself in order to ascertain the conduct that it criminalizes and to determine which offence created by the convention, if any, is disclosed by the conduct. The mischief addressed by the relevant UN convention is given effect in the United Kingdom by 'offence creating' legislation.

**4.38**   Any request under the convention will be limited to the mischief intended by the relevant convention.[37] In the Algerian extradition request for *Ait Haddad*[38] under the Montreal Convention and Protocol 1971 and the Extradition Act 1989, the Secretary of State could not issue an authority to proceed for general acts of terrorism, as the Convention only governs terrorist activities at an airport serving international civil aviation.

**The ad hoc international criminal tribunals and the ICC**

**4.39**   The 2003 Act has no impact on a request for the surrender of a person to the two ad hoc tribunals created by the United Nations Security Council—the International Criminal Tribunal for the former Yugoslavia (ICTY) and the International Criminal Tribunal for Rwanda (ICTR). Nor does it impact upon a request from the ICC. The surrender of a person to these bodies will continue to be governed by the relevant Orders in Council for the ICTY and ICTR and by the International Criminal Court Act 2001 in relation to the ICC.

---

[37] Extradition Act 2003, s 193(4).
[38] *Ait Haddad* (unreported).

# 5

# THE EXTRADITION HEARING

## A. Introduction

The extradition hearing is a substantive hearing at which the sufficiency of the extradition **5.01** request or European Arrest Warrant (EAW) is examined. The hearing is conducted by the 'appropriate judge' who, in England and Wales, is a District Judge sitting at the City of Westminster Magistrates' Court.[1]

The Extradition Act 2003 ('the 2003 Act') is divided into two schemes: one for category 1 **5.02** territories (EAWs) and one for category 2 territories. Both schemes provide the District Judge with a roadmap setting out in sequence the statutory questions that he must consider.

Proceedings at first instance are divided into two stages: **5.03**

• the initial hearing (Part 1 cases)/first appearance (Part 2 cases); and
• the extradition hearing.

---

[1] Extradition Act 2003, ss 67(1)(a), 139(1)(a).

## B. The initial hearing/first appearance

**5.04** Following arrest on an EAW or extradition request the person sought must be brought before the appropriate judge as soon as practicable, except in Part 2 cases in which the arresting officer grants the person bail.[2] The person must be served with a copy of the EAW or arrest warrant as soon as practicable after his arrest. Failure to produce the person as soon as practicable must result in his discharge upon application.[3] Failure to serve the EAW or warrant may lead to the person's discharge upon application.[4]

**5.05** Whether or not a person has been produced as soon as practicable is a question of fact. In *Nikonovs* the court emphasized the fact that the criterion in the test was 'practicable' rather than the wider 'reasonably practicable'.[5] There is nothing improper in reissuing an EAW that has been discharged under section 4.[6]

**5.06** At the initial hearing in a Part 1 case the only statutory question the judge must decide is in relation to identification. Under section 7(2) and (3) of the 2003 Act, the appropriate judge must decide, on the balance of probabilities, whether the person brought before him is the person in respect of whom the EAW was issued. This decision is final and he is entitled to refuse to re-open the question of identity at the extradition hearing.[7] In Part 2 cases there are no statutory questions for the judge to consider at the first appearance.

**5.07** At the initial hearing or first appearance the appropriate judge will:

- set a date for the extradition hearing;[8]
- inform the person of the contents of the Part 1 warrant/extradition request;
- give the person the required information about consent; and
- remand the person in custody or on bail.

### Fix a date for the extradition hearing

**5.08** In Part 1 cases, the date for the extradition hearing must be within the permitted period (twenty-one days) starting from the date of arrest. Under section 8(5) of the 2003 Act the judge may fix a later date if he believes it to be in the interests of justice to do so, and may do so more than once.

**5.09** In Part 2 cases the permitted period is different depending on whether the person was arrested on a provisional warrant or not:

*Arrest following extradition request*—two months starting from the date on which the person first appears or is brought before the judge (section 75(2)).
*Provisional arrest*—two months starting from the date he receives the documents (section 76(3)).

---

[2] Extradition Act 2003, ss 4(3), 72(3), (4).
[3] Extradition Act 2003, ss 4(5) (Part 1), 72(6) (Part 2).
[4] Extradition Act 2003, ss 4(4) (Part 1), 72(5) (Part 2).
[5] *Nikonovs v Governor of HM Prison Brixton and anor* [2006] 1 WLR 1518 (DC).
[6] *Lopetas v Minister of Justice for Lithuania* [2007] EWHC 2407 (Admin) (DC).
[7] *Nur v Public Prosecutor* [2005] EWHC 1874 (Admin) (DC) at para 19.
[8] Except in provisional arrest cases under Part 2 of the 2003 Act when the judge sets the date for the extradition hearing once the request has been served (Extradition Act 2003, s 76).

The judge may fix a later date if he believes it to be in the interests of justice to do so, and may do so more than once.[9]

If neither party applies for an extension of time then the extradition hearing must proceed **5.10** on the date fixed. In the event that the matter does not proceed to a hearing in a Part 1 case the judge *must* order discharge under section 8(8) unless reasonable cause is shown for the delay. There is no provision for reasonable cause for delay under Part 2 and in those cases the judge *must* discharge the person under section 76(5) if the extradition hearing does not begin on or before the date fixed.[10]

### Inform the person of the contents of the Part 1 warrant/extradition request

It would appear that the purpose of this requirement, in conjunction with the requirement **5.11** to serve the warrant or request on the person,[11] is to ensure that the person understands the reason that he has been arrested.

### Give the person the required information about consent

The procedure relating to, and the effects of, consent are set out in sections 45 (Part 1) and **5.12** 127 (Part 2) of the 2003 Act. There are three major implications of consent to extradition:

- consent is irrevocable;
- the rule of specialty will not apply. The rule of specialty means that, after a person has been extradited, he may only be dealt with for the conduct set out in the EAW or request. By consenting to extradition a person waives their rights under this rule; and
- persons who consent have no right of appeal against extradition.

### Remand the person in custody/bail

Under section 198 of the 2003 Act accused persons in extradition proceedings have a right **5.13** to bail under section 4 of the Bail Act 1976 similar to that of defendants in domestic criminal proceedings. Section 4 does not apply to persons convicted in the requesting state and there is no presumption of bail in those cases.

Both the requested person and the prosecution may appeal the refusal or grant of bail to the **5.14** High Court.[12]

### Provisional arrest

*Part 1 cases*

Section 5(1) of the 2003 Act empowers a police officer to provisionally arrest any person **5.15** without a warrant if there are reasonable grounds to believe that an EAW has been, or will be, issued in respect of the person.

---

[9] Extradition Act 2003, ss 75(3) and 76(4).
[10] For a discussion of when an extradition hearing is deemed to have been called on, see *Gronostajski v Government of Poland* [2007] EWHC 3314 (Admin) (DC).
[11] Pursuant to ss 4(2), 72(7)(a) of the 2003 Act.
[12] Criminal Justice Act 1967, s 22(1A) (defence appeal); Extradition Act 2003, s 200 (as amended by the Police and Justice Act 2006, Sch 13, para 27) amending the Bail (Amendment) Act 1993, s 1(1A) (prosecution appeal).

**5.16**   Section 6 governs the procedure once a person has been provisionally arrested on an EAW. He must be produced in court within forty-eight hours[13] or the District Judge must order his discharge. The EAW and certificate must be produced to the District Judge within forty-eight hours, unless the judicial authority applies for, and is granted, a further forty-eight hour extension. Failure to produce either document to the judge in the required period will result in the person's discharge on application. If a person is discharged under section 6, he may not be provisionally arrested again in respect of the same EAW. If the person is not discharged, then the initial hearing proceeds as set out above.[14]

*Part 2 cases*

**5.17**   By section 73 of the 2003 Act a judge may issue a provisional arrest warrant in a Part 2 case in respect of a person accused or convicted before a court in a category 2 territory, where he is satisfied that the person is in the United Kingdom, or on his way to the United Kingdom.

**5.18**   The procedure for the first appearance in a Part 2 provisional arrest case is governed by section 74 of the 2003 Act. The person must be served with a copy of the arrest warrant, and brought before the District Judge, as soon as practicable after his arrest, unless he is granted bail by the arresting officer. Failure to serve the warrant as soon as practicable may result in the person's discharge on application. Failure to produce the person as soon as practicable must result in his discharge upon application.

**5.19**   When the person is brought before the District Judge he must be:

- informed that he is accused or convicted in the category 2 territory;
- informed of his right to consent to extradition;
- remanded in custody or on bail.

**5.20**   The extradition request and certificate must be served on the person within forty-five days, unless the requesting state has been designated by the Secretary of State in which case a different time period will apply.[15] In practice the District Judge will usually adjourn the case until the last court day before the time for the service of the request expires, on which occasion he will satisfy himself that the request has been served and set a date for the extradition hearing.[16]

**Domestic proceedings**

**5.21**   Section 22 of the 2003 Act gives precedence to domestic proceedings over extradition proceedings by requiring the judge to adjourn (effectively stay) the extradition proceedings until the domestic proceedings are completed. Anomalously, if the person consents to his extradition prior to the extradition hearing then section 22 does not apply and the extradition proceedings take precedence.[17]

---

[13] Not including any Saturday, Sunday, Christmas Day, Good Friday, or bank holidays (s 5(8)(a)).

[14] See 5.07–5.14 above.

[15] Extradition Act 2003, s 74(11). For a list of category 2 territories that have been designated by the Secretary of State and the relevant time limits, see Appendix 2.

[16] See 5.08–5.10 above.

[17] *Governor of HMP Wandsworth v Kinderis* [2008] QB 347 (DC), although see Beatson J (dissenting) at para 46ff.

# C. The extradition hearing

### Evidence in extradition hearings

Extradition proceedings are a special type of criminal proceedings. The judge should apply **5.22**
the normal rules of criminal evidence and procedure subject to the specific provisions under
the 2003 Act.[18] The Criminal Procedure Rules apply to extradition hearings to the extent
that they are relevant.[19] The hearsay rules contained in the Criminal Justice Act 2003 do not
apply to extradition proceedings.[20]

By section 206 of the 2003 Act any question as to the burden and standard of proof must be **5.23**
decided as if the extradition proceedings were domestic criminal proceedings and the person
was a defendant. This means that, unless the 2003 Act specifies otherwise, the matters that
must be established by the requesting state in extradition proceedings must be proved to the
criminal standard.[21]

A judge conducting an extradition hearing under Part 1 of the 2003 Act may request further **5.24**
information from the requesting judicial authority.[22] However, if the judge in a Part 1 case is
deciding whether an EAW meets the requirements of section 2 of the 2003 Act he must do
so on the basis of the information in the warrant alone and not from any further information.[23] A judge considering a case under Part 2 of the 2003 Act may also request or receive
further information which will be admissible under section 202 if it is duly authenticated in
accordance with that section.[24]

### Disclosure in extradition hearings[25]

The normal rules of disclosure, whether criminal or civil, do not apply to extradition hear- **5.25**
ings. It is for the requesting authority or government to decide what material it chooses to
place before the court subject to a presumption of good faith.[26] The judge at the extradition
hearing can request further information from a Part 1 judicial authority or requesting state
but he cannot compel them to provide it.[27]

---

[18] *R v The Governor of Brixton Prison ex p Levin* [1997] AC 741 at 746; *USA, R (on the application of) v Senior District Judge, Bow Street Magistrates' Court* [2007] 1 WLR 1157 (DC) at para 76.
[19] *USA, R (on the application of) v Senior District Judge, Bow Street Magistrates' Court* [2007] 1 WLR 1157 (DC) at para 76; *Hubner v District Court of Prostejov Czech Republic and anor* [2009] EWHC 2929 (Admin) (DC).
[20] *Friesel v Government of the United States of America* [2009] EWHC 1659 (Admin) (DC) at para 33.
[21] *Bentley v United States* [2005] EWHC 1078 (Admin) (DC) at para 16.
[22] *Dabas v High Court of Justice, Madrid* [2007] 2 AC 31 (HL) at para 49.
[23] *Pilecki v Circuit Court of Legnica, Poland* [2008] 1 WLR 325 (HL) at para 34.
[24] *Mauro v Government of the United States of America* [2009] EWHC 150 (Admin) (DC) at paras 19–20.
[25] As for disclosure in bail applications, see *Raissi, R (on the application of) v Secretary of State for the Home Department* [2008] QB 836 (DC) at para 140.
[26] *Serbeh v Governor of HMP Brixton* [2002] EWHC 2356 Admin (DC) approved in *Jenkins v Government of USA* [2005] EWHC 1051 (Admin) (DC).
[27] *USA, R (on the application of) v Senior District Judge, Bow Street Magistrates' Court* [2007] 1 WLR 1157 (DC) at para 85ff; *Central Examining Court of the National Court of Madrid v City of Westminster Magistrates' Court* [2007] EWHC 2059 (Admin) (DC).

**Authentication**

**5.26**   Section 202 of the 2003 Act sets out the criteria for authentication, and distinguishes EAWs from 'any other document'. The Act is silent as to the format of the EAW; that is determined by, and laid out in, the Framework Decision.

**5.27**   As far as 'any other document' submitted by a category 1 or category 2 territory is concerned, it is authenticated provided that one of two criteria is met:

• the document purports to be signed by a judge, magistrate or other judicial authority of the territory; or
• it purports to be authenticated by the oath or affirmation of a witness.

**5.28**   Section 202(1) provides that a Part 1 warrant (EAW) is not a 'document' within the meaning of section 202(2). Therefore it does not have to be authenticated. Section 202(5) states that:

> Subsections (2) and (3) do not prevent a document that is not duly authenticated from being received in evidence in proceedings under this Act.

Although either side may adduce unauthenticated documents pursuant to section 202(5), in practice the subsection is most helpful to the defence who commonly use it to rely on evidence such as human rights reports.

**Part 1 (European Arrest Warrant)**

*Initial stage of the extradition hearing (section 10 of the 2003 Act)*

**5.29**   The only issue that requires determination at this stage is whether the offence is an extradition offence. This is determined by the judge after hearing representations from the parties. Although there is nothing in the Act to prevent either party from calling evidence, in practice it is rarely required.

**5.30**   Once the extradition hearing has commenced, the District Judge has a discretion to adjourn it.[28] Although the 2003 Act provides a staged procedure through which the judge must consider the questions required of him at the extradition hearing, the Act does not preclude him from returning to a previous stage if appropriate.[29]

**5.31**   If the judge is satisfied that the offence is an extradition offence,[30] then he *must* proceed under section 11 of the 2003 Act.

*Bars to extradition (section 11 of the 2003 Act)*

**5.32**   Bars to extradition for category 1 territories are listed in section 11(1) and their interpretations are contained in sections 12 to 19A.[31] The onus of proof that a person's extradition is barred by any of the reasons set out in section 11 is on the defence.

---

[28] *Raffile v Government of the United States of America* [2005] 1 All ER 889 (DC) at para 17. For a discussion of the exercise of the discretion see *Germany v Kleinschmidt and anor* [2006] 1 WLR 1 (DC) at para 29.
[29] *Raffile v Government of the United States of America* [2005] 1 All ER 889 (DC) at para 33.
[30] For the law relating to extradition offences, see Chapter 4.
[31] For the law on bars to extradition, see Chapter 6.

The bars to extradition are: **5.33**

- the rule against double jeopardy;
- extraneous considerations;
- the passage of time;
- the person's age;
- hostage-taking considerations;
- specialty;
- the person's earlier extradition to the United Kingdom from another category 1 territory;
- the person's earlier extradition to the United Kingdom from a non-category 1 territory; and
- the person's earlier transfer to the United Kingdom by the International Criminal Court.

If the judge finds that any one of the bars applies, he must discharge the person. If not, then **5.34** he must proceed in one of two ways:

- Section 11(4): conviction cases must proceed under section 20.
- Section 11(5): accusation cases must proceed under section 21.

*Conviction cases (section 20)*

The purpose of section 20 is to ensure that where a person has been tried in their absence **5.35** through no fault of their own, they would be entitled to a retrial once extradited. The judge must therefore ask himself the following three questions:

- Was the person convicted in his presence? If so the person does not require any additional procedural safeguards and the judge is required to proceed to section 21 (as in accusation cases).
- If the person was convicted in his absence, did he deliberately absent himself from his trial? If so, then the person is considered to have waived the right to be present at his trial and the judge is required to proceed under section 21.
- If the person was not present at his trial, and did not deliberately absent himself, would he be entitled to some form of retrial in which he would enjoy certain specified procedural rights?[32] If so, then the judge must proceed under section 21. Otherwise, the judge is obliged to order the person's discharge.

*Human rights (section 21)*

The essence of section 21 is to ensure that the person's extradition would be compatible with **5.36** his rights under the European Convention of Human Rights. If the judge decides this question in the affirmative he must order the person's extradition and remand the person in custody or on bail to await extradition. If he decides the question in the negative then he must order the person's discharge.

*Physical or mental condition (section 25)*

If at any time during the course of the proceedings the judge is of the view that the physical **5.37** or mental condition of the person is such that it would be 'unjust or oppressive' to extradite him, then he *must* order his discharge or adjourn the hearing until it appears to him that the person has recovered and it would no longer be unjust or oppressive to extradite him.

---

[32] Set out in s 20(8).

**Part 2 (category 2 territories)**

*Initial stage of the extradition hearing (section 78)*

**5.38**   Under section 78(2) of the 2003 Act, the judge must decide whether the documents sent to him by the Secretary of State include:

- the documents referred to in section 70(9): the request and the certificate;
- particulars of the person sought;
- particulars of the offence specified in the request;
- in an accusation case, an arrest warrant or any other judicial document authorising his arrest, issued in that territory;
- in a conviction case, a certificate of the conviction and sentence.

**5.39**   The courts have given short shrift under the 2003 Act to purely technical arguments relating to the documents provided in an extradition request.[33]

**5.40**   Once the judge is satisfied that all the criteria in section 78(2) are met, then he must determine the following questions set out in section 78(4):

- Whether the person before him is the person requested in the extradition request.

- Whether the offence specified is an extradition offence.

- Whether copies of the documents have been served on the person. The requesting state should normally serve the documents prior to the commencement of the extradition hearing but, if it fails to do so, the documents may be served at the hearing itself.[34]

**5.41**   Once the appropriate judge is satisfied with all the issues that require determination under section 78, he must proceed to section 79.

*Bars to extradition (section 79)*

**5.42**   Section 79(1) of the 2003 Act sets out the four 'bars to extradition' for category 2 territories:

- the rule against double jeopardy;
- extraneous considerations;
- passage of time; and
- hostage-taking considerations.

**5.43**   In Part 2 cases, the issues of specialty and re-extradition are vested in the Secretary of State.

**5.44**   If the judge finds that any one of the bars applies, he must discharge the person. If not, then he must proceed in one of two ways:

Section 79(4): accusation cases must proceed under section 84 unless the category 2 territory to which extradition is requested has been designated by the Secretary of State,[35] in which case the judge must proceed to section 87;

Section 79(5): conviction cases must proceed under section 85.

---

[33] For example *Welsh and anor v Secretary of State for the Home Department and anor* [2007] 1 WLR 1281 (DC) and *Hashmi v Government of the United States of America* [2007] EWHC 564 (Admin) (DC).

[34] *Germany v Kleinschmidt and anor* [2006] 1 WLR 1 (DC).

[35] Extradition Act 2003 (Designation of Part 2 Territories) Order 2003, SI 2003/3334. For the Secretary of State's designations, see Appendix 2.

*Accusation cases (section 84)*

Section 84(1) requires the requesting state to adduce evidence sufficient to make a case to **5.45** answer in a summary trial, that is to establish a prima facie case. The rest of the section outlines what amounts to admissible evidence. Under section 84(1) 'evidence' is 'evidence available as material upon which a prosecution could rely at a summary trial of an information in domestic law'.[36] The court in *Brown (aka Vincent Bajinja) and others v Government of Rwanda and others* described the procedure under section 84(1) as follows:

> The question for the judge under s 84(1) was whether the [Government of Rwanda] had produced 'evidence which would be sufficient to make a case requiring an answer by [each appellant] if the proceedings were the summary trial of an information against him'. In answering that question the judge was obliged to reject any evidence which he considered to be 'worthless'; but if he concluded that the strength or weakness of the evidence against the appellants depended on 'the view to be taken of its reliability' he was entitled to take it into account.[37]

In considering whether a prima facie case has been established the following material may be **5.46** admissible evidence of a fact:

- A statement made by a witness to a police officer or another person charged with the duty of investigating offences or charging offenders where direct oral evidence by the person of the fact would be admissible (section 84(2)).

- A summary in a document of a statement made by a witness (section 84(4)).

In deciding whether to treat a statement as admissible under section 84(2), section 84(3) **5.47** provides that the judge must have regard to the following factors:

- the nature and source of the document;

- whether or not, having regard to the nature and source of the document and to any other circumstances that appear to the judge to be relevant, it is likely that the document is authentic;

- the extent to which the statement appears to supply evidence which would not be readily available if the statement were not treated as being admissible;

- the relevance of the evidence that the statement appears to supply to any issue likely to have to be determined by the judge in deciding whether a prima facie case has been established; and

- any risk that the admission or exclusion of the statement will result in unfairness to the person whose extradition is sought, having regard in particular to whether it is likely to be possible to controvert the statement if the person making it does not attend to give oral evidence in the proceedings.

Given that individual witnesses will not be available to give evidence at the extradition hearing, in the majority of extradition cases section 84(2) (statements to police officers) and (4) **5.48** (summary of a statement) provide the basis upon which the District Judge will determine most extradition applications.[38]

---

[36] *India v Rajarathinam and anor* [2007] 1 WLR 1593 (DC) at para 8.
[37] *Brown (aka Vincent Bajinja) and ors v Government of Rwanda and ors* [2009] EWHC 770 (Admin) (DC); see also *R v Governor of Pentonville Prison ex p Alves* [1993] AC 284 per Lord Goff at 292 B–D.
[38] See *India v Rajarathinam and anor* [2007] 1 WLR 1593 (DC) at para 8.

*Conviction cases (section 85)*

**5.49**  If the judge is required by section 79(5) of the 2003 Act to proceed under section 85, then he must decide the following matters:

- Was the person convicted in his presence or did he deliberately absent himself from his trial? If so, the judge must proceed to section 87 (as in accusation cases).
- If not, would the person be entitled to some form of retrial in which he would enjoy certain specified procedural rights? If so, the judge must proceed under section 86, unless the category 2 territory to which extradition is requested has been designated by the Secretary of State,[39] in which case the judge must proceed to section 87. If not, the person must be discharged.

*Conviction in person's absence (section 86)*

**5.50**  If the appropriate judge is required to proceed under section 86(1) he 'must decide whether there is evidence which would be sufficient to make a case to answer by the person if the proceedings were the summary trial of an information'—thus, it is put on the same footing as an accusation case.

**5.51**  The provisions relating to the admissibility of evidence are identical to those contained in section 84.

**5.52**  If the appropriate judge is satisfied that there is a prima facie case, he must proceed under section 87.

*Human rights (section 87)*

**5.53**  This section is identical to section 21 and therefore the same considerations apply. The only difference is that if the judge is satisfied that the person's extradition is compatible with his Convention rights, he must send the case to the Secretary of State for him to decide whether the person is to be extradited.

*Physical or mental condition (section 91)*

**5.54**  This is identical to section 25 of the 2003 Act, and so the same considerations apply.

*Case sent to the Secretary of State (section 92)*

**5.55**  Upon conclusion of the proceedings at the magistrates' court, the appropriate judge must send the case to the Secretary of State, but he must inform the person:

- that he has a right of appeal to the High Court; and
- if he exercises the right, the appeal will not be heard until the Secretary of State has made his decision.

The person is then remanded on bail or in custody.

---

[39] For the Secretary of State's designations, see Appendix 2.

# 6

## BARS TO EXTRADITION

## A. Introduction

There are a number of established grounds, known as bars to extradition, upon which a person can rely in his defence at the extradition hearing. Once a bar to extradition is established the person must be discharged. **6.01**

Although not technically a bar to extradition, the person may also rely on his mental or physical condition to resist extradition if he can establish that it would be unjust or oppressive to extradite him because of it.[1] In practice, arguments relating to a person's mental or physical condition are considered in the same way as the bars to extradition and therefore the law in relation to these arguments is considered at the end of this chapter. **6.02**

### Category 1 cases

Section 11(1) of the Extradition Act 2003 ('the 2003 Act') lists the bars to extradition in category 1 cases as follows:[2] **6.03**

- the rule against double jeopardy;
- extraneous considerations;
- the passage of time;
- the person's age;
- hostage-taking considerations;
- specialty;

---

[1] Extradition Act 2003, s 25 (Part 1); s 91 (Part 2).
[2] These are further expanded upon in ss 12–19A.

- the person's earlier extradition to the United Kingdom from another category 1 territory;
- the person's earlier extradition to the United Kingdom from a non-category 1 territory; and
- the person's earlier transfer to the United Kingdom by the International Criminal Court.

**6.04** If the District Judge decides that the person's extradition is barred by reason of any of the matters set out in section 11 then he must order the person's discharge.

### Category 2 cases

**6.05** In category 2 cases the bars to extradition are split into two groups and afforded consideration at separate stages of the extradition process either by the District Judge at the extradition hearing or by the Secretary of State in deciding whether to order extradition.[3]

**6.06** The bars to extradition considered by the District Judge at the extradition hearing are as follows:[4]

- the rule against double jeopardy;
- extraneous considerations;
- the passage of time; and
- hostage-taking considerations.

**6.07** The bars to extradition considered by the Secretary of State are as follows:[5]

- the death penalty;
- specialty;
- earlier extradition to the United Kingdom from another territory; and
- earlier transfer to the United Kingdom by the International Criminal Court.

**6.08** If the District Judge or the Secretary of State decide that any of the bars to extradition have been established then they must order the person's discharge.

## B. The bars to extradition

### The rule against double jeopardy

**6.09** A person's extradition to a category 1 territory is barred by reason of the rule against double jeopardy if (and only if) it appears that he would be entitled to be discharged under any rule of law relating to previous acquittal or conviction. The court is required to make two assumptions:[6]

(i) that the conduct constituting the extradition offence was an offence in the part of the United Kingdom where the judge exercises jurisdiction; and

(ii) that the person was charged with the extradition offence in that part of the United Kingdom.

---

[3] Sections 93–102 of the 2003 Act, which deal with the Secretary of State's consideration of the case, do not use the language of bars to extradition. However in practice the matters set out in ss 94–96A are treated as bars to extradition in all but name.
[4] Section 79(1). These are set out in detail at ss 80–83.
[5] Section 93(2). These are set out in detail at ss 94–96A.
[6] Section 12.

For Part 2 cases, a person's extradition to a category 2 territory is barred by reason of the rule **6.10** against double jeopardy, if (and only if) it appears that he would be entitled to be discharged under any rule of law relating to previous acquittal or conviction if he were charged with the extradition offence in the United Kingdom.[7] The tests are different because not all extradition offences in category 1 cases are criminal offences in the United Kingdom.

The fundamental principle is that a man cannot be prosecuted twice for the same crime.[8] The **6.11** Divisional Court in *Fofana* held that there are two circumstances in which the principle of double jeopardy is engaged:[9]

- Where a person is charged with an offence which is the same in fact and law as an offence of which he has previously been acquitted or convicted (*autrefois acquit or convict*).
- Where a person is charged with an offence which is founded on 'the same or substantially the same facts' as an offence for which he has been tried and where the court would normally consider it right to stay the prosecution as an abuse of process and/or unless the prosecution can show 'special circumstances' why another trial should take place.

The term 'double jeopardy' therefore includes the plea in bar of *autrefois acquit or convict* and **6.12** the court's inherent jurisdiction to stay proceedings as an abuse of process. This reflects the common law rule on double jeopardy laid down by the House of Lords in *Connelly*.[10] The abuse of process aspect of the definition requires the court to consider not only whether the second prosecution arises out of the same, or substantially the same, facts as the first, but also whether the charge(s) which it is now sought to pursue should have been pursued at the time of the first prosecution.[11]

### Extraneous considerations

A person's extradition is barred by reason of extraneous considerations if either: **6.13**

- the extradition request or Part 1 warrant was issued for the purpose of prosecuting or punishing him for the purpose of any of the statutory factors set out below;[12] or
- if extradited he might be prejudiced at his trial, punished, detained, or restricted in his personal liberty by reason of the statutory factors.[13]

The statutory factors are race, religion, nationality, gender, sexual orientation, or political opinion.

In order to successfully rely upon the bar of extraneous considerations, the person must show **6.14** a causal link between the issue of the European Arrest Warrant (EAW) or extradition request and the detention, prosecution, punishment, or prejudice at trial that he asserts he will suffer by reason of any of the statutory factors.

---

[7] Section 80.

[8] *Bohning v Government of the United States of America* [2007] 1 WLR 362 (DC) at para 21.

[9] *Fofana and anor v Deputy Prosecutor Thubin Tribunal De Grande Instance De Meaux, France* [2006] EWHC 744 (Admin) (DC) at para 18.

[10] *Connelly v Director of Public Prosecutions* [1964] AC 1254 (HL), in particular the nine principles enunciated by Lord Morris of Borth-y-Gest at 1305.

[11] *Maxwell-King v United States of America* [2006] EWHC 3033 (Admin) (DC) at paras 24–25.

[12] Extradition Act 2003, s 13(a) (Part 1) and s 81(a) (Part 2).

[13] Extradition Act 2003, s 13(b) and s 81(b).

**6.15** In the case of *Fernandez*,[14] Lord Diplock stated:

> I do not think that the test … is that the court must be satisfied that it is more likely than not that the fugitive will be detained or restricted if he is returned. A lesser degree of likelihood is, in my view, sufficient; … 'A reasonable chance,' 'substantial grounds for thinking,' 'a serious possibility'—I see no significant difference between these various ways of describing the degree of likelihood of the detention or restriction of the fugitive on his return.[15]

**6.16** It is not sufficient for a person to establish that, if returned, they would be at risk of suffering general prejudice as a result of one of the statutory factors. They must establish a 'reasonable chance' or a 'serious possibility' of their being prejudiced at their trial or punished, detained or restricted in their personal liberty by reason of one of those factors. However, while the relevant question is what may happen to the person in the future if they are extradited, it is relevant to look at what has happened to them in the past.[16]

**6.17** In considering extraneous considerations the court is not bound by the ordinary rules of evidence and the appellant may rely on any material in support of his submissions.[17]

**The passage of time**

**6.18** A person's extradition is barred if it appears that it would be unjust or oppressive to extradite him by reason of the passage of time either since he is alleged to have committed the extradition offence (in an accusation case) or since he has been unlawfully at large (in a conviction case).[18]

*The burden and standard of proof*

**6.19** The burden of proof is on the person to establish on the balance of probabilities that his extradition would be unjust or oppressive by reason of the passage of time. Where the requesting state alleges that he has brought the delay upon himself by deliberately fleeing the jurisdiction, the burden is on the state to prove this beyond reasonable doubt.[19]

*The relevant time period*

**6.20** The relevant period, sometimes referred to as the 'cradle of events', is the period between:

(i) the date of the offence in an accusation case, or the date at which the person became unlawfully at large in a conviction case; and

(ii) the extradition proceedings (including any appeal).[20]

Where the offence is a continuing one, or a series of offences, committed over a period of time, the court must have regard to the total passage of time in which the person is alleged to have committed the offence(s).[21]

---

[14] *Fernandez v The Government of Singapore* [1971] 1 WLR 987.

[15] *Fernandez v The Government of Singapore* [1971] 1 WLR 987 at 993–994, applied in *Hilali v The National Court, Madrid and anor* [2006] EWHC 1239 (Admin) (DC) at para 62.

[16] *Tamarevichute v The Russian Federation* [2008] EWHC 534 (Admin) (DC) at paras 99–100.

[17] *Schtraks v Government of Israel* [1964] AC 556; *Hilali v The National Court, Madrid and anor* [2006] EWHC 1239 (Admin) (DC) at para 63.

[18] Extradition Act 2003, s 14 (Part 1) and s 82 (Part 2).

[19] *Krzyzowski v Circuit Court In Gliwice, Poland* [2007] EWHC 2754 (Admin) (DC) at para 16.

[20] Extradition Act 2003, s 14(b) and s 82(b); *Colda v Romania* [2006] EWHC 1150 (Admin) (DC) at para 30; *Gomes v Trinidad and Tobago* [2009] 1 WLR 1038 (HL) at para 38.

[21] *Maxwell-King v United States of America* [2006] EWHC 3033 (Admin) (DC) at para 38.

*The case-law*

The test in respect of passage of time was formulated by Lord Diplock in the case of *Kakis*[22]   **6.21**
as follows:

> 'Unjust' I regard as directed primarily to the risk of prejudice to the accused in the conduct of
> the trial itself, 'oppressive' as directed to hardship to the accused resulting from changes in his
> circumstances that have occurred during the period to be taken into consideration; but there
> is room for overlapping, and between them they would cover all cases where to return him
> would not be fair. Delay in the commencement or conduct of extradition proceedings which
> is brought about by the accused himself by fleeing the country, concealing his whereabouts or
> evading arrest cannot, in my view, be relied upon as a ground for holding it to be either unjust
> or oppressive to return him … Save in the most exceptional circumstances it would be neither
> unjust nor oppressive that he should be required to accept them.

> As respects delay which is not brought about by the acts of the accused himself, however, the
> question of where responsibility lies for the delay is not generally relevant. What matters is not
> so much the cause of such delay as its effect …[23]

Many early passage of time cases under the 2003 Act were concerned with the question of   **6.22**
when, if ever, delay caused by the requesting state was relevant to oppression or injustice. In
*Gomes*[24] the House of Lords settled the question by holding that delay caused by the requesting state can only ever be relevant in cases in which the accused has not contributed to the
delay. Their Lordships emphasized once more that it was the effect of the delay rather than
its cause that was important.[25]

In *Krzyzowski* the Divisional Court held that the effect of *Kakis* was that a finding that the   **6.23**
person deliberately fled the requesting state will 'operate as an almost automatic bar to reliance on delay'.[26]

In considering whether a person's extradition is barred by reason of the passage of time the   **6.24**
court will have regard to all the circumstances of the case. In *La Torre* the Divisional Court
observed that 'an overall judgment on the merits is required, unshackled by rules with too
sharp edges'.[27]

*Injustice*

In respect of injustice the House of Lords in *Gomes* endorsed the five principles set down by   **6.25**
the Privy Council in *Knowles*:[28]

(i)  The question is not whether it would be unjust or oppressive to try the accused but
     whether it would be unjust or oppressive to extradite him.
(ii) If the court of the requesting state is bound to conclude that a fair trial is impossible
     then it would be unjust or oppressive for the requested state to return him.

---

[22] *Kakis v Government of the Republic of Cyprus* [1978] 1 WLR 779.
[23] *Kakis v Government of the Republic of Cyprus* [1978] 1 WLR 779 at 782–783.
[24] *Gomes v Trinidad and Tobago* [2009] 1 WLR 1038 (HL).
[25] *Gomes v Trinidad and Tobago* [2009] 1 WLR 1038 (HL) at paras 19, 23–24.
[26] *Krzyzowski v Circuit Court In Gliwice, Poland* [2007] EWHC 2754 (Admin) (DC) at para 16; *Gomes v
Trinidad and Tobago* [2009] 1 WLR 1038 (HL) at para 29.
[27] *La Torre v Italy* [2007] EWHC 1370 (Admin) (DC) at para 37.
[28] *Knowles v US Government* [2007] 1 WLR 47 at para 31. See also *Woodcock v The Government of
New Zealand* [2004] 1 WLR 1979.

(iii)  The court of the requested state must have regard to the safeguards which exist under the domestic law of the requesting state to protect the defendant against a trial rendered unjust or oppressive by the passage of time. [29]

(iv)  No rule of thumb can be applied to determine whether the passage of time has rendered a fair trial no longer possible: much will turn on the particular case.

(v)  There can be no cut-off point beyond which extradition must inevitably be regarded as unjust or oppressive.

*Oppression*

**6.26**  In order to rely on oppression by reason of the passage of time the person must establish that he will suffer greater personal or family hardship than that which is inevitably inherent in the act of extradition.[30]

**6.27**  In *Spanovic* the court observed that it was not unusual for a person sought for extradition to have established themselves respectably in a new country and, where the person has not brought about the delay himself, this will be one factor to be weighed against the public interest of honouring extradition treaties.[31]

### The person's age

**6.28**  A person's extradition to a category 1 territory is barred by reason of his age if it would be conclusively presumed because of his age that he could not be guilty of the extradition offence on the assumption that:

- The conduct constituting the extradition offence constituted an offence in the relevant part of the United Kingdom.
- The person carried out the conduct when the extradition offence was committed or alleged to have been committed.
- The person carried out the conduct in the relevant part of the United Kingdom.[32]

**6.29**  In England and Wales it is conclusively presumed that children under the age of 10 years cannot be guilty of a criminal offence.[33]

**6.30**  There is no bar of age in Part 2 cases.

### Hostage-taking considerations

**6.31**  A person's extradition to a category 1 or category 2 territory is barred by reason of hostage-taking considerations if the requesting state is a party to the Hostage-Taking Convention and it appears that: [34]

---

[29]  Category 1 territories and countries with judicial systems similar to our own (such as New Zealand and the United States) should 'readily be assumed capable of protecting an accused against an unjust trial'. Other category 2 territories should also be presumed to capable of ensuring that justice is done unless the person can establish the contrary: *Gomes v Trinidad and Tobago* [2009] 1 WLR 1038 (HL) at paras 35–36.

[30]  *Norris v United States* [2007] 1 WLR 1730 at para 154.

[31]  *Croatia v Spanovic* [2007] EWHC 1770 (Admin) (DC) at para 22.

[32]  Extradition Act 2003, s 15. The relevant part of the United Kingdom is the part of the United Kingdom in which the judge at the extradition hearing exercises jurisdiction.

[33]  Children and Young Person's Act 1933, s 50.

[34]  Extradition Act 2003, s 16 (Part 1) and s 83 (Part 2).

- if extradited he might be prejudiced at his trial because communication between him and the appropriate authorities[35] would not be possible; and

- the act or omission constituting the extradition offence also constitutes an offence under section 1 of the Taking of Hostages Act 1982 or an attempt to commit such an offence.

**6.32** A person relying on this bar to extradition must show that he is accused in the requesting state of conduct amounting to an offence of hostage-taking, or an attempt, and that he might be prejudiced at his trial because it will not be possible for him to exercise his right to consular access in the requesting state.

### Specialty[36]

**6.33** Specialty arrangements between states are designed to ensure that the person is dealt with in the requesting state only for those offences for which he has been extradited. A person's extradition to a category 1 or category 2 territory is barred by reason of specialty if there are no specialty arrangements between the United Kingdom and the requesting judicial authority or state.[37]

**6.34** In Part 1 cases there are specialty arrangements between a category 1 territory and the United Kingdom if under either the law of the territory, or arrangements[38] made between it and the United Kingdom, a person who is extradited to the territory may be dealt with for an offence committed before his extradition only if:[39]

- the offence is the offence in respect of which the person was extradited;
- the offence is an extradition offence disclosed by the same facts as the offence in respect of which the person was extradited;
- the offence is an extradition offence and the appropriate judge has given his consent under section 55 of the 2003 Act for the person to be dealt with in respect of it;
- the offence is not punishable with imprisonment or another form of detention;
- the offence is one in respect of which the person will not be detained in connection with his trial, sentence, or appeal;
- the person has waived his specialty rights;
- the person is given the opportunity to leave the category 1 territory and either does not do so within forty-five days, or he leaves and returns of his own volition.

**6.35** In Part 2 cases the question of specialty is considered by the Secretary of State. The Secretary of State must not order a person's extradition to a category 2 territory if there are no specialty arrangements in place, unless the person has consented to his extradition under section 127 of the 2003 Act.[40]

---

[35] The appropriate authorities are the authorities of the territory which are entitled to exercise rights of protection in relation to him: Extradition Act 2003, s 16(2).
[36] The Extradition Act 2003 uses the terminology 'speciality', however this work will use the traditional expression 'specialty'.
[37] Extradition Act 2003, s 17(10) (Part 1) and s 95 (Part 2).
[38] In considering whether undertakings amount to 'arrangements' for the purpose of the specialty provisions in the 2003 Act, the key question is whether the arrangements satisfy the criteria in the relevant sections (*Welsh and anor v Secretary of State for the Home Department and anor* [2007] 1 WLR 1281 (DC) at para 28).
[39] Extradition Act 2003, s 17, giving effect to Art 27 of the Framework Decision.
[40] Section 95(1) and (2).

**6.36**    There are specialty arrangements in place if under either the law of the category 2 territory or arrangements made between it and the United Kingdom, a person who is extradited to the territory from the United Kingdom may be dealt with for an offence committed before his extradition only in the circumstances specified in section 95(3) of the 2003 Act.

**6.37**    Although they are not set out in identical terms the same considerations apply in relation to the specialty provisions under both Part 1 and Part 2 of the 2003 Act.[41] The question is whether there are practical and effective arrangements in the requesting territory to ensure that the person will only be tried either for the offence for which he has been extradited or other offences disclosed by the same facts.[42]

**6.38**    The Secretary of State, or District Judge in a Part 1 case, must make up his own mind whether on any given scenario of law and fact in the requesting state, the person would on his return be 'dealt with' in conformity with the 2003 Act and may not simply adopt the requesting state's view of the reach of the specialty rule.[43] A person seeking to demonstrate that the requesting state is likely to act in breach of its specialty obligations will need to adduce compelling evidence to this effect.[44]

**6.39**    The rule against specialty applies to the charges that can be brought by the requesting state against a person who has been extradited. It does not limit the evidence which can be admitted to prove the extradition offence which is a matter for the trial judge in the requesting state.[45] The fact that another state takes broader considerations into account when sentencing, including conduct relevant to other offences which are not the subject of the order for extradition, or in respect of which extradition had been refused, does not mean that an extradited defendant would be 'dealt with' other than in accordance with section 95.[46]

**Earlier extradition to the United Kingdom from another territory**

**6.40**    A person's extradition to a category 1 or category 2 territory is barred, in certain circumstances,[47] if the person has earlier been extradited to the United Kingdom from another territory and that territory has not consented to the person's onward extradition.

**6.41**    In respect of onward extradition to category 1 territories, the 2003 Act distinguishes between cases in which a person has previously been extradited from a category 1 territory[48] and cases in which a person has previously been extradited from a category 2 territory.[49] This is because the Framework Decision expressly prohibits onward extradition between category 1 territories

---

[41] *Hilali v The National Court, Madrid and anor* [2006] EWHC 1239 (Admin) (DC) at para 45.
[42] *Hilali v The National Court, Madrid and anor* [2006] EWHC 1239 (Admin) (DC) at para 46.
[43] *Welsh and anor v Secretary of State for the Home Department and anor* [2007] 1 WLR 1281 (DC) at paras 135–139, applied by *Bermingham and ors v Director of the Serious Fraud Office and anor* [2007] QB 727 (DC).
[44] *Hilali v The National Court, Madrid and anor* [2006] EWHC 1239 (Admin) (DC) at para 52.
[45] *Welsh and anor v Secretary of State for the Home Department and anor* [2007] 1 WLR 1281 (DC) at para 89.
[46] *Bermingham and ors v Director of the Serious Fraud Office and anor* [2007] QB 727 (DC) at para 147; *Norris v Government of the United States of America and anor* [2009] EWHC 995 (Admin) (DC) at para 54.
[47] There must be arrangements in place between the United Kingdom and the extraditing territory requiring that territory's consent is required to the person's onward extradition: Extradition Act 2003, ss 18(b), 19(b), 96(b).
[48] Section 18.
[49] Section 19.

without the consent of the state who first surrendered the person.[50] In category 2 cases onward extradition is dealt with under the specialty rules unless the treaty or convention expressly provides for onward extradition.

### Earlier transfer by the International Criminal Court

Section 19A(1) of the 2003 Act[51] provides that a person's extradition to a category 1 territory **6.42** is barred by reason of his earlier transfer by the International Criminal Court if (and only if):

- the person was transferred to the United Kingdom to serve a sentence imposed by the Court;
- under arrangements between the United Kingdom and the Court, the consent of the Presidency of the Court is required to the person's extradition from the United Kingdom to the category 1 territory in respect of the extradition offence under consideration;
- that consent has not been given.

Subsection 19A(1) does not apply if the person has served the sentence imposed by the Court **6.43** and has subsequently either voluntarily remained in the United Kingdom for more than 30 days or has left the United Kingdom and returned to it.

Section 96A contains identical provisions in respect of Part 2 cases. **6.44**

### The death penalty

The Secretary of State must not order a person's extradition to a category 2 territory if he **6.45** could be, will be, or has been sentenced to death for the offence in the category 2 territory.[52]

If the Secretary of State receives a written assurance that he considers to be adequate that a **6.46** sentence of death will not be imposed, or will not be carried out if it is imposed, then extradition can be ordered.[53]

The procedure was explained by the Divisional Court in the case of *Al-Saadoon* as follows: **6.47**

> As is well known, HM Government is a signatory to the relevant protocol ... Protocol 13, to the European Convention which effectively bars capital punishment ... in extradition cases the government will always insist on an undertaking which it regards as binding that the death penalty will not be imposed if someone is to be extradited. That is normally an undertaking by the relevant administrative body concerned with the investigation that they will not seek a death penalty, but the effect is no death penalty.[54]

When considering any assurances provided the court will act on the fundamental assump- **6.48** tion that the requesting state is acting in good faith. The fact that a state has previously honoured assurances and undertakings given in extradition proceedings will be treated by the court as a 'sure guide' that any assurances given in the individual case will be honoured.[55] However, if a state seeks to rely on assurances that are given by a country with a record for

---

[50] Framework Decision on extradition, Art 28(4).
[51] Inserted by the Police and Justice Act 2006, Sch 13(1), para 3(2).
[52] Section 94(1).
[53] Section 94(2).
[54] *R (Al-Saadoon) v Secretary of State for Defence* [2008] EWHC 2391 (Admin) (DC).
[55] *R (Bary) v Secretary of State for the Home Department* [2009] EWHC 2068 (Admin) at para 83.

disregarding fundamental human rights it will need to show that there is good reason to treat the assurances as providing a reliable guarantee that such treatment will not occur in each individual case.[56]

### Other 'bars'

*Forum*

**6.49**   Under previous legislation the question of forum (sometimes referred to as *forum conveniens* or 'exorbitant jurisdiction') was a matter of discretion for the Secretary of State.[57] In the controversial 'NatWest Three' case[58] the court ruled that there was no bar of forum under the 2003 Act but the court could consider the issue when considering whether the person's extradition would be compatible with his human rights under sections 21 and 87 of the 2003 Act.[59]

**6.50**   Following the 'NatWest Three' case the Attorney General published a protocol agreed between the United States and the United Kingdom as to forum[60] and Guidelines to be applied by the United Kingdom prosecuting authorities where there was concurrent jurisdiction.[61]

**6.51**   It was against this background that sections 19B and 83A were inserted into the 2003 Act although they have never been brought into force.[62] They provide in identical terms that a person's extradition to a category 1 or category 2 territory is barred by reason of forum if (and only if) it appears that:

(a) a significant part of the conduct alleged to constitute the extradition offence is conduct in the United Kingdom; and

(b) in view of that and all the other circumstances, it would not be in the interests of justice for the person to be tried for the offence in the requesting territory.

**6.52**   During the debates in the Commons on the passage of the Police and Justice Bill the government made it clear that sections 19B and 83A were subject to so-called sunset clauses which meant that the provisions would never in fact be brought into force.[63] The position therefore remains that the only means by which a requested person can rely on the question of forum to resist extradition is in the context of whether his extradition would be compatible with his human rights.[64]

---

[56]   *RB (Algeria) v Secretary of State for the Home Department* [2009] 2 WLR 512 at para 114.

[57]   *R (Al Fawwaz and ors) v Governor of Brixton Prison and ors* [2002] 2 WLR 101 (HL) at para 147.

[58]   *Bermingham and ors v Director of the Serious Fraud Office and anor* [2007] QB 727 (DC).

[59]   *Boudhiba v Central Examining Court No 5 of the National Court of Justice Madrid Spain* [2006] 3 All ER 574 (DC) at para 43.
    *Bermingham and ors v Director of the Serious Fraud Office and anor* [2007] QB 727 (DC) at para 59.

[60]   *Guidance for handling criminal cases with concurrent jurisdiction between the United Kingdom and the United States of America*, January 2007.

[61]   *Attorney General's Domestic Guidance for handling criminal cases affecting both England, Wales or Northern Ireland and the United States of America*, 18 January 2007.

[62]   Police and Justice Act 2006, Sch 13(1), para 4.

[63]   *Hansard*, col 626, 6 November 2006.

[64]   See for example *Onwuzulike v Government of the United States of America* [2009] EWHC 1395 (Admin) (DC).

Under previous legislation there was a bar of triviality under which the court had a discretion   **6.53**
to discharge the person if, by reason of the triviality of the offence, it would be unjust or
oppressive to extradite him.[65] There is no such bar under the 2003 Act. The only question for
the court is whether the statutory conditions for an extradition offence[66] have been met.[67]

## C. Mental or physical condition

If at any time in the extradition hearing it appears to the judge that the physical or mental   **6.54**
condition of the person is such that it would be unjust or oppressive to extradite him, he
must either order the person's discharge, or adjourn the extradition hearing until it appears
to him that it would no longer be unjust or oppressive to order extradition.[68]

The words 'unjust or oppressive' derive from their earlier statutory use and therefore the   **6.55**
principles set out by Lord Diplock in the case of *Kakis* apply.[69]

There are three key cases on a person's mental or physical condition:   **6.56**

* *R (Warren) v Secretary of State for the Home Department*;[70]
* *Boudhiba v Central Examining Court No 5 of the National Court of Justice, Madrid, Spain*;[71]
  and
* *Government of the United States of America v Tollman*.[72]

If there is no dispute between the parties that the person is unfit to stand trial then it would   **6.57**
be oppressive to extradite him.[73] However, where fitness to stand trial is in issue, the court in
*Warren* held that:

> The starting point, in my view, must be the proposition that it is part of the trial process that
> there should be a determination, where such an issue arises by the court, of the question
> whether a defendant is fit to be tried ... In the context of extradition proceedings, it is for the
> courts of the requesting State to determine those issues ... provided, of course, always that
> there exist proper procedures which are fair to an accused for the determination of such
> issues.[74]

In *Boudhiba* the court held that, when considering whether to discharge a person under sec-   **6.58**
tions 25 or 91, the court should 'keep its eye firmly' on the statutory question. The question
is not whether the person is suffering from a mental or physical illness, but whether by reason
of his mental or physical condition it would be unjust or oppressive to extradite him.[75]

---

[65] Extradition Act 1989, s 11(3)(a).
[66] Extradition Act 2003, ss 64–65 (Part 1) and ss 137–138 (Part 2).
[67] *Sandru v Government of Romania* [2009] EWHC 2879 (Admin) (DC); *Hubner v District Court of Prostejov Czech Republic and anor* [2009] EWHC 2929 (Admin) (DC).
[68] Extradition Act 2003, s 25 (Part 1) and s 91 (Part 2).
[69] *Kakis v The Government of the Republic of Cyprus* [1978] 1 WLR 779 (HL) at 782; *Prancs v Rezekne Court of Latvia* [2006] EWHC 2573 (Admin) (DC) at para 10. See paragraph 6.21.
[70] [2003] EWHC 1177 (Admin) (DC).
[71] [2007] 1 WLR 124 at para 65.
[72] [2008] EWHC 184 (Admin) (DC).
[73] *Davies, Re Application For A Writ Of Habeas Corpus* [1997] EWHC 733 (Admin) (DC).
[74] [2003] EWHC 1177 (Admin) (DC).
[75] *Boudhiba v Central Examining Court No 5 of the National Court of Justice, Madrid, Spain* [2007] 1 WLR 124 (DC) at para 65.

**6.59**   In *Tollman* the way in which the courts of the requesting state would consider the defendant's fitness to plead and health matters was said to be relevant to, but not determinative of, the way in which the United Kingdom courts should judge the issues arising under section 91.[76]

**6.60**   The courts have recognized that in practice 'a high threshold has to be reached' in order to succeed in an argument under section 25.[77] Further, the nature of the offence will be relevant as to whether oppression is made out. The more serious the offence for which the person is sought, the greater the public interest in returning him to stand trial or serve a sentence of imprisonment.[78]

---

[76] [2008] EWHC 184 (Admin) (DC).

[77] *R (Ahsan) v Government of the United States of America and anor* [2008] EWHC 666 (Admin) (DC) at para 108.

[78] *Hutton v Government of Australia* [2009] EWHC 564 (Admin) (DC); *Spanovic v Government of Croatia and anor* [2009] EWHC 723 (Admin) (DC) at para 39.

# 7

## CONVICTIONS IN ABSENCE

## A. Introduction

Generally speaking, extradition requests fall into two categories—'accusation' and 'conviction' requests. There are, however, occasions when a fugitive has been convicted in his absence (*in absentia*) in the requesting state and his return is sought from the United Kingdom. Convictions in absence may arise where the fugitive deliberately puts himself out of the jurisdiction, thereby evading justice. It may also be that the fugitive was wholly unaware of the criminal proceedings against him in the requesting state. **7.01**

The Extradition Act 2003 ('the 2003 Act') has created specific procedural provisions in order to deal with requests in respect of persons convicted in their absence. The procedure is governed by section 20 of the 2003 Act in respect of category 1 territories and sections 85 and 86 of the 2003 Act in respect of category 2 territories. **7.02**

## B. Category 1 territories

Section 20 of the 2003 Act states: **7.03**

(1) If the judge is required to proceed under this section (by virtue of section 11) he must decide whether the person was convicted in his presence.

(2) If the judge decides the question in subsection (1) in the affirmative he must proceed under section 21.

(3) If the judge decides that question in the negative he must decide whether the person deliberately absented himself from his trial.

(4) If the judge decides the question in subsection (3) in the affirmative he must proceed under section 21.

(5) If the judge decides that question in the negative he must decide whether the person would be entitled to a retrial or (on appeal) to a review amounting to a retrial.

(6) If the judge decides the question in subsection (5) in the affirmative he must proceed under section 21.

(7) If the judge decides that question in the negative he must order the person's discharge.

(8) The judge must not decide the question in subsection (5) in the affirmative unless, in any proceedings that it is alleged would constitute a retrial or a review amounting to a retrial, the person would have these rights—

(a) the right to defend himself in person or through legal assistance of his own choosing or, if he had not sufficient means to pay for legal assistance, to be given it free when the interests of justice so required;

(b) the right to examine or have examined witnesses against him and to obtain the attendance and examination of witnesses on his behalf under the same conditions as witnesses against him.

**7.04**    The procedure laid down by section 20 is, therefore, as follows:

- Was the person convicted in his presence? If yes, then proceed directly to section 21 ('Human rights'). If the appropriate judge, ie the District Judge, determines that the person was not convicted in his presence, the next step is section 20(3).

- Section 20(3)—the appropriate judge must decide if the person deliberately absented himself from the trial. If yes, then no further issue arises under section 20 and the appropriate judge will proceed to human rights considerations under section 21. If, however, the appropriate judge decides that the person did not deliberately absent himself, then the next step is section 20(5).

- Section 20(5)—would the person, if returned, be entitled to a retrial or a review tantamount to a retrial? In order to determine that issue, the appropriate judge must also be satisfied that the person would have his rights to a fair trial protected in accordance with section 20(8) of the 2003 Act. It is only after he is so satisfied that he may proceed to the human rights considerations under section 21. Clearly if the judge is not satisfied that the person would be entitled to a retrial or a review tantamount to a retrial, then the person will be discharged.

## C.  Category 2 territories

**7.05**    Under section 85 of the 2003 Act, the appropriate judge will follow identical steps to those under section 20 save for category 2 territories that are required to adduce a prima facie case. In those cases, the appropriate judge will proceed under section 86 of the 2003 Act to decide whether there is 'evidence which would be sufficient to make a case requiring an answer by the person if the proceedings were the summary trial of an information against him'.

**7.06**    Thus, under the 2003 Act the procedures and criteria in 'conviction in absence' cases are strictly laid down—this has had the effect of removing some of the uncertainties that existed under the 1989 Act's procedures in such cases.

## D. Principles

### Deliberate absence from trial

The question posed in sections 20 and 85 of the 2003 Act is whether the person 'deliberately **7.07** absented himself from his *trial*'. It has been held that since the word 'trial' is used rather than a wider phrase such as 'legal process', the 2003 Act contemplated a specific event, not the entire process.[1] Thus in *Bleta,* while the court was satisfied that the person had deliberately absented himself from Albania, there was no evidence that he knew of the existence of a trial or of any proceedings which might lead to a trial. Since the court was unable to conclude, upon examination of the Albanian provisions and the explanations given for them, that Bleta would be entitled to a retrial or review amounting to a retrial in Albania, he was discharged under section 85(7) of the 2003 Act.

When considering the question of whether the person deliberately absented himself from his **7.08** trial, the District Judge must apply the criminal standard of proof.[2]

### Entitlement to a retrial

Where a person had been convicted in their absence and had not deliberately absented **7.09** himself from the trial, the next question is whether he would be entitled to a retrial (sections 20(5) and 85(5) of the 2003 Act). In *Da An Chen*, the appellant, who had been tried and sentenced in Romania in his absence, submitted that it was necessary to look at what Romanian law affords *in practice*, and whether the legal remedy was effective. This submission was rejected. The court held that it should look first and foremost at the law of the requesting state in deciding the question of whether or not the person was entitled to a retrial. The law of Romania was clear: the appellant would in law be entitled to a retrial. His appeal on this ground was, therefore, dismissed.

Where the requesting state is a member of the Council of Europe, and thus a signatory to the **7.10** European Convention on Human Rights (ECHR)—as are all category 1 territories and some category 2 territories (for example, Albania, Croatia, and Russia)—the court construes the evidence that the person would have a right to a retrial in light of the state's obligation to ensure a fair trial under Article 6 of the ECHR.[3] That may be sufficient prima facie evidence of the right to a retrial which the person would then have to call evidence to rebut.

It is important that the court, when construing statutory material from other countries in **7.11** extradition cases, such as that applicable to the question of whether those convicted in their absence in a foreign country would enjoy the right to a retrial, should decide issues on the best material that could be produced. This is consistent with the emphasis given in extradition cases to the importance of international comity and to courts not being overly technical when considering applications by foreign governments.[4]

---

[1] *Bleta v Government of the Republic of Albania (No 2)* [2005] EWHC 475 (Admin), [2005] Extradition LR 47 ('*Bleta*').

[2] *Mitoi v Government of Romania* [2006] EWHC 1977 (Admin), [2006] Extradition LR 168.

[3] *Benko v Law Enforcement Division of Veszprem County Court, Hungary (a Hungarian Judicial Authority)* [2009] EWHC 3530 (Admin).

[4] *Bogdani v Government of the Republic of Albania* [2008] EWHC 2065 (Admin).

**Whether hearing in absence was a 'trial'**

**7.12**  In *Wade*,[5] the person was present at this trial, at which he was acquitted, but absent from his appeal, at which he was convicted. In that case, it was held that the appeal hearing was the 'trial' for the purposes of section 20 of the 2003 Act. As Wade was held not to have deliberately absented from the appeal hearing, and he would not have a retrial upon return, he was discharged under section 20(7) of the 2003 Act.

**7.13**  *Wade* was, however, distinguished in *Atkinson and Binnington v Supreme Court of Cyprus* [2009] EWHC 1579 (Admin), where on similar facts (the persons had been acquitted in their presence, in the Assize Court, and convicted in their absence, by the Supreme Court, and would not have the right to a retrial upon return), the court held that the trial in Cyprus was a continuing process which included both the proceedings before the Assize Court and before the Supreme Court. For the purposes of section 20, it was the whole of that continuing process which had to be considered. Atkinson and Binnington had deliberately absented themselves from part of the trial, namely the proceedings before the Supreme Court. Therefore they were not entitled to be discharged on the basis that they would not have a retrial.

**7.14**  A hearing at which the person's sentence is increased,[6] or at which a suspended or deferred sentence is reactivated,[7] does not constitute a 'trial' for the purposes of sections 20 and 85 of the 2003 Act.

**Accusation case or conviction case**

**7.15**  Convictions in absence where the person has the right to a retrial pose difficulties for the 2003 Act's classification of all extradition requests as either 'accusation' or 'conviction' cases.

**7.16**  Thus in *Caldarelli*,[8] the question arose of whether the European Arrest Warrant (EAW) was rightly characterized as an accusation warrant when the arrestee had been convicted in his absence but proceedings had not been finalized. The House of Lords, applying *Migliorelli*[9] and *La Torre*,[10] dismissed the appeal, holding that the Divisional Court had been correct to conclude that the EAW was an accusation warrant. Caldarelli was not being sought for the purpose of executing a custodial sentence or order, because no enforceable order had yet been made. He was being sought for the purpose of a criminal prosecution. Despite the stage which the process had reached in Italy, where a trial was a continuing process, he could properly be regarded as an accused person in the Italian system and so section 11(5) of the 2003 Act applied to him. Although Caldarelli lacked the safeguards of section 20(5) and (7) of the 2003 Act, despite having been convicted *in absentia* and having no right to a retrial or equivalent, he still had the safeguard of section 21 of the 2003 Act that his extradition would have to be compatible with his Convention rights.

---

[5] *Deputy Public Prosecutor of the Court of Appeal of Montpellier v Wade* [2006] EWHC 1909 (Admin), [2006] Extradition LR 204.
[6] *Virciglio v The Judicial Authority of the Graz High Court, Austria* [2006] EWHC 3197 (Admin), [2006] Extradition LR 238.
[7] *Raimondas Baksys v Ministry of Justice of the Republic of Lithuania* [2007] EWHC 2838 (Admin), [2008] Extradition LR 1.
[8] *Caldarelli v Court of Naples* [2008] UKHL 51, [2008] Extradition LR 300.
[9] *Migliorelli v Government of Italy* [2006] EWHC 243 (Admin), [2006] Extradition LR 7.
[10] *La Torre v HM Advocate* 2006 SCCR 503.

**The increasing willingness of the courts to order the extradition of defendants convicted in their absence**

As Pill LJ observed in *Bleta*,[11] 'in this jurisdiction, the appearance of a criminal defendant at  **7.17** his trial remains a matter of "capital importance" as does the requirement that a defendant be notified of the proceedings against him'. Traditionally, under the 1989 Act and before, this meant that English courts were reluctant to order extradition in cases where the fugitive had been tried in his absence and would not have a right to a retrial upon his return. Under the 2003 Act, however, it appears that the courts are increasingly prepared to order extradition in such cases, by virtue of the trust placed in the legal systems of foreign states, particularly category 1 territories, to provide defendants with retrial rights upon return which are compatible with Article 6 of the ECHR, or where they have found that the fugitive deliberately absented himself from his trial (or some part of it, as in *Atkinson and Binnington*). Consequently a criminal defendant who evades any part of his trial does so at his peril, even (indeed especially) when he has been acquitted at trial in his presence.

---

[11] [2005] EWHC 475 (Admin) at para 47.

# 8

## THE DECISION OF THE SECRETARY OF STATE

### A. Introduction

Traditionally the Secretary of State played a prominent role in extradition proceedings. One **8.01** of the major changes under Part 1 of the Extradition Act 2003 ('the 2003 Act') was the 'judicialization' of extradition between European Arrest Warrant (EAW) countries through the creation of a system of surrender between judicial authorities. This means that the Secretary of State now plays no part in extradition to category 1 territories.

Under Part 2 of the 2003 Act the Secretary of State is involved at the beginning of the **8.02** extradition process by certifying that the request is valid, and at the end by making the order for extradition.

### B. Certification

Under section 70(1) of the 2003 Act the Secretary of State must issue a certificate if he **8.03** receives a valid request for the extradition of a person to a category 2 territory unless one of the conditions in section 70(2) applies.

Section 70(3), (4), and (4A) of the 2003 Act provides that a request for extradition is valid if **8.04** the following requirements are satisfied:

- It contains a statement that the person is accused in the category 2 territory of the commission of an offence specified in the request (in an accusation case); or a statement that the person has been convicted of an offence specified in the request by a court in the category 2 territory (in a conviction case).

- It is made in the approved way.

**8.05**   In general, a request is made in the approved way if it is made by an authority of the territory that the Secretary of State believes has the function of making requests for extradition in that territory, or by a person recognized by the Secretary of State as a diplomatic or consular representative of the territory.[1]

**8.06**   In deciding whether the request contains the statements in section 70(4) and (4A) the Secretary of State is entitled to look at the request as a whole to see whether the statements can be inferred.[2]

**8.07**   The conditions in section 70(2) under which the Secretary of State may refuse to issue a certificate are as follows:

- he has power under section 126 to order that proceedings on the request be deferred;[3]
- the person whose extradition is requested has been recorded by the Secretary of State as a refugee within the meaning of the Refugee Convention, or
- the person whose extradition is requested has been granted leave to enter or remain in the United Kingdom on the grounds that it would be a breach of Articles 2 or 3 of the European Convention on Human Rights to remove him to the territory to which extradition is requested.

**8.08**   There is no statutory appeal against the decision of the Secretary of State to issue a certificate under section 70(1) of the 2003 Act. The correct means of challenge is by an application for judicial review.[4]

## C.  Order for extradition

**8.09**   If the District Judge decides at the extradition hearing of a Part 2 request to send the case to the Secretary of State, the Secretary of State must then decide whether to order the person's extradition.

**8.10**   Under section 93 of the 2003 Act the Secretary of State must first decide whether he is prohibited from ordering the person's extradition under any of the following sections:

- Section 94 (death penalty);
- Section 95 (speciality);
- Section 96 (earlier extradition to the United Kingdom from another territory); or
- Section 96A (earlier transfer to the United Kingdom by the International Criminal Court).

---

[1] Extradition Act 2003, s 70(7). Special provision is made in the 2003 Act for British overseas territories (s 70(5)) and the Hong Kong Special Administrative Region of the People's Republic of China (s 70(6)).
[2] *R (Bleta) (on the application of) v Secretary of State for the Home Department* [2005] 1 WLR 3194 (DC) at paras 13–14.
[3] Section 126 applies to competing extradition requests.
[4] *Akaroglu v Government of Romania and anor* [2008] 1 All ER 27 (DC) at paras 36–38.

If the Secretary of State decides that he is prohibited from ordering the person's extradition  **8.11**
under sections 94 to 96A then he must order the person's discharge.[5] In all other cases he
must order the person's extradition, unless:[6]

- he is informed that the request has been withdrawn;
- he makes an order for the proceedings to be deferred; or
- he orders the person's discharge under section 208 on the basis that extradition would not
  be in the interests of national security.

The person has four weeks from the date on which the District Judge sends the case to the  **8.12**
Secretary of State to make representations. The Secretary of State is not obliged to consider
any representations received after that date.[7] The Secretary of State must make his decision
within two months of the case being sent to him or the person is entitled to be discharged.[8]

Where a person faces criminal charges in the United Kingdom the Secretary of State must  **8.13**
not make a decision to order extradition until the domestic proceedings are at an end.[9] In
cases in which the person is serving a sentence of imprisonment in the United Kingdom, the
Secretary of State may defer ordering extradition until the sentence has been served.[10]

In Part 2 requests,[11] it is for the Secretary of State to decide on competing requests,[12] consent  **8.14**
to other offences being dealt with,[13] and re-extradition to a category 1 or 2 territory.[14]

### Other issues for consideration by the Secretary of State

The Secretary of State has the power under section 208(6) of the 2003 Act to issue a certifi-  **8.15**
cate directing that the request is not to be proceeded with provided the following conditions
under subsections (2) to (4) are satisfied:

(i)  the person's extradition is sought or will be sought;
(ii)  either that:
    a.  in engaging in the conduct alleged the person was acting for the purpose of assisting
       in the exercise of a function conferred by or imposed under an enactment; or
    b.  following an authorisation given by the Secretary of State the person is not liable
       under the criminal law of the UK;
(iii)  the person's extradition would be against the interests of national security.

---

[5] Extradition Act 2003, s 93(3).
[6] Extradition Act 2003, s 93(4).
[7] Extradition Act 2003, ss 93(5) and (6) and 102(7).
[8] Extradition Act 2003, s 99.
[9] Extradition Act 2003, s 97(2).
[10] Extradition Act 2003, s 97(3).
[11] By contrast to Part 1 under which these matters are decided by the District Judge.
[12] Extradition Act 2003, ss 126 and 179.
[13] Extradition Act 2003, s 129.
[14] Extradition Act 2003, ss 130 and 131.

## D. Post-appeal consideration of human rights

**8.16** The 2003 Act keeps a strict separation between the decisions of the District Judge and those of the Secretary of State. As the question of the compatibility of a person's extradition with his Convention rights is considered by the District Judge, the Secretary of State is not required, and indeed is not permitted, to reconsider those arguments when deciding whether to order extradition.[15]

**8.17** However, the Secretary of State is a public authority bound by section 6 of the Human Rights Act 1998. This means that if, exceptionally, there is a material change of circumstance (such as a supervening illness affecting the subject's ability to travel or face trial) after the person has exhausted their rights of appeal in respect of an order for extradition, that person may make representations to the Secretary of State to reconsider extradition on human rights grounds. An adverse decision by the Secretary of State in response to those representations may be challenged by means of judicial review.[16]

---

[15] *McKinnon v United States of America and ors* [2007] Extradition LR 117 (DC).

[16] *McKinnon v United States of America and ors* [2007] Extradition LR 117 (DC) at paras 61–63; *Nisbet v Secretary of State and ors* [2007] Extradition LR 198 (DC) at paras 4–5; *Taylor v HMP Wandsworth and ors* [2009] EWHC 1020 (Admin) (DC) at para 12.

# 9

# APPEALS, JUDICIAL REVIEW, AND HABEAS CORPUS

## A. Introduction

The Extradition Act 2003 ('the 2003 Act') provides for a streamlined statutory appeal process intended to remove the potential for multiple challenges, and the consequential delay, that had been inherent in the previous system.   **9.01**

The 2003 Act provides that a decision of the District Judge or the Secretary of State may only be challenged by means of an appeal under that Act.[1] However, the courts have held on a number of occasions that, in certain situations discussed below, decisions by the District Judge and Secretary of State may be challenged outside of the statutory appeal process by application for judicial review or habeas corpus.[2]   **9.02**

## B. Appeals under Part 1 of the 2003 Act (category 1 territories: European Arrest Warrant)

### Appeal to the High Court

*Procedural requirements*

Notice of appeal must be filed and served within seven days, starting with the day on which the order for extradition is made ('the permitted period').[3] The High Court has no power to extend the statutory time limit.[4]   **9.03**

---

[1] Extradition Act 2003, ss 34 and 116.
[2] See 9.33–9.36 below.
[3] Extradition Act 2003, ss 26(4) and 28(5).
[4] *Vilnius City, The District Court of v Barcys* [2007] 1 WLR 3249 (DC); *R (on the application of Mendy) v Crown Prosecution Service* [2007] EWHC 1765; *Mucelli v Government of Albania* [2009] 1 WLR 276 (HL).

**9.04**  The deeming provisions in the Civil Procedure Rules (CPR), rule 6.7 do not apply to appeals under the 2003 Act. Where the recipient's office is closed during the whole of the last day of the period for service, the notice will be validly filed or served if it is given at any time during the first succeeding day on which the office is open (ie the next business day).[5] The court has power under the CPR to approve an irregularity in the manner of service or filing so long as it is within the seven-day period.[6]

**9.05**  The High Court must commence the appeal hearing within forty days ('the relevant period') starting from the date on which the person was arrested on the European Arrest Warrant (EAW).[7] The High Court may extend the relevant period in the interests of justice.

**9.06**  If the High Court does not commence the appeal hearing before the end of the relevant period, then in accordance with section 31(6) of the 2003 Act, the appeal will be deemed to have been determined in favour of the person. However section 31(5) of the 2003 Act allows the High Court to extend the relevant period even after it has expired, so in practice a person is unlikely to be discharged unless he can show prejudice.[8]

*The appeal*

**9.07**  A person may appeal against an order for his extradition on a question of fact or law.[9] However, no appeal can lie if the person has consented to his return under sections 46 or 48 of the 2003 Act.

**9.08**  The 2003 Act sets out the conditions for a successful appeal in section 27(3) and (4). Section 27(3) sets out two conditions which must be met:

- the appropriate judge ought to have decided a question differently; and
- had he decided the question differently he would have been required to discharge the person.

**9.09**  Section 27(4) sets out three conditions which must be met:

- an issue is raised at the High Court that was not raised at the extradition hearing, or evidence is available that was not available at the extradition hearing;
- the issue or evidence would have led to the appropriate judge deciding a question before him differently; and
- it would have led to the person's discharge.

**9.10**  Section 28 allows the issuing authority (ie the category 1 territory) to lodge an appeal on a question of fact or law where a person has been discharged. Once the order for discharge is made, the legal representative for the category 1 territory must inform the court immediately of their intention to appeal.[10] No right of appeal exists if a warrant is withdrawn.

---

[5]  *Mucelli v Government of Albania* [2009] 1 WLR 276 (HL) at paras 80–84.
[6]  *Sciezka v The Court In Sad Okregowy, Kielce, Poland* [2009] EWHC 2259 (Admin) (DC) at para 23.
[7]  Extradition Act 2003, s 31(1) and (2); Practice Direction Supplementing CPR Pt 52 (Appeals), para 22.6A(3)(c).
[8]  See, eg, *Moulai v Deputy Public Prosecutor of Creteil, France* [2009] EWHC 1030 (Admin) (DC).
[9]  Extradition Act 2003, s 26.
[10]  Extradition Act 2003, s 30.

The conditions for allowing an appeal are identical to those set out in section 27 of the 2003 **9.11**
Act. At the conclusion of a successful appeal, the High Court must:

- quash the discharge order;
- remit the case; and
- direct the appropriate judge to proceed as he would have been required to do if he had decided the relevant question differently at the extradition hearing.

In *Fenyvesi* the Divisional Court defined 'evidence which was not available at the extradition **9.12**
hearing' as follows:

> Evidence which either did not exist at the time of the extradition hearing, or which was not at the disposal of the party wishing to adduce it and which he could not with reasonable diligence have obtained.[11]

However, where new evidence may establish that the person's Convention rights would be **9.13**
engaged if he were to be returned, then the court may admit fresh evidence notwithstanding
that the strict requirements of the 2003 Act have not been met.[12] The High Court will only
admit evidence that would require a full hearing in 'quite exceptional' circumstances.[13]

In practice the High Court is extremely wary of new points taken for the first time on appeal **9.14**
and will very rarely go behind a District Judge's finding of fact, especially where he or she has
heard evidence.[14]

### Appeal to the Supreme Court

Either party may appeal to the Supreme Court. An application for leave to appeal must be **9.15**
made to the High Court within fourteen days of the decision being appealed,[15] or to the
Supreme Court within fourteen days of the High Court refusing leave to appeal (the 'permitted period').[16]

Leave to appeal may only be granted if:[17] **9.16**

- the High Court has certified there is a point of law of general public importance; and
- it appears to the court granting leave that the point is one that ought to be considered by the Supreme Court.

Where leave is granted, the appeal must be brought within twenty-eight days starting with **9.17**
the day on which leave is granted (the 'permitted period').[18]

---

[11] *Szombathely City Court and ors v Fenyvesi and anor* [2009] 4 All ER 324 (DC) at para 32; *Kalniets v District Court of Ogre in Latvia* [2009] EWHC 534.
[12] *Szombathely City Court and ors v Fenyvesi and anor* [2009] 4 All ER 324 (DC) at para 34.
[13] *Szombathely City Court and ors v Fenyvesi and anor* [2009] 4 All ER 324 (DC) at para 33.
[14] *Wiejak v Olsztyn Circuit Court of Poland* [2007] EWHC 2123 (Admin) (DC) at para 23; *Pilecki v Circuit Court of Legnica, Poland* [2007] EWHC 2080 (Admin) (DC).
[15] Extradition Act 2003, s 32(5).
[16] Extradition Act 2003, s 32(6).
[17] Extradition Act 2003, s 32(3) and (4).
[18] Extradition Act 2003, s 32(7).

**9.18**   Section 33 sets out the powers of the Supreme Court on appeal:

- Allow the appeal or dismiss the appeal.
- Order the person's discharge and quash the order for extradition (successful appeal by the person).[19]
- Quash the order for discharge and order the person's extradition (successful appeal by the issuing judicial authority against order for discharge made by the High Court under section 26).[20]
- Quash the order for discharge and either (i) order the person's extradition, or (ii) remit the case to the District Judge (successful appeal by the issuing judicial authority against refusal of appeal against discharge under section 28).[21]

**Surrender**

**9.19**   The person is deemed to be extraditable at the conclusion of the judicial proceedings and must be surrendered within the required period. This is further broken down into two parts:

- instances where the person does not appeal (section 35); and
- cases in which an appeal is lodged (section 36).

**9.20**   Where a person does not lodge an appeal following the making of an extradition order, he must be extradited to the category 1 territory within ten days starting from the date of the order unless the judge and the issuing authority agree a later date, in which case it is ten days starting from the date agreed (the 'required period').[22]

**9.21**   If a person has not been extradited by the end of the required period, he may apply to the appropriate judge to be discharged and the judge must order his discharge unless reasonable cause is shown for the delay.

**9.22**   The same time period applies where a person lodges an appeal, in which case the ten days commence from the date that the decision of the relevant court becomes final.[23]

**9.23**   Section 39 provides that no extradition may take place where the person lodges an asylum claim, until the outcome of that application. A person may claim asylum at any time from the commencement of the proceedings up until the final stage. It will only be upon the conclusion of the asylum application that the person may be extradited to the category 1 territory. However, if the person is granted refugee status this constitutes a valid objection to their extradition.[24]

---

[19]   Extradition Act 2003, s 33(2), (3).
[20]   Extradition Act 2003, s 33(4), (5).
[21]   Extradition Act 2003, s 32(6), (7), (8).
[22]   Extradition Act 2003, s 35.
[23]   Extradition Act 2003, s 36(3). As to when the required period begins to run when the High Court refuses to certify a question, see *In re Owens* [2010] 1 WLR 17 (DC).
[24]   *The District Court in Ostroleka, Second Criminal Division (A Polish Judicial Authority) v Dytlow and anor* [2009] EWHC 1009 (Admin) (DC) at paras 28–31.

## C.  Appeals under Part 2 of the 2003 Act (category 2 territories)

### Appeal to the High Court

**9.24** Under Part 2 of the 2003 Act both the decision of the District Judge at the extradition hearing and the decision of the Secretary of State can be appealed to the High Court.[25] The appeal procedure and the relevant criteria for category 2 territories are set out in sections 103 to 116 of the 2003 Act and are identical to those under Part 1, except as set out below.

*Procedural requirements*

**9.25** At the end of the extradition hearing the District Judge must inform the person of his right to appeal to the High Court and that any appeal will not be heard until the Secretary of State has decided whether or not he is to be extradited.[26]

**9.26** Under section 100(1)(a) of the 2003 Act, the Secretary of State must notify the person of his decision to order extradition and at the same time inform him of his right of appeal to the High Court.[27] The duty under section 100 on the Secretary of State to inform the person that an order for his extradition has been made may be discharged by writing to the person's solicitor.[28]

**9.27** Notice of appeal must be filed and served within fourteen days starting with the day on which the Secretary of State informs the person that his extradition has been ordered, or the person is discharged.[29]

**9.28** Appeals under Part 2 of the 2003 Act must be heard within seventy-six days of the Appellant's Notice being filed or, for appeals under section 103, the date on which the Secretary of State informs the person of his decision if this is later (the 'relevant period').[30] In both cases the High Court has the power to extend the relevant period, even after it has expired, if it believes it to be in the interests of justice to do so.[31]

*The appeal*

**9.29** The powers of the High Court on an appeal under Part 2 of the 2003 Act are the same as those under Part 1 except that, in an appeal by the person under section 103, the High Court has an additional power to direct the judge to decide again a question (or questions) which he decided at the extradition hearing (section 104(1)(b)).

**9.30** The conditions for allowing an appeal are the same as under Part 1 of the 2003 Act.[32]

---

[25] Extradition Act 2003, ss 103–106 (appeal against District Judge); ss 108–111 (appeal against decision of the Secretary of State).

[26] Extradition Act 2003, s 92(2).

[27] Extradition Act 2003, ss 92(2)(b) and 103(5).

[28] *Mucelli v Government of Albania* [2008] 1 WLR 2437 (DC) at para 57.

[29] Extradition Act 2003, s 103(9).

[30] PD 52, para 22.6A(9).

[31] Extradition Act 2003, ss 31(4) and 113(3); PD 52, para 22.6A(4) and (11); *Moulai v Deputy Public Prosecutor of Creteil, France* [2009] EWHC 1030 (Admin) (DC) at para 14.

[32] Extradition Act 2003, ss 104(3), (4), 106(4), (5).

**9.31** Where a question is remitted to the District Judge under section 104(1)(b) he must confine himself to consideration of the remitted question(s) rather than treating the proceedings as a resumed extradition hearing.[33] If he comes to the same decision again the decision is not amenable to further appeal or review by the High Court unless an appeal lies to the Supreme Court.[34]

**9.32** The 'required period' for extradition to a category 2 territory is twenty-eight days starting from the date of the relevant decision, and failure to surrender within that time frame will lead to the discharge of the person unless reasonable cause is shown for the delay.[35]

## D. Habeas corpus and judicial review

**9.33** Sections 34 and 116 of the 2003 Act provide that the decisions of the District Judge in the extradition hearing, and in Part 2 cases the decisions of the Secretary of State in ordering extradition, may only be challenged by means of an appeal under that Act. Therefore the remedies of habeas corpus and judicial review are not available for decisions in respect of which there is a statutory right of appeal.[36] The validity of the extradition request or EAW may be challenged at the extradition hearing or on appeal because it founds the jurisdiction of the court.[37]

**9.34** A decision against which there is no appeal under the 2003 Act may be challenged by an application for habeas corpus or judicial review,[38] for example:

- a decision by the Serious Organised Crime Agency to certify an EAW;[39]
- a decision of the District Judge at the initial hearing;[40]
- a decision of the District Judge on a remitted question under section 104;[41]
- a decision of the District Judge to consent to a person being dealt with by the requesting state for other offences where the person has a valid human rights objection.[42]

---

[33] *Chen v Government of Romania* [2009] 1 WLR 257 (DC) at para 53.

[34] Extradition Act 2003, s 104(7); *Okandeji v Bow Street Magistrates Court and ors* [2006] 1 WLR 674 (DC); *Chen v Government of Romania* [2009] 1 WLR 257 (DC) at para 20.

[35] This provision is identical to that applicable to category 1 territories except for the time period of twenty-eight days.

[36] *Chen v Government of Romania* [2009] 1 WLR 257 (DC) at para 19.

[37] *Boudhiba v Central Examining Court No 5 of the National Court of Justice Madrid Spain* [2007] 1 WLR 124 (DC), para 15.

[38] *Nikonovs v HM Prison Brixton and anor* [2006] 1 WLR 1518 (DC) at para 18. *In re Owens* [2010] 1 WLR 17 (DC) at paras 12–13 and *Gronostajski v Government of Poland* [2007] EWHC 3314 (Admin) at para 8, suggests that judicial review will usually be the most appropriate remedy.

[39] *Boudhiba v Central Examining Court No 5 of the National Court of Justice Madrid Spain* [2007] 1 WLR 124 (DC) at para 15.

[40] *Nikonovs v HM Prison Brixton and anor* [2006] 1 WLR 1518 (DC); *Hilali v Governor of HMP Whitemoor and anor* [2007] 3 WLR 621 (DC) at para 28.

[41] *Chen v Government of Romania* [2009] 1 WLR 257 (DC) at para 61.

[42] Sections 54–58 and 129–131 of the Extradition Act 2003 deal with post-extradition consent to deal with the person for other matters or for his onward extradition. *Chyba v District Court in Strakonice* [2008] EWHC 3292 (Admin) at para 10.

Exceptionally, a change of circumstance may occur after the person's extradition has been **9.35**
ordered and the appeal process has been exhausted so as to render his extradition inconsistent
with his human rights. The courts have considered this issue in three key cases:

- *Hilali*;[43]
- *Ignaoua and others*;[44] and
- *Taylor*.[45]

In *Hilali* the court held that in principle an application for habeas corpus would be available **9.36**
in such a scenario.[46] However, in *Ignaoua* the court held that the better course of action in
Part 1 cases would be to apply to reopen the decision of the court under CPR, rule 52.17.[47]
In *Taylor* the court indicated that in Part 2 cases the appellant should make further representations to the Secretary of State and challenge any refusal by way of judicial review.[48]

---

[43] *Hilali v Governor of HMP Whitemoor and anor* [2007] 3 WLR 621 (DC); *R (Hilali) v Governor of
Whitemoor Prison and anor* [2008] 1 AC 805 (HL).
[44] *Ignaoua and ors v The Judicial Authority of the Courts of Milan and ors* [2008] EWHC 2619 (Admin) at
paras 22–24.
[45] *Taylor v HMP Wandsworth and ors* [2009] EWHC 1020 (Admin) (DC).
[46] *Hilali v Governor of Whitemoor Prison* [2008] 1 AC 805 (HL).
[47] *Ignaoua and ors v The Judicial Authority of the Courts of Milan and ors* [2008] EWHC 2619 (Admin) at
paras 22–24.
[48] *Taylor v HMP Wandsworth and ors* [2009] EWHC 1020 (Admin) (DC) at para 34.

# 10

## EXTRADITION AND HUMAN RIGHTS

## A. Introduction

While international human rights law does not recognize a 'right not to be extradited',[1] it has **10.01** long been recognized that human rights law applies to extradition generally.

Article 5 of the European Convention on Human Rights (ECHR) specifically recognizes **10.02** extradition as one of the justifications for depriving a person of their liberty:

> (1) Everyone has the right to liberty and security of the person. No-one shall be deprived of his liberty save in the following cases and in accordance with a procedure prescribed by law:
>
> ...
>
> (f) the lawful arrest or detention of a person to prevent his effecting an unauthorised entry into the country or of a person against whom action is being taken with a view to deportation *or extradition*.[2]

The European Court of Human Rights (ECtHR) has also recognized that extraditing a **10.03** person to a state where their human rights will or may be violated constitutes a breach by the requested state of its human rights obligations.[3] 'Disguised extradition', that is, ostensibly deporting a person with a view to effecting their extradition, has also been found by the ECtHR to violate the deportee's human rights.[4] Thus extradition inevitably involves a host of human rights issues, most commonly in relation to Articles 2, 3, 5, 6, and 8 of the ECHR.

---

[1] *EGM v Luxembourg* (1994) DR 144: 'Extradition is not, as such, among the matters covered by the Convention (ECHR). Similarly, the rights and freedoms recognised in the Convention and its Protocols do not include any right not to be extradited.'

[2] Emphasis added.

[3] *Soering v United Kingdom* (1989) 11 EHRR 439.

[4] *Bozano v Italy* (1987) 9 EHRR 428.

## B. Historical development

**10.04**    Even before the entry into force of the Human Rights Act 1998 (HRA 1998), on 2 October 2000, the United Kingdom had an obligation to ensure that a person's extradition from the United Kingdom did not violate their human rights, and to ensure that the extradition proceedings themselves were compatible with the ECHR, simply by virtue of the United Kingdom being a signatory to the ECHR. It was not, however, for the court of committal to consider whether extradition would breach the ECHR. The issue arose only once the Secretary of State took the decision to order extradition.[5]

**10.05**    With the entry into force of the HRA 1998, however, it became 'unlawful for a public authority to act in a way which is incompatible with a Convention right'.[6] Thus the courts and the Secretary of State, in deciding upon an extradition request from another state, have to act compatibly with the requested person's human rights under the ECHR, unless unable to do so by virtue of primary legislation.[7]

**10.06**    With the entry into force of the Extradition Act 2003 ('the 2003 Act') on 1 January 2004, the requirement that a person's extradition be compatible with their human rights has been placed on an explicit statutory footing for the first time. The preceding extradition acts—the Extradition Act 1870 and the Extradition Act 1989 (which repealed the 1870 Act)—did not specifically mention human rights, although provisions in those acts barring extradition where it was unjust or oppressive to do so[8] provided similar protection to the person whose extradition was sought.

**10.07**    The 2003 Act for the first time explicitly sets out that a person may not be extradited if their extradition is incompatible with their human rights.[9]

## C. Human rights under the 2003 Act

**10.08**    There is express provision in both Part 1 and Part 2 of the 2003 Act for deciding whether or not the person's extradition is compatible with their human rights (defined in terms of their 'Convention rights within the meaning of the Human Rights Act 1998').

**10.09**    Section 21 of the 2003 Act, applicable to Part 1 territories, provides as follows:

21. Human rights

   (1) If the judge is required to proceed under this section (by virtue of section 11 or 20) he must decide whether the person's extradition would be compatible with the Convention rights within the meaning of the Human Rights Act 1998.
   (2) If the judge decides the question in subsection (1) in the negative he must order the person's discharge.
   (3) If the judge decides that question in the affirmative he must order the person to be extradited to the category 1 territory in which the warrant was issued.

---

[5] *R (St John) v Governor of Brixton Prison* [2002] QB 613 at 624.
[6] HRA 1998, s 6(1).
[7] HRA 1998, s 6(2).
[8] See, for example, s 11(3) of the Extradition Act 1989.
[9] Extradition Act 2003, ss 21 and 87.

Section 87 of the 2003 Act, applicable to Part 2 territories is, in substance, in the same **10.10** terms.

With respect to both category 1 and category 2 territories, therefore, the core human rights **10.11** issue is the same: persons may not be extradited if their extradition would be incompatible with their Convention rights, which are defined by reference to the HRA 1998. If their extradition is incompatible with their human rights, they must be discharged, ie the extradition proceedings will be at an end and they will be released.

Typically, however, the consideration of a claimed human rights bar to extradition may differ **10.12** where the territory in question is a category 1 territory. The premise of the European Arrest Warrant (EAW) scheme is mutual trust for other EU states. It follows that courts in the United Kingdom may be less willing to find a prospective human rights breach in a Part 1 territory, which is by definition a partner to the EAW scheme and a signatory to the ECHR, than in a state which is not.

Thus the Administrative Court stated in *Hilali*, at paragraph 77: **10.13**

> It seems to us that the courts should give great weight to the fact that Spain is a western democracy, subject to the rule of law, a signatory of the European Convention of Human Rights and a party to the Framework Decision; it is a country which has and which applies the same human rights standards and is subject to the same international obligations as the UK. These surely are highly relevant matters which strongly militate against refusing extradition on the grounds of the risk of violating those standards and obligations.[10]

As Keene LJ noted in *Lisowski*,[11] at paragraph 26, there would be no need for section 21 of **10.14** the 2003 Act if it were automatically assumed that signatories to the ECHR would never breach a person's human rights:

> in my judgment, one needs to be careful about how far the issue of injustice in a European Arrest Warrant case can be determined merely by the fact that the requesting state is a signatory to the European Convention on Human Rights. Section 14 of the 2003 Act imposes a duty upon this court to make its own decision as to whether it would be unjust or oppressive to extradite someone by reason of the passage of time. The fact that the requesting state is a signatory to the ECHR is a relevant factor but I do not myself see it as being determinative of this issue in the absence of other evidence about the legal processes in that state. After all, states do not always comply with their Convention obligations in every case. It is a matter of record that many signatory states have been found to have breached Art 6 of that convention from time to time.[12]

The House of Lords, however, has recently both re-emphasised the assumptions made in **10.15** favour of Council of Europe countries and disapproved the *Lisowski* judgment to the extent that it suggests the contrary. In *Gomes and Goodyer*,[13] their Lordships stated, at paragraphs 35 to 36:

> 35 ... Council of Europe countries ... present no problem. *All are subject to Article 6 of the Convention and should readily be assumed capable of protecting an accused against an unjust*

---

[10] *Hilali v Central Court of Criminal Proceedings Number 5 of the National Court, Madrid, and Senior District Judge, Bow Street Magistrates' Court* [2006] EWHC 1239 (Admin), [2006] Extradition LR 154.

[11] *Lisowski v Regional Court of Bialystok, Poland* [2006] EWHC 3227 (Admin), [2006] Extradition LR 272.

[12] See also *Hilali* at para 74.

[13] *Gomes and Goodyer v Government of Trinidad and Tobago* [2009] UKHL 21, [2009] 1 WLR 1038.

*trial*—whether by an abuse of process jurisdiction like ours or in some other way. Insofar as Keene LJ's judgment in *Lisowski v Regional Court of Bialystok (Poland)* [2006] EWHC 3227 (Admin) suggests the contrary, it should not be followed …

36 … The extradition process, it must be remembered, is only available for returning suspects to friendly foreign states with whom this country has entered into multi-lateral or bilateral treaty obligations involving mutually agreed and reciprocal commitments. The arrangements are founded on mutual trust and respect. There is a strong public interest in respecting such treaty obligations. As has repeatedly been stated, international co-operation in this field is ever more important to bring to justice those accused of serious cross-border crimes and to ensure that fugitives cannot find safe havens abroad.[14]

**10.16**    The position nonetheless remains that even with regard to category 1 territories, it may be, and is indeed routinely argued, that extradition is incompatible with the person's human rights, and that discharge must therefore be ordered pursuant to section 21(2) of the Act. The most common arguments concern the right to family life under Article 8 (for example, where extradition involves separation from close family members) or Article 3 where the threat to the person emanates from non-state actors (for example, threats from 'mafia figures' or fellow prisoners in the foreign state). It has to be acknowledged, however, that the 'success rate' for such arguments in category 1 cases is extremely low.

## D. Specific human rights

**10.17**    The responsibility of an extraditing state for extraditing a person to a state where there is a risk that his human rights would be violated generally arose, following *Soering,* with respect to potential breaches of Article 3 of the ECHR. However, as the House of Lords made clear in *Ullah*,[15] the issue could arise with respect to other Convention rights:

24. While the Strasbourg jurisprudence does not preclude reliance on articles other than Art 3 as a ground for resisting extradition or expulsion, it makes it quite clear that *successful reliance demands presentation of a very strong case.* In relation to Art 3 it is necessary to show strong grounds for believing that the person, if returned, faces a real risk of being subjected to torture or to inhuman or degrading treatment or punishment … In *Dehwari*, para 61 … the Commission doubted whether a real risk was enough to resist removal under Art 2, suggesting the loss of life must be shown to be a 'near-certainty'. Where reliance is placed on Art 6 it must be shown that a person has suffered or risks suffering a flagrant denial of a fair trial in the receiving state … Successful reliance on Art 5 would have to meet no less exacting a test. *The lack of success of applicants relying on Arts 2, 5 and 6 before the Strasbourg court highlights the difficulty of meeting the stringent test which the court imposes.* This difficulty will not be less where reliance is placed on articles such as 8 or 9, which provide for the striking of a balance between the right of the individual and the wider interests of the community even in a case where a serious interference is shown.[16]

---

[14]  Emphasis added. To similar effect, see also *Benko v Law Enforcement Division of Veszprem County Court, Hungary (a Hungarian Judicial Authority)* [2009] EWHC 3530 (Admin) at paras 17 and 20.

[15]  *Ullah* [2004] 2 AC 323. Mr Ullah was an Ahmadi from Pakistan who wanted to spread his beliefs by preaching. In his asylum appeal before an adjudicator, it was accepted that the ability of Ahmadis to practice their religion was restricted by the law and by societal attitudes. Accordingly, he raised, in addition to the question of a breach of his rights under Art 3 of the ECHR, a potential breach under Art 9 (freedom of thought, conscience and religion) of the ECHR.

[16]  Emphasis added. See also *Government of the USA v Montgomery* [2004] 1 WLR 2241 per Lord Carswell at 2251.

Thus the person may rely on articles other than Article 3 of the ECHR as a ground for resist- **10.18** ing his extradition, but 'successful reliance demands presentation of a very strong case'. We will see below how this has been applied in practice in the English courts.

### Article 2

Article 2 of the ECHR provides that: **10.19**

> Everyone's right to life shall be protected by law. No one shall be deprived of his life intention- ally save in the execution of a sentence of a court following his conviction for a crime for which this penalty is provided by law.

There is a split in the jurisprudence of the ECtHR as to whether the test in relation to a **10.20** breach of Article 2 of the ECHR requires 'an almost certainty' of the applicant being killed[17] or requires only 'a real risk', in line with the threshold applied to Article 3 of the ECHR.[18] Without deciding the issue, the Court in *McLean v High Court of Dublin, Ireland* [2008] EWHC 547 (Admin) expressed its preference for the latter test:

> 10. The adoption of essentially the same test in relation to Art 2 as in relation to Art 3 has obvi- ous attractions to it. It is very unsatisfactory to apply a higher threshold in the case of a risk to life than in a case where the risk is of less serious harm (albeit sufficiently serious to fall within Art 3). True, the point may be devoid of practical significance since *Launder* shows that Art 3 can be relied on even where the risk is to life; but it is strange to have to rely on Art 3 where the subject matter falls more naturally under Art 2.

The test to be applied with regard to Article 2 claims, therefore, remains to a certain extent **10.21** unresolved. Indeed it is unlikely to be resolved until a case presents itself with the unusual feature of a person who faces a real risk of loss of life but without an accompanying risk of inhuman or degrading treatment or punishment.

The death penalty is one area where a clear risk to life arises. However the 2003 Act explicitly **10.22** provides that a person may not be extradited to a territory or state where he has been or will be sentenced to death for the offence concerned.

As regards Part 1 of the 2003 Act, section 1 prevents a state from being designated as a cate- **10.23** gory 1 territory 'if a person found guilty in the territory of a criminal offence may be sen- tenced to death for the offence under the general criminal law of the territory'.

As regards Part 2 of the 2003 Act, and category 2 territories, section 94 (Death penalty) **10.24** provides in compulsory terms that:

(1) The Secretary of State must not order a person's extradition to a category 2 territory if he could be, will be or has been sentenced to death for the offence concerned in the category 2 territory.
(2) Subsection (1) does not apply if the Secretary of State receives a written assurance which he considers adequate that a sentence of death –
    (a) will not be imposed, or
    (b) will not be carried out (if imposed).

---

[17] *Osman v UK* (1998) 29 EHRR 245; *Soering v UK* (1989) 11 EHRR 439; *Launder v UK* Application 27279/95, decision of 8 December 1997, pp 19–20.
[18] *Bader v Sweden* Application 13284/04, European Court of Human Rights, judgment of 8 August 2006, paras 41, 42 and 48.

**10.25**  Therefore where a state which imposes the death penalty for the offence in question seeks a person's extradition from the United Kingdom, it must give satisfactory assurances that the death penalty will not be imposed, or if the person has been sentenced to death, that the penalty will not be carried out.

**10.26**  The issue has been particularly litigated in UK extradition cases in relation to the United States, given that it is a frequent 'extradition partner' of the United Kingdom, but one where the death penalty still exists both federally and in several states.

**10.27**  The UK courts have consistently held that the United States may be relied upon not to impose the death penalty. In *Harkins v Government of the USA* [2007] EWHC 639 (Admin), Lloyd Jones J, in rejecting the appellant's claim that the United States could not be trusted in relation to its assurance that the death penalty would not be imposed or carried out, stated:

> There is an assumption in extradition cases that the requesting state is acting in good faith. There is no evidence to support any suggestion that the United States of America in providing this assurance is not acting in good faith. Moreover, as Laws LJ expressed the matter in *Ahmad*, we are here concerned with an assurance given by a mature democracy. The United States is a State with which the United Kingdom has entered into five substantial treaties on extradition over a continuous period of more than 150 years. Over this period there is no instance of any assurance given by the United States as the requesting State pursuant to an extradition treaty having been dishonoured.
>
> 62. This court in *Ahmad* referred to the critical importance of the integrity of diplomatic notes. That is a view to which I should certainly subscribe. In the present case the United States authorities will be well aware of the importance attached by the Secretary of State to the assurance which he has received and will appreciate that it is on the basis of that assurance that he is prepared to order the surrender of the claimant. Moreover, the United States' authorities will be in no doubt as to the importance which this court attaches to the undertakings given.

**10.28**  Article 2 also arises where it is claimed that death will result from the acts of 'non-state actors'. It is well-established that a person may resist removal from the United Kingdom (whether by expulsion, deportation, or extradition) on the grounds that non-state actors in the home state pose a threat to the person's life or limb and that the state is unwilling or unable to provide a reasonable level of protection against that threat.[19]

**10.29**  In *Bagdanavicius*,[20] the House of Lords affirmed that 'the State's failure to provide reasonable protection' against violent treatment by non-state agents would amount to Article 3 ill treatment (speech of Lord Brown of Eaton-under-Heywood, paragraph 24). Hence, extraditing the person in those circumstances would, on the *Soering* principle, constitute a breach of Article 3 by the requested State.

**Article 3**

**10.30**  Article 3 of the ECHR provides:

> No one shall be subjected to torture or to inhuman or degrading treatment or punishment.

---

[19]  *Horvath v Secretary of State for the Home Department* [2001] 1 AC 489.
[20]  *R v Secretary of State for the Home Department ex parte Bagdanavicius (FC) and anor* [2005] UKHL 38.

The right to be free from torture or inhuman or degrading treatment or punishment is a **10.31**
fundamental, non-derogable right[21] and the prohibition on torture is a norm of *jus cogens*.[22]

It is well established that it is a violation of the prohibition on torture and inhuman or **10.32**
degrading treatment or punishment for a state to extradite a person to another state where
they will be subjected to such treatment.[23]

As noted above, the test is whether the person faces a 'real risk' of treatment in violation of **10.33**
Article 3. As Lord Bingham said in *Ullah*: [24]

> In relation to Article 3 it is necessary to show strong grounds for believing that the person if
> returned faces a real risk of being subjected to torture or to inhuman or degrading treatment
> or punishment.

The courts have also consistently emphasized the need for a *minimum level of severity* of ill- **10.34**
treatment in order to reach the threshold of Article 3.[25]

The 'real risk' test has been consistently applied by the UK courts and is well established. **10.35**

The relevant authorities were recently reviewed in-depth by the Divisional Court (Scott **10.36**
Baker LJ, David Clarke J) in *Bary and Al Fawwaz*,[26] at paragraphs to 44 to 70. In that case,
the court had to consider, inter alia, whether the harsh conditions of solitary confinement
in the United States's federal 'Supermax' facility in Florence, Colorado ('ADX Florence'),
where the appellants faced life imprisonment without parole if convicted of terrorist offences,
were such as to create a real risk of a breach of Article 3 of the ECHR. Lord Justice Scott Baker
summarized the factors to consider, at paragraph 69, thus:

> I draw the following principles from the authorities that I regard as material in assessing
> whether in ordering the extradition of the claimants to the United States there is a real risk of
> violation of article 3.
>
> − The test is a stringent one and the burden of proof on the claimants.
> − The claimants must not be extradited to the United States unless the safeguards they will
>   enjoy there are as effective as the convention standard.
> − It is a matter for the United States' authorities where and in what circumstances they detain
>   the claimants both pre trial and post conviction.
> − The importance of international cooperation and maintaining our treaty obligations is an
>   important factor.
> − It is essential to focus on what is likely to happen to the claimants in their particular
>   circumstances.
> − Punishment that would be regarded as inhuman or degrading in the domestic field will not
>   necessarily be so regarded where the alternative to extradition is that the person sought to
>   be extradited will escape justice altogether.

---

[21] *UK v Ireland* (1979–80) 2 EHRR 25.
[22] See United Nations Convention against Torture, Art 2(2); see also the International Criminal Tribunal for
the former Yugoslavia's *Čelebići* Trial Judgement, para 454.
[23] *Soering v United Kingdom* (1989) 11 EHRR 439; *Ng v Canada*, Human Rights Committee,
Communication No 469/1991, (1993) 1 IHRR 161.
[24] [2004] 2 AC 323 at 352B.
[25] *Ibid.*
[26] *R (on the application of Bary and Al Fawwaz) v Secretary of State for the Home Department* [2009] EWHC
2068 (Admin).

    – Complete sensory isolation coupled with total social isolation cannot be justified whatever the circumstances.

**10.37**  In the event, the court concluded that the prison conditions at ADX Florence, although very harsh, did not amount to inhuman or degrading treatment either on their own or in combination with Special Administrative Measures and in the context of a whole life sentence. The case is currently before the ECtHR, along with other extradition cases from the United Kingdom which have raised the same issue in relation to ADX Florence (*Ahmad and Aswat, Abu Hamza*).

**10.38**  The penultimate point referred to by the court in *Bary and Al Fawwaz* above—'Punishment that would be regarded as inhuman or degrading in the domestic field will not necessarily be so regarded where the alternative to extradition is that the person sought to be extradited will escape justice altogether'—derives from the House of Lords' judgment in *Wellington*,[27] in which a majority of the House of Lords espoused a 'relativist' approach to what constituted inhuman or degrading treatment (although not to torture which attracts such abhorrence that a relativist approach may not be adopted).

**10.39**  The opinion of the majority (Lord Hoffmann, Baroness Hale, and Lord Carswell) was that punishment which would be regarded as inhuman and degrading in the domestic field will not necessarily be so regarded when the choice between either extraditing or allowing a fugitive offender to evade justice altogether is taken into account. Lord Hoffmann cited the statement of the ECtHR in *Soering* at paragraph 86 that the beneficial purpose of extradition in preventing fugitive offenders from evading justice could not be ignored in determining the scope of application of the Convention and of Article 3 in particular. He then said at paragraph 22 that Article 3:

> applies only in a modified form which takes into account the desirability of arrangements for extradition ...

**10.40**  Lord Scott of Foscote and Lord Brown of Eaton-Under-Heywood, whilst agreeing that the appeal should be dismissed, took a more absolutist approach on this point. Lord Scott observed that the language of Article 3 provided no basis for the majority's approach. Lord Brown said at 76E, paragraph 87:

> Whilst, however, I readily accept that there is a good deal of flexibility in the concept of inhuman and degrading treatment and punishment with many factors in play in determining whether it attains the minimum standard required and whether the risk of such ill-treatment is satisfied, I cannot accept that the expelling state's desire to extradite the person concerned (legitimate though clearly it is) can itself properly be one such factor.

**10.41**  It remains to be seen whether the ECtHR endorses the 'relativist' approach, as expressed in *Wellington*, when it decides that case and the ADX Florence cases.

**10.42**  Diplomatic assurances that the person will not be detained under conditions which would breach Article 3 may play an important role in the UK court's decision that the person's extradition is compatible with the ECHR.

---

[27]  *R (Wellington) v Secretary of State for the Home Department* [2009] 2 WLR 55.

In *Ahmad*,[28] the appellants maintained that, if extradited, there was a real prospect that, **10.43**
among other things, they would be held at the United States's detention facilities at
Guantánamo Bay, where their rights under Articles 5 and 6 of the ECHR would be violated,
that they would be subject to 'extraordinary rendition' to countries where they would be
tortured, and/or that they would be subjected to Special Administrative Measures (SAMs)
while detained in the USA, which would be imposed on them on a discriminatory basis as
Muslims.

The court rejected these claims, largely on the basis of assurances from the United States **10.44**
contained in diplomatic notes, and on the basis of the 'fundamental assumption that the
requesting state is acting in good faith', as well as the fact that the United States, in an unin-
terrupted 150-year history of extradition relations, had never dishonoured an assurance
which it had given.[29]

Diplomatic assurances provide the courts with a knotty issue. They are intrinsically political, **10.45**
and do not provide a legal safeguard as such. Accordingly, whether or not an assurance is
considered acceptable will largely depend on the state offering the assurance and its history
of honouring its diplomatic commitments in the past. Thus the United States, which has, as
stated above, apparently never dishonoured a diplomatic assurance is, in short, to be trusted.
The same may not be true where states with a history of human rights abuses are
concerned.[30]

Potential breaches of Article 3 thus arise in a number of different contexts: for example, risk **10.46**
of reprisals to an informer from other prisoners,[31] a conviction being allegedly based on
confessions extracted by torture,[32] prison conditions,[33] and life imprisonment without
parole.[34]

A person who relies on his mental health as a ground for resisting extradition may rely on **10.47**
section 25 (for Part 1 cases) and section 91 (for Part 2 cases) of the 2003 Act. It would be a
rare case where a person relying on his mental condition as making it unjust or oppressive
to extradite him would be unable to succeed under section 25 of the 2003 Act, but could
successfully invoke Article 3 of the ECHR in respect of the same facts.[35]

Where the risk of treatment in violation of Article 3 of the ECHR comes from non-state **10.48**
actors, as discussed above in relation to Article 2 of the ECHR, the question will be whether
the state in question is willing and able to offer sufficient protection to the extraditee from
those individuals.[36]

---

[28] *Ahmad and Aswat v USA* [2006] EWHC 2927 (Admin), [2006] Extradition LR 276.
[29] *Ibid* at paras 74–75.
[30] See, eg, *DD and AS v Secretary of State for the Home Department* [2007] UKSIAC 42/2005.
[31] *Miklis v Deputy Prosecutor General of Lithuania* [2006] EWHC 1032 (Admin), [2006] Extradition LR
146.
[32] *Prenga v Republic of Albania* [2006] EWHC 1616 (Admin), [2006] Extradition LR 200.
[33] See, eg *Gomes* and *Bary and Al Fawwaz*, both cited above, and *Deya v Government of Kenya* [2008] EWHC
2914 (Admin).
[34] See, eg *Wellington*, cited above.
[35] *Prancs v Rezekne Court of Latvia* [2006] EWHC 2573 (Admin), [2006] Extradition LR 234 at para 20.
[36] *R v Secretary of State for the Home Department ex parte Bagdanavicius (FC) and anor* [2006] UKHL 38.

### Article 5

**10.49** Article 5 of the ECHR is engaged in two ways by extradition proceedings. First, if the person is being detained under Article 5(1)(f), then he has the right under Article 5(4) to challenge the lawfulness of the deprivation of his liberty, which has been found to entail jurisdiction to discharge a defendant on the grounds of an abuse of process.[37]

**10.50** Secondly, if the requested person will be returned to a state where there is a real risk of a flagrant violation of his Article 5 rights, then that will operate as a bar to his or her extradition. Thus in *Virciglio*,[38] the person unsuccessfully argued that, if returned to Austria, he would be punished for breaching a ten-year residence ban, which would amount to arbitrary deprivation of his liberty. The argument was rejected on its facts. In *Ceausescu*,[39] it was argued that the absolute prohibition on bail upon return to Romania would violate Article 5. This was rejected by the court on the basis that, since Ceausescu had been convicted in Romania, his case fell under Article 5(1)(a), not Article 5(1)(c) and 5(3), of the ECHR, and accordingly there was no right under the ECHR to seek bail.

**10.51** Applying Article 5, the ECtHR has held that detention for the purposes of extradition has to be in good faith. If extradition is achieved through deportation or some other form of 'disguised extradition', then it will be unlawful.[40] Equally, extradition has to be conducted with due diligence or it will cease to be lawful.[41] Extradition proceedings may, however, become protracted due to the person pursuing all avenues of appeal. That will not mean that the requesting state has failed to act with due diligence.[42] It is difficult to provide examples of what will count as 'due diligence', as each case is fact-specific, and in many cases, extradition proceedings have gone on for a great many years.[43]

### Article 6

**10.52** Since extradition proceedings do not constitute the 'determination of any criminal charge' against the fugitive, Article 6(2) and (3) of the ECHR does not apply to the proceedings themselves.[44]

**10.53** Where reliance is placed on Article 6 of the ECHR to resist extradition, it must be shown that the person whose extradition is sought has suffered or risks suffering 'a flagrant denial of a fair trial in the receiving state'.[45]

---

[37] *R (Kashamu) v Governor of Brixton Prison* [2002] QB 887.

[38] *Virciglio v The Judicial Authority of the Graz High Court, Austria* [2006] EWHC 3197 (Admin), [2006] Extradition LR 238 at paras 29–30.

[39] *Government of Romania v Ceausescu* [2006] EWHC 2615 (Admin), [2006] Extradition LR 255.

[40] *Quinn v France* (1995) 21 EHRR 529.

[41] *Lymas v Switzerland* (1976) 6 DR 141.

[42] *Osman v United Kingdom* Application 15933/89 (second application).

[43] For example, the case of *Al Fawwaz* took more than eight years to progress through the English courts (*R (Al Fawwaz) v Governor of HM Prison Brixton* [2001] 1 WLR 1234 and [2002] AC 556).

[44] In *H v Spain* (1983) 37 DR 93, the European Commission held that the phrase, 'determination … of any criminal charge' in Art 6 of the ECHR refers to the 'full process of the examination of an individual's guilt or innocence of an offence and not the mere process of determining whether a person can be extradited to another country'. See also *Farmakopoulos v Greece* (1990) 64 DR 52 and *R (Al Fawwaz) v Governor of Brixton Prison* [2002] AC 556 at para 87.

[45] *Ullah* [2004] 2 AC 323 at para 24.

In Part 1 cases, where the requesting state is always a party to the ECHR, it is particularly **10.54** difficult successfully to argue that there will be or has been a flagrant denial of a fair trial, given that the requesting state is itself bound to ensure a fair trial by virtue of Article 6 of the ECHR, and is expected to do so.[46] Even in Part 2 cases, however, it is often said by the courts that it is for the domestic court of the requesting state to ensure that there is a fair trial,[47] and the courts in the United Kingdom will be slow to find a substantial risk of an unfair trial in the requesting state.

One of the few cases in which Article 6 has been successfully raised to resist extradition is **10.55** *Brown and others v Government of Rwanda*.[48] In that case, Rwanda sought the defendants' extradition for genocide committed in Rwanda in 1994. They resisted, inter alia, on the grounds that they would not receive a fair trial in Rwanda.

Their appeals to the High Court were allowed and they were discharged on the basis that the **10.56** evidence demonstrated a real risk that many potential defence witnesses—whether presently inside or outside Rwanda—would be so frightened of reprisals that they would not willingly testify. This was not mitigated by the possible use of video-link facilities to enable defence witnesses to testify, as there was on the evidence at least a substantial risk that such facilities would not be available. Accordingly, and taken together with the court's real concerns about the Rwandan judiciary's impartiality and independence, if the appellants were extradited to face trial in the High Court of Rwanda, there was a real risk that they would suffer a flagrant denial of justice.

Violations of Article 6 could also arise by virtue of lack of procedural due process protections **10.57** in the requesting state, and also from provisions of domestic law, for example placing a legal burden on the defendant in a criminal trial.[49]

### Article 8

Article 8 of the ECHR (right to respect for a person's private and family life) provides as **10.58** follows:

1.  Everyone has the right to respect for his private and family life, his home and his correspondence.
2.  There shall be no interference by a public authority with the exercise of this right except as is in accordance with the law and is necessary in a democratic society in the interests of national security, public safety or the economic well-being of the country, for the prevention of disorder or crime, for the protection of health or morals, or for the protection of the rights and freedoms of others.

Article 8 is thus one of the qualified rights under the ECHR, ie a right expressly made subject **10.59** to limitations or restrictions set out in the ECHR.

---

[46] Potential breaches of Art 6 were unsuccessfully argued in, among others: *Boudhiba* [2006] 3 All ER 574 (DC) (in relation to the conditions under which defence lawyers in Spain have to work and trial within a reasonable period); *Cebelis v Prosecutor-General's Office of the Republic of Lithuania* [2006] EWHC 3201 (Admin), [2006] Extradition LR 261 (claimed absence of adequate legal aid at trial).

[47] *Raffile v Government of the USA* [2004] EWHC 2913 (Admin), [2005] Extradition LR 29 at para 32 ('The necessary qualification for extradition is a fair trial. That is an obligation manifestly accepted by the US. How a fair trial is to be achieved is for consideration by the court of trial').

[48] *Brown and ors v Government of Rwanda* [2009] EWHC 770 (Admin).

[49] *Okendeji v Government of the Commonwealth of Australia and Bow Street Magistrates' Court* [2005] EWHC 471 (Admin), [2005] Extradition LR 57.

**10.60**   Strasbourg jurisprudence establishes beyond dispute that extradition 'invades the primary Article 8 right and has to be shown to be in accordance with the law and necessary in a democratic society—that is to say, in the Court's long-established jurisprudence, proportionate'.[50]

**10.61**   In *Launder*,[51] the European Commission on Human Rights, at paragraph 3, considered:

> that it is only in exceptional circumstances that the extradition of a person to face trial on charges of serious offences committed in the requesting State would be held to be an unjustified or disproportionate interference with the right to respect for family life.

**10.62**   The House of Lords recognised in *Ullah*[52] that Article 8 may be engaged by extradition proceedings:

> Enough has been said to demonstrate that on principles repeatedly affirmed by the European Court, Article 8 may be engaged in cases of a real risk of a flagrant violation of an individual's Article 8 rights.[53]

**10.63**   In most cases, extradition will constitute an interference with the person's rights under Article 8, but it will be 'in accordance with the law' and will be sought in pursuit of a legitimate aim, namely 'the prevention of … crime'. The only issue then remaining will be whether it would be a proportionate interference.

**10.64**   The test on Article 8 which was applied until recently was that set out by Dyson LJ in *Jaso*,[54] at paragraph 57 of the judgment:

> What is required is that the court should decide whether the interference with a person's right to respect of his private or (as the case may be) family life which would result from his or her extradition is proportionate to the legitimate aim of honouring extradition treaties with other states. It is clear that great weight should be accorded to the legitimate aim of honouring extradition treaties made with other states. Thus, although it is wrong to apply an exceptionality test, in an extradition case *there will have to be striking and unusual facts to lead to the conclusion that it is disproportionate to interfere with an extraditee's article 8 rights.*[55]

**10.65**   The Supreme Court, in *Norris v Government of the USA*,[56] has, however, expounded a slightly different test. The court held that, rather than saying that interference with Article 8 rights could only outweigh the importance of extradition in 'exceptional circumstances', it was more accurate and helpful to say that the consequences of interference with Article 8 rights had to be *exceptionally serious* before they could outweigh the importance of extradition.

**10.66**   The court also held, applying *Beoku-Betts v Secretary of State for the Home Department*,[57] that the person's family unit had to be considered as a whole when weighing whether the interference with Article 8 was proportionate or not. The effect of extradition on innocent members of an individual's family might well be a cogent consideration, particularly where

---

[50] *Bentley v Government of the USA* [2005] EWHC 1078 (Admin), [2005] Extradition LR 69 per Sedley LJ at para 24.

[51] *Launder v UK* Application 27279/95 (1997).

[52] *R (Ullah) v Special Adjudicator* [2004] 3 WLR 23.

[53] Per Lord Steyn (at 51). See also *Schmidt v Secretary of State for the Home Department* [2005] EWHC 959 (Admin), [2005] Extradition LR 70 at para 11.

[54] *Zigor Ruiz Jaso, Ana Isabel Lopez, Inigo Maria Albisu Hernandez v Central Criminal Court No 2, Spain* [2008] 1 WLR 2798.

[55] Emphasis added.

[56] [2010] UKSC 9.

[57] [2008] UKHL 39, [2009] 1 AC 115.

extradition was sought for an offence of no great gravity and the individual had sole responsibility for an incapacitated family member.

Finally, the court also held that extradition proceedings should not become the occasion for **10.67** a debate about the most convenient forum for criminal proceedings. Rarely, if ever, on an issue of proportionality, could the possibility of bringing criminal proceedings in the United Kingdom be capable of tipping the scales against extradition in accordance with the United Kingdom's treaty obligations. Unless the judge reached the conclusion that the scales were finely balanced, he should not enter into an enquiry as to the possibility of prosecution in the United Kingdom.

It follows from the foregoing, and is illustrated by the lack of success in cases where Article 8 **10.68** has been argued, that there is a very high threshold to reach before a person will succeed in establishing that their extradition is incompatible with Article 8 of the ECHR.

# 11

## THE RELATIONSHIP BETWEEN EXTRADITION LAW AND ASYLUM LAW

## A. Introduction

Extradition law and asylum and immigration law both involve the potential removal of persons from the United Kingdom. Both areas of law therefore commonly engage similar issues, in particular issues of the human rights of the person to be removed, deported, or extradited. Despite this, however, most extradition practitioners do not regularly practice in immigration law, and most immigration practitioners do not regularly practice in extradition. Consequently, in those cases where the person also has immigration matters (for example, an outstanding asylum claim), he is often represented by different firms of solicitors and different counsel in his extradition and immigration matters, resulting in a situation where 'the left hand doesn't know what the right hand is doing', clearly an undesirable state of affairs.  **11.01**

As a result of the above, the cross-fertilization of law that one would expect in two closely related areas of law has progressed more slowly than one would have expected.  **11.02**

This short chapter is therefore intended to set out the key concepts of asylum law for the extradition practitioner.  **11.03**

## B. The bases upon which asylum can be granted

When we refer to a person as having been granted asylum (sometimes referred to as 'political asylum'), it refers to their status as a *refugee* in terms of the Convention relating to the Status of Refugees done at Geneva on 28 July 1951 and its Protocol ('the Refugee Convention').  **11.04**

The Refugee Convention, as applied by the 1967 Protocol, defines a refugee in Article 1A(2) as any person who:  **11.05**

> owing to a well-founded fear of being persecuted for reasons of race, religion, nationality, membership of a particular social group or political opinion, is outside his country of

nationality and is unable or, owing to such fear, unwilling to avail himself of the protection of that country ...

**11.06** It is clear from this definition, therefore, that there are three basic elements to being a refugee:

(1) The person must be outside his country of nationality.
(2) He must have a well-founded fear of persecution in his country of nationality on one of the Refugee Convention grounds, ie for reasons of:
    a. race;
    b. religion;
    c. nationality;
    d. membership of a particular social group; or
    e. political opinion.
(3) He must be unwilling or unable to avail himself of the protection of his country of nationality.

**11.07** Thus asylum may be granted on a number of grounds—race, religion, nationality, membership of a particular social group, or political opinion. However, it can only be granted on one of those grounds.

**11.08** Since asylum can be granted on several grounds other than political grounds, it is something of a misnomer to refer to 'political asylum', unless asylum was granted specifically on political grounds.

## C. The differences between asylum and indefinite leave to remain

**11.09** A *refugee* is thus a person who has been recognized as being outside his country of nationality and as having a well-founded fear of persecution for a Convention reason.

**11.10** There is, of course, an important difference between those seeking asylum (but whose claim may end up being refused) and those who have been granted asylum.

**11.11** One of the reasons why asylum is so eagerly sought is because the consequence of being recognized as a refugee is that the person cannot then be returned, or *refouled*, to their home country. The *non-refoulement* obligation on states is one of the most important principles in the Refugee Convention and in asylum law and practice. Article 33 of the Refugee Convention provides that:

> (1) No contracting state shall expel or return ('refouler') a refugee in any manner whatsoever to the frontiers of territories where his life or freedom would be threatened on account of his race, religion, nationality, membership of a particular social group or political opinion.

**11.12** The United Kingdom is a party to the Refugee Convention and therefore has a duty not to return refugees to their country of nationality, where there is a real risk of persecution.

**11.13** Refugee status is, therefore, one thing. The *consequences* of being granted refugee status is another. In the United Kingdom, refugees (but not only refugees) are granted indefinite leave to remain (ILR) in the United Kingdom, upon being recognized as refugees.

**11.14** ILR is one form of leave to remain in the United Kingdom. It basically confers a permanent right of residence in the United Kingdom. There is also exceptional leave to remain (ELR), which is usually granted for a finite period, for example, two years, and various other forms of leave to enter (for example, entry on a visit visa for six months). ELR can, and usually does lead to ILR, so that a person granted ELR can then apply for ILR after, say two years. All British citizens have a right to reside in the United Kingdom; but a person may have ILR without being a British citizen.

**11.15** A common misunderstanding, therefore, both on the parts of clients (who are sometimes themselves unclear as to the basis upon which they were permitted to remain in the United Kingdom) and extradition practitioners alike, is that a person who has sought asylum and been granted ILR must, therefore, have been recognized as a refugee. That is simply incorrect. The asylum seeker may have sought asylum and been refused, but nonetheless been permitted to remain in the United Kingdom on some other basis. Only if he has been granted asylum, would it operate as a bar to extradition, by virtue of the principle set out in *Dytlow and Dytlow*.[1]

**11.16** It is critical, therefore, where a person claims to have been granted asylum in the United Kingdom, to obtain a copy of the official document from the Home Office confirming that asylum has been granted.

## D. The appeal procedures available in immigration cases

**11.17** Asylum procedure may be briefly summarized as follows. The asylum seeker applies to the Secretary of State for the Home Department for asylum. He is interviewed in-depth in relation to his claim. If the Secretary of State decides to grant asylum, that is the end of the matter. If he refuses, then the person may appeal to what was until recently called the Asylum and Immigration Tribunal (AIT), and is now (as of 15 February 2010) called the First-tier Tribunal (Immigration and Asylum Chamber). The appeal is heard before an Immigration Judge, with both parties usually represented, the asylum seeker by a legal representative, and the Home Office by a Home Office Presenting Officer. A typical asylum hearing would last for two to four hours. The Immigration Judge is obliged to write up his judgment, referred to as his *determination*, within ten days of the hearing.

**11.18** The Immigration Judge will either allow the appeal or dismiss it. The losing party, ie either the appellant (asylum seeker) or the respondent (the Secretary of State) may appeal to the Upper Tier Tribunal (Immigration and Asylum Chamber).

## E. Those instances in which leave to remain can be revoked and the procedure for so doing

**11.19** The grant of asylum may be revoked on any of the grounds set out in paragraph 339A of the Immigration Rules (HC 395):

Revocation or refusal to renew a grant of asylum

---

[1] *District Court in Ostroleka, second Criminal Division (a Polish Judicial Authority) v Dytlow and Dytlow* [2009] EWHC 1009 (Admin).

339A. A person's grant of asylum under paragraph 334 will be revoked or not renewed if the Secretary of State is satisfied that:

  (i)   he has voluntarily re-availed himself of the protection of the country of nationality;

  (ii)  having lost his nationality, he has voluntarily re-acquired it; or

  (iii) he has acquired a new nationality, and enjoys the protection of the country of his new nationality;

  (iv)  he has voluntarily re-established himself in the country which he left or outside which he remained owing to a fear of persecution;

  (v)   he can no longer, because the circumstances in connection with which he has been recognised as a refugee have ceased to exist, continue to refuse to avail himself of the protection of the country of nationality;

  (vi)  being a stateless person with no nationality, he is able, because the circumstances in connection with which he has been recognised a refugee have ceased to exist, to return to the country of former habitual residence;

  (vii) he should have been or is excluded from being a refugee in accordance with regulation 7 of The Refugee or Person in Need of International Protection (Qualification) Regulations 2006;

 (viii) his misrepresentation or omission or facts, including the use of false documents, were decisive for the grant of asylum;

  (ix)  there are reasonable grounds for regarding him as a danger to the security of the United Kingdom; or

  (x)   having been convicted by a final judgment of a particularly serious crime he constitutes danger to the community of the United Kingdom.

In considering (v) and (vi), the Secretary of State shall have regard to whether the change of circumstances is of such a significant and non-temporary nature that the refugee's fear of persecution can no longer be regarded as well-founded.

Where an application for asylum was made on or after the 21st October 2004, the Secretary of State will revoke or refuse to renew a person's grant of asylum where he is satisfied that at least one of the provisions in sub-paragraph (i)–(vi) apply.

**11.20**  If a person's grant of asylum is revoked, any limited leave which they have may be curtailed (paragraph 339B of the Immigration Rules). That would, of course, give a right of appeal to the First-tier Tribunal (Immigration and Asylum Chamber).

**11.21**  The procedure for revoking a person's refugee status is set out in paragraph 339BA of the Immigration Rules:

339BA. Where the Secretary of State is considering revoking refugee status in accordance with these Rules, the person concerned shall be informed in writing that the Secretary of State is reconsidering his qualification for refugee status and the reasons for the reconsideration. That person shall be given the opportunity to submit, in a personal interview or in a written statement, reasons as to why his refugee status should not be revoked. If there is a personal interview, it shall be subject to the safeguards set out in these Rules.

**11.22**  As the Divisional Court remarked in *Dytlow*, after a review of the authorities:

22. So the decision to revoke a person's refugee status is not something to be undertaken either lightly or on the basis of what may prove to be merely temporary changes in the country from which that person has fled. All this has implications for the procedures to be followed if revocation is contemplated. English domestic law deals with those procedures by way of the Immigration Rules. Paragraph 339A of those Rules empowers the Secretary of State to revoke a grant of asylum, broadly speaking, in the circumstances set out in Article 1C of the Refugee

Convention, replicating paragraph (v) of Article 1C in paragraph 339A(v) of the Rules. But the Rules then add this:

'In considering (v) and (vi), the Secretary of State shall have regard to whether the change of circumstances is of such a significant and nontemporary nature that the refugee's fear of persecution can no longer be regarded as well-founded.'

23. Any decision by the Secretary of State to revoke a grant of asylum status would normally carry with it a revocation of the respondent's indefinite leave to remain, and would give rise to a right of appeal to the Asylum and Immigration Tribunal, a right required by Article 39(1)(e) of the Council Directive 2005/85/EC.

## F. The effect of asylum on extradition

The effect of asylum on extradition depends on when the claim was made, and of course on the outcome.  **11.23**

Where the person has made a successful asylum claim before extradition proceedings are commenced, then the Secretary of State may refuse to certify the extradition request for immigration reasons.  **11.24**

If an asylum claim is made in the course of extradition proceedings, then the proceedings have to be adjourned until the asylum claim is determined. The relevant provisions are sections 39 (for category 1 territories) and 121 (for category 2 territories) of the Act. They provide as follows:  **11.25**

**Section 39 Asylum claim**

(1) This section applies if—

    (a) a person in respect of whom a Part 1 warrant is issued makes an asylum claim at any time in the relevant period;

    (b) an order is made under this Part for the person to be extradited in pursuance of the warrant.

(2) The relevant period is the period—

    (a) starting when a certificate is issued under section 2 in respect of the warrant;

    (b) ending when the person is extradited in pursuance of the warrant.

(3) The person must not be extradited in pursuance of the warrant before the asylum claim is finally determined; and sections 35, 36, 47 and 49 have effect subject to this.

(4) Subsection (3) is subject to section 40.

(5) If the Secretary of State allows the asylum claim, the claim is finally determined when he makes his decision on the claim.

(6) If the Secretary of State rejects the asylum claim, the claim is finally determined—

    (a) when the Secretary of State makes his decision on the claim, if there is no right to appeal against the Secretary of State's decision on the claim;

    (b) when the period permitted for appealing against the Secretary of State's decision on the claim ends, if there is such a right but there is no such appeal;

    (c) when the appeal against that decision is finally determined or is withdrawn or abandoned, if there is such an appeal.

(7) An appeal against the Secretary of State's decision on an asylum claim is not finally determined for the purposes of subsection (6) at any time when a further appeal or an application for leave to bring a further appeal—

(a) has been instituted and has not been finally determined or withdrawn or abandoned, or

(b) may be brought.

(8) The remittal of an appeal is not a final determination for the purposes of subsection (7).

(9) The possibility of an appeal out of time with leave must be ignored for the purposes of subsections (6) and (7).

...

**121 Asylum claim**

(1) This section applies if—

   (a) a person whose extradition is requested makes an asylum claim at any time in the relevant period;

   (b) an order is made under this Part for the person to be extradited in pursuance of the request.

(2) The relevant period is the period—

   (a) starting when a certificate is issued under section 70 in respect of the request;

   (b) ending when the person is extradited in pursuance of the request.

(3) The person must not be extradited in pursuance of the request before the asylum claim is finally determined; and sections 117 and 118 have effect subject to this.

(4) If the Secretary of State allows the asylum claim, the claim is finally determined when he makes his decision on the claim.

(5) If the Secretary of State rejects the asylum claim, the claim is finally determined—

   (a) when the Secretary of State makes his decision on the claim, if there is no right to appeal against the Secretary of State's decision on the claim;

   (b) when the period permitted for appealing against the Secretary of State's decision on the claim ends, if there is such a right but there is no such appeal;

   (c) when the appeal against that decision is finally determined or is withdrawn or abandoned, if there is such an appeal.

(6) An appeal against the Secretary of State's decision on an asylum claim is not finally determined for the purposes of subsection (5) at any time when a further appeal or an application for leave to bring a further appeal—

   (a) has been instituted and has not been finally determined or withdrawn or abandoned, or

   (b) may be brought.

(7) The remittal of an appeal is not a final determination for the purposes of subsection (6).

(8) The possibility of an appeal out of time with leave must be ignored for the purposes of subsections (5) and (6).

**11.26**  If the asylum application is unsuccessful, then it follows that asylum cannot operate as a bar to extradition. If the application is successful, and the requesting state is the state against which the person has successfully claimed asylum, then it follows that he cannot be extradited there as it would breach the *non-refoulement* principle. As Lord Justice Keene stated in *Dytlow*:

> 11. ... It seems to me clearly implicit that if the asylum claim is eventually granted, the refugee cannot then be extradited ...
>
> [...]
>
> 15. ... subject to that possibility of cessation, the position generally is that Article 33.1 [of the Refugee Convention] would prevent the extradition of a person to his home territory (or indeed any other territory) where his life or freedom would be threatened on account of his race or other factor there referred to (essentially the Refugee Convention grounds).
>
> [...]
>
> 31. To order the extradition of a person or persons enjoying the status of refugees in this country would, for the reasons I have set out earlier, amount to an abuse of process. It follows that the District Judge in the present case was right to order the discharge of the respondents, albeit that he arrived at that conclusion for somewhat different reasons.

## G. The relevance of immigration and asylum law in case preparation

Where the person seeks to argue that his extradition is barred, either by reason of extraneous **11.27** considerations or human rights, or some other reason, by virtue of conditions in the requesting state, it may be useful to consider the so-called *Country Guidance* (CG) cases issued by the AIT and now the Upper Tier Tribunal (Immigration and Asylum Chamber),[2] as there may a CG case dealing with the precise issue which the person seeks to raise (for example, prison conditions in Ukraine, treatment of Roma in former Eastern Bloc countries, etc).

Likewise, the country reports, such as those compiled by the US State Department, Human **11.28** Rights Watch, Amnesty International, and others, which are routinely relied upon by immigration practitioners, provide a useful source of material for extradition practitioners and it is, therefore, well worthwhile for the latter to be familiar with the websites where those materials have been assembled, in particular the Electronic Immigration Network or EIN (www.ein.org.uk/). Finally, country experts who often provide reports in asylum cases are a useful resource for potential experts in extradition cases.

In summary, there is considerable overlap between extradition and immigration and asylum **11.29** law, and it is indispensable for extradition practitioners to have a working knowledge of the latter, including its source materials, case-law, and research methods.

---

[2] The website to consult for the Immigration and Asylum Chamber's case-law is <http://www.tribunals.gov. uk/ImmigrationAsylum/utiac/CaseLaw/CaseLaw.htm>.

# Part II

## MULTILATERAL AND REGIONAL DIMENSIONS

# 12

## TRANSFER TO INTERNATIONAL CRIMINAL COURTS AND TRIBUNALS

## A. Introduction

Since the establishment of the International Criminal Tribunal for the former Yugoslavia (ICTY) in 1993,[1] a whole host of international tribunals have come into existence as part of the post-conflict peace and reconciliation processes.[2] Thus the International Criminal Tribunal for Rwanda (ICTR) was established in 1994,[3] the International Criminal Court (ICC) in 1998,[4] the East Timor Special Panel (ETSP) for Serious Crimes in 2000,[5] the Special Court for Sierra Leone (SCSL) in 2002,[6] the Extraordinary Chambers in the Courts of Cambodia (ECCC) in 2006, and the Special Tribunal for Lebanon (STL) in 2007.[7] **12.01**

Broadly speaking, these courts and tribunals have jurisdiction to prosecute persons for international crimes, ie genocide, crimes against humanity, and war crimes. **12.02**

---

[1] The ICTY was established by UN Security Council Resolution 827 of 25 May 1993.

[2] For an overview of the establishment of these tribunals, and a review of the rules of procedure and evidence, and jurisprudence, see John RWD Jones and Steven Powles, *International Criminal Practice* (3rd edn, Oxford University Press/Transnational Publishers, 2003).

[3] The ICTR was established by UN Security Council Resolution 955 of 8 November 1994.

[4] The ICC was established following the Rome Conference in 1998.

[5] The Serious Crimes Panel of the Dili District Court was established by Regulation 2000/15 of the United Nations Transitional Administration in East Timor (UNTAET).

[6] The SCSL is a mixed international-national tribunal, established by agreement between the Sierra Leone Government and the United Nations, in order to try persons allegedly bearing 'the greatest responsibility' for crimes committed during the conflict in Sierra Leone between the SL Government and Civil Defence Forces (CDF), Revolutionary United Front (RUF) and AFRC (Armed Forces Revolutionary Council).

[7] By UN Security Council resolution 1757 of 30 May 2007, the Statute of the Special Tribunal for Lebanon entered into force on 10 June 2007.

## B. The international criminal courts and tribunals

### The ICTY and ICTR

**12.03** The ICTY and ICTR were established by the United Nations following the atrocities committed in the former Yugoslavia and Rwanda, respectively. As these bodies were created under Chapter VII of the United Nations Charter,[8] all member states have an obligation to surrender persons indicted by these tribunals and these proceedings take precedence over any other domestic or extradition request from any other country.

### The ICC

**12.04** The ICC was established by treaty at the United Nations Diplomatic Conference of Plenipotentiaries on the Establishment of an International Criminal Court in Rome on 17 July 1998. The Rome Statute received the requisite sixty ratifications on 11 April 2002 and, accordingly, pursuant to Article 126 of the Rome Statute, it entered into force on 1 July 2002. The ICC therefore only has jurisdiction over crimes committed after 1 July 2002.

### The SCSL and the ETSP

**12.05** With regard to the SCSL and the ETSP, these courts were not created by the UN acting under Chapter VII of the UN Charter. The SCSL was established by an Agreement between the Government of Sierra Leone and the United Nations. The East Timor Special Panel was created by regulations adopted by the United Nations Transitional Administration in East Timor (UNTAET). In these cases, therefore, there is no binding obligation on member states to cooperate with these courts or to comply with their orders and requests. The fact that these courts were not created under Chapter VII of the UN Charter does not, however, mean that states should not surrender persons indicted by these courts. Given the nature of the crimes over which these courts exercise jurisdiction, it would be unusual for a state not to comply with a request emanating from those courts for a person's surrender, provided that a legal procedure was available.

## C. Transfer of persons to the jurisdiction of the international courts and tribunals

**12.06** The legal basis for transferring an individual from the United Kingdom to the jurisdiction of international courts and tribunals is very different from ordinary extradition procedures. The procedure is not, formally speaking, *extradition* at all, since extradition applies to the surrender of a person from one *state* to another.

**12.07** The procedure for transferring persons indicted by the ICTY and ICTR is governed by Orders in Council, that is by executive instruments, rather than by the Extradition Act 2003 ('the 2003 Act'), in which no reference is made to these bodies.

**12.08** In the case of the ICTY, the procedure is governed by the United Nations (International Tribunal) (Former Yugoslavia) Order 1996, SI 1996/716 (as amended). In the case of the

---

[8] The ICTY was created by UN Security Council Resolution 827 (1993) and given effect in the UK by SI 1996/716. The ICTR was created by UN Security Council Resolution 955 (1994) and given effect in the UK by SI 1996/1296.

ICTR, the procedure is governed by the United Nations (International Tribunal) (Rwanda) Order 1996, SI 1996/1296 (as amended). Both operate as a 'backing of warrants' system, and there is very little scope for resisting transfer. The UK court may only look at one issue— identity. Thus there is no provision in the Orders that transfer may be resisted on the grounds that it would be incompatible with the indictee's human rights.

The position is similar with respect to the ICC. The transfer of a person arrested in the United Kingdom to the ICC is governed by the International Criminal Court Act 2001 ('the ICC Act'). The delivery up of persons is governed by Part 2 of the ICC Act. As with the ICTY and ICTR, the system is essentially a backing of warrants scheme, ie the UK court simply establishes that the warrant has been duly issued by the ICC and that the person brought before the court is the person sought, and the person is then delivered up to the ICC's custody.[9] The court is precluded from entering into any enquiry as to evidentiary sufficiency and there is no scope for the person to argue that their transfer would be incompatible with their human rights. **12.09**

Since the SCSL is a mixed national-international court, a person arrested pursuant to a warrant issued by the SCSL would—unlike those arrested on warrants issued by the ICTY, ICTR, or ICC—be delivered to the state itself, ie Sierra Leone, rather than the court. Sierra Leone is a category 2 territory for the purposes of the Extradition Act 2003. Therefore, pursuant to section 87 of the 2003 Act, the judge in the United Kingdom will have to 'decide whether the person's extradition would be compatible with the Convention rights within the meaning of the Human Rights Act 1998' and, if not, to discharge him. The court will also consider all the other bars to extradition as set out in the 2003 Act. **12.10**

Thus, alone of the international or mixed national-international tribunals, a person sought by the SCSL will be able to raise human rights arguments (among others) to resist his surrender. **12.11**

---

[9] ICC Act, s 2.

# 13

## EXTRADITION LAW AND PRACTICE IN OTHER JURISDICTIONS

## A. Introduction

This chapter provides an overview of the extradition laws and practice in a number of jurisdictions and is aimed at providing the reader with a general understanding of the practice in countries other than the United Kingdom.                                                13.01

The law and practice from the following jurisdictions is considered:                           13.02

- the Caribbean region, in particular, Trinidad and Tobago;
- India;

- South Africa; and
- the United States.

## B. Extradition procedure in the Caribbean[1]

### Introduction

**13.03** The legal systems of the Caribbean jurisdictions, which are former British colonies, are based on the common law. In some instances, such as extradition, they have also 'inherited' UK legislation, namely the Extradition Act of 1870 (UK) (governing extradition with foreign states) and the Fugitive Offenders Acts 1881 and 1967 (governing extradition between Commonwealth jurisdictions). These laws guide some of the Caribbean national law on extradition to allow for extradition between foreign and commonwealth states.[2] To that extent, therefore, the procedure governing extradition to and from Caribbean countries closely follows the previous UK position under the 1989 Act.

**13.04** In fact the vast majority of the Caribbean countries passed their extradition legislation following a meeting in London of Commonwealth Law Ministers in 1966 when the 'Scheme for the Rendition of Fugitive Offenders within the Commonwealth' was adopted. However, given the onerous obligation under the Scheme to submit a prima facie case, some Caribbean countries have sought to simplify this requirement in response to the increase in transnational crime. For example, in 2004 Trinidad and Tobago amended its Extradition Act to remove the need for duly authenticated affidavits (similar to Canada's Extradition Act) and replace it with a 'record of the case'. This is signed by a judicial or prosecuting authority of the requesting state certifying that the 'evidence summarized or contained in the record of the case or supplementary record of the case is in a form that would be admissible at the trial and was gathered according to the law of that territory; or is sufficient under the law of that territory to justify prosecution'.[3]

**13.05** More recently, to improve regional security, Caribbean Governments have agreed in principle to introduce an approach similar to the European Union of mutual recognition of judicial decisions and judgments to enhance judicial cooperation in criminal matters. In July 2008 Antigua and Barbuda, Suriname, and Trinidad and Tobago signed the Caricom Arrest Warrant Treaty (CAWT), followed by Saint Lucia in March 2009. To date only Trinidad and Tobago has ratified the CAWT and it is anticipated that other Caribbean jurisdictions will soon follow.

### Extradition requests

**13.06** Most Caribbean jurisdictions have a Central Authority Unit or a dedicated department within the Ministry of the Attorney General that deals with extradition and Mutual Legal Assistance requests.

---

[1] Contributed by David West, Consultant, Central Authority for Trinidad and Tobago.
[2] See Table 13.1 at 13.53 below.
[3] Trinidad and Tobago: Extradition Act 1985, Act No 36 of 1985 as amended by Act No 12 of 2004, s 19A(5).

There are two types of request. The first is a request for the provisional arrest of the person. The second is a request for a full warrant of arrest based on a request that is accompanied by the relevant documentary evidence to prove the extraditable offence (sometimes referred to as 'full order' requests).[4] In the latter case the documents are submitted through diplomatic channels and upon receipt the relevant Minister issues an Authority to Proceed (ATP) if satisfied that there are no bars to extradition. Following this the magistrate may issue a warrant of arrest.

### Provisional warrant of arrest

In general, there are two types of warrants that may be issued by a magistrate, namely:    **13.07**

- a provisional warrant of arrest; or
- a full warrant of arrest.

However Barbados, Dominica, and Saint Lucia do not distinguish between provisional and full arrest warrants.

Where a provisional arrest warrant is issued, the majority of the Caribbean countries require    **13.08** the magistrate issuing it to send a copy of the warrant and evidence to the Minister or Attorney General forthwith. The following information must be put before the magistrate when considering a request for provisional arrest:

- a description of the person;
- the location of the person;
- a brief statement of the facts of the case, including, if possible, the time and location of the offence;
- the relevant law;
- a statement of the existence of a warrant of arrest or a finding of guilt or judgment of conviction against the person;
- a statement that a request for extradition for the person will follow.

This information does not need to be authenticated or certified according to the Extradition    **13.09** Act, and a fax copy of the documents will suffice. As in other jurisdictions, a request for provisional arrest is not required to be transmitted through diplomatic channels and can be received directly from the Central Authority of the requesting state.[5]

### Full warrant

When considering a 'full' warrant, the magistrate will have before him the ATP and the duly    **13.10** authenticated or certified extradition request. The ATP will cite the extradition offences and the warrant of arrest should mirror the offences listed in the ATP. The magistrate must be satisfied that there is 'evidence as would in his opinion justify the issue of a warrant for the arrest of a person accused or, as the case may be, convicted within his jurisdiction and it appears to him that the conduct alleged would constitute an extradition crime'.[6]

---

[4] Table 13.1 at 13.53 below.
[5] Application for Judicial Review filed by Zimmern Beharry (Trinidad and Tobago) applying *Government of the Federal Republic of Germany v Sotiriadis and another* [1979] 1 AC 25.
[6] See Table 13.1 at 13.53 below.

**Representations before warrant/ATP issued**

**13.11** The legislation does not make provision for defence representations at this initial stage.[7] However, if they have knowledge of the request, they can invite the relevant Minister or magistrate to refrain from issuing the warrant or ATP.

**Role of the magistrate**

**13.12** As in the United Kingdom, a magistrate in extradition proceedings in the Caribbean, shall have like jurisdiction and powers, 'as nearly as may be', to a magistrate acting under a preliminary enquiry.[8]

**13.13** Where a person has been arrested on a provisional warrant the magistrate will set a date for the receipt of the ATP. If the ATP is not issued by the relevant date the person will be discharged, although they may later be re-arrested if a further request is issued.[9] The time period for the receipt of the ATP is usually governed by treaty and domestic law but, in the absence of a treaty, the normal practice is to allow twenty-eight days and extensions may be granted if justified.

**13.14** When the ATP is signed by the relevant Minister the extradition proceedings are commenced and the person must be brought before the magistrate as soon as is reasonably practicable. Where a person is arrested under a provisional warrant it is good practice that he should be re-arrested under a 'full' warrant once the ATP has been signed by the relevant Minister, even if the person is in custody.[10]

**13.15** The requesting state is usually represented by the prosecuting authorities in the requested state, but practice varies in the region. For example, in Trinidad and Tobago all extradition requests and representation in court are conducted by counsel for the Central Authority Unit of the Ministry of the Attorney General, whilst in Jamaica, the department of the Director of Public Prosecutions represents the requesting state.

**13.16** Counsel representing the requesting state is required to serve on the person:

- the request;
- a copy of the warrant of arrest;
- a copy of the certificate of specialty (signed by the relevant Minister); and
- a copy of the corresponding charges so that he knows what charges he has to meet.[11]

However, in the Privy Council decision of *Charron v Government of the United States of America and Another* their Lordships held that:

> failure to list the offences with which a person is charged and to set out particulars of those offences for consideration by the magistrates does not necessarily invalidate the proceedings ...[12]

---

[7] *R v Secretary of State for the Home Department, ex p Norgen* [2000] 3 WLR 181.
[8] See Table 13.1 at 13.53 below.
[9] *Leon Paul Williams v The State* HCA No 3388 of 2000.
[10] *Ibrahim Noumeh v The State* HCA No 1160 of 1998.
[11] *In re Naghdi* [1990] 1 All ER 257.
[12] (2000) 56 WIR 27 (PC).

In practice a copy of the ATP is also provided to the fugitive which cites the extradition **13.17**
offences.[13]

At the extradition hearing in Trinidad and Tobago, two witnesses are called on behalf of **13.18**
the requesting state: the permanent secretary in the Ministry of the Attorney General and the
arresting officer. The permanent secretary is called to tender the extradition package (as
the extradition documents have been transmitted via diplomatic channels) and the certificate of specialty which is in terms of section 8(3) of the Extradition Act of Trinidad and
Tobago.[14] The arresting officer is called to formally identify the fugitive and also tenders into
evidence the warrant of arrest which should have his certificate on the back of the warrant
attesting to the arrest and anything that was said and done by the fugitive on arrest. The
request and ATP (as court exhibits) are tendered before the court.

Defence counsel then has the opportunity to make submissions on the sufficiency of evi- **13.19**
dence (discussed below), following which the magistrate rules on whether the requesting
state has made out a prima facie case. If he is so satisfied he will commit the fugitive to be
returned, otherwise the fugitive is discharged forthwith.[15]

There is provision in some of the extradition Acts of the Caribbean to allow a person, if he so **13.20**
wishes, to consent to his extradition.[16] In such circumstances, a fugitive is well advised to
seek the same specialty protection afforded to him, as if he were committed by the
magistrate.

### Bail

Extradition proceedings are akin to committal proceedings so magistrates have jurisdiction **13.21**
to hear an application for bail. It is for the requesting state to satisfy the court, on a balance
of probabilities, that there are substantial grounds for denying bail and the test for the magistrate is whether or not the fugitive will appear for his hearing.[17]

In *R v Phillips* Lord Hewitt CJ stated that an important factor to be considered in bail appli- **13.22**
cations is that the Caribbean jurisdiction has entered into a treaty with the foreign state and
a failure to surrender the fugitive because he absconded may be regarded as a failure to fulfil
its treaty obligations.[18] Likewise in *Knowles and others v Superintendent of Her Majesty's Prison,
Fox Hill and others* the Privy Council made the following observations when considering a
judge's decision to grant bail in extradition proceedings:

> The Board considers that there is much force in these criticisms and the judge did not appear
> to give sufficient weight either to the nature of the crimes alleged or to the risk of, and the
> advantage of, their fleeing. It is important that in this particular type of case these consider-
> ations should be taken fully into account and it should only be in exceptional cases that bail as
> a matter of discretion is granted.[19]

---

[13] Jamaica and Guyana list the foreign offences in the ATP.
[14] For other jurisdictions see Table 13.1 at 13.53 below.
[15] Table 13.1 at 13.53 below.
[16] Table 13.1 at 13.53 below.
[17] *R v Governor of Canterbury Prison, ex p Craig* [1991] 1 QB 195 per Watkins LJ at 205F; *Re Gordon Young,
Belize Law Reports*, Volume 1, p 220.
[18] [1921–25] Cox CC 332, 335.
[19] [2005] UKPC 17 at para 27.

**13.23**   There is some dispute as to whether bail may be granted prior to an application for habeas corpus. In the case of *Ishwar Galbaransingh and Steve Ferguson v The Commissioner of Prisons*, Justice Pemberton held that the 'application for and grant of bail cannot predate the application for habeas corpus'.[20] However, in *Launder v Governor of Brixton Prison*, Mance J was of the view that habeas corpus was available to a person even though granted bail.[21] On appeal in *Ishwar Galbaransingh and Steve Ferguson v The Commissioner of Prisons*, Smith JA agreed with the decision of Mance J.[22]

**13.24**   In both Antigua and Barbuda and Grenada the relevant legislation provides for the grant of bail immediately after the committal stage.[23]

### Disclosure

**13.25**   Disclosure in extradition proceedings has been the subject of judicial comment and more recently has grown in importance within Caribbean jurisdictions. In the Trinidad and Tobago case of *Michael Harroo v Commissioner of Prisons*, Justice Pemberton analysed the law relating to disclosure and stated:

> The learning is clear. There is a duty of candour on the Requesting State in extradition proceedings. This duty extends to material that may be inimical to the case against the person to be extradited. Failure to observe this duty should render an Extradition Order obtained tainted. When a person to be extradited raises the issue of material non-disclosure, he must bring evidence to show that the Requesting State had knowledge of the evidence and of its suppression. That to my mind is the first step.

> The next step … is that the court must examine the evidence to assess whether its non-disclosure severely 'destroys or undermines' the evidence upon which the Requesting State relies to secure an Order.[24]

**13.26**   In *Ralston Wellington v The Government of the United States of America* Justice Mitting set out six propositions governing disclosure in extradition proceedings, as follows:

- It is for the requesting state alone to determine the evidence upon which it relies to seek a committal.

- The requesting state is not under any general duty of disclosure similar to that imposed on the prosecution at any stage in domestic criminal proceedings.

- The magistrates' court has the right to protect its process from abuse of process and the requesting state has a duty not to abuse that process. That is no different from saying that the requesting state must fulfil the duty which it has always had of candour in making applications for extradition.

- In fulfilment of that duty, the requesting state must disclose any evidence which would render worthless the evidence on which it relies to seek committal.

- It is for the person subject to the extradition process to establish that the requesting state is abusing the process of the court.

---

[20]   CV 2008-02848 and CV 2008-02849 High Court Trinidad and Tobago.
[21]   [1998] EWHC 214 (Admin).
[22]   Civil Appeal No 108 of 2009 TT.
[23]   Antigua and Barbuda, Extradition Act, 1993, s 11(9); Grenada: Act No 22 of 1998, s 11(9).
[24]   Claim No CV 2006-03583 at para 9.

- The requested state may be given power to request further evidence under the relevant Order in Council but, in the absence of evidence of abuse, the court is entitled to, and should generally, refuse to request the UK authorities to exercise that power or to adjourn to permit it to be exercised.[25]

### Admissibility of evidence

The documents in support of an extradition request cannot be admitted unless they comply with the Extradition Act.[26] All the Caribbean jurisdictions (with the exception of Trinidad and Tobago) have provisions similar to that of the Extradition Act (UK) 1989 relating to the formal conditions of admissibility of evidence; that is, the dual need for proper certification and authentication. In *Ramcharan v Commissioner of Correctional Services and anor* the court said:     **13.27**

> Authentication under the Act has therefore a dual purpose, namely;
>
> (a) certification, by the relevant judicial or diplomatic authority of the requesting state, vouching for the genuineness of the documents as being either originals or true copies of originals, and
>
> (b) authentication, by the oath of the witness or the formal affixing of a seal by the relevant minister in the requesting state. This is in essence a subsidiary authentication.[27]

By contrast, in 2004 Trinidad and Tobago followed the Canadian model by inserting section 19A into the Extradition Act which simplified the admissibility requirements and removed the dual requirements of certification and authentication.     **13.28**

This section allows evidence that would 'not otherwise be admissible under the laws of Trinidad and Tobago', such as hearsay evidence, once the documents are signed by a judicial, prosecuting or penal authority of the requesting state. In *Steve Ferguson & Ishwar Galbaransingh v Attorney General of Trinidad and Tobago and Chief Magistrate* the court considered whether an Assistant United States Attorney or an Assistant District Attorney was a prosecuting authority. Justice N Bereaux stated:     **13.29**

> In my judgement, it is sufficient for the purposes of section 19A(3) that the certificate states on the face of the record that 'I am a prosecuting authority' ... Once the document recites that the official is a prosecuting authority on its face it is admissible.[28]

The law has now been settled that an Assistant United States Attorney would be a prosecuting authority for the purposes of the Extradition Act. By the same token, a lawyer in the Crown Prosecution Service (UK) or in the Director of Public Prosecutions Department would be considered a prosecuting authority.     **13.30**

### Conviction cases

In requests relating to convicted persons, the requesting state must prove that the person was convicted of an extraditable offence and is 'unlawfully at large'. The term unlawfully at large is not defined in the Extradition Acts of Caribbean jurisdictions and is wide enough to     **13.31**

---

[25] [2004] EWHC 418 (Admin); *Samuel Knowles Jr v The Government of USA and ors* [PC] Nos 64 of 2004 and 70 of 2005.

[26] Table 13.1 at 13.53 below.

[27] 73 WIR 312, 321.

[28] CV 2006-2959 (TT), p 29.

include persons who have escaped custody, persons who have failed to answer bail, and persons who have failed to appear for sentence. There must be direct evidence of the person being unlawfully at large.[29]

13.32 Where a person has been convicted in their absence and the conviction is not final the request is treated, in almost all Caribbean jurisdictions, as a request for a person accused rather than convicted.

**Test for committal[30]**

13.33 Once the magistrate has heard the evidence he will decide whether he is satisfied that there is a prima facie case. All Caribbean jurisdictions have the same test for committal.

13.34 The first step is to determine whether or not the relevant Minister has signed the ATP. The ATP has two functions as outlined by Dambrot J in *United States v Drysdale*:

> It appears to me that the authority to proceed has two functions in the extradition process. First, it is analogous to the information or indictment in a domestic prosecution, and thus gives notice to the person sought of what is alleged against him or her, and forms the basis of an order committing the person for extradition where such an order is made. Second, the authority to proceed ensures that the Minister's decision to authorize the seeking of committal on behalf of the requesting state is made in a timely way, in order to ensure that a person arrested provisionally does not languish in custody, or continue to have his or her liberty constrained by a judicial release order for an unnecessarily prolonged period of time ...[31]

13.35 In all the Caribbean jurisdictions, except Jamaica and Guyana, the offences listed in the ATP are the equivalent local offences. In Jamaica and Guyana the ATP can list the foreign offences. In the Jamaican case of *Emmanuel v Commissioner of Correctional Services and another* Harrison P stated:

> Nowhere in this section or under any other provision in the Act is the Minister required in his authority to proceed, to translate offences framed in terms of foreign law in a requesting state's indictment, in terms of Jamaican law.[32]

> Harrison P went on to state that it is up to the magistrate to determine whether the offences charged in the foreign indictment are translatable into corresponding offences under Jamaican law.

13.36 The second step for the magistrate is to determine whether the offences in the ATP relate to an extraditable offence.[33] The criteria to determine what amounts to an extradition offence varies in the Caribbean. Barbados, Belize, Dominica, Saint Lucia, and Saint Vincent use a list system to determine what amounts to an extradition offence. Other Caribbean jurisdictions adopt a conduct based approach.

13.37 Once the magistrate has considered the preliminary issues, he then has to decide if there is a prima facie case against the accused person. The test applied by the magistrate is the same as in ordinary preliminary enquiries, namely whether there is evidence upon which a jury properly directed could convict the accused of the charges (the *Galbraith* test).[34]

---

[29] *Urru v The Governor of HMP Brixton and the Government of Italy* CO/4009/99 DC.
[30] See Table 13.1 at 13.53 below.
[31] (2000) 32 CR (5th) 163 (Ont SJC) at 180.
[32] 73 WIR 291.
[33] See Table 13.1 at 13.53 below.
[34] *R v Galbraith* [1981] 1 WLR 1039, 73 Cr App R 124 (CA) per Lane CJ at 127.

The person may, if he wishes, give evidence on his own behalf or call witnesses.[35] However, **13.38** any inconsistencies or contradictions in the evidence of the extradition offences are a matter for the trial court. A magistrate is not concerned with the credibility of a witness nor can he compare one witness with the other.[36]

Finally, the identity of the person must be established on the extradition documents. **13.39** Identification is usually proved by photographs or fingerprints contained in the request. Trinidad and Tobago amended its legislation to make it easier to prove the identity of the person. If the person's name is similar to the name in the request or the physical characteristics of the person before the court are similar to those evidenced in the photograph, then identity would prima facie be proven.[37]

If the magistrate is satisfied that there is a prima facie case he must commit the accused in **13.40** custody to await the warrant of the Minister for his return. If the magistrate is not satisfied that there is a prima facie case he must discharge the fugitive.

### Application for habeas corpus

All Caribbean jurisdictions have legislation dealing with applications for habeas corpus.[38] **13.41** A magistrate on committing a person to await the decision of the relevant Minister must inform the fugitive that he may apply for habeas corpus within fifteen days. The High Court is given additional, albeit limited, powers to discharge a fugitive from custody. The additional grounds are:

- the trivial nature of the extraditable offence;
- the passage of time;
- the accusation was not made in good faith;
- it would be unfair or oppressive to surrender him; and
- any other sufficient cause.[39]

The function of the High Court when dealing with an application for habeas corpus was **13.42** described by Viscount Radcliffe in *Schtraks v Government of Israel & Ors* as follows:

> I think that it is clear that in habeas corpus proceedings ... the court does not rehear the case that was before the magistrate, nor does it hear an appeal from his order. Its function ... is to see that the prisoner is lawfully detained by his gaoler. I think that the distinction was accurately drawn by Lord Russell of Killowen CJ in *In re Galwey* when he said; 'The prisoner then, having been taken into custody under the warrant of the chief magistrate, was brought before him, and we should, after the order of committal, be entitled to review the magistrate's decisions, not in the sense of entertaining an appeal from it, but in a sense of determining whether there was evidence enough to give him jurisdiction to make the order of committal ...' It seems to me that the only ground on which this habeas corpus can be successfully maintained is that the committal order was made without jurisdiction and was illegal.

---

[35] *Re Gross* [1999] QB 538.

[36] *Ishwar Galbaransingh and Steve Ferguson (Trinidad and Tobago); R v Governor of Pentonville Prison, ex p Alves* [1993] AC 294 (HL).

[37] Trinidad and Tobago Extradition Act, 1985 as amended, by Act No 12 of 2004, s 19B.

[38] Table 13.1 at 13.53 below.

[39] Only in the Extradition Acts of Trinidad and Tobago and Guyana. Barbados, Dominica, Saint Lucia, and Saint Vincent have a general section on appeals to the Divisional Court.

### Order for return[40]

**13.43**  Where an application for habeas corpus is dismissed, the person may lodge an appeal to the Court of Appeal and thereafter to the Privy Council, providing the laws of the requested state allow. For Guyana, Barbados, and Saint Lucia the final court of appeal is the Caribbean Court of Justice. Jamaica's court of final resort is the Jamaican Court of Appeal. All other Caribbean jurisdictions retain the Privy Council.

**13.44**  Once all appeals have been heard, the relevant Minister must decide whether return is prohibited by any specialty provision or whether it appears to him that it would be unjust or oppressive to return the fugitive. If the Minister decides both of these questions in the negative he may issue a warrant for the return of the fugitive. Notice of the issue of the warrant should be given to the fugitive forthwith.

**13.45**  Section 15(2) of Antigua's extradition legislation specifically provides that a person who is the subject of an order for return can make representations to the Minister at any time within fifteen days commencing on the date when the notice for return was given. Section 15(6) allows the fugitive to judicially review the Minister's decision and section 15(7) states that once judicial review proceedings are pending, he may not be returned.[41]

**13.46**  In *Steve Ferguson and Ishwar Galbaransingh v The Attorney General of Trinidad and Tobago and Chief Magistrate*, the appellants were indicted in the United States for fraud and money laundering charges. The United States submitted a request for extradition and the Attorney General duly signed the ATP in 2006. The appellants argued that the ATP should not have been issued, and therefore no order for extradition could be made, because in 2004 they had been charged in Trinidad with criminal offences arising out of the same conduct as that charged in the United States. The court held that section 16(2) of Trinidad and Tobago's Extradition Act, which makes provision for extradition while local charges are pending, provided a complete answer to the argument. The court held that the question of forum should be decided after the Attorney General had made an order for return. Justice Bureaux stated:

> In my judgment unless the criminal proceedings have concluded with a verdict of guilt or innocence, criminal proceedings can be discontinued at any stage to facilitate extradition, unless it shows that such discontinuance is effected to obstruct or forestall a likely acquittal (which may become apparent during a trial)... Until such trial is concluded the order to proceed can be issued and the committal proceedings commence.[42]

### Assurances

**13.47**  In certain instances, for example cases involving the death penalty, the requested state may require diplomatic assurances from the requesting state. The following cases illustrate the effect of diplomatic assurances.

**13.48**  In *Abdul Kadir, Kareem Ibrahim and Abdul Nur v The Commissioner of Prisons*, the extradition of the applicants was sought by the United States in respect of charges of terrorism. They were arrested in Trinidad, the Attorney General issued his ATP, and the applicants were

---

[40]  Table 13.1 at 13.53 below.
[41]  Extradition Act No 12 of 1993 (Antigua and Barbuda).
[42]  Civil Appeal No 60 of 2007, p 39.

committed pursuant to section 12(4) of the Extradition Act. On appeal the applicants contended that it would be unjust and oppressive to extradite them because inter alia, 'The USA has not given any assurances to the Government of Trinidad and Tobago that the applicants are not or will not become subject to the [Military Commissions Act 2006]'. Justice Bereaux, applied the case of *Ahmad and Aswat v The Government of the United States of America*,[43] and made the following observations:

> the provision of a diplomatic assurance from the United States Embassy to the Government of Trinidad and Tobago that the applicants would be prosecuted before a Federal Court and would not be subject to the Military Commissions Act of 2006 ... pre-empted any holding by this court that the applicants were at risk of an unfair trial before such a military commission ...

> I am not aware of any previous assurance given by the USA to the Trinidad and Tobago Government in other extradition requests which may have come up in litigation. However, I too shall proceed on the basis that the USA is acting in good faith and that the assurance provided by the US Ambassador in Port of Spain is sufficient to bind the USA. That assurance makes it unnecessary to decide on the merits of the applicants' contention on this issue ...[44]

The second case in which an assurance was given to the Government of Trinidad and Tobago **13.49** by the United States involved an allegation of 'hostage-taking resulting in death'. This charge carried the death penalty in the United States but not under the law of Trinidad and Tobago. Before agreeing to order extradition the Government of Trinidad and Tobago sought and received an assurance that, if the fugitives were extradited, they would not be eligible for the death penalty.

### Constitutionality of the Caribbean Extradition Acts

In recent times there have been constitutional challenges to the Extradition Acts of Jamaica **13.50** and Trinidad and Tobago.

In the Jamaican case of *Trevor Forbes v The DPP and Commissioner of Prisons,* the applicant **13.51** argued that section 16 of the Constitution, which provided Jamaican citizens with immunity from expulsion from Jamaica, was inconsistent with the Extradition Act. The Privy Council held that section 16(3)(e) of the Extradition Act provided an exception to the rights under section 16 of the Constitution which applied in extradition cases.[45]

In *Steve Ferguson and Ishwar Galbaransingh* (Trinidad and Tobago), the appellants filed a **13.52** constitutional motion on the basis that the Extradition Act is unconstitutional, in particular, they are challenging the provisions of section 19A. This matter is currently being heard.[46]

In Canada there was a similar challenge to section 32(1)(a) and (b) and section 33 of the **13.53** Canadian extradition legislation, equivalent to section 19A of the Trinidad and Tobago Extradition Act. In that case McLachlin CJ held that these provisions were constitutional.[47]

---

[43] [2006] EWHC 2972 (Admin).
[44] CV 2007-3062/3 (Trinidad and Tobago) at paras 15 and 17.
[45] [2007] UKPC 61 (PC).
[46] CV 2008-00639.
[47] *United States of America v Ferras* [2006] 2 SCR 77.

Table 13.1 Key extradition provisions (Caribbean countries)

| | Request either provisional arrest or full order | Criteria for a full warrant | Powers of the magistrate | Certificate of specialty | Prima facie case | Consent to extradition | Admissibility of evidence | Test for committal | Extradition offence | Habeas corpus | Order for return |
|---|---|---|---|---|---|---|---|---|---|---|---|
| Antigua & Barbuda: Extradition Act No 12 of 1993 | s 10(b) | s 10(2) | s 11(2) | s 8(4) | s 11(10) | s 16 | ss 28–29 | s 11(7) | s 4 | s 13 | ss 14–15 |
| Bahamas: Act No 8 of 1994 | s 9(1)(b) | s 9(2) | s 10(1) | s 7(3) | s 10(5) | s 17 | s 14 | s 10(5) | s 5 | s 11 | s 12 |
| Barbados: Cap 189 Act No 21 of 1979 | s 10 | s 10(1) | s 13(3) | s 7(2) | s 18 | n/a | ss 15–16 | s 17(1) | s 4 | s 19 | ss 26–27 |
| Belize: Extradition Act, Cap 112 Revised Edition 2000 | s 6 | s 6(1) | s 3 | s 3 | s 3 | s 3 | s 3 (and art 7 of the US Treaty) | s 3 | s 3 (and art 3 of the US Treaty) | s 3 | s 3 |
| Dominica: Act No 6 of 1981 | s 10 | s 10(1) | s 13(3) | s 7(2) | s 18 | n/a | ss 15–16 | s 17(1) | s 4 | s 19 | ss 26–27 |
| Grenada: Act No 22 of 1998 | s 10(b) | s 10 | s 11(2) | s 8(4) | s 11(1) | s 14 | ss 30–31 | s 11(7) | s 4 | s 13 | ss 15–16 |
| Guyana: Fugitive Offenders Act 1988, Act No 15 of 1998 | s 13(2) | s 13(3) | s 15(2) | s 8(3) | s 15(4) | s 14 | s 24 | s 15(4) | s 5 | s 16 | s 26 |
| Jamaica: Extradition Act 1991, Act No 7 of 1991 | s 9(b) | s 9(2) | s 10(1) | s 7(3) | s 10(5) | s 17 | s 14 | s 10(5) | s 5 | s 11 | s 12 |
| Saint Lucia: Extradition Act 1986, Act No 12 of 1986 | s 9 | s 9(1) | s 12(3) | s 6(2) | s 17 | n/a | ss 14–15 | s 16(1) | s 3 | s 18 | ss 25–26 |
| Saint Kitts and Nevis: Extradition Act 1870 | s 8 | s 8 | s 9 | s 3(2) | s 10 | n/a | ss 14–15 | s 10 | s 26 | s 11 | s 11 |
| Saint Vincent and the Grenadines: Extradition Act No 50 of 1898 | s 11(b) | s 10(2) | s 12(2) | s 7(3) | s 12(4) | s 13 | s 26 | s 12(4) | s 6 | s 14 | ss 16–20 |
| Trinidad and Tobago: Extradition Act 1985, Act No 36 of 1985 | s 10(b) | s 10(2) | s 12(2) | s 8(3) | s 12(4) | s 11 | s 19A | s 12(4) | s 6 | s 13 | s 16 |

## C.  Extradition procedure in India[48]

**Introduction**

India's Extradition Act 1962 ('the 1962 Act') supplements India's treaty obligations and specifies the procedures for their implementation. The 1962 Act initially assigned a major role to government officers, and left the courts with the very restricted role of inquiring into the judicial and penal conditions in the requesting state.    **13.54**

Intended to repeal and replace both the Indian Extradition Act 1903 and the Fugitive Offenders Act 1881, the 1962 Act originally distinguished between those extraditions entered into by India with certain Commonwealth states (Chapter III) and those entered into with all other foreign states, including all Commonwealth states that did not fall under Chapter III (Chapter II).    **13.55**

However, in 1993 the 1962 Act was amended, effectively removing any explicit reference to Commonwealth states. Chapter III now applies to any foreign state that has entered into an extradition treaty with India, and in respect of which the Indian Government considers it expedient to apply the Chapter III procedure rather than the Chapter II procedure.[49]    **13.56**

The 1962 Act came into force in January 1963. It governs the extradition of a person from India to a foreign state and vice versa. This may be based on a treaty between India and the foreign state or an extradition arrangement. Under section 3 the Government of India can issue a notification for the application of the 1962 Act to any state or states.    **13.57**

**Definition of 'extradition' and 'extradition offence'**

While the 1962 Act does not explicitly define extradition, the Supreme Court of India has defined it to be the 'surrender by one State to another of a person desired to be dealt with for crimes which he has been accused or convicted which are justiciable in the Court of other State'.[50] In another case before the Supreme Court, Justice Kuldip Singh described extradition as:    **13.58**

> the process whereby under a concluded treaty one State surrenders to any other State at its request, a person accused or convicted of a criminal offence committed against the laws of the requesting State, such requesting State being competent to try the alleged offender.[51]

The extradition of a person to a foreign state under the 1962 Act can only be made in respect of an 'extradition offence'. Section 2 defines an extradition offence as follows:    **13.59**

> (i)  In relation to a foreign State, being a treaty State an offence provided for in the extradition treaty with the State;

> (ii)  In relation to a foreign State other than a treaty State an offence punishable with imprisonment for a term which shall not be less than one year under the laws of India or of a foreign State and includes a composite offence.

---

[48] Contributed by Arun Gupta.
[49] VK Bansal, *Law of Extradition in India* (Lexis Nexis Butterworths Wadhwa Nagpur, 2008) pp 4–5.
[50] *State of West Bengal v Jugal Kishor and ors* AIR 1969 SC 1171.
[51] *George Kutty Kuncheria v Union of India and ors* (1994) SCC 80.

**13.60**   In addition, section 26 provides:

> A fugitive criminal who is accused or convicted of abetting, conspiring, attempting to commit, inciting or participating as an accomplice in the commission of any extradition offence shall be deemed for the purposes of this Act to be accused or convicted of having committed such offence and shall be liable to be arrested and surrendered accordingly.

**13.61**   Most of the treaties define an extradition offence as an offence that under the law of both states is punishable by imprisonment or the denial of liberty for a period of at least one year. However, there are exceptions. The treaty between India and France, for instance, provides that the offence must be punishable with imprisonment of at least two years, while others, such as those with Nepal, Russia, Bhutan, the United States, Poland, and Ukraine, do not specify a sentence threshold.

**13.62**   In respect of extradition requests for conviction cases, the sentence threshold varies, for example, the United Kingdom and Ireland provide for the imposition of a sentence of imprisonment or other order for a minimum of four months or more; while the sentence threshold with Canada, Kuwait, Bahrain, Republic of Korea, Germany, Hong Kong, Spain, Canada, and the UAE is greater than six months.

**13.63**   Other treaties, such as those with Nepal, Hong Kong, and others, have adopted the list approach to define extradition offences.

**13.64**   The 1962 Act envisages two categories of foreign states: those with which the Government of India has entered into an extradition treaty, and those with which an extradition arrangement exists. Section 3(4) also provides that where there is no extradition treaty between India and a foreign state the government may, by means of a notified order, treat any Convention to which India and the foreign state are parties as an extradition treaty made between India and that foreign state. Extradition under section 3(4) is in respect of the offences specified in the relevant Convention. Therefore, extradition is possible even where there is no extradition treaty in existence provided that the offence committed is one that is specified in a Convention to which the requesting state and India are both signatories.

**The extradition procedure**

**13.65**   The procedure for submitting an extradition request to India is set out in section 4 of the 1962 Act:

> A requisition for the surrender of a fugitive criminal of a foreign State may be made to the Central Government
>
> (a)  By a diplomatic representative of the foreign State at Delhi; or
>
> (b)  By the Government of that foreign State communicating with the Central Government through its diplomatic representative in that State, and if neither of these modes is convenient, the requisition shall be made in such other mode as is settled by arrangement made by the Government of the foreign State the Government of India.

**13.66**   Chapter II of the 1962 Act details the procedure for the return of persons to foreign states with which India has entered into an extradition treaty. Chapter III deals with foreign states in respect of which India has extradition arrangements.

**13.67**   Upon receipt of a request from a foreign state the 1962 Act provides that extradition proceedings be initiated by the appointment of a magistrate by the Central Government to instigate an enquiry.

The 1962 Act lays out the different stages of the extradition process as follows:  **13.68**

- extradition request by a foreign state to the Central Government of India;
- order to a magistrate to issue warrant(s);
- issue of warrant(s) by the magistrate;
- arrest of the fugitive, and
- production of the fugitive before the magistrate to determine whether there is sufficient evidence against him.[52]

### The request

The 1962 Act does not prescribe the format of the extradition request or the documents to  **13.69** be submitted in the request. This is addressed in the relevant extradition treaties or arrangements. However, it is general practice for a request to contain the following:

- details of the offence(s);
- details of the sentence provided for each offence;
- the arrest warrant;
- witness statements and scientific reports (if any); and
- in the case of convicted persons, a copy of the judgment and the sentence passed.

### The magistrate's role

The appointment and jurisdiction of the magistrate is addressed in section 5 of the 1962 Act.  **13.70** Where an extradition request is made the Central Government may, if it thinks fit, issue an order to any magistrate who would have had jurisdiction to inquire into the offence if it had been an offence committed within the local limits of his jurisdiction, directing him to inquire into the case.

The word 'may' clearly stipulates that Central Government is not obliged to act upon the  **13.71** receipt of a request to appoint a magistrate to commence extradition proceedings.

In *Pragnesh Desai v Union Of India & others*, the High Court has held that the scheme of the  **13.72** 1962 Act does not require Central Government to initiate a detailed enquiry before appointing a magistrate to initiate extradition proceedings.[53]

In *Nina Pillai & others v Union Of India & others*, section 5 of the 1962 Act was challenged  **13.73** on the grounds that the failure to allow a hearing prior to the commencement of extradition proceedings was a violation of natural justice. The High Court held that although the 1962 Act did not provide for a preliminary hearing the Act contained sufficient safeguards to ensure the protection of the fugitive.[54]

The Central Government can appoint any magistrate with jurisdiction to conduct an enquiry  **13.74** into the offences. For the purposes of the 1962 Act any offence in the extradition request is deemed to have been committed within the local limits of the magistrate's jurisdiction.[55] In *Flemming Ludin Larsen v Union of India*, the court held that effect of section 7(1) of the 1962

---

[52] VK Bansal, *Law of Extradition in India* (Lexis Nexis Butterworths Wadhwa Nagpur, 2008) pp 45–46.
[53] (2004) ILR I Del95 (DB).
[54] (1997) CrLJ 2358 (Del).
[55] *Rosiline George v Union of India* (1994) 2 SCC 80.

Act was that the magistrate in extradition proceedings has the same jurisdiction and power as if the case were one triable by a court of session or High Court.[56]

**13.75** Section 6 makes it mandatory for the magistrate to issue a warrant of arrest once the Central Government has decided to initiate proceedings and appointed him as magistrate.

**13.76** The magistrate on receipt of the order of appointment, and after perusing the documents submitted to him, shall issue the warrant of arrest for the person or for their production if the person is already in his custody. The magistrate must issue an arrest warrant in order to prevent the person from frustrating the extradition proceedings by absconding. In India, a police officer can execute a warrant for extradition at any place on Indian Territory and the person can be produced before the nearest magistrate having jurisdiction in that area. It is not necessary that the person should be brought before the magistrate appointed under section 5.

**The extradition hearing**

**13.77** Section 7 deals with the procedure before the magistrate and subsection (1) provides as follows:

> When the fugitive criminal appears or is brought before the magistrate, the magistrate shall inquire into the case in the same manner and, shall have, the same jurisdiction and powers, as nearly as may be, as if the case was one trialable by a Court of Session or High Court.

**13.78** Extradition enquiries are similar to that of a trial. The magistrate may receive evidence from the requesting state and the fugitive although there is no requirement to call witnesses. Significantly, and in contrast to section 273 of the Indian Code of Criminal Procedure, evidence submitted in the absence of the fugitive is admissible in extradition proceedings.

**13.79** Section 7(2) allows the magistrate to:

> in particular, take such evidence as may be produced in support of the requisition of the foreign State and on behalf of the fugitive criminal, including any evidence to show that the offence of which the fugitive criminal is accused or has been convicted is an offence of political character or is not an extradition offence.

**13.80** Although the 1962 Act uses the word 'evidence', in *Sarabjit Rick Singh v Union of India*, the Apex Court ruled that:

> the word 'information' occurring in Section 7 could not mean an evidence which has been brought on record upon strict application of the provisions of the Evidence Act. The term 'information' contained therein has a positive meaning. It may in a sense be wider than the words 'documents and the evidence', but when a document is not required to be strictly proved upon applying the provisions of the Indian Evidence Act or when an evidence is not required to be adduced strictly in terms thereof, the use of the word 'information' in Section 10 of the Extradition Act as also Article 9(2) and 9(3) of the Treaty becomes relevant.[57]

**13.81** Although section 7(2) provides that the magistrate will take into account the evidence produced by both the requesting state and the defence, in *Union of India v Maninder Pal Singh Kohli*, the High Court ruled that the defence does not have an absolute right to adduce evidence. The judgment followed a petition by a fugitive subject to an extradition request from

---

[56] (1999) 105 CrLJ 526 (Del).
[57] (2008) I AD (SC) 481.

the United Kingdom who sought to examine, in India, the testimony of seven UK-based witnesses.[58]

In addition an extradition request should also provide evidence that the requesting state has **13.82** jurisdiction over the extradition offences. This is particularly relevant where the conduct alleged occurs in a number of jurisdictions and the requesting state asserts extra-territorial jurisdiction. Recent extradition treaties have reflected this change as they now explicitly cover offences which are not committed within the territory of the requesting state. For instance, the treaty between India and Bahrain asserts that extradition shall be granted in respect of extraditable offences committed outside the territory of the requesting state if it has jurisdiction to try the offence(s). Similar provisions are included in India's treaties with the United States and Canada which provide that extradition shall be granted in respect of extradition offences regardless of where the act or acts that constitute the offence were committed. The main purpose of these provisions is to tackle the rise in international terrorism and offences committed over the internet.

When conducting an extradition enquiry it is for the magistrate rather than the executive to **13.83** decide whether the request relates to a political offence. In such instances, the magistrate must receive evidence from both the requesting state and the person. The fugitive may adduce evidence that the offences of which he is accused or convicted are not extraditable because they are offences of a political character.

If the magistrate is satisfied that the offence is an extraditable offence the person will be com- **13.84** mitted, otherwise he will be discharged. By section 8 the Central Government may, after receipt of the report from the magistrate, deliver the fugitive to the requested state at a place and to a person named in the extradition request. During this period the Central Government may issue a warrant for the custody of the fugitive pending his surrender to the requested state.

Under Section 29, the Central Government has wide powers to discharge the fugitive, or to **13.85** cancel any warrant issued, if it finds that the request has not been made in good faith. It may also discharge the fugitive in the interests of justice or for political reasons if it would be unjust or inexpedient to surrender or return him.

### The issuance of arrest warrants

The High Court in *Flemming Lunding Larsen v Union of India and Others* held that there are **13.86** three provisions under the scheme of the 1962 Act by which a person can be placed under arrest: [59]

- section 6: pursuant to an order under section 5 from the Central Government to the magistrate to inquire into the offence. The magistrate thereafter proceeds under section 7;
- section 9: when it appears to a magistrate that a person within the local limits of his or her jurisdiction is a fugitive criminal of a foreign State. The magistrate must then await an order made by the Central Government under section 5; and
- section 34B: provisional arrest on receipt of an urgent request from a foreign state for the immediate arrest of a fugitive criminal.

---

[58] (2007) V AD (Del) 575.
[59] (1998) 72 DLT.

**13.87**   Only a magistrate nominated under section 5 may issue an arrest warrant under section 6. However, any magistrate may issue a warrant under section 9 which provides:

> Where it appears to any magistrate that a person within the local limits of his jurisdiction is a fugitive criminal of a foreign State he may, if he thinks fit, issue a warrant for the arrest of that person on such information and on such evidence as would, in his opinion, justify the issue of a warrant if the offence of which the person is accused or has been convicted had been committed within the local limits of his jurisdiction.

**13.88**   Following the issue of a warrant under section 9, the magistrate must immediately report it to the Central Government while forwarding the information and evidence, or certified copies thereof. If the Central Government does not make an order under section 5 within three months of the arrest of a person under section 9, that person must be released.[60]

**13.89**   There is also a power under section 41(1)(g) of the Criminal Procedure Code to arrest foreign fugitives in India if there is credible information, or even a reasonable suspicion, that he is concerned with any conduct which, if committed in India, would be punishable as an offence.

**13.90**   Where the Central Government receives a request from a foreign state for the urgent apprehension of a fugitive, it may request the magistrate having competent jurisdiction to issue a provisional arrest warrant under section 34B. Any application for provisional arrest must be supported with information setting out the reasons for the urgency. If the request for extradition is not made within sixty days of provisional arrest the fugitive must be discharged under section 34B(2).

**The receipt of evidence**

**13.91**   Section 10 of the 1962 Act relates to the admission of exhibits, depositions, and other documents as evidence in support of a request. A request for extradition must be supported by the following documents:

- A warrant issued by a court of the requesting state (accusation cases), or the certificate of conviction (conviction cases).
- The depositions or statements taken on oath by any court of justice outside India, or their photocopies. These must be duly authenticated before being received as evidence.
- A letter from the foreign state requesting extradition and setting out a short summary of the allegations. This should be made available to the magistrate at the outset.

**13.92**   While the law does not prescribe any particular form for the letter of request it is advisable to give brief particulars of the fugitive to establish identity, particulars of the extradition offences, and details of the evidence tendered.[61] If the fugitive has already been convicted, the letter of request may simply set out the offence, a certified copy of the sentencing document, and if appropriate, that part of the sentence which remains to be served.

---

[60]   Extradition Act 1962, s 9(2) and (3).
[61]   VK Bansal, *Law of Extradition in India* (Lexis Nexis Butterworths Wadhwa Nagpur, 2008) p 74.

## Chapter III of the 1962 Act

Section 12 of the 1962 Act deals with foreign states with whom the Government of India has **13.93** extradition arrangements and provides as follows:

(1) This Chapter [Chapter III] shall apply only to any such State to which, by reason of an extradition arrangement entered into with that State, it may seem expedient to the Central Government to apply the same.

(2) Every such application shall be by notified order, and the Central Government may, by the same or any subsequent notified order, direct that this Chapter and Chapters I, IV and V shall, in relation to any such foreign state, apply subject to such modifications, exceptions, conditions and qualifications as it may think fit to specify in the order for the purpose of implementing the arrangements.

Under this section, the Central Government will issue a notification specifying restrictions, **13.94** conditions and clarifications which have to be observed while deciding an application for surrender. Such notification is to be issued every time an application is made by a foreign state with which the Union of India has an extradition arrangement.

Section 13 provides that where a fugitive from any state with which India has an extradition **13.95** arrangement is found in India, he shall be apprehended and surrendered following the procedure prescribed in Chapter III.

Under Section 14 any fugitive on Indian territory is liable to be apprehended if he is subject **13.96** to either an endorsed warrant (section 15) or a provisional warrant (section 16).

Endorsed warrants are those issued in a foreign state and sent to the Government of India for **13.97** execution. The Central Government may endorse any such warrant if satisfied that:

- The fugitive is, or is suspected to be, in India.
- The warrant was issued by a person with lawful authority to do so.

Unlike under Chapter II (above), a person arrested on a provisional warrant under section **13.98** 16 can be remanded from time to time until an endorsed warrant is received, but not for more than seven days at a time. This section does not provide an upper limit during which time an endorsed warrant must be received.

Following arrest, the proceedings are governed by section 17 of the 1962 Act. The appointed **13.99** magistrate must be satisfied that the warrant is duly authenticated and that the offence for which warrant is issued is an extradition offence. If satisfied, he will then commit the person in custody and inform the Central Government. Although this Chapter does not explicitly require a magistrate to examine the offence and whether the request relates to a political offence, the overall scheme of the 1962 Act would seem to imply that the magistrate may conduct such an enquiry.

### The rule of speciality

Section 21 of the 1962 Act provides for the rule of speciality where a person is extradited to **13.100** India:

Whenever any person accused or convicted of an offence, which, if committed in India would be an extradition offence, is surrendered or returned by a foreign State, such person shall not, until he has been restored or has had an opportunity of returning to that State, be tried in India for an offence other than

(a) the extradition offence in relation to which he was surrendered or returned; or

(b) any lesser offence disclosed by the facts proved for the purposes of securing his surrender or return other than an offence in relation to which an order for his surrender or return could not be lawfully made; or

(c) the offence in respect of which the foreign State has given its consent.

**13.101** Both the Supreme Court and the High Court have confirmed that a person returned to India can only be tried for the offence(s) for which he was surrendered.[62] In *Prem Swarup v Delhi Administration*, the High Court held that section 21 operates as a bar to the trial of an extradited person for any previous offences until the condition of restoration is satisfied or the fugitive has been given an opportunity to return.[63] However, under the Amendment Act of 1993, a person can be tried for a lesser offence without the consent of the foreign state.

### Restrictions on surrender

**13.102** Restrictions on surrender to a foreign state are addressed in section 31(1), which provides as follows:

A fugitive criminal shall not be surrendered or returned to a foreign State:

(a) If the offence in respect of which his surrender is sought is of a political character or if he proves to the satisfaction of the magistrate or court before whom he may be produced or of the Central Government that the requisition or warrant for his surrender has, in fact, been made with a view to try or punish him for an offence of a political character;

(b) If prosecution for the offence in respect of which his surrender is sought is according to the law of that State or State barred by time;

(c) Unless provision is made by that law of the foreign State or in the extradition treaty with the foreign State that the fugitive criminal shall not be determined or tried in that State for an offence other than

(i) The extradition offence in relation to which he is to be surrendered or returned;

(ii) any lesser offence disclosed by the facts proved for the purposes of securing his surrender or return other than an offence in relation to which an order for his surrender or return could not be lawfully made; or

(iii) The offence in respect of which the Central Government has given its consent;

(d) if he has been accused of some offence in India, not being the offence for which his surrender or return is sought, or is undergoing sentence under any conviction in India until after he has been discharged, whether by acquittal or on expiration of his sentence or otherwise;

(e) until after the expiration of fifteen days from the date of his being committed to prison by the magistrate.

**13.103** Section 31(2) provides that, for the purposes of subsection (1), the offences specified in the Schedule to the Act shall not be regarded as offences of a political character.

**13.104** Additional grounds for refusal may include military offences,[64] double jeopardy, exhaustion of the relevant limitation period,[65] the person's health or age, extraneous considerations (extradition on the basis of the person's nationality, sex, or race),[66] and the death penalty.

---

[62] *Daya Singh Lahoria v Union of India and Union of India and ors* AIR 2001 SC 1716.

[63] (1980) Raj LR Note 54.

[64] The treaties with UAE, Hong Kong and Bhutan do not provide for refusal on the grounds of military offence.

[65] In India the law prohibits prosecution after a prescribed time limit (s 468 of CrPC 1973).

[66] Applies in extradition to South Africa, Hong Kong, the UK, Tunisia, and the Republic of Korea.

However, where a request for extradition is refused, India may consider initiating criminal **13.105** proceeding in its courts in compliance with the 'extradite or prosecute' principle set out in section 34A of the 1963 Act. Under this section the Government of India may apply to the requesting state to provide the evidence and the Indian courts will try the matter as if the crime has been committed in India. To date this right has not been exercised in India.

## D. Extradition procedure in South Africa[67]

### Introduction

In *Mohamed and Another v President of the Republic of South Africa and Others (Society for the* **13.106** *Abolition of the Death Penalty in South Africa and Another Intervening)*, the Constitutional Court of South Africa recognized that extradition essentially involves three aspects: first, acts of sovereignty on the part of two states; secondly, a request by one state to another state for the delivery to it of an alleged criminal; and thirdly, the delivery of the person requested for the purposes of trial or sentence in the territory of the requesting state.[68]

The need for effective extradition procedures has become increasingly acute as the mobility **13.107** of those accused or convicted of national crimes increases, and to reduce the temptation of law enforcement agencies to establish informal and unfair procedures for rendition.[69]

Historically South Africa has been party to very few extradition treaties. Its withdrawal from **13.108** the Commonwealth in 1961 resulted in the lapse of many of its extradition treaties with other Commonwealth states. In subsequent years, foreign states were reluctant to enter into any new extradition treaties with South Africa, largely because of its racist policies of apartheid.

South Africa, having emerged from isolation in 1994 after its first democratic elections, has **13.109** increasingly entered into more extradition treaties.[70]

### Domestic sources of South African extradition law

All law or conduct that is inconsistent with the supreme law of South Africa, the Constitution **13.110** of the Republic of South Africa 1996 ('the Constitution'), is invalid to the extent of the inconsistency.[71] Thus, any law or any executive or judicial conduct concerning extradition must satisfy the requirements of the Constitution, including the Bill of Rights.[72]

The prerogative powers held by the head of state which existed prior to the coming **13.111** into operation of the interim Constitution in 1994 no longer exist.[73] Accordingly, the only

---

[67] Contributed by Anton Katz SC, Cape Town Bar.
[68] 2001 (3) 893 (CC) ('*Mohamed*') at para 28.
[69] *President of the Republic of South Africa v Quagliani and Two Similar Cases* 2009 (2) SA 466 (CC) ('*Quagliani*') at para 41.
[70] See *Quagliani* at para 9, footnote 13; and more generally the information available from the South African Department of Home Affairs at www.dfa.gov.za/foreign/.
[71] Sections 1(c), 2 and 172(1)(a) of the Constitution. The Constitution must be distinguished from the 1994 interim Constitution that existed during the negotiations that ended the apartheid regime.
[72] Chapter 2 of the Constitution (ss 7–38) constitutes the Bill of Rights.
[73] Constitution of the Republic of South Africa, Act 200 of 1993; *President of the Republic of South Africa and Another v Hugo* 1997 (4) SA 1 (CC) at para 8, *Mohamed* at paras 31–32.

powers the South African Government, and particularly the head of state, may exercise are those that are found in the Constitution or legislation.[74]

**13.112** The Constitution itself does not provide for the sending or receiving of extradition requests, but it does regulate the process upon which international agreements, such as extradition agreements, may be entered into and by whom.

**13.113** In South Africa, extradition is governed by the provisions of the Extradition Act No 67 of 1962 ('the Extradition Act') and only addresses requests for extradition by foreign states to South Africa and not vice versa.

### Forms of extradition

**13.114** The Extradition Act makes provision for three situations in which extradition from South Africa may take place.

**13.115** The first is governed by the provisions of section 3(1) of the Extradition Act and applies to any person who is accused or convicted of an extraditable offence committed in the jurisdiction of a foreign state which is a party to an extradition agreement with South Africa.

**13.116** The second basis for extradition is governed by the provisions of section 3(2) of the Extradition Act, which allows for the extradition of a person to a state which is not a party to an extradition agreement with South Africa if the President has in writing consented to that person's surrender.

**13.117** The third scenario is one in which a person is liable to be extradited when the foreign state which requests the surrender has been 'designated' by the President.[75] To date, the President has designated the United Kingdom, Ireland, Zimbabwe, and Namibia as states for the purposes of section 3(3) of the Extradition Act.

**13.118** It is therefore not necessary for there to be an extradition agreement between the requesting state and South Africa for the extradition of requested persons to occur.[76] An individual may be extradited from South Africa to a foreign state, which is not a party to an extradition agreement with South Africa, under the second and third scenarios above where the President consents in writing or if the President has designated the foreign state.

### Extradition procedures

**13.119** The Act provides for two types of extradition procedure: one for 'associated states' and one for all other foreign states. By section 6 (read with section 1) of the Extradition Act, an 'associated state' is an African state with whom South Africa has an extradition treaty. Malawi and Botswana have been held to qualify as associated states, and Swaziland has been held not to qualify.[77]

---

[74] *Fedsure Life Assurance Ltd and ors v Greater Johannesburg Transitional Metropolitan Council and ors* 1999 (1) SA 374 (CC) at paras 56–59.

[75] *Government Gazettes* 478/23321/6 of 19 April 2002 and 188/18663/14 of 13 February 1998.

[76] *Harksen* at para 3; *Geuking v President of the Republic of South Africa and ors* 2003 (3) SA 34 (CC) at para 5.

[77] *S v Bull* 1967 (2) SA 636 (T) at 640H; *S v Williams* 1988 (4) SA 40 (W) at 51(B); *Minister of Justice v Bagattini* 1975 (4) SA 252 (T) at 256C; see generally *S v Eliasov* 1967 (4) SA 583 (A) at 592A–B.

*Associated states*

The procedure governing extradition from South Africa pursuant to requests by associated **13.120** states is simpler and intended to be more expeditious than the procedure concerning non-associated states. The simplified procedure consists of two phases.

The first is provided for by section 4 (read with section 9) of the Extradition Act and consists **13.121** of the administrative phase, in which a request for extradition is received by the South African authorities and processed until such time as the person is arrested and brought before the court.[78]

The second phase is the judicial phase, in which an extradition enquiry is held before a mag- **13.122** istrate under section 12 of the Extradition Act. The magistrate then determines whether the person should be surrendered in extradition to the requesting state. If the magistrate orders that the person is to be surrendered to the foreign state, the person has a right to appeal that decision to the High Court under section 13.

The enquiry before the magistrate is to determine whether the order for surrender is to be **13.123** issued and, subject to the grounds contained in section 12(2)(c), a magistrate must make the order for surrender under section 12(1) of the Extradition Act. The grounds contained in section 12(2)(c) are as follows:

• by reason of the trivial nature of the offence or by reason of the surrender not being acquired in good faith or in the interests of justice, or that for any other reason it would, having regard for the distance, the facilities for communication and to all the circum-stances of the case, be unjust or unreasonable or too severe a punishment to surrender the person concerned;

• the person concerned will be prosecuted or punished or prejudiced at his or her trial in the associated state by reason of his or her gender, race, religion, nationality or political opinion.

*Non-associated states*

Those requesting states which are not associated states are governed by a three-phase **13.124** process.

First there is the administrative phase, which is not dissimilar to that which relates to requests **13.125** by associated states.[79]

The second phase is the judicial phase.[80] The judicial phase consists of a magistrate's court **13.126** enquiry, where the magistrate is required to determine whether the person should be com-mitted to prison or not. Unlike in cases concerning associated states, the magistrate does not decide whether the person should be surrendered. In cases concerning non-associated states, it is the Minister of Justice who makes the decision to surrender.

---

[78] *Abel v Minister of Justice and Constitutional Development* ('*Abel*') 2001 (1) SA 1230 (C).

[79] *Abel; S v Thornhill* 1997 (2) SACR 626 (C).

[80] In *Minister of Justice and Constitutional Development and anor v Additional Magistrate, Cape Town* 2001 (2) SACR 49 (C), the court held that an extradition enquiry before a magistrate constitutes a judicial enquiry.

**13.127**  During the judicial phase the magistrate must consider two issues.[81] First whether the person is liable to be surrendered to the requesting state and, in accusation cases, whether there is sufficient evidence to warrant a prosecution for the offence in the foreign state concerned.

**13.128**  For the purpose of satisfying himself that there is sufficient evidence to warrant a prosecution in the requesting state, the magistrate shall accept as conclusive proof a certificate which appears to him to be issued by an appropriate authority in charge of the prosecution in the foreign state concerned, stating that it has sufficient evidence at its disposal to warrant the prosecution of the person concerned.[82]

**13.129**  If the magistrate is satisfied that the person concerned is liable to extradition and, where the person is an accused, that there is sufficient evidence to warrant the prosecution, the magistrate has no discretion but to commit the person to prison to await the decision of the Minister of Justice as to surrender.[83] When the magistrate issues the order of committal, he must immediately forward to the Minister a copy of the record of proceedings together with such report as he considers necessary.[84]

**13.130**  The third phase is the executive phase in which the Minister of Justice decides whether the person should be surrendered at all or at some later point.[85] Where the person is facing criminal proceedings and/or a term of imprisonment in South Africa, extradition may be delayed until such proceedings and any sentence are concluded.[86]

**13.131**  The Minister of Justice may refuse to issue an order of surrender at all, if satisfied that any of the grounds in section 11(b)(iii) of the Extradition Act are made out. These grounds are in the same terms as those under section 12(2)(c) (above). Finally, the Minister may refuse to issue an order of surrender if the person concerned will be prosecuted or punished or prejudiced at his or her trial in the associated state by reason of his or her gender, race, religion, nationality, or political opinion.

### Bail

**13.132**  Any person arrested under the Extradition Act must, under the Constitution, be brought before a court.[87] At the person's first appearance the magistrate has the power to grant the detained person bail in a similar manner to other arrested and detained persons.[88]

**13.133**  A person who has lodged an appeal under subsection 13(1) may, at any time before the appeal has been disposed of, apply to the magistrate who issued the order to be released on

---

[81]  *Geuking v President of the Republic of South Africa and Others ('Geuking')* 2003 (3) SA 34 (CC); *Director of Public Prosecutions, Cape of Good Hope v Robinson* 2005 (4) SA 1 (CC).

[82]  Section 10(2) of the Extradition Act; a constitutional challenge to the validity of s 10(2) did not succeed, see *Geuking*.

[83]  *Harksen v Director of Public Prosecutions and ors* [2002] 1 All SA 284 (C).

[84]  Section 10(4) of the Extradition Act; see also *Garrido v Director of Public Prosecutions, Witwatersrand Local Division and ors* 2007 (1) SACR 1 (SCA) for the proposition that the person brought before the magistrate is entitled to adduce evidence before the magistrate which could influence the Minister's surrender decision.

[85]  Section 11 of the Extradition Act; *Robinson v Minister of Justice and Constitutional Development* 2006 (6) SA 214 (C); *Harksen v Minister of Justice and Constitutional Development of the RSA and ors* [2002] 4 All SA 642 (C).

[86]  Section 11(b)(i) and (ii) of the Extradition Act.

[87]  Section 35(1) of the Constitution.

[88]  Section 9(2) of the Extradition Act; *S v Thornhill* (2) 1998 (1) SACR 177 (C).

bail on various conditions.[89] In respect of orders of surrender by either or both the magistrate and/or the Minister, any such order shall not be executed before the period allowed for an appeal has expired unless the person has in writing waived his right of appeal, or before such an appeal has been disposed of.[90]

Bail should be granted if it is in the interests of justice.[91] The key question to be answered is whether it is more likely that the accused will stand his trial than that he will abscond and forfeit his bail. The following factors are relevant: **13.134**

- how deep are the person's emotional, occupational and family roots within the country where he is to stand trial;
- what are his assets in that country;
- what are the means that he has to flee from the country;
- how much can he afford the forfeiture of the bail money;
- the availability of travel documents to enable him to leave the country;
- what arrangements exist or may later exist to extradite him if he flees to another country;
- how inherently serious is the offence in respect of which he is charged;
- how strong is the case against him and how much inducement there would therefore be for him to avoid standing trial;
- how severe is the punishment likely to be if he is found guilty; and
- how stringent are the conditions of his bail and how difficult would it be for him to evade effective policing of his movements.[92]

In addition, the court must take into account how prejudicial it might be for the person in all the circumstances to be kept in custody by being denied bail. This would involve again an examination of other issues such as, for example: **13.135**

- the duration of the period for which he has already been incarcerated, if any;
- the duration of the period during which he will have to be in custody before his trial is completed;
- the cause of any delay in the completion of his trial and whether or not the accused is partially or wholly to be blamed for such a delay;
- the extent to which the accused needs to continue working in order to meet his financial obligations;
- the extent to which he might be prejudiced in engaging legal assistance for his defence and in effectively preparing for his defence if he remains in custody; and
- the health of the accused.[93]

### Appeals

In respect of both associated and non-associated states, the person against whom an order for surrender or committal has been issued under sections 10 or 12 of the Extradition Act may, **13.136**

---

[89] Section 13(3) of the Extradition Act.
[90] Section 14(a) and (b) of the Extradition Act.
[91] Section 35(1)(f) of the Constitution; *S v Thornhill (2)* 1998 (1) SACR 177 (C) at 181.
[92] *S v Acheson* 1991 (2) SA 805 (Nm); see s 60 of the Criminal Procedure Act 51 of 1977.
[93] See *Robinson v Minister of Justice and Constitutional Development* 2006 (6) SA 214 (C) relying on *Warren (R) v Secretary of State for the Home Department* [2003] EWHC 1177 (Admin) at para 23.

within fifteen days, appeal to the High Court and the High Court may make such order as it deems fit.[94]

**13.137**   No order by the Minister for the surrender of any person shall be executed if the High Court, after reasonable notice to the Minister, orders the person's discharge on the grounds that there is insufficient cause for further detention. Such an order must be made within two months of the issue of the order of committal where there has been no appeal, or from the date that any appeal is dismissed.[95]

**13.138**   In the case of an order of a magistrate, a High Court may make a similar order of discharge within one month of the order of the magistrate becoming operative. No order for surrender shall thereafter be executed.[96]

**13.139**   Whether or not an order of discharge by a magistrate or by the High Court constitutes res judicata and the person can thereafter no longer be subject to an extradition enquiry in respect of the same charges, depends upon the basis of the discharge.[97] If the discharge is on the merits of the proceedings before the magistrate or High Court, the discharge order would be regarded as res judicata between the person concerned and the foreign state. However, if the person was discharged on the basis that the required evidence is not forthcoming within a reasonable time,[98] the discharge order would not be regarded as res judicata.

**13.140**   If the magistrate commits the person to prison, the Minister has a discretion as to whether to order the committed person to be surrendered or to order that the person shall not be surrendered. The courts have accepted that in general, a rule of non-enquiry has been developed in deference to the sovereignty of the requesting state.[99]

**13.141**   However, the Minister is permitted to make a limited enquiry when norms of international human rights are invoked. If the person complains that he has been tortured or suffered a similar violation of his human rights, this would constitute a flagrant denial of justice by the requesting state. The Minister would then be required to consider the validity of a complaint by the person that he would suffer a flagrant denial of justice by the requesting state if he were to be surrendered.[100]

**Special considerations**

*Death penalty*

**13.142**   South Africa has abolished the death penalty. Therefore, in keeping with international practice, assurances must be sought from the requesting state if extradition is sought for an offence that attracts the death penalty. The Constitutional Court in *Mohamed* has ruled that it would be unlawful and unconstitutional to extradite any person to face the possibility of

---

[94]   Section 13(1) and (2) of the Extradition Act.
[95]   Section 14(e) of the Extradition Act.
[96]   Section 14(f) of the Extradition Act.
[97]   *S v McCarthy* 1995 (3) SA 731 (A).
[98]   Section 10(3) of the Extradition Act.
[99]   *Robinson v Minister of Justice and Constitutional Development* ('*Robinson (High Court)*') 2006 (6) SA 214 (C) at 229.
[100]   *Robinson (High Court)* 2006 (6) SA 214 (C).

the death penalty without first securing an assurance that he or she would not be sentenced to death, or if so sentenced, would not be executed.[101]

### Sentence in absentia

In *Robinson (High Court)*, the court dealt with the issue of R being sentenced *in absentia* by the Canadian Court after having been present and represented during his trial. The court considered decisions of the US and Canadian courts, and the European Court of Human Rights, and found that in the circumstances, it did not necessarily constitute a flagrant denial of justice that R had been sentenced *in absentia*, and the Minister's surrender decision was not set aside.[102]    **13.143**

### Speciality

The rule of speciality provides that the requesting state is not permitted to prosecute an extradited individual for acts committed before his extradition and for which extradition was not sought. In *S v Stokes* the appellant was extradited from the United States to South Africa.[103] After his arrival he was served with an indictment containing a count of theft and three counts of fraud (all of which were allegedly committed before his extradition). He contended that he could not be charged with the aforementioned crimes, since they were not the crimes in respect of which his extradition from the United States was sought and granted. The court in applying the doctrine of speciality confirmed that:    **13.144**

> the person surrendered shall be tried and punished exclusively for offences for which extradition had been requested and granted (not sought), except after the fugitive offender has been given an opportunity to return to the extraditing country.[104]

### Double criminality

It is a requirement of the extradition process that the offence for which the person is sought constitutes an offence either as contemplated by the relevant extradition agreement or in respect of the laws of the requested state.[105]    **13.145**

### Non bis in idem

A person may not be extradited in respect of an offence of which he has already been acquitted or convicted by the requested state. This principle, which confirms the principle of *autrefois acquit* or *convict*, is not included in the Extradition Act, but appears in most extradition agreements.[106]    **13.146**

### Political offenders

The Extradition Act recognizes the political offence exception, and section 15 empowers the Minister of Justice to intervene at any stage during extradition proceedings in order to release    **13.147**

---

[101] *Mohamed* at paras 52–54.
[102] See *Robinson (High Court)* generally.
[103] *S v Stokes* ('*Stokes*') 2008 (2) SACR 307 (SCA), 2008 (5) SA 644 (SCA).
[104] *Stokes* at para 10. See s 19 of the Extradition Act.
[105] See *Abel v Minister of Justice* 2001 (1) SA 1230 (C); *Abel v Additional Magistrate, Cape Town and ors* 2002 (2) SACR 83 at 92C; *S v Bell* [1997] 2 All SA 692(e) at 699b–c; *S v Thornhill* 1997 (2) SACR 626 (C) at 636e; *Harksen v President of the RSA* 1998 (2) SA 1011 (C) at 1038H–I.
[106] See s 19 of the Extradition Act.

a fugitive if satisfied that the offence in respect of which extradition is sought is 'an offence of a political character'.

**13.148** In the context of the political offence exception, international terrorism presents a particular problem. In 2004 the Extradition Act was amended in an attempt to prevent terrorists from successfully relying on the political offence exception.[107] Section 22 of the Extradition Act now states that a request for extradition based on offences contemplated by the Protection of Constitutional Democracy Against Terrorist and Related Activities Act 33 of 2004 may not be refused on the sole ground that it concerns a political offence, an offence connected with a political offence, an offence inspired by political motives, or that it is a fiscal offence.[108] However, the general human rights considerations contained in sections 11 and 12 of the Extradition Act still apply in such cases.[109]

## E. Extradition procedure in the United States[110]

### Introduction

**13.149** Extradition requests received by the United States are first considered by the State Department prior to any judicial determination. The State Department is responsible for reviewing the request to ensure compliance with the relevant treaty and domestic law. It must consider whether the request is properly certified, the offence meets the dual criminality test, and whether the request contains the charging document and arrest warrant in relation to the offences for which extradition is sought.

**13.150** If satisfied that these requirements are met, the State Department's Office of the Legal Adviser prepares a declaration asserting these facts together with confirmation that there is a treaty in force between the United States and the requesting state. The request together with the declaration is sent to the Department of Justice's (DOJ) Office of International Affairs (OIA), in the Criminal Division, for review and execution. If the State Department considers the request to be deficient in any way, it will usually submit the request to the OIA for a detailed review. If the considered view of the OIA is that further information is required before the request can be executed, the State Department then returns the request, with comments, to the requesting state for clarification or for supplementary information.

### The role of the DOJ's Office of International Affairs and the review process

**13.151** Upon receipt of an extradition request from the State Department, the OIA conducts an in-depth review to ensure that the request complies with the requirements of the treaty namely:

- the request contains the documents required by the terms of the treaty (text of the relevant law, arrest warrant, charging document, if any, judgment, or memorandum of conviction);
- the request relates to an extraditable offence;

---

[107] Section 27(1) of Act No 33 of 2004.
[108] Section 22 of the Extradition Act. For the fiscal offence issue, see *Thornhill (1)* at 636.
[109] *Tantoush v Refugee Appeal Board* 2008 (1) SA 232 (T).
[110] Contributed by Jason E Carter, US–UK Liaison Officer.

- particulars of identity of the offender; and
- information establishing probable cause to believe that an extraditable offence has been committed and that the person whose extradition is sought committed the offence.

United States law does not require that an extradition request from a requesting state be **13.152** accompanied by sufficient evidence that would justify a conviction for a domestic offence. Thus, proof beyond a reasonable doubt, the standard for conviction in a US domestic prosecution, is not required.

Extradition requests to the United States must therefore only meet the 'probable cause' stan- **13.153** dard, which is the same standard as required by the US Constitution for the issuance of any warrant of arrest, including warrants issued in connection with a domestic prosecution. This Constitutional requirement is one that all countries must satisfy when making requests for extradition.

Following a review of the request the OIA sends the documents, if they are complete, to the **13.154** US Attorney's Office (federal prosecutor/USAO) in the federal district where the person is believed to be located.

The prosecutor then conducts a further review of the request and accompanying evidence **13.155** and prepares a complaint which is filed with the court to obtain the arrest warrant. Once the warrant is issued, it is delivered to a US law enforcement agency (generally the US Marshal's Service) for execution.

In urgent cases, a request provisional arrest prior to the receipt of a formal extradition request **13.156** can be submitted; however, a request for provisional arrest must set out reasons for the urgency and the following information must be included:

- a description of the person and possible location, including, to the extent known, the name and aliases, citizenship, place and date of birth, physical description, distinguishing features, and passport number. If available, a copy of the fugitive's photograph or fingerprints;
- a description of the document charging the person with criminal conduct, including the date issued, the issuing court, and a list of offences charged, including citations to the laws violated;
- a description of the arrest warrant, including the date issued, the issuing court, and a list of offences charged, including citations to the laws violated;
- a brief but thorough chronological statement of the alleged crime, identifying key participants and their specific acts in furtherance of the offence. The sources from which these facts are known, and the reason for believing these sources to be reliable, should be identified; and
- a statement that a formal request for extradition will be submitted in the time required by the applicable treaty.

As a matter of best practice, foreign states preparing extradition documents designed to meet **13.157** the probable cause standard should ensure that the request contains, first, a complete statement of facts that clearly and carefully shows the person's involvement in the commission of each offence for which extradition is requested and, secondly, references to the sources and reliability of evidence supporting the person's involvement in each such offence.

### Contents of an extradition request

**13.158** An extradition request should contain a case summary. This is a sworn statement by the foreign authority making the extradition request (for example a public prosecutor or investigating magistrate) and should include the following:

- name and title of the author;
- identification of the fugitive, including citizenship and a physical description (referring to photographs, fingerprints, or other forms of identification attached as exhibits);
- information on the fugitive's location;
- a detailed statement of the facts of the case and the source of evidence establishing these facts as described above (referring to witness statements or other relevant evidentiary documents attached as exhibits);
- the procedural history of the case including an explanation of any unusual practice or procedure (referring to relevant procedural documents attached as exhibits);
- a list of offences for which extradition is sought and the maximum penalty for each (referring to statutes or penal code provisions attached as exhibits);
- in the event that the fugitive has spent time in custody for the offence in question, a statement of the remaining time to be spent in custody;
- depending on the provisions of the applicable treaty, a statement that the statute of limitations does not bar prosecution or imposition of sentence (referring to statutes or penal code provisions attached as exhibits); and
- a list of exhibits (these should be identified and referred to in the case summary).

**13.159** The exhibits should be clearly marked and properly certified, for example, where the identification information includes a detailed physical description of the fugitive, photographs, fingerprints etc, there must be a nexus between the details provided and the person to show that he is indeed the person charged in the requesting country.

**13.160** An extradition request should also include the text of the relevant statutes (including the sections of the relevant penal code, the penalty provisions, and any applicable statute of limitations or period of prescription, if required by the applicable treaty).

**13.161** Where a request relates to a person convicted, the request must include an authenticated copy of the judgment of conviction and confirmation of the prison term to be served. However, a conviction *in absentia*, is generally treated as an 'accusation' case and therefore the request must include the same supporting materials as are required for a person charged and not convicted. In addition, the courts will require a detailed explanation of a person's rights to retrial or appeal.

### Certification of an extradition request

**13.162** Unless a different authentication procedure is specified in the applicable treaty, the US Embassy in the requesting country must certify all documents submitted in support of an extradition request in order for the documents to be admissible in a US court. The US Embassy certifies that the documents have been authenticated in accordance with the laws of the requesting state in a manner that would entitle them to be received for similar purposes in the courts of the requesting country. Once certified, the US Embassy will return the documents to the requesting state's foreign ministry to forward to the United States via the diplomatic channel, or as otherwise specified in the applicable treaty. In addition to the authenticated set of documents the requesting state should include at least one complete unbound set of the documents.

### Proceedings in court

Once a person has been arrested for the purposes of extradition, he is brought before a federal judge who informs the person of the reason for his arrest and sets a date for the extradition hearing. At this stage, or at any time before the hearing, the person may move to be released on bail. However, there is a strong presumption against bail in extradition cases.

**13.163**

The court then sets a date for the extradition hearing. As in most jurisdictions, the purpose of extradition proceedings in the United States is not to determine guilt or innocence. In most cases therefore no live evidence is called and the court makes a determination on the documents submitted. However, the court retains its discretion to call live testimony in instances where it is considered appropriate.

**13.164**

In deciding whether the person should be committed for extradition, the court must be satisfied of the following matters:

**13.165**

- Is the judge or court authorized to conduct the extradition proceedings?
- Does it have jurisdiction over the person?
- Is the applicable treaty in full force and effect?
- Are the crimes for which extradition is requested covered by the applicable treaty?
- Is the person before the court, in fact, the person whose extradition is sought?
- Is there sufficient evidence to support a finding of probable cause in respect of the charges for which extradition is sought?

'Probable cause' is a lower standard of proof than that which is required for conviction in a US court, and is in fact a much lower standard of proof than the prima facie standard required in extradition proceedings in some common law systems. The test for 'probable cause' is a reasonable basis to believe that the person whose extradition is requested committed the offences for which extradition is sought. The extradition documents must demonstrate that reliable evidence exists in the requesting state to prove that the fugitive committed each offence for which extradition is requested. This means more than just a statement of the facts: the specific source of evidence for the facts must also be described or included so that the US judge can evaluate its reliability. Hearsay evidence may be included.

**13.166**

If the person is found extraditable, the court will issue an order certifying that finding to the Secretary of State. The court will also order that the fugitive remain in custody pending issuance of the Secretary's surrender warrant.

**13.167**

Extradition decisions are not subject to appeal, either by the person or the US Government. However, within thirty days of the court's order, the fugitive can file a writ of habeas corpus seeking review of his continuing custody and the court's finding in favour of extradition. Thereafter, the person can appeal a denial of the habeas corpus petition through the appellate process, up to the Supreme Court.

**13.168**

US courts have repeatedly held that the extradition laws and treaties of the United States are to be interpreted liberally in order to effect extradition, and that the scope of defences that a

**13.169**

person is permitted to raise in opposition to extradition is severely limited. Matters outside the scope of the hearing include consideration of the defendant's affirmative defences and attacks on the credibility of the requesting government's witnesses.

### Consent/waiver

**13.170**  If the person consents to extradition, the court similarly will issue an order of 'extraditability' and the person is held in custody pending issuance of the Secretary of State's surrender warrant.

**13.171**  Equally, the person may also waive extradition at any time after he has been arrested. In such instances, the court does not have to make a determination of 'extraditability' and neither is the matter referred to the Secretary of State for the surrender order. Instead, the court commits the person into custody of the US Marshals who arrange his return to the requesting state.

### The State Department and the surrender phase

**13.172**  The United States has two calendar months to remove the person once the judicial proceedings have concluded.

**13.173**  The State Department must review the documents from the court, consider any humanitarian arguments that may be raised against surrender, and issue the surrender warrant. The US Marshals, in cooperation with the requesting state, must then remove the fugitive within the two-month period.

# 14

## THE POLITICAL OFFENCE EXCEPTION

## A. Introduction

Despite its previous importance as a doctrine of extradition law, in the United Kingdom the **14.01** Extradition Act 2003 ('the 2003 Act') removed reference to the political offence exception entirely. Instead the 2003 Act bars extradition where there are substantial grounds to believe that the request has been made for the purpose of prosecuting or punishing a person on account of their race, religion, nationality, ethnic origin, or political opinion (known as 'extraneous considerations').[1]

However, the political offence exception continues to play a role in other jurisdictions, and **14.02** indeed has received renewed attention in international instruments, most particularly the counter-terrorism conventions. Many regional instruments and arrangements, such as the London Scheme for Extradition within the Commonwealth, contain the political offence exception.[2]

The move under the 2003 Act away from the political offence exception to extraneous con- **14.03** siderations may reflect the approach in a number of international and regional conventions, in particular, the counter-terrorism conventions, which have prohibited the application of the exception. For example, the Terrorist Bombing Convention 1997 is the first interna- tional instrument in which the political offence exception is explicitly excluded.[3] Article 11 of that Convention provides:

> None of the offences set forth in Article 2 shall be regarded, for the purposes of extradition or mutual legal assistance, as a political offence or as an offence connected with a political offence

---

[1] Extradition Act 2003, ss 11, 13, 79 and 81. For a more detailed consideration of extraneous considerations see 6.14–6.18 above.

[2] Article 12 of the Commonwealth Scheme for the Rendition of Fugitive Offenders sets out the Political Offence Exception which is identical in terms with other extradition treaties and international instruments. The full text of the London Scheme (as amended in 1990) can be found at <http://www.thecommonwealth.org/Internal/38061/documents/>.

[3] This has been echoed in the subsequent conventions.

or as an offence inspired by political motives. Accordingly, a request for extradition or for mutual legal assistance based on such an offence may not be refused on the sole ground that it concerns a political offence or an offence connected with a political offence or an offence inspired by political motives.

14.04 In practice, even in its heyday, the cases in which states refused to extradite a fugitive on the basis of the political offence exception were few and far between. However, given the historical significance of this principle, and its continued application in foreign jurisdictions, this chapter looks at its historical development, analyses some of the leading cases in which the political offence exception was raised, and examines its modern day application in the international context.[4]

## B. What does political offence exception mean?

14.05 Despite its common usage both in extradition and refugee law, there is no definition or agreed meaning of this phrase. Treaties, whether bilateral, regional, or international have all remained silent. It has been largely left to national courts to interpret the term, assisted, to some extent, by the general comments and interpretation guidance issued by human rights committees and commissions.

14.06 Historically, the political offence exception has constituted a ground for refusal of extradition in many countries. That exception was based upon a desire to provide political asylum to persons accused of offences arising out of political activity directed against the government of another state, such as treason, sedition, or attempts to force a ruling group to change or adopt certain policies, otherwise referred to as 'pure' offences. This approach is fairly straightforward and clear, however the difficulty arises in respect of 'relative' offences, that is, conduct that alleges criminality but is also linked with political activity. It is this latter range of offences that national courts and international bodies have sought to grapple with.

14.07 The starting point must, therefore, be a determination by the court as to whether the offence falls within the exception and, if so, whether is it a 'pure' offence or a 'relative' offence. Once that is determined, it then becomes a matter for the court to decide if the particular facts lend themselves to the application of the exception.

### 'Pure' offences

14.08 Turning first to the 'pure' political offence, an illustration of the application of the exception is a case from Botswana called *The Republic of Namibia v Kakaena Likunga Alfred & others*.[5]

14.09 The case related to a request by the Republic of Namibia for the extradition of a group of individuals in respect of offences alleged to have been committed by them in the Caprivi region of that country. It was alleged that they were members of an organisation known as the Caprivi Liberation Army (CLA) which was seeking secession from Namibia. The CLA had set up training camps in Namibia securing arms and ammunitions. It was alleged that two of the group had shot and killed a person who was attempting to escape from the

---

[4] For a more detailed discussion readers are referred to Arvinder Sambei, Anton du Plessis, and Martin Polaine, *Counter-Terrorism Law and Practice: An International Handbook* (Oxford University Press, 2009) Ch 9.

[5] Court of Appeal, Botswana 64/03 (July 2004).

training camp. It was further alleged that the group had planned an attack on Namibia and, to that end, some of them had participated in an attack on government installations killing a number of people. The group had then fled to neighbouring Botswana.

Namibia sought extradition in respect of two charges, namely high treason and the unlawful **14.10** possession of arms and ammunition. All of the accused were arrested in August 2000 and were ruled extraditable by the magistrate the following year. The accused appealed to the High Court and were discharged on the grounds that the offences of which they were accused were caught by the political offence exception. In upholding this decision, the Court of Appeal held:

> The extradition application in respect of [the persons] had to be refused on the high treason charges because these were offences of a political character. This finding is made (a) because treason is per se a political offence and (b) because the actions of the [persons] ... were, in light of the background of them committed in the course of a political struggle against the Government of Namibia in pursuance of [the persons'] political aims ... [T]hey were therefore offences of a political character ... The possession by the [persons] of arms and ammunition was part of those actions and offences arising from such possession are therefore also offences of a political character.

The application of the exception in 'pure' offences is relatively straightforward and poses **14.11** little difficulty. As stated above, the range of offences that fall within the category of 'pure' offences are limited indeed. By far, the more common instances are those where the offence alleged may exhibit political tones but do not fall within the narrow category of treason or sedition; such offences are commonly referred to as 'relative' offences.

### 'Relative' offences

There has been a gradual development of the jurisprudence with respect to 'relative' offences, **14.12** and readers are urged to consider decisions from a range of jurisdictions when considering the application of the principle. The authorities show that the exception will always apply in cases involving 'pure' offences, but where the court is considering a 'relative' offence, the position is less than clear.

We will now examine the historical approach of the UK courts in determining the application **14.13** of the exception in cases that fall within 'relative' offences. The first of such cases was determined in *Re Castioni* which expounded the 'incidence' test in respect of relative offences.[6] This has been widely adopted and modified by various jurisdictions. It may assist to consider some of the cases illustrating the distillation of that test.

### *Re Castioni and the incidence test*

On 11 September 1890 a number of citizens, one of whom was the applicant Castioni, seized **14.14** the arsenal of a town in Switzerland, detained several people connected to the government and made them march to the municipal palace. The backdrop to this event was the general dissatisfaction in the town with the government administration. Upon arrival at the palace, the victim and another member of the government refused entry to the crowd. The applicant, who was armed, shot the victim. There was no evidence to suggest that the applicant

---

[6] [1891] 1 QB 149.

knew the victim prior to the incident. The palace was occupied and several members of the government were imprisoned.

**14.15** The Swiss Government sought the extradition of Castioni in respect of the murder and he contended that he should not be surrendered as the offence was 'one of a political character'.

**14.16** The magistrate rejected that argument and Castioni was committed. He lodged a petition for a writ of habeas corpus and the High Court in allowing the appeal considered the meaning of 'offence of a political nature':

> I think that in order to bring the case within the words of the Act and to exclude extradition for such an act as murder, which is one of the extradition offences, *it must at least be shewn that the act is done in furtherance of, done with intention of assistance, as a sort of overt act in the course of acting in a political matter, a political uprising, or a dispute between two parties in the State as to which is to have the government in its hands, before it can be brought within the meaning of the words used in the Act* … I do not think it is intended that a scrap of a prima facie case on the one side should have the effect of throwing upon the other side the onus of proving or disproving his position … there is nothing said as to upon whom is the onus probandi, or that it shall be made to appear by one side or the other in such a case. It is a restriction upon the surrender of a fugitive criminal … wholly irrespective of any doctrine of onus on the one side or the other, that is within the restriction, and he cannot be surrendered … I think it follows that this Court must have the power to go into the whole matter, and in some cases … might take a different view of the matter from that taken by the magistrate. It seems to me that it is a question of mixed law and fact—mainly indeed fact—as to whether the facts are such as to bring the case within s.3 and to shew that it was an offence of a political character …[7] (emphasis added)

**14.17** Therefore the incidence test has two limbs:

- the alleged crimes must be committed in the course of, and incidental to, a political disturbance such as war, revolution, or rebellion; and
- there must be a nexus between the crime and the alleged political objective.

*The application of the incidence test*

**14.18** The incidence test was followed in *Re Meunier*, a request to the United Kingdom from France for an anarchist who had caused an explosion.[8] The court rejected the applicant's argument that the conduct fell within the exception on the basis that the crime was committed towards private citizens.

**14.19** In *R v Governor of Brixton Prison ex parte Schtraks*, Israel sought the extradition of Schtraks from the United Kingdom to stand trial on charges of perjury and child stealing allegedly committed in Jerusalem. He was committed to await extradition to Israel.[9]

**14.20** Lord Reid introduced a subjective element in the determination of the exception, namely the 'motive and purpose of the accused in committing the offence must be relevant and may be decisive'.[10] This cast some doubt on the previously rigid incidence test which required proof of a nexus to violent political uprising or insurrection.

---

[7] Per Denman J (emphasis added).
[8] [1894] 2 QB 415.
[9] [1894] 2 QB 415.
[10] At 583–584.

This approach was the subject of comment in the case of *Tzu-Tsai Cheng v Governor of* **14.21**
*Pentonville Prison*.[11] The cases so far had concerned conduct in the requesting state; however,
in *Cheng* the court considered the question of whether the political offence exception applied
where the conduct alleged had no political nexus to the requesting state, in this case the
United States.

The applicant Cheng was convicted of murder in the United States. He was the executive **14.22**
secretary of a political group (WUFI) which promoted as one its aims the exposure of the
corruption and oppression of the Chiand Kai-Shek regime in Taiwan. On 24 April 1970,
Kai-Shek's son visited New York and WUFI planned a demonstration. During the course of
the demonstration a shot was fired and the applicant was arrested. He subsequently travelled
to the United Kingdom.

In extradition proceedings in the United Kingdom, the applicant submitted that he had **14.23**
been convicted of an offence of a 'political character'. It was accepted that he was not engaged
in any political activity against the United States. The issue that arose was whether an offence
committed within the jurisdiction of the requesting state can amount to an offence of a
political character where (1) the offence was committed in the course of a dispute between
the governing party of a state other than the requesting state, on the one hand, and a movement dedicated to its overthrow; and (2) the offence was committed directly to further the
purpose of that movement and for no other purpose, or for any other motive. The House of
Lords held that 'political character' in its context connoted opposition to the requesting state
on some issue connected with the political control or government of that state. As the applicant was not taking political action against the US Government the offence was not one of a
political character within the meaning of the relevant legislation. In dismissing the appeal
their Lordships reiterated the incidence test.

*The application of the exception in other jurisdictions*

In the United States the political offence exception has been raised in both deportation and **14.24**
extradition matters, with the courts adopting a similar approach to that of the United
Kingdom. The US Court of Appeals for the Fourth Circuit in the recent case of *Wilmer
Yarleque Ordinola v John Hackman* very helpfully sets out the position and historical develop-
ment of the exception by the US courts.[12] In the leading case of *Barapind v Enomoto* the US
Court of Appeals held:

> ... the indiscriminate killing of civilians and police officers cannot and must not qualify for
> the political offense exception to extradition, even if 'politically motivated'. To hold otherwise
> is to open the door for our country to turn into 'a social jungle and an encouragement to ter-
> rorists everywhere' [Eain, 641 F.2d at 520]. In international affairs and multi-lateral situa-
> tions, one cannot ignore the principle of reciprocity: what goes around comes around.

In Canada, the exception was examined in *Gil v Canada (Minister of Employment and* **14.25**
*Immigration) (CA)* in the context of refugee law, in particular the application and interpretation of Article 1F(b) of the United Nations Convention Relating to the Status of Refugees
1951. This Article excludes the application of the Convention in cases where the applicant

---

[11] [1973] AC 931.
[12] US Court of Appeals for the Fourth Circuit No 06-6126 (22 December 2007).

has committed a serious non-political crime outside the country of refuge prior to his admission to that country as a refugee.[13]

**14.26**   During the time of the Khomeini regime in Iran in 1979, Gil, an Iranian citizen and supporter of the Shah, was engaged in incidents of bombing and arson against supporters of the regime. The incidents occurred in crowded bazaars, consequently leading to the death and injury of innocent people. Gil subsequently left for Canada in 1986 and his refugee status was determined in 1991. The Immigration Board found that Gil had a well-founded fear of persecution if he were to be returned to Iran; however, given the nature of the allegations against him, he could not avail himself of the protection under the Convention under Article 1F(b).

**14.27**   The Court of Appeal, in dismissing the application, examined the nature of 'political offence' and whether the meaning as understood under extradition law was mutatis mutandis applicable under refugee law. The court held:

> Although the concept of 'political crime' is not normally thought of as known to Canadian criminal law, in two respects at least the laws of Canada recognize that the consequences of an otherwise criminal act may vary if that act can be characterized as political … The two exceptions are found in the law of refugee status and extradition law. Although they are said to be but two sides of the same coin and serve to complement one another, there are important differences between the two.

**14.28**   More recently, in Thailand a court dismissed a US request for extradition in the case of Viktor Bout, an alleged arms dealer and representative of the FARC (Revolutionary Armed Forces of Columbia). The request was refused on the grounds that the allegations amounted to an offence of a political nature as Thailand did not recognize the FARC as a terrorist organization and therefore it did not see itself as bound by the prohibition on the political offence exception said to apply in terrorism cases.[14]

## C.  Concluding remarks

**14.29**   The authorities show that, in jurisdictions where the exception applies, pure offences attract an absolute prohibition for the purposes of extradition. Whether a relative offence attracts protection will depend on the principles outlined above.

**14.30**   The move away from the political offence exception in the United Kingdom reflected the general trend in some international conventions and the reasons behind it can be seen in the 1996 judgment of Lord Mustill in an asylum case:[15]

> during the 19th century those who used violence to challenge despotic regimes often occupied the high moral ground, and were welcomed in foreign countries as true patriots and democrats. Now, much has changed. The authors of violence are more ruthless, their methods more destructive and undiscriminating; their targets are no longer ministers and heads of state but the populace at large; and their aims and ideals are frequently no more congenial to the countries in which they take refuge than those of the regimes whom they seek to displace. The

---

[13]  [1995] 1 FC 508.

[14]  11 August 2009. Following the decision of the Bangkok Criminal Court, the prosecuting authorities lodged an appeal and the matter is yet to be determined.

[15]  *T v Immigration Officer* [1996] AC 742 (HL) at 752–753.

unsympathetic call them terrorists, and their presence is seen as both an affront and a danger. These fundamental changes in method and perception have not been matched by changes in the parallel, although not identical, laws of extradition and asylum. These laws were conceived at a time when political struggles could be painted in clear primary colours largely inappropriate today; and the so-called 'political exception' which forms part of these laws, and which is the subject of this appeal, was a product of Western European and North American liberal democratic ideals which no longer give a full account of political struggles in the modern world. What I regard as the exceptional difficulty of this appeal is that the courts here, as in other legal systems, must struggle to apply a concept which is out of date.

Whether the political offence exception is to survive the increasing restrictions on its application, or whether other jurisdictions will adopt the more limited 'extraneous considerations' approach to so-called political offences, remains to be seen.     **14.31**

# Part III

## MUTUAL LEGAL ASSISTANCE

# 15

# MUTUAL LEGAL ASSISTANCE AND OTHER EUROPEAN COUNCIL FRAMEWORK DECISIONS

## A. Introduction

The term 'mutual legal assistance' refers to formal cooperation between sovereign states in criminal investigations and proceedings. Mutual legal assistance includes the provision of information and evidence to other jurisdictions and making witnesses available to foreign trial courts. Many mutual legal assistance treaties (often referred to as 'MLATs') also include provision for service of legal documents and for freezing and recovery of assets. **15.01**

Mutual legal assistance is sometimes distinguished from informal assistance, or administrative assistance, such as police to police enquiries. Informal assistance is often available even where mutual legal assistance is not available from the requested state. Requests for intelligence or information may be made under MLATs, but most states can provide information which will not be used as evidence in court without any need for a formal request for assistance, and some (including the United Kingdom) can carry out investigative steps which do not require the use of coercive powers or court orders. **15.02**

Most MLATs do not cover arrest and extradition, appropriate forum and transfer of criminal proceedings, or repatriation of prisoners. **15.03**

### Historical background

**15.04**  International cooperation in the investigation and prosecution of crime was extremely limited until the second half of the twentieth century, lagging at least a half-century behind cooperation in civil and commercial litigation, and still longer behind extradition. To the extent that assistance was granted at all, requests were based on principles of comity between nations and presented through diplomatic channels. This typically requires that letters of request issued by a local court be transmitted via justice and foreign affairs ministries to a foreign embassy. The embassy asks the foreign government to transmit it in turn through its own civil service, accumulating, as one commentator has put it, 'various certifications and waxen seals along the way',[1] to be executed by the police or a court which would send any response through the same route. Under this system, assistance is slow and the potential for misunderstanding between legal systems with no tradition of cooperation is high. For example, judges in civil law systems, for whom all proceedings following the institution of a suit are part of the 'trial', may regard pre-trial evidence-gathering requests as ineligible for judicial cooperation.

**15.05**  With the explosive growth in serious cross-border crime in the last half-century, particularly trafficking in guns, drugs, and humans and international terrorism, new measures were needed. From the first modern international agreement, the European Convention on Mutual Assistance in Criminal Matters of 1959,[2] there developed a body of international and domestic provisions intended to enable greater assistance and improve efficiency. Following the adoption of the Commonwealth's Harare Scheme[3] in 1986 and enactment of a statutory scheme in 1990,[4] the United Kingdom began regularly to pursue and conclude bilateral agreements and continues to do so.

### Fundamental principles

**15.06**  Although assistance through diplomatic or consular channels remains a possibility in default of other mechanisms, most MLATs are based on a system of 'Central Authorities', which operate (among other functions) as clearing houses for letters of request and communicate directly with one another, expediting the process.[5] Authorities designated as competent to do so may initiate requests for assistance which are transmitted to the Central Authorities: typically the competent authorities are government departments, prosecuting agencies, or courts.

**15.07**  The role of the Central Authority upon receipt of a request typically includes determining whether the request meets the requirements of its domestic law and deciding whether it will, in its discretion, execute the request. In some cases it may negotiate with the requesting state for a contribution towards the cost of providing assistance. The Central Authority is also responsible for considering the best means of executing the request, ensuring that execution

---

[1]  E A Nadelmann, 'Negotiations in Criminal Law Assistance Treaties' (1985) 33 Am J Comp L 465.

[2]  ETS No 030: hereafter the European Convention of 1959.

[3]  Scheme Relating to Mutual Assistance in Criminal Matters within the Commonwealth, Commonwealth Secretariat, London, LMN (86) 13.

[4]  Criminal Justice (International Co-operation) Act 1990 (now largely repealed).

[5]  See, eg, United Nations Model Treaty on Mutual Assistance in Criminal Matters, adopted by UN General Assembly resolution 45/117 (the template for many bilateral treaties; hereafter 'the United Nations Model Treaty'), Art 3.

is completed within an appropriate timescale, and transmitting evidence where this is not done directly.

The foundation of many MLATs is a provision, first found in the European Convention of 1959, that contracting states should afford each other the 'widest measure of mutual assistance …'.[6] Nevertheless, the extent to which mutual legal assistance is available in law and in practice varies widely from state to state, and the international obligations which apply vary from treaty to treaty.  **15.08**

### Relevant instruments

The United Kingdom attaches great importance to combating international crime through the provision of mutual legal assistance. It is a party to multilateral instruments dealing with mutual legal assistance within the Council of Europe, the European Union, the Commonwealth, and the United Nations, and has also, since the 1990s, pursued bilateral agreements where possible.  **15.09**

Europe has led the global trend towards increasing levels of assistance. The European Convention of 1959 (to which non-EU Council of Europe members and certain non-European states including the United States, Canada, Japan, and South Africa are also parties) remains in use over fifty years on. This has been built on by measures within the European Union, most notably the EU Convention of 2000.[7] The trend within the European Union is now towards eliminating traditional mutual legal assistance between member states through harmonization of procedures and mutual recognition of evidence, proceedings, and orders.[8]  **15.10**

The Harare Scheme was adopted between members of the Commonwealth in 1986 and takes a very different approach.[9] It is a 'scheme', not a treaty, and assistance under it is voluntary, it being recognized that it depends for its implementation upon the domestic law of participating states. Many countries have given legislative effect to it and its provisions are generally respected.  **15.11**

There is no United Nations treaty which deals with mutual legal assistance generally. However, a number of United Nations treaties make provision for mutual legal assistance in relation to particular areas.[10] Additionally, the UN model treaty adopted in 1990 has formed the basis for many bilateral agreements.[11]  **15.12**

An up-to-date list of bilateral treaties concluded by the United Kingdom is maintained at the website of the Foreign and Commonwealth Office.[12] As at June 2010, the countries with whom the United Kingdom has a bilateral treaty currently in force are Algeria, Antigua and  **15.13**

---

[6] This provision forms Art 1.1 of the United Nations Model Treaty.
[7] The Convention on Mutual Legal Assistance in Criminal Matters (2000/C197/01) and Protocol (2001/C326/01).
[8] See 15.40 and 15.63 below.
[9] See n 3 above.
[10] UN Convention on Narcotic Drugs, New York in 1961, and Additional Protocol, New York, 1972; UN Convention Against Illicit Traffic in Narcotic Drugs and Psychotropic Substances, Vienna, 1988; UN Convention against Transnational Organised Crime 2000; UN Convention against Corruption 2003.
[11] See n 5 above.
[12] See <http://www.fco.gov.uk/en/about-us/publications-and-documents/treaties/lists-treaties/bilateral-mutual-legal>.

Barbuda, Argentina, Australia, the Bahamas, Bahrain, Barbados, Bolivia, Canada, the Cayman Islands, Chile, Colombia, Ecuador, Grenada, Guyana, Hong Kong, India, Ireland, Italy, Libya, Malaysia, Mexico, the Netherlands, Nigeria, Panama, Paraguay, Romania, Saudi Arabia, South Africa, Spain, Sweden, Thailand, Trinidad and Tobago, Ukraine, the United Arab Emirates, the United States, Uruguay, and Vietnam. Some of these treaties are limited to assistance in relation to drug trafficking or restraint and confiscation.

**15.14** The United Kingdom's domestic legislation on mutual legal assistance is now principally found in the Crime (International Co-operation) Act 2003 (CICA). The practitioner is also encouraged to consult the 'Mutual Assistance Guidelines for the United Kingdom' ('MLA Guidelines'), published and regularly updated by the Home Office.[13]

## B. Obtaining assistance from overseas

**15.15** In any case where evidence is required from overseas, a formal request for mutual legal assistance should be considered: direct enquiries which would be lawful in the United Kingdom may be seen as a violation of sovereignty by foreign states and it is a criminal offence in some countries to contact individuals within the jurisdiction in the course of a criminal investigation before a letter of request has been sent in due form. Equally, it is often permissible, and indeed simpler and quicker, to approach witnesses directly by telephone, engage private overseas agents, or conduct police-to-police enquiries. For example, a request for a prosecution witness's foreign record of convictions could in principle be provided through a defence letter of request, but is likely in practice to be more expeditiously obtained through an informal police request with the assistance of the prosecution.

**15.16** Formal assistance is available in principle from most jurisdictions, although there are certain states which cannot provide assistance without a governing treaty, and there is a possibility that the request will be refused or will not be complied with within a reasonable time frame. Some jurisdictions are also more wary of requests initiated by the defence than those from the prosecution, even where the request is routed through the courts of the United Kingdom, since they conceptualize mutual legal assistance as cooperation between state authorities.

**15.17** An advantage to the defence of requesting mutual legal assistance rather than engaging private investigators or agents overseas is that any costs are usually borne by the requested state: no application for legal aid funding is typically required.

**15.18** There is no generally applicable mandatory format for letters of request, although the templates attached to the MLA guidance relating to incoming requests may also serve as a general guide for the pattern of outgoing requests. Requests should set out in summary form the factual allegations and the principal evidence upon which they are based, together with a precise explanation of the evidence to be obtained and its relevance to the case. The details required necessarily vary depending on the assistance sought. While (for obvious reasons) it is not necessary to show a prima facie case if proceedings have not been instituted, it is often necessary to satisfy the requested state that there is a reasonable suspicion that the conduct

---

[13] As at June 2010, the current version is the Eighth Edition dated 1 April 2010, available at <http://www. homeoffice.gov.uk/police/mutual-legal-assistance/Assistance-from-UK/>.

alleged would constitute an offence in its jurisdiction (see dual criminality at 15.57 below), and the request should annex the relevant law.

The principal legislative provision governing a request for evidence to be provided by another **15.19** state is section 7 of CICA. Requests may only be made directly by certain named prosecuting authorities.[14] Other prosecuting authorities and defendants must apply to a court to request evidence for their use in the proceedings on their behalf. In all cases, it is an essential precondition that the authority making the request (whether the court or a prosecuting authority directly) is satisfied of two matters:

(a) that an offence has been committed or that there are reasonable grounds for suspecting that an offence has been committed, and
(b) that proceedings in respect of the offence have been instituted (if the request is made directly by a prosecuting authority, then by that authority) or that the offence is being investigated.

Section 7(3)(c) makes clear that a person suspected of an offence may only apply to a court to request assistance if proceedings have been instituted against him.

The request is for 'any evidence specified in the request for use in the proceedings or investi- **15.20** gation'. Such evidence may include testimony of witnesses or documents and articles. It is up to the requested state to determine how best to obtain the evidence (for example whether a search warrant is required) although provisions or concepts of domestic law which may affect admissibility in the United Kingdom should be set out. Most notably, practitioners should bear in mind that in countries which do not share the common law tradition, there may be no direct equivalent to a witness statement and no perceived difficulty with the admission of hearsay.

Section 9 of CICA provides that evidence received under a request for assistance may not, **15.21** once provided, be used for 'any purpose other than that specified in the request' without the consent of the overseas authority;[15] however, the Court of Appeal held in *BOC Ltd v Barlow* that an earlier version of this provision restricted only use in other criminal proceedings.[16]

## C. Requests for evidence to be provided by the United Kingdom

The United Kingdom is unusual in that it has several Central Authorities. In England, Wales, **15.22** and Northern Ireland mutual legal assistance is the responsibility of the United Kingdom Central Authority, part of the Judicial Cooperation Unit of the Home Office. In Scotland it is dealt with by the Scottish Crown Office (which represents the Lord Advocate). Her Majesty's Revenue and Customs is also a Central Authority in relation to a limited category

---

[14] Set out in the Crime (International Co-operation) Act 2003 (Designation of Prosecuting Authorities) Order 2004, SI 2004/1034. Currently, these are the Crown Prosecution Service in England and Wales and the Public Prosecution Service in Northern Ireland, the Lord Advocate and Procurator Fiscal in Scotland, the Attorneys General for England and Wales and Northern Ireland, the Revenue and Customs Prosecutions Office, the Financial Services Authority, the Serious Fraud Office, and the Department for Business, Innovation and Skills.
[15] With consent, however, there is no limitation on use: see, for example, *Magnetic Services Limited v HMRC* [2009] UKFTT 391 (TC).
[16] [2002] QB 537. The court was considering the Criminal Justice (International Co-operation) Act 1990, s 3, now replaced by s 9 of CICA.

of offences including indirect taxation, alcohol and tobacco smuggling, though not including the importation of illegal drugs.

15.23   The United Kingdom does not require that there be in place any bilateral or multilateral agreement, exchange of letters or other prior arrangement in order for it to make or entertain a request for mutual legal assistance. A wide range of assistance can be provided informally, including:

- interviews of cooperative witnesses, unless their evidence needs to be taken on oath;
- information and intelligence concerning investigations into offences committed in the United Kingdom, unless this is for use in overseas proceedings;
- publicly available documents and certain other records;
- details of previous convictions; and
- asset tracing enquiries.

15.24   The principal provisions governing formal requests for assistance in obtaining evidence in the United Kingdom are found in Part 1, Chapter 2 of CICA. Section 13 of CICA sets out the bodies which may request assistance. These are:

- a court exercising criminal jurisdiction, or a prosecuting authority, in a country outside the United Kingdom,
- any other authority in such a country which appears to the territorial authority to have the function of making such requests for assistance,
- the International Criminal Police Organisation,
- any other body or person competent to make a request under provisions adopted under the Treaty on European Union.

15.25   Upon receipt of a request, the first question is whether statutory conditions for the grant of assistance are met. These vary depending on the nature of the request. In the case of a request for assistance in obtaining evidence to be received by a court in the United Kingdom, for example, the conditions are found in sections 13 and 14 of CICA: the request must be made by a competent body in connection with certain types of proceedings set out in section 14(1), and in most cases the authority considering the request must be satisfied that an offence under the law of the requested state has been committed or there are reasonable grounds for suspecting that it has, and that an investigation or proceedings are being conducted in that state (section 14(2)). If the relevant statutory conditions are not met, the request must be returned. The second question is whether to comply with the request for assistance. This is in the discretion of the territorial authority, although it must take into account any relevant treaty grounds for refusal. There is an obligation to act lawfully, rationally, and in a procedurally fair way when considering the discretion to assist, and a person affected by the grant of assistance may challenge it by way of judicial review.

15.26   The suspect in foreign enquiries is not generally entitled to know that a request has been made, and the United Kingdom Central Authority will usually treat requests as confidential. However, this is not based on any statutory bar to disclosure, and the courts have held that there are circumstances in which fairness requires that the letter of request is gisted or an interested person is invited to make representations.[17] Moreover, the suspect may become

---

[17]   *R (Evans) v Director of the Serious Fraud Office* [2003] 1 WLR 299; *R (Abacha) v Secretary of State for the Home Department* [2001] EWHC 787 (Admin).

aware of a request upon execution (for example, where searches are conducted). If any legal objection is raised prior to transmission, the Secretary of State should not forward the material until the question has been resolved.[18]

### Execution

CICA permits evidence to be obtained in two ways: first, it provides (under section 15) for evidence in relation to the proceedings to be received by a court in the United Kingdom to be nominated by the Secretary of State and secondly, it extends powers of search and seizure to cover mutual legal assistance requests (under sections 16–18). **15.27**

Where a court is nominated under section 15, Schedule 1 has effect. This provides powers for securing the attendance of witnesses. It also provides that witnesses cannot be compelled to give any evidence which they could not be compelled to give in the United Kingdom, or which the requesting state concedes they could not be required to give in its domestic proceedings. This ensures protection of legal professional privilege and the privilege against self-incrimination. **15.28**

Section 16 applies the powers of entry search and seizure in Part 2 of the Police and Criminal Evidence Act 1984 to requests for mutual legal assistance. Section 17 permits a justice of the peace to issue a search warrant in a case in which an arrest has taken place or proceedings have begun overseas in respect of an offence which would be indictable in England or arrestable in Northern Ireland. Section 18 extends powers of search in Scotland. All three sections are subject to a requirement of dual criminality. **15.29**

The evidence may then be transmitted to the requesting state either directly or indirectly. The United Kingdom requires an undertaking regarding collateral use before transmission. **15.30**

## D. Other forms of assistance

Mutual legal assistance is not limited to requests for evidence. This section considers other requests which may be made and received. **15.31**

### Service of process and procedural documents

Foreign states may serve procedural documents directly on individuals within the United Kingdom without requesting assistance. Home Office guidelines state that the United Kingdom strongly encourages direct transmission of procedural documents by post, unless this is not legally possible under the domestic law of the requesting state.[19] **15.32**

Section 1 of CICA also provides for the Secretary of State to serve process on behalf of a foreign government. Documents should be originals or certified copies or translations as appropriate. Unless another form of service, such as personal service, is specifically requested, the United Kingdom will give effect to such requests by using recorded delivery post. **15.33**

A person upon whom foreign process or other documents are served is not put under any obligation under the law of the United Kingdom as a result, regardless of the method of **15.34**

---

[18] *Gross v Southwark Crown Court*, 24 July 1998 (CO/1759/98).
[19] MLA Guidelines, p 13.

service and the involvement of the authorities of the United Kingdom in effecting transmission. Section 2(3) of CICA provides that any foreign process served by the United Kingdom which requires a person to appear as a party or attend as a witness in a foreign court must contain a notice to the effect that:

(a) service of the document does not impose any obligation to comply under the law of the relevant part of the United Kingdom;

(b) the recipient may wish to seek advice as to the possible consequences of failing to comply under the law of the foreign country;

(c) under that law he may not be entitled to the same rights and privileges as he would have in similar circumstances in the relevant part of the United Kingdom.

**15.35** Sections 3–6[20] of CICA provide that a court may serve process in criminal proceedings in the United Kingdom on a person outside the United Kingdom, either by direct post or by letter of request.[21] The statute makes clear that there is no obligation upon the overseas recipient to comply and no sanction (such as the risk of proceedings for contempt of court) for failing to do so. The process may however subsequently be re-served on the person in question in the United Kingdom in the event of his return and the usual consequences for non-compliance will then follow.

### Temporary transfer of prisoners

**15.36** Where a serving prisoner in another country is required to assist in an investigation or prosecution, it may be possible to arrange a temporary transfer in custody in order that the prisoner can assist or give evidence in person. (This process is to be distinguished from prisoner repatriation agreements.) The United Kingdom's provisions are found in the Criminal Justice (International Co-operation) Act 1990 where the transfer is for the purposes of giving evidence, and in sections 47 and 48 of CICA where it is for the purpose of assisting in an investigation within the European Union.[22] Transfer of prisoners under both Acts is conditional on the prisoner's consent.

### Video and telephone conferencing

**15.37** Arrangements may also be made for a witness in one country to give evidence in proceedings in another by means of video or telephone link. This form of assistance is provided for in the EU Convention[23] and in the second additional protocol to the European Convention of 1959,[24] as well as some bilateral agreements. The two conventions take nearly identical approaches:

(a) requests should only be made where it is not desirable or possible for the witness to appear in the requesting state in person,[25] and the request should set out the reasons for this;[26]

---

[20] Sections 3 and 4 applicable to England and Wales and Northern Ireland; ss 5 and 6 applicable to Scotland.

[21] The EU Convention provides that direct postal transmission is the appropriate method of service to persons in EU states: Art 5.1.

[22] This implements Art 9 of the EU Convention.

[23] Articles 10 and 11.

[24] Strasbourg, 2001, ETS 182, Arts 9 and 10.

[25] EU Convention Art 10.1; Second Additional Protocol 9.1.

[26] EU Convention Art 10.3; Second Additional Protocol 9.3.

(b) the witness is summoned to attend by the judicial authority of the requested state;[27]

(c) the hearing is conducted directly by the requesting state in accordance with its own procedures,[28] but a judicial authority of the requested state is present with the witness during the hearing and is responsible for ensuring the identification of the person to be heard and respect for the fundamental principles of law of the requested state;[29]

(d) the witness may claim any right not to testify which he or she would have in either state;[30]

(e) hearings involving a suspect or accused may only be carried out with his or her consent;[31]

(f) telephone hearings may only take place with the consent of the witness;[32]

(g) other measures for the protection of the witness may be agreed;[33] and

(h) the requested state must be in a position to bring proceedings for any refusal to testify or false testimony.[34]

**15.38** In relation to outgoing requests, these provisions have been implemented in England and Wales by section 32 of the Criminal Justice Act 1988 for the purposes of trials on indictment and in the Youth Court, appeals to the Criminal Division of the Court of Appeal and hearings of references under section 9 of the Criminal Appeal Act 1995.[35] Section 32(3) has the effect of applying section 1 of the Perjury Act 1911 to the overseas witness. Procedural rules as to interpreters and record keeping are found in the Criminal Procedure Rules, rule 32.6–8.

**15.39** In relation to incoming requests, the EU Convention was implemented by sections 30 and 31 of CICA. The Secretary of State will nominate a court in which the witness is to be heard,[36] and the law of perjury and contempt of court applies as though the evidence was given in proceedings in this country.[37] The court will intervene where it considers it necessary to safeguard the rights of the witness, who is not to be compelled to give any evidence which he could not be compelled to give in proceedings in the relevant part of the United Kingdom or which prejudices the security of the United Kingdom.[38]

### Freezing orders

**15.40** An EU framework decision on the execution in the EU of orders freezing property or evidence[39] provides for mutual recognition of 'freezing orders' within the EU, and is a notable example of increasing convergence of law and procedure under the 'third pillar'.[40]

---

[27] EU Convention Art 10.4, Second Additional Protocol 9.4.

[28] EU Convention Art 10.5(c), Second Additional Protocol 9.5(c).

[29] EU Convention Art 10.5(a), Second Additional Protocol 9.5(a).

[30] EU Convention Art 10.5(e), Second Additional Protocol 9.5(e).

[31] EU Convention Art 10.9; Second Additional Protocol 9.8.

[32] Articles 11.2 and 11.6 of the EU Convention and 10.2 and 10.6 of the Second Additional Protocol.

[33] EU Convention Art 10.5(b), Second Additional Protocol 9.5(b).

[34] EU Convention Art 10.8; Second Additional Protocol 9.7.

[35] In Scotland, TV link evidence can be used in cases prosecuted on indictment: Criminal Procedure (Scotland) Act 1995.

[36] Section 30(3).

[37] Section 30(4).

[38] Schedule 2, paras 5 and 9(1)–(3).

[39] 2003/577/JHA, 22 July 2003; *Official Journal*, L 196, 2 August 2003.

[40] See the 'Report from the Commission based on Article 14 of the Council Framework Decision 2003/577/JHA of 22 July 2003 on the execution in the European Union of orders freezing property or evidence' for a critique of member states' implementing legislation.

EU members are required to give effect to freezing orders made in other member states without further formality, although there remain some limitations (such as a requirement of dual criminality, subject to a framework list).

**15.41**  The name 'freezing order' may give a misleading impression to English lawyers. 'Freezing orders' in this context are orders issued for the purposes of securing evidence or the subsequent confiscation of property, and are executed through a warrant of search and seizure. The intention is that there should be direct transmission between judicial authorities and immediate execution. The framework decision has been given legislative effect by sections 10 (the making of freezing orders to have effect overseas) and 20–27 (the recognition and execution of freezing orders in the United Kingdom) of CICA, which should be consulted for the details of implementation, including the grounds for postponement, non-recognition and non-execution.

**15.42**  Where a request is received by the United Kingdom, it is transmitted to a court nominated by the Secretary of State by notice,[41] which will in general consider it no later than the next business day.[42] The Secretary of State will also notify the chief police officer of the area, who will be given an opportunity to make representations before a judge, if appropriate, issues a warrant.

**15.43**  Application for a freezing order to be executed overseas may be made in the United Kingdom by a constable.[43] There are a number of conditions, including that the evidence is likely to be of substantial value to the proceedings or investigation and that it is likely to be admissible in evidence at a trial.[44] Freezing orders are not available to the defence.

### Banking information

**15.44**  Some countries still have robust bank secrecy laws, although recent multilateral MLATs prohibit or circumscribe refusal of requests on these grounds,[45] and there are detailed measures for provision of banking information within the European Union in the 2001 Protocol to the EU Convention.[46] Part 1, Chapter 4 of CICA ('Information about banking transactions') implements this Protocol in relation to both incoming and outgoing requests within 'participating' states (EU member states and other states designated by Parliament): orders are available in relation to 'serious criminal conduct' as defined in the Protocol and may be for information or monitoring. Dual criminality is required. It is an offence under section 42 of CICA to disclose the existence of such a request.

### Telephone intercept

**15.45**  Article 18.3 of the EU Convention covers the provision of telephone intercept material. Although not used in evidence criminal proceedings in the United Kingdom, telephone

---

[41]  CICA, s 21(3).

[42]  CPR, r 32.10(2).

[43]  CICA, s 10(4); in Scotland, by the Lord Advocate or a procurator fiscal.

[44]  See CICA, s 10.

[45]  See Art 4.2 of the UN model treaty, Art 46.8 of the UN Convention Against Corruption, Art 18 of the UN Convention Against Transnational Organised Crime. The Convention Against Corruption also invites states to consider setting up financial intelligence units responsible for 'receiving, analysing and disseminating … reports of suspicious financial transactions': Art 58.

[46]  See n 7 above.

intercept material is relied on in many other jurisdictions. The Regulation of Investigatory Powers Act 2000 contains provision for the necessary interception warrant to be authorized for the purposes of a request.[47] A request for interception may be refused where the requested measure would not be taken in a similar national case,[48] and under domestic legislation the Secretary of State is required to ensure that restrictions are in place which would prevent disclosure in proceedings overseas which would not be made in the United Kingdom.[49]

The Convention on Cybercrime[50] contains detailed provisions for mutual legal assistance in relation to evidence in electronic form, including intercepted evidence. Provisions relating to interception of communications have also been proposed for inclusion in the revised Harare Scheme. **15.46**

### Restraint and confiscation

A number of MLATs provide for assistance in restraint and confiscation of the proceeds of crime.[51] Although the relevant statutory provisions are complex, the assistance sought can be very simple. Requests may be a considerable advantage to the requested state, since under most MLATs it retains any confiscated assets. **15.47**

References to 'property' under the Proceeds of Crime Act 2002 (POCA) are to 'all property, wherever situated'[52] and a confiscation order made in the United Kingdom may therefore reflect available assets overseas. Assistance may be sought by prosecutors in the United Kingdom to restrain or realise property pursuant to such an order under section 74 of POCA. Assistance may only be requested where the conditions for making a domestic restraint order[53] are satisfied. Although assets confiscated by the requested state are not likely to be returned to the United Kingdom, a certificate should be requested which sets out the amount realised and the 'date of realisation'. A sum equal to the sterling value of this must then be subtracted from the amount outstanding under the confiscation order. **15.48**

Evidence to be adduced at a confiscation hearing may also be requested in the usual way under section 7 of CICA. Where evidence may be relevant to both trial and subsequent confiscation proceedings, the evidence should be requested for the purposes of both proceedings as there is otherwise a risk that the prohibition on collateral use in section 9 will apply.[54] **15.49**

The United Kingdom is also able to restrain assets at the request of foreign states and give effect to foreign confiscation orders under the provisions of the Proceeds of Crime Act 2002 (External Requests and Orders) Order 2005. In relation to both restraint and confiscation, the request will be referred by the Secretary of State to either the Director of Public **15.50**

---

[47] Sections 5(3)(c) and 6(2)(j). Competent authorities of requesting states are persons to whom disclosure is permitted: s 19(2)(a).
[48] Article 18.5(b).
[49] Section 15(7)(b) of the Regulation of Investigatory Powers Act 2000.
[50] ETS No 185.
[51] Provisions are found in the Harare Scheme and in a number of UN treaties such as the UN Convention against Illicit Traffic in Narcotic Drugs and Psychotropic Substances. There is also a European Convention on Laundering, Search Seizure and Confiscation of the Proceeds of Crime.
[52] Section 84(1).
[53] Found in s 40 of POCA: see s 74(1) of POCA.
[54] See, eg, *Gooch* [1999] 1 Cr App R (S) 283, a case in which the count specified in the request was not proceeded with by the Crown at retrial.

Prosecutions or the Director of Revenue and Customs Prosecutions, who will apply to a Crown Court for an order giving effect to the request. Applications may be made ex parte, but there is provision for any person affected by them to make an application to discharge or vary them. This safeguards not only the rights of the defence but also those of bona fide third parties. Orders made under these provisions may only relate to assets held within the United Kingdom.[55]

15.51 The United Kingdom is able to provide assistance through its system of civil recovery.

# E. Grounds for refusal

15.52 Although there is a general discretion to refuse assistance, the United Kingdom rarely declines incoming requests, and with both incoming and outgoing requests, delay is a more frequent problem than refusal. Consultation is encouraged: it is often possible to attach conditions to the grant of assistance rather than declining altogether, and reasons should be given for any refusal. In some circumstances (such as where enquiries may prejudice an ongoing domestic investigation), execution of the request may be postponed.

15.53 CICA does not attempt to define the grounds on which the United Kingdom will refuse an incoming request for assistance, though it must take into account any grounds in an applicable treaty.[56] Different MLATs may contain different grounds for refusal, and different states take different approaches to the same grounds. This section accordingly deals with some common grounds for refusal, whether applicable to incoming or outgoing requests. It is not exhaustive and reference must always be made to any applicable MLAT.

15.54 It is important to note that many MLATs permit a country to refuse a request on the grounds that to comply would be contrary to its domestic law.[57] In these circumstances, grounds for refusal may be found not only in applicable MLATs but also in the implementing legislation of requested states.

### Public interest and human rights

15.55 Most MLATs allow for refusal of assistance which, as the United Nations model treaty puts it,[58] 'if granted would prejudice [the] sovereignty, security, public order *(ordre public)* or other essential public interest' of the requested country (or other similar wording). The authorities in the United Kingdom which request, transmit and execute requests are also public authorities within the meaning of the Human Rights Act 1998, and are therefore bound to act compatibly with the Convention whether or not this is a specific ground of refusal in the relevant MLAT. Most notably, any investigative measure must constitute a proportionate interference with individuals' Article 8 rights, and where a case may result in a penalty of death, assistance will only be provided if an assurance is given that the death penalty will not be imposed, or if imposed will not be carried out. Whether or not they have

---

[55] *King v Serious Fraud Office* [2009] 1 WLR 718.
[56] *R v Secretary of State for the Home Department, ex p Fininvest Spa* [1997] 1 WLR 743.
[57] This applies in particular to UN instruments: see for example the UN Convention Against Corruption (Art 46.2), and the UN Convention Against Transnational Organised Crime (Art 18.2). It also applies to the Harare Scheme, which is non-binding.
[58] Article 4.1(a).

human rights obligations in international law, many states will refuse to comply with a request made for the purpose of prosecuting a person on account of their race, sex, religion, nationality, ethnic origin, or political opinions, or where a person's position may be prejudiced for those reasons.[59]

### Reciprocity

The United Kingdom will provide assistance even where no international agreement applies **15.56** and the requesting state would not be in a position to afford it assistance in similar circumstances.[60] Other states may not.[61] Where no agreement covers an outgoing request, the requested state may have no legal power to provide assistance, and even if it can do so this is dependent upon its good will and friendly relations with the United Kingdom, as well as the time and resources it is able to devote to the request. It is important to bear in mind that the costs of execution are usually to be borne by the requested state. The global imbalance in requests for assistance is even greater than in requests for extradition: some states, particularly those which are financial centres, are overwhelmed by requests although others have never received a request for assistance.

### Dual criminality

The United Kingdom is also able to provide most forms of assistance in the absence of dual **15.57** criminality, though not assistance with search and seizure, restraint and confiscation, or requests for banking evidence. Section 14 of CICA requires the territorial authority to refuse a request for assistance which relates to a fiscal offence in respect of which proceedings have not been instituted in the absence of dual criminality, unless the requesting state is a member of the Commonwealth or makes the request pursuant to a treaty to which the United Kingdom is a party.

Despite encouragement to abandon it,[62] dual criminality (with all its attendant problems) is **15.58** required by many other states. It is an express discretionary ground for refusal under the Harare Scheme.[63]

### Double jeopardy

The United Kingdom has always declined to execute requests where a trial in the requesting **15.59** country would involve double jeopardy, regardless of the country in which the previous trial took place, and requests are unlikely to be met until satisfactory details are given of any previous prosecutions or proceedings. Double jeopardy is a ground for refusal under most MLATs.[64]

---

[59] A provision to this effect is found in Art 4.1(c) of the UN Model Treaty and a similar provision in para 8(2)(b) of the Harare Scheme.

[60] MLA guidelines, p 5.

[61] For instance, the absence of reciprocal arrangements is a discretionary ground of refusal under the Harare Scheme: para 8(3).

[62] Article 46.9(c) of the UN Convention Against Corruption provides: 'Each State Party may consider adopting such measures as may be necessary to enable it to provide a wider scope of assistance ... in the absence of dual criminality.'

[63] Paragraph 8(1)(a).

[64] It is found, for example, in Art 4.1(d) of the UN Model Treaty.

### Triviality

**15.60**   Understandably, many states feel that that the good will upon which international co-operation relies is abused if assistance is requested in relation to a trivial offence (although the level at which an offence is regarded as trivial may vary from country to country). If assistance is agreed in principle, it is unlikely to be a priority for the police. Where an offence is so trivial that it would not be prosecuted at all in the United Kingdom, the United Kingdom has occasionally refused to provide assistance.

### Political offences

**15.61**   As with extradition, many states decline to provide assistance in relation to offences which they regard as of a political character. This is found as a discretionary ground of refusal in the European Convention of 1959,[65] the Harare Scheme,[66] and the UN model treaty[67] among others.

### Offences under military law

**15.62**   Many states will not assist in relation to offences arising only under military law.[68]

## F. Current developments

**15.63**   It had always been intended that the European Arrest Warrant should be partnered by a 'European Evidence Warrant', based on the same principle of mutual recognition of judicial decisions within an area of freedom, security, and justice.[69] This was finally effected by a framework decision[70] which came into force on 19 January 2009; the deadline for transposition into the domestic law of member states is 19 January 2011. The central conceit of the European Evidence Warrant is a standard form warrant (appended to the framework decision, much like the European Arrest Warrant) which may be executed 'without any further formality';[71] the state's general discretion to refuse a request is removed. The decision is intended to operate together with the freezing order framework decision,[72] and whilst member states are effecting the transition to the European Evidence Warrant system, will also operate in parallel with mutual legal assistance under the EU Convention.

**15.64**   The Harare Scheme is currently at an advanced stage of revision, with an updated scheme due to be submitted to senior officials of Commonwealth member states in late 2010 to be recommended to their Law Ministers for adoption.

---

[65] Article 2(b).
[66] Paragraph 8(1)(b).
[67] Article 4.1(b).
[68] See, eg, UN Model Treaty, Art 4.1(f).
[69] Following the conclusions of the Tampere European Council of 15 and 16 October 1999.
[70] Council Framework Decision 2008/978/JHA of 18 December 2008 on the European evidence warrant for the purpose of obtaining objects, documents and data for use in proceedings in criminal matters.
[71] Article 11.
[72] See 15.40 above.

# Appendices

# A Guide for Duty Solicitors: the First Appearance in Extradition Cases

*Fadi Daoud*

## Introduction

Although extradition cases used to be rare, the advent of the Extradition Act 2003 ('the 2003 Act') and, in particular the European Arrest Warrant (EAW), have greatly increased the chances that a duty solicitor will be required to represent a person arrested in extradition proceedings. This appendix deals with 'surviving' the first hearing as a duty solicitor, focusing in particular on cases involving EAWs.

If you do not have experience of extradition cases, you should remember that the number of extradition judges sitting at City of Westminster Magistrates' Court (CWMC) is currently under ten which means that they will know if you do not appear before them regularly. The best approach is to be candid with the court and to limit yourself to those issues that must be dealt with there and then. The style of advocacy, both with the court and the CPS, is less adversarial than in regular criminal proceedings.

All extradition cases are governed by the 2003 Act which is divided into two parts. Part 1 is based on the European Framework Decision on extradition and governs EAW cases. Part 2 cases are extradition requests that are not EAWs. The procedure under the two parts is not always identical. This appendix focuses on EAW cases, but includes a section on Part 2 cases.

## Terminology

The terminology in extradition cases is slightly different from domestic cases. Below are the key terms:

- The *appropriate judge* or *District Judge* is a judge who is qualified to hear extradition cases.
- The 'prosecution' is the *judicial authority* (EAW cases) or the *requesting state* (Part 2 cases), and in both cases is represented by the CPS or counsel instructed on their behalf.
- The 'defendant' is formally referred to as *the requested person*, although in practice the two terms are interchangeable. The 2003 Act uses the term '*person*' which is adopted in this appendix.
- The first appearance is referred to as the *initial hearing* in EAW cases and the *first appearance* in Part 2 cases.
- The *extradition hearing* is the hearing at which the District Judge considers whether the statutory requirements for extradition have been established.
- *Consent to extradition* is the process by which a person agrees to their extradition without the need for an extradition hearing and thereby waives their specialty protection.
- *Specialty* is the doctrine of extradition law that means that a person may only be dealt with after their extradition for the conduct contained in the EAW or extradition request.
- An *uncontested extradition hearing* is a short extradition hearing at which no objections to extradition are raised but the person's extradition is ordered while preserving his speciality protection.
- *Bars to extradition* are statutory grounds upon which the court may refuse to extradite the person.

## Initial hearing

The first appearance in EAW cases is provided for in sections 4–8 of the 2003 Act. The District Judge is required to determine the following issues at this hearing:

*Section 4: service of warrant and production at court*
- Was the person served with a copy of the EAW as soon as practicable?
- Was the person produced at court as soon as practicable?

*Section 7: identity*

- Is the person who has been arrested in fact the person named in the EAW?

If any of the above questions are determined in the negative the District Judge may, or in some cases must, discharge the person. The court cannot usually adjourn to deal with these issues, so the District Judge will give judgment at the initial hearing. If you are successful in obtaining the discharge of your client from the EAW, you should remember that the judicial authority may simply issue a new warrant upon which your client will be liable to arrest. However, discharge from the EAW can buy your client some time to deal with the matter if it is capable of amicable resolution, for example by voluntary return; or instructing lawyers or payment of a fine in the requesting country.

Having determined these issues the court then goes on to do the following:

*Section 8*

- Set a date for the extradition hearing
- Inform the person of the contents of the EAW
- Give the person the required information about consent
- Remand the person in custody or on bail.

## Section 4 of the 2003 Act

Under section 4 of the 2003 Act the District Judge must decide whether the person has been served with the EAW as soon as practicable (section 4(2)) and, if so, whether he has been produced at court as soon as practicable (section 4(3)). If the first question is decided in the negative the District Judge 'may' discharge the person. If the second question is decided in the negative then the District Judge 'must' discharge the person.

The meaning of 'as soon as practicable' was considered by the High Court in the case of *Nikonovs v HMP Brixton and Latvia* [2005] EWHC 2405 (Admin). The court held that the test was narrower than '*as soon as reasonably practicable*' and whether something was done as soon as practicable was a question of fact in each case.

### Burden of proof

The burden of proof under section 4, as set out in section 206 of the 2003 Act, is on the judicial authority. This is usually discharged by means of a witness statement from the arresting officer. The statement gives a timeline from arrest to service of the EAW, and the arrangement of transportation to the court. You should read the statements carefully. If in doubt, contact the police and find out what happened from the custody sergeant. You would be surprised at the number of inaccuracies that arise in these witness statements. Of course, you should also take instructions from the client.

The police rarely breach the obligation to produce the person as soon as practicable because they routinely delay arresting on an EAW until arrangements are in place to take the person to court. A more common occurrence is that the police merely show the person the EAW rather than serving it as required under the 2003 Act.

### Service of the EAW as soon as practicable

Section 4(2) of the 2003 Act provides that '*a copy of the warrant must be given to the person as soon as practicable after his arrest*'. The warrant referred to here is the EAW.

Failure to serve the EAW as soon as practicable *may* result in the person's discharge. In practice this rarely happens unless you can show that your client has been prejudiced in some way by the late service. The court will consider the following factors when assessing whether late service ought to result in discharge:

- The length of time it took to serve the EAW
- Whether the person understood the reasons for his arrest, particularly if he does not speak English
- Any other factors specific to the individual person.

### Production before the judge as soon as practicable

Section 4(3) of the 2003 Act provides that: '*The person must be brought as soon as practicable before the appropriate judge.*'

When considering whether your client has been produced as soon as practicable, you should consider the following issues:

- Following arrest, was the client brought to court as soon as they could be? For example, if he were arrested in London in the early hours of the morning, then he ought to be at court that same day. The closer you get to lunchtime, however, the weaker the argument that he ought to be there on the same day becomes, bearing in mind the practicalities of arrest, and the logistics of processing the arrested person at the police station and organizing transport to court. Should his place of arrest be, say, Cornwall, then arrival at court on the day after arrest may well be as soon as practicable, although it will be a matter of fact in each case.
- Was the client taken somewhere else before he was brought to court? On occasion, a person is arrested on an EAW but first dealt with for domestic matters (that is for crimes committed in England and Wales). Some police forces do not receive guidance and presume that the person must be taken to, for example, the Crown Court to execute a bench warrant first, as this would normally take priority. In fact, production at court on the EAW must take priority.

Failure to produce the person as soon as practicable *must* result in his discharge.

## Provisional arrest

On occasion you may come across a case in which the person has been arrested on a provisional arrest warrant. In EAW cases a police officer may provisionally arrest any person without a warrant if there are reasonable grounds to believe that an EAW has been, or will be, issued in respect of the person.

Section 6(2) of the 2003 Act provides that the following must occur within *48 hours* of provisional arrest:

- The person must be brought before the District Judge
- The EAW and certificate must be produced to the District Judge.

Failure to do either of these things within 48 hours *must* result in the person's discharge.

Under section 6(5) the person must be served with a copy of the EAW as soon as practicable after his arrest (see above for a discussion of 'as soon as practicable'). Failure to do so *may* result in the person's discharge.

## Section 7 of the 2003 Act

Under section 7 the District Judge must decide whether the person brought before him is the person in respect of whom the EAW or provisional warrant was issued. The judge must decide the question on the balance of probabilities.

In practice, issues as to identity are relatively common. Previous cases have included brothers using each other's identities, people having similar or similar-sounding names and/or similar dates of birth, or confusion over places of birth.

Usually there will some evidence of identity because the person has been arrested, for example because he was using the name of the person in the warrant. Therefore, in most cases where identity is in issue, it will be necessary for the person to give evidence or to produce documents to show that he is not in fact the person named in the warrant. Once identity is challenged, the judicial authority will often fax or email fingerprints or photographs of the person named in the warrant. If the judge finds that identity has not been established on the balance of probabilities, then he *must* discharge the person.

It is worth noting that spurious denials of identity may well undermine the client's credibility in the eyes of the court, with potentially an adverse knock-on effect when he raises other issues at the extradition hearing (see, for example, *Stefan v Government of Albania* [2007] EWHC 3267 (Admin) and [2008] EWHC 2600 (Admin)).

## Section 8: consent to extradition

A person may choose to consent to his extradition. The key points about consent to extradition are as follows:

- Consent is voluntary
- Consent to extradition results in a truncated timetable that should result in the person being returned more quickly, usually within ten days

- By consenting to extradition the person waives their specialty protection (see below)
- Consent is irrevocable
- A person who consents to extradition has no right of appeal.

## Specialty

Specialty (sometimes spelt 'speciality' but pronounced 'specialty') is an important concept in extradition law and is dealt with fully elsewhere in this book. In EAW cases specialty is defined in section 17 of the 2003 Act which provides (so far as relevant) as follows:

(2)  … a person who is extradited to the territory from the United Kingdom may be dealt with in the territory for an offence committed before his extradition only if—

    (a)  the offence is one falling within subsection (3), or

    (b)  the condition in subsection (4) is satisfied.

(3)  The offences are—

    (a)  the offence in respect of which the person is extradited;

    (b)  an extradition offence disclosed by the same facts as that offence;

    (c)  an extradition offence in respect of which the appropriate judge gives his consent under section 55 to the person being dealt with;

    (d)  an offence which is not punishable with imprisonment or another form of detention;

    (e)  an offence in respect of which the person will not be detained in connection with his trial, sentence or appeal;

    (f)  an offence in respect of which the person waives the right that he would have (but for this paragraph) not to be dealt with for the offence.

(4)  The condition is that the person is given an opportunity to leave the category 1 territory and—

    (a)  he does not do so before the end of the permitted period, or

    (b)  if he does so before the end of the permitted period, he returns there.

(5)  The permitted period is 45 days starting with the day on which the person arrives in the category 1 territory.

In essence, the rule of specialty means that a person may only be dealt with (prosecuted, sentenced, or required to serve a sentence of imprisonment) in respect of the conduct set out in the EAW or extradition request. For example, if the EAW states that the person is wanted for murder, then the authorities in the category 1 territory may also deal with him for manslaughter on those same facts. However, they would not be permitted to deal with him, for example, for theft if this were a separate factual allegation unless they gave him the opportunity to leave the jurisdiction first.

Specialty protection is not absolute because under the EAW scheme the judicial authority may apply to the UK court for consent to deal with a person for other offences. In practice, consent is often given.

## Part 2 cases

These cases are less common than EAW cases but duty solicitors do, on occasion, have to deal with them. The procedure under Part 2 is broadly similar to Part 1/EAW cases but not identical. Set out below are the key differences with respect to the first appearance which is provided for in sections 71–76 of the 2003 Act. The main difference is that *identity is not determined at the first appearance* in Part 2 cases, but instead at the extradition hearing.

### Full requests

Under Part 2 of the 2003 Act extradition is sought by means of an extradition request rather than an EAW. An extradition request is first sent to the Secretary of State who then sends it to the District Judge who may issue an arrest warrant in respect of the person. These cases are called *full request* cases.

The judge at the first appearance in a full request case must do the following things:

- Establish that the person has been served with a copy of the arrest warrant as soon as practicable after arrest
- Establish that he has been brought before the District Judge as soon as practicable unless he has been granted bail by the arresting officer
- Inform the person of the contents of the extradition request
- Inform him of his right to consent to extradition
- Set a date for the extradition hearing
- Remand him in custody or on bail.

After a person has been arrested on a full request he must be served with a copy of the arrest warrant and brought before the District Judge as soon as practicable, unless the arresting officer granted him bail (section 72(1) and (3) of the 2003 Act). Failure to do the former *may* result in the person's discharge, failure to do the latter *must* result in the person's discharge. See above for a full discussion of 'as soon as practicable' and the matters to take into consideration when applying for discharge.

The District Judge must set a date for the extradition hearing which must be within two months of the date of the first appearance, unless the judge grants an application by either party for a later date. Failure to start the extradition hearing on or before the date set *must* result in the person's discharge.

### Provisional arrest

Unlike EAW cases, provisional arrest under Part 2 still requires an arrest warrant issued by a domestic court. A provisional arrest warrant is issued where a judge is satisfied that the person is either in the United Kingdom, or is on his way to the United Kingdom, and he is either accused or convicted before a court in a category 2 territory (section 73 of the 2003 Act). These cases are called *provisional arrest cases*.

The judge at the first appearance in a provisional arrest case must do the following things (section 74):

- Establish that the person has been served with the provisional arrest warrant as soon as practicable
- Establish that he has either been produced in court as soon as practicable or granted bail by the arresting officer
- Inform the person that he is accused or convicted in the requesting state
- Inform the person of his right to consent to extradition
- Remand the person on bail or in custody.

A person who is provisionally arrested must be served with a copy of the provisional arrest warrant as soon as practicable after his arrest (section 74(2) of the 2003 Act). Failure to do this *may* result in his discharge. He must also be brought before the District Judge as soon as practicable (section 74(3) of the 2003 Act) unless he has been granted bail by the arresting officer. Where the person is not granted bail and is not produced as soon as practicable he *must* be discharged. See above for a full discussion of 'as soon as practicable' and the matters to take into consideration when applying for discharge.

The full request must be served on the person within 45 days of the person's arrest unless the requesting state has been designated by the Secretary of State as being permitted a longer period. See Appendix 2 for category 2 territories that have been so designated. If the request is not served within this period the person *must* be discharged.

In practice in provisional arrest cases, the court will usually adjourn the case at the first appearance until the nearest court day prior to the expiry of the forty-five days (or whatever the period that has been designated) when the District Judge will satisfy himself that the request has been served and will set a date for the extradition hearing. This must be within two months of the date on which the judge received the extradition request (section 76(3) of the 2003 Act) unless he grants an application by either side for a later date. If the extradition hearing does not begin on or before the date fixed then the person *must* be discharged.

## Instructions/advising your client

In extradition cases you will need to advise your client on the following matters:

- That in extradition cases the judge is not deciding guilt or innocence but whether the conditions for extradition as set out in the 2003 Act have been met

- The timescale (see below)
- His right to consent to extradition and the consequences of so doing (see above)
- His right to bail.

In respect of the final point, extradition cases usually concern foreign nationals and therefore bail conditions such as reporting, securities and sureties, and retention of travel documents are the norm. It is therefore helpful to obtain instructions on the following matters:

- Personal details
- The location of any travel documents (identity card or passport). If these have not been seized by the police on arrest, can arrangements be made for family members or friends to bring them to court?
- What is the nearest police station (for a possible reporting condition)?
- Can your client provide a security or a surety and, if so, how much? You should note that some judges only allow sureties from British citizens or residents
- Working hours—to allow for electronic tag or a curfew
- Family structure—are there children of the family and, if so, what are their ages? This has an impact on the availability of money and curfew times, as well as community ties
- Was the client present during the proceedings in the foreign jurisdiction?
- Did the client have any notice of proceedings in the foreign jurisdiction?
- Has the client instructed a lawyer in the foreign jurisdiction and are there any current applications?

## Right to bail

An application for bail can be pursued in all cases. The presumptions on bail are the same as in domestic criminal cases, namely:

- If the person is accused of the offences in the EAW or request, then he has a right to bail
- If he has been convicted of the offences in the EAW or request, then there is no right to bail.

It goes without saying that if the client is detained under immigration legislation, or is a serving prisoner, then there is usually little point in applying for bail.

## Indication of issues

It is common for the judge at the initial hearing to ask for an indication of the likely issues to be raised at the extradition hearing. It is equally common for duty solicitors to respond that they are not experienced in extradition and have not yet considered the issues.

Some issues that are frequently identified at initial hearings are the following:

1. Section 2 arguments (arguments about the EAW's formal validity, in particular that it contains insufficient or inaccurate information). This may include the argument that the person is not in fact wanted for prosecution but only as a witness or suspect in an investigation
2. Human Rights arguments under section 21 of the 2003 Act (usually Articles 3, 6 and/or 8 of the ECHR)
3. Section 25 (physical or mental condition).

## Timetable

In EAW cases a full hearing must be listed within twenty-one days of the date of arrest (for Part 2 cases see above). The court is under a duty to resolve extradition cases expeditiously and will expect your co-operation in achieving this. Some of the most experienced District Judges deal with extradition cases and they usually welcome the raising of arguable points of law and/or fact, particularly if they are novel or otherwise interesting.

## Legal aid

Extradition proceedings are a type of criminal proceeding and therefore you should apply for legal aid, where appropriate, in the usual way.

## Time spent on remand

In extradition proceedings the client is often, understandably, concerned about whether any time spent in custody in this jurisdiction will count towards any sentence imposed or required to be served abroad.

In EAW cases, Article 26 of the Framework Decision states that all periods of detention arising from the execution of an EAW are to be counted towards any sentence to be served once the person is extradited. Whether or not this in fact happens will depend on whether the requesting judicial authority abides by Article 26. Anecdotal evidence suggests that many category 1 territories do not in fact take time spent on remand awaiting extradition into account, even though they are required to do so under Article 26.

The UK authorities have a duty to communicate the period of detention to the requesting authorities. However there are things that you can do to help the process. You can ask the District Judge to record the number of days spent on remand on the order for extradition. You can also write to the judicial authority to inform them of the time spent on remand and to remind them of their obligation under Article 26 of the Framework Decision.

## Conclusion

Although extradition can seem daunting to those who have little experience of it, once you get used to the procedures and the terminology you should find that it is a very interesting and fulfilling area in which to practice. This appendix should provide you with the basics required to represent clients at the initial hearing and for a more in-depth discussion of the law and practice you are referred to the rest of this book.

# Extradition Arrangements by Country

| Country | Status under 2003 Act | Required to show a prima facie case or not | Multilateral or bilateral treaty | Order in Council |
|---|---|---|---|---|
| Afghanistan | Party to international conventions | Yes | Multilateral | 2005 No 46 |
| Albania | Category 2 | No | European Convention on Extradition (ECE) | 2003 No 3334 |
| Algeria | Category 2 | Yes | Bilateral and multilateral | 2003 No 3334 2005 No 46 |
| Andorra | Category 2 | No | ECE | 2003 No 3334 |
| Angola | Party to international conventions | Yes | Multilateral | 2005 No 46 |
| Antigua and Barbuda | Category 2 | Yes | | 2003 No 3334 |
| Argentina | Category 2 | Yes | Bilateral | 2003 No 3334 |
| Armenia | Category 2 | No | ECE | 2003 No 3334 |
| Australia | Category 2 | No | | 2003 No 3334 |
| Austria | Category 1 (EAW) | No | ECE | 2004 No 1898 |
| Azerbaijan | Category 2 | No | ECE | 2003 No 3334 |
| The Bahamas | Category 2 | Yes | | 2003 No 3334 |
| Bahrain | Party to international conventions | Yes | Multilateral | 2005 No 46 |
| Bangladesh | Category 2 | Yes | | 2003 No 3334 |
| Barbados | Category 2 | Yes | | 2003 No 3334 |
| Belarus | Party to international conventions | Yes | Multilateral | 2005 No 46 |
| Belgium | Category 1 (EAW) | No | ECE | 2003 No 3333 |
| Belize | Category 2 | Yes | | 2003 No 3334 |
| Benin | Party to international conventions | Yes | Multilateral | 2005 No 46 |
| Bhutan | Party to international conventions | Yes | Multilateral | 2005 No 46 |
| Bolivia | Category 2 | Yes | Bilateral | 2003 No 3334 |
| Bosnia and Herzegovina | Category 2 | Yes | ECE | 2003 No 3334 |
| Botswana | Category 2 | Yes | | 2003 No 3334 |

| Country | Status under 2003 Act | Required to show a prima facie case or not | Multilateral or bilateral treaty | Order in Council |
|---|---|---|---|---|
| Brazil | Category 2 | Yes | Bilateral | 2003 No 3334 |
| Brunei | Category 2 | Yes | | 2003 No 3334 |
| Bulgaria | Category 2 | No | ECE | 2006 No 3451 |
| Burkina Faso | Party to international conventions | Yes | Multilateral | 2005 No 46 |
| Burundi | Party to international conventions | Yes | Multilateral | 2005 No 46 |
| Cambodia | Party to international conventions | Yes | Multilateral | 2005 No 46 |
| Cameroon | Party to international conventions | Yes | Multilateral | 2005 No 46 |
| Canada | Category 2 | No | | 2003 No 3334 |
| Cape Verde | Party to international conventions | Yes | Multilateral | 2005 No 46 |
| Central African Republic | Party to international conventions | Yes | Multilateral | 2005 No 46 |
| Chad | Party to international conventions | Yes | Multilateral | 2005 No 46 |
| Chile | Category 2 | Yes | Bilateral | 2003 No 3334 |
| China | Party to international conventions | Yes | Multilateral | 2005 No 46 |
| Colombia | Category 2 | Yes | Bilateral | 2003 No 3334 |
| Comoros | Party to international conventions | Yes | Multilateral | 2005 No 46 |
| Congo | Party to international conventions | Yes | Multilateral | 2005 No 46 |
| Cook Islands | Category 2 | Yes | | 2003 No 3334 |
| Costa Rica | Party to international conventions | Yes | Multilateral | 2005 No 46 |
| Cote d'Ivoire | Party to international conventions | Yes | Multilateral | 2005 No 46 |
| Croatia | Category 2 | No | ECE | 2003 No 3334 |
| Cuba | Category 2 | Yes | Bilateral | 2003 No 3334 |
| Cyprus | Category 1 (EAW) | No | ECE | 2004 No 1898 |
| Czech Republic | Category 1 (EAW) | No | ECE | 2005 No 365 |
| Democratic People's Republic of Korea (North Korea) | Party to international conventions | Yes | Multilateral | 2005 No 46 |
| Denmark | Category 1 (EAW) | No | ECE | 2003 No 3333 |

| Country | Status under 2003 Act | Required to show a prima facie case or not | Multilateral or bilateral treaty | Order in Council |
|---|---|---|---|---|
| Djibouti | Party to international conventions | Yes | Multilateral | 2005 No 46 |
| Dominica | Category 2 | Yes | | 2003 No 3334<br>2005 No 46 |
| Dominican Republic | Party to international conventions | Yes | Multilateral | 2005 No 46 |
| Ecuador | Category 2 | Yes | Bilateral | 2003 No 3334 |
| Egypt | Party to international conventions | Yes | Multilateral | 2005 No 46 |
| El Salvador | Category 2 | Yes | Bilateral | 2003 No 3334 |
| Equatorial Guinea | Party to international conventions | Yes | Multilateral | 2005 No 46 |
| Estonia | Category 1 (EAW) | No | ECE | 2005 No 365 |
| Ethiopia | Party to international conventions | Yes | Multilateral | 2005 No 46 |
| Fiji | Category 2 | Yes | | 2003 No 3334 |
| Finland | Category 1 (EAW) | No | ECE | 2003 No 3333 |
| France | Category 1 (EAW) | No | ECE | 2004 No 1898 |
| Gabon | Party to international conventions | Yes | Multilateral | 2005 No 46 |
| The Gambia | Category 2 | Yes | | 2003 No 3334 |
| Georgia | Category 2 | No | ECE | 2003 No 3334 |
| Germany | Category 1 (EAW) | No | ECE | 2005 No 365 |
| Ghana | Category 2 | Yes | | 2003 No 3334 |
| Gibraltar | Category 1 (EAW) | No | | 2007 No 2238 |
| Greece | Category 1 (EAW) | No | ECE | 2005 No 365 |
| Grenada | Category 2 | Yes | | 2003 No 3334 |
| Guatemala | Category 2 | Yes | Bilateral | 2003 No 3334 |
| Guinea | Party to international conventions | Yes | Multilateral | 2005 No 46 |
| Guinea-Bissau | Party to international conventions | Yes | Multilateral | 2005 No 46 |
| Guyana | Category 2 | Yes | | 2003 No 3334 |
| Haiti | | | Bilateral | |
| Honduras | Party to international conventions | Yes | Multilateral | 2005 No 46 |
| Hong Kong Special Administrative Region (HKSAR) | Category 2 | No | | 2003 No 3334<br>2005 No 365 |
| Haiti | Category 2 | Yes | | 2003 No 3334 |
| Hungary | Category 1 (EAW) | No | ECE | 2004 No 1898 |
| Iceland | Category 2 | No | | 2003 No 3334 |
| India | Category 2 | Yes | Bilateral | 2003 No 3334 |

| Country | Status under 2003 Act | Required to show a prima facie case or not | Multilateral or bilateral treaty | Order in Council |
|---|---|---|---|---|
| Indonesia | Party to international conventions | Yes | Multilateral | 2005 No 46 |
| Iraq | Category 2 | Yes | Bilateral | 2003 No 3334 |
| Ireland | Category 1 (EAW) | No | ECE | 2003 No 3333 |
| Islamic Republic of Iran | Party to international conventions | Yes | Multilateral | 2005 No 46 |
| Israel | Category 2 | No | | 2003 No 3334 |
| Italy | Category 1 (EAW) | No | ECE | 2005 No 2036 |
| Jamaica | Category 2 | Yes | | 2003 No 3334 |
| Japan | Party to international conventions | Yes | Multilateral | 2005 No 46 |
| Jordan | Party to international conventions | Yes | Multilateral | 2005 No 46 |
| Kazakhstan | Party to international conventions | Yes | Multilateral | 2005 No 46 |
| Kenya | Category 2 | Yes | | 2003 No 3334 |
| Kiribati | Category 2 | Yes | | 2003 No 3334 |
| Korea, Republic of | Party to international conventions | Yes | Multilateral | 2005 No 46 |
| Kuwait | Party to international conventions | Yes | Multilateral | 2005 No 46 |
| Kyrgyzstan | Party to international conventions | Yes | Multilateral | 2005 No 46 |
| Lao People's Democratic Republic | Party to international conventions | Yes | Multilateral | 2005 No 46 |
| Latvia | Category 1 (EAW) | No | ECE | 2004 No 1898 |
| Lebanon | Party to international conventions | Yes | Multilateral | 2005 No 46 |
| Lesotho | Category 2 | Yes | | 2003 No 3334 |
| Liberia | Category 2 | Yes | Bilateral | 2003 No 3334 |
| Libyan Arab Jamahiriya (Libya) | Category 2 territory | Yes | Bilateral and Multilateral | Extradition Act 2003 (Amendment to Designations) Order 2010 |
| Liechtenstein | Category 2 | No | ECE | 2003 No 3334 |
| Lithuania | Category 1 (EAW) | No | ECE | 2004 No 1898 |
| Luxembourg | Category 1 (EAW) | No | ECE | 2004 No 1898 |
| Macedonia, FYR | Category 2 | No | ECE | 2003 No 3334 |
| Madagascar | Party to international conventions | Yes | Multilateral | 2005 No 46 |
| Malawi | Category 2 | Yes | | 2003 No 3334 |

| Country | Status under 2003 Act | Required to show a prima facie case or not | Multilateral or bilateral treaty | Order in Council |
| --- | --- | --- | --- | --- |
| Malaysia | Category 2 | Yes | | 2003 No 3334 |
| Maldives | Category 2 | Yes | | 2003 No 3334 |
| Mali | Party to international conventions | Yes | Multilateral | 2005 No 46 |
| Malta | Category 1 (EAW) | No | ECE | 2004 No 1898 |
| Marshall Islands | Party to international conventions | Yes | Multilateral | 2005 No 46 |
| Mauritania | Party to international conventions | Yes | Multilateral | 2005 No 46 |
| Mauritius | Category 2 | Yes | | 2003 No 3334 |
| Mexico | Category 2 | Yes | Bilateral | 2003 No 3334 |
| Micronesia, Federated States of | Party to international conventions | Yes | Multilateral | 2005 No 46 |
| Moldova | Category 2 | No | ECE | 2003 No 3334 |
| Monaco | Category 2 | Yes | ECE, Bilateral | 2003 No 3334 |
| Mongolia | Party to international conventions | Yes | Multilateral | 2005 No 46 |
| Montenegro | Category 2 | No | ECE | 2003 No 3334 2006 No 3451 |
| Morocco | Party to international conventions | Yes | Multilateral | 2005 No 46 |
| Mozambique | Party to international conventions | Yes | Multilateral | 2005 No 46 |
| Myanmar (Burma) | Party to international conventions | Yes | Multilateral | 2005 No 46 |
| Namibia | Party to international conventions | Yes | Multilateral | 2005 No 46 |
| Nauru | Category 2 | Yes | | 2003 No 3334 |
| Nepal | Party to international conventions | Yes | Multilateral | 2005 No 46 |
| The Netherlands | Category 1 (EAW) | No | ECE | 2004 No 1898 |
| New Zealand | Category 2 | No | | 2003 No 3334 |
| Nicaragua | Category 2 | Yes | Bilateral | 2003 No 3334 |
| Niger | Party to international conventions | Yes | Multilateral | 2005 No 46 |
| Nigeria | Category 2 | Yes | | 2003 No 3334 |
| Norway | Category 2 | No | ECE | 2003 No 3334 |
| Oman | Party to international conventions | Yes | Multilateral | 2005 No 46 |

| Country | Status under 2003 Act | Required to show a prima facie case or not | Multilateral or bilateral treaty | Order in Council |
|---|---|---|---|---|
| Pakistan | Party to international conventions | Yes | Multilateral | 2005 No 46 |
| Palau | Party to international conventions | Yes | Multilateral | 2005 No 46 |
| Panama | Category 2 | Yes | Bilateral | 2003 No 3334 |
| Papua New Guinea | Category 2 | Yes | | 2003 No 3334 |
| Paraguay | Category 2 | Yes | Bilateral | 2003 No 3334 |
| Peru | Category 2 | Yes | Bilateral | 2003 No 3334 |
| Philippines | Party to international conventions | Yes | Multilateral | 2005 No 46 |
| Poland | Category 1 (EAW) | No | ECE | 2004 No 1898 |
| Portugal | Category 1 (EAW) | No | | 2003 No 3333 |
| Qatar | Party to international conventions | Yes | Multilateral | 2005 No 46 |
| Romania | Category 2 | No | ECE | 2006 No 3451 |
| Russian Federation | Category 2 | No | ECE | 2003 No 3334 |
| Rwanda | Party to international conventions | Yes | Multilateral | 2005 No 46 |
| Saint Christopher and Nevis | Category 2 | Yes | | 2003 No 3334 |
| Saint Lucia | Category 2 | Yes | | 2003 No 3334 |
| Saint Vincent and the Grenadines | Category 2 | Yes | | 2003 No 3334 |
| San Marino | Category 2 | Yes | ECE, Bilateral | 2003 No 3334 |
| Sao Tome and Principe | Party to international conventions | Yes | Multilateral | 2005 No 46 |
| Saudi Arabia | Party to international conventions | Yes | Multilateral | 2005 No 46 |
| Senegal | Party to international conventions | Yes | Multilateral | 2005 No 46 |
| Serbia | Category 2 | No | ECE, Bilateral | 2003 No 3334 2006 No 3451 |
| Seychelles | Category 2 | Yes | | 2003 No 3334 |
| Sierra Leone | Category 2 | Yes | | 2003 No 3334 |
| Singapore | Category 2 | Yes | | 2003 No 3334 |
| Slovakia | Category 1 (EAW) | No | ECE | 2005 No 365 |
| Slovenia | Category 1 (EAW) | No | ECE | 2004 No 1898 |
| Solomon Islands | Category 2 | Yes | | 2003 No 3334 |
| South Africa | Category 2 | No | | 2003 No 3334 |
| Spain | Category 1 (EAW) | No | ECE | 2003 No 3333 |
| Sri Lanka | Category 2 | Yes | | 2003 No 3334 |
| Sudan | Party to international conventions | Yes | Multilateral | 2005 No 46 |

| Country | Status under 2003 Act | Required to show a prima facie case or not | Multilateral or bilateral treaty | Order in Council |
|---|---|---|---|---|
| Suriname | Party to international conventions | Yes | Multilateral | 2005 No 46 |
| Swaziland | Category 2 | Yes | | 2003 No 3334 |
| Sweden | Category 1 (EAW) | No | ECE | 2003 No 3333 |
| Switzerland | Category 2 | No | ECE | 2003 No 3334 |
| Syrian Arab Republic | Party to international conventions | Yes | Multilateral | 2005 No 46 |
| Tajikistan | Party to international conventions | Yes | Multilateral | 2005 No 46 |
| Tanzania | Category 2 | Yes | | 2003 No 3334 |
| Thailand | Category 2 | Yes | Bilateral | 2003 No 3334 |
| Togo | Party to international conventions | Yes | Multilateral | 2005 No 46 |
| Tonga | Category 2 | Yes | | 2003 No 3334 |
| Tunisia | Party to international conventions | Yes | Multilateral | 2005 No 46 |
| Turkmenistan | Party to international conventions | Yes | Multilateral | 2005 No 46 |
| Trinidad and Tobago | Category 2 | Yes | | 2003 No 3334 |
| Turkey | Category 2 | No | ECE | 2003 No 3334 |
| Tuvalu | Category 2 | Yes | | 2003 No 3334 |
| Uganda | Category 2 | Yes | | 2003 No 3334 |
| Ukraine | Category 2 | No | ECE | 2003 No 3334 |
| United Arab Emirates | Category 2 | Yes | Bilateral | 2008 No 1589 |
| United States of America | Category 2 | No | Bilateral | 2003 No 3334 |
| Uruguay | Category 2 | Yes | Bilateral | 2003 No 3334 |
| Uzbekistan | Party to international conventions | Yes | Multilateral | 2005 No 46 |
| Vanuatu | Category 2 | Yes | | 2003 No 3334 |
| Venezuela | Party to international conventions | Yes | Multilateral | 2005 No 46 |
| Vietnam | Party to international conventions | Yes | Multilateral | 2005 No 46 |
| Western Samoa | Category 2 | Yes | | 2003 No 3334 |
| Yemen | Party to international conventions | Yes | Multilateral | 2005 No 46 |
| Zambia | Category 2 | Yes | | 2003 No 3334 |
| Zimbabwe | Category 2 | Yes | | 2003 No 3334 |

## APPENDIX 3

# Subject Matter Guide to Case Law

### Abbreviations

ECHR    European Convention on Human Rights

EA 2003  Extradition Act 2003

EAW     European Arrest Warrant

SOCA    Serious Organised Crime Agency

## Requests for extradition—whether formal requirements satisfied (including domestic warrants in Part 2 cases)

| Case Name | Citation | Issue(s) |
|---|---|---|
| *Bleta v SSHD (No 1)* | [2004] EWHC 2034 (Admin); [2005] Extradition LR 17 | Whether, in a conviction case under the EA 2003, it was necessary for the request to state that the person sought was 'unlawfully at large' and whether that could be inferred from the request and accompanying documents |
| *Pinto v Governor of HMP Brixton and the First Section of the First Criminal Court of Lisbon* | [2004] EWHC 2986 (Admin); [2005] Extradition LR 35 | Whether the EAW was invalid because it did not make clear that the person sought was unlawfully at large and if so, whether that invalidated all the steps taken under the EA 2003 pursuant to the EAW |
| *Kleinschmidt and Dewar v Government of Germany* | [2005] EWHC 1373 (Admin); [2005] Extradition LR 89 | By when and by whom the documents specified in s 70(9) of the EA 2003, in particular the relevant Order in Council, are to be served |
| *Enander v Governor of HMP Brixton and Swedish National Police Board* | [2005] EWHC 3036 (Admin); [2005] Extradition LR 135 | Whether the Swedish National Police Board was a 'Judicial Authority' for the purposes of the EA 2003 |
| *Dabas v High Court of Justice, Madrid, Spain* | [2006] EWHC 971 (Admin); [2006] Extradition LR 123 | Whether the EAW satisfied the requirements of the EA 2003, whether a separate certificate was required to certify that the conduct fell within the European Framework list |
| *Dabas v High Court of Justice, Madrid, Spain (House of Lords)* | [2007] UKHL 6; [2007] Extradition LR 69 | Whether a separate certificate was required in addition to the EAW to certify that the conduct fell within the European Framework list; whether the requirement of double criminality was satisfied in this case; and whether the EAW had to set out the text of the relevant law of the requesting judicial authority |

| Case Name | Citation | Issue(s) |
|---|---|---|
| *Kuprevicius v Vice Minister of Justice, Ministry of Justice, Lithuania* | [2006] EWHC 1518 (Admin); [2006] Extradition LR 151 | Whether the EAW met the requirements of s 2 of the EA 2003 in stating that K was unlawfully at large following conviction |
| *Barnard v Commonwealth of Australia and SSHD* | [2007] EWHC 1080 (Admin); [2007] Extradition LR 39 | Whether the extradition request was invalidated by inaccuracies in the warrants issued for B's arrest |
| *Hashmi v Government of the USA* | [2007] EWHC 564 (Admin); [2007] Extradition LR 102 | Whether the contents of the warrants satisfied the EA 2003; whether the United States was claiming exorbitant jurisdiction; and whether the conduct was properly described in the request |

## Secretary of State's powers

| Case Name | Citation | Issue(s) |
|---|---|---|
| *Akaroglu v Government of Romania* | [2007] EWHC 367 (Admin); [2007] Extradition LR 83 | Whether the Secretary of State's decision to certify under s 70 of the EA 2003 was challengeable by appeal or judicial review |
| *Vincent Brown and others v (1) Governor of HMP Belmarsh, (2) SSHD, (3) The Republic of Rwanda* | [2007] EWHC 498 (Admin); [2007] Extradition LR 88 | Whether the power conferred by s 194(4)(b) of the EA 2003 permits the Secretary of State to extend the required period under s 74(11)(a) from 45 days to 95 days. |

## Section 2 of the EA 2003 (person wanted as a suspect, or for questioning, and not for prosecution)

| Case Name | Citation | Issue(s) |
|---|---|---|
| *Vey v The Office of the Public Prosecutor of the County Court of Mountluçon, France* | [2006] EWHC 760 (Admin); [2006] Extradition LR 110 | Whether V was sought for interrogation or prosecution in France |
| *Hilali v Central Court of Criminal Proceedings Number 5 of the National Court, Madrid, and Senior District Judge, Bow Street Magistrates' Court* | [2006] EWHC 1239 (Admin); [2006] Extradition LR 154 | Whether H was accused of an offence in Spain or merely suspected |
| *Akaroglu v Government of Romania* | [2007] EWHC 367 (Admin); [2007] Extradition LR 83 | Whether A was sought as an accused or convicted person |
| *Paschayan v Government of Switzerland* | [2008] EWHC 388 (Admin); [2008] Extradition LR 144 | Whether P's extradition was sought as an accused person or merely as a suspect |
| *McCormack v Tribunal de Grande Instance, Quimper, France* | [2008] EWHC 1453 (Admin); [2008] Extradition LR 252 | Whether M's extradition was sought as an accused person or merely as a suspect |

## Section 2(3) of the EA 2003 (the statement required under s 2(3) of the EA 2003)

| Case Name | Citation | Issue(s) |
| --- | --- | --- |
| *Hunt v The Court at First Instance, Antwerp, Belgium* | [2006] EWHC 165 (Admin); [2006] Extradition LR 16 | Whether the EAW contained the statement required by s 2(3) of the EA 2003 that the person was accused in Belgium of the commission of an offence specified in EAW |
| *Glica v Regional Court of Bydgoszcz, Poland* | [2008] EWHC 1111 (Admin); [2008] Extradition LR 235 | Whether an EAW complied with s 2 of the EA 2003; whether the English translation was inaccurate and, if so, whether that precluded extradition |

## Section 2(4)(b) of the EA 2003 (particulars of any other warrant)

| Case Name | Citation | Issue(s) |
| --- | --- | --- |
| *Jaso, Lopez and Albisu Hernandez v Central Criminal Court No 2 Madrid* | [2007] EWHC 2983 (Admin); [2008] Extradition LR 35 | Whether the EAWs were defective in not containing the particulars required by s 2 of the EA 2003 |

## Section 2(4)(c) of the EA 2003 (whether sufficient particulars of the accusation)

| Case Name | Citation | Issue(s) |
| --- | --- | --- |
| *Palar v Court of First Instance Brussels* | [2005] EWHC 915 (Admin); [2005] Extradition LR 62 | Whether the EAW provided sufficient particulars of the person's alleged conduct |
| *Hunt v The Court at First Instance, Antwerp, Belgium* | [2006] EWHC 165 (Admin); [2006] Extradition LR 16 | Whether the EAW contained the information required by s 2(4) of the EA 2003 citing the provision of Belgian law under which the conduct was alleged to constitute an offence |
| *Hall v Government of Germany* | [2006] EWHC 462 (Admin); [2006] Extradition LR 94 | Whether an EAW was valid in the absence of information as to the legal provisions which the conduct was said to have violated |
| *Pahlen v Government of Austria* | [2006] EWHC 1672 (Admin); [2006] Extradition LR 197 | Whether an EAW was invalid for want of particulars |
| *Cebelis v the Prosecutor-General's Office of the Republic of Lithuania* | [2006] EWHC 3201 (Admin); [2006] Extradition LR 261 | Whether the EAW was invalid because the conduct allegedly did not correspond to the provisions of foreign law cited in the EAW |
| *Crean v Government of Ireland* | [2007] EWHC 814 (Admin); [2007] Extradition LR 109 | Whether the EAW was sufficiently particularised to meet the requirements of s 2(4)(c) of the EA 2003 |
| *Sidlauskaite v The Prosecutor General's Office of the Republic of Lithuania* | [2006] EWHC 3486 (Admin); [2007] Extradition LR 160 | Whether the EAW provided sufficient particulars of the alleged conduct |

| Case Name | Citation | Issue(s) |
| --- | --- | --- |
| *Iqtidar Mahmood Dara v Public Prosecutor's Office at the Regional Court of Marburg, Germany* | [2007] EWHC 1678 (Admin); [2007] Extradition LR 195 | Whether, in an extradition request from Germany alleging the obtaining of components for making nuclear weapons in Pakistan, the conduct was sufficiently particularised |
| *Haynes v The Court of Magistrates, Malta* | [2007] EWHC 2651 (Admin); [2007] Extradition LR 295 | Whether the EAW met the requirements of s 2 of the EA 2003 |
| *Gilbert Ektor v National Public Prosecutor of Holland* | [2007] EWHC 3106 (Admin); [2008] Extradition LR 28 | Whether the EAW provided sufficient particulars of the alleged conduct to satisfy the requirements of s 2(4)(c) of the EA 2003 |
| *Harvey v Judicial Authority of Portugal— Tribunal Judicial de Albufeira* | [2007] EWHC 3282 (Admin); [2008] Extradition LR 31 | Whether the EAW contained sufficient particulars to meet the requirements of s 2 of the EA 2003 |
| *Saeed Aryantash v Tribunal de Grand Instance, Lille, France* | [2008] EWHC 2115 (Admin); [2008] Extradition LR 279 | Whether typographical errors in an EAW regarding dates rendered it invalid |

## Section 2(6)(b) of the EA 2003 (sufficient particulars)

| Case Name | Citation | Issue(s) |
| --- | --- | --- |
| *Zakowski v Regional Court in Szczecin, Poland* | [2008] EWHC 1389 (Admin); [2008] Extradition LR 249 | Whether the EAW contained sufficient particulars of the conviction for the purposes of s 2(6)(b) of the EA 2003 |

## Section 2(6)(c) of the EA 2003 (particulars of 'any other warrant')

| Case Name | Citation | Issue(s) |
| --- | --- | --- |
| *Zakowski v Regional Court in Szczecin, Poland* | [2008] EWHC 1389 (Admin); [2008] Extradition LR 249 | Whether the reference in s 2(6)(c) of the 2003 Act to '*any other warrant*' referred to any other domestic warrant or any other EAW |

## Section 2(6)(e) of the EA 2003 (particulars of sentence)

| Case Name | Citation | Issue(s) |
| --- | --- | --- |
| *Trepac v Presiding Judge, County Court in Trencin, Slovak Republic* | [2006] EWHC 3346 (Admin); [2006] Extradition LR 265 | Whether the EAW has to specify the sentence imposed with respect to each offence of which a person had been convicted |
| *Pilecki v the Circuit Court of Legnica, Poland* | [2007] EWHC 2080 (Admin); [2007] Extradition LR 266 | Whether an EAW which provided an aggregate sentence in respect of multiple offences failed to comply with s 2(6)(e) of the EA 2003, and whether the District Judge had been entitled to find that P had deliberately absented himself from his trial in Poland |

| Case Name | Citation | Issue(s) |
| --- | --- | --- |
| *Wiercinski v 2nd Division of the Criminal Circuit in Olsztyn, Poland* | [2008] EWHC 200 (Admin); [2008] Extradition LR 55 | Whether W could be extradited to serve an aggregate sentence imposed for three offences one of which was not an extradition offence, where there was no indication as to the sentence imposed in respect of the other two, extraditable, offences |
| *Pilecki v Circuit Court of Legnica, Poland (House of Lords)* | [2008] UKHL 7; [2008] Extradition LR 78 | Whether an EAW which referred to an aggregate sentence in respect of multiple offences failed to comply with s 2(6)(e) of the EA 2003; whether it had to be shown that the sentence that was imposed in respect of each offence, taken on its own, was at least 4 months |
| *Palinski v The Regional Court of Bydgoszcz, Poland* | [2007] EWHC 732 (Admin); [2008] Extradition LR 141 | Whether an EAW which provided an aggregate sentence in respect of multiple offences failed to comply with s 2(6)(e) of the EA 2003 and whether the offences were 'extradition offences' |
| *Kucera v District Court of Karvina, Czech Republic* | [2008] EWHC 414 (Admin); [2008] Extradition LR 149 | Whether, when an aggregate sentence had been imposed for two offences, of which one was not an extradition offence, an EAW was valid; whether theft was an extradition offence in the absence of an indication of a separate sentence for it |
| *Pietrzak v Regional Court of Wloclawek, Poland* | [2008] EWHC 2138 (Admin); [2008] Extradition LR 256 | Whether the EAW was invalid because it misstated the remaining term of imprisonment to be served |

## Consent to extradition

| Case Name | Citation | Issue(s) |
| --- | --- | --- |
| *Governor of HMP Wandsworth v Antanas Kinderis; Prosecutor General's Office of the Republic of Lithuania and Crown Prosecution Service, Cambridgeshire* | [2007] EWHC 998 (Admin); [2007] Extradition LR 136 | Whether, when the requested person consents to his extradition, the duty to deliver him for extradition took priority over any duty to deliver him for trial in domestic criminal proceedings |
| *Darius Skruodys v Siauliai City District Court, Lithuania* | [2007] EWHC 1192 (Admin); [2007] Extradition LR 135 | Whether the Court had power to allow a person to return voluntarily to the requesting state using his own international travel document |

## Identity (s 7 of the EA 2003)

| Case Name | Citation | Issue(s) |
| --- | --- | --- |
| *Nur v Public Prosecutor Van der Valk* | [2005] EWHC 1874 (Admin); [2005] Extradition LR 109 | Whether the District Judge had been right not to allow N to re-open the issue of identity at the extradition hearing after it had been decided against him at the initial hearing |

| Case Name | Citation | Issue(s) |
|---|---|---|
| *Hilali v Central Court of Criminal Proceedings Number 5 of the National Court, Madrid, and Senior District Judge, Bow Street Magistrates' Court* | [2006] EWHC 1239 (Admin) | Whether H's identity had been proved |
| *Franco Stefan v Government of Albania* | [2007] EWHC 3267 (Admin); [2008] Extradition LR 49 | Whether the District Judge had been entitled to conclude, on a balance of probabilities, that S was the person sought by the Government of Albania |

## Time limits for the extradition hearing to begin (s 8 of the EA 2003)

| Case Name | Citation | Issue(s) |
|---|---|---|
| *Convery v High Court of Rotterdam* | [2005] EWHC 566 (Admin); [2005] Extradition LR 42 | Whether there had been a failure to comply with the time limits laid down in the EA 2003 |
| *Gronostajski v Government of Poland* | [2007] EWHC 3314 (Admin); [2007] Extradition LR 299 | Whether, when non-production or late production of a prisoner causes an extradition hearing to be put off until the following day, delay to the hearing can be said to have a 'reasonable cause' for the purposes of s 8(7) of the EA 2003 |

## Extradition offence/double criminality (ss 10 and 78(4)(b) of the EA 2003)

| Case Name | Citation | Issue(s) |
|---|---|---|
| *Office of the King's Prosecutor, Brussels v Armas and Bow Street Magistrates' Court* | [2004] EWHC 2019 (Admin); [2005] Extradition LR 22 | Whether an extradition request fell within s 65 of the EA 2003 |
| *Office of the King's Prosecutor, Brussels v Armas and others (House of Lords)* | [2005] UKHL 67; [2005] Extradition LR 139 | Whether an extradition request fell within s 65 of the EA 2003 |
| *Convery v High Court of Rotterdam* | [2005] EWHC 566 (Admin) | Whether the offences in respect of which extradition was sought were 'extradition offences' under the Act |
| *Bentley v Government of the USA* | [2005] EWHC 1078 (Admin); [2005] Extradition LR 65 | Whether extradition should be refused by virtue of the fact that the US government had not proved that MDMA was a banned substance at the material time in the United States and/or that the conduct relied on did not take place in the United States |
| *Derevianko v Government of Lithuania and Governor of HMP Brixton* | [2005] EWHC 1212 (Admin); [2005] Extradition LR 75 | Whether an offence was an '*extradition crime*' under the Extradition Act 1989 |
| *Kadre v Government of France; Governor of Belmarsh Prison* | [2005] EWHC 1712 (Admin); [2005] Extradition LR 104 | Whether the request disclosed extradition crimes and/or whether it disclosed sufficient conduct |

| Case Name | Citation | Issue(s) |
| --- | --- | --- |
| *Beresford v Government of the Commonwealth of Australia* | [2005] EWHC 2175 (Admin); [2005] Extradition LR 113 | Whether lack of clarity in the evidence meant that it was not shown that there was an extradition offence |
| *Mariotti v Government of Italy and Others* | [2005] EWHC 2745 (Admin); [2005] Extradition LR 162 | Whether the request disclosed an extradition offence in relation to an Italian conviction for murder |
| *Fofana and Belise v Deputy Prosecutor, Tribunal de Grande Instance de Meaux, France* | [2006] EWHC 744 (Admin); [2006] Extradition LR 102 | Whether extradition was barred by double jeopardy by virtue of criminal proceedings in the United Kingdom, and whether the EAW accurately or adequately described commission by F and B of an extradition offence |
| *Hosseini, Ahmed and Zada v Head of the Prosecution Department of the Courts of Higher Instance, Paris, France* | [2006] EWHC 1333 (Admin); [2006] Extradition LR 176 | Whether the EAWs set out extradition offences |
| *Norris v The Government of the USA and others* | [2007] EWHC 71 (Admin); [2007] Extradition LR 1 | Whether price-fixing at the relevant time was an extradition offence in the United Kingdom |
| *Dabas v High Court of Justice, Madrid, Spain (House of Lords)* | [2007] UKHL 6; [2007] Extradition LR 69 | Whether the requirement of double criminality was met |
| *Sidlauskaite v The Prosecutor General's Office of the Republic of Lithuania* | [2006] EWHC 3486 (Admin); [2007] Extradition LR 160 | Whether the requirement of 'double criminality' in s 64(3)(c) of the EA 2003 was met |
| *Iqtidar Mahmood Dara v Public Prosecutor's Office at the Regional Court of Marburg, Germany* | [2007] EWHC 1678 (Admin); [2007] Extradition LR 195 | Whether, in an extradition request from Germany alleging the obtaining of components for making nuclear weapons in Pakistan, the conduct amounted to an extradition offence |
| *Osunta v Public Prosecutor's Office in Dusseldorf* | [2007] EWHC 1562 (Admin); [2007] Extradition LR 200 | Whether geographical excision from the EAW was permissible in order that the conduct should constitute an extradition offence |
| *Mitchell v High Court of Boulogne sur mer* | [2007] EWHC 2006 (Admin); [2007] Extradition LR 222 | Whether M's extradition to France was barred because no part of the conduct took place in France |
| *Edwards v Government of the USA* | [2007] EWHC 1877 (Admin); [2007] Extradition LR 262 | Whether, in deciding whether the dual criminality requirement is met in a case under Part 2 of the EA 2003, the domestic court is limited to what is set out in the foreign indictment, together with any document which it incorporates by express reference, or whether it may take into account any narrative or explanation tendered by the requesting state |
| *Haynes v The Court of Magistrates, Malta* | [2007] EWHC 2651 (Admin); [2007] Extradition LR 295 | Whether the requirements of s 64 of the EA 2003 were met |

| Case Name | Citation | Issue(s) |
|-----------|----------|----------|
| *Zak v Regional Court of Bydgoszcz, Poland* | [2008] EWHC 470 (Admin); [2008] Extradition LR 134 | Whether the conduct set out in an EAW amounted to an extradition offence, when it did not specify the *mens rea* that would be required for the corresponding offences in English law |
| *Norris v Government of the USA and others (House of Lords)* | [2008] UKHL 16; [2008] Extradition LR 159 | Whether price-fixing at the relevant time was an extradition offence in the United Kingdom |
| *R (Ahsan) v DPP and Government of the USA (interested party); Ahsan v Government of the USA and SSHD; Tajik v Government of the USA and SSHD* | [2008] EWHC 666 (Admin); [2008] Extradition LR 207 | Whether offences were extradition offences |

## Passage of time—whether extradition would be oppressive or unjust by reason of the passage of time (ss 14 and 82 of the EA 2003)

| Case Name | Citation | Issue(s) |
|-----------|----------|----------|
| *Raffile v Government of the USA* | [2004] EWHC 2913 (Admin); [2005] Extradition LR 29 | Whether extradition was barred by reason of the passage of time |
| *Schmidt v SSHD* | [2005] EWHC 959 (Admin); [2005] Extradition LR 70 | Whether extradition was barred by reason of the passage of time |
| *Derevianko v Government of Lithuania and Governor of HMP Brixton* | [2005] EWHC 1212 (Admin); [2005] Extradition LR 75 | Whether extradition was barred by reason of the passage of time |
| *Cook v Government of Spain and Governor of HMP Brixton* | [2005] EWHC 1388 (Admin); [2005] Extradition LR 83 | Whether extradition was barred by reason of the passage of time |
| *Guven v Government of France and Governor of HMP Brixton* | [2005] EWHC 1391 (Admin); [2005] Extradition LR 86 | Whether extradition was barred by reason of the passage of time |
| *Zigmund v Government of Slovakia and SSHD* | [2005] EWHC 2507 (Admin); [2005] Extradition LR 100 | Whether extradition was barred by reason of the passage of time |
| *Beresford v Government of the Commonwealth of Australia* | [2005] EWHC 2175 (Admin) | Whether extradition was barred by reason of the passage of time |
| *Sirvelis v Governor of HM Prison Brixton and Government of Lithuania* | [2005] EWHC 2611 (Admin); [2005] Extradition LR 118 | Whether extradition was barred by reason of the passage of time |
| *Owalabi v Court Number 4 at the High Court of Justice in Spain* | [2005] EWHC 2849 (Admin); [2005] Extradition LR 132 | Whether extradition was barred by reason of the passage of time |
| *Mariotti v Government of Italy and Others* | [2005] EWHC 2745 (Admin); [2005] Extradition LR 162 | Whether extradition was barred by reason of the passage of time |

| Case Name | Citation | Issue(s) |
| --- | --- | --- |
| *Kociukow v District Court of Bialystok III Penal Division (a Polish Judicial Authority* | [2006] EWHC 56 (Admin); [2006] Extradition LR 4 | Whether extradition was barred by reason of the passage of time |
| *Hunt v The Court at First Instance, Antwerp, Belgium* | [2006] EWHC 165 (Admin) | Whether extradition was barred by reason of the passage of time |
| *Colda v Government of Romania* | [2006] EWHC 1150 (Admin); [2006] Extradition LR 118 | Whether extradition was barred by reason of the passage of time |
| *Dziedic v Government of Germany* | [2006] EWHC 1750 (Admin); [2006] Extradition LR 185 | Whether extradition was barred by reason of the passage of time |
| *Da An Chen v Government of Romania* | [2006] EWHC 1752 (Admin); [2006] Extradition LR 192 | Whether extradition was barred by reason of the passage of time |
| *Pahlen v Government of Austria* | [2006] EWHC 1672 (Admin); [2006] Extradition LR 197 | Whether extradition was barred by reason of the passage of time |
| *Prancs v Rezekne Court of Latvia* | [2006] EWHC 2573 (Admin); [2006] Extradition LR 234 | Whether extradition was barred by reason of the passage of time |
| *Azcarate v Government of the USA* | [2006] EWHC 2526 (Admin); [2006] Extradition LR 246 | Whether extradition was barred by reason of the passage of time |
| *Calder v The Public Prosecutor's Office of Landshut, Germany* | [2006] EWHC 2921 (Admin); [2006] Extradition LR 249 | Whether extradition was barred by reason of the passage of time |
| *Filipczak v Provincial Court (5th Criminal District) Warsaw-Praga, Poland* | [2006] EWHC 2700 (Admin); [2006] Extradition LR 252 | Whether extradition was barred by reason of the passage of time |
| *Yarrow and Tonge v Public Prosecutor's Office of Appeal of Crete* | [2006] EWHC 3388 (Admin); [2006] Extradition LR 269 | Whether extradition was barred by reason of the passage of time |
| *Lisowski v Regional Court of Bialystok (Poland)* | [2006] EWHC 3227 (Admin); [2006] Extradition LR 272 | Whether extradition was barred by reason of the passage of time |
| *Maxwell-King v Government of the USA* | [2006] EWHC 3033 (Admin); [2006] Extradition LR 297 | Whether extradition was barred by reason of the passage of time |
| *Norris v The Government of the USA and others* | [2007] EWHC 71 (Admin); [2007] Extradition LR 1 | Whether extradition was barred by reason of the passage of time |
| *Falanga v Office of the State Prosecutor, Court of Navara, Italy* | [2007] EWHC 268 (Admin); [2007] Extradition LR 29 | Whether extradition was barred by reason of the passage of time |
| *Senkus v District Court of Kaunas, Lithuania* | [2007] EWHC 345 (Admin); [2007] Extradition LR 36 | Whether extradition was barred by reason of the passage of time |
| *Harkins v SSHD* | [2007] EWHC 639 (Admin); [2007] Extradition LR 41 | Whether extradition was barred by reason of the passage of time |
| *Crean v Government of Ireland* | [2007] EWHC 814 (Admin); [2007] Extradition LR 109 | Whether extradition was barred by reason of the passage of time |

| Case Name | Citation | Issue(s) |
| --- | --- | --- |
| *Gary McKinnon v (1) Government of the USA and (2) SSHD* | [2007] EWHC 762 (Admin); [2007] Extradition LR 117 | Whether extradition was barred by reason of the passage of time |
| *Toafike Chababe v Bonn Public Prosecutor's Office* | [2007] EWHC 288 (Admin); [2007] Extradition LR 162 | Whether extradition was barred by reason of the passage of time (offences committed in 1989) |
| *Prus v District Court of Bialystok* | [2007] EWHC 934 (Admin); [2007] Extradition LR 165 | Whether extradition was barred by reason of the passage of time |
| *La Torre v Republic of Italy* | [2007] EWHC 1370 (Admin); [2007] Extradition LR 185 | Whether extradition was barred by reason of the passage of time |
| *Tomasz Piotrowski v District Court of Slupsk, Poland* | [2007] EWHC 1982 (Admin); [2007] Extradition LR 204 | Whether extradition was barred by reason of the passage of time |
| *Mitchell v High Court of Boulogne sur mer* | [2007] EWHC 2006 (Admin); [2007] Extradition LR 222 | Whether extradition was barred by reason of the passage of time |
| *Mariusz Artur Wiejak v Olsztyn Circuit Court of Poland* | [2007] EWHC 2123 (Admin); [2007] Extradition LR 252 | Whether extradition was barred by reason of the passage of time |
| *Government of Croatia v Milan Spanovic* | [2007] EWHC 1770 (Admin); [2007] Extradition LR 255 | Whether the District Judge had been entitled to hold that S's extradition to Croatia on war crimes charges was barred due to the passage of time |
| *Goodyer and Gomes v Government of Trinidad and Tobago* | [2007] EWHC 2012 (Admin); [2007] Extradition LR 271 | Whether the District Judge had been entitled to hold that extradition was barred due to the passage of time |
| *Zielinski v District Court Legnica (a Polish Judicial Authority)* | [2007] EWHC 2645 (Admin); [2007] Extradition LR 303 | Whether the District Judge had been entitled to hold that extradition was barred due to the passage of time |
| *David Charles Watson v Public Prosecutor M Bonheur (a Dutch Judicial Authority)* | [2007] EWHC 2975 (Admin); [2008] Extradition LR 17 | Whether the District Judge had been entitled to hold that extradition was barred due to the passage of time |
| *Harvey v Judicial Authority of Portugal— Tribunal Judicial de Albufeira* | [2007] EWHC 3282 (Admin); [2008] Extradition LR 31 | Whether the District Judge had been entitled to hold that extradition was barred due to the passage of time |
| *Tuvia Stern v Government of the USA* | [2007] EWHC 3266 (Admin); [2008] Extradition LR 52 | Whether the District Judge had been entitled to hold that extradition was barred due to the passage of time |
| *Geary v Government of Canada* | [2008] EWHC 304 (Admin); [2008] Extradition LR 67 | Whether the District Judge had been entitled to hold that extradition was barred due to the passage of time |
| *Davis and Griffiths v Court of Instruction No 2 Benidorm, Alicante, Spain* | [2008] EWHC 853 (Admin); [2008] Extradition LR 71 | Whether it would be unjust or oppressive to extradite D and G to Spain for murder by reason of the passage of time; whether a requested person may rely upon the passage of time bar when he has fled from the authorities in the country seeking extradition but not in order to evade prosecution for the offences in respect of which the extradition is sought |

| Case Name | Citation | Issue(s) |
| --- | --- | --- |
| *Jaworski v Regional Court Katowice, Poland* | [2008] EWHC 858 (Admin); [2008] Extradition LR 75 | Whether J's extradition was barred by reason of the passage of time having rendered his extradition unjust and/or oppressive |
| *Government of the USA v Stanley Tollman and Beatrice Tollman* | [2008] EWHC 184 (Admin); [2008] Extradition LR 85 | Whether the District Judge had been right to conclude that Mr T's extradition would be unjust and oppressive by reason of the passage of time |
| *Zak v Regional Court of Bydgoszcz, Poland* | [2008] EWHC 470 (Admin); [2008] Extradition LR 134 | Whether extradition was barred by reason of the passage of time |
| *Norris v Government of the USA and others (House of Lords)* | [2008] UKHL 16; [2008] Extradition LR 159 | Whether extradition was barred by reason of the passage of time |
| *Oraczko v District Court in Krakow* | [2008] EWHC 904 (Admin); [2008] Extradition LR 204 | Whether extradition was barred by reason of the passage of time |
| *R (Lakatus) v SSHD and the Government of the Republic of Poland (Interested Party)* | [2008] EWHC 887 (Admin); [2008] Extradition LR 231 | Whether the Secretary of State had erred in approaching the question of whether extradition would be oppressive by reason of the passage of time in terms of s 12(2)(a) of the Extradition Act 1989 |
| *Krompalcas v Prosecutor General's Office, Lithuania* | [2008] EWHC 1486 (Admin); [2008] Extradition LR 258 | Whether K was a fugitive from justice and so disentitled from relying on the passage of time as a bar to his extradition pursuant to ss 11 and 14 of the EA 2003 |
| *Mustafa Kamel Mustafa (otherwise Abu Hamza) v (1) Government of the USA, (2) SSHD* | [2008] EWHC 1357 (Admin); [2008] Extradition LR 263 | Whether extradition would be unjust or oppressive by reason of the passage of time since the alleged offences |

## The rule against double jeopardy (ss 12 and 80 of the EA 2003)

| Case Name | Citation | Issue(s) |
| --- | --- | --- |
| *Selbach v Government of Lithuania* | [2005] EWHC 1536 (Admin); [2005] Extradition LR 98 | Whether proceedings in Lithuania amounted to an adjudication on which S could rely to show that he had been acquitted of the offence and that his extradition was therefore barred by virtue of s 6(3) of the Extradition Act 1989 |
| *Bohning v Government of the USA* | [2005] EWHC 2613 (Admin); [2005] Extradition LR 121 | Whether extraditing B to the United States would amount to double jeopardy or abuse of process in light of the UK proceedings against him |
| *Fofana and Belise v Deputy Prosecutor, Tribunal de Grande Instance de Meaux, France* | [2006] EWHC 744 (Admin) | Whether extradition was barred by double jeopardy by virtue of criminal proceedings in the United Kingdom |
| *Maxwell-King v Government of the USA* | [2006] EWHC 3033 (Admin); [2006] Extradition LR 297 | Whether M's extradition was barred by double jeopardy |
| *John v Government of the USA* | [2006] EWHC 3512 (Admin); [2006] Extradition LR 305 | Whether J's extradition was barred by double jeopardy |
| *Mitchell v High Court of Boulogne sur mer* | [2007] EWHC 2006 (Admin); [2007] Extradition LR 222 | Whether M's extradition to France was barred because of double jeopardy |

## Extraneous considerations (ss 13 and 81 of the EA 2003)

| Case Name | Citation | Issue(s) |
| --- | --- | --- |
| *Gary McKinnon v (1) Government of the USA and (2) SSHD* | [2007] EWHC 762 (Admin); [2007] Extradition LR 117 | Whether M's extradition to the United States for trial on charges of having 'hacked' into US government computers and networks was barred by extraneous considerations |
| *Tamarevichute v Government of the Russian Federation* | [2008] EWHC 534 (Admin); [2008] Extradition LR 188 | Whether T's extradition was barred because of a real risk that she might be prejudiced at her trial on account of her Roma ethnicity |
| *R (Ahsan) v DPP and Government of the USA (interested party); Ahsan v Government of the USA and SSHD; Tajik v Government of the USA and SSHD* | [2008] EWHC 666 (Admin); [2008] Extradition LR 207 | Whether extradition was barred by extraneous considerations |

## Conviction in absence and right to a retrial (ss 20 and 85 of the EA 2003)

| Case Name | Citation | Issue(s) |
| --- | --- | --- |
| *Bleta v Government of the Republic of Albania (No 2)* | [2005] EWHC 475 (Admin); [2005] Extradition LR 47 | Whether B had deliberately absented himself from his trial in Albania and, if not, whether he would be entitled to a retrial |
| *Mariotti v Government of Italy and Others* | [2005] EWHC 2745 (Admin) | Whether M's extradition was barred by virtue of s 6(2) (conviction in absence) of the Extradition Act 1989 |
| *Migliorelli v SSHD* | [2006] EWHC 243 (Admin); [2006] Extradition LR 7 | Whether, considering that the appellant had been convicted in his absence, it would, in terms of s 6 of the Extradition Act 1989, be in the interests of justice to return him to Italy on the ground of that conviction |
| *Mitoi v Government of Romania* | [2006] EWHC 1977 (Admin); [2006] Extradition LR 168 | Whether the District Judge had been right to conclude that M had deliberately absented himself from trial, and to what standard of proof that had to be proved |
| *Da An Chen v Government of Romania* | [2006] EWHC 1752 (Admin); [2006] Extradition LR 192 | Whether D's extradition was barred by the fact that he was tried and sentenced *in absentia*, and had not deliberately absented himself from his trial |
| *Deputy Public Prosecutor of the Court of Appeal of Montpellier v Wade* | [2006] EWHC 1909 (Admin); [2006] Extradition LR 204 | Whether an appeal hearing at which W's acquittal was overturned was a trial; whether he had deliberately absented himself from his trial and whether his return would violate s 20 of the EA 2003 |
| *Virciglio v The Judicial Authority of the Graz High Court, Austria* | [2006] EWHC 3197 (Admin); [2006] Extradition LR 238 | Whether a hearing at which V's sentence was increased was a conviction in absence |
| *Falanga v Office of the State Prosecutor, Court of Navara, Italy* | [2007] EWHC 268 (Admin); [2007] Extradition LR 29 | Whether F's extradition was barred by the fact of trial *in absentia* |

| Case Name | Citation | Issue(s) |
| --- | --- | --- |
| *Prus v District Court of Bialystok* | [2007] EWHC 934 (Admin); [2007] Extradition LR 165 | Whether P had deliberately absented himself from his trial |
| *Caldarelli v The Court of Naples* | [2007] EWHC 1624 (Admin); [2007] Extradition LR 209 | Whether the EAW was rightly characterized as an accusation warrant when the arrestee had been convicted in his absence but proceedings had not been finalized; whether there was bad faith; and whether the EAW was unlawful in light of the dates of the conduct alleged |
| *Raimondas Baksys v Ministry of Justice of the Republic of Lithuania* | [2007] EWHC 2838 (Admin); [2008] Extradition LR 1 | Whether a ruling in which a deferred sentence was enforced constituted a ruling *in absentia* and so raised a bar under s 20 of the EA 2003, and on whom the burden lay of bringing proof in that regard |
| *Mucelli v Government of the Republic of Albania and SSHD (Interested Party)* | [2007] EWHC 2632 (Admin); [2008] Extradition LR 4 | (1) Whether M had deliberately absented himself from trial; (2) whether, having been convicted in his absence, M would be entitled to a retrial upon return to Albania; (3) whether M's extradition was barred by the passage of time; and (4) whether the notice of appeal was served out of time and, if so, whether the court had power to grant an extension of time for serving notice of appeal in extradition proceedings |
| *Bogdani v Government of the Republic of Albania* | [2007] EWHC 2065 (Admin); [2008] Extradition LR 284 | Whether, having been convicted in his absence, B would be entitled to a retrial upon return to Albania and whether new evidence from the Government of Albania should be admitted on that issue |
| *Caldarelli v Court of Naples (House of Lords)* | [2008] UKHL 51; [2008] Extradition LR 300 | Whether the EAW was rightly characterized as an accusation warrant when the arrestee had been convicted in his absence but proceedings had not been finalized |

## Human rights (ss 21 and 87 of the EA 2003)

| Case Name | Citation | Issue(s) |
| --- | --- | --- |
| *Raffile v Government of the USA* | [2004] EWHC 2913 (Admin) | Whether extradition would breach Arts 2, 3, 6, or 8 ECHR |
| *Okendeji v Government of the Commonwealth of Australia and Bow Street Magistrates' Court* | [2005] EWHC 471 (Admin); [2005] Extradition LR 57 | Whether O would receive a fair trial in Australia, in light of a claimed reversal of the legal burden of proof, and thus whether his extradition would be compatible with Art 6 ECHR |
| *Bentley v Government of the USA* | [2005] EWHC 1078 (Admin) | Whether extradition would violate B's rights under Art 8 ECHR |
| *Schmidt v SSHD* | [2005] EWHC 959 (Admin) | Whether return would breach Art 8 ECHR; and whether S would be prejudiced at trial by virtue of his membership of an evangelical Protestant group |
| *Ramda v SSHD and Government of France* | [2005] EWHC 2526 (Admin); [2005] Extradition LR 152 | Whether the Secretary of State's decision to order R's extradition was flawed by virtue of the risk of an unfair trial in France or ill-treatment in France or in Algeria if he were to be extradited |

| Case Name | Citation | Issue(s) |
| --- | --- | --- |
| *Labsi v SSHD and Government of France* | [2006] EWHC 2931 (Admin); [2005] Extradition LR 169 | Whether an extradition to France would arguably breach the right to a fair trial, be unjust or breach Art 3 ECHR |
| *Boudhiba v Central Examining Court No 5 of the National Court of Justice, Madrid, Spain* | [2006] EWHC 167 (Admin); [2006] Extradition LR 20 | Whether B's extradition was compatible with his human rights |
| *Bermingham and others v Director of the Serious Fraud Office, HM Attorney General, SSHD, Government of the USA* | [2006] EWHC 200 (Admin) | Whether extradition to the United States was compatible with the ECHR |
| *Arain v Government of Germany and SSHD* | [2006] EWHC 1702 (Admin) | Whether the District Judge should have heard argument that part of A's conduct was not criminal in the United Kingdom in relation to his arguments that his return would violate Art 8 of the ECHR |
| *Dabas v High Court of Justice, Madrid, Spain* | [2006] EWHC 971 (Admin) | Whether D's extradition was compatible with his Convention rights and whether he was at risk of refoulement |
| *Miklis v Deputy Prosecutor General of Lithuania* | [2006] EWHC 1032 (Admin); [2006] Extradition LR 146 | Whether M's extradition would breach his human rights |
| *Hilali v Central Court of Criminal Proceedings Number 5 of the National Court, Madrid, and Senior District Judge, Bow Street Magistrates' Court* | [2006] EWHC 1239 (Admin) | Whether H's extradition was barred on the basis that, as a suspected Islamic terrorist, he would be mistreated and not have a fair trial in Spain; whether the real purpose of the request was to deport H to Morocco, where he would be mistreated |
| *Hosseini, Ahmed and Zada v Head of the Prosecution Department of the Courts of Higher Instance, Paris, France* | [2006] EWHC 1333 (Admin) | Whether extradition would breach Art 8 ECHR |
| *Prenga v Republic of Albania* | [2006] EWHC 1616 (Admin); [2006] Extradition LR 200 | Whether P's conviction was the result of a confession or admission obtained by torture or other ill-treatment amounting to a breach of Art 3 ECHR, with the result that his extradition would be barred |
| *Prancs v Rezekne Court of Latvia* | [2006] EWHC 2573 (Admin); [2006] Extradition LR 234 | Whether P's return would breach Arts 3 or 6 ECHR |
| *Government of Romania v Ceausescu* | [2006] EWHC 2615 (Admin); [2006] Extradition LR 255 | Whether Art 5 ECHR would be breached by returning C to Romania following his *in absentia* conviction as he would not be eligible for bail pending retrial |
| *Cebelis v the Prosecutor-General's Office of the Republic of Lithuania* | [2006] EWHC 3201 (Admin); [2006] Extradition LR 261 | Whether C's extradition was compatible with his human rights |
| *Yarrow and Tonge v Public Prosecutor's Office of Appeal of Crete* | [2006] EWHC 3388 (Admin); [2006] Extradition LR 269 | Whether the extradition of Y and T would violate Arts 3 and/or 5 ECHR |

| Case Name | Citation | Issue(s) |
|---|---|---|
| *Ahmad and Aswat v Government of the USA* | [2006] EWHC 2927 (Admin); [2006] Extradition LR 276 | Whether, if the appellants were extradited to the United States, there was a real prospect that they would be held at Guantánamo Bay, made subject to '*extraordinary rendition*', subjected to Special Administrative Measures on a discriminatory basis or tried in a manner that would violate the ECHR and/or the Torture Convention |
| *Colda v Government of Romania* | [2006] EWHC 1150 (Admin); [2006] Extradition LR 118 | Whether C's extradition would violate Art 8 ECHR by virtue of disproportionate interference with her right to family life, in particular with her daughter |
| *Norris v Government of the USA and others* | [2007] EWHC 71 (Admin); [2007] Extradition LR 1 | Whether N's extradition to the United States was incompatible with the ECHR |
| *Falanga v Office of the State Prosecutor, Court of Navara, Italy* | [2007] EWHC 268 (Admin); [2007] Extradition LR 29 | Whether F's extradition was incompatible with his human rights |
| *Hashmi v Government of the USA* | [2007] EWHC 564 (Admin); [2007] Extradition LR 102 | Whether extradition would breach H's rights under Art 8 ECHR |
| *Crean v Government of Ireland* | [2007] EWHC 814 (Admin); [2007] Extradition LR 109 | Whether C's extradition would be incompatible with his rights under Art 8 ECHR |
| *Gary McKinnon v (1) Government of the USA and (2) SSHD* | [2007] EWHC 762 (Admin); [2007] Extradition LR 117 | Whether M's extradition to the United States for trial on charges of having 'hacked' into US government computers and networks was incompatible with his human rights |
| *Montvydas v District Court of Klaffadorys* | [2007] EWHC 1030 (Admin); [2007] Extradition LR 128 | Whether M had been informed of the hearing at which his conditional release from prison was revoked and if not, whether it amounted to a flagrant breach of M's human rights |
| *Ceausescu v SSHD and others* | [2007] EWHC 1423 (Admin); [2007] Extradition LR 146 | Whether C could raise Art 6 ECHR in an appeal against the decision of the Secretary of State; whether the fact that C was convicted in his absence in Romania violated Art 6 given that he could request a retrial |
| *Prus v District Court of Bialystok* | [2007] EWHC 934 (Admin); [2007] Extradition LR 165 | Whether P's extradition would violate his rights under Art 8 ECHR |
| *R (Wellington) v SSHD* | [2007] EWHC 1109 (Admin); [2007] Extradition LR 168 | Whether extraditing a person to a state where, if convicted, they would be mandatorily sentenced to life imprisonment, constituted a breach of Art 3 ECHR, and thus operated as a bar to their extradition |
| *La Torre v Republic of Italy* | [2007] EWHC 1370 (Admin); [2007] Extradition LR 185 | Whether return would breach LT's human rights |

| Case Name | Citation | Issue(s) |
|-----------|----------|----------|
| *Nisbet v SSHD and Government of Canada* | [2007] EWHC 1768; [2007] Extradition LR 198 | Whether it was wrong to appeal against the Secretary of State's decision in respect of alleged human rights bars, and whether N's extradition to Canada was barred by ill-health, by a disproportionate and unjustified interference with his right to private and family life under Art 8 ECHR and/or by the risk of a flagrant denial of a fair trial in Canada in breach of Art 6 ECHR |
| *Goodyer and Gomes v Government of Trinidad and Tobago* | [2007] EWHC 2012 (Admin); [2007] Extradition LR 271 | Whether, if returned, the prison conditions would be such as to make extradition incompatible with Art 3 ECHR |
| *Niescier v Circuit Court of Legnica III, Criminal Department, Poland* | [2007] EWHC 2367 (Admin); [2007] Extradition LR 276 | Whether N's extradition to serve a prison sentence was as a result of being resentenced for the same offence, in breach of Art 7 ECHR, and whether his extradition was, therefore, barred as being incompatible with his human rights |
| *Ogonowski v District Court of Bialystok, Poland* | [2007] EWHC 2445 (Admin); [2007] Extradition LR 278 | Whether the District Judge had been entitled to find that O would not be at risk of ill-treatment by Polish police on return such as would breach Art 3 ECHR |
| *Taylor v Government of the USA* | [2007] EWHC 2527 (Admin); [2007] Extradition LR 287 | Whether T's extradition to the United States would be oppressive by virtue of civil proceedings in the United States founded on the same facts having resulted in a judgment against T, thereby prejudicing him in his criminal trial, and whether return would violate Arts 3 or 8 ECHR due to his health condition |
| *Jaso, Lopez and Albisu Hernandez v Central Criminal Court No 2 Madrid* | [2007] EWHC 2983 (Admin); [2008] Extradition LR 35 | Whether the extradition of the appellants would violate their rights under Arts 3, 5, 6, or 8 ECHR |
| *Zak v Regional Court of Bydgoszcz, Poland* | [2008] EWHC 470 (Admin); [2008] Extradition LR 134 | Whether extradition was incompatible with Art 8 ECHR, given the relative triviality of the offence and the suspect's established family life in the United Kingdom |
| *Kucera v District Court of Karvina, Czech Republic* | [2008] EWHC 414 (Admin); [2008] Extradition LR 149 | Whether extradition was compatible with Art 8 ECHR |
| *Norris v Government of the USA and others (House of Lords)* | [2008] UKHL 16; [2008] Extradition LR 159 | Whether N's extradition to the United States was incompatible with his rights under the ECHR |
| *Slivka v District Court of Prague, Czech Republic* | [2008] EWHC 595 (Admin); [2008] Extradition LR 180 | Whether extradition was incompatible with Art 8 ECHR |
| *McLean v High Court of Dublin, Ireland* | [2008] EWHC 547 (Admin); [2008] Extradition LR 182 | Whether extradition was incompatible with Arts 2 and 3 ECHR on the basis that M's life was under threat from non-state agents in Ireland and that the Irish authorities would be unable to provide him with a reasonable level of protection in prison |
| *Tamarevichute v Government of the Russian Federation* | [2008] EWHC 534 (Admin); [2008] Extradition LR 188 | Whether T's extradition was barred because of a real risk that she might be prejudiced at her trial on account of her Roma ethnicity; whether extradition was compatible with her rights under Arts 3, 5, and/or 6 ECHR |

| Case Name | Citation | Issue(s) |
| --- | --- | --- |
| *R (Ahsan) v DPP and Government of the USA (interested party); Ahsan v Government of the USA and SSHD; Tajik v Government of the USA and SSHD* | [2008] EWHC 666 (Admin); [2008] Extradition LR 207 | Whether extradition breached Art 8 ECHR |
| *R (Lakatus) v SSHD and the Government of the Republic of Poland (Interested Party)* | [2008] EWHC 887 (Admin); [2008] Extradition LR 231 | Whether the Secretary of State had erred in approaching the question of whether extradition would breach L's Art 8 rights and/or be oppressive by reason of the passage of time or otherwise, in terms of s 12(2)(a) of the Extradition Act 1989 |
| *Mustafa Kamel Mustafa (otherwise Abu Hamza) v (1) Government of the USA, (2) SSHD* | [2008] EWHC 1357 (Admin); [2008] Extradition LR 263 | Whether extradition would be incompatible with M's rights under Arts 3, 6, and 8 ECHR |
| *Khemiri, Ignaoua and Chehidi v the Court of Milan, Italy* | [2008] EWHC 1988 (Admin); [2008] Extradition LR 290 | Whether return to Italy involved a real risk that K, I, and C would be removed to Tunisia, where they would suffer treatment in breach of Art 3 ECHR |
| *Stefan (being prosecuted as Nuri Seferi) v Government of the Republic of Albania* | [2008] EWHC 2600 (Admin); [2008] Extradition LR 315 | Whether S's return to Albania would be oppressive or breach Art 3 ECHR in light of his mental and physical health and conditions in Albanian prisons |

## Person serving a domestic sentence in the United Kingdom (s 23 of the EA 2003)

| Case Name | Citation | Issue(s) |
| --- | --- | --- |
| *Handa v Bow Street Magistrates' Court and the High Instance Court of Paris* | [2004] EWHC 3116 (Admin); [2005] Extradition LR 37 | Whether the District Judge should have adjourned the extradition hearing of a person serving a domestic sentence to a time closer to the person's earliest release date |
| *Slator v Bow Street Magistrates' Court (Defendant), High Court of Dublin (Interested Party)* | [2006] EWHC 2628 (Admin); [2006] Extradition LR 243 | Whether, when the person whose extradition is sought is serving a domestic sentence, the extradition hearing should be adjourned to a time closer to his earliest release date |

## Physical or mental condition (ss 25 and 91 of the EA 2003)

| Case Name | Citation | Issue(s) |
| --- | --- | --- |
| *Raffile v Government of the USA* | [2004] EWHC 2913 (Admin) | Whether extradition was barred because R was mentally unfit to stand trial |
| *McCaughey v Government of the USA and SSHD* | [2006] EWHC 248 (Admin); [2006] Extradition LR 1 | Whether the appellant's removal to the United States was barred by reason of his obese medical condition |
| *Miklis v Deputy Prosecutor General of Lithuania* | [2006] EWHC 1032 (Admin) | Whether it would be unjust or oppressive to extradite M by reason of his mental condition |
| *Prancs v Rezekne Court of Latvia* | [2006] EWHC 2573 (Admin); [2006] Extradition LR 234 | Whether it would be unjust or oppressive to extradite P by virtue of his mental condition |

| Case Name | Citation | Issue(s) |
| --- | --- | --- |
| *R (Niziol) v City of Westminster Magistrates' Court; Niziol v District Law Court in Tarnobrzeg, Poland* | [2007] EWHC 1257 (Admin); [2007] Extradition LR 133 | Whether the District Judge had been entitled to conclude that N's physical and/or mental health was not such as to make his return oppressive |
| *La Torre v Republic of Italy* | [2007] EWHC 1370 (Admin); [2007] Extradition LR 185 | Whether LT's extradition should have been refused on the grounds that his physical or mental condition made his return oppressive |
| *Taylor v Government of the USA* | [2007] EWHC 2527 (Admin); [2007] Extradition LR 287 | Whether T's extradition to the United States would be oppressive because of his chronic heart condition |
| *Government of the USA v Stanley Tollman and Beatrice Tollman* | [2008] EWHC 184 (Admin); [2008] Extradition LR 85 | Whether the District Judge had been right to conclude that Mr T's extradition would be unjust and oppressive by reason of the passage of time and that Mrs T's extradition was barred by reason of her mental condition |
| *R (Ahsan) v DPP and Government of the USA (interested party); Ahsan v Government of the USA and SSHD; Tajik v Government of the USA and SSHD* | [2008] EWHC 666 (Admin); [2008] Extradition LR 207 | Whether extradition was unjust or oppressive in light of T's physical and mental condition |
| *Jervis v Office of the Public Prosecutor of the Court of Appeal, Rennes, France* | [2008] EWHC 2011 (Admin); [2008] Extradition LR 282 | Whether it would be unjust or oppressive to extradite J by reason of his mental condition |

## Time limits for filing and/or serving notice of appeal (s 26 of the EA 2003)

| Case Name | Citation | Issue(s) |
| --- | --- | --- |
| *Amoako v Director of Public Prosecutions* | [2006] EWHC 1572 (Admin); [2006] Extradition LR 97 | Whether A's notice of appeal had been filed in time |
| *The District Court of Vilnius City v Barcys* | [2007] EWHC 615 (Admin); [2007] Extradition LR 112 | Whether the Court has jurisdiction to hear an appeal where notice has been given outside the time limits of the EA 2003 |
| *Mendy v Crown Prosecution Service* | [2007] EWHC 1765 (Admin); [2007] Extradition LR 219 | Whether the High Court had the power to extend time for filing and/or serving the notice of appeal in a statutory appeal under the EA 2003 |
| *Mucelli v Government of the Republic of Albania and SSHD (Interested Party)* | [2007] EWHC 2632 (Admin); [2008] Extradition LR 4 | Whether the notice of appeal was served out of time and, if so, whether the court had power to grant an extension of time for serving notice of appeal in extradition proceedings |
| *Re Mucelli* | [2008] EWHC 249 (Admin); [2008] Extradition LR 57 | Whether M's detention was unlawful where his statutory appeal had been dismissed on the basis of failure to comply with a statutory time limit but would have been allowed but for that failure |
| *Gercans v A Latvian Judicial Authority* | [2008] EWHC 884 (Admin); [2008] Extradition LR 138 | Whether the Court had jurisdiction to entertain an appeal when the application was filed and served out of time |
| *Moulai v Deputy Public Prosecutor in Creteil, France* | [2008] EWHC 1024 (Admin); [2008] Extradition LR 237 | Whether the High Court had jurisdiction to entertain an appeal when notice of appeal had been lodged out-of-time |

## Repatriation cases (s 63 of the EA 2003)

| Case Name | Citation | Issue(s) |
| --- | --- | --- |
| *Chalitovas v State Secretary of Ministry of Justice, Lithuania* | [2006] EWHC 1978 (Admin); [2006] Extradition LR 172 | Whether s 63 of the EA 2003 applied only to '*over the wall*' cases of escape from prison, or whether it could apply to a situation the person had been convicted and sentenced in another country and was unlawfully at large from the requesting state without ever having been imprisoned there |

## Prima facie case

| Case Name | Citation | Issue(s) |
| --- | --- | --- |
| *Harkins v SSHD* | [2007] EWHC 639 (Admin); [2007] Extradition LR 41 | Whether the evidence against H was insufficient to justify committal |

## Specialty/speciality (s 95 of the EA 2003)

| Case Name | Citation | Issue(s) |
| --- | --- | --- |
| *Welsh and Thrasher v SSHD and Government of the USA* | [2006] EWHC 156 (Admin); [2006] Extradition LR 31 | Whether the US government would breach the specialty rule and whether, therefore, the requirements of s 95 of the EA 2003 were not met |
| *Bermingham and others v Director of the Serious Fraud Office, HM Attorney General, SSHD, Government of the USA* | [2006] EWHC 200 (Admin); [2006] Extradition LR 52 | Whether effective specialty arrangements with the United States were in place for the purposes of s 95 of the EA 2003 |
| *Arain v Government of Germany and SSHD* | [2006] EWHC 1702 (Admin); [2006] Extradition LR 99 | Whether there was a risk of a breach of the specialty rule upon A's return to Germany |
| *Stepp v Government of the USA and SSHD* | [2006] EWHC 1033 (Admin) | Whether S's extradition was barred because specialty arrangements were allegedly not in place with the United States as required by s 95 of the EA 2003 |
| *Selami Cokaj (aka Valton Gashi) v SSHD and Government of Albania* | [2007] EWHC 238 (Admin); [2007] Extradition LR 51 | Whether the specialty principle would be breached by extraditing C to Albania where a merged sentence of 20 years had been imposed for murder and armed robbery, but where C's extradition had been ordered only in respect of the conviction for murder |
| *Jaso, Lopez and Albisu Hernandez v Central Criminal Court No 2 Madrid* | [2007] EWHC 2983 (Admin); [2008] Extradition LR 35 | Whether there was a risk of a breach by the Spanish authorities of the specialty rule |
| *Kucera v District Court of Karvina, Czech Republic* | [2008] EWHC 414 (Admin); [2008] Extradition LR 149 | Whether it would breach specialty if K might be required to serve a sentence in part attributable to a non-extradition offence |

| Case Name | Citation | Issue(s) |
| --- | --- | --- |
| *R (Ahsan) v DPP and Government of the USA (interested party); Ahsan v Government of the USA and SSHD; Tajik v Government of the USA and SSHD* | [2008] EWHC 666 (Admin); [2008] Extradition LR 207 | Whether extradition should have been refused for risk of a breach of speciality |

## Forum

| Case Name | Citation | Issue(s) |
| --- | --- | --- |
| *Bermingham and others v Director of the Serious Fraud Office, HM Attorney General, SSHD, Government of the USA* | [2006] EWHC 200 (Admin); [2006] Extradition LR 52 | Whether a trial should occur in England or the United States |
| *R (Ahsan) v DPP and Government of the USA (interested party); Ahsan v Government of the USA and SSHD; Tajik v Government of the USA and SSHD* | [2008] EWHC 666 (Admin); [2008] Extradition LR 207 | Whether the Attorney General's guidance on concurrent jurisdiction should have been considered by the DPP in deciding not to prosecute A in the United Kingdom |

## Triviality of the offence for which extradition is sought

| Case Name | Citation | Issue(s) |
| --- | --- | --- |
| *Derevianko v Government of Lithuania and Governor of HMP Brixton* | [2005] EWHC 1212 (Admin); [2005] Extradition LR 75 | Whether D should not be extradited due to the triviality of the offence |
| *Zak v Regional Court of Bydgoszcz, Poland* | [2008] EWHC 470 (Admin); [2008] Extradition LR 134 | Whether extradition was incompatible with Art 8 ECHR, given the relative triviality of the offence and the suspect's established family life in the United Kingdom |

## Offences becoming time-barred in the requesting state

| Case Name | Citation | Issue(s) |
| --- | --- | --- |
| *Atilla v Government of Turkey and the Secretary of State* | [2006] EWHC 1203 (Admin); [2006] Extradition LR 133 | Whether the offence for which A's extradition was sought had become time-barred under Turkish law and whether his extradition was therefore barred by Art 10 of the European Convention on Extradition Order 2001 |

## Asylum and immigration law, and extradition

| Case Name | Citation | Issue(s) |
| --- | --- | --- |
| *Guven v Government of France and Governor of HMP Brixton* | [2005] EWHC 1391 (Admin) | Whether risk of return to Turkey in breach of a grant of asylum |

| Case Name | Citation | Issue(s) |
| --- | --- | --- |
| *District Court in Ostroleka, second Criminal Division (a Polish Judicial Authority) v Dytlow and Dytlow* | [2009] EWHC 1009 (Admin) | What is the appropriate procedure where an EAW is received and duly certified under s 2 of the 2003 Act in respect of a person who has been granted refugee status in this country because of a well-founded fear of persecution for a Convention reason in the territory where the EAW was issued? |

### Rules of evidence in extradition proceedings

| Case Name | Citation | Issue(s) |
| --- | --- | --- |
| *Government of India v Rajarathinam* | [2006] EWHC 2615 (Admin); [2006] Extradition LR 255 | Whether an affidavit which was not clearly the summary of a statement made by another person constituted 'evidence' under s 84 of the EA 2003 |

### Disclosure in extradition proceedings

| Case Name | Citation | Issue(s) |
| --- | --- | --- |
| *Wellington v Governor of HMP Belmarsh and Government of the USA* | [2004] EWHC 418 (Admin); [2005] Extradition LR 1 | Whether a state requesting a person's extradition had a duty of disclosure similar to that of a prosecuting authority in domestic criminal proceedings |
| *USA v Stanley Tollman and Beatrice Tollman; Central Examining Court, Criminal Court of the National Court, Madrid v Sander and 6 other interested parties* | [2006] EWHC 2256 (Admin); [2006] Extradition LR 216 | The procedure to be adopted where disclosure was sought in relation to an allegation of abuse of process in extradition proceedings, and whether the Extradition Act 1989 or the EA 2003 applied when requests for extradition had first been made, and then withdrawn, before the commencement of the EA 2003 |

### Abuse of process/bad faith

| Case Name | Citation | Issue(s) |
| --- | --- | --- |
| *Castillo v Kingdom of Spain and Governor of HMP Belmarsh* | [2004] EWHC 1672 (Admin); [2005] Extradition LR 8 | Whether the request for extradition contained a fair description of the conduct alleged against C and whether it was made in good faith |
| *Schmidt v SSHD* | [2005] EWHC 959 (Admin) | Whether the request was in bad faith and/or whether the allegations were time-barred |
| *Jenkins and Benbow v Government of the USA* | [2005] EWHC 1051 (Admin); [2005] Extradition LR 78 | Whether the appellants had been entrapped by the US government to commit the offences and, if so, whether that was a bar to their extradition for those offences |

| Case Name | Citation | Issue(s) |
|---|---|---|
| *Kadre v Government of France; Governor of Belmarsh Prison* | [2005] EWHC 1712 (Admin); [2005] Extradition LR 104 | Whether the request disclosed extradition crimes, whether it disclosed sufficient conduct and whether the request was made in bad faith |
| *Ramda v SSHD and Government of France* | [2005] EWHC 2526 (Admin) | Whether the Secretary of State's decision to order R's extradition was flawed by virtue of bad faith on the part of the French authorities or by the risk of an unfair trial in France or ill-treatment in France or in Algeria if he were to be extradited |
| *Mariotti v Government of Italy and Others* | [2005] EWHC 2745 (Admin); [2005] Extradition LR 162 | Whether the accusation was made in good faith |
| *Boudhiba v Central Examining Court No 5 of the National Court of Justice, Madrid, Spain* | [2006] EWHC 167 (Admin) | Alleged abuse of process in relation to extradition to Spain for terrorist offences |
| *Stepp v Government of the USA and SSHD* | [2006] EWHC 1033 (Admin); [2006] Extradition LR 138 | Whether S's extradition was barred because the case against him was allegedly fabricated |
| *Hilali v Central Court of Criminal Proceedings Number 5 of the National Court, Madrid, and Senior District Judge, Bow Street Magistrates' Court* | [2006] EWHC 1239 (Admin) | Whether it would be an abuse of process to extradite H to Spain |
| *Carlyle-Clarke v SSHD* | [2006] EWHC 1438 (Admin); [2006] Extradition LR 187 | Whether fresh material indicated bad faith on the part of the United States, undermining prior decisions of the Secretary of State and the Divisional Court |
| *USA v Stanley Tollman and Beatrice Tollman; Central Examining Court, Criminal Court of the National Court, Madrid v Sander and 6 other interested parties* | [2006] EWHC 2256 (Admin); [2006] Extradition LR 216 | The procedure to be adopted where disclosure was sought in relation to an allegation of abuse of process in extradition proceedings, and whether the Extradition Act 1989 or the EA 2003 applied when requests for extradition had first been made, and then withdrawn, before the commencement of the 2003 Act |
| *Harkins v SSHD* | [2007] EWHC 639 (Admin); [2007] Extradition LR 41 | Whether the evidence obtained by the Prosecution in the United States was an abuse of process |
| *Gary McKinnon v (1) Government of the USA and (2) SSHD* | [2007] EWHC 762 (Admin); [2007] Extradition LR 117 | Whether M's extradition to the United States for trial on charges of having 'hacked' into US government computers and networks should be stayed as an abuse of process because of either deliberate delay on the part of the US authorities or the plea bargaining history |
| *Caldarelli v The Court of Naples* | [2007] EWHC 1624 (Admin); [2007] Extradition LR 209 | Whether there was bad faith; and whether the EAW was unlawful in light of the dates of the conduct alleged |

| Case Name | Citation | Issue(s) |
| --- | --- | --- |
| *Lopetas v Minister of Justice for Lithuania* | [2007] EWHC 2407 (Admin); [2007] Extradition LR 227 | Whether, due to procedural irregularities in the certification of an EAW in the extradition proceedings, and the subsequent detention of the requested person, the proceedings constituted an abuse of process |
| *Knowles v Government of the USA & Superintendent of Prisons of the Commonwealth of the Bahamas (Privy Council)* | [2006] UKPC 38; [2007] Extradition LR 230 | Whether K's extradition from the Bahamas to the United States on drug-trafficking charges was barred by reason of unfair trial, abuse of process, the request not being made in good faith, lapse of time and/or a failure of disclosure by the US government |
| *Central Examining Court of the National Court of Madrid v City of Westminster Magistrates' Court (Defendant) and Malkit Singh (first interested party)* | [2007] EWHC 2059 (Admin); [2007] Extradition LR 245 | Whether the CPS providing simple drafting assistance to an Issuing Judicial Authority is, in law, capable of constituting an abuse of process |
| *Haynes v The Court of Magistrates, Malta* | [2007] EWHC 2651 (Admin); [2007] Extradition LR 295 | Whether there had been an abuse of process by the requesting judicial authority |
| *Jaso, Lopez and Albisu Hernandez v Central Criminal Court No 2 Madrid* | [2007] EWHC 2983 (Admin); [2008] Extradition LR 35 | Whether the proceedings constituted an abuse of process |
| *R (Ahsan) v DPP and Government of the USA (interested party); Ahsan v Government of the USA and SSHD; Tajik v Government of the USA and SSHD* | [2008] EWHC 666 (Admin); [2008] Extradition LR 207 | Whether the extradition proceedings were an abuse of process |
| *Mustafa Kamel Mustafa (otherwise Abu Hamza) v (1) Government of the USA, (2) SSHD* | [2008] EWHC 1357 (Admin); [2008] Extradition LR 263 | Whether it would be an abuse of process to extradite M to face trial for the alleged offences in the United States because the request was founded on evidence obtained by torture or ill-treatment |
| *Gary McKinnon v (1) Government of the USA and (2) SSHD (House of Lords)* | [2008] UKHL 59; [2008] Extradition LR 309 | Whether M's extradition to the United States for trial on charges of having 'hacked' into US government computers and networks was barred by human rights considerations and/or whether the proceedings should be stayed as an abuse of process because of the plea bargaining history |

## Government assurances/undertakings

| Case Name | Citation | Issue(s) |
| --- | --- | --- |
| *Harkins v SSHD* | [2007] EWHC 639 (Admin); [2007] Extradition LR 41 | Whether the United States's undertaking in relation to the death penalty was adequate |

## Habeas corpus/Judicial review

| Case Name | Citation | Issue(s) |
| --- | --- | --- |
| *Nikonovs v Governor of HM Prison Brixton and Republic of Latvia* | [2005] EWHC 2405 (Admin); [2005] Extradition LR 125 | Whether habeas corpus was available in extradition proceedings under the EA 2003 and, if so, whether it should be granted in this case on the basis that N was not brought before the Court as soon as practicable, as required by the EA 2003 |
| *Hilali v Governor of HMP Whitemoor and Central Court of Committal Proceedings No 5, The High Court, Madrid and SSHD (Intervener)* | [2007] EWHC 939 (Admin); [2007] Extradition LR 149 | Whether habeas corpus is available when the statutory extradition process has been completed and, if so, whether it should be issued on the facts |
| *In the matter of Zygmund Adam Niziol* | [2007] EWHC 1483 (Admin); [2007] Extradition LR 183 | Whether N was entitled to the writ of habeas corpus on the grounds of his deteriorating mental state |
| *Knowles v Government of the USA & Superintendent of Prisons of the Commonwealth of the Bahamas (Privy Council)* | [2006] UKPC 38; [2007] Extradition LR 230 | Whether the Bahamian Court of Appeal had been able to hear an appeal from the grant of habeas corpus in extradition proceedings |
| *In re Hilali (House of Lords)* | [2008] UKHL 3; [2008] Extradition LR 61 | Whether habeas corpus is available when the statutory extradition process has been completed and, if so, whether it should be issued on the facts |
| *Olah v Regional Court in Plzen, Czech Republic* | [2008] EWHC 2701 (Admin); [2008] Extradition LR 278 | Whether the District Judge had been wrong to refuse to grant an adjournment for the defence to obtain psychiatric evidence in relation to a potential claim that O's mental condition rendered it unjust or oppressive to extradite him, and if so whether there was a remedy in a statutory appeal or judicial review |

## Appeals to the High Court, including raising new issues/admissibility of fresh evidence on appeal

| Case Name | Citation | Issue(s) |
| --- | --- | --- |
| *Okendeji v Government of the Commonwealth of Australia and Bow Street Magistrates Court (No 2)* | [2005] EWHC 2925 (Admin); [2005] Extradition LR 128 | Whether s 104(7) of the EA 2003 barred a second appeal to the High Court where the District Judge reached the same decision as at a hearing which had been appealed successfully and remitted for a further decision |
| *Da An Chen v Government of Romania and SSHD; Mitoi (No 2) v SSHD and Government of Romania* | [2007] EWHC 520 (Admin); [2007] Extradition LR 92 | What is the scope of any right of appeal or review following remittal by the High Court of a question under s 104(1)(b) of the EA 2003? |
| *Tuvia Stern v Government of the USA* | [2007] EWHC 3266 (Admin); [2008] Extradition LR 52 | Whether S could raise a bar to his extradition on appeal that he did not raise and in respect of which he did not adduce evidence in the court below |

| Case Name | Citation | Issue(s) |
| --- | --- | --- |
| *Bogdani v Government of the Republic of Albania* | [2007] EWHC 2065 (Admin); [2008] Extradition LR 284 | Whether, having been convicted in his absence, B would be entitled to a retrial upon return to Albania and whether new evidence from the Government of Albania should be admitted on that issue |

## Secretary of State's designation of categories

| Case Name | Citation | Issue(s) |
| --- | --- | --- |
| *Norris v SSHD* | [2006] EWHC 280 (Admin); [2006] Extradition LR 85 | Whether the Secretary of State was correct to continue to designate the United States as a territory not required to show a prima facie case given the United States's failure to ratify the 2003 US–UK Extradition Treaty, which had created asymmetry in the extradition arrangements between the two countries |
| *Oliver v SSHD* | [2006] EWHC 1847 (Admin); [2006] Extradition LR 207 | Whether the decision of the German Constitutional Court to declare the German European Arrest Warrant Act to be unconstitutional and void in its entirety meant that the Secretary of State had to change the designation of Germany as a category 1 (EAW) territory under the EA 2003 |

## Time for extradition

| Case Name | Citation | Issue(s) |
| --- | --- | --- |
| *Niziol v District Law Court in Tarnobrzeg, Poland* | [2007] EWCA Civ 596; [2007] Extradition LR 181 | Whether the Court of Appeal (Civil Division) has jurisdiction to consider an application to delay a person's extradition due to their ill-health |
| *Keith Stuart Ashley Wood v (i) City of Westminster Magistrates Court, (ii) SSHD and (iii) Government of the USA* | [2007] EWHC 2058 (Admin); [2007] Extradition LR 260 | Whether the time for extradition could be extended where the High Court had declined to certify a point of law of general public importance |
| *Tomasz Szklanny v City of Westminster Magistrates' Court and Government of Poland* | [2007] EWHC 2646 (Admin); [2007] Extradition LR 291 | Whether s 35(4)(b) of the EA 2003 allowed an extension of time to be granted for extraditing the requested person only where the need for the extension arose due to circumstances beyond the control of the member states concerned |

## Privy Council

| Case Name | Citation | Issue(s) |
| --- | --- | --- |
| *Roberts and Others v Minister of Foreign Affairs, Superintendent of Prisons (Fox Hill), Attorney General of the Commonwealth of the Bahamas (Privy Council)* | [2007] UKPC 56; [2007] Extradition LR 281 | Whether extradition arrangements between the Bahamas and the United States were unconstitutional, null and void |
| *Forbes v Director of Public Prosecutions & Commissioner of Correctional Services (Privy Council)* | [2007] UKPC; [2008] Extradition LR 3 | Whether the Jamaican Extradition Act 1991 was inconsistent with the Jamaican Constitution |

## Miscellaneous

| Case Name | Citation | Issue(s) |
| --- | --- | --- |
| *Srama v District Court of Bydgoszsz* | [2007] EWHC 666 (Admin); [2007] Extradition LR 33 | Whether the District Judge had misunderstood for which offence the Polish Judicial Authority sought S's extradition, and the consequences of that misunderstanding |
| *R (Raissi) v SSHD* | [2007] EWHC 243 (Admin); [2007] Extradition LR 58 | Whether the Home Secretary's scheme for making ex gratia payments to those wrongly detained applied to persons detained in connection with extradition proceedings; if so, whether the claimant had been 'completely exonerated' for the purposes of the scheme, or the Home Secretary was unreasonable in not finding the case to be wholly exceptional |
| *R (Ahmad) v SSHD* | [2007] EWHC 3217 (Admin); [2008] Extradition LR 25 | Whether permission should be granted to judicially review the Secretary of State's decision ordering A's extradition to the United States on terrorism charges on the grounds that extradition would deprive A of his right to conduct civil litigation against the Metropolitan Police in relation to an alleged assault |
| *R (Raissi) v SSHD* | [2008] EWCA Civ 72; [2008] Extradition LR 109 | Whether the Home Secretary's scheme for making ex gratia payments to those wrongly detained applied to persons detained in connection with extradition proceedings; if so, whether the claimant had been 'completely exonerated' for the purposes of the scheme, or the Home Secretary was unreasonable in not finding the case to be wholly exceptional |

# Extradition Act 2003 (as amended)

The Act is printed as amended by subsequent legislation.

# 2003 CHAPTER 41

An Act to make provision about extradition.

[20th November 2003]

BE IT ENACTED by the Queen's most Excellent Majesty, by and with the advice and consent of the Lords Spiritual and Temporal, and Commons, in this present Parliament assembled, and by the authority of the same, as follows:—

## PART 1

## EXTRADITION TO CATEGORY 1 TERRITORIES

### Introduction

**1 Extradition to category 1 territories**

(1) This Part deals with extradition from the United Kingdom to the territories designated for the purposes of this Part by order made by the Secretary of State.

(2) In this Act references to category 1 territories are to the territories designated for the purposes of this Part.

(3) A territory may not be designated for the purposes of this Part if a person found guilty in the territory of a criminal offence may be sentenced to death for the offence under the general criminal law of the territory.

**2 Part 1 warrant and certificate**

(1) This section applies if the designated authority receives a Part 1 warrant in respect of a person.

(2) A Part 1 warrant is an arrest warrant which is issued by a judicial authority of a category 1 territory and which contains—

    (a) the statement referred to in subsection (3) and the information referred to in subsection (4), or

    (b) the statement referred to in subsection (5) and the information referred to in subsection (6).

(3) The statement is one that—

    (a) the person in respect of whom the Part 1 warrant is issued is accused in the category 1 territory of the commission of an offence specified in the warrant, and

    (b) the Part 1 warrant is issued with a view to his arrest and extradition to the category 1 territory for the purpose of being prosecuted for the offence.

(4) The information is—

    (a) particulars of the person's identity;

(b) particulars of any other warrant issued in the category 1 territory for the person's arrest in respect of the offence;

(c) particulars of the circumstances in which the person is alleged to have committed the offence, including the conduct alleged to constitute the offence, the time and place at which he is alleged to have committed the offence and any provision of the law of the category 1 territory under which the conduct is alleged to constitute an offence;

(d) particulars of the sentence which may be imposed under the law of the category 1 territory in respect of the offence if the person is convicted of it.

(5) The statement is one that—

(a) the person in respect of whom the Part 1 warrant is issued [has been convicted] of an offence specified in the warrant by a court in the category 1 territory, and

(b) the Part 1 warrant is issued with a view to his arrest and extradition to the category 1 territory for the purpose of being sentenced for the offence or of serving a sentence of imprisonment or another form of detention imposed in respect of the offence.

(6) The information is—

(a) particulars of the person's identity;

(b) particulars of the conviction;

(c) particulars of any other warrant issued in the category 1 territory for the person's arrest in respect of the offence;

(d) particulars of the sentence which may be imposed under the law of the category 1 territory in respect of the offence, if the person has not been sentenced for the offence;

(e) particulars of the sentence which has been imposed under the law of the category 1 territory in respect of the offence, if the person has been sentenced for the offence.

(7) The designated authority may issue a certificate under this section if it believes that the authority which issued the Part 1 warrant has the function of issuing arrest warrants in the category 1 territory.

(8) A certificate under this section must certify that the authority which issued the Part 1 warrant has the function of issuing arrest warrants in the category 1 territory.

(9) The designated authority is the authority designated for the purposes of this Part by order made by the Secretary of State.

(10) An order made under subsection (9) may—

(a) designate more than one authority;

(b) designate different authorities for different parts of the United Kingdom.

## Arrest

### 3 Arrest under certified Part 1 warrant

(1) This section applies if a certificate is issued under section 2 in respect of a Part 1 warrant issued in respect of a person.

(2) The warrant may be executed by a constable or a customs officer in any part of the United Kingdom.

[(3) The warrant may be executed by a service policeman anywhere, but only if the person is subject to service law or is a civilian subject to service discipline.]

(5) The warrant may be executed even if neither the warrant nor a copy of it is in the possession of the person executing it at the time of the arrest.

(6) [...]

## 4  Person arrested under Part 1 warrant

(1)  This section applies if a person is arrested under a Part 1 warrant.

(2)  A copy of the warrant must be given to the person as soon as practicable after his arrest.

(3)  The person must be brought as soon as practicable before the appropriate judge.

(4)  If subsection (2) is not complied with and the person applies to the judge to be discharged, the judge may order his discharge.

(5)  If subsection (3) is not complied with and the person applies to the judge to be discharged, the judge must order his discharge.

(6)  A person arrested under the warrant must be treated as continuing in legal custody until he is brought before the appropriate judge under subsection (3) or he is discharged under subsection (4) or (5).

## 5  Provisional arrest

(1)  A constable, a customs officer or a service policeman may arrest a person without a warrant if he has reasonable grounds for believing—

    (a)  that a Part 1 warrant has been or will be issued in respect of the person by an authority of a category 1 territory, and

    (b)  that the authority has the function of issuing arrest warrants in the category 1 territory.

(2)  A constable or a customs officer may arrest a person under subsection (1) in any part of the United Kingdom.

[(3)  A service policeman may arrest a person under subsection (1) only if the person is subject to service law or is a civilian subject to service discipline.

(4)  If a service policeman has power to arrest a person under subsection (1) he may exercise the power anywhere.]

## 6  Person arrested under section 5

(1)  This section applies if a person is arrested under section 5.

[(2)  The person must be brought before the appropriate judge within 48 hours starting with the time when the person is arrested.

(2A)  The documents specified in subsection (4) must be produced to the judge within 48 hours starting with the time when the person is arrested but this is subject to any extension under subsection (3B).

(2B)  Subsection (3) applies if—

    (a)  the person has been brought before the judge in compliance with subsection (2); but

    (b)  documents have not been produced to the judge in compliance with subsection (2A).

(3)  The person must be brought before the judge when the documents are produced to the judge.

(3A)  While the person is before the judge in pursuance of subsection (2), the authority of the category 1 territory may apply to the judge for an extension of the 48 hour period mentioned in subsection (2A) by a further 48 hours.

(3B)  The judge may grant an extension if the judge decides that subsection (2A) could not reasonably be complied with within the initial 48 hour period.

(3C)  The judge must decide whether that subsection could reasonably be so complied with on a balance of probabilities.

(3D)  Notice of an application under subsection (3A) must be given in accordance with rules of court.]

(4) The documents are—

    (a) a Part 1 warrant in respect of the person;

    (b) a certificate under section 2 in respect of the warrant.

(5) A copy of the warrant must be given to the person as soon as practicable after his arrest.

[(5A) Subsection (5B) applies if—

    (a) the person is before the judge in pursuance of subsection (2); and

    (b) the documents specified in subsection (4) have not been produced to the judge.

(5B) The judge must remand the person in custody or on bail (subject to subsection (6)).]

(6) If subsection (2) [, (2A) or (3)]7 is not complied with and the person applies to the judge to be discharged, the judge must order his discharge.

(7) If subsection (5) is not complied with and the person applies to the judge to be discharged, the judge may order his discharge.

(8) The person must be treated as continuing in legal custody until he is brought before the appropriate judge under subsection (2) or he is discharged under subsection (6) or (7).

[(8A) In calculating a period of 48 hours for the purposes of this section no account is to be taken of—

    (a) any Saturday or Sunday;

    (b) Christmas Day;

    (c) Good Friday; or

    (d) any day falling within subsection (8B).

(8B) The following days fall within this subsection—

    (a) in Scotland, any day prescribed under section 8(2) of the Criminal Procedure (Scotland) Act 1995 as a court holiday in the court of the appropriate judge;

    (b) in any part of the United Kingdom, any day that is a bank holiday under the Banking and Financial Dealings Act 1971 in that part of the United Kingdom.]

(9) Subsection (10) applies if—

    (a) a person is arrested under section 5 on the basis of a belief that a Part 1 warrant has been or will be issued in respect of him;

    (b) the person is discharged under subsection (6) or (7).

(10) The person must not be arrested again under section 5 on the basis of a belief relating to the same Part 1 warrant.

## The initial hearing

### 7 Identity of person arrested

(1) This section applies if—

    (a) a person arrested under a Part 1 warrant is brought before the appropriate judge under section 4(3), or

    (b) a person [arrested under section 5 is brought before the appropriate judge under section 6 and section 6(2A)] is complied with in relation to him.

(2) The judge must decide whether the person brought before him is the person in respect of whom—

    (a) the warrant referred to in subsection (1)(a) was issued, or

    (b) the warrant referred to in section 6(4) was issued.

(3) The judge must decide the question in subsection (2) on a balance of probabilities.

(4) If the judge decides the question in subsection (2) in the negative he must order the person's discharge.

(5) If the judge decides that question in the affirmative he must proceed under section 8.

(6) In England and Wales, the judge has the same powers (as nearly as may be) as a magistrates' court would have if the proceedings were the summary trial of an information against the person.

(7) In Scotland—

(a) the judge has the same powers (as nearly as may be) as if the proceedings were summary proceedings in respect of an offence alleged to have been committed by the person; but

(b) in his making any decision under subsection (2) evidence from a single source shall be sufficient.

(8) In Northern Ireland, the judge has the same powers (as nearly as may be) as a magistrates' court would have if the proceedings were the hearing and determination of a complaint against the person.

(9) If the judge exercises his power to adjourn the proceedings he must remand the person in custody or on bail.

(10) [If the person is remanded in custody, the appropriate judge may] later grant bail.

### 8 Remand etc.

(1) If the judge is required to proceed under this section he must—

(a) fix a date on which the extradition hearing is to begin;

(b) inform the person of the contents of the Part 1 warrant;

(c) give the person the required information about consent;

(d) remand the person in custody or on bail.

(2) [If the person is remanded in custody, the appropriate judge may] later grant bail.

(3) The required information about consent is—

(a) that the person may consent to his extradition to the category 1 territory in which the Part 1 warrant was issued;

(b) an explanation of the effect of consent and the procedure that will apply if he gives consent;

(c) that consent must be given before the judge and is irrevocable.

(4) The date fixed under subsection (1) must not be later than the end of the permitted period, which is 21 days starting with the date of the arrest referred to in section 7(1)(a) or (b).

(5) If before the date fixed under subsection (1) (or this subsection) a party to the proceedings applies to the judge for a later date to be fixed and the judge believes it to be in the interests of justice to do so, he may fix a later date; and this subsection may apply more than once.

(6) Subsections (7) and (8) apply if the extradition hearing does not begin on or before the date fixed under this section.

(7) If the person applies to the judge to be discharged the judge must order his discharge, unless reasonable cause is shown for the delay.

(8) If no application is made under subsection (7) the judge must order the person's discharge on the first occasion after the date fixed under this section when the person appears or is brought before the judge, unless reasonable cause is shown for the delay.

### [8A Person charged with offence in United Kingdom before extradition hearing

(1) This section applies if—

(a) a person has been brought before the appropriate judge under section 4(3) or 6(2) but the extradition hearing has not begun; and

(b) the judge is informed that the person is charged with an offence in the United Kingdom.

(2) The judge must order further proceedings in respect of the extradition to be adjourned until one of these occurs—

    (a) the charge is disposed of;

    (b) the charge is withdrawn;

    (c) proceedings in respect of the charge are discontinued;

    (d) an order is made for the charge to lie on the file, or in relation to Scotland, the diet is deserted *pro loco et tempore.*

(3) If a sentence of imprisonment or another form of detention is imposed in respect of the offence charged, the judge may order further proceedings in respect of the extradition to be adjourned until the person is released from detention pursuant to the sentence (whether on licence or otherwise).]

### [8B Person serving sentence in United Kingdom before extradition hearing

(1) This section applies if—

    (a) a person has been brought before the appropriate judge under section 4(3) or 6(2) but the extradition hearing has not begun; and

    (b) the judge is informed that the person is in custody serving a sentence of imprisonment or another form of detention in the United Kingdom.

(2) The judge may order further proceedings in respect of the extradition to be adjourned until the person is released from detention pursuant to the sentence (whether on licence or otherwise).

(3) In a case where further proceedings in respect of the extradition are adjourned under subsection (2)—

    (a) section 131 of the Magistrates' Courts Act 1980 (remand of accused already in custody) has effect as if a reference to 28 clear days in subsection (1) or (2) of that section were a reference to six months;

    (b) Article 47(2) of the Magistrates' Courts (Northern Ireland) Order 1981 (period of remand in custody) has effect as if a reference to 28 days in—

        (i) sub-paragraph (a)(iii), or
        (ii) the words after sub-paragraph (b),

    were a reference to six months.]

## The extradition hearing

### 9 Judge's powers at extradition hearing

(1) In England and Wales, at the extradition hearing the appropriate judge has the same powers (as nearly as may be) as a magistrates' court would have if the proceedings were the summary trial of an information against the person in respect of whom the Part 1 warrant was issued.

(2) In Scotland, at the extradition hearing the appropriate judge has the same powers (as nearly as may be) as if the proceedings were summary proceedings in respect of an offence alleged to have been committed by the person in respect of whom the Part 1 warrant was issued.

(3) In Northern Ireland, at the extradition hearing the appropriate judge has the same powers (as nearly as may be) as a magistrates' court would have if the proceedings were the hearing and determination of a complaint against the person in respect of whom the Part 1 warrant was issued.

(4) If the judge adjourns the extradition hearing he must remand the person in custody or on bail.

(5) [If the person is remanded in custody, the appropriate judge may] later grant bail.

## 10 Initial stage of extradition hearing

(1) This section applies if a person in respect of whom a Part 1 warrant is issued appears or is brought before the appropriate judge for the extradition hearing.

(2) The judge must decide whether the offence specified in the Part 1 warrant is an extradition offence.

(3) If the judge decides the question in subsection (2) in the negative he must order the person's discharge.

(4) If the judge decides that question in the affirmative he must proceed under section 11.

## 11 Bars to extradition

(1) If the judge is required to proceed under this section he must decide whether the person's extradition to the category 1 territory is barred by reason of—

(a) the rule against double jeopardy;

(b) extraneous considerations;

(c) the passage of time;

(d) the person's age;

(e) hostage-taking considerations;

(f) speciality;

(g) the person's earlier extradition to the United Kingdom from another category 1 territory;

(h) the person's earlier extradition to the United Kingdom from a non-category 1 territory [;]

[(i) the person's earlier transfer to the United Kingdom by the International Criminal Court.]

(2) [Sections 12 to 19A] apply for the interpretation of subsection (1).

(3) If the judge decides any of the questions in subsection (1) in the affirmative he must order the person's discharge.

(4) If the judge decides those questions in the negative and the person is alleged to be unlawfully at large after conviction of the extradition offence, the judge must proceed under section 20.

(5) If the judge decides those questions in the negative and the person is accused of the commission of the extradition offence but is not alleged to be unlawfully at large after conviction of it, the judge must proceed under section 21.

## 12 Rule against double jeopardy

A person's extradition to a category 1 territory is barred by reason of the rule against double jeopardy if (and only if) it appears that he would be entitled to be discharged under any rule of law relating to previous acquittal or conviction on the assumption—

(a) that the conduct constituting the extradition offence constituted an offence in the part of the United Kingdom where the judge exercises jurisdiction;

(b) that the person were charged with the extradition offence in that part of the United Kingdom.

## 13 Extraneous considerations

A person's extradition to a category 1 territory is barred by reason of extraneous considerations if (and only if) it appears that—

(a) the Part 1 warrant issued in respect of him (though purporting to be issued on account of the extradition offence) is in fact issued for the purpose of prosecuting or punishing him on account of his race, religion, nationality, gender, sexual orientation or political opinions, or

(b) if extradited he might be prejudiced at his trial or punished, detained or restricted in his personal liberty by reason of his race, religion, nationality, gender, sexual orientation or political opinions.

**14 Passage of time**

A person's extradition to a category 1 territory is barred by reason of the passage of time if (and only if) it appears that it would be unjust or oppressive to extradite him by reason of the passage of time [since he is alleged to have–]

[(a) committed the extradition offence (where he is accused of its commission), or

(b) become unlawfully at large (where he is alleged to have been convicted of it).]

**15 Age**

A person's extradition to a category 1 territory is barred by reason of his age if (and only if) it would be conclusively presumed because of his age that he could not be guilty of the extradition offence on the assumption—

(a) that the conduct constituting the extradition offence constituted an offence in the part of the United Kingdom where the judge exercises jurisdiction;

(b) that the person carried out the conduct when the extradition offence was committed (or alleged to be committed);

(c) that the person carried out the conduct in the part of the United Kingdom where the judge exercises jurisdiction.

**16 Hostage-taking considerations**

(1) A person's extradition to a category 1 territory is barred by reason of hostage-taking considerations if (and only if) the territory is a party to the Hostage-taking Convention and it appears that—

(a) if extradited he might be prejudiced at his trial because communication between him and the appropriate authorities would not be possible, and

(b) the act or omission constituting the extradition offence also constitutes an offence under section 1 of the Taking of Hostages Act 1982 (c. 28) or an attempt to commit such an offence.

(2) The appropriate authorities are the authorities of the territory which are entitled to exercise rights of protection in relation to him.

(3) A certificate issued by the Secretary of State that a territory is a party to the Hostage-taking Convention is conclusive evidence of that fact for the purposes of subsection (1).

(4) The Hostage-taking Convention is the International Convention against the Taking of Hostages opened for signature at New York on 18 December 1979.

**17 Speciality**

(1) A person's extradition to a category 1 territory is barred by reason of speciality if (and only if) there are no speciality arrangements with the category 1 territory.

(2) There are speciality arrangements with a category 1 territory if, under the law of that territory or arrangements made between it and the United Kingdom, a person who is extradited to the territory from the United Kingdom may be dealt with in the territory for an offence committed before his extradition only if—

(a) the offence is one falling within subsection (3), or

(b) the condition in subsection (4) is satisfied.

(3) The offences are—

(a) the offence in respect of which the person is extradited;

(b) an extradition offence disclosed by the same facts as that offence;

(c) an extradition offence in respect of which the appropriate judge gives his consent under section 55 to the person being dealt with;

(d) an offence which is not punishable with imprisonment or another form of detention;

(e) an offence in respect of which the person will not be detained in connection with his trial, sentence or appeal;

(f) an offence in respect of which the person waives the right that he would have (but for this paragraph) not to be dealt with for the offence.

(4) The condition is that the person is given an opportunity to leave the category 1 territory and—

(a) he does not do so before the end of the permitted period, or

(b) if he does so before the end of the permitted period, he returns there.

(5) The permitted period is 45 days starting with the day on which the person arrives in the category 1 territory.

(6) Arrangements made with a category 1 territory which is a Commonwealth country or a British overseas territory may be made for a particular case or more generally.

(7) A certificate issued by or under the authority of the Secretary of State confirming the existence of arrangements with a category 1 territory which is a Commonwealth country or a British overseas territory and stating the terms of the arrangements is conclusive evidence of those matters.

## 18  Earlier extradition to United Kingdom from category 1 territory

A person's extradition to a category 1 territory is barred by reason of his earlier extradition to the United Kingdom from another category 1 territory if (and only if)—

(a) the person was extradited to the United Kingdom from another category 1 territory (the extraditing territory);

(b) under arrangements between the United Kingdom and the extraditing territory, that territory's consent is required to the person's extradition from the United Kingdom to the category 1 territory in respect of the extradition offence under consideration;

(c) that consent has not been given on behalf of the extraditing territory.

## 19  Earlier extradition to United Kingdom from non-category 1 territory

A person's extradition to a category 1 territory is barred by reason of his earlier extradition to the United Kingdom from a non-category 1 territory if (and only if)—

(a) the person was extradited to the United Kingdom from a territory that is not a category 1 territory (the extraditing territory);

(b) under arrangements between the United Kingdom and the extraditing territory, that territory's consent is required to the person's being dealt with in the United Kingdom in respect of the extradition offence under consideration;

(c) consent has not been given on behalf of the extraditing territory to the person's extradition from the United Kingdom to the category 1 territory in respect of the extradition offence under consideration.

## [19A Earlier transfer to United Kingdom by International Criminal Court

(1) A person's extradition to a category 1 territory is barred by reason of his earlier transfer by the International Criminal Court if (and only if)–

(a) the person was transferred to the United Kingdom to serve a sentence imposed by the Court;

(b) under arrangements between the United Kingdom and the Court, the consent of the Presidency of the Court is required to the person's extradition from the United Kingdom to the category 1 territory in respect of the extradition offence under consideration;

(c) that consent has not been given.

(2) Subsection (1) does not apply if the person has served the sentence imposed by the Court and has subsequently–

(a) remained voluntarily in the United Kingdom for more than 30 days, or

(b) left the United Kingdom and returned to it.]

### 20  Case where person has been convicted

(1)  If the judge is required to proceed under this section (by virtue of section 11) he must decide whether the person was convicted in his presence.

(2)  If the judge decides the question in subsection (1) in the affirmative he must proceed under section 21.

(3)  If the judge decides that question in the negative he must decide whether the person deliberately absented himself from his trial.

(4)  If the judge decides the question in subsection (3) in the affirmative he must proceed under section 21.

(5)  If the judge decides that question in the negative he must decide whether the person would be entitled to a retrial or (on appeal) to a review amounting to a retrial.

(6)  If the judge decides the question in subsection (5) in the affirmative he must proceed under section 21.

(7)  If the judge decides that question in the negative he must order the person's discharge.

(8)  The judge must not decide the question in subsection (5) in the affirmative unless, in any proceedings that it is alleged would constitute a retrial or a review amounting to a retrial, the person would have these rights—

    (a)  the right to defend himself in person or through legal assistance of his own choosing or, if he had not sufficient means to pay for legal assistance, to be given it free when the interests of justice so required;

    (b)  the right to examine or have examined witnesses against him and to obtain the attendance and examination of witnesses on his behalf under the same conditions as witnesses against him.

### 21  Human rights

(1)  If the judge is required to proceed under this section (by virtue of section 11 or 20) he must decide whether the person's extradition would be compatible with the Convention rights within the meaning of the Human Rights Act 1998 (c. 42).

(2)  If the judge decides the question in subsection (1) in the negative he must order the person's discharge.

(3)  If the judge decides that question in the affirmative he must order the person to be extradited to the category 1 territory in which the warrant was issued.

(4)  If the judge makes an order under subsection (3) he must remand the person in custody or on bail to wait for his extradition to the category 1 territory.

(5)  [If the person is remanded in custody, the appropriate judge may] later grant bail.

## Matters arising before end of extradition hearing

### 22  Person charged with offence in United Kingdom

(1)  This section applies if at any time in the extradition hearing the judge is informed that the person in respect of whom the Part 1 warrant is issued is charged with an offence in the United Kingdom.

(2)  The judge must adjourn the extradition hearing until one of these occurs—

    (a)  the charge is disposed of;

    (b)  the charge is withdrawn;

(c)  proceedings in respect of the charge are discontinued;

(d)  an order is made for the charge to lie on the file, or in relation to Scotland, the diet is deserted *pro loco et tempore*.

(3)  If a sentence of imprisonment or another form of detention is imposed in respect of the offence charged, the judge may adjourn the extradition hearing until [the person is released from detention pursuant to the sentence (whether on licence or otherwise)].

(4)  If before he adjourns the extradition hearing under subsection (2) the judge has decided under section 11 whether the person's extradition is barred by reason of the rule against double jeopardy, the judge must decide that question again after the resumption of the hearing.

### 23  Person serving sentence in United Kingdom

(1)  This section applies if at any time in the extradition hearing the judge is informed that the person in respect of whom the Part 1 warrant is issued is [in custody] serving a sentence of imprisonment or another form of detention in the United Kingdom.

(2)  The judge may adjourn the extradition hearing until [the person is released from detention pursuant to the sentence (whether on licence or otherwise)].

[(3)  In a case where an extradition hearing is adjourned under subsection (2)–

(a)  section 131 of the Magistrates' Courts Act 1980 (remand of accused already in custody) has effect as if a reference to 28 clear days in subsection (1) or (2) of that section were a reference to six months;

(b)  Article 47(2) of the Magistrates' Courts (Northern Ireland) Order 1981 (S.I. 1981/1675 (N.I. 26)) (period of remand in custody) has effect as if a reference to 28 days in–

(i)  paragraph (a)(iii), or

(ii)  the words after paragraph (b),

were a reference to six months].]

### 24  Extradition request

(1)  This section applies if at any time in the extradition hearing the judge is informed that—

(a)  a certificate has been issued under section 70 in respect of a request for the person's extradition;

(b)  the request has not been disposed of;

(c)  an order has been made under section 179(2) for further proceedings on the warrant to be deferred until the request has been disposed of.

(2)  The judge must remand the person in custody or on bail.

(3)  [If the person is remanded in custody, the appropriate judge may] later grant bail.

### 25  Physical or mental condition

(1)  This section applies if at any time in the extradition hearing it appears to the judge that the condition in subsection (2) is satisfied.

(2)  The condition is that the physical or mental condition of the person in respect of whom the Part 1 warrant is issued is such that it would be unjust or oppressive to extradite him.

(3)  The judge must—

(a)  order the person's discharge, or

(b)  adjourn the extradition hearing until it appears to him that the condition in subsection (2) is no longer satisfied.

## Appeals

**26  Appeal against extradition order**

(1)  If the appropriate judge orders a person's extradition under this Part, the person may appeal to the High Court against the order.

(2)  But subsection (1) does not apply if the order is made under section 46 or 48.

(3)  An appeal under this section may be brought on a question of law or fact.

(4)  Notice of an appeal under this section must be given in accordance with rules of court before the end of the permitted period, which is 7 days starting with the day on which the order is made.

**27  Court's powers on appeal under section 26**

(1)  On an appeal under section 26 the High Court may—

  (a)  allow the appeal;

  (b)  dismiss the appeal.

(2)  The court may allow the appeal only if the conditions in subsection (3) or the conditions in subsection (4) are satisfied.

(3)  The conditions are that—

  (a)  the appropriate judge ought to have decided a question before him at the extradition hearing differently;

  (b)  if he had decided the question in the way he ought to have done, he would have been required to order the person's discharge.

(4)  The conditions are that—

  (a)  an issue is raised that was not raised at the extradition hearing or evidence is available that was not available at the extradition hearing;

  (b)  the issue or evidence would have resulted in the appropriate judge deciding a question before him at the extradition hearing differently;

  (c)  if he had decided the question in that way, he would have been required to order the person's discharge.

(5)  If the court allows the appeal it must—

  (a)  order the person's discharge;

  (b)  quash the order for his extradition.

**28  Appeal against discharge at extradition hearing**

(1)  If the judge orders a person's discharge at the extradition hearing the authority which issued the Part 1 warrant may appeal to the High Court against the relevant decision.

(2)  But subsection (1) does not apply if the order for the person's discharge was under section 41.

(3)  The relevant decision is the decision which resulted in the order for the person's discharge.

(4)  An appeal under this section may be brought on a question of law or fact.

(5)  Notice of an appeal under this section must be given in accordance with rules of court before the end of the permitted period, which is 7 days starting with the day on which the order for the person's discharge is made.

**29  Court's powers on appeal under section 28**

(1)  On an appeal under section 28 the High Court may—

  (a)  allow the appeal;
  (b)  dismiss the appeal.

(2) The court may allow the appeal only if the conditions in subsection (3) or the conditions in subsection (4) are satisfied.

(3) The conditions are that—

(a) the judge ought to have decided the relevant question differently;

(b) if he had decided the question in the way he ought to have done, he would not have been required to order the person's discharge.

(4) The conditions are that—

(a) an issue is raised that was not raised at the extradition hearing or evidence is available that was not available at the extradition hearing;

(b) the issue or evidence would have resulted in the judge deciding the relevant question differently;

(c) if he had decided the question in that way, he would not have been required to order the person's discharge.

(5) If the court allows the appeal it must—

(a) quash the order discharging the person;

(b) remit the case to the judge;

(c) direct him to proceed as he would have been required to do if he had decided the relevant question differently at the extradition hearing.

(6) A question is the relevant question if the judge's decision on it resulted in the order for the person's discharge.

[(7) If the court allows the appeal it must remand the person in custody or on bail.

(8) If the court remands the person in custody it may later grant bail.]

### 30 Detention pending conclusion of appeal under section 28

(1) This section applies if immediately after the judge orders the person's discharge the judge is informed by the authority which issued the Part 1 warrant that it intends to appeal under section 28.

(2) The judge must remand the person in custody or on bail while the appeal is pending.

(3) [If the person is remanded in custody, the appropriate judge may] later grant bail.

(4) An appeal under section 28 ceases to be pending at the earliest of these times—

(a) when the proceedings on the appeal are discontinued;

[(b) when the High Court–

(i) allows the appeal, or

(ii) dismisses the appeal,

unless, where the appeal is dismissed, the authority immediately informs the court that it intends to apply for leave to appeal to the [Supreme Court] ;]

(c) at the end of the permitted period, which is 28 days starting with the day on which leave to appeal to the [Supreme Court] against the decision of the High Court on the appeal is granted [, if no appeal to the [Supreme Court] is brought before the end of that period];

(d) when there is no further step that can be taken by the authority which issued the Part 1 warrant in relation to the appeal (ignoring any power of a court to grant leave to take a step out of time).

(5) The preceding provisions of this section apply to Scotland with these modifications—

(a) in subsection (4)(b) omit the words from ["unless"] to the end;

(b) omit subsection (4)(c).

**31  Appeal to High Court: time limit for start of hearing**

(1)  Rules of court must prescribe the period (the relevant period) within which the High Court must begin to hear an appeal under section 26 or 28.

(2)  Rules of court must provide for the relevant period to start with the date on which the person in respect of whom a Part 1 warrant is issued—

    (a)  was arrested under section 5, if he was arrested under that section;

    (b)  was arrested under the Part 1 warrant, if he was not arrested under section 5.

(3)  The High Court must begin to hear the appeal before the end of the relevant period.

(4)  The High Court may extend the relevant period if it believes it to be in the interests of justice to do so; and this subsection may apply more than once.

(5)  The power in subsection (4) may be exercised even after the end of the relevant period.

(6)  If subsection (3) is not complied with and the appeal is under section 26—

    (a)  the appeal must be taken to have been allowed by a decision of the High Court;

    (b)  the person whose extradition has been ordered must be taken to have been discharged by the High Court;

    (c)  the order for the person's extradition must be taken to have been quashed by the High Court.

(7)  If subsection (3) is not complied with and the appeal is under section 28 the appeal must be taken to have been dismissed by a decision of the High Court.


**32  Appeal to [Supreme Court]**

(1)  An appeal lies to the [Supreme Court] from a decision of the High Court on an appeal under section 26 or 28.

(2)  An appeal under this section lies at the instance of—

    (a)  the person in respect of whom the Part 1 warrant was issued;

    (b)  the authority which issued the Part 1 warrant.

(3)  An appeal under this section lies only with the leave of the High Court or the [Supreme Court].

(4)  Leave to appeal under this section must not be granted unless—

    (a)  the High Court has certified that there is a point of law of general public importance involved in the decision, and

    (b)  it appears to the court granting leave that the point is one which ought to be considered by the [Supreme Court] .

(5)  An application to the High Court for leave to appeal under this section must be made before the end of the permitted period, which is 14 days starting with the day on which the court makes its decision on the appeal to it.

(6)  An application to the [Supreme Court] for leave to appeal under this section must be made before the end of the permitted period, which is 14 days starting with the day on which the High Court refuses leave to appeal.

(7)  If leave to appeal under this section is granted, the appeal must be brought before the end of the permitted period, which is 28 days starting with the day on which leave is granted.

(8)  If subsection (7) is not complied with—

    (a)  the appeal must be taken to have been brought;

    (b)  the appeal must be taken to have been dismissed by the [Supreme Court] immediately after the end of the period permitted under that subsection.

(9) These must be ignored for the purposes of subsection (8)(b)—

    (a) any power of a court to extend the period permitted for bringing the appeal;

    (b) any power of a court to grant leave to take a step out of time.

[(10) The High Court may grant bail to a person appealing under this section, or applying for leave to appeal under this section, against the dismissal of his appeal under section 26.]

(11) Section 5 of the Appellate Jurisdiction Act 1876 (c. 59) (composition of House of Lords for hearing and determination of appeals) applies in relation to an appeal under this section or an application for leave to appeal under this section as it applies in relation to an appeal under that Act.

(12) An order of the House of Lords which provides for an application for leave to appeal under this section to be determined by a committee constituted in accordance with section 5 of the Appellate Jurisdiction Act 1876 may direct that the decision of the committee is taken on behalf of the House.

(13) The preceding provisions of this section do not apply to Scotland.

**33 Powers of [Supreme Court] on appeal under section 32**

(1) On an appeal under section 32 the [Supreme Court] may—

    (a) allow the appeal;

    (b) dismiss the appeal.

(2) Subsection (3) applies if—

    (a) the person in respect of whom the Part 1 warrant was issued brings an appeal under section 32, and

    (b) the [Supreme Court] allows the appeal.

(3) The [Supreme Court] must—

    (a) order the person's discharge;

    (b) quash the order for his extradition, if the appeal was against a decision of the High Court to dismiss an appeal under section 26.

(4) Subsection (5) applies if—

    (a) the High Court allows an appeal under section 26 by the person in respect of whom the Part 1 warrant was issued,

    (b) the authority which issued the warrant brings an appeal under section 32 against the decision of the High Court, and

    (c) the [Supreme Court] allows the appeal.

(5) The [Supreme Court] must—

    (a) quash the order of the High Court under section 27(5) discharging the person;

    (b) order the person to be extradited to the category 1 territory in which the warrant was issued.

(6) Subsections (7) and (8) apply if—

    (a) the High Court dismisses an appeal under section 28 against a decision made by the judge at the extradition hearing,

    (b) the authority which issued the Part 1 warrant brings an appeal under section 32 against the decision of the High Court, and

    (c) the [Supreme Court] allows the appeal.

(7) If the judge would have been required to order the person in respect of whom the warrant was issued to be extradited had he decided the relevant question differently, the [Supreme Court] must—

    (a) quash the order of the judge discharging the person;

    (b) order the person to be extradited to the category 1 territory in which the warrant was issued.

(8) In any other case, the [Supreme Court] must—

(a) quash the order of the judge discharging the person in respect of whom the warrant was issued;

(b) remit the case to the judge;

(c) direct him to proceed as he would have been required to do if he had decided the relevant question differently at the extradition hearing.

(9) A question is the relevant question if the judge's decision on it resulted in the order for the person's discharge.

[(10) In a case where–

(a) subsection (5) applies, or

(b) subsections (7) and (8) apply,

the [Supreme Court] must remand, in custody or on bail, the person in respect of whom the warrant was issued.

(11) If the [Supreme Court] remands the person in custody the High Court may later grant bail.]

**[33A Detention pending conclusion of certain appeals under section 32**

(1) This section applies if immediately after the High Court orders the person's discharge the court is informed by the authority which issued the Part 1 warrant that it intends to appeal under section 32.

(2) The court must remand the person in custody or on bail while the appeal under section 32 is pending.

(3) If the court remands the person in custody it may later grant bail.

(4) An appeal under section 32 ceases to be pending at the earliest of these times–

(a) when the proceedings on the appeal are discontinued;

(b) at the end of the permitted period, which is 28 days starting with the day on which leave to appeal to the [Supreme Court] against the decision of the High Court on the appeal under section 26 is granted, if no appeal to the [Supreme Court] is brought before the end of that period;

(c) when there is no further step that can be taken by the authority which issued the Part 1 warrant in relation to the appeal (ignoring any power of a court to grant leave to take a step out of time).

(5) The preceding provisions of this section do not apply to Scotland.]

**34 Appeals: general**

A decision of the judge under this Part may be questioned in legal proceedings only by means of an appeal under this Part.

# Time for extradition

**35 Extradition where no appeal**

(1) This section applies if—

(a) the appropriate judge orders a person's extradition to a category 1 territory under this Part, and

(b) no notice of an appeal under section 26 is given before the end of the period permitted under that section.

(2) But this section does not apply if the order is made under section 46 or 48.

(3) The person must be extradited to the category 1 territory before the end of the required period.

(4) The required period is—

(a) 10 days starting with [the first day after the period permitted under section 26 for giving notice of appeal against the judge's order], or

(b) if the judge and the authority which issued the Part 1 warrant agree a later date, 10 days starting with the later date.

(5) If subsection (3) is not complied with and the person applies to the appropriate judge to be discharged the judge must order his discharge, unless reasonable cause is shown for the delay.

(6) These must be ignored for the purposes of subsection (1)(b)—

(a) any power of a court to extend the period permitted for giving notice of appeal;

(b) any power of a court to grant leave to take a step out of time.

## 36 Extradition following appeal

(1) This section applies if—

(a) there is an appeal to the High Court under section 26 against an order for a person's extradition to a category 1 territory, and

(b) the effect of the decision of the relevant court on the appeal is that the person is to be extradited there.

(2) The person must be extradited to the category 1 territory before the end of the required period.

(3) The required period is—

(a) 10 days starting with the day on which the decision of the relevant court on the appeal becomes final or proceedings on the appeal are discontinued, or

(b) if the relevant court and the authority which issued the Part 1 warrant agree a later date, 10 days starting with the later date.

(4) The relevant court is—

(a) the High Court, if there is no appeal to the [Supreme Court] against the decision of the High Court on the appeal;

(b) the [Supreme Court], if there is such an appeal.

(5) The decision of the High Court on the appeal becomes final—

(a) when the period permitted for applying to the High Court for leave to appeal to the [Supreme Court] ends, if there is no such application;

(b) when the period permitted for applying to the [Supreme Court] for leave to appeal to it ends, if the High Court refuses leave to appeal and there is no application to the [Supreme Court] for leave to appeal;

(c) when the [Supreme Court] refuses leave to appeal to it;

(d) at the end of the permitted period, which is 28 days starting with the day on which leave to appeal to the [Supreme Court] is granted, if no such appeal is brought before the end of that period.

(6) These must be ignored for the purposes of subsection (5)—

(a) any power of a court to extend the period permitted for applying for leave to appeal;

(b) any power of a court to grant leave to take a step out of time.

(7) The decision of the [Supreme Court] on the appeal becomes final when it is made.

(8) If subsection (2) is not complied with and the person applies to the appropriate judge to be discharged the judge must order his discharge, unless reasonable cause is shown for the delay.

(9) The preceding provisions of this section apply to Scotland with these modifications—

(a) in subsections (1) and (3) for "relevant court" substitute "High Court";

(b) omit subsections (4) to (7).

### 37  Undertaking in relation to person serving sentence in United Kingdom

(1)  This section applies if—

(a)  the appropriate judge orders a person's extradition to a category 1 territory under this Part;

(b)  the person is serving a sentence of imprisonment or another form of detention in the United Kingdom [, either–]

[(i)  in custody, or

(ii)  on licence.]

(2)  But this section does not apply if the order is made under section 46 or 48.

(3)  The judge may make the order for extradition subject to the condition that extradition is not to take place before he receives an undertaking given on behalf of the category 1 territory in terms specified by him.

(4)  The terms which may be specified by the judge in relation to a person [within subsection (1)(b)(i) who is] accused in a category 1 territory of the commission of an offence include terms—

(a)  that the person be kept in custody until the conclusion of the proceedings against him for the offence and any other offence in respect of which he is permitted to be dealt with in the category 1 territory;

(b)  that the person be returned to the United Kingdom to serve the remainder of his sentence on the conclusion of those proceedings.

(5)  The terms which may be specified by the judge in relation to a person alleged to be unlawfully at large after conviction of an offence by a court in a category 1 territory include terms that the person be returned to the United Kingdom to serve the remainder of his sentence after serving any sentence imposed on him in the category 1 territory for—

(a)  the offence, and

(b)  any other offence in respect of which he is permitted to be dealt with in the category 1 territory.

(6)  Subsections (7) and (8) apply if the judge makes an order for extradition subject to a condition under subsection (3).

(7)  If the judge does not receive the undertaking before the end of the period of 21 days starting with the day on which he makes the order and the person applies to the appropriate judge to be discharged, the judge must order his discharge.

(8)  If the judge receives the undertaking before the end of that period—

(a)  in a case where section 35 applies, the required period for the purposes of section 35(3) is 10 days starting with the day on which the judge receives the undertaking;

(b)  in a case where section 36 applies, the required period for the purposes of section 36(2) is 10 days starting with the day on which the decision of the relevant court on the appeal becomes final (within the meaning of that section) or (if later) the day on which the judge receives the undertaking.

[Paragraph (a) applies only if the day mentioned in that paragraph is later than the day mentioned in section 35(4)(a).]

### 38  Extradition following deferral for competing claim

(1)  This section applies if—

(a)  an order is made under this Part for a person to be extradited to a category 1 territory in pursuance of a Part 1 warrant;

(b)  before the person is extradited to the territory an order is made under section 44(4)(b) or 179(2)

(b)  for the person's extradition in pursuance of the warrant to be deferred;

(c)  the appropriate judge makes an order under section 181(2) for the person's extradition in pursuance of the warrant to cease to be deferred.

(2)  But this section does not apply if the order for the person's extradition is made under section 46 or 48.

(3)  In a case where section 35 applies, the required period for the purposes of section 35(3) is 10 days starting with the day on which the order under section 181(2) is made. [This subsection applies only if the day on which the order is made is later than the day mentioned in section 35(4)(a).]

(4)  In a case where section 36 applies, the required period for the purposes of section 36(2) is 10 days starting with the day on which the decision of the relevant court on the appeal becomes final (within the meaning of that section) or (if later) the day on which the order under section 181(2) is made.

### 39  Asylum claim

(1)  This section applies if—

(a)  a person in respect of whom a Part 1 warrant is issued makes an asylum claim at any time in the relevant period;

(b)  an order is made under this Part for the person to be extradited in pursuance of the warrant.

(2)  The relevant period is the period—

(a)  starting when a certificate is issued under section 2 in respect of the warrant;

(b)  ending when the person is extradited in pursuance of the warrant.

(3)  The person must not be extradited in pursuance of the warrant before the asylum claim is finally determined; and sections 35, 36, 47 and 49 have effect subject to this.

(4)  Subsection (3) is subject to section 40.

(5)  If the Secretary of State allows the asylum claim, the claim is finally determined when he makes his decision on the claim.

(6)  If the Secretary of State rejects the asylum claim, the claim is finally determined—

(a)  when the Secretary of State makes his decision on the claim, if there is no right to appeal against the Secretary of State's decision on the claim;

(b)  when the period permitted for appealing against the Secretary of State's decision on the claim ends, if there is such a right but there is no such appeal;

(c)  when the appeal against that decision is finally determined or is withdrawn or abandoned, if there is such an appeal.

(7)  An appeal against the Secretary of State's decision on an asylum claim is not finally determined for the purposes of subsection (6) at any time when a further appeal or an application for leave to bring a further appeal—

(a)  has been instituted and has not been finally determined or withdrawn or abandoned, or

(b)  may be brought.

(8)  The remittal of an appeal is not a final determination for the purposes of subsection (7).

(9)  The possibility of an appeal out of time with leave must be ignored for the purposes of subsections (6) and (7).

### 40  Certificate in respect of asylum claimant

(1)  Section 39(3) does not apply in relation to a person if the Secretary of State has certified that the conditions in subsection (2) or the conditions in subsection (3) are satisfied in relation to him.

(2)  The conditions are that—

(a)  the category 1 territory to which the person's extradition has been ordered has accepted that, under standing arrangements, it is the responsible State in relation to the person's asylum claim;

(b)  in the opinion of the Secretary of State, the person is not a national or citizen of the territory.

(3) The conditions are that, in the opinion of the Secretary of State—

(a) the person is not a national or citizen of the category 1 territory to which his extradition has been ordered;

(b) the person's life and liberty would not be threatened in that territory by reason of his race, religion, nationality, political opinion or membership of a particular social group;

(c) the government of the territory would not send the person to another country otherwise than in accordance with the Refugee Convention.

(4) In this section—

"the Refugee Convention" has the meaning given by section 167(1) of the Immigration and Asylum Act 1999 (c. 33);

"standing arrangements" means arrangements in force between the United Kingdom and the category 1 territory for determining which State is responsible for considering applications for asylum.

## Withdrawal of Part 1 warrant

### 41 Withdrawal of warrant before extradition

(1) This section applies if at any time in the relevant period the appropriate judge is informed by the designated authority that a Part 1 warrant issued in respect of a person has been withdrawn.

(2) The relevant period is the period—

(a) starting when the person is first brought before the appropriate judge following his arrest under this Part;

(b) ending when the person is extradited in pursuance of the warrant or discharged.

(3) The judge must order the person's discharge.

(4) If the person is not before the judge at the time the judge orders his discharge, the judge must inform him of the order as soon as practicable.

### 42 Withdrawal of warrant while appeal to High Court pending

(1) This section applies if at any time in the relevant period the High Court is informed by the designated authority that a Part 1 warrant issued in respect of a person has been withdrawn.

(2) The relevant period is the period—

(a) starting when notice of an appeal to the court is given by the person or the authority which issued the warrant;

(b) ending when proceedings on the appeal are discontinued or the court makes its decision on the appeal.

(3) The court must—

(a) if the appeal is under section 26, order the person's discharge and quash the order for his extradition;

(b) if the appeal is under section 28, dismiss the appeal.

(4) If the person is not before the court at the time the court orders his discharge, the court must inform him of the order as soon as practicable.

### 43 Withdrawal of warrant while appeal to [Supreme Court] pending

(1) This section applies if at any time in the relevant period the [Supreme Court] is informed by the designated authority that a Part 1 warrant issued in respect of a person has been withdrawn.

(2) The relevant period is the period—

    (a) starting when leave to appeal to the [Supreme Court] is granted to the person or the authority which issued the warrant;

    (b) ending when proceedings on the appeal are discontinued or the [Supreme Court] makes its decision on the appeal.

(3) If the appeal is brought by the person in respect of whom the warrant was issued the [Supreme Court] must—

    (a) order the person's discharge;

    (b) quash the order for his extradition, in a case where the appeal was against a decision of the High Court to dismiss an appeal under section 26.

(4) If the appeal is brought by the authority which issued the warrant the [Supreme Court] must dismiss the appeal.

(5) If the person is not before the [Supreme Court] at the time it orders his discharge, the [Supreme Court] must inform him of the order as soon as practicable.

## Competing Part 1 warrants

### 44 Competing Part 1 warrants

(1) This section applies if at any time in the relevant period the conditions in subsection (3) are satisfied in relation to a person in respect of whom a Part 1 warrant has been issued.

(2) The relevant period is the period—

    (a) starting when the person is first brought before the appropriate judge following his arrest under this Part;

    (b) ending when the person is extradited in pursuance of the warrant or discharged.

(3) The conditions are that—

    (a) the judge is informed that another Part 1 warrant has been issued in respect of the person;

    (b) the other warrant falls to be dealt with by the judge or by a judge who is the appropriate judge in another part of the United Kingdom;

    (c) the other warrant has not been disposed of.

(4) The judge may—

    (a) order further proceedings on the warrant under consideration to be deferred until the other warrant has been disposed of, if the warrant under consideration has not been disposed of;

    (b) order the person's extradition in pursuance of the warrant under consideration to be deferred until the other warrant has been disposed of, if an order for his extradition in pursuance of the warrant under consideration has been made.

(5) If the judge makes an order under subsection (4) and the person is not already remanded in custody or on bail, the judge must remand the person in custody or on bail.

(6) [If the person is remanded in custody, the appropriate judge may] later grant bail.

(7) In applying subsection (4) the judge must take account in particular of these matters—

    (a) the relative seriousness of the offences concerned;

    (b) the place where each offence was committed (or was alleged to have been committed);

    (c) the date on which each warrant was issued;

    (d) whether, in the case of each offence, the person is accused of its commission (but not alleged to have been convicted) or is alleged to be unlawfully at large after conviction.

## Consent to extradition

### 45 Consent to extradition

(1) A person arrested under a Part 1 warrant may consent to his extradition to the category 1 territory in which the warrant was issued.

(2) A person arrested under section 5 may consent to his extradition to the category 1 territory referred to in subsection (1) of that section.

(3) If a person consents to his extradition under this section he must be taken to have waived any right he would have (apart from the consent) not to be dealt with in the category 1 territory for an offence committed before his extradition.

(4) Consent under this section—

    (a) must be given before the appropriate judge;

    (b) must be recorded in writing;

    (c) is irrevocable.

(5) A person may not give his consent under this section unless—

    (a) he is legally represented before the appropriate judge at the time he gives consent, or

    (b) he is a person to whom subsection (6) applies.

(6) This subsection applies to a person if—

    (a) he has been informed of his right to apply for legal aid and has had the opportunity to apply for legal aid, but he has refused or failed to apply;

    (b) he has applied for legal aid but his application has been refused;

    (c) he was granted legal aid but the legal aid was withdrawn.

(7) In subsection (6) "legal aid" means—

    (a) in England and Wales, a right to representation funded by the Legal Services Commission as part of the Criminal Defence Service;

    (b) in Scotland, such legal aid as is available by virtue of section 183(a) of this Act;

    (c) in Northern Ireland, such free legal aid as is available by virtue of sections 184 and 185 of this Act.

(8) For the purposes of subsection (5) a person is to be treated as legally represented before the appropriate judge if (and only if) he has the assistance of counsel or a solicitor to represent him in the proceedings before the appropriate judge.

### 46 Extradition order following consent

(1) This section applies if a person consents to his extradition under section 45.

(2) The judge must remand the person in custody or on bail.

(3) [If the person is remanded in custody, the appropriate judge may] later grant bail.

(4) If the judge has not fixed a date under section 8 on which the extradition hearing is to begin he is not required to do so.

(5) If the extradition hearing has begun the judge is no longer required to proceed or continue proceeding under sections 10 to 25.

(6) The judge must within the period of 10 days starting with the day on which consent is given order the person's extradition to the category 1 territory.

(7) Subsection (6) has effect subject to sections 48 and 51.

(8)  If subsection (6) is not complied with and the person applies to the judge to be discharged the judge must order his discharge.

### 47  Extradition to category 1 territory following consent

(1)  This section applies if the appropriate judge makes an order under section 46(6) for a person's extradition to a category 1 territory.

(2)  The person must be extradited to the category 1 territory before the end of the required period.

(3)  The required period is—

(a)  10 days starting with the day on which the order is made, or

(b)  if the judge and the authority which issued the Part 1 warrant agree a later date, 10 days starting with the later date.

(4)  If subsection (2) is not complied with and the person applies to the judge to be discharged the judge must order his discharge, unless reasonable cause is shown for the delay.

(5)  If before the person is extradited to the category 1 territory the judge is informed by the designated authority that the Part 1 warrant has been withdrawn—

(a)  subsection (2) does not apply, and

(b)  the judge must order the person's discharge.

### 48  Other warrant issued following consent

(1)  This section applies if—

(a)  a person consents under section 45 to his extradition to a category 1 territory, and

(b)  the conditions in subsection (2) are satisfied before the judge orders his extradition under section 46(6).

(2)  The conditions are that—

(a)  the judge is informed that another Part 1 warrant has been issued in respect of the person;

(b)  the warrant falls to be dealt with by the judge or by a judge who is the appropriate judge in another part of the United Kingdom;

(c)  the warrant has not been disposed of.

(3)  Section 46(6) does not apply but the judge may—

(a)  order the person's extradition in pursuance of his consent, or

(b)  order further proceedings on the warrant under consideration to be deferred until the other warrant has been disposed of.

(4)  Subsection (3) is subject to section 51.

(5)  In applying subsection (3) the judge must take account in particular of these matters—

(a)  the relative seriousness of the offences concerned;

(b)  the place where each offence was committed (or was alleged to have been committed);

(c)  the date on which each warrant was issued;

(d)  whether, in the case of each offence, the person is accused of its commission (but not alleged to have been convicted) or is alleged to be unlawfully at large after conviction.

### 49  Other warrant issued: extradition to category 1 territory

(1)  This section applies if the appropriate judge makes an order under section 48(3)(a) for a person's extradition to a category 1 territory.

(2)  The person must be extradited to the category 1 territory before the end of the required period.

(3) The required period is—

    (a) 10 days starting with the day on which the order is made, or

    (b) if the judge and the authority which issued the Part 1 warrant agree a later date, 10 days starting with the later date.

(4) If subsection (2) is not complied with and the person applies to the judge to be discharged the judge must order his discharge, unless reasonable cause is shown for the delay.

(5) If before the person is extradited to the category 1 territory the judge is informed by the designated authority that the Part 1 warrant has been withdrawn—

    (a) subsection (2) does not apply, and

    (b) the judge must order the person's discharge.

### 50 Other warrant issued: proceedings deferred

(1) This section applies if the appropriate judge makes an order under section 48(3)(b) for further proceedings on a Part 1 warrant to be deferred.

(2) The judge must remand the person in respect of whom the warrant was issued in custody or on bail.

(3) [If the person is remanded in custody, the appropriate judge may] later grant bail.

(4) If an order is made under section 180 for proceedings on the warrant to be resumed, the period specified in section 46(6) must be taken to be 10 days starting with the day on which the order under section 180 is made.

### 51 Extradition request following consent

(1) This section applies if—

    (a) a person in respect of whom a Part 1 warrant is issued consents under section 45 to his extradition to the category 1 territory in which the warrant was issued, and

    (b) the condition in subsection (2) is satisfied before the judge orders his extradition under section 46(6) or 48(3)(a).

(2) The condition is that the judge is informed that—

    (a) a certificate has been issued under section 70 in respect of a request for the person's extradition;

    (b) the request has not been disposed of.

(3) The judge must not make an order under section 46(6) or 48(3) until he is informed what order has been made under section 179(2).

(4) If the order under section 179(2) is for further proceedings on the warrant to be deferred until the request has been disposed of, the judge must remand the person in custody or on bail.

(5) [If the person is remanded in custody, the appropriate judge may] later grant bail.

(6) If—

    (a) the order under section 179(2) is for further proceedings on the warrant to be deferred until the request has been disposed of, and

    (b) an order is made under section 180 for proceedings on the warrant to be resumed, the period specified in section 46(6) must be taken to be 10 days starting with the day on which the order under section 180 is made.

(7) If the order under section 179(2) is for further proceedings on the request to be deferred until the warrant has been disposed of, the period specified in section 46(6) must be taken to be 10 days starting with the day on which the judge is informed of the order.

## 52  Undertaking in relation to person serving sentence

(1)  This section applies if—

(a)  the appropriate judge makes an order under section 46(6) or 48(3)(a) for a person's extradition to a category 1 territory;

(b)  the person is serving a sentence of imprisonment or another form of detention in the United Kingdom [, either–]

[(i)  in custody, or

(ii)  on licence.]

(2)  The judge may make the order for extradition subject to the condition that extradition is not to take place before he receives an undertaking given on behalf of the category 1 territory in terms specified by him.

(3)  The terms which may be specified by the judge in relation to a person [within subsection (1)(b)(i) who is] accused in a category 1 territory of the commission of an offence include terms—

(a)  that the person be kept in custody until the conclusion of the proceedings against him for the offence and any other offence in respect of which he is permitted to be dealt with in the category 1 territory;

(b)  that the person be returned to the United Kingdom to serve the remainder of his sentence on the conclusion of those proceedings.

[(3A) The terms which may be specified by the judge in relation to a person within subsection (1)(b)(ii) who is accused in a category 1 territory of the commission of an offence include terms that the person be returned to the United Kingdom to serve the remainder of his sentence after serving any sentence imposed on him in the category 1 territory for–

(a)  the offence, and

(b)  any other offence in respect of which he is permitted to be dealt with in the category 1 territory.]

(4)  The terms which may be specified by the judge in relation to a person alleged to be unlawfully at large after conviction of an offence by a court in a category 1 territory include terms that the person be returned to the United Kingdom to serve the remainder of his sentence after serving any sentence imposed on him in the category 1 territory for—

(a)  the offence, and

(b)  any other offence in respect of which he is permitted to be dealt with in the category 1 territory.

(5)  If the judge makes an order for extradition subject to a condition under subsection (2) the required period for the purposes of sections 47(2) and 49(2) is 10 days starting with the day on which the judge receives the undertaking.

## 53  Extradition following deferral for competing claim

(1)  This section applies if—

(a)  an order is made under section 46(6) or 48(3)(a) for a person to be extradited to a category 1 territory in pursuance of a Part 1 warrant;

(b)  before the person is extradited to the territory an order is made under section 44(4)(b) or 179(2) (b) for the person's extradition in pursuance of the warrant to be deferred;

(c)  the appropriate judge makes an order under section 181(2) for the person's extradition in pursuance of the warrant to cease to be deferred.

(2)  The required period for the purposes of sections 47(2) and 49(2) is 10 days starting with the day on which the order under section 181(2) is made.

## Post-extradition matters

### 54 Request for consent to other offence being dealt with

(1) This section applies if—

(a) a person is extradited to a category 1 territory in respect of an offence in accordance with this Part;

(b) the appropriate judge receives a request for consent to the person being dealt with in the territory for another offence;

(c) the request is certified under this section by the designated authority.

(2) The designated authority may certify a request for consent under this section if it believes that the authority making the request—

(a) is a judicial authority of the territory, and

(b) has the function of making requests for the consent referred to in subsection (1)(b) in that territory.

(3) A certificate under subsection (2) must certify that the authority making the request falls within paragraphs (a) and (b) of that subsection.

(4) The judge must serve notice on the person that he has received the request for consent, unless he is satisfied that it would not be practicable to do so.

(5) The consent hearing must begin before the end of the required period, which is 21 days starting with the day on which the request for consent is received by the designated authority.

(6) The judge may extend the required period if he believes it to be in the interests of justice to do so; and this subsection may apply more than once.

(7) The power in subsection (6) may be exercised even after the end of the required period.

(8) If the consent hearing does not begin before the end of the required period and the judge does not exercise the power in subsection (6) to extend the period, he must refuse consent.

(9) The judge may at any time adjourn the consent hearing.

(10) The consent hearing is the hearing at which the judge is to consider the request for consent.

### 55 Questions for decision at consent hearing

(1) At the consent hearing under section 54 the judge must decide whether consent is required to the person being dealt with in the territory for the offence for which consent is requested.

(2) If the judge decides the question in subsection (1) in the negative he must inform the authority making the request of his decision.

(3) If the judge decides that question in the affirmative he must decide whether the offence for which consent is requested is an extradition offence.

(4) If the judge decides the question in subsection (3) in the negative he must refuse consent.

(5) If the judge decides that question in the affirmative he must decide whether he would order the person's extradition under sections 11 to 25 if—

(a) the person were in the United Kingdom, and

(b) the judge were required to proceed under section 11 in respect of the offence for which consent is requested.

(6) If the judge decides the question in subsection (5) in the affirmative he must give consent.

(7) If the judge decides that question in the negative he must refuse consent.

(8)  Consent is not required to the person being dealt with in the territory for the offence if the person has been given an opportunity to leave the territory and—

(a)  he has not done so before the end of the permitted period, or

(b)  if he did so before the end of the permitted period, he has returned there.

(9)  The permitted period is 45 days starting with the day on which the person arrived in the territory following his extradition there in accordance with this Part.

(10)  Subject to subsection (8), the judge must decide whether consent is required to the person being dealt with in the territory for the offence by reference to what appears to him to be the law of the territory or arrangements made between the territory and the United Kingdom.

### 56  Request for consent to further extradition to category 1 territory

(1)  This section applies if—

(a)  a person is extradited to a category 1 territory (the requesting territory) in accordance with this Part;

(b)  the appropriate judge receives a request for consent to the person's extradition to another category 1 territory for an offence;

(c)  the request is certified under this section by the designated authority.

(2)  The designated authority may certify a request for consent under this section if it believes that the authority making the request—

(a)  is a judicial authority of the requesting territory, and

(b)  has the function of making requests for the consent referred to in subsection (1)(b) in that territory.

(3)  A certificate under subsection (2) must certify that the authority making the request falls within paragraphs (a) and (b) of that subsection.

(4)  The judge must serve notice on the person that he has received the request for consent, unless he is satisfied that it would not be practicable to do so.

(5)  The consent hearing must begin before the end of the required period, which is 21 days starting with the day on which the request for consent is received by the designated authority.

(6)  The judge may extend the required period if he believes it to be in the interests of justice to do so; and this subsection may apply more than once.

(7)  The power in subsection (6) may be exercised even after the end of the required period.

(8)  If the consent hearing does not begin before the end of the required period and the judge does not exercise the power in subsection (6) to extend the period, he must refuse consent.

(9)  The judge may at any time adjourn the consent hearing.

(10)  The consent hearing is the hearing at which the judge is to consider the request for consent.

### 57  Questions for decision at consent hearing

(1)  At the consent hearing under section 56 the judge must decide whether consent is required to the person's extradition to the other category 1 territory for the offence.

(2)  If the judge decides the question in subsection (1) in the negative he must inform the authority making the request of his decision.

(3)  If the judge decides that question in the affirmative he must decide whether the offence is an extradition offence in relation to the category 1 territory referred to in section 56(1)(b).

(4)  If the judge decides the question in subsection (3) in the negative he must refuse consent.

(5) If the judge decides that question in the affirmative he must decide whether he would order the person's extradition under sections 11 to 25 if—

(a) the person were in the United Kingdom, and

(b) the judge were required to proceed under section 11 in respect of the offence for which consent is requested.

(6) If the judge decides the question in subsection (5) in the affirmative he must give consent.

(7) If the judge decides that question in the negative he must refuse consent.

(8) Consent is not required to the person's extradition to the other territory for the offence if the person has been given an opportunity to leave the requesting territory and—

(a) he has not done so before the end of the permitted period, or

(b) if he did so before the end of the permitted period, he has returned there.

(9) The permitted period is 45 days starting with the day on which the person arrived in the requesting territory following his extradition there in accordance with this Part.

(10) Subject to subsection (8), the judge must decide whether consent is required to the person's extradition to the other territory for the offence by reference to what appears to him to be the arrangements made between the requesting territory and the United Kingdom.

**58  Consent to further extradition to category 2 territory**

(1) This section applies if—

(a) a person is extradited to a category 1 territory (the requesting territory) in accordance with this Part;

(b) the Secretary of State receives a request for consent to the person's extradition to a category 2 territory for an offence;

(c) the request is certified under this section by the designated authority.

(2) The designated authority may certify a request for consent under this section if it believes that the authority making the request—

(a) is a judicial authority of the requesting territory, and

(b) has the function of making requests for the consent referred to in subsection (1)(b) in that territory.

(3) A certificate under subsection (2) must certify that the authority making the request falls within paragraphs (a) and (b) of that subsection.

(4) The Secretary of State must serve notice on the person that he has received the request for consent, unless he is satisfied that it would not be practicable to do so.

(5) The Secretary of State must decide whether the offence is an extradition offence within the meaning given by section 137 in relation to the category 2 territory.

(6) If the Secretary of State decides the question in subsection (5) in the negative he must refuse consent.

(7) If the Secretary of State decides that question in the affirmative he must decide whether the appropriate judge would send the case to him (for his decision whether the person was to be extradited) under sections 79 to 91 if—

(a) the person were in the United Kingdom, and

(b) the judge were required to proceed under section 79 in respect of the offence for which the Secretary of State's consent is requested.

(8) If the Secretary of State decides the question in subsection (7) in the negative he must refuse his consent.

(9) If the Secretary of State decides that question in the affirmative he must decide whether, if the person were in the United Kingdom, his extradition to the category 2 territory in respect of the offence would be prohibited under section 94, 95 or 96.

(10)  If the Secretary of State decides the question in subsection (9) in the negative he may give consent.

(11)  If the Secretary of State decides that question in the affirmative he must refuse consent.

(12)  This section applies in relation to any function which falls under this section to be exercised in relation to Scotland only as if the references in this section to the Secretary of State were to the Scottish Ministers.

**[59 Return of person to serve remainder of sentence**

(1)  This section applies if—

    (a)  a person who is serving a sentence of imprisonment or another form of detention in the United Kingdom is extradited to a category 1 territory in accordance with this Part;

    (b)  the person is returned to the United Kingdom to serve the remainder of the sentence or the person otherwise returns to the United Kingdom.

(2)  Time during which the person was outside the United Kingdom as a result of the extradition does not count as time served by the person as part of the sentence.

(3)  But subsection (2) does not apply if—

    (a)  the person was extradited for the purpose of being prosecuted for an offence, and

    (b)  the person has not been convicted of the offence or of any other offence in respect of which the person was permitted to be dealt with in the category 1 territory.

(4)  In a case falling within subsection (3), time during which the person was outside the United Kingdom as a result of the extradition counts as time served by the person as part of the sentence if (and only if) it was spent in custody in connection with the offence or any other offence in respect of which the person was permitted to be dealt with in the territory.

(5)  In a case where the person is not entitled to be released from detention pursuant to the sentence—

    (a)  the person is liable to be detained in pursuance of the sentence, and

    (b)  if at large, the person must be treated as being unlawfully at large.

(6)  In a case where the person is entitled to be released from detention on licence pursuant to the sentence—

    (a)  if the person was released on licence at the time of extradition, the licence is suspended until the person's return;

    (b)  if the person was not released on licence at that time, subsections (7) to (10) apply in relation to the person ("the offender").

(7)  The offender is liable to be detained, on return, in any place in which the offender could have been detained pursuant to the sentence before the time of extradition.

(8)  A constable or immigration officer may—

    (a)  take the offender into custody, and

    (b)  convey the offender to the place mentioned in subsection (7).

(9)  The offender must be released on licence within the period of 5 days beginning when the offender is taken (or retaken) into custody under this section.

(10)  In calculating a period of 5 days for the purposes of subsection (9) no account is to be taken of—

    (a)  any Saturday or Sunday,

    (b)  Christmas Day,

    (c)  Good Friday, or

    (d)  in any part of the United Kingdom, any day that is a bank holiday under the Banking and Financial Dealings Act 1971 in that part of the United Kingdom.

(11) A person is entitled to be released from detention if there is—

(a) a duty to release the person under section 33(1), (1A) or (2) of the Criminal Justice Act 1991,

(b) a duty to release the person under section 244 of the Criminal Justice Act 2003 (other than temporarily on licence pursuant to an intermittent custody order under section 183(1)(b) of the Criminal Justice Act 2003),

(c) a duty to release the person under section 1, 1AA or 7(1) of the Prisoners and Criminal Proceedings (Scotland) Act 1993 or section 5, 11(2), 13, 19 or 23 of the Custodial Sentences and Weapons (Scotland) Act 2007, or

(d) a duty to release the person under section 1 of the Northern Ireland (Remission of Sentences) Act 1995, Article 26 of the Criminal Justice (Northern Ireland) Order 1996 or Article 17 or 18(8) of the Criminal Justice (Northern Ireland) Order 2008.

(12) The powers conferred on a constable by subsection (8) are exercisable in any part of the United Kingdom.

(13) An immigration officer is a person who is an immigration officer within the meaning of the Immigration Act 1971.]


## Costs

### 60  Costs where extradition ordered

(1) This section applies if any of the following occurs in relation to a person in respect of whom a Part 1 warrant is issued—

(a) an order for the person's extradition is made under this Part;

(b) the High Court dismisses an appeal under section 26;

(c) the High Court or the [Supreme Court] dismisses an application for leave to appeal to the [Supreme Court] under section 32, if the application is made by the person;

(d) the [Supreme Court] dismisses an appeal under section 32, if the appeal is brought by the person.

(2) In a case falling within subsection (1)(a), the appropriate judge may make such order as he considers just and reasonable with regard to the costs to be paid by the person.

(3) In a case falling within subsection (1)(b), (c) or (d), the court by which the application or appeal is dismissed may make such order as it considers just and reasonable with regard to the costs to be paid by the person.

(4) An order for costs under this section—

(a) must specify their amount;

(b) may name the person to whom they are to be paid.

### 61  Costs where discharge ordered

(1) This section applies if any of the following occurs in relation to a person in respect of whom a Part 1 warrant is issued—

(a) an order for the person's discharge is made under this Part;

(b) the person is taken to be discharged under this Part;

(c) the High Court dismisses an appeal under section 28;

(d) the High Court or the [Supreme Court] dismisses an application for leave to appeal to the [Supreme Court] under section 32, if the application is made by the authority which issued the warrant;

(e) the [Supreme Court] dismisses an appeal under section 32, if the appeal is brought by the authority which issued the warrant.

(2) In a case falling within subsection (1)(a), an order under subsection (5) in favour of the person may be made by—

    (a)  the appropriate judge, if the order for the person's discharge is made by him;

    (b)  the High Court, if the order for the person's discharge is made by it;

    (c)  the [Supreme Court], if the order for the person's discharge is made by it.

(3) In a case falling within subsection (1)(b), the appropriate judge may make an order under subsection (5) in favour of the person.

(4) In a case falling within subsection (1)(c), (d) or (e), the court by which the application or appeal is dismissed may make an order under subsection (5) in favour of the person.

(5) An order under this subsection in favour of a person is an order for a payment of the appropriate amount to be made to the person out of money provided by Parliament.

(6) The appropriate amount is such amount as the judge or court making the order under subsection

(5) considers reasonably sufficient to compensate the person in whose favour the order is made for any expenses properly incurred by him in the proceedings under this Part.

(7) But if the judge or court making an order under subsection (5) is of the opinion that there are circumstances which make it inappropriate that the person in whose favour the order is made should recover the full amount mentioned in subsection (6), the judge or court must—

    (a)  assess what amount would in his or its opinion be just and reasonable;

    (b)  specify that amount in the order as the appropriate amount.

(8) Unless subsection (7) applies, the appropriate amount—

    (a)  must be specified in the order, if the court considers it appropriate for it to be so specified and the person in whose favour the order is made agrees the amount;

    (b)  must be determined in accordance with regulations made by the Lord Chancellor for the purposes of this section, in any other case.

### 62 Costs where discharge ordered: supplementary

(1) In England and Wales, subsections (1) and (3) of section 20 of the Prosecution of Offences Act 1985 (c. 23) (regulations for carrying Part 2 of that Act into effect) apply in relation to section 61 as those subsections apply in relation to Part 2 of that Act.

(2) As so applied those subsections have effect as if an order under section 61(5) were an order under Part 2 of that Act for a payment to be made out of central funds.

(3) In Northern Ireland, section 7 of the Costs in Criminal Cases Act (Northern Ireland) 1968 (c.10) (rules relating to costs) applies in relation to section 61 as that section applies in relation to sections 2 to 5 of that Act.

## Repatriation cases

### 63 Persons serving sentences outside territory where convicted

(1) This section applies if an arrest warrant is issued in respect of a person by an authority of a category 1 territory and the warrant contains the statement referred to in subsection (2).

(2) The statement is one that—

    (a)  the person is alleged to be unlawfully at large from a prison in one territory (the imprisoning territory) in which he was serving a sentence after conviction of an offence specified in the warrant by a court in another territory (the convicting territory), and

(b) the person was serving the sentence in pursuance of international arrangements for prisoners sentenced in one territory to be repatriated to another territory in order to serve their sentence, and

(c) the warrant is issued with a view to his arrest and extradition to the category 1 territory for the purpose of serving a sentence or another form of detention imposed in respect of the offence.

(3) If the category 1 territory is either the imprisoning territory or the convicting territory, section 2(2)(b) has effect as if the reference to the statement referred to in subsection (5) of that section were a reference to the statement referred to in subsection (2) of this section.

(4) If the category 1 territory is the imprisoning territory—

(a) section 2(6)(e) has effect as if "the category 1 territory" read "the convicting territory";

(b) section 10(2) has effect as if "an extradition offence" read "an extradition offence in relation to the convicting territory";

(c) section 20(5) has effect as if after "entitled" there were inserted "in the convicting territory";

(d) section 37(5) has effect as if "a category 1 territory" read "the convicting territory" and as if "the category 1 territory" in both places read "the convicting territory";

(e) section 52(4) has effect as if "a category 1 territory" read "the convicting territory" and as if "the category 1 territory" in both places read "the convicting territory";

(f) section 65(1) has effect as if "a category 1 territory" read "the convicting territory";

(g) section 65(2) has effect as if "the category 1 territory" in the opening words and paragraphs (a) and (c) read "the convicting territory" and as if "the category 1 territory" in paragraph (b) read "the imprisoning territory";

(h) in section 65, subsections (3), (4), (5), (6) and (8) have effect as if "the category 1 territory" in each place read "the convicting territory".

## Interpretation

### 64 Extradition offences: person not sentenced for offence

(1) This section applies in relation to conduct of a person if—

(a) he is accused in a category 1 territory of the commission of an offence constituted by the conduct, or

(b) he is alleged to be unlawfully at large after conviction by a court in a category 1 territory of an offence constituted by the conduct and he has not been sentenced for the offence.

(2) The conduct constitutes an extradition offence in relation to the category 1 territory if these conditions are satisfied—

(a) the conduct occurs in the category 1 territory and no part of it occurs in the United Kingdom;

(b) a certificate issued by an appropriate authority of the category 1 territory shows that the conduct falls within the European framework list;

(c) the certificate shows that the conduct is punishable under the law of the category 1 territory with imprisonment or another form of detention for a term of 3 years or a greater punishment.

(3) The conduct also constitutes an extradition offence in relation to the category 1 territory if these conditions are satisfied—

(a) the conduct occurs in the category 1 territory;

(b) the conduct would constitute an offence under the law of the relevant part of the United Kingdom if it occurred in that part of the United Kingdom;

(c) the conduct is punishable under the law of the category 1 territory with imprisonment or another form of detention for a term of 12 months or a greater punishment (however it is described in that law).

(4) The conduct also constitutes an extradition offence in relation to the category 1 territory if these conditions are satisfied—

(a) the conduct occurs outside the category 1 territory;

(b) the conduct is punishable under the law of the category 1 territory with imprisonment or another form of detention for a term of 12 months or a greater punishment (however it is described in that law);

(c) in corresponding circumstances equivalent conduct would constitute an extra-territorial offence under the law of the relevant part of the United Kingdom punishable with imprisonment or another form of detention for a term of 12 months or a greater punishment.

(5) The conduct also constitutes an extradition offence in relation to the category 1 territory if these conditions are satisfied—

(a) the conduct occurs outside the category 1 territory and no part of it occurs in the United Kingdom;

(b) the conduct would constitute an offence under the law o the relevant part of the United Kingdom punishable with imprisonment or another form of detention for a term of 12 months or a greater punishment if it occurred in that part of the United Kingdom;

(c) the conduct is so punishable under the law of the category 1 territory (however it is described in that law).

(6) The conduct also constitutes an extradition offence in relation to the category 1 territory if these conditions are satisfied—

(a) the conduct occurs outside the category 1 territory and no part of it occurs in the United Kingdom;

(b) the conduct is punishable under the law of the category 1 territory with imprisonment or another form of detention for a term of 12 months or a greater punishment (however it is described in that law);

(c) the conduct constitutes or if committed in the United Kingdom would constitute an offence mentioned in subsection (7).

(7) The offences are—

(a) an offence under section 51 or 58 of the International Criminal Court Act 2001 (c. 17) (genocide, crimes against humanity and war crimes);

(b) an offence under section 52 or 59 of that Act (conduct ancillary to genocide etc. committed outside the jurisdiction);

(c) an ancillary offence, as defined in section 55 or 62 of that Act, in relation to an offence falling within paragraph (a) or (b);

(d) an offence under section 1 of the International Criminal Court (Scotland) Act 2001 (asp 13) (genocide, crimes against humanity and war crimes);

(e) an offence under section 2 of that Act (conduct ancillary to genocide etc. committed outside the jurisdiction);

(f) an ancillary offence, as defined in section 7 of that Act, in relation to an offence falling within paragraph (d) or (e).

(8) For the purposes of subsections (3)(b), (4)(c) and (5)(b)—

(a) if the conduct relates to a tax or duty, it is immaterial that the law of the relevant part of the United Kingdom does not impose the same kind of tax or duty or does not contain rules of the same kind as those of the law of the category 1 territory;

(b) if the conduct relates to customs or exchange, it is immaterial that the law of the relevant part of the United Kingdom does not contain rules of the same kind as those of the law of the category 1 territory.

(9) This section applies for the purposes of this Part.

**65 Extradition offences: person sentenced for offence**

(1) This section applies in relation to conduct of a person if—

(a) he is alleged to be unlawfully at large after conviction by a court in a category 1 territory of an offence constituted by the conduct, and

(b) he has been sentenced for the offence.

(2) The conduct constitutes an extradition offence in relation to the category 1 territory if these conditions are satisfied—

(a) the conduct occurs in the category 1 territory and no part of it occurs in the United Kingdom;

(b) a certificate issued by an appropriate authority of the category 1 territory shows that the conduct falls within the European framework list;

(c) the certificate shows that a sentence of imprisonment or another form of detention for a term of 12 months or a greater punishment has been imposed in the category 1 territory in respect of the conduct.

(3) The conduct also constitutes an extradition offence in relation to the category 1 territory if these conditions are satisfied—

(a) the conduct occurs in the category 1 territory;

(b) the conduct would constitute an offence under the law of the relevant part of the United Kingdom if it occurred in that part of the United Kingdom;

(c) a sentence of imprisonment or another form of detention for a term of 4 months or a greater punishment has been imposed in the category 1 territory in respect of the conduct.

(4) The conduct also constitutes an extradition offence in relation to the category 1 territory if these conditions are satisfied—

(a) the conduct occurs outside the category 1 territory;

(b) a sentence of imprisonment or another form of detention for a term of 4 months or a greater punishment has been imposed in the category 1 territory in respect of the conduct;

(c) in corresponding circumstances equivalent conduct would constitute an extra-territorial offence under the law of the relevant part of the United Kingdom punishable with imprisonment or another form of detention for a term of 12 months or a greater punishment.

(5) The conduct also constitutes an extradition offence in relation to the category 1 territory if these conditions are satisfied—

(a) the conduct occurs outside the category 1 territory and no part of it occurs in the United Kingdom;

(b) the conduct would constitute an offence under the law of the relevant part of the United Kingdom punishable with imprisonment or another form of detention for a term of 12 months or a greater punishment if it occurred in that part of the United Kingdom;

(c) a sentence of imprisonment or another form of detention for a term of 4 months or a greater punishment has been imposed in the category 1 territory in respect of the conduct.

(6) The conduct also constitutes an extradition offence in relation to the category 1 territory if these conditions are satisfied—

(a) the conduct occurs outside the category 1 territory and no part of it occurs in the United Kingdom;

(b) a sentence of imprisonment or another form of detention for a term of 4 months or a greater punishment has been imposed in the category 1 territory in respect of the conduct;

(c) the conduct constitutes or if committed in the United Kingdom would constitute an offence mentioned in subsection (7).

(7) The offences are—

(a) an offence under section 51 or 58 of the International Criminal Court Act 2001 (c. 17) (genocide, crimes against humanity and war crimes);

(b) an offence under section 52 or 59 of that Act (conduct ancillary to genocide etc. committed outside the jurisdiction);

(c) an ancillary offence, as defined in section 55 or 62 of that Act, in relation to an offence falling within paragraph (a) or (b);

(d) an offence under section 1 of the International Criminal Court (Scotland) Act 2001 (asp 13) (genocide, crimes against humanity and war crimes);

(e) an offence under section 2 of that Act (conduct ancillary to genocide etc. committed outside the jurisdiction);

(f) an ancillary offence, as defined in section 7 of that Act, in relation to an offence falling within paragraph (d) or (e).

(8) For the purposes of subsections (3)(b), (4)(c) and (5)(b)—

(a) if the conduct relates to a tax or duty, it is immaterial that the law of the relevant part of the United Kingdom does not impose the same kind of tax or duty or does not contain rules of the same kind as those of the law of the category 1 territory;

(b) if the conduct relates to customs or exchange, it is immaterial that the law of the relevant part of the United Kingdom does not contain rules of the same kind as those of the law of the category 1 territory.

(9) This section applies for the purposes of this Part.

## 66 Extradition offences: supplementary

(1) Subsections (2) to (4) apply for the purposes of sections 64 and 65.

(2) An appropriate authority of a category 1 territory is a judicial authority of the territory which the appropriate judge believes has the function of issuing arrest warrants in that territory.

(3) The law of a territory is the general criminal law of the territory.

(4) The relevant part of the United Kingdom is the part of the United Kingdom in which the relevant proceedings are taking place.

(5) The relevant proceedings are the proceedings in which it is necessary to decide whether conduct constitutes an extradition offence.

## 67 The appropriate judge

(1) The appropriate judge is—

(a) in England and Wales, a District Judge (Magistrates' Courts) designated for the purposes of this Part [by the Lord Chief Justice of England and Wales after consulting the Lord Chancellor];

(b) in Scotland, the sheriff of Lothian and Borders;

(c) in Northern Ireland, such county court judge or resident magistrate as is designated for the purposes of this Part [by the Lord Chief Justice of Northern Ireland after consulting the Lord Chancellor].

(2) A designation under subsection (1) may be made for all cases or for such cases (or cases of such description) as the designation stipulates.

(3) More than one designation may be made under subsection (1).

[(3A) The use of the expression "the judge" in a section containing a previous reference to "the appropriate judge" or "the judge" does not in itself require both references to be read as referring to the same individual.]

(4) This section applies for the purposes of this Part.

[(5) The Lord Chief Justice of England and Wales may nominate a judicial office holder (as defined in section 109(4) of the Constitutional Reform Act 2005) to exercise his functions under subsection (1)(a).

(6) The Lord Chief Justice of Northern Ireland may nominate any of the following to exercise his functions under subsection (1)(c)–

(a) the holder of one of the offices listed in Schedule 1 to the Justice (Northern Ireland) Act 2002;

(b) a Lord Justice of Appeal (as defined in section 88 of that Act).]

### 68 The extradition hearing

(1) The extradition hearing is the hearing at which the appropriate judge is to decide whether a person in respect of whom a Part 1 warrant was issued is to be extradited to the category 1 territory in which it was issued.

(2) This section applies for the purposes of this Part.

### [68A Unlawfully at large

(1) A person is alleged to be unlawfully at large after conviction of an offence if–

(a) he is alleged to have been convicted of it, and

(b) his extradition is sought for the purpose of his being sentenced for the offence or of his serving a sentence of imprisonment or another form of detention imposed in respect of the offence.

(2) This section applies for the purposes of this Part, other than sections 14 and 63.]

## PART 2

# EXTRADITION TO CATEGORY 2 TERRITORIES

## Introduction

### 69 Extradition to category 2 territories

(1) This Part deals with extradition from the United Kingdom to the territories designated for the purposes of this Part by order made by the Secretary of State.

(2) In this Act references to category 2 territories are to the territories designated for the purposes of this Part.

### 70 Extradition request and certificate

(1) The Secretary of State must [(subject to subsection (2))] issue a certificate under this section if he receives a valid request for the extradition [of a person to a category 2 territory].

[(2) The Secretary of State may refuse to issue a certificate under this section if–

(a) he has power under section 126 to order that proceedings on the request be deferred,

(b) the person whose extradition is requested has been recorded by the Secretary of State as a refugee within the meaning of the Refugee Convention, or

(c) the person whose extradition is requested has been granted leave to enter or remain in the United Kingdom on the ground that it would be a breach of Article 2 or 3 of the Human Rights Convention to remove him to the territory to which extradition is requested.

(2A) In subsection (2)–

"Refugee Convention" has the meaning given by section 167(1) of the Immigration and Asylum Act 1999;

"Human Rights Convention" has the meaning given to "the Convention" by section 21(1) of the Human Rights Act 1998.]

(3) A request for a person's extradition is valid if—

(a) it contains the statement referred to in subsection (4) [or the statement referred to in subsection (4A)], and

(b) it is made in the approved way.

[(4) The statement is one that–

(a) the person is accused in the category 2 territory of the commission of an offence specified in the request, and

(b) the request is made with a view to his arrest and extradition to the category 2 territory for the purpose of being prosecuted for the offence.

(4A) The statement is one that–

(a) the person has been convicted of an offence specified in the request by a court in the category 2 territory, and

(b) the request is made with a view to his arrest and extradition to the category 2 territory for the purpose of being sentenced for the offence or of serving a sentence of imprisonment or another form of detention imposed in respect of the offence.]

(5) A request for extradition to a category 2 territory which is a British overseas territory is made in the approved way if it is made by or on behalf of the person administering the territory.

(6) A request for extradition to a category 2 territory which is the Hong Kong Special Administrative Region of the People's Republic of China is made in the approved way if it is made by or on behalf of the government of the Region.

(7) A request for extradition to any other category 2 territory is made in the approved way if it is made—

(a) by an authority of the territory which the Secretary of State believes has the function of making requests for extradition in that territory, or

(b) by a person recognised by the Secretary of State as a diplomatic or consular representative of the territory.

(8) [A certificate under this section must—

(a) certify that the request is made in the approved way, and

(b) identify the order by which the territory in question is designated as a category 2 territory.]

[(9) If a certificate is issued under this section the Secretary of State must send the request and the certificate to the appropriate judge.]

## Arrest

### 71 Arrest warrant following extradition request

(1) This section applies if the Secretary of State sends documents to the appropriate judge under section 70.

(2) The judge may issue a warrant for the arrest of the person whose extradition is requested if the judge has reasonable grounds for believing that—

(a) the offence in respect of which extradition is requested is an extradition offence, and

(b) there is evidence falling within subsection (3).

(3) The evidence is—

(a) evidence that would justify the issue of a warrant for the arrest of a person accused of the offence within the judge's jurisdiction, if the person whose extradition is requested is accused of the commission of the offence;

(b) evidence that would justify the issue of a warrant for the arrest of a person unlawfully at large after conviction of the offence within the judge's jurisdiction, if the person whose extradition is requested is alleged to be unlawfully at large after conviction of the offence.

(4) But if the category 2 territory to which extradition is requested is designated for the purposes of this section by order made by the Secretary of State, subsections (2) and (3) have effect as if "evidence" read "information".

(5) A warrant issued under this section may—

(a) be executed by any person to whom it is directed or by any constable or customs officer;

(b) be executed even if neither the warrant nor a copy of it is in the possession of the person executing it at the time of the arrest.

[(6) If a warrant issued under this section–

(a) is directed to a service policeman, and

(b) is in respect of a person subject to service law or a civilian subject to service discipline, it may be executed anywhere.]

(7) In any other case, a warrant issued under this section may be executed in any part of the United Kingdom.

(8) [...]


**72 Person arrested under section 71**

(1) This section applies if a person is arrested under a warrant issued under section 71.

(2) A copy of the warrant must be given to the person as soon as practicable after his arrest.

(3) The person must be brought as soon as practicable before the appropriate judge.

(4) But subsection (3) does not apply if—

(a) the person is granted bail by a constable following his arrest, or

(b) the Secretary of State decides under section 126 that the request for the person's extradition is not to be proceeded with.

(5) If subsection (2) is not complied with and the person applies to the judge to be discharged, the judge may order his discharge.

(6) If subsection (3) is not complied with and the person applies to the judge to be discharged, the judge must order his discharge.

(7) When the person first appears or is brought before the appropriate judge, the judge must—

(a) inform him of the contents of the request for his extradition;

(b) give him the required information about consent;

(c) remand him in custody or on bail.

(8) The required information about consent is—

(a) that the person may consent to his extradition to the category 2 territory to which his extradition is requested;

(b) an explanation of the effect of consent and the procedure that will apply if he gives consent;

(c) that consent must be given in writing and is irrevocable.

(9) [If the person is remanded in custody, the appropriate judge may] later grant bail.

(10) Subsection (4)(a) applies to Scotland with the omission of the words "by a constable".

## 73 Provisional warrant

(1) This section applies if a justice of the peace is satisfied on information in writing and on oath that a person within subsection (2)—

(a) is or is believed to be in the United Kingdom, or

(b) is or is believed to be on his way to the United Kingdom.

(2) A person is within this subsection if—

(a) he is accused in a category 2 territory of the commission of an offence, or

(b) he is alleged to be unlawfully at large after conviction of an offence by a court in a category 2 territory.

(3) The justice may issue a warrant for the arrest of the person (a provisional warrant) if he has reasonable grounds for believing that—

(a) the offence of which the person is accused or has been convicted is an extradition offence, and

(b) there is written evidence falling within subsection (4).

(4) The evidence is—

(a) evidence that would justify the issue of a warrant for the arrest of a person accused of the offence within the justice's jurisdiction, if the person in respect of whom the warrant is sought is accused of the commission of the offence;

(b) evidence that would justify the issue of a warrant for the arrest of a person unlawfully at large after conviction of the offence within the justice's jurisdiction, if the person in respect of whom the warrant is sought is alleged to be unlawfully at large after conviction of the offence.

(5) But if the category 2 territory is designated for the purposes of this section by order made by the Secretary of State, subsections (3) and (4) have effect as if "evidence" read "information".

(6) A provisional warrant may—

(a) be executed by any person to whom it is directed or by any constable or customs officer;

(b) be executed even if neither the warrant nor a copy of it is in the possession of the person executing it at the time of the arrest.

[(7) If a warrant issued under this section–

(a) is directed to a service policeman, and

(b) is in respect of a person subject to service law or a civilian subject to service discipline,

it may be executed anywhere.]

(8) In any other case, a warrant issued under this section may be executed in any part of the United Kingdom.

(9) [...]

(10) The preceding provisions of this section apply to Scotland with these modifications—

(a) in subsection (1) for "justice of the peace is satisfied on information in writing and on oath" substitute "sheriff is satisfied, on an application by a procurator fiscal,";

(b) in subsection (3) for "justice" substitute "sheriff";

(c) in subsection (4) for "justice's", in paragraphs (a) and (b), substitute "sheriff's". (11) Subsection (1) applies to Northern Ireland with the substitution of "a complaint" for "information".

## 74 Person arrested under provisional warrant

(1) This section applies if a person is arrested under a provisional warrant.

(2) A copy of the warrant must be given to the person as soon as practicable after his arrest.

(3) The person must be brought as soon as practicable before the appropriate judge.

(4) But subsection (3) does not apply if—

    (a) the person is granted bail by a constable following his arrest, or

    (b) in a case where the Secretary of State has received a valid request for the person's extradition, the Secretary of State decides under section 126 that the request is not to be proceeded with.

(5) If subsection (2) is not complied with and the person applies to the judge to be discharged, the judge may order his discharge.

(6) If subsection (3) is not complied with and the person applies to the judge to be discharged, the judge must order his discharge.

(7) When the person first appears or is brought before the appropriate judge, the judge must—

    (a) inform him that he is accused of the commission of an offence in a category 2 territory or that he is alleged to be unlawfully at large after conviction of an offence by a court in a category 2 territory;

    (b) give him the required information about consent;

    (c) remand him in custody or on bail.

(8) The required information about consent is—

    (a) that the person may consent to his extradition to the category 2 territory in which he is accused of the commission of an offence or is alleged to have been convicted of an offence;

    (b) an explanation of the effect of consent and the procedure that will apply if he gives consent;

    (c) that consent must be given in writing and is irrevocable.

(9) [If the person is remanded in custody, the appropriate judge may] later grant bail.

(10) The judge must order the person's discharge if the documents referred to in section 70(9) are not received by the judge within the required period.

(11) The required period is—

    (a) 45 days starting with the day on which the person was arrested, or

    (b) if the category 2 territory is designated by order made by the Secretary of State for the purposes of this section, any longer period permitted by the order.

(12) Subsection (4)(a) applies to Scotland with the omission of the words "by a constable".

## The extradition hearing

### 75 Date of extradition hearing: arrest under section 71

(1) When a person arrested under a warrant issued under section 71 first appears or is brought before the appropriate judge, the judge must fix a date on which the extradition hearing is to begin.

(2) The date fixed under subsection (1) must not be later than the end of the permitted period, which is 2 months starting with the date on which the person first appears or is brought before the judge.

(3) If before the date fixed under subsection (1) (or this subsection) a party to the proceedings applies to the judge for a later date to be fixed and the judge believes it to be in the interests of justice to do so, he may fix a later date; and this subsection may apply more than once.

(4) If the extradition hearing does not begin on or before the date fixed under this section and the person applies to the judge to be discharged, the judge must order his discharge.

### 76 Date of extradition hearing: arrest under provisional warrant

(1) Subsection (2) applies if—

(a) a person is arrested under a provisional warrant, and

(b) the documents referred to in section 70(9) are received by the appropriate judge within the period required under section 74(10).

(2) The judge must fix a date on which the extradition hearing is to begin.

(3) The date fixed under subsection (2) must not be later than the end of the permitted period, which is 2 months starting with the date on which the judge receives the documents.

(4) If before the date fixed under subsection (2) (or this subsection) a party to the proceedings applies to the judge for a later date to be fixed and the judge believes it to be in the interests of justice to do so, he may fix a later date; and this subsection may apply more than once.

(5) If the extradition hearing does not begin on or before the date fixed under this section and the person applies to the judge to be discharged, the judge must order his discharge.

**[76A Person charged with offence in United Kingdom before extradition hearing**

(1) This section applies if—

(a) a person has been brought before the appropriate judge under section 72(3) or 74(3) but the extradition hearing has not begun; and

(b) the judge is informed that the person is charged with an offence in the United Kingdom.

(2) The judge must order further proceedings in respect of the extradition to be adjourned until one of these occurs—

(a) the charge is disposed of;

(b) the charge is withdrawn;

(c) proceedings in respect of the charge are discontinued;

(d) an order is made for the charge to lie on the file, or in relation to Scotland, the diet is deserted *pro loco et tempore*.

(3) If a sentence of imprisonment or another form of detention is imposed in respect of the offence charged, the judge may order further proceedings in respect of the extradition to be adjourned until the person is released from detention pursuant to the sentence (whether on licence or otherwise).]

**[76B Person serving sentence in United Kingdom before extradition hearing**

(1) This section applies if—

(a) a person has been brought before the appropriate judge under section 72(3) or 74(3) but the extradition hearing has not begun; and

(b) the judge is informed that the person is in custody serving a sentence of imprisonment or another form of detention in the United Kingdom.

(2) The judge may order further proceedings in respect of the extradition to be adjourned until the person is released from detention pursuant to the sentence (whether on licence or otherwise).

(3) In a case where further proceedings in respect of the extradition are adjourned under subsection (2)—

(a) section 131 of the Magistrates' Courts Act 1980 (remand of accused already in custody) has effect as if a reference to 28 clear days in subsection (1) or (2) of that section were a reference to six months;

(b) Article 47(2) of the Magistrates' Courts (Northern Ireland) Order 1981 (period of remand in custody) has effect as if a reference to 28 days in—

(i) sub-paragraph (a)(iii), or

(ii) the words after sub-paragraph (b),

were a reference to six months.]

### 77 Judge's powers at extradition hearing

(1) In England and Wales, at the extradition hearing the appropriate judge has the same powers (as nearly as may be) as a magistrates' court would have if the proceedings were the summary trial of an information against the person whose extradition is requested.

(2) In Scotland—

(a) at the extradition hearing the appropriate judge has the same powers (as nearly as may be) as if the proceedings were summary proceedings in respect of an offence alleged to have been committed by the person whose extradition is requested; but

(b) in his making any decision under section 78(4)(a) evidence from a single source shall be sufficient.

(3) In Northern Ireland, at the extradition hearing the appropriate judge has the same powers (as nearly as may be) as a magistrates' court would have if the proceedings were the hearing and determination of a complaint against the person whose extradition is requested.

(4) If the judge adjourns the extradition hearing he must remand the person in custody or on bail.

(5) [If the person is remanded in custody, the appropriate judge may] later grant bail.

### 78 Initial stages of extradition hearing

(1) This section applies if a person alleged to be the person whose extradition is requested appears or is brought before the appropriate judge for the extradition hearing.

(2) The judge must decide whether the documents sent to him by the Secretary of State consist of (or include)—

(a) the documents referred to in section 70(9);

(b) particulars of the person whose extradition is requested;

(c) particulars of the offence specified in the request;

(d) in the case of a person accused of an offence, a warrant for his arrest issued in the category 2 territory;

(e) in the case of a person alleged to be unlawfully at large after conviction of an offence, a certificate issued in the category 2 territory of the conviction and (if he has been sentenced) of the sentence.

(3) If the judge decides the question in subsection (2) in the negative he must order the person's discharge.

(4) If the judge decides that question in the affirmative he must decide whether—

(a) the person appearing or brought before him is the person whose extradition is requested;

(b) the offence specified in the request is an extradition offence;

(c) copies of the documents sent to the judge by the Secretary of State have been served on the person.

(5) The judge must decide the question in subsection (4)(a) on a balance of probabilities.

(6) If the judge decides any of the questions in subsection (4) in the negative he must order the person's discharge.

(7) If the judge decides those questions in the affirmative he must proceed under section 79.

(8) The reference in subsection (2)(d) to a warrant for a person's arrest includes a reference to a judicial document authorising his arrest.

### 79 Bars to extradition

(1) If the judge is required to proceed under this section he must decide whether the person's extradition to the category 2 territory is barred by reason of—

(a) the rule against double jeopardy;

(b) extraneous considerations;

(c) the passage of time;

(d) hostage-taking considerations.

(2) Sections 80 to 83 apply for the interpretation of subsection (1).

(3) If the judge decides any of the questions in subsection (1) in the affirmative he must order the person's discharge.

(4) If the judge decides those questions in the negative and the person is accused of the commission of the extradition offence but is not alleged to be unlawfully at large after conviction of it, the judge must proceed under section 84.

(5) If the judge decides those questions in the negative and the person is alleged to be unlawfully at large after conviction of the extradition offence, the judge must proceed under section 85.

## 80 Rule against double jeopardy

A person's extradition to a category 2 territory is barred by reason of the rule against double jeopardy if (and only if) it appears that he would be entitled to be discharged under any rule of law relating to previous acquittal or conviction if he were charged with the extradition offence in the part of the United Kingdom where the judge exercises his jurisdiction.

## 81 Extraneous considerations

A person's extradition to a category 2 territory is barred by reason of extraneous considerations if (and only if) it appears that—

(a) the request for his extradition (though purporting to be made on account of the extradition offence) is in fact made for the purpose of prosecuting or punishing him on account of his race, religion, nationality, gender, sexual orientation or political opinions, or

(b) if extradited he might be prejudiced at his trial or punished, detained or restricted in his personal liberty by reason of his race, religion, nationality, gender, sexual orientation or political opinions.

## 82 Passage of time

[A person's extradition to a category 2 territory is barred by reason of the passage of time if (and only if) it appears that it would be unjust or oppressive to extradite him by reason of the passage of time since he is alleged to have–

(a) committed the extradition offence (where he is accused of its commission), or

(b) become unlawfully at large (where he is alleged to have been convicted of it).]

## 83 Hostage-taking considerations

(1) A person's extradition to a category 2 territory is barred by reason of hostage-taking considerations if (and only if) the territory is a party to the Hostage-taking Convention and it appears that—

(a) if extradited he might be prejudiced at his trial because communication between him and the appropriate authorities would not be possible, and

(b) the act or omission constituting the extradition offence also constitutes an offence under section 1 of the Taking of Hostages Act 1982 (c. 28) or an attempt to commit such an offence.

(2) The appropriate authorities are the authorities of the territory which are entitled to exercise rights of protection in relation to him.

(3) A certificate issued by the Secretary of State that a territory is a party to the Hostage-taking Convention is conclusive evidence of that fact for the purposes of subsection (1).

(4) The Hostage-taking Convention is the International Convention against the Taking of Hostages opened for signature at New York on 18 December 1979.

### 84 Case where person has not been convicted

(1) If the judge is required to proceed under this section he must decide whether there is evidence which would be sufficient to make a case requiring an answer by the person if the proceedings were the summary trial of an information against him.

(2) In deciding the question in subsection (1) the judge may treat a statement made by a person in a document as admissible evidence of a fact if—

(a) the statement is made by the person to a police officer or another person charged with the duty of investigating offences or charging offenders, and

(b) direct oral evidence by the person of the fact would be admissible.

(3) In deciding whether to treat a statement made by a person in a document as admissible evidence of a fact, the judge must in particular have regard—

(a) to the nature and source of the document;

(b) to whether or not, having regard to the nature and source of the document and to any other circumstances that appear to the judge to be relevant, it is likely that the document is authentic;

(c) to the extent to which the statement appears to supply evidence which would not be readily available if the statement were not treated as being admissible evidence of the fact;

(d) to the relevance of the evidence that the statement appears to supply to any issue likely to have to be determined by the judge in deciding the question in subsection (1);

(e) to any risk that the admission or exclusion of the statement will result in unfairness to the person whose extradition is sought, having regard in particular to whether it is likely to be possible to controvert the statement if the person making it does not attend to give oral evidence in the proceedings.

(4) A summary in a document of a statement made by a person must be treated as a statement made by the person in the document for the purposes of subsection (2).

(5) If the judge decides the question in subsection (1) in the negative he must order the person's discharge.

(6) If the judge decides that question in the affirmative he must proceed under section 87.

(7) If the judge is required to proceed under this section and the category 2 territory to which extradition is requested is designated for the purposes of this section by order made by the Secretary of State—

(a) the judge must not decide under subsection (1), and

(b) he must proceed under section 87.

(8) Subsection (1) applies to Scotland with the substitution of "summary proceedings in respect of an offence alleged to have been committed by the person (except that for this purpose evidence from a single source shall be sufficient)" for "the summary trial of an information against him".

(9) Subsection (1) applies to Northern Ireland with the substitution of "the hearing and determination of a complaint" for "the summary trial of an information".

### 85 Case where person has been convicted

(1) If the judge is required to proceed under this section he must decide whether the person was convicted in his presence.

(2) If the judge decides the question in subsection (1) in the affirmative he must proceed under section 87.

(3) If the judge decides that question in the negative he must decide whether the person deliberately absented himself from his trial.

(4) If the judge decides the question in subsection (3) in the affirmative he must proceed under section 87.

(5)  If the judge decides that question in the negative he must decide whether the person would be entitled to a retrial or (on appeal) to a review amounting to a retrial.

(6)  If the judge decides the question in subsection (5) in the affirmative he must proceed under section 86.

(7)  If the judge decides that question in the negative he must order the person's discharge.

(8)  The judge must not decide the question in subsection (5) in the affirmative unless, in any proceedings that it is alleged would constitute a retrial or a review amounting to a retrial, the person would have these rights—

(a)  the right to defend himself in person or through legal assistance of his own choosing or, if he had not sufficient means to pay for legal assistance, to be given it free when the interests of justice so required;

(b)  the right to examine or have examined witnesses against him and to obtain the attendance and examination of witnesses on his behalf under the same conditions as witnesses against him.

## 86  Conviction in person's absence

(1)  If the judge is required to proceed under this section he must decide whether there is evidence which would be sufficient to make a case requiring an answer by the person if the proceedings were the summary trial of an information against him.

(2)  In deciding the question in subsection (1) the judge may treat a statement made by a person in a document as admissible evidence of a fact if—

(a)  the statement is made by the person to a police officer or another person charged with the duty of investigating offences or charging offenders, and

(b)  direct oral evidence by the person of the fact would be admissible.

(3)  In deciding whether to treat a statement made by a person in a document as admissible evidence of a fact, the judge must in particular have regard—

(a)  to the nature and source of the document;

(b)  to whether or not, having regard to the nature and source of the document and to any other circumstances that appear to the judge to be relevant, it is likely that the document is authentic;

(c)  to the extent to which the statement appears to supply evidence which would not be readily available if the statement were not treated as being admissible evidence of the fact;

(d)  to the relevance of the evidence that the statement appears to supply to any issue likely to have to be determined by the judge in deciding the question in subsection (1);

(e)  to any risk that the admission or exclusion of the statement will result in unfairness to the person whose extradition is sought, having regard in particular to whether it is likely to be possible to controvert the statement if the person making it does not attend to give oral evidence in the proceedings.

(4)  A summary in a document of a statement made by a person must be treated as a statement made by the person in the document for the purposes of subsection (2).

(5)  If the judge decides the question in subsection (1) in the negative he must order the person's discharge.

(6)  If the judge decides that question in the affirmative he must proceed under section 87.

(7)  If the judge is required to proceed under this section and the category 2 territory to which extradition is requested is designated for the purposes of this section by order made by the Secretary of State—

(a)  the judge must not decide under subsection (1), and

(b)  he must proceed under section 87.

(8)  Subsection (1) applies to Scotland with the substitution of "summary proceedings in respect of an offence alleged to have been committed by the person (except that for this purpose evidence from a single source shall be sufficient)" for "the summary trial of an information against him".

(9) Subsection (1) applies to Northern Ireland with the substitution of "the hearing and determination of a complaint" for "the summary trial of an information".

### 87 Human rights

(1) If the judge is required to proceed under this section (by virtue of section 84, 85 or 86) he must decide whether the person's extradition would be compatible with the Convention rights within the meaning of the Human Rights Act 1998 (c. 42).

(2) If the judge decides the question in subsection (1) in the negative he must order the person's discharge.

(3) If the judge decides that question in the affirmative he must send the case to the Secretary of State for his decision whether the person is to be extradited.

### 88 Person charged with offence in United Kingdom

(1) This section applies if at any time in the extradition hearing the judge is informed that the person is charged with an offence in the United Kingdom.

(2) The judge must adjourn the extradition hearing until one of these occurs—

(a) the charge is disposed of;

(b) the charge is withdrawn;

(c) proceedings in respect of the charge are discontinued;

(d) an order is made for the charge to lie on the file, or in relation to Scotland, the diet is deserted *pro loco et tempore.*

(3) If a sentence of imprisonment or another form of detention is imposed in respect of the offence charged, the judge may adjourn the extradition hearing until [the person is released from detention pursuant to the sentence (whether on licence or otherwise)].

(4) If before he adjourns the extradition hearing under subsection (2) the judge has decided under section 79 whether the person's extradition is barred by reason of the rule against double jeopardy, the judge must decide that question again after the resumption of the hearing.

### 89 Person serving sentence in United Kingdom

(1) This section applies if at any time in the extradition hearing the judge is informed that the person is [in custody] serving a sentence of imprisonment or another form of detention in the United Kingdom.

(2) The judge may adjourn the extradition hearing until [the person is released from detention pursuant to the sentence (whether on licence or otherwise)].

[(3) In a case where an extradition hearing is adjourned under subsection (2)–

(a) section 131 of the Magistrates' Courts Act 1980 (remand of accused already in custody) has effect as if a reference to 28 clear days in subsection (1) or (2) of that section were a reference to six months;

(b) Article 47(2) of the Magistrates' Courts (Northern Ireland) Order 1981 (S.I. 1981/1675 (N.I. 26)) (period of remand in custody) has effect as if a reference to 28 days in–

(i) paragraph (a)(iii), or

(ii) the words after paragraph (b),

were a reference to six months.]

### 90 Competing extradition claim

(1) This section applies if at any time in the extradition hearing the judge is informed that the conditions in subsection (2) or (3) are met.

(2) The conditions are that—

(a) the Secretary of State has received another valid request for the person's extradition to a category 2 territory;

(b) the other request has not been disposed of;

(c) the Secretary of State has made an order under section 126(2) for further proceedings on the request under consideration to be deferred until the other request has been disposed of.

(3) The conditions are that—

(a) a certificate has been issued under section 2 in respect of a Part 1 warrant issued in respect of the person;

(b) the warrant has not been disposed of;

(c) the Secretary of State has made an order under section 179(2) for further proceedings on the request to be deferred until the warrant has been disposed of.

(4) The judge must remand the person in custody or on bail.

(5) [If the person is remanded in custody, the appropriate judge may] later grant bail.

**91  Physical or mental condition**

(1) This section applies if at any time in the extradition hearing it appears to the judge that the condition in subsection (2) is satisfied.

(2) The condition is that the physical or mental condition of the person is such that it would be unjust or oppressive to extradite him.

(3) The judge must—

(a) order the person's discharge, or

(b) adjourn the extradition hearing until it appears to him that the condition in subsection (2) is no longer satisfied.

**92  Case sent to Secretary of State**

(1) This section applies if the appropriate judge sends a case to the Secretary of State under this Part for his decision whether a person is to be extradited.

(2) The judge must inform the person in ordinary language that—

(a) he has a right to appeal to the High Court;

(b) if he exercises the right the appeal will not be heard until the Secretary of State has made his decision.

(3) But subsection (2) does not apply if the person has consented to his extradition under section 127.

(4) The judge must remand the person in custody or on bail—

(a) to wait for the Secretary of State's decision, and

(b) to wait for his extradition to the territory to which extradition is requested (if the Secretary of State orders him to be extradited).

(5) [If the person is remanded in custody, the appropriate judge may] later grant bail.

## Secretary of State's functions

**93  Secretary of State's consideration of case**

(1) This section applies if the appropriate judge sends a case to the Secretary of State under this Part for his decision whether a person is to be extradited.

(2) The Secretary of State must decide whether he is prohibited from ordering the person's extradition under any of these sections—

    (a) section 94 (death penalty);

    (b) section 95 (speciality);

    (c) section 96 (earlier extradition to United Kingdom from other territory) [;]

    [(d) section 96A (earlier transfer to United Kingdom by International Criminal Court).]

(3) If the Secretary of State decides any of the questions in subsection (2) in the affirmative he must order the person's discharge.

(4) If the Secretary of State decides those questions in the negative he must order the person to be extradited to the territory to which his extradition is requested unless—

    (a) he is informed that the request has been withdrawn,

    (b) he makes an order under section 126(2) or 179(2) for further proceedings on the request to be deferred and the person is discharged under section 180, or

    (c) he orders the person's discharge under section 208.

(5) In deciding the questions in subsection (2), the Secretary of State is not required to consider any representations received by him after the end of the permitted period.

(6) The permitted period is the period of [4 weeks] starting with the appropriate day.

[(7) In the case of a person who has consented under section 127 to his extradition, the Secretary of State is not required–

    (a) to wait until the end of the permitted period before ordering the person's extradition, or

    (b) to consider any representations received after the order is made.]

## 94 Death penalty

(1) The Secretary of State must not order a person's extradition to a category 2 territory if he could be, will be or has been sentenced to death for the offence concerned in the category 2 territory.

(2) Subsection (1) does not apply if the Secretary of State receives a written assurance which he considers adequate that a sentence of death—

    (a) will not be imposed, or

    (b) will not be carried out (if imposed).

## 95 Speciality

(1) The Secretary of State must not order a person's extradition to a category 2 territory if there are no speciality arrangements with the category 2 territory.

(2) But subsection (1) does not apply if the person consented to his extradition under section 127 before his case was sent to the Secretary of State.

(3) There are speciality arrangements with a category 2 territory if (and only if) under the law of that territory or arrangements made between it and the United Kingdom a person who is extradited to the territory from the United Kingdom may be dealt with in the territory for an offence committed before his extradition only if—

    (a) the offence is one falling within subsection (4), or

    (b) he is first given an opportunity to leave the territory.

(4) The offences are—

    (a) the offence in respect of which the person is extradited;

    (b) an extradition offence disclosed by the same facts as that offence, other than one in respect of which a sentence of death could be imposed;

(c)  an extradition offence in respect of which the Secretary of State consents to the person being dealt with;

(d)  an offence in respect of which the person waives the right that he would have (but for this paragraph) not to be dealt with for the offence.

(5)  Arrangements made with a category 2 territory which is a Commonwealth country or a British overseas territory may be made for a particular case or more generally.

(6)  A certificate issued by or under the authority of the Secretary of State confirming the existence of arrangements with a category 2 territory which is a Commonwealth country or a British overseas territory and stating the terms of the arrangements is conclusive evidence of those matters.

### 96  Earlier extradition to United Kingdom from other territory

The Secretary of State must not order a person's extradition to a category 2 territory if—

(a)  the person was extradited to the United Kingdom from another territory (the extraditing territory);

(b)  under arrangements between the United Kingdom and the extraditing territory, that territory's consent is required to the person's extradition from the United Kingdom to the category 2 territory in respect of the extradition offence under consideration;

(c)  that consent has not been given on behalf of the extraditing territory.

### [96A  Earlier transfer to United Kingdom by International Criminal Court

(1)  The Secretary of State must not order a person's extradition to a category 2 territory if–

(a)  the person was transferred to the United Kingdom to serve a sentence imposed by the International Criminal Court;

(b)  under arrangements between the United Kingdom and the Court, the consent of the Presidency of the Court is required to the person's extradition from the United Kingdom to the category 2 territory in respect of the extradition offence under consideration;

(c)  that consent has not been given.

(2)  Subsection (1) does not apply if the person has served the sentence imposed by the Court and has subsequently–

(a)  remained voluntarily in the United Kingdom for more than 30 days, or

(b)  left the United Kingdom and returned to it.]

### 97  Deferral: person charged with offence in United Kingdom

(1)  This section applies if—

(a)  the appropriate judge sends a case to the Secretary of State under this Part for his decision whether a person is to be extradited;

(b)  the person is charged with an offence in the United Kingdom.

(2)  The Secretary of State must not make a decision with regard to the person's extradition until one of these occurs—

(a)  the charge is disposed of;

(b)  the charge is withdrawn;

(c)  proceedings in respect of the charge are discontinued;

(d)  an order is made for the charge to lie on the file or, in relation to Scotland, the diet is deserted *pro loco et tempore.*

(3)  If a sentence of imprisonment or another form of detention is imposed in respect of the offence charged, the Secretary of State may defer making a decision with regard to the person's extradition until [the person is released from detention pursuant to the sentence (whether on licence or otherwise)].

**98  Deferral: person serving sentence in United Kingdom**

(1)  This section applies if—

(a)  the appropriate judge sends a case to the Secretary of State under this Part for his decision whether a person is to be extradited;

(b)  the person is [in custody] serving a sentence of imprisonment or another form of detention in the United Kingdom.

(2)  The Secretary of State may defer making a decision with regard to the person's extradition until [the person is released from detention pursuant to the sentence (whether on licence or otherwise)].

**99  Time limit for order for extradition or discharge**

(1)  This section applies if—

(a)  the appropriate judge sends a case to the Secretary of State under this Part for his decision whether a person is to be extradited;

(b)  within the required period the Secretary of State does not make an order for the person's extradition or discharge.

(2)  If the person applies to [the appropriate judge] to be discharged, [the judge] must order his discharge.

(3)  The required period is the period of 2 months starting with the appropriate day.

(4)  If before the required period ends the Secretary of State [applies to the appropriate judge] for it to be extended [the judge may] make an order accordingly; and this subsection may apply more than once.

**100  Information**

(1)  If the Secretary of State orders a person's extradition under this Part he must—

(a)  inform the person of the order;

(b)  inform him in ordinary language that he has a right of appeal to the High Court;

(c)  inform a person acting on behalf of the category 2 territory of the order.

(2)  But subsection (1)(b) does not apply if the person has consented to his extradition under section 127.

(3)  If the Secretary of State orders a person's extradition under this Part and he has received an assurance such as is mentioned in section 94(2), he must give the person a copy of the assurance when he informs him under subsection (1) of the order.

(4)  If the Secretary of State orders a person's discharge under this Part he must—

(a)  inform him of the order;

(b)  inform a person acting on behalf of the category 2 territory of the order.

**101  Making of order for extradition or discharge**

(1)  An order to which this section applies must be made under the hand of one of these—

(a)  the Secretary of State;

(b)  a Minister of State;

(c)  a Parliamentary Under-Secretary of State;

(d)  a senior official.

(2)  But, in relation to Scotland, an order to which this section applies must be made under the hand of one of these—

(a)  a member of the Scottish Executive or a junior Scottish Minister;

(b)  a senior official who is a member of the staff of the Scottish Administration.

(3) This section applies to—

  (a) an order under section 93 for a person's extradition;

  (b) an order under section 93 or 123 for a person's discharge.

(4) A senior official is—

  (a) a member of the Senior Civil Service;

  (b) a member of the Senior Management Structure of Her Majesty's Diplomatic Service.

(5) If it appears to the Secretary of State that it is necessary to do so in consequence of any changes to the structure or grading of the home civil service or diplomatic service, he may by order make such amendments to subsection (4) as appear to him appropriate to preserve (so far as practicable) the effect of that subsection.

### 102 The appropriate day

(1) This section applies for the purposes of sections 93 and 99 if the appropriate judge sends a case to the Secretary of State under this Part for his decision whether a person is to be extradited.

(2) If the person is charged with an offence in the United Kingdom, the appropriate day is the day on which one of these occurs—

  (a) the charge is disposed of;

  (b) the charge is withdrawn;

  (c) proceedings in respect of the charge are discontinued;

  (d) an order is made for the charge to lie on the file, or in relation to Scotland, the diet is deserted *pro loco et tempore*.

(3) If under section 97(3) or 98(2) the Secretary of State defers making a decision [, the appropriate day is the day on which the person is released from detention pursuant to the sentence (whether on licence or otherwise)].

(4) If section 126 applies in relation to the request for the person's extradition (the request concerned) the appropriate day is—

  (a) the day on which the Secretary of State makes an order under that section, if the order is for proceedings on the other request to be deferred;

  (b) the day on which an order under section 180 is made, if the order under section 126 is for proceedings on the request concerned to be deferred and the order under section 180 is for the proceedings to be resumed.

(5) If section 179 applies in relation to the request for the person's extradition, the appropriate day is—

  (a) the day on which the Secretary of State makes an order under that section, if the order is for proceedings on the warrant to be deferred;

  (b) the day on which an order under section 180 is made, if the order under section 179 is for proceedings on the request to be deferred and the order under section 180 is for the proceedings to be resumed.

(6) If more than one of subsections (2) to (5) applies, the appropriate day is the latest of the days found under the subsections which apply.

(7) In any other case, the appropriate day is the day on which the judge sends the case to the Secretary of State for his decision whether the person is to be extradited.

## Appeals

### 103 Appeal where case sent to Secretary of State

(1) If the judge sends a case to the Secretary of State under this Part for his decision whether a person is to be extradited, the person may appeal to the High Court against the relevant decision.

(2) But subsection (1) does not apply if the person consented to his extradition under section 127 before his case was sent to the Secretary of State.

(3) The relevant decision is the decision that resulted in the case being sent to the Secretary of State.

(4) An appeal under this section may be brought on a question of law or fact.

(5) If an appeal is brought under this section before the Secretary of State has decided whether the person is to be extradited the appeal must not be heard until after the Secretary of State has made his decision.

(6) If the Secretary of State orders the person's discharge the appeal must not be proceeded with.

(7) No appeal may be brought under this section if the Secretary of State has ordered the person's discharge.

(8) If notice of an appeal under section 110 against the decision which resulted in the order for the person's discharge is given in accordance with subsection (5) of that section—

(a) subsections (6) and (7) do not apply;

(b) no appeal may be brought under this section if the High Court has made its decision on the appeal.

(9) Notice of an appeal under this section must be given in accordance with rules of court before the end of the permitted period, which is 14 days starting with the day on which the Secretary of State informs the person under section 100(1) or (4) of the order he has made in respect of the person.

**104  Court's powers on appeal under section 103**

(1) On an appeal under section 103 the High Court may—

(a) allow the appeal;

(b) direct the judge to decide again a question (or questions) which he decided at the extradition hearing;

(c) dismiss the appeal.

(2) The court may allow the appeal only if the conditions in subsection (3) or the conditions in subsection (4) are satisfied.

(3) The conditions are that—

(a) the judge ought to have decided a question before him at the extradition hearing differently;

(b) if he had decided the question in the way he ought to have done, he would have been required to order the person's discharge.

(4) The conditions are that—

(a) an issue is raised that was not raised at the extradition hearing or evidence is available that was not available at the extradition hearing;

(b) the issue or evidence would have resulted in the judge deciding a question before him at the extradition hearing differently;

(c) if he had decided the question in that way, he would have been required to order the person's discharge.

(5) If the court allows the appeal it must—

(a) order the person's discharge;

(b) quash the order for his extradition.

(6) If the judge comes to a different decision on any question that is the subject of a direction under subsection (1)(b) he must order the person's discharge.

(7) If the judge comes to the same decision as he did at the extradition hearing on the question that is (or all the questions that are) the subject of a direction under subsection (1)(b) the appeal must be taken to have been dismissed by a decision of the High Court.

[(8) If the court makes a direction under subsection (1)(b) it must remand the person in custody or on bail.

(9) If the court remands the person in custody it may later grant bail.]

### 105 Appeal against discharge at extradition hearing

(1) If at the extradition hearing the judge orders a person's discharge, an appeal to the High Court may be brought on behalf of the category 2 territory against the relevant decision.

(2) But subsection (1) does not apply if the order for the person's discharge was under section 122.

(3) The relevant decision is the decision which resulted in the order for the person's discharge.

(4) An appeal under this section may be brought on a question of law or fact.

(5) Notice of an appeal under this section must be given in accordance with rules of court before the end of the permitted period, which is 14 days starting with the day on which the order for the person's discharge is made.

### 106 Court's powers on appeal under section 105

(1) On an appeal under section 105 the High Court may—

    (a) allow the appeal;

    (b) direct the judge to decide the relevant question again;

    (c) dismiss the appeal.

(2) A question is the relevant question if the judge's decision on it resulted in the order for the person's discharge.

(3) The court may allow the appeal only if the conditions in subsection (4) or the conditions in subsection (5) are satisfied.

(4) The conditions are that—

    (a) the judge ought to have decided the relevant question differently;

    (b) if he had decided the question in the way he ought to have done, he would not have been required to order the person's discharge.

(5) The conditions are that—

    (a) an issue is raised that was not raised at the extradition hearing or evidence is available that was not available at the extradition hearing;

    (b) the issue or evidence would have resulted in the judge deciding the relevant question differently;

    (c) if he had decided the question in that way, he would not have been required to order the person's discharge.

(6) If the court allows the appeal it must—

    (a) quash the order discharging the person;

    (b) remit the case to the judge;

    (c) direct him to proceed as he would have been required to do if he had decided the relevant question differently at the extradition hearing.

(7) If the court makes a direction under subsection (1)(b) and the judge decides the relevant question differently he must proceed as he would have been required to do if he had decided that question differently at the extradition hearing.

(8) If the court makes a direction under subsection (1)(b) and the judge does not decide the relevant question differently the appeal must be taken to have been dismissed by a decision of the High Court.

[(9) If the court–

    (a) allows the appeal, or

    (b) makes a direction under subsection (1)(b),

it must remand the person in custody or on bail.

(10) If the court remands the person in custody it may later grant bail.]

### 107 Detention pending conclusion of appeal under section 105

(1) This section applies if immediately after the judge orders the person's discharge the judge is informed on behalf of the category 2 territory of an intention to appeal under section 105.

(2) The judge must remand the person in custody or on bail while the appeal is pending.

(3) [If the person is remanded in custody, the appropriate judge may] later grant bail.

(4) An appeal under section 105 ceases to be pending at the earliest of these times—

    (a) when the proceedings on the appeal are discontinued;

    [(b) when the High Court–

        (i) allows the appeal,

        (ii) makes a direction under section 106(1)(b), or

        (iii) dismisses the appeal,

unless, where the appeal is dismissed, the court is immediately informed on behalf of the category 2 territory of an intention to apply for leave to appeal to the [Supreme Court];]

    (c) at the end of the permitted period, which is 28 days starting with the day on which leave to appeal to the [Supreme Court] against the decision of the High Court on the appeal is granted [, if no appeal to the [Supreme Court] is brought before the end of that period];

    (d) when there is no further step that can be taken on behalf of the category 2 territory in relation to the appeal (ignoring any power of a court to grant leave to take a step out of time).

(5) The preceding provisions of this section apply to Scotland with these modifications—

    (a) in subsection (4)(b) omit the words from " [unless]" to the end;

    (b) omit subsection (4)(c).

### 108 Appeal against extradition order

(1) If the Secretary of State orders a person's extradition under this Part, the person may appeal to the High Court against the order.

(2) But subsection (1) does not apply if the person has consented to his extradition under section 127.

(3) An appeal under this section may be brought on a question of law or fact.

(4) Notice of an appeal under this section must be given in accordance with rules of court before the end of the permitted period, which is 14 days starting with the day on which the Secretary of State informs the person of the order under section 100(1).

### 109 Court's powers on appeal under section 108

(1) On an appeal under section 108 the High Court may—

    (a) allow the appeal;

    (b) dismiss the appeal.

(2) The court may allow the appeal only if the conditions in subsection (3) or the conditions in subsection (4) are satisfied.

(3) The conditions are that—

(a) the Secretary of State ought to have decided a question before him differently;

(b) if he had decided the question in the way he ought to have done, he would not have ordered the person's extradition.

(4) The conditions are that—

(a) an issue is raised that was not raised when the case was being considered by the Secretary of State or information is available that was not available at that time;

(b) the issue or information would have resulted in the Secretary of State deciding a question before him differently;

(c) if he had decided the question in that way, he would not have ordered the person's extradition.

(5) If the court allows the appeal it must—

(a) order the person's discharge;

(b) quash the order for his extradition.

## 110 Appeal against discharge by Secretary of State

(1) If the Secretary of State makes an order for a person's discharge under this Part, an appeal to the High Court may be brought on behalf of the category 2 territory against the relevant decision.

(2) But subsection (1) does not apply if the order for the person's discharge was under section 123.

(3) The relevant decision is the decision which resulted in the order for the person's discharge.

(4) An appeal under this section may be brought on a question of law or fact.

(5) Notice of an appeal under this section must be given in accordance with rules of court before the end of the permitted period, which is 14 days starting with the day on which (under section 100(4)) the Secretary of State informs a person acting on behalf of the category 2 territory of the order.

## 111 Court's powers on appeal under section 110

(1) On an appeal under section 110 the High Court may—

(a) allow the appeal;

(b) dismiss the appeal.

(2) The court may allow the appeal only if the conditions in subsection (3) or the conditions in subsection (4) are satisfied.

(3) The conditions are that—

(a) the Secretary of State ought to have decided a question before him differently;

(b) if he had decided the question in the way he ought to have done, he would have ordered the person's extradition.

(4) The conditions are that—

(a) an issue is raised that was not raised when the case was being considered by the Secretary of State or information is available that was not available at that time;

(b) the issue or information would have resulted in the Secretary of State deciding a question before him differently;

(c) if he had decided the question in that way, he would have ordered the person's extradition.

(5) If the court allows the appeal it must—

(a) quash the order discharging the person;

(b) order the person's extradition.

[(6) If the court allows the appeal it must remand the person in custody or on bail.

(7) If the court remands the person in custody it may later grant bail.]

**[112 Detention pending conclusion of appeal under section 110**

(1) This section applies in a case where the Secretary of State orders the person's discharge under this Part.

(2) Subject to subsection (3)–

(a) the order made by the appropriate judge under section 92(4) ("the remand order") remains in force until the end of the period of three days beginning with the day on which the person's discharge is ordered;

(b) if within that period the Secretary of State is informed in writing on behalf of the category 2 territory of an intention to appeal under section 110, the remand order remains in force while the appeal is pending.

(3) If the person is remanded in custody under section 92(4), the appropriate judge may grant bail.

(4) An appeal under section 110 ceases to be pending at the earliest of these times–

(a) when the proceedings on the appeal are discontinued;

(b) when the High Court–

(i) allows the appeal, or

(ii) dismisses the appeal,

unless, where the appeal is dismissed, the court is immediately informed on behalf of the category 2 territory of an intention to apply for leave to appeal to the [Supreme Court];

(c) at the end of the permitted period, which is 28 days starting with the day on which leave to appeal to the [Supreme Court] against the decision of the High Court on the appeal is granted, if no appeal to the [Supreme Court] is brought before the end of that period;

(d) when there is no further step that can be taken on behalf of the category 2 territory in relation to the appeal (ignoring any power of a court to grant leave to take a step out of time).

(5) The preceding provisions of this section apply to Scotland with these modifications–

(a) in subsection (4)(b) omit the words from "unless" to the end;

(b) omit subsection (4)(c).]

**113 Appeal to High Court: time limit for start of hearing**

(1) Rules of court must prescribe the period (the relevant period) within which the High Court must begin to hear an appeal under section 103, 105, 108 or 110.

(2) The High Court must begin to hear the appeal before the end of the relevant period.

(3) The High Court may extend the relevant period if it believes it to be in the interests of justice to do so; and this subsection may apply more than once.

(4) The power in subsection (3) may be exercised even after the end of the relevant period.

(5) If subsection (2) is not complied with and the appeal is under section 103 or 108—

(a) the appeal must be taken to have been allowed by a decision of the High Court;

(b) the person whose extradition has been ordered must be taken to have been discharged by the High Court;

(c) the order for the person's extradition must be taken to have been quashed by the High Court.

(6) If subsection (2) is not complied with and the appeal is under section 105 or 110 the appeal must be taken to have been dismissed by a decision of the High Court.

**114  Appeal to [Supreme Court]**

(1)  An appeal lies to the [Supreme Court] from a decision of the High Court on an appeal under section 103, 105, 108 or 110.

(2)  An appeal under this section lies at the instance of—

(a)  the person whose extradition is requested;

(b)  a person acting on behalf of the category 2 territory.

(3)  An appeal under this section lies only with the leave of the High Court or the [Supreme Court].

(4)  Leave to appeal under this section must not be granted unless—

(a)  the High Court has certified that there is a point of law of general public importance involved in the decision, and

(b)  it appears to the court granting leave that the point is one which ought to be considered by the [Supreme Court].

(5)  An application to the High Court for leave to appeal under this section must be made before the end of the permitted period, which is 14 days starting with the day on which the court makes its decision on the appeal to it.

(6)  An application to the [Supreme Court] for leave to appeal under this section must be made before the end of the permitted period, which is 14 days starting with the day on which the High Court refuses leave to appeal.

(7)  If leave to appeal under this section is granted, the appeal must be brought before the end of the permitted period, which is 28 days starting with the day on which leave is granted.

(8)  If subsection (7) is not complied with—

(a)  the appeal must be taken to have been brought;

(b)  the appeal must be taken to have been dismissed by the [Supreme Court] immediately after the end of the period permitted under that subsection.

(9)  These must be ignored for the purposes of subsection (8)(b)—

(a)  any power of a court to extend the period permitted for bringing the appeal;

(b)  any power of a court to grant leave to take a step out of time.

[(10)  The High Court may grant bail to a person appealing under this section, or applying for leave to appeal under this section, against the dismissal of his appeal under section 103 or 108.]

(11)  Section 5 of the Appellate Jurisdiction Act 1876 (c. 59) (composition of House of Lords for hearing and determination of appeals) applies in relation to an appeal under this section or an application for leave to appeal under this section as it applies in relation to an appeal under that Act.

(12)  An order of the House of Lords which provides for an application for leave to appeal under this section to be determined by a committee constituted in accordance with section 5 of the Appellate Jurisdiction Act 1876 may direct that the decision of the committee is taken on behalf of the House.

(13)  The preceding provisions of this section do not apply to Scotland.

**115  Powers of [Supreme Court] on appeal under section 114**

(1)  On an appeal under section 114 the [Supreme Court] may—

(a)  allow the appeal;

(b)  dismiss the appeal.

(2)  Subsection (3) applies if—

(a)  the person whose extradition is requested brings an appeal under section 114, and

(b)  the [Supreme Court] allows the appeal.

(3) The [Supreme Court] must—

(a) order the person's discharge;

(b) quash the order for his extradition, if the appeal was against a decision of the High Court to dismiss an appeal under section 103 or 108 or to allow an appeal under section 110.

(4) Subsection (5) applies if—

(a) the High Court allows an appeal under section 103 or 108 by the person whose extradition is requested or dismisses an appeal under section 110 by a person acting on behalf of the category 2 territory,

(b) a person acting on behalf of the category 2 territory brings an appeal under section 114 against the decision of the High Court, and

(c) the [Supreme Court] allows the appeal.

(5) The [Supreme Court] must—

(a) quash the order discharging the person made by the High Court under section 104(5) or 109(5) or by the Secretary of State under this Part;

(b) order the person to be extradited to the category 2 territory.

(6) Subsection (7) applies if—

(a) the High Court dismisses an appeal under section 105 against a decision made by the judge at the extradition hearing,

(b) a person acting on behalf of the category 2 territory brings an appeal under section 114 against the decision of the High Court, and

(c) the [Supreme Court] allows the appeal.

(7) The [Supreme Court] must—

(a) quash the order of the judge discharging the person whose extradition is requested;

(b) remit the case to the judge;

(c) direct him to proceed as he would have been required to do if he had decided the relevant question differently at the extradition hearing.

(8) A question is the relevant question if the judge's decision on it resulted in the order for the person's discharge.

[(9) In a case where subsection (5) or (7) applies, the [Supreme Court] must remand, in custody or on bail, the person whose extradition is requested.

(10) If the [Supreme Court] remands the person in custody the High Court may later grant bail.]

**[115A Detention pending conclusion of certain appeals under section 114**

(1) This section applies if–

(a) on an appeal under section 103 or 108 the High Court orders the person's discharge;

(b) immediately after it does so, the court is informed on behalf of the category 2 territory of an intention to appeal under section 114.

(2) The court must remand the person in custody or on bail while the appeal is pending.

(3) If the court remands the person in custody it may later grant bail.

(4) An appeal under section 114 ceases to be pending at the earliest of these times–

(a) when the proceedings on the appeal are discontinued;

(b) at the end of the permitted period, which is 28 days starting with the day on which leave to appeal to the [Supreme Court] against the decision of the High Court on the appeal under section

103 or 108 is granted, if no appeal to the [Supreme Court] is brought before the end of that period;

(c) when there is no further step that can be taken on behalf of the category 2 territory in relation to the appeal (ignoring any power of a court to grant leave to take a step out of time).

(5) The preceding provisions of this section do not apply to Scotland.]

**116 Appeals: general**

A decision under this Part of the judge or the Secretary of State may be questioned in legal proceedings only by means of an appeal under this Part.

## Time for extradition

**117 Extradition where no appeal**

(1) This section applies if—

(a) the Secretary of State orders a person's extradition to a category 2 territory under this Part, and

(b) no notice of an appeal under section 103 or 108 is given before the end of the permitted period, which is 14 days starting with the day on which the Secretary of State informs the person under section 100(1) that he has ordered his extradition.

(2) The person must be extradited to the category 2 territory before the end of the required period, which is 28 days starting with the day on which the Secretary of State makes the order.

(3) If subsection (2) is not complied with and the person applies to the appropriate judge to be discharged the judge must order his discharge, unless reasonable cause is shown for the delay.

(4) These must be ignored for the purposes of subsection (1)(b)—

(a) any power of a court to extend the period permitted for giving notice of appeal;

(b) any power of a court to grant leave to take a step out of time.

**118 Extradition following appeal**

(1) This section applies if—

(a) there is an appeal to the High Court under section 103, 108 or 110 against a decision or order relating to a person's extradition to a category 2 territory, and

(b) the effect of the decision of the relevant court on the appeal is that the person is to be extradited there.

(2) The person must be extradited to the category 2 territory before the end of the required period, which is 28 days starting with—

(a) the day on which the decision of the relevant court on the appeal becomes final, or

(b) the day on which proceedings on the appeal are discontinued.

(3) The relevant court is—

(a) the High Court, if there is no appeal to the [Supreme Court] against the decision of the High Court on the appeal;

(b) the [Supreme Court], if there is such an appeal.

(4) The decision of the High Court on the appeal becomes final—

(a) when the period permitted for applying to the High Court for leave to appeal to the [Supreme Court] ends, if there is no such application;

(b) when the period permitted for applying to the [Supreme Court] for leave to appeal to it ends, if the High Court refuses leave to appeal and there is no application to the [Supreme Court] for leave to appeal;

(c)  when the [Supreme Court] refuses leave to appeal to it;

(d)  at the end of the permitted period, which is 28 days starting with the day on which leave to appeal to the [Supreme Court] is granted, if no such appeal is brought before the end of that period.

(5)  These must be ignored for the purposes of subsection (4)—

(a)  any power of a court to extend the period permitted for applying for leave to appeal;

(b)  any power of a court to grant leave to take a step out of time.

(6)  The decision of the [Supreme Court] on the appeal becomes final when it is made.

(7)  If subsection (2) is not complied with and the person applies to the appropriate judge to be discharged the judge must order his discharge, unless reasonable cause is shown for the delay.

(8)  The preceding provisions of this section apply to Scotland with these modifications—

(a)  in subsections (1) and (2) for "relevant court" substitute "High Court";

(b)  omit subsections (3) to (6).

## 119  Undertaking in relation to person serving sentence in United Kingdom

(1)  This section applies if—

(a)  the Secretary of State orders a person's extradition to a category 2 territory under this Part;

(b)  the person is serving a sentence of imprisonment or another form of detention in the United Kingdom [, either–]

[(i) in custody, or

(ii)  on licence.]

(2)  The Secretary of State may make the order for extradition subject to the condition that extradition is not to take place before he receives an undertaking given on behalf of the category 2 territory in terms specified by him.

(3)  The terms which may be specified by the Secretary of State in relation to a person [within subsection (1)(b)(i) who is] accused in a category 2 territory of the commission of an offence include terms—

(a)  that the person be kept in custody until the conclusion of the proceedings against him for the offence and any other offence in respect of which he is permitted to be dealt with in the category 2 territory;

(b)  that the person be returned to the United Kingdom to serve the remainder of his sentence on the conclusion of those proceedings.

[(3A) The terms which may be specified by the Secretary of State in relation to a person within subsection (1)(b)(ii) who is accused in a category 2 territory of the commission of an offence include terms that the person be returned to the United Kingdom to serve the remainder of his sentence after serving any sentence imposed on him in the category 2 territory for–

(a)  the offence, and

(b)  any other offence in respect of which he is permitted to be dealt with in the category 2 territory.]

(4)  The terms which may be specified by the Secretary of State in relation to a person alleged to be unlawfully at large after conviction of an offence by a court in a category 2 territory include terms that the person be returned to the United Kingdom to serve the remainder of his sentence after serving any sentence imposed on him in the category 2 territory for—

(a)  the offence, and

(b)  any other offence in respect of which he is permitted to be dealt with in the category 2 territory.

(5) Subsections (6) and (7) apply if the Secretary of State makes an order for extradition subject to a condition under subsection (2).

(6) If the Secretary of State does not receive the undertaking before the end of the period of 21 days starting with the day on which he makes the order and the person applies to the High Court to be discharged, the court must order his discharge.

(7) If the Secretary of State receives the undertaking before the end of that period—

(a) in a case where section 117 applies, the required period for the purposes of section 117(2) is 28 days starting with the day on which the Secretary of State receives the undertaking;

(b) in a case where section 118 applies, the required period for the purposes of section 118(2) is 28 days starting with the day on which the decision of the relevant court on the appeal becomes final (within the meaning of that section) or (if later) the day on which the Secretary of State receives the undertaking.

### 120 Extradition following deferral for competing claim

(1) This section applies if—

(a) an order is made under this Part for a person to be extradited to a category 2 territory in pursuance of a request for his extradition;

(b) before the person is extradited to the territory an order is made under section 126(2) or 179(2) for the person's extradition in pursuance of the request to be deferred;

(c) the appropriate judge makes an order under section 181(2) for the person's extradition in pursuance of the request to cease to be deferred.

(2) In a case where section 117 applies, the required period for the purposes of section 117(2) is 28 days starting with the day on which the order under section 181(2) is made.

(3) In a case where section 118 applies, the required period for the purposes of section 118(2) is 28 days starting with the day on which the decision of the relevant court on the appeal becomes final (within the meaning of that section) or (if later) the day on which the order under section 181(2) is made.

### 121 Asylum claim

(1) This section applies if—

(a) a person whose extradition is requested makes an asylum claim at any time in the relevant period;

(b) an order is made under this Part for the person to be extradited in pursuance of the request.

(2) The relevant period is the period—

(a) starting when a certificate is issued under section 70 in respect of the request;

(b) ending when the person is extradited in pursuance of the request.

(3) The person must not be extradited in pursuance of the request before the asylum claim is finally determined; and sections 117 and 118 have effect subject to this.

(4) If the Secretary of State allows the asylum claim, the claim is finally determined when he makes his decision on the claim.

(5) If the Secretary of State rejects the asylum claim, the claim is finally determined—

(a) when the Secretary of State makes his decision on the claim, if there is no right to appeal against the Secretary of State's decision on the claim;

(b) when the period permitted for appealing against the Secretary of State's decision on the claim ends, if there is such a right but there is no such appeal;

(c) when the appeal against that decision is finally determined or is withdrawn or abandoned, if there is such an appeal.

(6) An appeal against the Secretary of State's decision on an asylum claim is not finally determined for the purposes of subsection (5) at any time when a further appeal or an application for leave to bring a further appeal—

    (a) has been instituted and has not been finally determined or withdrawn or abandoned, or

    (b) may be brought.

(7) The remittal of an appeal is not a final determination for the purposes of subsection (6).

(8) The possibility of an appeal out of time with leave must be ignored for the purposes of subsections (5) and (6).

## Withdrawal of extradition request

### 122 Withdrawal of request before end of extradition hearing

(1) This section applies if at any time in the relevant period the appropriate judge is informed by the Secretary of State that a request for a person's extradition has been withdrawn.

(2) The relevant period is the period—

    (a) starting when the person first appears or is brought before the appropriate judge following his arrest under this Part;

    (b) ending when the judge orders the person's discharge or sends the case to the Secretary of State for his decision whether the person is to be extradited.

(3) The judge must order the person's discharge.

(4) If the person is not before the judge at the time the judge orders his discharge, the judge must inform him of the order as soon as practicable.

### 123 Withdrawal of request after case sent to Secretary of State

(1) This section applies if at any time in the relevant period the Secretary of State is informed that a request for a person's extradition has been withdrawn.

(2) The relevant period is the period—

    (a) starting when the judge sends the case to the Secretary of State for his decision whether the person is to be extradited;

    (b) ending when the person is extradited in pursuance of the request or discharged.

(3) The Secretary of State must order the person's discharge.

### 124 Withdrawal of request while appeal to High Court pending

(1) This section applies if at any time in the relevant period the High Court is informed by the Secretary of State that a request for a person's extradition has been withdrawn.

(2) The relevant period is the period—

    (a) starting when notice of an appeal to the court is given by the person whose extradition is requested or by a person acting on behalf of the category 2 territory to which his extradition is requested;

    (b) ending when proceedings on the appeal are discontinued or the court makes its decision on the appeal.

(3) If the appeal is under section 103 or 108, the court must—

    (a) order the person's discharge;

    (b) quash the order for his extradition, if the Secretary of State has ordered his extradition.

(4) If the appeal is under section 105 or 110, the court must dismiss the appeal.

(5) If the person is not before the court at the time the court orders his discharge, the court must inform him of the order as soon as practicable.

**125 Withdrawal of request while appeal to [Supreme Court] pending**

(1) This section applies if at any time in the relevant period the [Supreme Court] is informed by the Secretary of State that a request for a person's extradition has been withdrawn.

(2) The relevant period is the period—

(a) starting when leave to appeal to the [Supreme Court] is granted to the person whose extradition is requested or a person acting on behalf of the category 2 territory to which his extradition is requested;

(b) ending when proceedings on the appeal are discontinued or the [Supreme Court] makes its decision on the appeal.

(3) If the appeal is brought by the person whose extradition is requested the [Supreme Court] must—

(a) order the person's discharge;

(b) quash the order for his extradition, in a case where the appeal was against a decision of the High Court to dismiss an appeal under section 103 or 108.

(4) If the appeal is brought by a person acting on behalf of the category 2 territory the [Supreme Court] must dismiss the appeal.

(5) If the person whose extradition is requested is not before the [Supreme Court] at the time it orders his discharge, the [Supreme Court] must inform him of the order as soon as practicable.

## Competing extradition requests

**126 Competing extradition requests**

(1) This section applies if—

(a) the Secretary of State receives a valid request for a person's extradition to a category 2 territory;

(b) the person is in the United Kingdom;

(c) before the person is extradited in pursuance of the request or discharged, the Secretary of State receives another valid request for the person's extradition.

(2) The Secretary of State may—

(a) order proceedings (or further proceedings) on one of the requests to be deferred until the other one has been disposed of, if neither of the requests has been disposed of;

(b) order the person's extradition in pursuance of the request under consideration to be deferred until the other request has been disposed of, if an order for his extradition in pursuance of the request under consideration has been made.

(3) In applying subsection (2) the Secretary of State must take account in particular of these matters—

(a) the relative seriousness of the offences concerned;

(b) the place where each offence was committed (or was alleged to have been committed);

(c) the date when each request was received;

(d) whether, in the case of each offence, the person is accused of its commission (but not alleged to have been convicted) or is alleged to be unlawfully at large after conviction.

## Consent to extradition

**127 Consent to extradition: general**

(1) A person arrested under a warrant issued under section 71 may consent to his extradition to the category 2 territory to which his extradition is requested.

(2)  A person arrested under a provisional warrant may consent to his extradition to the category 2 territory in which he is accused of the commission of an offence or is alleged to have been convicted of an offence.

(3)  Consent under this section—

(a)  must be given in writing;

(b)  is irrevocable.

(4)  Consent under this section which is given by a person before his case is sent to the Secretary of State for the Secretary of State's decision whether he is to be extradited must be given before the appropriate judge.

(5)  Consent under this section which is given in any other case must be given to the Secretary of State.

(6)  A person may not give his consent under this section before the appropriate judge unless—

(a)  he is legally represented before the appropriate judge at the time he gives consent, or

(b)  he is a person to whom subsection (7) applies.

(7)  This subsection applies to a person if—

(a)  he has been informed of his right to apply for legal aid and has had the opportunity to apply for legal aid, but he has refused or failed to apply;

(b)  he has applied for legal aid but his application has been refused;

(c)  he was granted legal aid but the legal aid was withdrawn.

(8)  In subsection (7) "legal aid" means—

(a)  in England and Wales, a right to representation funded by the Legal Services Commission as part of the Criminal Defence Service;

(b)  in Scotland, such legal aid as is available by virtue of section 183(a) of this Act;

(c)  in Northern Ireland, such free legal aid as is available by virtue of sections 184 and 185 of this Act.

(9)  For the purposes of subsection (6) a person is to be treated as legally represented before the appropriate judge if (and only if) he has the assistance of counsel or a solicitor to represent him in the proceedings before the appropriate judge.

### 128  Consent to extradition before case sent to Secretary of State

(1)  This section applies if a person gives his consent under section 127 to the appropriate judge.

(2)  If the judge has not fixed a date under section 75 or 76 on which the extradition hearing is to begin he is not required to do so.

(3)  If the extradition hearing has begun the judge is no longer required to proceed or continue proceeding under sections 78 to 91.

(4)  The judge must send the case to the Secretary of State for his decision whether the person is to be extradited.

(5)  The person must be taken to have waived any right he would have (apart from the consent) not to be dealt with in the category 2 territory for an offence committed before his extradition.

## Post-extradition matters

### 129  Consent to other offence being dealt with

(1)  This section applies if—

(a)  a person is extradited to a category 2 territory in accordance with this Part;

(b) the Secretary of State receives a valid request for his consent to the person being dealt with in the territory for an offence other than the offence in respect of which he was extradited.

(2) A request for consent is valid if it is made by an authority which is an authority of the territory and which the Secretary of State believes has the function of making requests for the consent referred to in subsection (1)(b) in that territory.

(3) The Secretary of State must serve notice on the person that he has received the request for consent, unless he is satisfied that it would not be practicable to do so.

(4) The Secretary of State must decide whether the offence is an extradition offence.

(5) If the Secretary of State decides the question in subsection (4) in the negative he must refuse his consent.

(6) If the Secretary of State decides that question in the affirmative he must decide whether the appropriate judge would send the case to him (for his decision whether the person was to be extradited) under sections 79 to 91 if—

(a) the person were in the United Kingdom, and

(b) the judge were required to proceed under section 79 in respect of the offence for which the Secretary of State's consent is requested.

(7) If the Secretary of State decides the question in subsection (6) in the negative he must refuse his consent.

(8) If the Secretary of State decides that question in the affirmative he must decide whether, if the person were in the United Kingdom, his extradition in respect of the offence would be prohibited under section 94, 95 or 96.

(9) If the Secretary of State decides the question in subsection (8) in the affirmative he must refuse his consent.

(10) If the Secretary of State decides that question in the negative he may give his consent.

### 130 Consent to further extradition to category 2 territory

(1) This section applies if—

(a) a person is extradited to a category 2 territory (the requesting territory) in accordance with this Part;

(b) the Secretary of State receives a valid request for his consent to the person's extradition to another category 2 territory for an offence other than the offence in respect of which he was extradited.

(2) A request for consent is valid if it is made by an authority which is an authority of the requesting territory and which the Secretary of State believes has the function of making requests for the consent referred to in subsection (1)(b) in that territory.

(3) The Secretary of State must serve notice on the person that he has received the request for consent, unless he is satisfied that it would not be practicable to do so.

(4) The Secretary of State must decide whether the offence is an extradition offence in relation to the category 2 territory referred to in subsection (1)(b).

(5) If the Secretary of State decides the question in subsection (4) in the negative he must refuse his consent.

(6) If the Secretary of State decides that question in the affirmative he must decide whether the appropriate judge would send the case to him (for his decision whether the person was to be extradited) under sections 79 to 91 if—

(a) the person were in the United Kingdom, and

(b) the judge were required to proceed under section 79 in respect of the offence for which the Secretary of State's consent is requested.

(7) If the Secretary of State decides the question in subsection (6) in the negative he must refuse his consent.

(8) If the Secretary of State decides that question in the affirmative he must decide whether, if the person were in the United Kingdom, his extradition in respect of the offence would be prohibited under section 94, 95 or 96.

(9) If the Secretary of State decides the question in subsection (8) in the affirmative he must refuse his consent.

(10) If the Secretary of State decides that question in the negative he may give his consent.

### 131  Consent to further extradition to category 1 territory

(1) This section applies if—

(a) a person is extradited to a category 2 territory (the requesting territory) in accordance with this Part;

(b) the Secretary of State receives a valid request for his consent to the person's extradition to a category 1 territory for an offence other than the offence in respect of which he was extradited.

(2) A request for consent is valid if it is made by an authority which is an authority of the requesting territory and which the Secretary of State believes has the function of making requests for the consent referred to in subsection (1)(b) in that territory.

(3) The Secretary of State must serve notice on the person that he has received the request for consent, unless he is satisfied that it would not be practicable to do so.

(4) The Secretary of State must decide whether the offence is an extradition offence within the meaning given by section 64 in relation to the category 1 territory.

(5) If the Secretary of State decides the question in subsection (4) in the negative he must refuse his consent.

(6) If the Secretary of State decides that question in the affirmative he must decide whether the appropriate judge would order the person's extradition under sections 11 to 25 if—

(a) the person were in the United Kingdom, and

(b) the judge were required to proceed under section 11 in respect of the offence for which the Secretary of State's consent is requested.

(7) If the Secretary of State decides the question in subsection (6) in the affirmative he must give his consent.

(8) If the Secretary of State decides that question in the negative he must refuse his consent.

### [132 Return of person to serve remainder of sentence

(1) This section applies if—

(a) a person who is serving a sentence of imprisonment or another form of detention in the United Kingdom is extradited to a category 2 territory in accordance with this Part;

(b) the person is returned to the United Kingdom to serve the remainder of the sentence or the person otherwise returns to the United Kingdom.

(2) Time during which the person was outside the United Kingdom as a result of the extradition does not count as time served by the person as part of the sentence.

(3) But subsection (2) does not apply if—

(a) the person was extradited for the purpose of being prosecuted for an offence, and

(b) the person has not been convicted of the offence or of any other offence in respect of which the person was permitted to be dealt with in the category 2 territory.

(4) In a case falling within subsection (3), time during which the person was outside the United Kingdom as a result of the extradition counts as time served by the person as part of the sentence if (and only if) it was spent in custody in connection with the offence or any other offence in respect of which the person was permitted to be dealt with in the territory.

(5) In a case where the person is not entitled to be released from detention pursuant to the sentence—

(a) the person is liable to be detained in pursuance of the sentence, and

(b) if at large, the person must be treated as being unlawfully at large.

(6) In a case where the person is entitled to be released from detention on licence pursuant to the sentence—

(a) if the person was released on licence at the time of extradition, the licence is suspended until the person's return,

(b) if the person was not released on licence at that time, subsections (7) to (10) apply in relation to the person ("the offender").

(7) The offender is liable to be detained, on return, in any place in which the offender could have been detained pursuant to the sentence before the time of extradition.

(8) A constable or immigration officer may—

(a) take the offender into custody, and

(b) convey the offender to the place mentioned in subsection (7).

(9) The offender must be released on licence within the period of 5 days beginning when the offender is taken (or retaken) into custody under this section.

(10) In calculating a period of 5 days for the purposes of subsection (9) no account is to be taken of any day mentioned in any of paragraphs (a) to (d) of section 59(10).

(11) A person is entitled to be released from detention if there is—

(a) a duty to release the person under section 33(1), (1A) or (2) of the Criminal Justice Act 1991,

(b) a duty to release the person under section 244 of the Criminal Justice Act 2003 (other than temporarily on licence pursuant to an intermittent custody order under section 183(1)(b) of the Criminal Justice Act 2003),

(c) a duty to release the person under section 1, 1AA or 7(1) of the Prisoners and Criminal Proceedings (Scotland) Act 1993 or section 5, 11(2), 13, 19 or 23 of the Custodial Sentences and Weapons (Scotland) Act 2007, or

(d) a duty to release the person under section 1 of the Northern Ireland (Remission of Sentences) Act 1995, Article 26 of the Criminal Justice (Northern Ireland) Order 1996 or Article 17 or 18(8) of the Criminal Justice (Northern Ireland) Order 2008.

(12) The powers conferred on a constable by subsection (8) are exercisable in any part of the United Kingdom.

(13) An immigration officer is a person who is an immigration officer within the meaning of the Immigration Act 1971.]

## Costs

### 133  Costs where extradition ordered

(1) This section applies if any of the following occurs in relation to a person whose extradition is requested under this Part—

(a) an order for the person's extradition is made under this Part;

(b) the High Court dismisses an appeal under section 103 or 108;

(c) the High Court or the [Supreme Court] dismisses an application for leave to appeal to the [Supreme Court] under section 114, if the application is made by the person;

(d) the [Supreme Court] dismisses an appeal under section 114, if the appeal is brought by the person.

(2) In a case falling within subsection (1)(a), the appropriate judge may make such order as he considers just and reasonable with regard to the costs to be paid by the person.

(3) In a case falling within subsection (1)(b) by virtue of section 104(7), the judge who decides the question that is (or all the questions that are) the subject of a direction under section 104(1)(b) may make such order as he considers just and reasonable with regard to the costs to be paid by the person.

(4) In any other case falling within subsection (1)(b), the High Court may make such order as it considers just and reasonable with regard to the costs to be paid by the person.

(5) In a case falling within subsection (1)(c) or (d), the court by which the application or appeal is dismissed may make such order as it considers just and reasonable with regard to the costs to be paid by the person.

(6) An order for costs under this section—

(a) must specify their amount;

(b) may name the person to whom they are to be paid.

### 134 Costs where discharge ordered

(1) This section applies if any of the following occurs in relation to a person whose extradition to a category 2 territory is requested under this Part—

(a) an order for the person's discharge is made under this Part;

(b) the person is taken to be discharged under this Part;

(c) the High Court dismisses an appeal under section 105 or 110;

(d) the High Court or the [Supreme Court] dismisses an application for leave to appeal to the [Supreme Court] under section 114, if the application is made on behalf of the category 2 territory;

(e) the [Supreme Court] dismisses an appeal under section 114, if the appeal is brought on behalf of the category 2 territory.

(2) In a case falling within subsection (1)(a), an order under subsection (5) in favour of the person may be made by—

(a) the appropriate judge, if the order for the person's discharge is made by him or by the Secretary of State;

(b) the High Court, if the order for the person's discharge is made by it;

(c) the [Supreme Court], if the order for the person's discharge is made by it.

(3) In a case falling within subsection (1)(b), the appropriate judge may make an order under subsection (5) in favour of the person.

(4) In a case falling within subsection (1)(c), (d) or (e), the court by which the application or appeal is dismissed may make an order under subsection (5) in favour of the person.

(5) An order under this subsection in favour of a person is an order for a payment of the appropriate amount to be made to the person out of money provided by Parliament.

(6) The appropriate amount is such amount as the judge or court making the order under subsection (5) considers reasonably sufficient to compensate the person in whose favour the order is made for any expenses properly incurred by him in the proceedings under this Part.

(7) But if the judge or court making an order under subsection (5) is of the opinion that there are circumstances which make it inappropriate that the person in whose favour the order is made should recover the full amount mentioned in subsection (6), the judge or court must—

(a) assess what amount would in his or its opinion be just and reasonable;

(b) specify that amount in the order as the appropriate amount.

(8) Unless subsection (7) applies, the appropriate amount—

(a) must be specified in the order, if the court considers it appropriate for it to be so specified and the person in whose favour the order is made agrees the amount;

(b) must be determined in accordance with regulations made by the Lord Chancellor for the purposes of this section, in any other case.

### 135  Costs where discharge ordered: supplementary

(1) In England and Wales, subsections (1) and (3) of section 20 of the Prosecution of Offences Act 1985 (c. 23) (regulations for carrying Part 2 of that Act into effect) apply in relation to section 134 as those subsections apply in relation to Part 2 of that Act.

(2) As so applied those subsections have effect as if an order under section 134(5) were an order under Part 2 of that Act for a payment to be made out of central funds.

(3) In Northern Ireland, section 7 of the Costs in Criminal Cases Act (Northern Ireland) 1968 (c.10) (rules relating to costs) applies in relation to section 134 as that section applies in relation to sections 2 to 5 of that Act.

## Repatriation cases

### 136  Persons serving sentences outside territory where convicted

(1) This section applies if—

(a) a request is made for a person's extradition to a category 2 territory and the request contains the statement referred to in subsection (2), or

(b) a provisional warrant for a person's arrest is sought on behalf of a category 2 territory and the information laid before the justice contains the statement referred to in subsection (2).

(2) The statement is one that the person—

(a) is alleged to be unlawfully at large from a prison in one territory (the imprisoning territory) in which he was serving a sentence after conviction of an offence specified in the request by a court in another territory (the convicting territory), and

(b) was serving the sentence in pursuance of international arrangements for prisoners sentenced in one territory to be repatriated to another territory in order to serve their sentence.

(3) If the category 2 territory is either the imprisoning territory or the convicting territory—

(a) section 70(3) has effect as if the reference to the statement referred to in subsection (4) of that section were a reference to the statement referred to in subsection (2) of this section;

(b) section 73(1) has effect as if the reference to a person within subsection (2) of that section were a reference to the person referred to in subsection (1)(b) of this section.

(4) If the category 2 territory is the imprisoning territory—

(a) sections 71(2)(a), 73(3)(a) and 78(4)(b) have effect as if "an extradition offence" read "an extradition offence in relation to the convicting territory";

(b) sections 74(8)(a) and 127(2) have effect as if "the category 2 territory in which he is accused of the commission of an offence or is alleged to have been convicted of an offence" read "the imprisoning territory";

273

(c)  section 74(11)(b) has effect as if "the category 2 territory" read "the imprisoning territory";

(d)  section 78(2)(e) has effect as if "the category 2 territory" read "the convicting territory";

(e)  section 85(5) has effect as if after "entitled" there were inserted "in the convicting territory";

(f)  section 119(4) has effect as if "a category 2 territory" read "the convicting territory" and as if "the category 2 territory" in both places read "the convicting territory";

(g)  section 138(1) has effect as if "a category 2 territory" read "the convicting territory";

(h)  in section 138, subsections (2), (3), (4), (5) and (7) have effect as if "the category 2 territory" read "the convicting territory".

(5)  Subsection (1)(b) applies to Scotland with the substitution of "application by the procurator fiscal sets out the matters referred to in paragraphs (a) and (b) of subsection (2)" for "information laid by the justice contains the statement referred to in subsection (2)".

(6)  Subsection (1)(b) applies to Northern Ireland with the substitution of "the complaint made to" for "the information laid before".

## Interpretation

### 137  Extradition offences: person not sentenced for offence

(1)  This section applies in relation to conduct of a person if—

(a)  he is accused in a category 2 territory of the commission of an offence constituted by the conduct, or

(b)  he is alleged to be unlawfully at large after conviction by a court in a category 2 territory of an offence constituted by the conduct and he has not been sentenced for the offence.

(2)  The conduct constitutes an extradition offence in relation to the category 2 territory if these conditions are satisfied—

(a)  the conduct occurs in the category 2 territory;

(b)  the conduct would constitute an offence under the law of the relevant part of the United Kingdom punishable with imprisonment or another form of detention for a term of 12 months or a greater punishment if it occurred in that part of the United Kingdom;

(c)  the conduct is so punishable under the law of the category 2 territory (however it is described in that law).

(3)  The conduct also constitutes an extradition offence in relation to the category 2 territory if these conditions are satisfied—

(a)  the conduct occurs outside the category 2 territory;

(b)  the conduct is punishable under the law of the category 2 territory with imprisonment or another form of detention for a term of 12 months or a greater punishment (however it is described in that law);

(c)  in corresponding circumstances equivalent conduct would constitute an extra-territorial offence under the law of the relevant part of the United Kingdom punishable with imprisonment or another form of detention for a term of 12 months or a greater punishment.

(4)  The conduct also constitutes an extradition offence in relation to the category 2 territory if these conditions are satisfied—

(a)  the conduct occurs outside the category 2 territory and no part of it occurs in the United Kingdom;

(b)  the conduct would constitute an offence under the law of the relevant part of the United Kingdom punishable with imprisonment or another form of detention for a term of 12 months or a greater punishment if it occurred in that part of the United Kingdom;

(c)  the conduct is so punishable under the law of the category 2 territory (however it is described in that law).

(5) The conduct also constitutes an extradition offence in relation to the category 2 territory if these conditions are satisfied—

(a) the conduct occurs outside the category 2 territory and no part of it occurs in the United Kingdom;

(b) the conduct is punishable under the law of the category 2 territory with imprisonment for a term of 12 months or another form of detention or a greater punishment (however it is described in that law);

(c) the conduct constitutes or if committed in the United Kingdom would constitute an offence mentioned in subsection (6).

(6) The offences are—

(a) an offence under section 51 or 58 of the International Criminal Court Act 2001 (c. 17) (genocide, crimes against humanity and war crimes);

(b) an offence under section 52 or 59 of that Act (conduct ancillary to genocide etc. committed outside the jurisdiction);

(c) an ancillary offence, as defined in section 55 or 62 of that Act, in relation to an offence falling within paragraph (a) or (b);

(d) an offence under section 1 of the International Criminal Court (Scotland) Act 2001 (asp 13) (genocide, crimes against humanity and war crimes);

(e) an offence under section 2 of that Act (conduct ancillary to genocide etc. committed outside the jurisdiction);

(f) an ancillary offence, as defined in section 7 of that Act, in relation to an offence falling within paragraph (d) or (e).

(7) If the conduct constitutes an offence under the military law of the category 2 territory but does not constitute an offence under the general criminal law of the relevant part of the United Kingdom it does not constitute an extradition offence; and subsections (1) to (6) have effect subject to this.

(8) The relevant part of the United Kingdom is the part of the United Kingdom in which—

(a) the extradition hearing took place, if the question of whether conduct constitutes an extradition offence is to be decided by the Secretary of State;

(b) proceedings in which it is necessary to decide that question are taking place, in any other case.

(9) Subsections (1) to (7) apply for the purposes of this Part.

**138 Extradition offences: person sentenced for offence**

(1) This section applies in relation to conduct of a person if—

(a) he is alleged to be unlawfully at large after conviction by a court in a category 2 territory of an offence constituted by the conduct, and

(b) he has been sentenced for the offence.

(2) The conduct constitutes an extradition offence in relation to the category 2 territory if these conditions are satisfied—

(a) the conduct occurs in the category 2 territory;

(b) the conduct would constitute an offence under the law of the relevant part of the United Kingdom punishable with imprisonment or another form of detention for a term of 12 months or a greater punishment if it occurred in that part of the United Kingdom;

(c) a sentence of imprisonment or another form of detention for a term of 4 months or a greater punishment has been imposed in the category 2 territory in respect of the conduct.

(3) The conduct also constitutes an extradition offence in relation to the category 2 territory if these conditions are satisfied—

(a) the conduct occurs outside the category 2 territory;

(b) a sentence of imprisonment or another form of detention for a term of 4 months or a greater punishment has been imposed in the category 2 territory in respect of the conduct;

(c) in corresponding circumstances equivalent conduct would constitute an extra-territorial offence under the law of the relevant part of the United Kingdom punishable with imprisonment or another form of detention for a term of 12 months or a greater punishment.

(4) The conduct also constitutes an extradition offence in relation to the category 2 territory if these conditions are satisfied—

(a) the conduct occurs outside the category 2 territory and no part of it occurs in the United Kingdom;

(b) the conduct would constitute an offence under the law of the relevant part of the United Kingdom punishable with imprisonment or another form of detention for a term of 12 months or a greater punishment if it occurred in that part of the United Kingdom;

(c) a sentence of imprisonment or another form of detention for a term of 4 months or a greater punishment has been imposed in the category 2 territory in respect of the conduct.

(5) The conduct also constitutes an extradition offence in relation to the category 2 territory if these conditions are satisfied—

(a) the conduct occurs outside the category 2 territory and no part of it occurs in the United Kingdom;

(b) a sentence of imprisonment or another form of detention for a term of 4 months or a greater punishment has been imposed in the category 2 territory in respect of the conduct;

(c) the conduct constitutes or if committed in the United Kingdom would constitute an offence mentioned in subsection (6).

(6) The offences are—

(a) an offence under section 51 or 58 of the International Criminal Court Act 2001 (c. 17) (genocide, crimes against humanity and war crimes);

(b) an offence under section 52 or 59 of that Act (conduct ancillary to genocide etc. committed outside the jurisdiction);

(c) an ancillary offence, as defined in section 55 or 62 of that Act, in relation to an offence falling within paragraph (a) or (b);

(d) an offence under section 1 of the International Criminal Court (Scotland) Act 2001 (asp 13) (genocide, crimes against humanity and war crimes);

(e) an offence under section 2 of that Act (conduct ancillary to genocide etc. committed outside the jurisdiction);

(f) an ancillary offence, as defined in section 7 of that Act, in relation to an offence falling within paragraph (d) or (e).

(7) If the conduct constitutes an offence under the military law of the category 2 territory but does not constitute an offence under the general criminal law of the relevant part of the United Kingdom it does not constitute an extradition offence; and subsections (1) to (6) have effect subject to this.

(8) The relevant part of the United Kingdom is the part of the United Kingdom in which—

(a) the extradition hearing took place, if the question of whether conduct constitutes an extradition offence is to be decided by the Secretary of State;

(b) proceedings in which it is necessary to decide that question are taking place, in any other case.

(9) Subsections (1) to (7) apply for the purposes of this Part.

### 139 The appropriate judge

(1) The appropriate judge is—

(a) in England and Wales, a District Judge (Magistrates' Courts) designated for the purposes of this Part [by the Lord Chief Justice of England and Wales after consulting the Lord Chancellor];

(b)  in Scotland, the sheriff of Lothian and Borders;

(c)  in Northern Ireland, such county court judge or resident magistrate as is designated for the purposes of this Part by the [Lord Chief Justice of Northern Ireland after consulting the Lord Chancellor].

(2)  A designation under subsection (1) may be made for all cases or for such cases (or cases of such description) as the designation stipulates.

(3)  More than one designation may be made under subsection (1).

[(3A) The use of the expression "the judge" in a section containing a previous reference to "the appropriate judge" or "the judge" does not in itself require both references to be read as referring to the same individual.]

(4)  This section applies for the purposes of this Part.

[(5)  The Lord Chief Justice of England and Wales may nominate a judicial office holder (as defined in section 109(4) of the Constitutional Reform Act 2005) to exercise his functions under subsection (1)(a).

(6)  The Lord Chief Justice of Northern Ireland may nominate any of the following to exercise his functions under subsection (1)(c)–

(a)  the holder of one of the offices listed in Schedule 1 to the Justice (Northern Ireland) Act 2002;

(b)  a Lord Justice of Appeal (as defined in section 88 of that Act).]

### 140  The extradition hearing

(1)  The extradition hearing is the hearing at which the appropriate judge is to deal with a request for extradition to a category 2 territory.

(2)  This section applies for the purposes of this Part.

### [140A Unlawfully at large

(1)  A person is alleged to be unlawfully at large after conviction of an offence if–

(a)  he is alleged to have been convicted of it, and

(b)  his extradition is sought for the purpose of his being sentenced for the offence or of his serving a sentence of imprisonment or another form of detention imposed in respect of the offence.

(2)  This section applies for the purposes of this Part, other than sections 82 and 136.]

### 141  Scotland: references to Secretary of State

(1)  This Part applies in relation to any function which falls under this Part to be exercised in relation to Scotland only as if references in this Part to the Secretary of State were to the Scottish Ministers.

(2)  Subsection (1) does not apply to the references to the Secretary of State [in paragraph (b) of section 70(2), in paragraph (c) of section 93(4) and] in sections 83(3), 101(5) and 121.

## PART 3

# EXTRADITION TO THE UNITED KINGDOM

### Extradition from category 1 territories

#### 142  Issue of Part 3 warrant

(1)  The appropriate judge may issue a Part 3 warrant in respect of a person if—

    (a)  a constable or an appropriate person applies to the judge for a Part 3 warrant, and

    (b)  the condition in subsection (2) [, or the condition in subsection (2A),] is satisfied.

[(2)  The condition is that–

    (a)  there are reasonable grounds for believing that the person has committed an extradition offence, and

    (b)  a domestic warrant has been issued in respect of the person.

(2A)  The condition is that–

    (a)  there are reasonable grounds for believing that the person is unlawfully at large after conviction of an extradition offence by a court in the United Kingdom, and

    (b)  either a domestic warrant has been issued in respect of the person or the person may (if unlawfully at large as mentioned in paragraph (a)) be arrested without a warrant.]

(3)  A Part 3 warrant is an arrest warrant which contains—

    (a)  the statement referred to in subsection (4) or the statement referred to in subsection (5), and

    (b)  the certificate referred to in subsection (6).

(4)  The statement is one that—

    (a)  the person in respect of whom the warrant is issued is accused in the United Kingdom of the commission of an extradition offence specified in the warrant, and

    (b)  the warrant is issued with a view to his arrest and extradition to the United Kingdom for the purpose of being prosecuted for the offence.

(5)  The statement is one that—

    (a)  the person in respect of whom the warrant is issued [has been convicted] of an extradition offence specified in the warrant by a court in the United Kingdom, and

    (b)  the warrant is issued with a view to his arrest and extradition to the United Kingdom for the purpose of being sentenced for the offence or of serving a sentence of imprisonment or another form of detention imposed in respect of the offence.

(6)  The certificate is one certifying—

    (a)  whether the conduct constituting the extradition offence specified in the warrant falls within the European framework list;

    (b)  whether the offence is an extra-territorial offence;

    (c)  what is the maximum punishment that may be imposed on conviction of the offence or (if the person has been sentenced for the offence) what sentence has been imposed.

(7)  The conduct which falls within the European framework list must be taken for the purposes of subsection (6)(a) to include conduct which constitutes—

    (a)  an attempt, conspiracy or incitement to carry out conduct falling within the list, or

    (b)  aiding, abetting, counselling or procuring the carrying out of conduct falling within the list.

[(8) A domestic warrant is a warrant for the arrest or apprehension of a person which is issued under any of the provisions referred to in subsection (8A), or at common law by a Crown Court judge in Northern Ireland.

(8A) The provisions are–

(a) section 72 of the Criminal Justice Act 1967;

(b) section 7 of the Bail Act 1976;

(c) section 51 of the Judicature (Northern Ireland) Act 1978;

(d) section 1 of the Magistrates' Courts Act 1980;

(e) Article 20 or 25 of the Magistrates' Courts (Northern Ireland) Order 1981 (S.I. 1981/1675 (N.I. 26));

(f) the Criminal Procedure (Scotland) Act 1995.]

(9) An appropriate person is a person of a description specified in an order made by the Secretary of State for the purposes of this section.

(10) Subsection (1)(a) applies to Scotland with the substitution of "a procurator fiscal" for "a constable or an appropriate person".

**143** [...]

**144** [...]

### 145 Service of sentence in territory executing Part 3 warrant

(1) This section applies if—

(a) a Part 3 warrant is issued in respect of a person;

(b) the certificate contained in the warrant certifies that a sentence has been imposed;

(c) an undertaking is given on behalf of a category 1 territory that the person will be required to serve the sentence in the territory;

(d) on the basis of the undertaking the person is not extradited to the United Kingdom from the category 1 territory.

(2) The [sentence for the offence must be treated as served] but the person's conviction for the offence must be treated as a conviction for all other purposes.

### 146 Dealing with person for other offences

(1) This section applies if a person is extradited to the United Kingdom from a category 1 territory in pursuance of a Part 3 warrant.

(2) The person may be dealt with in the United Kingdom for an offence committed before his extradition only if—

(a) the offence is one falling within subsection (3), or

(b) the condition in subsection (4) is satisfied.

(3) The offences are—

(a) the offence in respect of which the person is extradited;

(b) an offence disclosed by the information provided to the category 1 territory in respect of that offence;

(c) an extradition offence in respect of which consent to the person being dealt with is given on behalf of the territory [in response to a request made by the appropriate judge];

(d) an offence which is not punishable with imprisonment or another form of detention;

(e) an offence in respect of which the person will not be detained in connection with his trial, sentence or appeal;

(f) an offence in respect of which the person waives the right that he would have (but for this paragraph) not to be dealt with for the offence.

(4) The condition is that the person has been given an opportunity to leave the United Kingdom and—

(a) he has not done so before the end of the permitted period, or

(b) he has done so before the end of the permitted period and has returned to the United Kingdom.

(5) The permitted period is 45 days starting with the day on which the person arrives in the United Kingdom.

### 147 Effect of consent to extradition to the United Kingdom

(1) This section applies if—

(a) a person is extradited to the United Kingdom from a category 1 territory in pursuance of a Part 3 warrant;

(b) the person consented to his extradition to the United Kingdom in accordance with the law of the category 1 territory.

(2) Section 146(2) does not apply if the conditions in subsection (3) or the conditions in subsection (4) are satisfied.

(3) The conditions are that—

(a) under the law of the category 1 territory, the effect of the person's consent is to waive his right under section 146(2);

(b) the person has not revoked his consent in accordance with that law, if he is permitted to do so under that law.

(4) The conditions are that—

(a) under the law of the category 1 territory, the effect of the person's consent is not to waive his right under section 146(2);

(b) the person has expressly waived his right under section 146(2) in accordance with that law;

(c) the person has not revoked his consent in accordance with that law, if he is permitted to do so under that law;

(d) the person has not revoked the waiver of his right under section 146(2) in accordance with that law, if he is permitted to do so under that law.

### 148 Extradition offences

(1) Conduct constitutes an extradition offence in relation to the United Kingdom if these conditions are satisfied—

(a) the conduct occurs in the United Kingdom;

(b) the conduct is punishable under the law of the relevant part of the United Kingdom with imprisonment or another form of detention for a term of 12 months or a greater punishment.

(2) Conduct also constitutes an extradition offence in relation to the United Kingdom if these conditions are satisfied—

(a) the conduct occurs outside the United Kingdom;

(b) the conduct constitutes an extra-territorial offence punishable under the law of the relevant part of the United Kingdom with imprisonment or another form of detention for a term of 12 months or a greater punishment.

(3) But subsections (1) and (2) do not apply in relation to conduct of a person if—

    (a) he [has been convicted] by a court in the United Kingdom of the offence constituted by the conduct, and

    (b) he has been sentenced for the offence.

(4) Conduct also constitutes an extradition offence in relation to the United Kingdom if these conditions are satisfied—

    (a) the conduct occurs in the United Kingdom;

    (b) a sentence of imprisonment or another form of detention for a term of 4 months or a greater punishment has been imposed in the United Kingdom in respect of the conduct.

(5) Conduct also constitutes an extradition offence in relation to the United Kingdom if these conditions are satisfied—

    (a) the conduct occurs outside the United Kingdom;

    (b) the conduct constitutes an extra-territorial offence;

    (c) a sentence of imprisonment or another form of detention for a term of 4 months or a greater punishment has been imposed in the United Kingdom in respect of the conduct.

(6) The relevant part of the United Kingdom is the part of the United Kingdom in which the relevant proceedings are taking place.

(7) The relevant proceedings are the proceedings in which it is necessary to decide whether conduct constitutes an extradition offence.

(8) Subsections (1) to (5) apply for the purposes of sections 142 to 147.

### 149 The appropriate judge

(1) The appropriate judge is—

    (a) in England and Wales, a District Judge (Magistrates' Courts), a justice of the peace or a judge entitled to exercise the jurisdiction of the Crown Court;

    (b) in Scotland, a sheriff;

    (c) in Northern Ireland, a justice of the peace, a resident magistrate or a Crown Court judge.

(2) This section applies for the purposes of sections 142 to 147.

## Extradition from category 2 territories

### 150 Dealing with person for other offences: Commonwealth countries etc.

(1) This section applies if—

    (a) a person is extradited to the United Kingdom from a category 2 territory under law of the territory corresponding to Part 2 of this Act, and

    (b) the territory is a Commonwealth country, a British overseas territory or the Hong Kong Special Administrative Region of the People's Republic of China.

(2) The person may be dealt with in the United Kingdom for an offence committed before his extradition only if—

    (a) the offence is one falling within subsection (3), or

    (b) the condition in subsection (6) is satisfied.

(3) The offences are—

    (a) the offence in respect of which the person is extradited;

(b) a lesser offence disclosed by the information provided to the category 2 territory in respect of that offence;

(c) an offence in respect of which consent to the person being dealt with is given by or on behalf of the relevant authority.

(4) An offence is a lesser offence in relation to another offence if the maximum punishment for it is less severe than the maximum punishment for the other offence.

(5) The relevant authority is—

(a) if the person has been extradited from a Commonwealth country, the government of the country;

(b) if the person has been extradited from a British overseas territory, the person

administering the territory;

(c) if the person has been extradited from the Hong Kong Special Administrative Region of the People's Republic of China, the government of the Region.

(6) The condition is that the protected period has ended.

(7) The protected period is 45 days starting with the first day after his extradition to the United Kingdom on which the person is given an opportunity to leave the United Kingdom.

(8) A person is dealt with in the United Kingdom for an offence if—

(a) he is tried there for it;

(b) he is detained with a view to trial there for it.

**151 [...]**

# General

**[151A Dealing with person for other offences**

(1) This section applies if a person is extradited to the United Kingdom from a territory which is not—

(a) a category 1 territory, or

(b) a territory falling within section 150(1)(b).

(2) The person may be dealt with in the United Kingdom for an offence committed before the person's extradition only if—

(a) the offence is one falling within subsection (3), or

(b) the condition in subsection (4) is satisfied.

(3) The offences are—

(a) the offence in respect of which the person is extradited;

(b) an offence disclosed by the information provided to the territory in respect of that offence;

(c) an offence in respect of which consent to the person being dealt with is given on behalf of the territory.

(4) The condition is that—

(a) the person has returned to the territory from which the person was extradited, or

(b) the person has been given an opportunity to leave the United Kingdom.

(5) A person is dealt with in the United Kingdom for an offence if—

(a) the person is tried there for it;

(b) the person is detained with a view to trial there for it.]

**152  Remission of punishment for other offences**

(1)  This section applies if—

    (a)  a person is extradited to the United Kingdom [from a territory;]

        (i)–(ii) […]

    (b)  before his extradition he has been convicted of an offence in the United Kingdom;

    (c)  he has not been extradited in respect of that offence.

(2)  The [sentence for the offence must be treated as served] but the person's conviction for the offence must be treated as a conviction for all other purposes.

**153  Return of person acquitted or not tried**

(1)  This section applies if—

    (a)  a person is accused in the United Kingdom of the commission of an offence;

    (b)  the person is extradited to the United Kingdom in respect of the offence [from a territory;]

        (i)–(ii) […]

    (c)  the condition in subsection (2) or the condition in subsection (3) is satisfied.

(2)  The condition is that—

    (a)  proceedings against the person for the offence are not begun before the end of the required period, which is 6 months starting with the day on which the person arrives in the United Kingdom on his extradition, and

    (b)  before the end of the period of 3 months starting immediately after the end of the required period the person asks the Secretary of State to return him to the territory from which he was extradited.

(3)  The condition is that—

    (a)  at his trial for the offence the person is acquitted or is discharged under any of the provisions specified in subsection (4), and

    (b)  before the end of the period of 3 months starting immediately after the date of his acquittal or discharge the person asks the Secretary of State to return him to the territory from which he was extradited.

(4)  The provisions are—

    (a)  section 12(1) of the Powers of Criminal Courts (Sentencing) Act 2000 (c. 6);

    (b)  section 246(1), (2) or (3) of the Criminal Procedure (Scotland) Act 1995 (c. 46);

    (c)  Article 4(1) of the Criminal Justice (Northern Ireland) Order 1996 (S.I. 1996/3160 (N.I. 24)).

(5)  The Secretary of State must arrange for him to be sent back, free of charge and with as little delay as possible, to the territory from which he was extradited to the United Kingdom in respect of the offence.

(6)  If the accusation in subsection (1)(a) relates to the commission of an offence in Scotland, subsections (2)(b), (3)(b) and (5) apply as if the references to the Secretary of State were references to the Scottish Ministers.

**[153A  Undertaking in relation to person serving sentence**

(1)  This section applies if—

    (a)  a person is accused in the United Kingdom of the commission of an offence or has been convicted of an offence by or before a court in the United Kingdom;

    (b)  a Part 3 warrant is issued in respect of the person or the Secretary of State makes a request for the extradition of the person;

(c)  the person is serving a sentence of imprisonment or another form of detention in a territory;

(d)  the person's extradition to the United Kingdom from the territory in pursuance of the warrant or request is made subject to a condition that an undertaking is given by or on behalf of the United Kingdom with regard to the person's treatment in the United Kingdom or return to the territory (or both).

(2)  The Secretary of State may give an undertaking to a person acting on behalf of the territory with regard to either or both of these things—

(a)  the treatment in the United Kingdom of the person in respect of whom the warrant is issued or the request for extradition is made;

(b)  the return of that person to the territory.

(3)  The terms which may be included by the Secretary of State in an undertaking given under subsection (2) in relation to a person accused in the United Kingdom of the commission of an offence include terms—

(a)  that the person be kept in custody until the conclusion of the proceedings against the person for the offence and any other offence in respect of which the person is permitted to be dealt with in the United Kingdom;

(b)  that the person be returned to the territory to serve the remainder of the sentence on the conclusion of those proceedings.

(4)  The terms which may be included by the Secretary of State in an undertaking given under subsection (2) in relation to a person who has been convicted of an offence by or before a court in the United Kingdom include terms that the person be returned to the territory to serve the remainder of the sentence after the person would otherwise be released from detention pursuant to the sentence imposed in the United Kingdom (whether or not on licence).

(5)  If a person is to be returned to a territory by virtue of an undertaking given under subsection (2), the undertaking is sufficient authority for a constable—

(a)  to remove the person from any prison or other institution where the person is detained;

(b)  to keep the person in custody until returned;

(c)  to convey the person to the territory.]

### [153B Return of person in pursuance of undertaking

(1)  This section applies if—

(a)  an undertaking is given under section 153A(2) as to the return of a person to a territory;

(b)  the person is returned to the territory in pursuance of the undertaking;

(c)  the person is returned to the United Kingdom to serve the remainder of any sentence imposed in the United Kingdom or the person otherwise returns to the United Kingdom.

(2)  Time during which the person was outside the United Kingdom as a result of the undertaking given under section 153A(2) does not count as time served by the person as part of the sentence.

(3)  If the person is not entitled to be released from detention pursuant to the sentence—

(a)  the person is liable to be detained in pursuance of the sentence, and

(b)  if at large, the person must be treated as being unlawfully at large.

(4)  If the person is entitled to be released from detention on licence pursuant to the sentence—

(a)  if the person was released on licence at the time of return to the territory, the licence is suspended until the person's return to the United Kingdom;

(b)  if the person was not released on licence at that time, subsections (5) to (8) apply in relation to the person ("the offender").

(5) The offender is liable to be detained, on return to the United Kingdom, in any place in which the offender could have been detained pursuant to the sentence before the time of return to the territory.

(6) A constable or immigration officer may—

(a) take the offender into custody, and

(b) convey the offender to the place mentioned in subsection (5).

(7) The offender must be released on licence within the period of 5 days beginning when the offender is taken (or retaken) into custody under this section.

(8) In calculating a period of 5 days for the purposes of subsection (7) no account is to be taken of any day mentioned in any of paragraphs (a) to (d) of section 59(10).

(9) The powers conferred on a constable by subsection (6) are exercisable in any part of the United Kingdom.

(10) For the purposes of this section—

(a) a person is entitled to be released from detention if there is—

(i) a duty to release the person under section 33(1), (1A) or (2) of the Criminal Justice Act 1991,

(ii) a duty to release the person under section 244 of the Criminal Justice Act 2003 (other than temporarily on licence pursuant to an intermittent custody order under section 183(1)(b) of the Criminal Justice Act 2003),

(iii) a duty to release the person under section 1, 1AA or 7(1) of the Prisoners and Criminal Proceedings (Scotland) Act 1993 or section 5, 11(2), 13, 19 or 23 of the Custodial Sentences and Weapons (Scotland) Act 2007, or

(iv) a duty to release the person under section 1 of the Northern Ireland (Remission of Sentences) Act 1995, Article 26 of the Criminal Justice (Northern Ireland) Order 1996 or Article 17 or 18(8) of the Criminal Justice (Northern Ireland) Order 2008;

(b) an immigration officer is a person who is an immigration officer within the meaning of the Immigration Act 1971.]

## [153C Return to extraditing territory to serve sentence

(1) This section applies if—

(a) a person is extradited to the United Kingdom from a territory for the purposes of being prosecuted for an offence;

(b) the person's extradition is made subject to a condition that an undertaking is given by or on behalf of the United Kingdom as to the person's return to the territory.

(2) The Secretary of State may give an undertaking to a person acting on behalf of the territory as to the person's return to the territory.

(3) The terms which may be included by the Secretary of State in an undertaking given under subsection (2) in relation to a person include terms that if the person is convicted of the offence and a sentence of imprisonment or another form of detention is imposed in respect of it, the person is to be returned to the territory to serve the sentence.

(4) A person who is to be returned to a territory by virtue of an undertaking given under subsection (2) must be returned as soon as is reasonably practicable after the sentence is imposed and any other proceedings in respect of the offence are concluded.

(5) If subsection (4) is complied with the sentence for the offence is treated as served but the person's conviction for the offence must be treated as a conviction for all other purposes.

(6) The sentence for the offence is treated as served under subsection (5) only in so far as it consists of the sentence of imprisonment or another form of detention mentioned in subsection (3).

(7) Subsection (8) applies if—

    (a) subsection (4) is not complied with, and

    (b) the person applies to the court which imposed the sentence to expedite return to the territory.

(8) The court must order return by such date as is specified in the order unless reasonable cause is shown for the delay.

(9) If a person is to be returned by virtue of an undertaking given under subsection (2), a constable may—

    (a) remove the person from any prison or other institution where the person is detained;

    (b) keep the person in custody until returned;

    (c) convey the person to the territory to which the person is to be returned.]

### [153D Sections 153A and 153C etc: supplementary

(1) Nothing in section 153A or 153C requires the return of a person to a territory in a case in which the Secretary of State is not satisfied that the return is compatible with the Convention rights within the meaning of the Human Rights Act 1998 or with the United Kingdom's obligations under the Refugee Convention.

(2) References in sections 153A and 153C and subsection (1) above to the Secretary of State are to be read as references to the Scottish Ministers in a case in which—

    (a) a Part 3 warrant was issued in respect of the person to be returned, and

    (b) the warrant was issued by a sheriff.

(3) The reference in subsection (1) to the Refugee Convention is to the Convention relating to the Status of Refugees done at Geneva on 28 July 1951 and the Protocol to the Convention.]

### 154 Restriction on bail where undertaking given by Secretary of State

(1) This section applies in relation to a person if—

    (a) the Secretary of State has given an undertaking in connection with the person's extradition to the United Kingdom, and

    (b) the undertaking includes terms that the person be kept in custody until the conclusion of any proceedings against him in the United Kingdom for an offence.

(2) A court, judge or justice of the peace may grant bail to the person in the proceedings only if the court, judge or justice of the peace considers that there are exceptional circumstances which justify it.

### 155 Service personnel

The Secretary of State may by order provide for the preceding provisions of this Part to have effect with specified modifications in relation to a case where the person whose extradition is sought or ordered is subject to [service law.]

### [155A Category 1 territories not applying framework decision to old cases

(1) This section applies to a category 1 territory that deals with European extradition requests otherwise than in accordance with the system provided for in the European framework decision if they relate to acts committed before a particular date ("the relevant date").

(2) In the case of a territory to which this section applies, the Secretary of State has the same powers to request a person's extradition in relation to acts committed before the relevant date as he would have in the case of a category 2 territory.

(3) The Secretary of State may by order provide that, in the case of an extradition request which–

(a) is made to a specified category 1 territory to which this section applies, and

(b) relates to acts committed before the relevant date,

this Part is to have effect as if that territory were a category 2 territory, and with such modifications as may be specified.

(4) In this section–

"European extradition request" means a request for extradition made by the United Kingdom or a category 1 territory;

"European framework decision" means the framework decision of the Council of the European Union made on 13 June 2002 on the European arrest warrant and the surrender procedures between member states (2002/584/JHA);

"specified", in relation to an order under this section, means specified in the order.]

# PART 4

# POLICE POWERS

## Warrants and orders

### 156 Search and seizure warrants

(1) A justice of the peace may, on an application made to him by a constable, issue a search and seizure warrant if he is satisfied that the requirements for the issue of a search and seizure warrant are fulfilled.

(2) The application for a search and seizure warrant must state that—

(a) the extradition of a person specified in the application is sought under Part 1 or Part 2;

(b) the warrant is sought in relation to premises specified in the application;

(c) the warrant is sought in relation to material, or material of a description, specified in the application;

(d) that material, or material of that description, is believed to be on the premises.

(3) If the application states that the extradition of the person is sought under Part 1, the application must also state that the person is accused in a category 1 territory specified in the application of the commission of an offence—

(a) which is specified in the application, and

(b) which is an extradition offence within the meaning given by section 64.

(4) If the application states that the extradition of the person is sought under Part 2, the application must also state that the person is accused in a category 2 territory specified in the application of the commission of an offence—

(a) which is specified in the application, and

(b) which is an extradition offence within the meaning given by section 137.

(5) A search and seizure warrant is a warrant authorising a constable—

(a) to enter and search the premises specified in the application for the warrant, and

(b) to seize and retain any material found there which falls within subsection (6).

(6) Material falls within this subsection if—

(a) it would be likely to be admissible evidence at a trial in the relevant part of the United Kingdom for the offence specified in the application for the warrant (on the assumption that conduct constituting that offence would constitute an offence in that part of the United Kingdom), and

(b) it does not consist of or include items subject to legal privilege, excluded material or special procedure material.

(7) The relevant part of the United Kingdom is the part of the United Kingdom where the justice of the peace exercises jurisdiction.

(8) The requirements for the issue of a search and seizure warrant are that there are reasonable grounds for believing that—

(a) the offence specified in the application has been committed by the person so specified;

(b) the person is in the United Kingdom or is on his way to the United Kingdom;

(c) the offence is an extradition offence within the meaning given by section 64 (if subsection (3) applies) or section 137 (if subsection (4) applies);

(d) there is material on premises specified in the application which falls within subsection (6);

(e) any of the conditions referred to in subsection (9) is satisfied.

(9) The conditions are—

(a) that it is not practicable to communicate with a person entitled to grant entry to the premises;

(b) that it is practicable to communicate with a person entitled to grant entry to the premises but it is not practicable to communicate with a person entitled to grant access to the material referred to in subsection (8)(d);

(c) that entry to the premises will not be granted unless a warrant is produced;

(d) that the purpose of a search may be frustrated or seriously prejudiced unless a constable arriving at the premises can secure immediate entry to them.

(10) The preceding provisions of this section apply to Scotland with these modifications—

(a) in subsections (1) and (7) for "justice of the peace" substitute "sheriff";

(b) in subsection (1) for "constable" substitute "procurator fiscal";

(c) for "search and seizure warrant" substitute "warrant to search";

(d) in subsection (6)(b) omit the words ", excluded material or special procedure material";

(e) subsections (8)(e) and (9) are omitted.

### 157 Production orders

(1) A judge may, on an application made to him by a constable, make a production order if he is satisfied that the requirements for the making of a production order are fulfilled.

(2) The application for a production order must state that—

(a) the extradition of a person specified in the application is sought under Part 1 or Part 2;

(b) the order is sought in relation to premises specified in the application;

(c) the order is sought in relation to material, or material of a description, specified in the application;

(d) the material is special procedure material or excluded material;

(e) a person specified in the application appears to be in possession or control of the material.

(3) If the application states that the extradition of the person is sought under Part 1, the application must also state that the person is accused in a category 1 territory specified in the application of the commission of an offence—

(a) which is specified in the application, and

(b) which is an extradition offence within the meaning given by section 64.

(4)  If the application states that the extradition of the person is sought under Part 2, the application must also state that the person is accused in a category 2 territory specified in the application of the commission of an offence—

(a)  which is specified in the application, and

(b)  which is an extradition offence within the meaning given by section 137.

(5)  A production order is an order either—

(a)  requiring the person the application for the order specifies as appearing to be in possession or control of special procedure material or excluded material to produce it to a constable (within the period stated in the order) for him to take away, or

(b)  requiring that person to give a constable access to the special procedure material or excluded material within the period stated in the order.

(6)  The period stated in a production order must be a period of 7 days starting with the day on which the order is made, unless it appears to the judge by whom the order is made that a longer period would be appropriate.

(7)  Production orders have effect as if they were orders of the court.

(8)  In this section "judge"—

(a)  in England and Wales, means a circuit judge;

(b)  in Northern Ireland, means a Crown Court judge.

### 158  Requirements for making of production order

(1)  These are the requirements for the making of a production order.

(2)  There must be reasonable grounds for believing that—

(a)  the offence specified in the application has been committed by the person so specified;

(b)  the person is in the United Kingdom or is on his way to the United Kingdom;

(c)  the offence is an extradition offence within the meaning given by section 64 (if section 157(3) applies) or section 137 (if section 157(4) applies);

(d)  there is material which consists of or includes special procedure material or excluded material on premises specified in the application;

(e)  the material would be likely to be admissible evidence at a trial in the relevant part of the United Kingdom for the offence specified in the application (on the assumption that conduct constituting that offence would constitute an offence in that part of the United Kingdom).

(3)  The relevant part of the United Kingdom is the part of the United Kingdom where the judge exercises jurisdiction.

(4)  It must appear that other methods of obtaining the material—

(a)  have been tried without success, or

(b)  have not been tried because they were bound to fail.

(5)  It must be in the public interest that the material should be produced or that access to it should be given.

### 159  Computer information

(1)  This section applies if any of the special procedure material or excluded material specified in an application for a production order consists of information stored in any electronic form.

(2)  If the order is an order requiring a person to produce the material to a constable for him to take away, it has effect as an order to produce the material in a form—

(a)  in which it can be taken away by him;

(b)  in which it is visible and legible or from which it can readily be produced in a visible and legible form.

(3)  If the order is an order requiring a person to give a constable access to the material, it has effect as an order to give him access to the material in a form—

(a)  in which it is visible and legible, or

(b)  from which it can readily be produced in a visible and legible form.

### 160  Warrants: special procedure material and excluded material

(1)  A judge may, on an application made to him by a constable, issue a warrant under this section if he is satisfied that—

(a)  the requirements for the making of a production order are fulfilled, and

(b)  the further requirement for the issue of a warrant under this section is fulfilled.

(2)  The application for a warrant under this section must state that—

(a)  the extradition of a person specified in the application is sought under Part 1 or Part 2;

(b)  the warrant is sought in relation to premises specified in the application;

(c)  the warrant is sought in relation to material, or material of a description, specified in the application;

(d)  the material is special procedure material or excluded material.

(3)  If the application states that the extradition of the person is sought under Part 1, the application must also state that the person is accused in a category 1 territory specified in the application of the commission of an offence—

(a)  which is specified in the application, and

(b)  which is an extradition offence within the meaning given by section 64.

(4)  If the application states that the extradition of the person is sought under Part 2, the application must also state that the person is accused in a category 2 territory specified in the application of the commission of an offence—

(a)  which is specified in the application, and

(b)  which is an extradition offence within the meaning given by section 137.

(5)  A warrant under this section authorises a constable to enter and search the premises specified in the application for the warrant and—

(a)  to seize and retain any material found there which falls within subsection (6) and which is special procedure material, if the application for the warrant states that the warrant is sought in relation to special procedure material;

(b)  to seize and retain any material found there which falls within subsection (6) and which is excluded material, if the application for the warrant states that the warrant is sought in relation to excluded material.

(6)  Material falls within this subsection if it would be likely to be admissible evidence at a trial in the relevant part of the United Kingdom for the offence specified in the application for the warrant (on the assumption that conduct constituting that offence would constitute an offence in that part of the United Kingdom).

(7)  The relevant part of the United Kingdom is the part of the United Kingdom where the judge exercises jurisdiction.

(8)  The further requirement for the issue of a warrant under this section is that any of these conditions is satisfied—

(a)  it is not practicable to communicate with a person entitled to grant entry to the premises;

(b)  it is practicable to communicate with a person entitled to grant entry to the premises but it is not practicable to communicate with a person entitled to grant access to the material referred to in section 158(2)(d);

(c) the material contains information which is subject to a restriction on disclosure or an obligation of secrecy contained in an enactment (including one passed after this Act) and is likely to be disclosed in breach of the restriction or obligation if a warrant is not issued.

(9) In this section "judge"—

(a) in England and Wales, means a circuit judge;

(b) in Northern Ireland, means a Crown Court judge.

## Search and seizure without warrant

### 161 Entry and search of premises for purposes of arrest

(1) This section applies if a constable has power to arrest a person under an extradition arrest power.

(2) A constable may enter and search any premises for the purpose of exercising the power of arrest if he has reasonable grounds for believing that the person is on the premises.

(3) The power to search conferred by subsection (2) is exercisable only to the extent that is reasonably required for the purpose of exercising the power of arrest.

(4) A constable who has entered premises in exercise of the power conferred by subsection (2) may seize and retain anything which is on the premises if he has reasonable grounds for believing—

(a) that it has been obtained in consequence of the commission of an offence or it is evidence in relation to an offence, and

(b) that it is necessary to seize it in order to prevent it being concealed, lost, damaged, altered or destroyed.

(5) An offence includes an offence committed outside the United Kingdom.

(6) If the premises contain 2 or more separate dwellings, the power conferred by subsection (2) is a power to enter and search only—

(a) any parts of the premises which the occupiers of any dwelling comprised in the premises use in common with the occupiers of any other dwelling comprised in the premises, and

(b) any dwelling comprised in the premises in which the constable has reasonable grounds for believing that the person may be.

### 162 Entry and search of premises on arrest

(1) This section applies if a person has been arrested under an extradition arrest power at a place other than a police station.

(2) A constable may enter and search any premises in which the person was at the time of his arrest or immediately before his arrest if he has reasonable grounds for believing—

(a) if the person has not been convicted of the relevant offence, that there is on the premises evidence (other than items subject to legal privilege) relating to the relevant offence;

(b) in any case, that there is on the premises evidence (other than items subject to legal privilege) relating to the identity of the person.

(3) The relevant offence is the offence—

(a) referred to in the Part 1 warrant, if the arrest was under a Part 1 warrant;

(b) in respect of which the constable has reasonable grounds for believing that a Part 1 warrant has been or will be issued, if the arrest was under section 5;

(c) in respect of which extradition is requested, if the arrest was under a warrant issued under section 71;

(d) of which the person is accused, if the arrest was under a provisional warrant.

(4) The power to search conferred by subsection (2)—

(a) if the person has not been convicted of the relevant offence, is a power to search for evidence (other than items subject to legal privilege) relating to the relevant offence;

(b) in any case, is a power to search for evidence (other than items subject to legal privilege) relating to the identity of the person.

(5) The power to search conferred by subsection (2) is exercisable only to the extent that it is reasonably required for the purpose of discovering evidence in respect of which the power is available by virtue of subsection (4).

(6) A constable may seize and retain anything for which he may search by virtue of subsections (4) and (5).

(7) A constable who has entered premises in exercise of the power conferred by subsection (2) may seize and retain anything which is on the premises if he has reasonable grounds for believing—

(a) that it has been obtained in consequence of the commission of an offence or it is evidence in relation to an offence, and

(b) that it is necessary to seize it in order to prevent it being concealed, lost, damaged, altered or destroyed.

(8) An offence includes an offence committed outside the United Kingdom.

(9) If the premises contain 2 or more separate dwellings, the power conferred by subsection (2) is a power to enter and search only—

(a) any dwelling in which the arrest took place or in which the person was immediately before his arrest, and

(b) any parts of the premises which the occupier of any such dwelling uses in common with the occupiers of any other dwelling comprised in the premises.

### 163  Search of person on arrest

(1) This section applies if a person has been arrested under an extradition arrest power at a place other than a police station.

(2) A constable may search the person if he has reasonable grounds for believing that the person may present a danger to himself or others.

(3) A constable may search the person if he has reasonable grounds for believing that the person may have concealed on him anything—

(a) which he might use to assist him to escape from lawful custody;

(b) which might be evidence relating to an offence or to the identity of the person.

(4) The power to search conferred by subsection (3)—

(a) is a power to search for anything falling within paragraph (a) or (b) of that subsection;

(b) is exercisable only to the extent that is reasonably required for the purpose of discovering such a thing.

(5) The powers conferred by subsections (2) and (3)—

(a) do not authorise a constable to require a person to remove any of his clothing in public, other than an outer coat, jacket or gloves;

(b) authorise a search of a person's mouth.

(6) A constable searching a person in exercise of the power conferred by subsection (2) may seize and retain anything he finds, if he has reasonable grounds for believing that the person searched might use it to cause physical injury to himself or to any other person.

(7) A constable searching a person in exercise of the power conferred by subsection (3) may seize and retain anything he finds if he has reasonable grounds for believing—

(a) that the person might use it to assist him to escape from lawful custody;

(b) that it is evidence of an offence or of the identity of the person or has been obtained in consequence of the commission of an offence.

(8) An offence includes an offence committed outside the United Kingdom.

(9) Nothing in this section affects the power conferred by section 43 of the Terrorism Act 2000 (c. 11).

**164 Entry and search of premises after arrest**

(1) This section applies if a person has been arrested under an extradition arrest power.

(2) A constable may enter and search any premises occupied or controlled by the person if the constable has reasonable grounds for suspecting—

(a) if the person has not been convicted of the relevant offence, that there is on the premises evidence (other than items subject to legal privilege) relating to the relevant offence;

(b) in any case, that there is on the premises evidence (other than items subject to legal privilege) relating to the identity of the person.

(3) The relevant offence is the offence—

(a) referred to in the Part 1 warrant, if the arrest was under a Part 1 warrant;

(b) in respect of which the constable has reasonable grounds for believing that a Part 1 warrant has been or will be issued, if the arrest was under section 5;

(c) in respect of which extradition is requested, if the arrest was under a warrant issued under section 71;

(d) of which the person is accused, if the arrest was under a provisional warrant.

(4) The power to search conferred by subsection (2)—

(a) if the person has not been convicted of the relevant offence, is a power to search for evidence (other than items subject to legal privilege) relating to the relevant offence;

(b) in any case, is a power to search for evidence (other than items subject to legal privilege) relating to the identity of the person.

(5) The power to search conferred by subsection (2) is exercisable only to the extent that it is reasonably required for the purpose of discovering evidence in respect of which the power is available by virtue of subsection (4).

(6) A constable may seize and retain anything for which he may search by virtue of subsections (4) and (5).

(7) A constable who has entered premises in exercise of the power conferred by subsection (2) may seize and retain anything which is on the premises if he has reasonable grounds for believing—

(a) that it has been obtained in consequence of the commission of an offence or it is evidence in relation to an offence, and

(b) that it is necessary to seize it in order to prevent it being concealed, lost, damaged, altered or destroyed.

(8) An offence includes an offence committed outside the United Kingdom.

(9) The powers conferred by subsections (2) and (6) may be exercised only if a police officer of the rank of inspector or above has given written authorisation for their exercise.

(10) But the power conferred by subsection (2) may be exercised without authorisation under subsection (9) if—

(a) it is exercised before the person arrested is taken to a police station, and

(b) the presence of the person at a place other than a police station is necessary for the effective exercise of the power to search.

(11) Subsections (9) and (10) do not apply to Scotland.

### 165 Additional seizure powers

(1) The Criminal Justice and Police Act 2001 (c. 16) is amended as follows.

(2) In Part 1 of Schedule 1 (powers of seizure to which section 50 of that Act applies) at the end add—

"73D Extradition Act 2003 (c. 41)

The powers of seizure conferred by sections 156(5), 160(5), 161(4), 162(6) and (7) and 164(6) and (7) of the Extradition Act 2003 (seizure in connection with extradition)."

(3) In Part 2 of Schedule 1 (powers of seizure to which section 51 of that Act applies) at the end add—

"83A Extradition Act 2003 (c. 41)

The powers of seizure conferred by section 163(6) and (7) of the Extradition Act 2003 (seizure in connection with extradition)."

## Treatment following arrest

### 166 Fingerprints and samples

(1) This section applies if a person has been arrested under an extradition arrest power and is detained at a police station.

(2) Fingerprints may be taken from the person only if they are taken by a constable—

    (a) with the appropriate consent given in writing, or

    (b) without that consent, under subsection (4).

(3) A non-intimate sample may be taken from the person only if it is taken by a constable—

    (a) with the appropriate consent given in writing, or

    (b) without that consent, under subsection (4).

(4) Fingerprints or a non-intimate sample may be taken from the person without the appropriate consent only if a police officer of at least the rank of inspector authorises the fingerprints or sample to be taken.

### 167 Searches and examination

(1) This section applies if a person has been arrested under an extradition arrest power and is detained at a police station.

(2) If a police officer of at least the rank of inspector authorises it, the person may be searched or examined, or both, for the purpose of facilitating the ascertainment of his identity.

(3) An identifying mark found on a search or examination under this section may be photographed—

    (a) with the appropriate consent, or

    (b) without the appropriate consent, if that consent is withheld or it is not practicable to obtain it.

(4) The only persons entitled to carry out a search or examination, or take a photograph, under this section are—

    (a) constables;

    (b) persons designated for the purposes of this section by the appropriate police officer.

(5) A person may not under this section—

    (a) carry out a search or examination of a person of the opposite sex;

    (b) take a photograph of any part of the body (other than the face) of a person of the opposite sex.

(6) An intimate search may not be carried out under this section.

(7) Ascertaining a person's identity includes showing that he is not a particular person.

(8) Taking a photograph includes using a process by means of which a visual image may be produced; and photographing a person must be construed accordingly.

(9) Mark includes features and injuries and a mark is an identifying mark if its existence in a person's case facilitates the ascertainment of his identity.

(10) The appropriate police officer is—

(a) in England and Wales, the chief officer of police for the police area in which the police station in question is situated;

(b) in Northern Ireland, the Chief Constable of the Police Service of Northern Ireland.

## 168 Photographs

(1) This section applies if a person has been arrested under an extradition arrest power and is detained at a police station.

(2) The person may be photographed—

(a) with the appropriate consent, or

(b) without the appropriate consent, if that consent is withheld or it is not practicable to obtain it.

(3) A person proposing to take a photograph of a person under this section—

(a) may for the purpose of doing so require the removal of any item or substance worn on or over the whole or any part of the head or face of the person to be photographed, and

(b) if the requirement is not complied with may remove the item or substance himself.

(4) The only persons entitled to take a photograph under this section are—

(a) constables;

(b) persons designated for the purposes of this section by the appropriate police officer.

(5) Taking a photograph includes using a process by means of which a visual image may be produced; and photographing a person must be construed accordingly.

(6) The appropriate police officer is—

(a) in England and Wales, the chief officer of police for the police area in which the police station in question is situated;

(b) in Northern Ireland, the Chief Constable of the Police Service of Northern Ireland.

## 169 Evidence of identity: England and Wales

(1) The Police and Criminal Evidence Act 1984 (c. 60) is amended as follows.

(2) In section 54A (searches and examination to ascertain identity) at the end insert—

"(13) Nothing in this section applies to a person arrested under an extradition arrest power."

(3) In section 61 (fingerprinting) at the end insert—

"(10) Nothing in this section applies to a person arrested under an extradition arrest power."

(4) In section 63 (non-intimate samples) at the end insert—

"(11) Nothing in this section applies to a person arrested under an extradition arrest power."

(5) In section 64A (photographing of suspects etc.) at the end insert—

"(7) Nothing in this section applies to a person arrested under an extradition arrest power."

(6) In section 65 (interpretation of Part 5) after the definition of "drug trafficking" and "drug trafficking offence" insert—

""extradition arrest power" means any of the following—

(a) a Part 1 warrant (within the meaning given by the Extradition Act 2003) in respect of which a certificate under section 2 of that Act has been issued;

(b) section 5 of that Act;

(c) a warrant issued under section 71 of that Act;

(d) a provisional warrant (within the meaning given by that Act)."

### 170  Evidence of identity: Northern Ireland

(1) The Police and Criminal Evidence (Northern Ireland) Order 1989 (S.I. 1989/1341 (N.I. 12)) is amended as follows.

(2) In Article 55A (searches and examination to ascertain identity) at the end insert—

"(13) Nothing in this Article applies to a person arrested under an extradition arrest power."

(3) In Article 61 (fingerprinting) at the end insert—

"(10) Nothing in this Article applies to a person arrested under an extradition arrest power."

(4) In Article 63 (non-intimate samples) at the end insert—

"(12) Nothing in this Article applies to a person arrested under an extradition arrest power."

(5) In Article 64A (photographing of suspects etc.) at the end insert—

"(7) Nothing in this Article applies to a person arrested under an extradition arrest power."

(6) In Article 53 (interpretation) after the definition of "drug trafficking" and "drug trafficking offence" insert—

""extradition arrest power" means any of the following—

(a) a Part 1 warrant (within the meaning given by the Extradition Act 2003) in respect of which a certificate under section 2 of that Act has been issued;

(b) section 5 of that Act;

(c) a warrant issued under section 71 of that Act;

(d) a provisional warrant (within the meaning given by that Act)."

### 171  Other treatment and rights

(1) This section applies in relation to cases where a person—

(a) is arrested under an extradition arrest power at a police station;

(b) is taken to a police station after being arrested elsewhere under an extradition arrest power;

(c) is detained at a police station after being arrested under an extradition arrest power.

(2) In relation to those cases the Secretary of State may by order apply the provisions mentioned in sub-sections (3) and (4) with specified modifications.

(3) The provisions are these provisions of the Police and Criminal Evidence Act 1984 (c. 60)—

(a) section 54 (searches of detained persons);

(b) section 55 (intimate searches);

(c) section 56 (right to have someone informed when arrested);

(d) section 58 (access to legal advice).

(4) The provisions are these provisions of the Police and Criminal Evidence (Northern Ireland) Order 1989 (S.I. 1989/1341 (N.I. 12))—

(a) Article 55 (searches of detained persons);

(b) Article 56 (intimate searches);

(c) Article 57 (right to have someone informed when arrested);

(d) Article 59 (access to legal advice).

## Delivery of seized property

**172 Delivery of seized property**

(1) This section applies to—

(a) anything which has been seized or produced under this Part, or

(b) anything which has been seized under section 50 or 51 of the Criminal Justice and Police Act 2001 (c. 16) in reliance on a power of seizure conferred by this Part.

(2) A constable may deliver any such thing to a person who is or is acting on behalf of an authority if the constable has reasonable grounds for believing that the authority—

(a) is an authority of the relevant territory, and

(b) has functions such that it is appropriate for the thing to be delivered to it.

(3) If the relevant seizure power was a warrant issued under this Part, or the thing was produced under an order made under this Part, the relevant territory is the category 1 or category 2 territory specified in the application for the warrant or order.

(4) If the relevant seizure power was section 161(4), 162(6) or (7), 163(6) or (7) or 164(6) or (7), the relevant territory is—

(a) the territory in which the Part 1 warrant was issued, in a case where the applicable extradition arrest power is a Part 1 warrant in respect of which a certificate under section 2 has been issued;

(b) the territory in which a constable has reasonable grounds for believing that a Part 1 warrant has been or will be issued, in a case where the applicable extradition arrest power is section 5;

(c) the territory to which a person's extradition is requested, in a case where the applicable extradition arrest power is a warrant issued under section 71;

(d) the territory in which a person is accused of the commission of an offence or has been convicted of an offence, in a case where the applicable extradition arrest power is a provisional warrant.

(5) The applicable extradition arrest power is—

(a) the extradition arrest power under which a constable had a power of arrest, if the relevant seizure power was section 161(4);

(b) the extradition arrest power under which a person was arrested, if the relevant seizure power was section 162(6) or (7), 163(6) or (7) or 164(6) or (7).

(6) The relevant seizure power is—

(a) the power under which the thing was seized, or

(b) the power in reliance on which the thing was seized under section 50 or 51 of the Criminal Justice and Police Act 2001 (c. 16).

(7) Subsection (1)(a) applies to Scotland with the insertio after "Part" of "(so far as it applies to Scotland) or for the purposes of this Act (as it so applies) by virtue of any enactment or rule of law".

(8) Subsection (2) applies to Scotland with the substitution of "procurator fiscal" for "constable".

(9) In subsection (7) "enactment" includes an enactment comprised in, or in an instrument made under, an Act of the Scottish Parliament.

## Codes of practice

**173 Codes of practice**

(1) The Secretary of State must issue codes of practice in connection with—

    (a) the exercise of the powers conferred by this Part;

    (b) the retention, use and return of anything seized or produced under this Part;

    (c) access to and the taking of photographs and copies of anything so seized or produced;

    (d) the retention, use, disclosure and destruction of fingerprints, a sample or a photograph taken under this Part.

(2) If the Secretary of State proposes to issue a code of practice under this section he must—

    (a) publish a draft of the code;

    (b) consider any representations made to him about the draft;

    (c) if he thinks it appropriate, modify the draft in the light of any such representations.

(3) The Secretary of State must lay the code before Parliament.

(4) When he has done so he may bring the code into operation by order.

(5) The Secretary of State may revise the whole or any part of a code issued under this section and issue the code as revised; and subsections (2) to (4) apply to such a revised code as they apply to the original code.

(6) A failure by a constable to comply with a provision of a code issued under this section does not of itself make him liable to criminal or civil proceedings.

(7) A code issued under this section is admissible in evidence in proceedings under this Act and must be taken into account by a judge or court in determining any question to which it appears to the judge or the court to be relevant.

(8) If the Secretary of State publishes a draft code of practice in connection with a matter specified in subsection (1) before the date on which this section comes into force—

    (a) the draft is as effective as one published under subsection (2) on or after that date;

    (b) representations made to the Secretary of State about the draft before that date are as effective as representations made to him about it after that date;

    (c) modifications made by the Secretary of State to the draft in the light of any such representations before that date are as effective as any such modifications made by him on or after that date.

## General

**174 Interpretation**

(1) Subsections (2) to (8) apply for the purposes of this Part.

(2) Each of these is an extradition arrest power—

    (a) a Part 1 warrant in respect of which a certificate under section 2 has been issued;

    (b) section 5;

    (c) a warrant issued under section 71;

    (d) a provisional warrant.

(3) "Excluded material"—

    (a) in England and Wales, has the meaning given by section 11 of the 1984 Act;

    (b) in Northern Ireland, has the meaning given by Article 13 of the 1989 Order.

(4)  "Items subject to legal privilege"—

    (a)  in England and Wales, has the meaning given by section 10 of the 1984 Act;

    (b)  in Scotland, has the meaning given by section 412 of the 2002 Act;

    (c)  in Northern Ireland, has the meaning given by Article 12 of the 1989 Order.

(5)  "Premises"—

    (a)  in England and Wales, has the meaning given by section 23 of the 1984 Act;

    (b)  in Scotland, has the meaning given by section 412 of the 2002 Act;

    (c)  in Northern Ireland, has the meaning given by Article 25 of the 1989 Order.

(6)  "Special procedure material"—

    (a)  in England and Wales, has the meaning given by section 14 of the 1984 Act;

    (b)  in Northern Ireland, has the meaning given by Article 16 of the 1989 Order.

(7)  The expressions in subsection (8) have the meanings given—

    (a)  in England and Wales, by section 65 of the 1984 Act;

    (b)  in Northern Ireland, by Article 53 of the 1989 Order.

(8)  The expressions are—

    (a)  appropriate consent;

    (b)  fingerprints;

    (c)  intimate search;

    (d)  non-intimate sample.

(9)  The 1984 Act is the Police and Criminal Evidence Act 1984 (c. 60).

(10)  The 1989 Order is the Police and Criminal Evidence (Northern Ireland) Order 1989 (S.I. 1989/1341 (N.I. 12)).

(11)  The 2002 Act is the Proceeds of Crime Act 2002 (c. 29).

### 175  Customs officers

The Treasury may by order provide for any provision of this Part which applies in relation to police officers or persons arrested by police officers to apply with specified modifications in relation to customs officers or persons arrested by customs officers.

### 176  Service policemen

The Secretary of State may by order provide for any provision of this Part which applies in relation to police officers or persons arrested by police officers to apply with specified modifications in relation to service policemen or persons arrested by service policemen.

# PART 5

# MISCELLANEOUS AND GENERAL

## British overseas territories

### 177  Extradition from British overseas territories

(1)  This section applies in relation to extradition—

    (a)  from a British overseas territory to a category 1 territory;

    (b)  from a British overseas territory to the United Kingdom;

(c) from a British overseas territory to a category 2 territory;

(d) from a British overseas territory to any of the Channel Islands or the Isle of Man.

(2) An Order in Council may provide for any provision of this Act applicable to extradition from the United Kingdom to apply to extradition in a case falling within subsection (1)(a) or (b).

(3) An Order in Council may provide for any provision of this Act applicable to extradition from the United Kingdom to a category 2 territory to apply to extradition in a case falling within subsection (1)(c) or (d).

(4) An Order in Council under this section may provide that the provision applied has effect with specified modifications.

### 178  Extradition to British overseas territories

(1) This section applies in relation to extradition—

(a) to a British overseas territory from a category 1 territory;

(b) to a British overseas territory from the United Kingdom;

(c) to a British overseas territory from a category 2 territory;

(d) to a British overseas territory from any of the Channel Islands or the Isle of Man.

(2) An Order in Council may provide for any provision of this Act applicable to extradition to the United Kingdom to apply to extradition in a case falling within subsection (1)(a) or (b).

(3) An Order in Council may provide for any provision of this Act applicable to extradition to the United Kingdom from a category 2 territory to apply to extradition in a case falling within subsection (1)(c) or (d).

(4) An Order in Council under this section may provide that the provision applied has effect with specified modifications.

## Competing extradition claims

### 179  Competing claims to extradition

(1) This section applies if at the same time—

(a) there is a Part 1 warrant in respect of a person, a certificate has been issued under section 2 in respect of the warrant, and the person has not been extradited in pursuance of the warrant or discharged, and

(b) there is a request for the same person's extradition, a certificate has been issued under section 70 in respect of the request, and the person has not been extradited in pursuance of the request or discharged.

(2) The Secretary of State may—

(a) order proceedings (or further proceedings) on one of them (the warrant or the request) to be deferred until the other one has been disposed of, if neither the warrant nor the request has been disposed of;

(b) order the person's extradition in pursuance of the warrant to be deferred until the request has been disposed of, if an order for his extradition in pursuance of the warrant has been made;

(c) order the person's extradition in pursuance of the request to be deferred until the warrant has been disposed of, if an order for his extradition in pursuance of the request has been made.

(3) In applying subsection (2) the Secretary of State must take account in particular of these matters—

(a) the relative seriousness of the offences concerned;

(b) the place where each offence was committed (or was alleged to have been committed);

(c)  the date when the warrant was issued and the date when the request was received;

(d)  whether, in the case of each offence, the person is accused of its commission (but not alleged to have been convicted) or is alleged to be unlawfully at large after conviction.

(4)  If both the certificates referred to in subsection (1) are issued in Scotland, the preceding provisions of this section apply as if the references to the Secretary of State were to the Scottish Ministers.

[(5)  For the purposes of this section a person is alleged to be unlawfully at large after conviction of an offence if–

(a)  he is alleged to have been convicted of it, and

(b)  his extradition is sought for the purpose of his being sentenced for the offence or of his serving a sentence of imprisonment or another form of detention imposed in respect of the offence.]

### 180  Proceedings on deferred warrant or request

(1)  This section applies if—

(a)  an order is made under this Act deferring proceedings on an extradition claim in respect of a person (the deferred claim) until another extradition claim in respect of the person has been disposed of, and

(b)  the other extradition claim is disposed of.

(2)  The judge may make an order for proceedings on the deferred claim to be resumed.

(3)  No order under subsection (2) may be made after the end of the required period.

(4)  If the person applies to the appropriate judge to be discharged, the judge may order his discharge.

(5)  If the person applies to the appropriate judge to be discharged, the judge must order his discharge if—

(a)  the required period has ended, and

(b)  the judge has not made an order under subsection (2) or ordered the person's discharge.

(6)  The required period is 21 days starting with the day on which the other extradition claim is disposed of.

(7)  If the proceedings on the deferred claim were under Part 1, section 67 applies for determining the appropriate judge.

(8)  If the proceedings on the deferred claim were under Part 2, section 139 applies for determining the appropriate judge.

(9)  An extradition claim is made in respect of a person if—

(a)  a Part 1 warrant is issued in respect of him;

(b)  a request for his extradition is made.

### 181  Proceedings where extradition deferred

(1)  This section applies if—

(a)  an order is made under this Act deferring a person's extradition in pursuance of an extradition claim (the deferred claim) until another extradition claim in respect of him has been disposed of;

(b)  the other extradition claim is disposed of.

(2)  The judge may make an order for the person's extradition in pursuance of the deferred claim to cease to be deferred.

(3)  No order under subsection (2) may be made after the end of the required period.

(4)  If the person applies to the appropriate judge to be discharged, the judge may order his discharge.

(5) If the person applies to the appropriate judge to be discharged, the judge must order his discharge if—

    (a) the required period has ended, and

    (b) the judge has not made an order under subsection (2) or ordered the person's discharge.

(6) The required period is 21 days starting with the day on which the other extradition claim is disposed of.

(7) If the person's extradition in pursuance of the deferred claim was ordered under Part 1, section 67 applies for determining the appropriate judge.

(8) If the person's extradition in pursuance of the deferred claim was ordered under Part 2, section 139 applies for determining the appropriate judge.

(9) An extradition claim is made in respect of a person if—

    (a) a Part 1 warrant is issued in respect of him;

    (b) a request for his extradition is made.

# Legal aid

### 182 Legal advice, assistance and representation: England and Wales

In section 12(2) of the Access to Justice Act 1999 (c. 22) (meaning of "criminal proceedings") for paragraph (c) substitute—

    "(c) proceedings for dealing with an individual under the Extradition Act 2003,".

### 183 Legal aid: Scotland

The provisions of the Legal Aid (Scotland) Act 1986 (c. 47) apply—

    (a) in relation to proceedings in Scotland before the appropriate judge under Part 1, 2 or 5 of this Act as those provisions apply in relation to summary proceedings;

    (b) in relation to any proceedings on appeal arising out of such proceedings before the appropriate judge as those provisions apply in relation to appeals in summary proceedings.

### 184 Grant of free legal aid: Northern Ireland

(1) The appropriate judge may grant free legal aid to a person in connection with proceedings under Part 1 or Part 2 before the judge or the High Court.

(2) A judge of the High Court may grant free legal aid to a person in connection with proceedings under Part 1 or Part 2 before the High Court or the [Supreme Court].

(3) If the appropriate judge refuses to grant free legal aid under subsection (1) in connection with proceedings before the High Court the person may appeal to the High Court against the judge's decision.

(4) A judge of the High Court may grant free legal aid to a person in connection with proceedings on an appeal under subsection (3).

(5) Free legal aid may be granted to a person under subsection (1), (2) or (4) only if it appears to the judge that—

    (a) the person's means are insufficient to enable him to obtain legal aid, and

    (b) it is desirable in the interests of justice that the person should be granted free legal aid.

(6) On an appeal under subsection (3) the High Court may—

    (a) allow the appeal;

    (b) dismiss the appeal.

(7) The High Court may allow an appeal under subsection (3) only if it appears to the High Court that—

(a) the person's means are insufficient to enable him to obtain legal aid, and

(b) it is desirable in the interests of justice that the person should be granted free legal aid.

(8) If the High Court allows an appeal under subsection (3) it must grant free legal aid to the person in connection with the proceedings under Part 1 or Part 2 before it.

(9) If on a question of granting free legal aid under this section or of allowing an appeal under subsection (3) there is a doubt as to whether—

(a) the person's means are insufficient to enable him to obtain legal aid, or

(b) it is desirable in the interests of justice that the person should be granted free legal aid, the doubt must be resolved in favour of granting him free legal aid.

(10) References in this section to granting free legal aid to a person are to assigning to him—

(a) a solicitor and counsel, or

(b) a solicitor only, or

(c) counsel only.


### 185 Free legal aid: supplementary

(1) The provisions of the Legal Aid, Advice and Assistance (Northern Ireland) Order 1981 (S.I. 1981/228 (N.I. 8)) listed in subsection (2) apply in relation to free legal aid under section 184 in connection with proceedings before the appropriate judge or the High Court as they apply in relation to free legal aid under Part III of the Order.

(2) The provisions are—

(a) Article 32 (statements of means);

(b) Article 36(1) (payment of legal aid);

(c) Article 36(3) and (4) (rules);

(d) Article 36A (solicitors excluded from legal aid work);

(e) Article 37 (remuneration of solicitors and counsel);

(f) Article 40 (stamp duty exemption).

(3) As so applied those Articles have effect as if—

(a) a person granted free legal aid under section 184 had been granted a criminal aid certificate under Part III of the Order;

(b) section 184 were contained in Part III of the Order.

(4) The fees of any counsel, and the expenses and fees of any solicitor, assigned to a person under section 184 in connection with proceedings before the [Supreme Court] must be paid by the Lord Chancellor.

(5) The fees and expenses paid under subsection (4) must not exceed the amount [allowed] [by the Supreme Court or under Supreme Court Rules.]

(a)–(b) […]

(6) For the purposes of section 184 and this section the appropriate judge is—

(a) such county court jude or resident magistrate as is designated for the purposes of Part 1 [under section 67], if the proceedings are under Part 1;

(b) such county court judge or resident magistrate as is designated for the purposes of Part 2 [under section 139], if the proceedings are under Part 2.

## Re-extradition

### 186 Re-extradition: preliminary

(1) Section 187 applies in relation to a person if the conditions in subsections (2) to (6) are satisfied.

(2) The first condition is that the person was extradited to a territory in accordance with Part 1 or Part 2.

(3) The second condition is that the person was serving a sentence of imprisonment or another form of detention in the United Kingdom (the UK sentence) before he was extradited.

(4) The third condition is that—

(a) if the person was extradited in accordance with Part 1, the Part 1 warrant in pursuance of which he was extradited contained a statement that it was issued with a view to his extradition for the purpose of being prosecuted for an offence;

(b) if the person was extradited in accordance with Part 2, the request in pursuance of which the person was extradited contained a statement that the person was accused of the commission of an offence.

(5) The fourth condition is that a certificate issued by a judicial authority of the territory shows that—

(a) a sentence of imprisonment or another form of detention for a term of 4 months or a greater punishment (the overseas sentence) was imposed on the person in the territory;

(b) the overseas sentence was imposed on him in respect of—

(i) the offence specified in the warrant or request, or

(ii) any other offence committed before his extradition in respect of which he was permitted to be dealt with in the territory.

(6) The fifth condition is that before serving the overseas sentence the person was returned to the United Kingdom to serve the remainder of the UK sentence.

### 187 Re-extradition hearing

(1) If this section applies in relation to a person, as soon as practicable after the relevant time the person must be brought before the appropriate judge for the judge to decide whether the person is to be extradited again to the territory in which the overseas sentence was imposed.

(2) The relevant time is the time at which the person would otherwise be released from detention pursuant to the UK sentence (whether or not on licence).

(3) If subsection (1) is not complied with and the person applies to the judge to be discharged, the judge must order his discharge.

(4) The person must be treated as continuing in legal custody until he is brought before the appropriate judge under subsection (1) or he is discharged under subsection (3).

(5) If the person is brought before the appropriate judge under subsection (1) the judge must decide whether the territory in which the overseas sentence was imposed is—

(a) a category 1 territory;

(b) a category 2 territory;

(c) neither a category 1 territory nor a category 2 territory.

(6) If the judge decides that the territory is a category 1 territory, section 188 applies.

(7) If the judge decides that the territory is a category 2 territory, section 189 applies.

(8) If the judge decides that the territory is neither a category 1 territory nor a category 2 territory, he must order the person's discharge.

(9) A person's discharge as a result of this section or section 188 or 189 does not affect any conditions on which he is released from detention pursuant to the UK sentence.

[(10) Section 139 applies for the purposes of this section as it applies for the purposes of Part 2.]

**188  Re-extradition to category 1 territories**

(1)  If this section applies, this Act applies as it would if—

(a)  a Part 1 warrant had been issued in respect of the person;

(b)  the warrant contained a statement that—

(i)  the person [had been convicted] of the relevant offence, and

(ii)  the warrant was issued with a view to the person's arrest and extradition to the territory for the purpose of serving a sentence imposed in respect of the relevant offence;

(c)  the warrant were issued by the authority of the territory which issued the certificate referred to in section 186(5);

(d)  the relevant offence were specified in the warrant;

(e)  the judge were the appropriate judge for the purposes of Part 1;

(f)  the hearing at which the judge is to make the decision referred to in section 187(1) were the extradition hearing;

(g)  the proceedings before the judge were under Part 1.

(2)  As applied by subsection (1) this Act has effect with the modifications set out in Part 1 of Schedule 1.

(3)  The relevant offence is the offence in respect of which the overseas sentence is imposed.

**189  Re-extradition to category 2 territories**

(1)  If this section applies, this Act applies as it would if—

(a)  a valid request for the person's extradition to the territory had been made;

(b)  the request contained a statement that the person [had been convicted] of the relevant offence;

(c)  the relevant offence were specified in the request;

(d)  the hearing at which the appropriate judge is to make the decision referred to in section 187(1) were the extradition hearing;

(e)  the proceedings before the judge were under Part 2.

(2)  As applied by subsection (1) this Act has effect with the modifications set out in Part 2 of Schedule 1.

(3)  The relevant offence is the offence in respect of which the overseas sentence is imposed.

## Conduct of extradition proceedings

**190  Crown Prosecution Service: role in extradition proceedings**

(1)  The Prosecution of Offences Act 1985 (c. 23) is amended as follows.

(2)  In section 3 (functions of the Director) in subsection (2) after paragraph (e) insert—

"(ea)  to have the conduct of any extradition proceedings;

(eb)  to give, to such extent as he considers appropriate, and to such persons as he considers appropriate, advice on any matters relating to extradition proceedings or proposed extradition proceedings;".

(3) In section 3 after subsection (2) insert—

"(2A) Subsection (2)(ea) above does not require the Director to have the conduct of any extradition proceedings in respect of a person if he has received a request not to do so and—

(a) in a case where the proceedings are under Part 1 of the Extradition Act 2003, the request is made by the authority which issued the Part 1 warrant in respect of the person;

(b) in a case where the proceedings are under Part 2 of that Act, the request is made on behalf of the territory to which the person's extradition has been requested."

(4) In section 5(1) (conduct of prosecutions on behalf of Crown Prosecution Service) after "criminal proceedings" insert "or extradition proceedings".

(5) In section 14 (control of fees and expenses etc paid by the Service) in subsection (1)(a) after "criminal proceedings" insert "or extradition proceedings".

(6) In section 15(1) (interpretation of Part 1) in the appropriate place insert—

""extradition proceedings" means proceedings under the Extradition Act 2003;".

**191  Lord Advocate: role in extradition proceedings**

(1) The Lord Advocate must—

(a) conduct any extradition proceedings in Scotland;

(b) give, to such extent as he considers appropriate, and to such persons as he considers appropriate, advice on any matters relating to extradition proceedings or proposed extradition proceedings, in Scotland.

(2) Subsection (1)(a) does not require the Lord Advocate to conduct any extradition proceedings in respect of a person if he has received a request not to do so and—

(a) in a case where the proceedings are under Part 1, the request is made by the authority which issued the Part 1 warrant in respect of the person;

(b) in a case where the proceedings are under Part 2, the request is made on behalf of the territory to which the person's extradition has been requested.

**192  Northern Ireland DPP and Crown Solicitor: role in extradition proceedings**

(1) The Prosecution of Offences (Northern Ireland) Order 1972 (S.I. 1972/538 (N.I. 1)) is amended as set out in subsections (2) to (4).

(2) In article 2(2) (interpretation) in the appropriate place insert—

""extradition proceedings" means proceedings under the Extradition Act 2003;".

(3) In article 4(7) (conduct of prosecutions on behalf of DPP) after "prosecution" insert "or extradition proceedings".

(4) In article 5 (functions of DPP) after paragraph (1) insert—

"(1A) The Director may—

(a) have the conduct of any extradition proceedings in Northern Ireland;

(b) give to such persons as appear to him appropriate such advice as appears to him appropriate on matters relating to extradition proceedings, or proposed extradition proceedings, in Northern Ireland."

(5) The Justice (Northern Ireland) Act 2002 (c. 26) is amended as set out in subsections (6) to (8).

(6) After section 31 insert—

"31A Conduct of extradition proceedings

(1) The Director may have the conduct of any extradition proceedings in Northern Ireland.

(2) The Director may give to such persons as appear to him appropriate such advice as appears to him appropriate on matters relating to extradition proceedings, or proposed extradition proceedings, in Northern Ireland."

(7)  In section 36(2) (conduct of criminal proceedings on behalf of DPP) after "criminal proceedings" insert "or extradition proceedings".

(8)  In section 44 (interpretation) after subsection (6) insert—

"(7) For the purposes of this Part "extradition proceedings" means proceedings under the Extradition Act 2003."

(9)  The Crown Solicitor for Northern Ireland may—

(a)  have the conduct of any proceedings under this Act in Northern Ireland;

(b)  give to such persons as appear to him appropriate such advice as appears to him appropriate on matters relating to proceedings under this Act, or proposed proceedings under this Act, in Northern Ireland.

## Parties to international Conventions

### 193  Parties to international Conventions

(1)  A territory may be designated by order made by the Secretary of State if—

(a)  it is not a category 1 territory or a category 2 territory, and

(b)  it is a party to an international Convention to which the United Kingdom is a party.

(2)  This Act applies in relation to a territory designated by order under subsection (1) as if the territory were a category 2 territory.

(3)  As applied to a territory by subsection (2), this Act has effect as if—

(a)  sections 71(4), 73(5), 74(11)(b), 84(7), 86(7), 137 and 138 were omitted;

(b)  the conduct that constituted an extradition offence for the purposes of Part 2 were the conduct specified in relation to the territory in the order under subsection (1) designating the territory.

(4)  Conduct may be specified in relation to a territory in an order under subsection (1) designating the territory only if it is conduct to which the relevant Convention applies.

(5)  The relevant Convention is the Convention referred to in subsection (1)(b) which is specified in relation to the territory in the order under subsection (1) designating it.

## Special extradition arrangements

### 194  Special extradition arrangements

(1)  This section applies if the Secretary of State believes that—

(a)  arrangements have been made between the United Kingdom and another territory for the extradition of a person to the territory, and

(b)  the territory is not a category 1 territory or a category 2 territory.

(2)  The Secretary of State may certify that the conditions in paragraphs (a) and (b) of subsection (1) are satisfied in relation to the extradition of the person.

(3)  If the Secretary of State issues a certificate under subsection (2) this Act applies in respect of the person's extradition to the territory as if the territory were a category 2 territory.

(4)  As applied by subsection (3), this Act has effect—

(a)  as if sections 71(4), 73(5), 74(11)(b), 84(7) and 86(7) were omitted;

(b)  with any other modifications specified in the certificate.

(5)  A certificate under subsection (2) in relation to a person is conclusive evidence that the conditions in paragraphs (a) and (b) of subsection (1) are satisfied in relation to the person's extradition.

## Human rights

### 195 Human rights: appropriate tribunal

(1) The appropriate judge is the only appropriate tribunal in relation to proceedings under section 7(1) (a) of the Human Rights Act 1998 (c. 42) (proceedings for acts incompatible with Convention rights) if the proceedings relate to extradition under Part 1 or Part 2 of this Act.

(2) If the proceedings relate to extradition under Part 1, section 67 applies for determining the appropriate judge.

(3) If the proceedings relate to extradition under Part 2, section 139 applies for determining the appropriate judge.

## Genocide etc

### 196 Genocide, crimes against humanity and war crimes

(1) This section applies if—

(a) a Part 1 warrant in respect of a person is issued in respect of an offence mentioned in subsection (2), or

(b) a valid request for a person's extradition is made in respect of an offence mentioned in subsection (2).

(2) The offences are—

(a) an offence that if committed in the United Kingdom would be punishable as an offence under section 51 or 58 of the International Criminal Court Act 2001 (c. 17) (genocide, crimes against humanity and war crimes);

(b) an offence that if committed in the United Kingdom would be punishable as an offence under section 52 or 59 of that Act (conduct ancillary to genocide, etc. committed outside the jurisdiction);

(c) an offence that if committed in the United Kingdom would be punishable as an ancillary offence, as defined in section 55 or 62 of that Act, in relation to an offence falling within paragraph (a) or (b);

(d) an offence that if committed in the United Kingdom would be punishable as an offence under section 1 of the International Criminal Court (Scotland) Act 2001 (asp 13) (genocide, crimes against humanity and war crimes);

(e) an offence that if committed in the United Kingdom would be punishable as an offence under section 2 of that Act (conduct ancillary to genocide etc. committed outside the jurisdiction);

(f) an offence that if committed in the United Kingdom would be punishable as an ancillary offence, as defined in section 7 of that Act, in relation to an offence falling within paragraph (d) or (e);

(g) any offence punishable in the United Kingdom under section 1 of the Geneva

Conventions Act 1957 (c. 52) (grave breach of scheduled conventions).

(3) It is not an objection to extradition under this Act that the person could not have been punished for the offence under the law in force at the time when and in the place where he is alleged to have committed the act of which he is accused or of which he has been convicted.

## Custody and bail

### 197 Custody

(1) If a judge remands a person in custody under this Act, the person must be committed to the institution to which he would have been committed if charged with an offence before the judge.

(2) If a person in custody following his arrest under Part 1 or Part 2 [, or kept in custody by virtue of a power under Part 3,] escapes from custody, he may be retaken in any part of the United Kingdom in the same way as he could have been if he had been in custody following his arrest or apprehension under a relevant domestic warrant.

(3) A relevant domestic warrant is a warrant for his arrest or apprehension issued in the part of the United Kingdom in question in respect of an offence committed there.

(4) Subsection (5) applies if—

(a) a person is in custody in one part of the United Kingdom (whether under this Act or otherwise);

(b) he is required to be removed to another part of the United Kingdom after being remanded in custody under this Act;

(c) he is so removed by sea or air.

(5) The person must be treated as continuing in legal custody until he reaches the place to which he is required to be removed.

(6) An order for a person's extradition under this Act is sufficient authority for an appropriate person—

(a) to receive him;

(b) to keep him in custody until he is extradited under this Act;

(c) to convey him to the territory to which he is to be extradited under this Act.

(7) An appropriate person is—

(a) a person to whom the order is directed;

(b) a constable.

## [197A Extradition of serving prisoner

If an order is made under Part 1 or 2 for the extradition of a person who is [in custody] serving a sentence of imprisonment or another form of detention in the United Kingdom, the order is sufficient authority for the person to be removed from the prison or other institution where he is detained.]

## 198 Bail: England and Wales

(1) The Bail Act 1976 (c. 63) is amended as follows.

(2) In section 1(1) (meaning of "bail in criminal proceedings") after paragraph (b) insert—

", or

(c) bail grantable in connection with extradition proceedings in respect of an offence."

(3) In section 2(2) (other definitions) omit the definition of "proceedings against a fugitive offender" and in the appropriate places insert—

""extradition proceedings" means proceedings under the Extradition Act 2003;";

""prosecutor", in relation to extradition proceedings, means the person acting on behalf of the territory to which extradition is sought;".

(4) In section 4 (general right to bail) in subsection (2) omit the words "or proceedings against a fugitive offender for the offence".

(5) In section 4 after subsection (2) insert—

"(2A) This section also applies to a person whose extradition is sought in respect of an offence, when—

(a) he appears or is brought before a court in the course of or in connection with extradition proceedings in respect of the offence, or

(b) he applies to a court for bail or for a variation of the conditions of bail in connection with the proceedings.

(2B) But subsection (2A) above does not apply if the person is alleged to be unlawfully at large after conviction of the offence."

(6) In section 5B (reconsideration of decisions granting bail) for subsection (1) substitute—

"(A1) This section applies in any of these cases—

(a) a magistrates' court has granted bail in criminal proceedings in connection with an offence to which this section applies or proceedings for such an offence;

(b) a constable has granted bail in criminal proceedings in connection with

proceedings for such an offence;

(c) a magistrates' court or a constable has granted bail in connection with extradition proceedings.

(1) The court or the appropriate court in relation to the constable may, on application by the prosecutor for the decision to be reconsidered—

(a) vary the conditions of bail,

(b) impose conditions in respect of bail which has been granted unconditionally, or

(c) withhold bail."

(7) In section 7 (liability to arrest for absconding or breaking conditions of bail) after subsection (1) insert—

"(1A) Subsection (1B) applies if—

(a) a person has been released on bail in connection with extradition proceedings,

(b) the person is under a duty to surrender into the custody of a constable, and

(c) the person fails to surrender to custody at the time appointed for him to do so.

(1B) A magistrates' court may issue a warrant for the person's arrest."

(8) In section 7(4) omit the words from "In reckoning" to "Sunday".

(9) In section 7 after subsection (4) insert—

"(4A) A person who has been released on bail in connection with extradition proceedings and is under a duty to surrender into the custody of a constable may be arrested without warrant by a constable on any of the grounds set out in paragraphs (a) to (c) of subsection (3).

(4B) A person arrested in pursuance of subsection (4A) above shall be brought as soon as practicable and in any event within 24 hours after his arrest before a justice of the peace for the petty sessions area in which he was arrested."

(10) In section 7(5) after "subsection (4)" insert "or (4B)".

(11) In section 7 after subsection (6) insert—

"(7) In reckoning for the purposes of this section any period of 24 hours, no account shall be taken of Christmas Day, Good Friday or any Sunday."

(12) In Part 1 of Schedule 1 (defendants accused or convicted of imprisonable offences) for paragraph 1 substitute—

"1

The following provisions of this Part of this Schedule apply to the defendant if—

(a) the offence or one of the offences of which he is accused or convicted in the proceedings is punishable with imprisonment, or

(b) his extradition is sought in respect of an offence."

(13) In Part 1 of Schedule 1 after paragraph 2A insert—

"2B

The defendant need not be granted bail in connection with extradition proceedings if—

(a) the conduct constituting the offence would, if carried out by the defendant in England and Wales, constitute an indictable offence or an offence triable either way; and

(b)  it appears to the court that the defendant was on bail on the date of the offence."

(14)  In Part 1 of Schedule 1 in paragraph 6 after "the offence" insert "or the extradition proceedings".

## 199  Bail: Scotland

After section 24 of the Criminal Procedure (Scotland) Act 1995 (c. 46) (bail and bail conditions) insert—

"24A Bail: extradition proceedings

(1)  In the application of the provisions of this Part by virtue of section 9(2) or 77(2) of the Extradition Act 2003 (judge's powers at extradition hearing), those provisions apply with the modifications that—

(a)  references to the prosecutor are to be read as references to a person acting on behalf of the territory to which extradition is sought;

(b)  the right of the Lord Advocate mentioned in section 24(2) of this Act applies to a person subject to extradition proceedings as it applies to a person charged with any crime or offence;

(c)  the following do not apply—

(i)  paragraph (b) of section 24(3); and

(ii)  subsection (3) of section 30; and

(d)  sections 28(1) and 33 apply to a person subject to extradition proceedings as they apply to an accused.

(2)  Section 32 of this Act applies in relation to a refusal of bail, the amount of bail or a decision to allow bail or ordain appearance in proceedings under this Part as the Part applies by virtue of the sections of that Act of 2003 mentioned in subsection (1) above.

(3)  The Scottish Ministers may, by order, for the purposes of section 9(2) or 77(2) of the Extradition Act 2003 make such amendments to this Part as they consider necessary or expedient.

(4)  The order making power in subsection (3) above shall be exercisable by statutory instrument subject to annulment in pursuance of a resolution of the Scottish Parliament."

## 200  Appeal against grant of bail

(1)  Section 1 of the Bail (Amendment) Act 1993 (c. 26) (prosecution right of appeal against grant of bail) is amended as follows.

(2)  After subsection (1) insert—

"(1A) Where a magistrates' court grants bail to a person in connection with extradition proceedings, the prosecution may appeal to a judge of the Crown Court against the granting of bail."

(3)  In subsection (3) for "Such an appeal" substitute "An appeal under subsection (1) or (1A)".

(4)  In subsection (4)—

(a)  after subsection (1) insert "or (1A)";

(b)  for "magistrates' court" substitute "court which has granted bail";

(c)  omit "such".

(5)  In subsection (5) for "magistrates' court" substitute "court which has granted bail".

(6)  In subsection (6) for "magistrates' court" substitute "court which has granted bail".

(7)  In subsection (8)—

(a)  after "subsection (1)" insert "or (1A)";

(b)  omit "magistrates'".

(8)  In subsection (10)(b) for "reference in subsection (5) above to remand in custody is" substitute "references in subsections (6) and (9) above to remand in custody are".

(9) After subsection (11) insert—

"(12) In this section—

"extradition proceedings" means proceedings under the Extradition Act 2003;

"magistrates' court" and "court" in relation to extradition proceedings means a District Judge (Magistrates' Courts) designated for the purposes of Part 1 or Part 2 of the Extradition Act 2003 by the Lord Chancellor;

"prosecution" in relation to extradition proceedings means the person acting on behalf of the territory to which extradition is sought."

### 201 Remand to local authority accommodation

(1) Section 23 of the Children and Young Persons Act 1969 (c. 54) (remand to local authority accommodation) is amended as set out in subsections (2) to (11).

(2) In subsection (1) after "following provisions of this section" insert "(except subsection (1A))".

(3) After subsection (1) insert—

"(1A) Where a court remands a child or young person in connection with extradition proceedings and he is not released on bail the remand shall be to local authority accommodation."

(4) In subsection (4) after "subsections (5)" insert ", (5ZA)".

(5) In subsection (5) after "security requirement" insert "in relation to a person remanded in accordance with subsection (1) above".

(6) After subsection (5) insert—

"(5ZA) A court shall not impose a security requirement in relation to a person remanded in accordance with subsection (1A) above unless—

(a) he has attained the age of twelve and is of a prescribed description;

(b) one or both of the conditions set out in subsection (5ZB) below is satisfied; and

(c) the condition set out in subsection (5AA) below is satisfied.

(5ZB) The conditions mentioned in subsection (5ZA)(b) above are—

(a) that the conduct constituting the offence to which the extradition proceedings relate would if committed in the United Kingdom constitute an offence punishable in the case of an adult with imprisonment for a term of fourteen years or more;

(b) that the person has previously absconded from the extradition proceedings or from proceedings in the United Kingdom or the requesting territory which relate to the conduct constituting the offence to which the extradition proceedings relate.

(5ZC) For the purposes of subsection (5ZB) above a person has absconded from proceedings if in relation to those proceedings—

(a) he has been released subject to a requirement to surrender to custody at a particular time and he has failed to surrender to custody at that time, or

(b) he has surrendered into the custody of a court and he has at any time absented himself from the court without its leave."

(7) In subsection (5AA) for "subsection (5)" substitute "subsections (5) and (5ZA)".

(8) In subsection (12) for the definition of "relevant court" substitute—

""relevant court"—

(a) in relation to a person remanded to local authority accommodation under subsection (1) above, means the court by which he was so remanded, or any magistrates' court having jurisdiction in the place where he is for the time being;

(b) in relation to a person remanded to local authority accommodation under subsection (1A) above, means the court by which he was so remanded."

(9)  In subsection (12) in the appropriate places insert—

""extradition proceedings" means proceedings under the Extradition Act 2003;";

""requesting territory" means the territory to which a person's extradition is sought in extradition proceedings;".

(10)  In section 98(1) of the Crime and Disorder Act 1998 (c. 37) (modifications of section 23 of the Children and Young Persons Act 1969 (c. 54) in relation to 15 and 16 year old boys) after paragraph (b) insert

"; and

(c)  is not remanded in connection with proceedings under the Extradition Act 2003."

## Evidence

### 202  Receivable documents

(1)  A Part 1 warrant may be received in evidence in proceedings under this Act.

(2)  Any other document issued in a category 1 territory may be received in evidence in proceedings under this Act if it is duly authenticated.

(3)  A document issued in a category 2 territory may be received in evidence in proceedings under this Act if it is duly authenticated.

(4)  A document issued in a category 1 or category 2 territory is duly authenticated if (and only if) one of these applies—

(a)  it purports to be signed by a judge, magistrate or [officer] of the territory;

[(aa)  it purports to be certified, whether by seal or otherwise, by the Ministry or Department of the territory responsible for justice or for foreign affairs;]

(b)  it purports to be authenticated by the oath or affirmation of a witness.

(5)  Subsections (2) and (3) do not prevent a document that is not duly authenticated from being received in evidence in proceedings under this Act.

### 203  Documents sent by facsimile

(1)  This section applies if a document to be sent in connection with proceedings under this Act is sent by facsimile transmission.

(2)  This Act has effect as if the document received by facsimile transmission were the document used to make the transmission.

### [204  Warrant issued by category 1 territory: transmission by other electronic means

(1)  This section applies if—

(a)  an arrest warrant is issued by an authority of a category 1 territory in a case in which an article 26 alert is issued,

(b)  the information contained in the warrant and the alert are transmitted to the designated authority by electronic means, and

(c)  that information is received by the designated authority in a qualifying form.

(2)  This section also applies if—

(a)  an arrest warrant is issued by an authority of a category 1 territory in a case in which no article 26 alert is issued,

(b)  the information contained in the warrant is transmitted to the designated authority by electronic means, and

(c)  that information is received by the designated authority in a qualifying form.

(3) The reference in section 2(2) to an arrest warrant issued by a judicial authority of a category 1 territory is to be read as if it were a reference to the information received by the designated authority.

(4) The references in section 63(1) to an arrest warrant are to be read as if they were references to the information received by the designated authority.

(5) For the purposes of subsection (1), a reference to the information contained in the article 26 alert includes a reference to any information sent with that information relating to the case in question.

(6) For the purposes of this section—

(a) an article 26 alert is an alert issued pursuant to article 26 of the Council Decision on the establishment, operation and use of the second generation Schengen Information System of 12 June 2007,

(b) references to information being transmitted by electronic means do not include facsimile transmission, and

(c) information is received in a qualifying form if it is received in a form in which it is intelligible and which is capable of being used for subsequent reference.]

## 205 Written statements and admissions

(1) The provisions mentioned in subsection (2) apply in relation to proceedings under this Act as they apply in relation to proceedings for an offence.

(2) The provisions are—

(a) section 9 of the Criminal Justice Act 1967 (c. 80) (proof by written statement in criminal proceedings);

(b) section 10 of the Criminal Justice Act 1967 (proof by formal admission in criminal proceedings);

(c) section 1 of the Criminal Justice (Miscellaneous Provisions) Act (Northern Ireland) 1968 (c. 28) (proof by written statement in criminal proceedings);

(d) section 2 of the Criminal Justice (Miscellaneous Provisions) Act (Northern Ireland) 1968 (proof by formal admission in criminal proceedings).

(3) As applied by subsection (1) in relation to proceedings under this Act, section 10 of the Criminal Justice Act 1967 and section 2 of the Criminal Justice (Miscellaneous Provisions) Act (Northern Ireland) 1968 have effect as if—

(a) references to the defendant were to the person whose extradition is sought (or who has been extradited);

(b) references to the prosecutor were to the category 1 or category 2 territory concerned;

(c) references to the trial were to the proceedings under this Act for the purposes of which the admission is made;

(d) references to subsequent criminal proceedings were to subsequent proceedings under this Act.

## 206 Burden and standard of proof

(1) This section applies if, in proceedings under this Act, a question arises as to burden or standard of proof.

(2) The question must be decided by applying any enactment or rule of law that would apply if the proceedings were proceedings for an offence.

(3) Any enactment or rule of law applied under subsection (2) to proceedings under this Act must be applied as if—

(a) the person whose extradition is sought (or who has been extradited) were accused of an offence;

(b) the category 1 or category 2 territory concerned were the prosecution.

(4) Subsections (2) and (3) are subject to any express provision of this Act.

(5) In this section "enactment" includes an enactment comprised in, or in an instrument made under, an Act of the Scottish Parliament.

## [Live links]

### [206A Use of live links at certain hearings

(1) This section applies in relation to—

    (a) a hearing before the appropriate judge in proceedings under Part 1, other than—

        (i) an extradition hearing within the meaning of that Part;

        (ii) a hearing under section 54 or 56, and

    (b) a hearing before the appropriate judge in proceedings under Part 2, other than an extradition hearing within the meaning of that Part.

(2) If satisfied that the person affected by an extradition claim is likely to be in custody during the hearing, the appropriate judge may give a live link direction at any time before the hearing.

(3) A live link direction is a direction that, if the person is being held in custody at the time of the hearing, any attendance at the hearing is to be through a live link from the place at which the person is held.

(4) Such a direction—

    (a) may be given on the appropriate judge's own motion or on the application of a party to the proceedings, and

    (b) may be given in relation to all subsequent hearings to which this section applies, or to such hearing or hearings to which this section applies as may be specified or described in the direction.

(5) The appropriate judge may give such a direction only if satisfied that it is not contrary to the interests of justice to give the direction.

(6) A person affected by an extradition claim is to be treated as present in court when, by virtue of a live link direction, the person attends a hearing through a live link.]

### [206B Live links: supplementary

(1) The appropriate judge may rescind a live link direction at any time before or during a hearing to which it relates.

(2) The appropriate judge must not give a live link direction or rescind such a direction unless the parties to the proceedings have been given the opportunity to make representations.

(3) If a hearing takes place in relation to the giving or rescinding of a live link direction, the appropriate judge may require or permit any party to the proceedings who wishes to make representations to do so through a live link.

(4) If in a case where an appropriate judge has power to give a live link direction but decides not to do so, the appropriate judge must—

    (a) state in open court the reasons for not doing so, and

    (b) cause those reasons to be entered in the register of proceedings.

(5) Subsection (7) applies if—

    (a) an application for a live link direction is made under section 206A(4) in relation to a qualifying hearing but the application is refused, or

    (b) a live link direction is given in relation to a qualifying hearing but the direction is rescinded before the hearing takes place.

(6)  A hearing is a qualifying hearing—

(a)  in relation to proceedings under Part 1, if it is a hearing by virtue of which section 4(3) would be complied with;

(b)  in relation to proceedings under Part 2, if it is a hearing by virtue of which section 72(3) or 74(3) would be complied with.

(7)  The requirement in section 4(3), 72(3) or 74(3) (as the case requires) to bring the person as soon as practicable before the appropriate judge is to be read as a requirement to bring the person before that judge as soon as practicable after the application is refused or the direction is rescinded.]

### [206C Live links: interpretation

(1)  This section applies for the purposes of section 206A and subsections (2) and (3) also apply for the purposes of section 206B.

(2)  In relation to proceedings under Part 1, section 67 applies for determining the appropriate judge.

(3)  In relation to proceedings under Part 2, section 139 applies for determining the appropriate judge.

(4)  A person is affected by an extradition claim if—

(a)  a Part 1 warrant is issued in respect of the person;

(b)  the person is arrested under section 5;

(c)  a request for the person's extradition is made; or

(d)  a warrant under section 73 is issued in respect of the person.

(5)  References to being in custody include—

(a)  in England and Wales, references to being in police detention within the meaning of the Police and Criminal Evidence Act 1984;

(b)  in Northern Ireland, references to being in police detention within the meaning of the Police and Criminal Evidence (Northern Ireland) Order 1989;

(c)  in Scotland, references to detention under section 14 of the Criminal Procedure (Scotland) Act 1995.

(6)  "Live link" means an arrangement by which a person, while absent from the place where the hearing is being held, is able—

(a)  to see and hear the appropriate judge, and other persons,

(b)  to be seen and heard by the judge, other persons,

and for this purpose any impairment of eyesight or hearing is to be disregarded.]

## Other miscellaneous provisions

### 207  Extradition for more than one offence

The Secretary of State may by order provide for this Act to have effect with specified modifications in relation to a case where—

(a)  a Part 1 warrant is issued in respect of more than one offence;

(b)  a request for extradition is made in respect of more than one offence.

### 208  National security

(1)  This section applies if the Secretary of State believes that the conditions in subsections (2) to (4) are satisfied in relation to a person.

(2) The first condition is that the person's extradition is sought or will be sought under Part 1 or Part 2 in respect of an offence.

(3) The second condition is that—

(a) in engaging in the conduct constituting (or alleged to constitute) the offence the person was acting for the purpose of assisting in the exercise of a function conferred or imposed by or under an enactment, or

(b) as a result of an authorisation given by the Secretary of State the person is not liable under the criminal law of any part of the United Kingdom for the conduct constituting (or alleged to constitute) the offence.

(4) The third condition is that the person's extradition in respect of the offence would be against the interests of national security.

(5) The Secretary of State may certify that the conditions in subsections (2) to (4) are satisfied in relation to the person.

(6) If the Secretary of State issues a certificate under subsection (5) he may—

(a) direct that a Part 1 warrant issued in respect of the person and in respect of the offence is not to be proceeded with, or

(b) direct that a request for the person's extradition in respect of the offence is not to be proceeded with.

(7) If the Secretary of State issues a certificate under subsection (5) he may order the person's discharge (instead of or in addition to giving a direction under subsection (6)).

(8) These rules apply if the Secretary of State gives a direction under subsection (6)(a) in respect of a warrant—

(a) if the designated authority has not issued a certificate under section 2 in respect of the warrant it must not do so;

(b) if the person is arrested under the warrant or under section 5 there is no requirement for him to be brought before the appropriate judge and he must be discharged;

(c) if the person is brought before the appropriate judge under section 4 or 6 the judge is no longer required to proceed or continue proceeding under sections 7 and 8;

(d) if the extradition hearing has begun the judge is no longer required to proceed or continue proceeding under sections 10 to 25;

(e) if the person has consented to his extradition, the judge is no longer required to order his extradition;

(f) if an appeal to the High Court or [Supreme Court] has been brought, the court is no longer required to hear or continue hearing the appeal;

(g) if the person's extradition has been ordered there is no requirement for him to be extradited.

(9) These rules apply if the Secretary of State gives a direction under subsection (6)(b) in respect of a request—

(a) if he has not issued a certificate under section 70 in respect of the request he is no longer required to do so;

(b) if the person is arrested under a warrant issued under section 71 or under a provisional warrant there is no requirement for him to appear or be brought before the appropriate judge and he must be discharged;

(c) if the person appears or is brought before the appropriate judge the judge is no longer required to proceed or continue proceeding under sections 72, 74, 75 and 76;

(d) if the extradition hearing has begun the judge is no longer required to proceed or continue proceeding under sections 78 to 91;

(e) if the person has given his consent to his extradition to the appropriate judge, the judge is no longer required to send the case to the Secretary of State for his decision whether the person is to be extradited;

(f) if an appeal to the High Court or [Supreme Court]164 has been brought, the court is no longer required to hear or continue hearing the appeal;

(g) if the person's extradition has been ordered there is no requirement for him to be extradited.

(10) These must be made under the hand of the Secretary of State—

(a) a certificate under subsection (5);

(b) a direction under subsection (6);

(c) an order under subsection (7).

(11) The preceding provisions of this section apply to Scotland with these modifications—

(a) in subsection (9)(a) for "he has" substitute "the Scottish Ministers have" and for "he is" substitute "they are";

(b) in subsection (9)(e) for "Secretary of State for his" substitute "Scottish Ministers for their".

(12) In subsection (3) the reference to an enactment includes an enactment comprised in, or in an instrument made under, an Act of the Scottish Parliament.

## 209  Reasonable force

A person may use reasonable force, if necessary, in the exercise of a power conferred by this Act.

## 210  Rules of court

(1) Rules of court may make provision as to the practice and procedure to be followed in connection with proceedings under this Act.

(2) In Scotland any rules of court under this Act are to be made by Act of Adjournal.

## 211  Service of notices

Service of a notice on a person under section 54, 56, 58, 129, 130 or 131 may be effected in any of these ways—

(a) by delivering the notice to the person;

(b) by leaving it for him with another person at his last known or usual place of abode;

(c) by sending it by post in a letter addressed to him at his last known or usual place of abode.

## 212  Article 95 alerts: transitional provision

[(1) This section applies in a case where an article 95 alert is issued at the request of an authority of a category 1 territory.

(2) The reference in section 2(2) to an arrest warrant issued by a judicial authority of a category 1 territory is to be read—

(a) as if it were a reference to the alert issued at the request of the authority, and

(b) as if the alert included any information sent with it which relates to the case.

(2A) The references in section 63(1) to an arrest warrant are to be read in accordance with paragraphs (a) and (b) of subsection (2) above.]

(3) [In consequence of] subsection (2), this Act has effect with these modifications—

(a) in sections 2(7) and (8), 28(1), 30(1) and (4)(d), 32(2)(b), 33(6)(b), 35(4)(b), 36(3)(b), 47(3)(b), 49(3)(b), 190(3) and 191(2)(a) for "authority which issued the Part 1 warrant" substitute "authority at the request of which the alert was issued";

(b) omit section 5;

(c) in sections 33(4)(b), 42(2)(a), 43(2)(a) and (4) and 61(1)(d) and (e), for "authority which issued the warrant" substitute "authority at the request of which the alert was issued";

(d) in section 66(2), for the words from "believes" to the end substitute "believes is the authority at the request of which the alert was issued".

(4) An article 95 alert is an alert issued pursuant to article 95 of the Convention implementing the Schengen agreement of 14th June 1985.

## Interpretation

### 213 Disposal of Part 1 warrant and extradition request

(1) A Part 1 warrant issued in respect of a person is disposed of—

(a) when an order is made for the person's discharge in respect of the warrant and there is no further possibility of an appeal;

(b) when the person is taken to be discharged in respect of the warrant;

(c) when an order is made for the person's extradition in pursuance of the warrant and there is no further possibility of an appeal.

(2) A request for a person's extradition is disposed of—

(a) when an order is made for the person's discharge in respect of the request and there is no further possibility of an appeal;

(b) when the person is taken to be discharged in respect of the request;

(c) when an order is made for the person's extradition in pursuance of the request and there is no further possibility of an appeal.

(3) There is no further possibility of an appeal against an order for a person's discharge or extradition—

(a) when the period permitted for giving notice of an appeal to the High Court ends, if notice is not given before the end of that period;

(b) when the decision of the High Court on an appeal becomes final, if there is no appeal to the [Supreme Court] against that decision;

(c) when the decision of the [Supreme Court] on an appeal is made, if there is such an appeal.

(4) The decision of the High Court on an appeal becomes final—

(a) when the period permitted for applying to the High Court for leave to appeal to the [Supreme Court] ends, if there is no such application;

(b) when the period permitted for applying to the [Supreme Court] for leave to appeal to it ends, if the High Court refuses leave to appeal and there is no application to the [Supreme Court] for leave to appeal;

(c) when the [Supreme Court] refuses leave to appeal to it;

(d) at the end of the permitted period, which is 28 days starting with the day on which leave to appeal to the [Supreme Court] is granted, if no such appeal is brought before the end of that period.

(5) These must be ignored for the purposes of subsections (3) and (4)—

(a) any power of a court to extend the period permitted for giving notice of appeal or for applying for leave to appeal;

(b) any power of a court to grant leave to take a step out of time.

(6) Subsections (3) to (5) do not apply to Scotland.

### 214 Disposal of charge

(1) A charge against a person is disposed of—

(a) if the person is acquitted in respect of it, when he is acquitted;

(b) if the person is convicted in respect of it, when there is no further possibility of an appeal against the conviction.

(2) There is no further possibility of an appeal against a conviction—

(a) when the period permitted for giving notice of application for leave to appeal to the Court of Appeal against the conviction ends, if the leave of the Court of Appeal is required and no such notice is given before the end of that period;

(b) when the Court of Appeal refuses leave to appeal against the conviction, if the leave of the Court of Appeal is required and notice of application for leave is given before the end of that period;

(c) when the period permitted for giving notice of appeal to the Court of Appeal against the conviction ends, if notice is not given before the end of that period;

(d) when the decision of the Court of Appeal on an appeal becomes final, if there is no appeal to the [Supreme Court] against that decision;

(e) when the decision of the [Supreme Court] on an appeal is made, if there is such an appeal.

(3) The decision of the Court of Appeal on an appeal becomes final—

(a) when the period permitted for applying to the Court of Appeal for leave to appeal to the [Supreme Court] ends, if there is no such application;

(b) when the period permitted for applying to the [Supreme Court] for leave to appeal to it ends, if the Court of Appeal refuses leave to appeal and there is no application to the [Supreme Court] for leave to appeal;

(c) when the [Supreme Court] refuses leave to appeal to it;

(d) at the end of the permitted period, which is 28 days starting with the day on which leave to appeal to the [Supreme Court] is granted, if no such appeal is brought before the end of that period.

(4) These must be ignored for the purposes of subsections (2) and (3)—

(a) any power of a court to extend the period permitted for giving notice of appeal or of application for leave to appeal or for applying for leave to appeal;

(b) any power of a court to grant leave to take a step out of time.

(5) Subsections (2) to (4) do not apply to Scotland.

### 215 European framework list

(1) The European framework list is the list of conduct set out in Schedule 2.

(2) The Secretary of State may by order amend Schedule 2 for the purpose of ensuring that the list of conduct set out in the Schedule corresponds to the list of conduct set out in article 2.2 of the European framework decision.

(3) The European framework decision is the framework decision of the Council of the European Union made on 13 June 2002 on the European arrest warrant and the surrender procedures between member states (2002/584/JHA).

### 216 Other interpretative provisions

(1) References to a category 1 territory must be read in accordance with section 1.

(2) References to a category 2 territory must be read in accordance with section 69.

(3) References to the designated authority must be read in accordance with section 2(9).

(4) References to a Part 1 warrant must be read in accordance with section 2.

(5) References to a Part 3 warrant must be read in accordance with section 142.

(6) References to a valid request for a person's extradition must be read in accordance with section 70.

[(6A) References to releasing a person from detention pursuant to a sentence do not include releasing a person temporarily on licence pursuant to an intermittent custody order under section 183(1)(b) of the Criminal Justice Act 2003.]

(7) "Asylum claim" has the meaning given by section 113(1) of the Nationality, Immigration and Asylum Act 2002 (c. 41).

[(7A) "Civilian subject to service discipline" has the same meaning as in the Armed Forces Act 2006.]

(8) A customs officer is a person commissioned by the Commissioners of Customs and Excise under section 6(3) of the Customs and Excise Management Act 1979 (c. 2).

(9) "High Court" in relation to Scotland means the High Court of Justiciary.

(10) In relation to Scotland, references to an appeal being discontinued are to be construed as references to its being abandoned.

(11) "Police officer" in relation to Northern Ireland has the same meaning as in the Police (Northern Ireland) Act 2000 (c. 32).

(12) A provisional warrant is a warrant issued under section 73(3).

[(13) "Service policeman" means anyone who is, or by reason of section 375(5) of the Armed Forces Act 2006 is to be treated as, a service policeman for the purposes of that Act.

(13A) "Subject to service law" has the same meaning as in that Act.]

(15) This section and sections 213 to 215 apply for the purposes of this Act.

# General

### 217  Form of documents

The Secretary of State may by regulations prescribe the form of any document required for the purposes of this Act.

### 218  Existing legislation on extradition

These Acts shall cease to have effect—

    (a)  the Backing of Warrants (Republic of Ireland) Act 1965 (c. 45);

    (b)  the Extradition Act 1989 (c. 33).

### 219  Amendments

(1)  Schedule 3 contains miscellaneous and consequential amendments.

(2)  The Secretary of State may by order make—

    (a)  any supplementary, incidental or consequential provision, and

    (b)  any transitory, transitional or saving provision,

which he considers necessary or expedient for the purposes of, in consequence of, or for giving full effect to any provision of this Act.

(3)  An order under subsection (2) may, in particular—

    (a)  provide for any provision of this Act which comes into force before another such provision has come into force to have effect, until that other provision has come into force, with such modifications as are specified in the order, and

    (b)  amend, repeal or revoke any enactment other than one contained in an Act passed in a Session after that in which this Act is passed.

(4)  The amendments that may be made under subsection (3)(b) are in addition to those made by or under any other provision of this Act.

**220 Repeals**

Schedule 4 contains repeals.

**221 Commencement**

The preceding provisions of this Act come into force in accordance with provision made by the Secretary of State by order.

**222 Channel Islands and Isle of Man**

An Order in Council may provide for this Act to extend to any of the Channel Islands or the Isle of Man with the modifications (if any) specified in the Order.

**223 Orders and regulations**

(1) References in this section to subordinate legislation are to—

    (a) an order of the Secretary of State under this Act (other than an order within subsection (2));

    (b) an order of the Treasury under this Act;

    (c) regulations under this Act.

(2) The orders referred to in subsection (1)(a) are—

    (a) an order for a person's extradition or discharge;

    (b) an order deferring proceedings on a warrant or request;

    (c) an order deferring a person's extradition in pursuance of a warrant or request.

(3) Subordinate legislation—

    (a) may make different provision for different purposes;

    (b) may include supplementary, incidental, saving or transitional provisions.

(4) A power to make subordinate legislation is exercisable by statutory instrument.

(5) No order mentioned in subsection (6) may be made unless a draft of the order has been laid before Parliament and approved by a resolution of each House.

(6) The orders are—

    (a) an order under any of these provisions—

    section 1(1);

    section 69(1);

    section 71(4);

    section 73(5);

    section 74(11)(b);

    section 84(7);

    section 86(7);

    section 142(9);

    section 173(4);

    section 215(2);

    (b) an order under section 219(2) which contains any provision (whether alone or with other provisions) amending or repealing any Act or provision of an Act.

(7) A statutory instrument is subject to annulment in pursuance of a resolution of either House of Parliament if it contains subordinate legislation other than an order mentioned in subsection (6) or an order under section 221.

(8)  A territory may be designated by being named in an order made by the Secretary of State under this Act or by falling within a description set out in such an order.

(9)  An order made by the Secretary of State under section 1(1) or 69(1) may provide that this Act has effect in relation to a territory designated by the order with specified modifications.

## 224  Orders in Council

(1)  An Order in Council under section 177 or 178 is subject to annulment in pursuance of a resolution of either House of Parliament.

(2)  An Order in Council under this Act—

>    (a)  may make different provision for different purposes;

>    (b)  may include supplementary, incidental, saving or transitional provisions.

## 225  Finance

The following are to be paid out of money provided by Parliament—

>    (a)  any expenditure incurred by the Lord Chancellor under this Act;

>    (b)  any increase attributable to this Act in the sums payable out of money provided by Parliament under any other enactment.

## 226  Extent

(1)  Sections 157 to 160, 166 to 168, 171, 173 and 205 do not extend to Scotland.

(2)  Sections 154, 198, 200 and 201 extend to England and Wales only.

(3)  Sections 183 and 199 extend to Scotland only.

(4)  Sections 184 and 185 extend to Northern Ireland only.

## 227  Short title

This Act may be cited as the Extradition Act 2003.


SCHEDULE 1                                    Sections 188 and 189

RE-EXTRADITION: MODIFICATIONS


PART 1

# CATEGORY 1 TERRITORIES

**1**  In section 11(1), omit paragraphs (c), (g) and (h).

**2**  Omit sections 14, 18 and 19.

**3**  In section 21(3), for "must" substitute "may".

**4**  In section 31(2), for paragraphs (a) and (b) substitute "would (apart from section 187(1)) be released from detention pursuant to the UK sentence (whether or not on licence)".

5 In section 39(2)(a), for "a certificate is issued under section 2 in respect of the warrant" substitute "the person would (apart from section 187(1)) be released from detention pursuant to the UK sentence (whether or not on licence)".

6 In section 44(2)(a), for "following his arrest under this Part" substitute "under section 187(1)".

7 In section 45(1), for the words from "arrested" to "issued" substitute "brought before the appropriate judge under section 187(1) may consent to his extradition to the territory in which the overseas sentence was imposed".

PART 2

# CATEGORY 2 TERRITORIES

8 In section 78, omit subsections (2), (3), (5) and (8).

9 In section 78, for subsection (4) substitute—

"(4) The judge must decide whether the offence specified in the request is an extradition offence."

10 In section 78(6), for "any of the questions" substitute "the question".

11 In section 78(7), for "those questions" substitute "that question".

12 In section 79(1), omit paragraph (c).

13 Omit section 82.

14 In section 87(3), for the words from "must send the case" to "extradited" substitute "may order the person to be extradited to the category 2 territory".

15 In section 87, after subsection (3) insert—

"(4) If the judge makes an order under subsection (3) he must remand the person in custody or on bail to wait for his extradition to the territory.

(5) [If the person is remanded in custody, the appropriate judge may] later grant bail."

16 In section 103(1)—

(a) for the words from "sends a case" to "extradited" substitute "orders a person's extradition under this Part"; and

(b) for "the relevant decision" substitute "the order".

17 In section 103(2), for the words from "the person" to "the Secretary of State" substitute "the order is made under section 128".

18 In section 103, omit subsections (3), (5), (6), (7) and (8).

19 In section 103(9), for the words from "the Secretary of State" to "person" substitute "the order is made".

20 In section 104, omit subsections (1)(b), (6) and (7).

21 In section 106, omit subsections (1)(b), (7) and (8).

22 In section 117(1)(a), for "the Secretary of State" substitute "the appropriate judge".

23 In section 117(1)(b), for the words from "permitted period" to "extradition" substitute "period permitted under that section".

24 In section 117, after subsection (1) insert—

"(1A) But this section does not apply if the order is made under section 128."

25 In section 117(2), for "the Secretary of State" substitute "the judge".

26 In section 119(1)(a), for "the Secretary of State" substitute "the appropriate judge".

**27** In section 119, in subsections (2) to (6) and in each place in subsection (7), for "the Secretary of State" substitute "the judge".

**28** In section 120, after subsection (1) insert—

"(1A) But this section does not apply if the order for the person's extradition is made under section 128."

**29** In section 121(2)(a), for "a certificate is issued under section 70 in respect of the request" substitute "the person would (apart from section 187(1)) be released from detention pursuant to the UK sentence (whether or not on licence)".

**30** In section 127(1), for the words from "arrested" to "requested" substitute "brought before the appropriate judge under section 187(1) may consent to his extradition to the territory in which the overseas sentence was imposed".

**31** In section 127(3), before paragraph (a) insert—

"(aa) must be given before the appropriate judge;".

**32** In section 127, omit subsections (4) and (5).

**33** In section 128, after subsection (1) insert—

"(1A) The judge must remand the person in custody or on bail.

(1B) [If the person is remanded in custody, the appropriate judge may] later grant bail."

**34** In section 128(4), for the words from "send the case" to "extradited" substitute "within the period of 10 days starting with the day on which consent is given order the person's extradition to the category 2 territory".

**35** In section 128, after subsection (5) insert—

"(6) Subsection (4) has effect subject to section 128B.

(7) If subsection (4) is not complied with and the person applies to the judge to be discharged the judge must order his discharge."

**36** After section 128 insert—

"**128A Extradition to category 2 territory following consent**

(1) This section applies if the appropriate judge makes an order under section 128(4) for a person's extradition to a category 2 territory.

(2) The person must be extradited to the category 2 territory before the end of the required period, which is 28 days starting with the day on which the order is made.

(3) If subsection (2) is not complied with and the person applies to the judge to be discharged the judge must order his discharge, unless reasonable cause is shown for the delay.

**128B Extradition claim following consent**

(1) This section applies if—

(a) a person consents under section 127 to his extradition to a category 2 territory, and

(b) before the judge orders his extradition under section 128(4), the judge is informed that the conditions in subsection (2) or (3) are met.

(2) The conditions are that—

(a) the Secretary of State has received another valid request for the person's Extradition to a category 2 territory;

(b) the other request has not been disposed of.

(3) The conditions are that—

(a) a certificate has been issued under section 2 in respect of a Part 1 warrant issued in respect of the person;

(b) the warrant has not been disposed of.

(4)  The judge must not make an order under section 128(4) until he is informed what order has been made under section 126(2) or 179(2).

(5)  If the order under section 126(2) or 179(2) is for further proceedings on the request under consideration to be deferred until the other request, or the warrant, has been disposed of, the judge must remand the person in custody or on bail.

(6)  [If the person is remanded in custody, the appropriate judge may] later grant bail.

(7)  If—

(a)  the order under section 126(2) or 179(2) is for further proceedings on the request under consideration to be deferred until the other request, or the warrant, has been disposed of, and

(b)  an order is made under section 180 for proceedings on the request under consideration to be resumed, the period specified in section 128(4) must be taken to be 10 days starting with the day on which the order under section 180 is made.

(8)  If the order under section 126(2) or 179(2) is for further proceedings on the other request, or the warrant, to be deferred until the request under consideration has been disposed of, the period specified in section 128(4) must be taken to be 10 days starting with the day on which the judge is informed of the order.

**128C Extradition following deferral for competing claim**

(1)  This section applies if—

(a)  an order is made under section 128(4) for a person to be extradited to a category 2 territory in pursuance of a request for his extradition;

(b)  before the person is extradited to the territory an order is made under section 126(2) or 179(2) for the person's extradition in pursuance of the request to be deferred;

(c)  the appropriate judge makes an order under section 181(2) for the person's extradition in pursuance of the request to cease to be deferred.

(2)  The required period for the purposes of section 128A(2) is 28 days starting with the day on which the order under section 181(2) is made."

**SCHEDULE 2**                                                          **Section 215**

**EUROPEAN FRAMEWORK LIST**

1  Participation in a criminal organisation.

2  Terrorism.

3  Trafficking in human beings.

4  Sexual exploitation of children and child pornography.

5  Illicit trafficking in narcotic drugs and psychotropic substances.

6  Illicit trafficking in weapons, munitions and explosives.

7  Corruption.

8  Fraud, including that affecting the financial interests of the European Communities within the meaning of the Convention of 26 July 1995 on the protection of the European Communities' financial interests.

9  Laundering of the proceeds of crime.

10  Counterfeiting currency, including of the euro.

11  Computer-related crime.

12  Environmental crime, including illicit trafficking in endangered animal species and in endangered plant species and varieties.

13  Facilitation of unauthorised entry and residence.

14  Murder, grievous bodily injury.

15  Illicit trade in human organs and tissue.

16  Kidnapping, illegal restraint and hostage-taking.

17  Racism and xenophobia.

18  Organised or armed robbery.

19  Illicit trafficking in cultural goods, including antiques and works of art.

20  Swindling.

21  Racketeering and extortion.

22  Counterfeiting and piracy of products.

23  Forgery of administrative documents and trafficking therein.

24  Forgery of means of payment.

25  Illicit trafficking in hormonal substances and other growth promoters.

26  Illicit trafficking in nuclear or radioactive materials.

27  Trafficking in stolen vehicles.

28  Rape.

29  Arson.

30  Crimes within the jurisdiction of the International Criminal Court.

31  Unlawful seizure of aircraft/ships.

32  Sabotage.


**SCHEDULE 3**                              Section 219

**AMENDMENTS**

### Introduction

1  The amendments specified in this Schedule shall have effect.


### Parliamentary Commissioner Act 1967 (c. 13)

2  In Schedule 3 to the Parliamentary Commissioner Act 1967 (c. 13) (matters not subject to investigation) for paragraph 4 substitute—

"4 Action taken by the Secretary of State under the Extradition Act 2003."

## Criminal Justice Act 1967 (c. 80)

**3** Section 34 of the Criminal Justice Act 1967 (c. 80) (committal of persons under twenty-one accused of extradition crimes) shall cease to have effect.

## Suppression of Terrorism Act 1978 (c. 26)

**4** Sections 1 (offences not to be regarded as of a political character) and 2 (restrictions on return of criminal under Extradition Act 1870 or to Republic of Ireland) of the Suppression of Terrorism Act 1978 (c. 26) shall cease to have effect.

**5** For section 5 of the Suppression of Terrorism Act 1978 substitute—

**"5 Power to apply section 4 to non-convention countries**

(1) The Secretary of State may by order direct that section 4 above shall apply in relation to a country falling within subsection (2) below as it applies in relation to a convention country, subject to the exceptions (if any) specified in the order.

(2) A country falls within this subsection if—

(a) it is not a convention country; and

(b) it is a category 1 territory or a category 2 territory within the meaning of the Extradition Act 2003."

## Criminal Justice (International Co-operation) Act 1990 (c. 5)

**6** Section 22(1) of the Criminal Justice (International Co-operation) Act 1990 (c. 5) (offences to which an Order in Council under the Extradition Act 1870 can apply) shall cease to have effect.

## Computer Misuse Act 1990 (c. 18)

**7** Section 15 of the Computer Misuse Act 1990 (c. 18) (extradition where Schedule 1 to the Extradition Act 1989 applies) shall cease to have effect.

## Aviation and Maritime Security Act 1990 (c. 31)

**8** Section 49 of the Aviation and Maritime Security Act 1990 (c. 31) (extradition by virtue of Orders in Council under Extradition Act 1870) shall cease to have effect.

## Criminal Justice Act 1991 (c. 53)

**9** In section 47 of the Criminal Justice Act 1991 (c. 53) (persons extradited to the United Kingdom) subsection (4) shall cease to have effect.

## United Nations Personnel Act 1997 (c. 13)

**10** Section 6(1) of the United Nations Personnel Act 1997 (c. 13) (offences to which an Order in Council under section 2 of the Extradition Act 1870 can apply) shall cease to have effect.

## Terrorism Act 2000 (c. 11)

**11** Section 64(5) of the Terrorism Act 2000 (c. 11) (offences to which an Order in Council under section 2 of the Extradition Act 1870 can apply) shall cease to have effect.

## International Criminal Court Act 2001 (c. 17)

**12** Section 71 of the International Criminal Court Act 2001 (c. 17) (extradition: Orders in Council under the Extradition Act 1870) shall cease to have effect.

**13** (1) Part 2 of Schedule 2 to the International Criminal Court Act 2001 (delivery up to International Criminal Court of persons subject to extradition proceedings) is amended as follows.

(2) For paragraph 7 (meaning of "extradition proceedings") substitute—

"7 In this Part of this Schedule "extradition proceedings" means proceedings before a court or judge in the United Kingdom under the Extradition Act 2003."

(3) In paragraph 8 (extradition proceedings in England and Wales or Northern Ireland) after sub-paragraph (5) add—

"(6) References in this paragraph to a court include references to a judge."

(4) In paragraph 9 (extradition proceedings in Scotland) after sub-paragraph (3) add—

"(4) References in this paragraph to a court include references to a judge."

(5) In paragraph 10 (power to suspend or revoke warrant or order) for subparagraph (1) substitute—

"(1) Where a court makes a delivery order in respect of a person whose extradition has been ordered under the Extradition Act 2003, it may make any such order as is necessary to enable the delivery order to be executed."

(6) In paragraph 10(2) omit the words "by a court or judicial officer".

## Enterprise Act 2002 (c. 40)

**14** Section 191 of the Enterprise Act 2002 (c. 40) (offences to which an Order in Council under the Extradition Act 1870 can apply) shall cease to have effect.

SCHEDULE 4                                                                 Section 220

REPEALS

| Short title and chapter | Extent of repeal |
| --- | --- |
| Backing of Warrants (Republic of Ireland) Act 1965 (c. 45) | The whole Act. |
| Criminal Justice Act 1967 (c. 80) | Section 34. |
| Criminal Jurisdiction Act 1975 (c. 59) | In Schedule 3, paragraph 1. |
| Bail Act 1976 (c. 63) | In section 2(2) the definition of "proceedings against a fugitive offender". In section 4(2) the words "or proceedings against a fugitive offender for the offence". In section 7(4) the words from "In reckoning" to "Sunday". In Schedule 2, paragraph 33. |
| Criminal Law Act 1977 (c. 45) | In Schedule 12, in the entry for the Bail Act 1976, paragraph 4. |

| Short title and chapter | Extent of repeal |
|---|---|
| Suppression of Terrorism Act 1978 (c. 26) | Sections 1 and 2.<br>In section 8—<br>(a) subsection (5)(a);<br>(b) in subsection (6) the words from "an order made under section 1(4)" to "or". |
| Extradition Act 1989 (c. 33) | The whole Act. |
| Criminal Justice (International Co-operation) Act 1990 (c. 5) | Section 22. |
| Computer Misuse Act 1990 (c. 18) | Section 15. |
| Aviation and Maritime Security Act 1990 (c. 31) | Section 49. |
| Criminal Justice Act 1991 (c. 53) | Section 47(4). |
| Bail (Amendment) Act 1993 (c. 26) | In section 1—<br>(a) in subsection (4), the word "such";<br>(b) in subsection (8), the word "magistrates". |
| Criminal Justice Act 1993 (c. 36) | Section 72.<br>Section 79(7). |
| Criminal Justice and Public Order Act 1994 (c. 33) | Sections 158 and 159. |
| United Nations Personnel Act 1997 (c. 13) | Section 6. |
| Justices of the Peace Act 1997 (c. 25) | In Schedule 5, paragraph 9. |
| Access to Justice Act 1999 (c. 22) | In Schedule 11, paragraphs 18 and 31 to 36. |
| Powers of Criminal Courts (Sentencing) Act 2000 (c. 6) | In Schedule 9, paragraph 124. |
| Terrorism Act 2000 (c. 11) | Section 64. |
| International Criminal Court Act 2001 (c. 17) | Sections 71 to 73.<br>In paragraph 10(2) of Schedule 2, the words "by a court or judicial officer". |
| Proceeds of Crime Act 2002 (c. 29) | In Schedule 11, paragraph 18. |
| Enterprise Act 2002 (c. 40) | Section 191. |

---

## STATUTORY INSTRUMENTS

---

# 2003 No. 3150

# EXTRADITION

## The Extradition Act 2003 (Multiple Offences) Order 2003

| | |
|---|---|
| *Made* - - - - - | *4th December 2003* |
| Laid before Parliament | 11th December 2003 |
| *Coming into force* - - | *1st January 2004* |

The Secretary of State, in exercise of the powers conferred on him by sections 207 and 223(3) of the Extradition Act 2003[1], hereby makes the following Order:

1.  This Order may be cited as the Extradition Act 2003 (Multiple Offences) Order 2003 and shall come into force on 1st January 2004.

2.—(1)  In this Order "the Act" means the Extradition Act 2003.

(2)  The Act is to have effect with the modifications specified in the Schedule to this Order in relation to a case where—

 (a)  a Part 1 warrant is issued for more than one offence;

 (b)  a request for extradition is made in respect of more than one offence.

| | |
|---|---|
| Home Office | *Caroline Flint* |
| 4th December 2003 | Parliamentary Under-Secretary of State |

---

[1] 2003 c. 41.

SCHEDULE ARTICLE 2(2)

MODIFICATIONS TO THE ACT

**General modification**

**1.**—(1) Unless the context otherwise requires, any reference in the Act to an offence (including a reference to an extradition offence) is to be construed as a reference to offences (or extradition offences).

(2) Sub-paragraph (1) does not apply to any reference to an offence—
  (a) in a modification made by this Schedule; or
  (b) in a provision of the Act which is relevant to such a modification.

**Initial stage of extradition hearing**

**2.**—(1) Section 10 is modified as follows.

(2) In subsection (2) for "the offence" substitute "any of the offences".

(3) For subsection (3) substitute—

  "(3) If the judge decides the question in subsection (2) in the negative in relation to an offence, he must order the person's discharge in relation to that offence only.".

(4) For subsection (4) substitute—

  "(4) If the judge decides that question in the affirmative in relation to one or more offences he must proceed under section 11".

**Bars to extradition**

**3.**—(1) Section 11 is modified as follows.

(2) For subsection (3) substitute—

  "(3) If the judge decides any of the questions in subsection (1) in the affirmative in relation to an offence, he must order the person's discharge in relation to that offence only".

(3) For subsection (4) substitute—

  "(4) If the judge decides those questions in the negative in relation to an offence and the person is alleged to be unlawfully at large after conviction of the extradition offence, the judge must proceed under section 20."

(4) For subsection (5) substitute—

  "(5) If the judge decides those questions in the negative in relation to an offence and the person is accused of the commission of the extradition offence but is not alleged to be unlawfully at large after conviction of it, the judge must proceed under section 21".

**Case where person has been convicted**

**4.**—(1) Section 20 is modified as follows.

(2) In subsection (1) after "decide" insert "in relation to each offence".

(3) In subsection (2) after "section 21" insert "in relation to the offence in question".

(4) In subsection (3) after "decide" insert "in relation to each offence".

(5) In subsection (4) after "section 21" insert "in relation to the offence in question".

**Human rights**

**5.**—(1) Section 21 is modified as follows.

(2) In subsection (1) after "decide" insert "in relation to each offence".

(3) In subsection (2) after "discharge" insert "in relation to the offence in question".

(4) In subsection (3) after "extradited" insert "for the offence in question".

**Appeal against extradition order**

**6.**—(1) Section 26 is modified as follows.

(2) In subsection (1) after "extradition" insert "in relation to an offence".

### Court's powers on appeal under section 26

**7.**—(1) Section 27 is modified as follows.

(2) In subsection (5) after "it must" insert "in relation to the relevant offence only".

### Appeal against discharge at extradition hearing

**8.**—(1) Section 28 is modified as follows.

(2) In subsection (1) after "discharge" insert "in relation to an offence".

### Court's powers on appeal under section 28

**9.**—(1) Section 29 is modified as follows.

(2) In subsection (5) after "it must" insert "in relation to the relevant offence only".

### Detention pending conclusion of appeal under section 28

**10.**—(1) Section 30 is modified as follows.

(2) In subsection (1) after "discharge" insert "in relation to an offence".

### Appeal to House of Lords

**11.**—(1) Section 32 is modified as follows.

(2) In subsection (1) after "appeal" insert "in relation to each offence".

### Powers of House of Lords on appeal under section 32

**12.**—(1) Section 33 is modified as follows.

(2) In subsection (3) after "must" insert "in relation to the relevant offence only".

(3) In subsection (5) after "must" insert "in relation to the relevant offence only".

(4) In subsection (7) after "must" insert "in relation to the relevant offence only".

(5) In subsection (8) after "must" insert "in relation to the relevant offence only".

### Extradition where no appeal

**13.**—(1) Section 35 is modified as follows.

(2) In subsection (1)(a) after "extradition" insert "in relation to an offence".

(3) In subsection (4)(b) after the second "date" insert ", or

    (c) if proceedings are continuing in relation to other offences contained in the same Part 1 warrant, 10 days starting with the day on which the judge, the High Court or the House of Lords make the final order in relation to the last of the offences in respect of which the same Part 1 warrant was issued".

### Extradition following an appeal

**14.**—(1) Section 36 is modified as follows.

(2) In subsection (1)(a) after "territory" insert "in relation to an offence".

(3) In subsection (1)(b) after "there" insert "in relation to that offence".

(4) In subsection (3)(a)—

    (a) for "the decision of the relevant court on the appeal becomes" substitute "all decisions of the relevant court on any appeal in relation to any offence in respect of which the same Part 1 warrant was issued become";

    (b) for "the appeal are discontinued" insert "any appeal in relation to any offence in respect of which the same Part 1 warrant was issued are discontinued".

### Withdrawal of warrant before extradition

**15.**—(1) Section 41 is modified as follows.

(2) In subsection (1) for the words from "a Part 1 warrant" to the end substitute "they do not wish to proceed with their request for extradition in relation to an offence in respect of which the Part 1 warrant was issued".

(3)  In subsection (3) after "discharge" insert "in relation to that offence".

### Withdrawal of warrant while appeal to High Court pending

**16.**—(1)  Section 42 is modified as follows.

(2)  In subsection (1) for the words from "a Part 1 warrant" to the end substitute "they do not wish to proceed with their request for extradition in relation to an offence in respect of which the Part 1 warrant was issued".

(3)  In subsection (3)(a) after "extradition" insert "in relation to that offence".

(4)  In subsection (3)(b) after "appeal" insert "in relation to that offence".

### Withdrawal of warrant while appeal to House of Lords pending

**17.**—(1)  Section 43 is modified as follows.

(2)  In subsection (1) for the words from "a Part 1 warrant" to the end substitute "they do not wish to proceed with their request for extradition in relation to an offence in respect of which the Part 1 warrant was issued".

(3)  In subsection (3)(a) after "discharge" insert "in relation to that offence".

(4)  In subsection (3)(b) after "extradition" insert "in relation to that offence".

(5)  In subsection (4) after "appeal" insert "in relation to that offence".

### Consent to extradition

**18.**—(1)  Section 45 is modified as follows.

(2)  In subsection (1) after "issued" insert "in relation to any offence contained in the Part 1 warrant".

(3)  In subsection (2) after the second "section" insert "in relation to any offence contained in the Part 1 warrant".

(4)  In subsection (3) after "section" insert "to every offence contained in the Part 1 warrant".

### Extradition to category 1 territory following consent

**19.**—(1)  Section 47 is modified as follows.

(2)  In subsection (3)(b) after the second "date" insert ", or

    (c)  if proceedings are continuing in relation to other offences contained in the same Part 1 warrant, 10 days starting with the day on which the judge, the High Court or the House of Lords make the final order in relation to the last of the offences in respect of which the same Part 1 warrant was issued".

(3)  In subsection (5) for the words from "the Part 1 warrant" to the end substitute "they do not wish to proceed with their request for extradition in relation to an offence in respect of which the Part 1 warrant was issued".

(4)  In subsection (5)(b) after "discharge" insert "in relation to that offence".

### Other warrant issued: extradition to category 1 territory

**20.**—(1)  Section 49 is modified as follows.

(2)  In subsection (3)(b) after "date" insert ", or

    (c)  if proceedings are continuing in relation to other offences contained in the same Part 1 warrant, 10 days starting with the day on which the judge, the High Court or the House of Lords make the final order in relation to the last of the offences in respect of which the same Part 1 warrant was issued".

(3)  In subsection (5) for the words from "the Part 1 warrant" to the end substitute "they do not wish to proceed with their request for extradition in relation to an offence in respect of which the Part 1 warrant was issued".

(4)  In subsection (5)(b) after "discharge" insert "in relation to that offence".

### Arrest warrant following extradition request

**21.**—(1) Section 71 is modified as follows.

(2) For subsection (2)(a) substitute "any of the offences in respect of which extradition is requested are extradition offences".

(3) In subsection (2)(b) after "evidence" insert "in relation to that offence".

### Provisional warrant

**22.**—(1) Section 73 is modified as follows.

(2) For subsection (3)(a) substitute—

"(a) any of the offences in respect of which extradition is requested are extradition offences.".

(3) In subsection (3)(b) after "evidence" insert "in relation to that offence".

### Initial stages of extradition hearing

**23.**—(1) Section 78 is modified as follows.

(2) In subsection (2) after "(or include)" insert "in relation to each offence".

(3) In subsection (3) after "discharge" insert "in relation to the relevant offence only".

(4) In subsection (4)(b) for "the offence" substitute "each offence".

(5) In subsection (6) after "discharge" insert "in relation to that offence".

(6) For subsection (7) substitute—

"(7) If the judge decides those questions in the affirmative in relation to one or more offences he must proceed under section 79".

### Bars to extradition

**24.**—(1) Section 79 is modified as follows.

(2) For subsection (3) substitute—

"(3) If the judge decides any of the questions in subsection (1) in the affirmative in relation to any offence, he must order the person's discharge in relation to that offence only".

(3) For subsection (4) substitute—

"(4) If the judge decides those questions in the negative in relation to any offence and the person is accused of the commission of the extradition offences but is not alleged to be unlawfully at large after conviction of it, the judge must proceed under section 84 in relation to that offence".

(4) For subsection (5) substitute—

"(5) If the judge decides any of those questions in the negative in relation to any offence and the person is alleged to be unlawfully at large after conviction of it, the judge must proceed under section 85 in relation to that offence".

### Case where person has not been convicted

**25.**—(1) Section 84 is modified as follows.

(2) In subsection (1) after "evidence" insert "in relation to each offence".

(3) In subsection (5) after "discharge" insert "in relation to that offence".

(4) In subsections (6) and (7) after "section 87" insert "in relation to that offence".

### Case where person has been convicted

**26.**—(1) Section 85 is modified as follows.

(2) In subsection (1) after "decide" insert "in relation to each offence".

(3) In subsection (2) after "section 87" insert "in relation to the offence".

(4) In subsection (4) after "section 87" insert "in relation to the offence".

(5) In subsection (6) after "section 86" insert "in relation to the offence".

(6) In subsection (7) after "discharge" insert "in relation to the offence".

### Conviction in person's absence

**27.**—(1) Section 86 is modified as follows.

(2) In subsection (1) after "decide" insert "in relation to each offence".

(3) In subsection (5) after "discharge" insert "in relation to the offence".

(4) In subsection (6) after "section 87" insert "in relation to the offence".

(5) In subsection (7)(b) after "section 87" insert "in relation to the offence".

### Human rights

**28.**—(1) Section 87 is modified as follows.

(2) In subsection (1) after "decide" insert "in relation to each offence".

(3) In subsection (2) after "discharge" insert "in relation to the offence".

(4) In subsection (3) after "extradited" insert "for the offence in question".

### Case sent to the Secretary of State

**29.**—(1) Section 92 is modified as follows.

(2) In subsection (2)(a) after "High Court" insert "in relation to each relevant offence".

### Secretary of State's consideration of case

**30.**—(1) Section 93 is modified as follows.

(2) In subsection (2) after "decide" insert "in relation to each offence".

(3) In subsection (3) after "discharge" insert "in relation to the offence".

(4) In subsection (4)—

    (a) after "negative" insert "in relation to the offence in question" and
    (b) after "requested" insert "for that offence".

### Death penalty

**31.**—(1) Section 94 is modified as follows.

(2) In subsection (1) after the first "territory" insert "in relation to an offence".

(3) In subsection (2) after "assurance" insert "in relation to the relevant offence".

### Speciality

**32.**—(1) Section 95 is modified as follows.

(2) In subsection (2) after "section 127" insert "in relation to all offences contained in the extradition request".

### Information

**33.**—(1) Section 100 is modified as follows.

(2) In subsection (1)(b) after "High Court" insert "in relation to each relevant offence".

(3) In subsection (2) after "extradition" insert "in relation to the offence".

(4) In subsection (4) after "discharge" insert "in relation to an offence".

### Appeal where case sent to Secretary of State

**34.**—(1) Section 103 is modified as follows.

(2) In subsection (1) after "relevant decision" insert "in relation to each offence".

(3) In subsection (2) after "section 127" insert "in relation to the offence".

(4) In subsection (6) after "discharge" insert "in relation to the offence".

(5) In subsection (7) after "discharge" insert "in relation to the offence".

#### Court's powers on appeal under section 103

**35.**—(1) Section 104 is modified as follows.

(2) In subsection (5) after "it must" insert "in relation to the relevant offence only".

#### Appeal against discharge at extradition hearing

**36.**—(1) Section 105 is modified as follows.

(2) In subsection (1) after "discharge" insert "in relation to an offence".

#### Court's powers on appeal under section 105

**37.**—(1) Section 106 is modified as follows.

(2) In subsection (6) after "it must" insert "in relation to the relevant offence only".

#### Detention pending conclusion of appeal under section 105

**38.**—(1) Section 107 is modified as follows.

(2) In subsection (1) after "section 105" insert "in relation to at least one offence".

(3) In subsection (4) after "times" insert "taking all offences contained in the extradition request together".

#### Appeal against extradition order

**39.**—(1) Section 108 is modified as follows.

(2) In subsection (1) after "extradition" insert "in relation to an offence".

(3) In subsection (2) after "extradition" insert "in relation to the offence".

#### Court's powers on appeal under section 108

**40.**—(1) Section 109 is modified as follows.

(2) In subsection (5) after "it must" insert "in relation to the relevant offence only".

#### Appeal against discharge by Secretary of State

**41.**—(1) Section 110 is modified as follows.

(2) In subsection (1) after "discharge" insert "in relation to an offence".

#### Court's powers on appeal under section 110

**42.**—(1) Section 111 is modified as follows.

(2) In subsection (5) after "it must" insert "in relation to the relevant offence only".

#### Detention pending conclusion of appeal under section 110

**43.**—(1) Section 112 is modified as follows.

(2) In subsection (2) for "the appeal" substitute "any appeal".

#### Appeal to House of Lords

**44.**—(1) Section 114 is modified as follows.

(2) In subsection (1) after "High Court" insert "in relation to each offence".

#### Powers of House of Lords on appeal under section 114

**45.**—(1) Section 115 is modified as follows.

(2) In subsection (3) after "must" insert "in relation to the relevant offence only".

(3) In subsection (5) after "must" insert "in relation to the relevant offence only".

(4) In subsection (7) after "must" insert "in relation to the relevant offence only".

### Extradition where no appeal

**46.**—(1) Section 117 is modified as follows.

(2) In subsection (1)(a) after "extradition" insert "in relation to an offence".

(3) In subsection (2) after "order" insert "or if proceedings are continuing in relation to other offences contained in the extradition request, 10 days starting with the day on which the Secretary of State makes the final order in relation to the last of the offences in respect of which the same extradition request was made".

### Extradition following appeal

**47.**—(1) Section 118 is modified as follows.

(2) In subsection (2)(b) after "discontinued" insert ", or

(c) if there is more than one appeal outstanding in relation to offences contained in the same extradition request, the day on which the last decision of the relevant court becomes final or on which the last proceedings on the appeal are discontinued".

### Withdrawal of request before end of extradition hearing

**48.**—(1) Section 122 is modified as follows.

(2) In subsection (1) after "extradition" insert "in relation to an offence".

(3) In subsection (3) after "discharge" insert "in relation to the offence".

### Withdrawal of request after case sent to Secretary of State

**49.**—(1) Section 123 is modified as follows.

(2) In subsection (1) after "extradition" insert "in relation to an offence".

(3) In subsection (3) after "discharge" insert "in relation to the offence".

### Withdrawal of request while appeal to High Court pending

**50.**—(1) Section 124 is modified as follows.

(2) In subsection (1) after "extradition" insert "in relation to an offence".

(3) In subsection (3) after "must" insert "in relation to the offence".

(4) In subsection (4) after "appeal" insert "in relation to the offence".

### Withdrawal of request while appeal to House of Lords pending

**51.**—(1) Section 125 is modified as follows.

(2) In subsection (1) after "extradition" insert "in relation to an offence".

(3) In subsection (3) after "must" insert "in relation to the offence".

(4) In subsection (4) after "appeal" insert "in relation to the offence".

### Consent to extradition: general

**52.**—(1) Section 127 is modified as follows.

(2) In subsection (1) after "requested" insert "in relation to one or more offences contained within the extradition request".

(3) In subsection (2) after "extradition" insert "in relation to one or more offences contained within the extradition request".

**Consent to extradition before case sent to Secretary of State**

**53.**—(1)  Section 128 is modified as follows.

(2)  In subsection (2) after "so" insert "unless there are other offences contained within the extradition request in relation to which the person has not consented to his extradition".

(3)  In subsection (3) after "91" insert "unless there are other offences contained within the extradition request in relation to which the person has not consented to his extradition".

(4)  In subsection (5) after "extradition" insert "if he has consented to his extradition in relation to every offence contained within the extradition request".

**National security**

**54.**—(1)  Section 208 is modified as follows.

(2)  In subsection (2) for "an offence" substitute "more than one offence".

(3)  In subsection (3)(a) for "the offence" substitute "any of the offences".

(4)  In subsection (3)(b) for "the offence" substitute "the offence in question".

(5)  In subsection (4) after "the offence" insert "in question".

(6)  For subsection (6)(a) substitute—

"(a)  direct that proceedings in relation to an offence contained in the Part 1 warrant are not to be proceeded with".

(7)  In subsection (6)(b) after "the offence" insert "in question only".

(8)  In subsection (7) after "discharge" insert "in relation to the offence".

# EXPLANATORY NOTE

*(This note is not part of the Order)*

This Order provides for the Extradition Act 2003 to have effect with the modifications specified in the Schedule to the Order in relation to the following cases. Those cases are where a Part 1 warrant is issued in respect of more than one offence or where a request for extradition is made in respect of more than one offence.

In particular, the modifications are such as to allow for the partial execution of the Part 1 warrant or the request for extradition in cases where the judge and or the Secretary of State must consider more than one offence for which extradition is sought. It is possible that extradition will be refused in relation to some offences but not all, allowing for extradition to take place in relation to some offences only.

# APPENDIX 6

*(Acts adopted pursuant to Title VI of the Treaty on European Union)*

## COUNCIL FRAMEWORK DECISION
### of 13 June 2002

**on the European arrest warrant and the surrender procedures between Member States**

(2002/584/JHA)

THE COUNCIL OF THE EUROPEAN UNION,

Having regard to the Treaty on European Union, and in particular Article 31(a) and (b) and Article 34(2)(b) thereof,

Having regard to the proposal from the Commission[1],

Having regard to the opinion of the European Parliament[2],

Whereas:

(1) According to the Conclusions of the Tampere European Council of 15 and 16 October 1999, and in particular point 35 thereof, the formal extradition procedure should be abolished among the Member States in respect of persons who are fleeing from justice after having been finally sentenced and extradition procedures should be speeded up in respect of persons suspected of having committed an offence.

(2) The programme of measures to implement the principle of mutual recognition of criminal decisions envisaged in point 37 of the Tampere European Council Conclusions and adopted by the Council on 30 November 2000[3], addresses the matter of mutual enforcement of arrest warrants.

(3) All or some Member States are parties to a number of conventions in the field of extradition, including the European Convention on extradition of 13 December 1957 and the European Convention on the suppression of terrorism of 27 January 1977. The Nordic States have extradition laws with identical wording.

(4) In addition, the following three Conventions dealing in whole or in part with extradition have been agreed upon among Member States and form part of the Union acquis: the Convention of 19 June 1990 implementing the Schengen Agreement of 14 June 1985 on the gradual abolition of checks at their common borders[4] (regarding relations between the Member States which are parties to that Convention), the Convention of 10 March 1995 on simplified extradition procedure between the Member States of the European Union[5] and the Convention of 27 September 1996 relating to extradition between the Member States of the European Union[6].

(5) The objective set for the Union to become an area of freedom, security and justice leads to abolishing extradition between Member States and replacing it by a system of surrender between judicial authorities. Further, the introduction of a new simplified system of surrender of sentenced or suspected persons for the purposes of execution or prosecution of criminal sentences makes it possible to remove the complexity and potential for delay inherent in the present extradition procedures. Traditional cooperation

---

[1] OJ C 332 E, 27.11.2001, p. 305.
[2] Opinion delivered on 9 January 2002 (not yet published in the Official Journal).
[3] OJ C 12 E, 15.1.2001, p. 10.

[4] OJ L 239, 22.9.2000, p. 19.
[5] OJ C 78, 30.3.1995, p. 2.
[6] OJ C 313, 13.10.1996, p. 12.

relations which have prevailed up till now between Member States should be replaced by a system of free movement of judicial decisions in criminal matters, covering both pre-sentence and final decisions, within an area of freedom, security and justice.

(6) The European arrest warrant provided for in this Framework Decision is the first concrete measure in the field of criminal law implementing the principle of mutual recognition which the European Council referred to as the 'cornerstone' of judicial cooperation.

(7) Since the aim of replacing the system of multilateral extradition built upon the European Convention on Extradition of 13 December 1957 cannot be sufficiently achieved by the Member States acting unilaterally and can therefore, by reason of its scale and effects, be better achieved at Union level, the Council may adopt measures in accordance with the principle of subsidiarity as referred to in Article 2 of the Treaty on European Union and Article 5 of the Treaty establishing the European Community. In accordance with the principle of proportionality, as set out in the latter Article, this Framework Decision does not go beyond what is necessary in order to achieve that objective.

(8) Decisions on the execution of the European arrest warrant must be subject to sufficient controls, which means that a judicial authority of the Member State where the requested person has been arrested will have to take the decision on his or her surrender.

(9) The role of central authorities in the execution of a European arrest warrant must be limited to practical and administrative assistance.

(10) The mechanism of the European arrest warrant is based on a high level of confidence between Member States. Its implementation may be suspended only in the event of a serious and persistent breach by one of the Member States of the principles set out in Article 6(1) of the Treaty on European Union, determined by the Council pursuant to Article 7(1) of the said Treaty with the consequences set out in Article 7(2) thereof.

(11) In relations between Member States, the European arrest warrant should replace all the previous instruments concerning extradition, including the provisions of Title III of the Convention implementing the Schengen Agreement which concern extradition.

(12) This Framework Decision respects fundamental rights and observes the principles recognised by Article 6 of the Treaty on European Union and reflected in the Charter of Fundamental Rights of the European Union[7], in particular Chapter VI thereof. Nothing in this Framework Decision may be interpreted as prohibiting refusal to surrender a person for whom a European arrest warrant has been issued when there are reasons to believe, on the basis of objective elements, that the said arrest warrant has been issued for the purpose of prosecuting or punishing a person on the grounds of his or her sex, race, religion, ethnic origin, nationality, language, political opinions or sexual orientation, or that that person's position may be prejudiced for any of these reasons.

This Framework Decision does not prevent a Member State from applying its constitutional rules relating to due process, freedom of association, freedom of the press and freedom of expression in other media.

(13) No person should be removed, expelled or extradited to a State where there is a serious risk that he or she would be subjected to the death penalty, torture or other inhuman or degrading treatment or punishment.

(14) Since all Member States have ratified the Council of Europe Convention of 28 January 1981 for the protection of individuals with regard to automatic processing of personal data, the personal data processed in the context of the implementation of this Framework Decision should be protected in accordance with the principles of the said Convention,

---

[7] OJ C 364, 18.12.2000, p. 1.

HAS ADOPTED THIS FRAMEWORK DECISION:

## CHAPTER 1
## GENERAL PRINCIPLES
### Article 1
**Definition of the European arrest warrant and obligation to execute it**

1. The European arrest warrant is a judicial decision issued by a Member State with a view to the arrest and surrender by another Member State of a requested person, for the purposes of conducting a criminal prosecution or executing a custodial sentence or detention order.

2. Member States shall execute any European arrest warrant on the basis of the principle of mutual recognition and in accordance with the provisions of this Framework Decision.

3. This Framework Decision shall not have the effect of modifying the obligation to respect fundamental rights and fundamental legal principles as enshrined in Article 6 of the Treaty on European Union.

### Article 2
**Scope of the European arrest warrant**

1. A European arrest warrant may be issued for acts punishable by the law of the issuing Member State by a custodial sentence or a detention order for a maximum period of at least 12 months or, where a sentence has been passed or a detention order has been made, for sentences of at least four months.

2. The following offences, if they are punishable in the issuing Member State by a custodial sentence or a detention order for a maximum period of at least three years and as they are defined by the law of the issuing Member State, shall, under the terms of this Framework Decision and without verification of the double criminality of the act, give rise to surrender pursuant to a European arrest warrant:

   - participation in a criminal organisation,
   - terrorism,
   - trafficking in human beings,
   - sexual exploitation of children and child pornography,
   - illicit trafficking in narcotic drugs and psychotropic substances,
   - illicit trafficking in weapons, munitions and explosives,
   - corruption,
   - fraud, including that affecting the financial interests of the European Communities within the meaning of the Convention of 26 July 1995 on the protection of the European Communities' financial interests,
   - laundering of the proceeds of crime,
   - counterfeiting currency, including of the euro,
   - computer-related crime,
   - environmental crime, including illicit trafficking in endangered animal species and in endangered plant species and varieties,
   - facilitation of unauthorised entry and residence,
   - murder, grievous bodily injury,
   - illicit trade in human organs and tissue,
   - kidnapping, illegal restraint and hostage-taking,
   - racism and xenophobia,
   - organised or armed robbery,
   - illicit trafficking in cultural goods, including antiques and works of art,
   - swindling,
   - racketeering and extortion,
   - counterfeiting and piracy of products,
   - forgery of administrative documents and trafficking therein,
   - forgery of means of payment,
   - illicit trafficking in hormonal substances and other growth promoters,
   - illicit trafficking in nuclear or radioactive materials,
   - trafficking in stolen vehicles,
   - rape,
   - arson,
   - crimes within the jurisdiction of the International Criminal Court,
   - unlawful seizure of aircraft/ships,
   - sabotage.

3. The Council may decide at any time, acting unanimously after consultation of the European Parliament under the conditions laid down in Article 39(1) of the Treaty on European Union (TEU), to add other categories of offence to the list contained in paragraph 2. The Council shall examine, in the light of the report submitted by the Commission pursuant to Article 34(3), whether the list should be extended or amended.

4. For offences other than those covered by paragraph 2, surrender may be subject to the condition that the acts for which the

European arrest warrant has been issued constitute an offence under the law of the executing Member State, whatever the constituent elements or however it is described.

## Article 3
### Grounds for mandatory non-execution of the European arrest warrant

The judicial authority of the Member State of execution (hereinafter 'executing judicial authority') shall refuse to execute the European arrest warrant in the following cases:

1. if the offence on which the arrest warrant is based is covered by amnesty in the executing Member State, where that State had jurisdiction to prosecute the offence under its own criminal law;

2. if the executing judicial authority is informed that the requested person has been finally judged by a Member State in respect of the same acts provided that, where there has been sentence, the sentence has been served or is currently being served or may no longer be executed under the law of the sentencing Member State;

3. if the person who is the subject of the European arrest warrant may not, owing to his age, be held criminally responsible for the acts on which the arrest warrant is based under the law of the executing State.

## Article 4
### Grounds for optional non-execution of the European arrest warrant

The executing judicial authority may refuse to execute the European arrest warrant:

1. if, in one of the cases referred to in Article 2(4), the act on which the European arrest warrant is based does not constitute an offence under the law of the executing Member State; however, in relation to taxes or duties, customs and exchange, execution of the European arrest warrant shall not be refused on the ground that the law of the executing Member State does not impose the same kind of tax or duty or does not contain the same type of rules as regards taxes, duties and customs and exchange regulations as the law of the issuing Member State;

2. where the person who is the subject of the European arrest warrant is being prosecuted in the executing Member State for the same act as that on which the European arrest warrant is based;

3. where the judicial authorities of the executing Member State have decided either not to prosecute for the offence on which the European arrest warrant is based or to halt proceedings, or where a final judgment has been passed upon the requested person in a Member State, in respect of the same acts, which prevents further proceedings;

4. where the criminal prosecution or punishment of the requested person is statute-barred according to the law of the executing Member State and the acts fall within the jurisdiction of that Member State under its own criminal law;

5. if the executing judicial authority is informed that the requested person has been finally judged by a third State in respect of the same acts provided that, where there has been sentence, the sentence has been served or is currently being served or may no longer be executed under the law of the sentencing country;

6. if the European arrest warrant has been issued for the purposes of execution of a custodial sentence or detention order, where the requested person is staying in, or is a national or a resident of the executing Member State and that State undertakes to execute the sentence or detention order in accordance with its domestic law;

7. where the European arrest warrant relates to offences which:

   (a) are regarded by the law of the executing Member State as having been committed in whole or in part in the territory of the executing Member State or in a place treated as such; or

   (b) have been committed outside the territory of the issuing Member State and the law of the executing Member State does not allow prosecution for the same offences when committed outside its territory.

## Article 5
### Guarantees to be given by the issuing Member State in particular cases

The execution of the European arrest warrant by the executing judicial authority may, by the law of the executing Member State, be subject to the following conditions:

1. where the European arrest warrant has been issued for the purposes of executing a sentence or a detention order imposed by a decision rendered in absentia and if the person concerned has not been summoned in person or otherwise informed of the date and place of the hearing which led to the decision rendered in absentia, surrender may be subject to the condition that the issuing judicial authority gives an assurance deemed adequate to guarantee the person who is the subject of the European arrest warrant that he or she will have an opportunity to apply for a retrial of the case in the issuing Member State and to be present at the judgment;

2. if the offence on the basis of which the European arrest warrant has been issued is punishable by custodial life sentence or life-time detention order, the execution of the said arrest warrant may be subject to the condition that the issuing Member State has provisions in its legal system for a review of the penalty or measure imposed, on request or at the latest after 20 years, or for the application of measures of clemency to which the person is entitled to apply for under the law or practice of the issuing Member State, aiming at a non-execution of such penalty or measure;

3. where a person who is the subject of a European arrest warrant for the purposes of prosecution is a national or resident of the executing Member State, surrender may be subject to the condition that the person, after being heard, is returned to the executing Member State in order to serve there the custodial sentence or detention order passed against him in the issuing Member State.

### Article 6
### Determination of the competent judicial authorities

1. The issuing judicial authority shall be the judicial authority of the issuing Member State which is competent to issue a European arrest warrant by virtue of the law of that State.

2. The executing judicial authority shall be the judicial authority of the executing Member State which is competent to execute the European arrest warrant by virtue of the law of that State.

3. Each Member State shall inform the General Secretariat of the Council of the competent judicial authority under its law.

### Article 7
### Recourse to the central authority

1. Each Member State may designate a central authority or, when its legal system so provides, more than one central authority to assist the competent judicial authorities.

2. A Member State may, if it is necessary as a result of the organisation of its internal judicial system, make its central authority(ies) responsible for the administrative transmission and reception of European arrest warrants as well as for all other official correspondence relating thereto. Member State wishing to make use of the possibilities referred to in this Article shall communicate to the General Secretariat of the Council information relating to the designated central authority or central authorities. These indications shall be binding upon all the authorities of the issuing Member State.

### Article 8
### Content and form of the European arrest warrant

1. The European arrest warrant shall contain the following information set out in accordance with the form contained in the Annex:

   (a) the identity and nationality of the requested person;

   (b) the name, address, telephone and fax numbers and e-mail address of the issuing judicial authority;

   (c) evidence of an enforceable judgment, an arrest warrant or any other enforceable judicial decision having the same effect, coming within the scope of Articles 1 and 2;

   (d) the nature and legal classification of the offence, particularly in respect of Article 2;

   (e) a description of the circumstances in which the offence was committed, including the time, place and degree of participation in the offence by the requested person;

(f) the penalty imposed, if there is a final judgment, or the prescribed scale of penalties for the offence under the law of the issuing Member State;

(g) if possible, other consequences of the offence.

2. The European arrest warrant must be translated into the official language or one of the official languages of the executing Member State. Any Member State may, when this Framework Decision is adopted or at a later date, state in a declaration deposited with the General Secretariat of the Council that it will accept a translation in one or more other official languages of the Institutions of the European Communities.

## CHAPTER 2
## SURRENDER PROCEDURE

### *Article 9*
### Transmission of a European arrest warrant

1. When the location of the requested person is known, the issuing judicial authority may transmit the European arrest warrant directly to the executing judicial authority.

2. The issuing judicial authority may, in any event, decide to issue an alert for the requested person in the Schengen Information System (SIS).

3. Such an alert shall be effected in accordance with the provisions of Article 95 of the Convention of 19 June 1990 implementing the Schengen Agreement of 14 June 1985 on the gradual abolition of controls at common borders. An alert in the Schengen Information System shall be equivalent to a European arrest warrant accompanied by the information set out in Article 8(1).

For a transitional period, until the SIS is capable of transmitting all the information described in Article 8, the alert shall be equivalent to a European arrest warrant pending the receipt of the original in due and proper form by the executing judicial authority.

### *Article 10*
### Detailed procedures for transmitting a European arrest warrant

1. If the issuing judicial authority does not know the competent executing judicial

authority, it shall make the requisite enquiries, including through the contact points of the European Judicial Network[8], in order to obtain that information from the executing Member State.

2. If the issuing judicial authority so wishes, transmission may be effected via the secure telecommunications system of the European Judicial Network.

3. If it is not possible to call on the services of the SIS, the issuing judicial authority may call on Interpol to transmit a European arrest warrant.

4. The issuing judicial authority may forward the European arrest warrant by any secure means capable of producing written records under conditions allowing the executing Member State to establish its authenticity.

5. All difficulties concerning the transmission or the authenticity of any document needed for the execution of the European arrest warrant shall be dealt with by direct contacts between the judicial authorities involved, or, where appropriate, with the involvement of the central authorities of the Member States.

6. If the authority which receives a European arrest warrant is not competent to act upon it, it shall automatically forward the European arrest warrant to the competent authority in its Member State and shall inform the issuing judicial authority accordingly.

### *Article 11*
### Rights of a requested person

1. When a requested person is arrested, the executing competent judicial authority shall, in accordance with its national law, inform that person of the European arrest warrant and of its contents, and also of the possibility of consenting to surrender to the issuing judicial authority.

2. A requested person who is arrested for the purpose of the execution of a European arrest warrant shall have a right to be assisted by a legal counsel and by an interpreter in accordance with the national law of the executing Member State.

---

[8] Council Joint Action 98/428/JHA of 29 June 1998 on the creation of a European Judicial Network (OJ L 191, 7.7.1998, p. 4).

## Article 12
### Keeping the person in detention

When a person is arrested on the basis of a European arrest warrant, the executing judicial authority shall take a decision on whether the requested person should remain in detention, in accordance with the law of the executing Member State. The person may be released provisionally at any time in conformity with the domestic law of the executing Member State, provided that the competent authority of the said Member State takes all the measures it deems necessary to prevent the person absconding.

## Article 13
### Consent to surrender

1. If the arrested person indicates that he or she consents to surrender, that consent and, if appropriate, express renunciation of entitlement to the 'speciality rule', referred to in Article 27(2), shall be given before the executing judicial authority, in accordance with the domestic law of the executing Member State.

2. Each Member State shall adopt the measures necessary to ensure that consent and, where appropriate, renunciation, as referred to in paragraph 1, are established in such a way as to show that the person concerned has expressed them voluntarily and in full awareness of the consequences. To that end, the requested person shall have the right to legal counsel.

3. The consent and, where appropriate, renunciation, as referred to in paragraph 1, shall be formally recorded in accordance with the procedure laid down by the domestic law of the executing Member State.

4. In principle, consent may not be revoked. Each Member State may provide that consent and, if appropriate, renunciation may be revoked, in accordance with the rules applicable under its domestic law. In this case, the period between the date of consent and that of its revocation shall not be taken into consideration in establishing the time limits laid down in Article 17. A Member State which wishes to have recourse to this possibility shall inform the General Secretariat of the Council accordingly when this Framework Decision is adopted and shall specify the procedures whereby revocation of consent shall be possible and any amendment to them.

## Article 14
### Hearing of the requested person

Where the arrested person does not consent to his or her surrender as referred to in Article 13, he or she shall be entitled to be heard by the executing judicial authority, in accordance with the law of the executing Member State.

## Article 15
### Surrender decision

1. The executing judicial authority shall decide, within the time-limits and under the conditions defined in this Framework Decision, whether the person is to be surrendered.

2. If the executing judicial authority finds the information communicated by the issuing Member State to be insufficient to allow it to decide on surrender, it shall request that the necessary supplementary information, in particular with respect to Articles 3 to 5 and Article 8, be furnished as a matter of urgency and may fix a time limit for the receipt thereof, taking into account the need to observe the time limits set in Article 17.

3. The issuing judicial authority may at any time forward any additional useful information to the executing judicial authority.

## Article 16
### Decision in the event of multiple requests

1. If two or more Member States have issued European arrest warrants for the same person, the decision on which of the European arrest warrants shall be executed shall be taken by the executing judicial authority with due consideration of all the circumstances and especially the relative seriousness and place of the offences, the respective dates of the European arrest warrants and whether the warrant has been issued for the purposes of prosecution or for execution of a custodial sentence or detention order.

2. The executing judicial authority may seek the advice of Eurojust[9] when making the choice referred to in paragraph 1.

---

[9] Council Decision 2002/187/JHA of 28 February 2002 setting up Eurojust with a view to reinforcing the fight against serious crime (OJ L 63, 6.3.2002, p. 1).

3. In the event of a conflict between a European arrest warrant and a request for extradition presented by a third country, the decision on whether the European arrest warrant or the extradition request takes precedence shall be taken by the competent authority of the executing Member State with due consideration of all the circumstances, in particular those referred to in paragraph 1 and those mentioned in the applicable convention.

4. This Article shall be without prejudice to Member States' obligations under the Statute of the International Criminal Court.

*Article 17*
**Time limits and procedures for the decision to execute the European arrest warrant**

1. A European arrest warrant shall be dealt with and executed as a matter of urgency.

2. In cases where the requested person consents to his surrender, the final decision on the execution of the European arrest warrant should be taken within a period of 10 days after consent has been given.

3. In other cases, the final decision on the execution of the European arrest warrant should be taken within a period of 60 days after the arrest of the requested person.

4. Where in specific cases the European arrest warrant cannot be executed within the time limits laid down in paragraphs 2 or 3, the executing judicial authority shall immediately inform the issuing judicial authority thereof, giving the reasons for the delay. In such case, the time limits may be extended by a further 30 days.

5. As long as the executing judicial authority has not taken a final decision on the European arrest warrant, it shall ensure that the material conditions necessary for effective surrender of the person remain fulfilled.

6. Reasons must be given for any refusal to execute a European arrest warrant.

7. Where in exceptional circumstances a Member State cannot observe the time limits provided for in this Article, it shall inform Eurojust, giving the reasons for the delay. In addition, a Member State which has experienced repeated delays on the part of another Member State in the execution of European arrest warrants shall inform the Council with a view to evaluating the implementation of this Framework Decision at Member State level.

*Article 18*
**Situation pending the decision**

1. Where the European arrest warrant has been issued for the purpose of conducting a criminal prosecution, the executing judicial authority must:

   (a) either agree that the requested person should be heard according to Article 19;

   (b) or agree to the temporary transfer of the requested person.

2. The conditions and the duration of the temporary transfer shall be determined by mutual agreement between the issuing and executing judicial authorities.

3. In the case of temporary transfer, the person must be able to return to the executing Member State to attend hearings concerning him or her as part of the surrender procedure.

*Article 19*
**Hearing the person pending the decision**

1. The requested person shall be heard by a judicial authority, assisted by another person designated in accordance with the law of the Member State of the requesting court.

2. The requested person shall be heard in accordance with the law of the executing Member State and with the conditions determined by mutual agreement between the issuing and executing judicial authorities.

3. The competent executing judicial authority may assign another judicial authority of its Member State to take part in the hearing of the requested person in order to ensure the proper application of this Article and of the conditions laid down.

*Article 20*
**Privileges and immunities**

1. Where the requested person enjoys a privilege or immunity regarding jurisdiction or execution in the executing Member State, the time limits referred to in Article 17 shall not start running unless, and counting from the day when, the executing judicial authority is informed of the fact that the privilege or immunity has been waived.

The executing Member State shall ensure that the material conditions necessary for effective surrender are fulfilled when the person no longer enjoys such privilege or immunity.

2. Where power to waive the privilege or immunity lies with an authority of the executing Member State, the executing judicial authority shall request it to exercise that power forthwith. Where power to waive the privilege or immunity lies with an authority of another State or international organisation, it shall be for the issuing judicial authority to request it to exercise that power.

### Article 21
### Competing international obligations

This Framework Decision shall not prejudice the obligations of the executing Member State where the requested person has been extradited to that Member State from a third State and where that person is protected by provisions of the arrangement under which he or she was extradited concerning speciality. The executing Member State shall take all necessary measures for requesting forthwith the consent of the State from which the requested person was extradited so that he or she can be surrendered to the Member State which issued the European arrest warrant. The time limits referred to in Article 17 shall not start running until the day on which these speciality rules cease to apply. Pending the decision of the State from which the requested person was extradited, the executing Member State will ensure that the material conditions necessary for effective surrender remain fulfilled.

### Article 22
### Notification of the decision

The executing judicial authority shall notify the issuing judicial authority immediately of the decision on the action to be taken on the European arrest warrant.

### Article 23
### Time limits for surrender of the person

1. The person requested shall be surrendered as soon as possible on a date agreed between the authorities concerned.

2. He or she shall be surrendered no later than 10 days after the final decision on the execution of the European arrest warrant.

3. If the surrender of the requested person within the period laid down in paragraph 2 is prevented by circumstances beyond the control of any of the Member States, the executing and issuing judicial authorities shall immediately contact each other and agree on a new surrender date. In that event, the surrender shall take place within 10 days of the new date thus agreed.

4. The surrender may exceptionally be temporarily postponed for serious humanitarian reasons, for example if there are substantial grounds for believing that it would manifestly endanger the requested person's life or health. The execution of the European arrest warrant shall take place as soon as these grounds have ceased to exist. The executing judicial authority shall immediately inform the issuing judicial authority and agree on a new surrender date. In that event, the surrender shall take place within 10 days of the new date thus agreed.

5. Upon expiry of the time limits referred to in paragraphs 2 to 4, if the person is still being held in custody he shall be released.

### Article 24
### Postponed or conditional surrender

1. The executing judicial authority may, after deciding to execute the European arrest warrant, postpone the surrender of the requested person so that he or she may be prosecuted in the executing Member State or, if he or she has already been sentenced, so that he or she may serve, in its territory, a sentence passed for an act other than that referred to in the European arrest warrant.

2. Instead of postponing the surrender, the executing judicial authority may temporarily surrender the requested person to the issuing Member State under conditions to be determined by mutual agreement between the executing and the issuing judicial authorities. The agreement shall be made in writing and the conditions shall be binding on all the authorities in the issuing Member State.

### Article 25
### Transit

1. Each Member State shall, except when it avails itself of the possibility of refusal when the transit of a national or a resident is requested for the purpose of the execution

of a custodial sentence or detention order, permit the transit through its territory of a requested person who is being surrendered provided that it has been given information on:

(a) the identity and nationality of the person subject to the European arrest warrant;

(b) the existence of a European arrest warrant;

(c) the nature and legal classification of the offence;

(d) the description of the circumstances of the offence, including the date and place.

Where a person who is the subject of a European arrest warrant for the purposes of prosecution is a national or resident of the Member State of transit, transit may be subject to the condition that the person, after being heard, is returned to the transit Member State to serve the custodial sentence or detention order passed against him in the issuing Member State.

2. Each Member State shall designate an authority responsible for receiving transit requests and the necessary documents, as well as any other official correspondence relating to transit requests. Member States shall communicate this designation to the General Secretariat of the Council.

3. The transit request and the information set out in paragraph 1 may be addressed to the authority designated pursuant to paragraph 2 by any means capable of producing a written record. The Member State of transit shall notify its decision by the same procedure.

4. This Framework Decision does not apply in the case of transport by air without a scheduled stopover. However, if an unscheduled landing occurs, the issuing Member State shall provide the authority designated pursuant to paragraph 2 with the information provided for in paragraph 1.

5. Where a transit concerns a person who is to be extradited from a third State to a Member State this Article will apply **mutatis mutandis**. In particular the expression 'European arrest warrant' shall be deemed to be replaced by 'extradition request'.

## CHAPTER 3
## EFFECTS OF THE SURRENDER

### Article 26
**Deduction of the period of detention served in the executing Member State**

1. The issuing Member State shall deduct all periods of detention arising from the execution of a European arrest warrant from the total period of detention to be served in the issuing Member State as a result of a custodial sentence or detention order being passed.

2. To that end, all information concerning the duration of the detention of the requested person on the basis of the European arrest warrant shall be transmitted by the executing judicial authority or the central authority designated under Article 7 to the issuing judicial authority at the time of the surrender.

### Article 27
**Possible prosecution for other offences**

1. Each Member State may notify the General Secretariat of the Council that, in its relations with other Member States that have given the same notification, consent is presumed to have been given for the prosecution, sentencing or detention with a view to the carrying out of a custodial sentence or detention order for an offence committed prior to his or her surrender, other than that for which he or she was surrendered, unless in a particular case the executing judicial authority states otherwise in its decision on surrender.

2. Except in the cases referred to in paragraphs 1 and 3, a person surrendered may not be prosecuted, sentenced or otherwise deprived of his or her liberty for an offence committed prior to his or her surrender other than that for which he or she was surrendered.

3. Paragraph 2 does not apply in the following cases:

(a) when the person having had an opportunity to leave the territory of the Member State to which he or she has been surrendered has not done so within 45 days of his or her final discharge, or has returned to that territory after leaving it;

(b) the offence is not punishable by a custodial sentence or detention order;

(c) the criminal proceedings do not give rise to the application of a measure restricting personal liberty;

(d) when the person could be liable to a penalty or a measure not involving the deprivation of liberty, in particular a financial penalty or a measure in lieu thereof, even if the penalty or measure may give rise to a restriction of his or her personal liberty;

(e) when the person consented to be surrendered, where appropriate at the same time as he or she renounced the speciality rule, in accordance with Article 13;

(f) when the person, after his/her surrender, has expressly renounced entitlement to the speciality rule with regard to specific offences preceding his/her surrender. Renunciation shall be given before the competent judicial authorities of the issuing Member State and shall be recorded in accordance with that State's domestic law. The renunciation shall be drawn up in such a way as to make clear that the person has given it voluntarily and in full awareness of the consequences. To that end, the person shall have the right to legal counsel;

(g) where the executing judicial authority which surrendered the person gives its consent in accordance with paragraph 4.

4. A request for consent shall be submitted to the executing judicial authority, accompanied by the information mentioned in Article 8(1) and a translation as referred to in Article 8(2). Consent shall be given when the offence for which it is requested is itself subject to surrender in accordance with the provisions of this Framework Decision. Consent shall be refused on the grounds referred to in Article 3 and otherwise may be refused only on the grounds referred to in Article 4. The decision shall be taken no later than 30 days after receipt of the request.

For the situations mentioned in Article 5 the issuing Member State must give the guarantees provided for therein.

## *Article 28*
### Surrender or subsequent extradition

1. Each Member State may notify the General Secretariat of the Council that, in its relations with other Member States which have given the same notification, the consent for the surrender of a person to a Member State other than the executing Member State pursuant to a European arrest warrant issued for an offence committed prior to his or her surrender is presumed to have been given, unless in a particular case the executing judicial authority states otherwise in its decision on surrender.

2. In any case, a person who has been surrendered to the issuing Member State pursuant to a European arrest warrant may, without the consent of the executing Member State, be surrendered to a Member State other than the executing Member State pursuant to a European arrest warrant issued for any offence committed prior to his or her surrender in the following cases:

(a) where the requested person, having had an opportunity to leave the territory of the Member State to which he or she has been surrendered, has not done so within 45 days of his final discharge, or has returned to that territory after leaving it;

(b) where the requested person consents to be surrendered to a Member State other than the executing Member State pursuant to a European arrest warrant. Consent shall be given before the competent judicial authorities of the issuing Member State and shall be recorded in accordance with that State's national law. It shall be drawn up in such a way as to make clear that the person concerned has given it voluntarily and in full awareness of the consequences. To that end, the requested person shall have the right to legal counsel;

(c) where the requested person is not subject to the speciality rule, in accordance with Article 27(3)(a), (e), (f) and (g).

3. The executing judicial authority consents to the surrender to another Member State according to the following rules:

   (a) the request for consent shall be submitted in accordance with Article 9, accompanied by the information mentioned in Article 8(1) and a translation as stated in Article 8(2);

   (b) consent shall be given when the offence for which it is requested is itself subject to surrender in accordance with the provisions of this Framework Decision;

   (c) the decision shall be taken no later than 30 days after receipt of the request;

   (d) consent shall be refused on the grounds referred to in Article 3 and otherwise may be refused only on the grounds referred to in Article 4.

   For the situations referred to in Article 5, the issuing Member State must give the guarantees provided for therein.

4. Notwithstanding paragraph 1, a person who has been surrendered pursuant to a European arrest warrant shall not be extradited to a third State without the consent of the competent authority of the Member State which surrendered the person. Such consent shall be given in accordance with the Conventions by which that Member State is bound, as well as with its domestic law.

### Article 29
### Handing over of property

1. At the request of the issuing judicial authority or on its own initiative, the executing judicial authority shall, in accordance with its national law, seize and hand over property which:

   (a) may be required as evidence, or

   (b) has been acquired by the requested person as a result of the offence.

2. The property referred to in paragraph 1 shall be handed over even if the European arrest warrant cannot be carried out owing to the death or escape of the requested person.

3. If the property referred to in paragraph 1 is liable to seizure or confiscation in the territory of the executing Member State, the latter may, if the property is needed in connection with pending criminal proceedings, temporarily retain it or hand it over to the issuing Member State, on condition that it is returned.

4. Any rights which the executing Member State or third parties may have acquired in the property referred to in paragraph 1 shall be preserved. Where such rights exist, the issuing Member State shall return the property without charge to the executing Member State as soon as the criminal proceedings have been terminated.

### Article 30
### Expenses

1. Expenses incurred in the territory of the executing Member State for the execution of a European arrest warrant shall be borne by that Member State.

2. All other expenses shall be borne by the issuing Member State.

## CHAPTER 4
## GENERAL AND FINAL PROVISIONS

### Article 31
### Relation to other legal instruments

1. Without prejudice to their application in relations between Member States and third States, this Framework Decision shall, from 1 January 2004, replace the corresponding provisions of the following conventions applicable in the field of extradition in relations between the Member States:

   (a) the European Convention on Extradition of 13 December 1957, its additional protocol of 15 October 1975, its second additional protocol of 17 March 1978, and the European Convention on the suppression of terrorism of 27 January 1977 as far as extradition is concerned;

   (b) the Agreement between the 12 Member States of the European Communities on the simplification and modernisation of methods of transmitting extradition requests of 26 May 1989;

   (c) the Convention of 10 March 1995 on simplified extradition procedure between the Member States of the European Union;

   (d) the Convention of 27 September 1996 relating to extradition between the Member States of the European Union;

   (e) Title III, Chapter 4 of the Convention of 19 June 1990 implementing the Schengen Agreement of 14 June 1985 on the gradual abolition of checks at common borders.

2. Member States may continue to apply bilateral or multilateral agreements or arrangements in force when this Framework Decision is adopted in so far as such agreements or arrangements allow the objectives of this Framework Decision to be extended or enlarged and help to simplify or facilitate further the procedures for surrender of persons who are the subject of European arrest warrants.

   Member States may conclude bilateral or multilateral agreements or arrangements after this Framework Decision has come into force in so far as such agreements or arrangements allow the prescriptions of this Framework Decision to be extended or enlarged and help to simplify or facilitate further the procedures for surrender of persons who are the subject of European arrest warrants, in particular by fixing time limits shorter than those fixed in Article 17, by extending the list of offences laid down in Article 2(2), by further limiting the grounds for refusal set out in Articles 3 and 4, or by lowering the threshold provided for in Article 2(1) or (2).

   The agreements and arrangements referred to in the second subparagraph may in no case affect relations with Member States which are not parties to them.

   Member States shall, within three months from the entry into force of this Framework Decision, notify the Council and the Commission of the existing agreements and arrangements referred to in the first subparagraph which they wish to continue applying.

   Member States shall also notify the Council and the Commission of any new agreement or arrangement as referred to in the second subparagraph, within three months of signing it.

3. Where the conventions or agreements referred to in paragraph 1 apply to the territories of Member States or to territories for whose external relations a Member State is responsible to which this Framework Decision does not apply, these instruments shall continue to govern the relations existing between those territories and the other Members States.

## Article 32
**Transitional provision**

1. Extradition requests received before 1 January 2004 will continue to be governed by existing instruments relating to extradition. Requests received after that date will be governed by the rules adopted by Member States pursuant to this Framework Decision. However, any Member State may, at the time of the adoption of this Framework Decision by the Council, make a statement indicating that as executing Member State it will continue to deal with requests relating to acts committed before a date which it specifies in accordance with the extradition system applicable before 1 January 2004. The date in question may not be later than 7 August 2002. The said statement will be published in the *Official Journal of the European Communities*. It may be withdrawn at any time.

## Article 33
**Provisions concerning Austria and Gibraltar**

1. As long as Austria has not modified Article 12(1) of the 'Auslieferungs- und Rechtshilfegesetz' and, at the latest, until 31 December 2008, it may allow its executing judicial authorities to refuse the enforcement of a European arrest warrant if the requested person is an Austrian citizen and if the act for which the European arrest warrant has been issued is not punishable under Austrian law.

2. This Framework Decision shall apply to Gibraltar.

## Article 34
**Implementation**

1. Member States shall take the necessary measures to comply with the provisions of this Framework Decision by 31 December 2003.

2. Member States shall transmit to the General Secretariat of the Council and to the Commission the text of the provisions transposing into their national law the obligations imposed on them under this Framework Decision. When doing so, each Member State may indicate that it will apply immediately this Framework Decision in its relations with those Member States which have given the same notification.

   The General Secretariat of the Council shall communicate to the Member States and to the Commission the information received pursuant to Article 7(2), Article 8(2), Article 13(4) and Article 25(2). It shall also have the information published in the *Official Journal of the European Communities*.

3. On the basis of the information communicated by the General Secretariat of the Council, the Commission shall, by 31 December 2004 at the latest, submit a report to the European Parliament and to the Council on the operation of this Framework Decision, accompanied, where necessary, by legislative proposals.

4. The Council shall in the second half of 2003 conduct a review, in particular of the practical application, of the provisions of this Framework Decision by the Member States as well as the functioning of the Schengen Information System.

*Article 35*
**Entry into force**

This Framework Decision shall enter into force on the twentieth day following that of its publication in the *Official Journal of the European Communities*.

Done at Luxembourg, 13 June 2002.

*For the Council*
*The President*
M. RAJOY BREY

# ANNEX

## EUROPEAN ARREST WARRANT[10]

This warrant has been issued by a competent judicial authority. I request that the person mentioned below be arrested and surrendered for the purposes of conducting a criminal prosecution or executing a custodial sentence or detention order.

---

[10] This warrant must be written in, or translated into, one of the official languages of the executing Member State, when that State is known, or any other language accepted by that State.

(a) Information regarding the identity of the requested person: . . . . . . . . . . . . . . . . . . . . . .

    Name: . . . . . . . . . . . . . . . . . . . . . . . . . . . . . . . . . . . . . . . . . . . . . . . . . . . . . . . .

    Forename(s): . . . . . . . . . . . . . . . . . . . . . . . . . . . . . . . . . . . . . . . . . . . . . . . . . . . .

    Maiden name, where applicable: . . . . . . . . . . . . . . . . . . . . . . . . . . . . .. . . . . . . . . . .

    Aliases, where applicable: . . . . . . . . . . . . . . . . . . . . . . . . . . . . . . . . . . . . . . . . . . . .

    Sex: . . . . . . . . . . . . . . . . . . . . . . . . . . . . . . . . . . . .. . . . . . . . . . . . . . . . . . . . . . .

    Nationality: . . . . . . . . . . . . . . . . . . . . . . . . . . . . . . . . . . . . . . . . . . . . . . . . . . . . . .

    Date of birth: . . . . . . . . . . . . . . . . . . . . . . . . . . . . . . . . . . . . . . . . . . . . . . . . . .

    Place of birth: . . . . . . . . . . . . . . . . . . . . . . . . . . . . . . . . . . . . . . . . . . . . . . . . . .

    Residence and/or known address: . . . . . . . . . . . . . . . . . . . . . . . . . . . . . . . . . . . . .

    Language(s) which the requested person understands (if known): . . . . . . . . . . . . . . . . .. . .
    . . . . . . . . . . . . . . . . . . . . . . . . . . . . . . . . . . . . . . . . . . . . . . . . . . . . . . . . . . . .

    Distinctive marks/description of the requested person: . . . . . . . . . . . . . . . . . . . . . . . . .

    . . . . . . . . . . . . . . . . . . . . . . . . . . . . . .. . . . . . . . . . . . . . . . . . . . .. . . . . . . . . . . .

    Photo and fingerprints of the requested person, if they are available and can be transmitted, or contact details of the person to be contacted in order to obtain such information or a DNA profile (where this evidence can be supplied but has not been included)

(b) Decision on which the warrant is based:

1. Arrest warrant or judicial decision having the same effect: . . . . . . . . . . . . . . . . . . . . . .

    Type: . . . . . . . . . . . . . . . . . . . . . . . . . . . . . . . . . . . . . . . . . . . . . . . . . . . . . . . .

2. Enforceable judgement: . . . . . . . . . . . . . . . . . . . . . . . . . . . . . . . . . . . . . . . . . . . . ..

    . . . . . . . . . . . . . . . . . . . . . . . . . . . . . . . . . . . . . . . . . . . . . . . . . . . . . . . . . . . .

    Reference: . . . . . . . . . . . . . . . . . . . . . . . . . . . . . . . . . . . . . . . . . . . . . . . . . . . . .

(c) Indications on the length of the sentence:

1. Maximum length of the custodial sentence or detention order which may be imposed for the offence(s):

   . . . . . . . . . . . . . . . . . . . . . . . . . . . . . . . . . . . . . . . . . . . . . . . . . . . . . . . . . . . . . . . . . . . . .

   . . . . . . . . . . . . . . . . . . . . . . . . . . . . . . . . . . . . . . . . . . . . . . . . . . . . . . . . . . . . . . . . . . . . .

2. Length of the custodial sentence or detention order imposed:

   . . . . . . . . . . . . . . . . . . . . . . . . . . . . . . . . . . . . . . . . . . . . . . . . . . . . . . . . . . . . . . . . . . . . .

   Remaining sentence to be served: . . . . . . . . . . . . . . . . . . . . . . . . . . . . . . . . . . . . . . . . . . . . . . .

   . . . . . . . . . . . . . . . . . . . . . . . . . . . . . . . . . . . . . . . . . . . . . . . . . . . . . . . . . . . . . . . . . . . . .

   . . . . . . . . . . . . . . . . . . . . . . . . . . . . . . . . . . . . . . . . . . . . . . . . . . . . . . . . . . . . . . . . . . . . .

---

(d) Decision rendered in absentia and:

- the person concerned has been summoned in person or otherwise informed of the date and place of the hearing which led to the decision rendered in absentia,

  or

- the person concerned has not been summoned in person or otherwise informed of the date and place of the hearing which led to the decision rendered in absentia but has the following legal guarantees after surrender (such guarantees can be given in advance)

  Specify the legal guarantees

  . . . . . . . . . . . . . . . . . . . . . . . . . . . . . . . . . . . . . . . . . . . . . . . . . . . . . . . . . . . . . . . . . . . . .

  . . . . . . . . . . . . . . . . . . . . . . . . . . . . . . . . . . . . . . . . . . . . . . . . . . . . . . . . . . . . . . . . . . . . .

  . . . . . . . . . . . . . . . . . . . . . . . . . . . . . . . . . . . . . . . . . . . . . . . . . . . . . . . . . . . . . . . . . . . . .

(e) Offences:

This warrant relates to in total: . . . . . . . . . . . . . . . . . . . . . . . . . . . offences.

Description of the circumstances in which the offence(s) was (were) committed, including the time, place and degree of participation in the offence(s) by the requested person:

. . . . . . . . . . . . . . . . . . . . . . . . . . . . . . . . . . . . . . . . . . . . . . . . . . . . . . . . . .

. . . . . . . . . . . . . . . . . . . . . . . . . . . . . . . . . . . . . . . . . . . . . . . . . . . . . . . . . .

. . . . . . . . . . . . . . . . . . . . . . . . . . . . . . . . . . . . . . . . . . . . . . . . . . . . . . . . . .

Nature and legal classification of the offence(s) and the applicable statutory provision/code:

. . . . . . . . . . . . . . . . . . . . . . . . . . . . . . . . . . . . . . . . . . . . . . . . . . . . . . . . . .

. . . . . . . . . . . . . . . . . . . . . . . . . . . . . . . . . . . . . . . . . . . . . . . . . . . . . . . . . .

. . . . . . . . . . . . . . . . . . . . . . . . . . . . . . . . . . . . . . . . . . . . . . . . . . . . . . . . . .

. . . . . . . . . . . . . . . . . . . . . . . . . . . . . . . . . . . . . . . . . . . . . . . . . . . . . . . . . .

. . . . . . . . . . . . . . . . . . . . . . . . . . . . . . . . . . . . . . . . . . . . . . . . . . . . . . . . . .

I. If applicable, tick one or more of the following offences punishable in the issuing Member State by a custodial sentence or detention order of a maximum of at least 3 years as defined by the laws of the issuing Member State:

☐ participation in a criminal organisation;
☐ terrorism;
☐ trafficking in human beings;
☐ sexual exploitation of children and child pornography;
☐ illicit trafficking in narcotic drugs and psychotropic substances;
☐ illicit trafficking in weapons, munitions and explosives;
☐ corruption;
☐ fraud, including that affecting the financial interests of the European Communities within the meaning of the Convention of 26 July 1995 on the protection of European Communities' financial interests;
☐ laundering of the proceeds of crime;
☐ counterfeiting of currency, including the euro;
☐ computer-related crime;
☐ environmental crime, including illicit trafficking in endangered animal species and in endangered plant species and varieties;
☐ facilitation of unauthorised entry and residence;
☐ murder, grievous bodily injury;
☐ illicit trade in human organs and tissue;
☐ kidnapping, illegal restraint and hostage-taking;
☐ racism and xenophobia;
☐ organised or armed robbery;
☐ illicit trafficking in cultural goods, including antiques and works of art;
☐ swindling;
☐ racketeering and extortion;
☐ counterfeiting and piracy of products;
☐ forgery of administrative documents and trafficking therein;
☐ forgery of means of payment;
☐ illicit trafficking in hormonal substances and other growth promoters;
☐ illicit trafficking in nuclear or radioactive materials;
☐ trafficking in stolen vehicles;

☐   rape;
☐   arson;
☐   crimes within the jurisdiction of the International Criminal Court;
☐   unlawful seizure of aircraft/ships;
☐   sabotage.

II.   Full descriptions of offence(s) not covered by section I above:

. . . . . . . . . . . . . . . . . . . . . . . . . . . . . . . . . . . . . . . . . . . . . . . . . . . . . . . . . . . . . . . .

. . . . . . . . . . . . . . . . . . . . . . . . . . . . . . . . . . . . . . . . . . . . . . . . . . . . . . . . . . . . . . . .

(f)   Other circumstances relevant to the case (optional information):

(NB: *This could cover remarks on extraterritoriality, interruption of periods of time limitation and other consequences of the offence*)

. . . . . . . . . . . . . . . . . . . . . . . . . . . . . . . . . . . . . . . . . . . . . . . . . . . . . . . . . . . . . . . .

. . . . . . . . . . . . . . . . . . . . . . . . . . . . . . . . . . . . . . . . . . . . . . . . . . . . . . . . . . . . . . . .

(g)   This warrant pertains also to the seizure and handing over of property which may be required as evidence:

This warrant pertains also to the seizure and handing over of property acquired by the requested person as a result of the offence:

Description of the property (and location) (if known):

. . . . . . . . . . . . . . . . . . . . . . . . . . . . . . . . . . . . . . . . . . . . . . . . . . . . . . . . . . . . . . . .

. . . . . . . . . . . . . . . . . . . . . . . . . . . . . . . . . . . . . . . . . . . . . . . . . . . . . . . . . . . . . . . .

. . . . . . . . . . . . . . . . . . . . . . . . . . . . . . . . . . . . . . . . . . . . . . . . . . . . . . . . . . . . . . . .

(h)   The offence(s) on the basis of which this warrant has been issued is(are) punishable by/has(have) led to a custodial life sentence or lifetime detention order:

•   the legal system of the issuing Member State allows for a review of the penalty or measure imposed—on request or at least after 20 years—aiming at a non-execution of such penalty or measure,

•   and/or

•   the legal system of the issuing Member State allows for the application of measures of clemency to which the person is entitled under the law or practice of the issuing Member State, aiming at non-execution of such penalty or measure.

(i) The judicial authority which issued the warrant:

Official name:

Name of its representative[11]: . . . . . . . . . . . . . . . . . . . . . . . . . . . . . . . . . . . . . . .

. . . . . . . . . . . . . . . . . . . . . . . . . . . . . . . . . . . . . . . . . . . . . . . . . . . . . . . . . . . . . . .

Post held (title/grade): . . . . . . . . . . . . . . . . . . . . . . . . . . . . . . . . . . . . . . . . . . . .

. . . . . . . . . . . . . . . . . . . . . . . . . . . . . . . . . . . . . . . . . . . . . . . . . . . . . . . . . . . . . . .

File reference: . . . . . . . . . . . . . . . . . . . . . . . . . . . . . . . . . . . . . . . . . . . . . . . . . . .

Address: . . . . . . . . . . . . . . . . . . . . . . . . . . . . . . . . . . . . . . . . . . . . . . . . . . . . . . . .

. . . . . . . . . . . . . . . . . . . . . . . . . . . . . . . . . . . . . . . . . . . . . . . . . . . . . . . . . . . . . . .

Tel: (country code) (area/city code) (.) . . . . . . . . . . . . . . . . . . . . . . . . . . . . . . . .

Fax: (country code) (area/city code) (.) . . . . . . . . . . . . . . . . . . . . . . . . . . . . . . . .

E-mail: . . . . . . . . . . . . . . . . . . . . . . . . . . . . . . . . . . . . . . . . . . . . . . . . . . . . . . . . .

Contact details of the person to contact to make necessary practical arrangements for the surrender:
. . . . . . . . . . . . . . . . . . . . . . . . . . . . . . . . . . . . . . . . . . . . . . . . . . . . . . . . . . . . . . .

. . . . . . . . . . . . . . . . . . . . . . . . . . . . . . . . . . . . . . . . . . . . . . . . . . . . . . . . . . . . . . .

Where a central authority has been made responsible for the transmission and administrative reception of European arrest warrants:

Name of the central authority:

. . . . . . . . . . . . . . . . . . . . . . . . . . . . . . . . . . . . . . . . . . . . . . . . . . . . . . . . . . . . . . .

Contact person, if applicable (title/grade and name):

. . . . . . . . . . . . . . . . . . . . . . . . . . . . . . . . . . . . . . . . . . . . . . . . . . . . . . . . . . . . . . .

Address: . . . . . . . . . . . . . . . . . . . . . . . . . . . . . . . . . . . . . . . . . . . . . . . . . . . . . . . .

. . . . . . . . . . . . . . . . . . . . . . . . . . . . . . . . . . . . . . . . . . . . . . . . . . . . . . . . . . . . . . .

Tel: (country code) (area/city code) (.) . . . . . . . . . . . . . . . . . . . . . . . . . . . . . . . .

Fax: (country code) (area/city code) (.) . . . . . . . . . . . . . . . . . . . . . . . . . . . . . . . .

E-mail: . . . . . . . . . . . . . . . . . . . . . . . . . . . . . . . . . . . . . . . . . . . . . . . . . . . . . . . . .

[11] In the different language versions a reference to the 'holder' of the judicial authority will be included.

Signature of the issuing judicial authority and/or its representative:

. . . . . . . . . . . . . . . . . . . . . . . . . . . . . . . . . . . . . . . . . . . . . . . . . . . . . . . . . . . . . . . . . . . .

Name: . . . . . . . . . . . . . . . . . . . . . . . . . . . . . . . . . . . . . . . . . . . . . . . . . . . . . . . . .

Post held (title/grade): . . . . . . . . . . . . . . . . . . . . . . . . . . . . . . . . . . . . . . . . . . . . . . . .

Date: . . . . . . . . . . . . . . . . . . . . . . . . . . . . . . . . . . . . . . . . . . . . . . . . . . . . . . . . .


Official stamp (if available)

APPENDIX 7

COUNCIL CONSEIL
OF EUROPE DE L'EUROPE

*European Treaty Series - No. 24*

# EUROPEAN CONVENTION
# ON EXTRADITION

**Paris, 13.XII.1957**

The governments signatory hereto, being members of the Council of Europe,

Considering that the aim of the Council of Europe is to achieve a greater unity between its members;

Considering that this purpose can be attained by the conclusion of agreements and by common action in legal matters;

Considering that the acceptance of uniform rules with regard to extradition is likely to assist this work of unification,

Have agreed as follows:

### Article 1 – Obligation to extradite

The Contracting Parties undertake to surrender to each other, subject to the provisions and conditions laid down in this Convention, all persons against whom the competent authorities of the requesting Party are proceeding for an offence or who are wanted by the said authorities for the carrying out of a sentence or detention order.

### Article 2 – Extraditable offences

1   Extradition shall be granted in respect of offences punishable under the laws of the requesting Party and of the requested Party by deprivation of liberty or under a detention order for a maximum period of at least one year or by a more severe penalty. Where a conviction and prison sentence have occurred or a detention order has been made in the territory of the requesting Party, the punishment awarded must have been for a period of at least four months.

2   If the request for extradition includes several separate offences each of which is punishable under the laws of the requesting Party and the requested Party by deprivation of liberty or under a detention order, but of which some do not fulfil the condition with regard to the amount of punishment which may be awarded, the requested Party shall also have the right to grant extradition for the latter offences.

3   Any Contracting Party whose law does not allow extradition for certain of the offences referred to in paragraph 1 of this article may, in so far as it is concerned, exclude such offences from the application of this Convention.

4   Any Contracting Party which wishes to avail itself of the right provided for in paragraph 3 of this article shall, at the time of deposit of its instrument of ratification or accession, transmit to the Secretary General of the Council of Europe either a list of the offences for which extradition is allowed or a list of those for which it is excluded and shall at the same time indicate the legal provisions which allow or exclude extradition. The Secretary General of the Council shall forward these lists to the other signatories.

5   If extradition is subsequently excluded in respect of other offences by the law of a Contracting Party, that Party shall notify the Secretary General. The Secretary General shall inform the other signatories. Such notification shall not take effect until three months from the date of its receipt by the Secretary General.

6   Any Party which avails itself of the right provided for in paragraphs 4 or 5 of this article may at any time apply this Convention to offences which have been excluded from it. It shall inform the Secretary General of the Council of such changes, and the Secretary General shall inform the other signatories.

7   Any Party may apply reciprocity in respect of any offences excluded from the application of the Convention under this article.

### Article 3 – Political offences

1   Extradition shall not be granted if the offence in respect of which it is requested is regarded by the requested Party as a political offence or as an offence connected with a political offence.

2   The same rule shall apply if the requested Party has substantial grounds for believing that a request for extradition for an ordinary criminal offence has been made for the purpose of prosecuting or

punishing a person on account of his race, religion, nationality or political opinion, or that that person's position may be prejudiced for any of these reasons.

3   The taking or attempted taking of the life of a Head of State or a member of his family shall not be deemed to be a political offence for the purposes of this Convention.

4   This article shall not affect any obligations which the Contracting Parties may have undertaken or may undertake under any other international convention of a multilateral character.

## Article 4 – Military offences

Extradition for offences under military law which are not offences under ordinary criminal law is excluded from the application of this Convention.

## Article 5 – Fiscal offences

Extradition shall be granted, in accordance with the provisions of this Convention, for offences in connection with taxes, duties, customs and exchange only if the Contracting Parties have so decided in respect of any such offence or category of offences.

## Article 6 – Extradition of nationals

1   a   A Contracting Party shall have the right to refuse extradition of its nationals.
    b   Each Contracting Party may, by a declaration made at the time of signature or of deposit of its instrument of ratification or accession, define as far as it is concerned the term "nationals" within the meaning of this Convention.
    c   Nationality shall be determined as at the time of the decision concerning extradition. If, however, the person claimed is first recognised as a national of the requested Party during the period between the time of the decision and the time contemplated for the surrender, the requested Party may avail itself of the provision contained in sub-paragraph a of this article.

2   If the requested Party does not extradite its national, it shall at the request of the requesting Party submit the case to its competent authorities in order that proceedings may be taken if they are considered appropriate. For this purpose, the files, information and exhibits relating to the offence shall be transmitted without charge by the means provided for in Article 12, paragraph 1. The requesting Party shall be informed of the result of its request.

## Article 7 – Place of commission

1   The requested Party may refuse to extradite a person claimed for an offence which is regarded by its law as having been committed in whole or in part in its territory or in a place treated as its territory.

2   When the offence for which extradition is requested has been committed outside the territory of the requesting Party, extradition may only be refused if the law of the requested Party does not allow prosecution for the same category of offence when committed outside the latter Party's territory or does not allow extradition for the offence concerned.

## Article 8 – Pending proceedings for the same offences

The requested Party may refuse to extradite the person claimed if the competent authorities of such Party are proceeding against him in respect of the offence or offences for which extradition is requested.

## Article 9 – Non bis in idem

Extradition shall not be granted if final judgment has been passed by the competent authorities of the requested Party upon the person claimed in respect of the offence or offences for which extradition is requested. Extradition may be refused if the competent authorities of the requested Party have decided either not to institute or to terminate proceedings in respect of the same offence or offences.

### Article 10 – Lapse of time

Extradition shall not be granted when the person claimed has, according to the law of either the requesting or the requested Party, become immune by reason of lapse of time from prosecution or punishment.

### Article 11 – Capital punishment

If the offence for which extradition is requested is punishable by death under the law of the requesting Party, and if in respect of such offence the death-penalty is not provided for by the law of the requested Party or is not normally carried out, extradition may be refused unless the requesting Party gives such assurance as the requested Party considers sufficient that the death-penalty will not be carried out.

### Article 12 – The request and supporting documents

1 The request shall be in writing and shall be communicated through the diplomatic channel. Other means of communication may be arranged by direct agreement between two or more Parties.

2 The request shall be supported by:
   a the original or an authenticated copy of the conviction and sentence or detention order immediately enforceable or of the warrant of arrest or other order having the same effect and issued in accordance with the procedure laid down in the law of the requesting Party;
   b a statement of the offences for which extradition is requested. The time and place of their commission, their legal descriptions and a reference to the relevant legal provisions shall be set out as accurately as possible; and
   c a copy of the relevant enactments or, where this is not possible, a statement of the relevant law and as accurate a description as possible of the person claimed, together with any other information which will help to establish his identity and nationality.

### Article 13 – Supplementary information

If the information communicated by the requesting Party is found to be insufficient to allow the requested Party to make a decision in pursuance of this Convention, the latter Party shall request the necessary supplementary information and may fix a time-limit for the receipt thereof.

### Article 14 – Rule of speciality

1 A person who has been extradited shall not be proceeded against, sentenced or detained with a view to the carrying out of a sentence or detention order for any offence committed prior to his surrender other than that for which he was extradited, nor shall he be for any other reason restricted in his personal freedom, except in the following cases:
   a when the Party which surrendered him consents. A request for consent shall be submitted, accompanied by the documents mentioned in Article 12 and a legal record of any statement made by the extradited person in respect of the offence concerned. Consent shall be given when the offence for which it is requested is itself subject to extradition in accordance with the provisions of this Convention;
   b when that person, having had an opportunity to leave the territory of the Party to which he has been surrendered, has not done so within 45 days of his final discharge, or has returned to that territory after leaving it.

2 The requesting Party may, however, take any measures necessary to remove the person from its territory, or any measures necessary under its law, including proceedings by default, to prevent any legal effects of lapse of time.

3 When the description of the offence charged is altered in the course of proceedings, the extradited person shall only be proceeded against or sentenced in so far as the offence under its new description is shown by its constituent elements to be an offence which would allow extradition.

### Article 15 – Re-extradition to a third state

Except as provided for in Article 14, paragraph 1.b, the requesting Party shall not, without the consent of the requested Party, surrender to another Party or to a third State a person surrendered to the requesting

Party and sought by the said other Party or third State in respect of offences committed before his surrender. The requested Party may request the production of the documents mentioned in Article 12, paragraph 2.

### Article 16 – Provisional arrest

1   In case of urgency the competent authorities of the requesting Party may request the provisional arrest of the person sought. The competent authorities of the requested Party shall decide the matter in accordance with its law.

2   The request for provisional arrest shall state that one of the documents mentioned in Article 12, paragraph 2.a, exists and that it is intended to send a request for extradition. It shall also state for what offence extradition will be requested and when and where such offence was committed and shall so far as possible give a description of the person sought.

3   A request for provisional arrest shall be sent to the competent authorities of the requested Party either through the diplomatic channel or direct by post or telegraph or through the International Criminal Police Organisation (Interpol) or by any other means affording evidence in writing or accepted by the requested Party. The requesting authority shall be informed without delay of the result of its request.

4   Provisional arrest may be terminated if, within a period of 18 days after arrest, the requested Party has not received the request for extradition and the documents mentioned in Article 12. It shall not, in any event, exceed 40 days from the date of such arrest. The possibility of provisional release at any time is not excluded, but the requested Party shall take any measures which it considers necessary to prevent the escape of the person sought.

5   Release shall not prejudice re-arrest and extradition if a request for extradition is received subsequently.

### Article 17 – Conflicting requests

If extradition is requested concurrently by more than one State, either for the same offence or for different offences, the requested Party shall make its decision having regard to all the circumstances and especially the relative seriousness and place of commission of the offences, the respective dates of the requests, the nationality of the person claimed and the possibility of subsequent extradition to another State.

### Article 18 – Surrender of the person to be extradited

1   The requested Party shall inform the requesting Party by the means mentioned in Article 12, paragraph 1, of its decision with regard to the extradition.

2   Reasons shall be given for any complete or partial rejection.

3   If the request is agreed to, the requesting Party shall be informed of the place and date of surrender and of the length of time for which the person claimed was detained with a view to surrender.

4   Subject to the provisions of paragraph 5 of this article, if the person claimed has not been taken over on the appointed date, he may be released after the expiry of 15 days and shall in any case be released after the expiry of 30 days. The requested Party may refuse to extradite him for the same offence.

5   If circumstances beyond its control prevent a Party from surrendering or taking over the person to be extradited, it shall notify the other Party. The two Parties shall agree a new date for surrender and the provisions of paragraph 4 of this article shall apply.

### Article 19 – Postponed or conditional surrender

1   The requested Party may, after making its decision on the request for extradition, postpone the surrender of the person claimed in order that he may be proceeded against by that Party or, if he has already been convicted, in order that he may serve his sentence in the territory of that Party for an offence other than that for which extradition is requested.

2    The requested Party may, instead of postponing surrender, temporarily surrender the person claimed to the requesting Party in accordance with conditions to be determined by mutual agreement between the Parties.

### Article 20 – Handing over of property

1    The requested Party shall, in so far as its law permits and at the request of the requesting Party, seize and hand over property:

    a  which may be required as evidence, or

    b  which has been acquired as a result of the offence and which, at the time of the arrest, is found in the possession of the person claimed or is discovered subsequently.

2    The property mentioned in paragraph 1 of this article shall be handed over even if extradition, having been agreed to, cannot be carried out owing to the death or escape of the person claimed.

3    When the said property is liable to seizure or confiscation in the territory of the requested Party, the latter may, in connection with pending criminal proceedings, temporarily retain it or hand it over on condition that it is returned.

4    Any rights which the requested Party or third parties may have acquired in the said property shall be preserved. Where these rights exist, the property shall be returned without charge to the requested Party as soon as possible after the trial.

### Article 21 – Transit

1    Transit through the territory of one of the Contracting Parties shall be granted on submission of a request by the means mentioned in Article 12, paragraph 1, provided that the offence concerned is not considered by the Party requested to grant transit as an offence of a political or purely military character having regard to Articles 3 and 4 of this Convention.

2    Transit of a national, within the meaning of Article 6, of a country requested to grant transit may be refused.

3    Subject to the provisions of paragraph 4 of this article, it shall be necessary to produce the documents mentioned in Article 12, paragraph 2.

4    If air transport is used, the following provisions shall apply:

    a  when it is not intended to land, the requesting Party shall notify the Party over whose territory the flight is to be made and shall certify that one of the documents mentioned in Article 12, paragraph 2.a exists. In the case of an unscheduled landing, such notification shall have the effect of a request for provisional arrest as provided for in Article 16, and the requesting Party shall submit a formal request for transit;

    b  when it is intended to land, the requesting Party shall submit a formal request for transit.

5    A Party may, however, at the time of signature or of the deposit of its instrument of ratification of, or accession to, this Convention, declare that it will only grant transit of a person on some or all of the conditions on which it grants extradition. In that event, reciprocity may be applied.

6    The transit of the extradited person shall not be carried out through any territory where there is reason to believe that his life or his freedom may be threatened by reason of his race, religion, nationality or political opinion.

### Article 22 – Procedure

Except where this Convention otherwise provides, the procedure with regard to extradition and provisional arrest shall be governed solely by the law of the requested Party.

### Article 23 – Language to be used

The documents to be produced shall be in the language of the requesting or requested Party. The requested Party may require a translation into one of the official languages of the Council of Europe to be chosen by it.

**Article 24 – Expenses**

1  Expenses incurred in the territory of the requested Party by reason of extradition shall be borne by that Party.

2  Expenses incurred by reason of transit through the territory of a Party requested to grant transit shall be borne by the requesting Party.

3  In the event of extradition from a non-metropolitan territory of the requested Party, the expenses occasioned by travel between that territory and the metropolitan territory of the requesting Party shall be borne by the latter. The same rule shall apply to expenses occasioned by travel between the non-metropolitan territory of the requested Party and its metropolitan territory.

**Article 25 – Definition of "detention order"**

For the purposes of this Convention, the expression "detention order" means any order involving deprivation of liberty which has been made by a criminal court in addition to or instead of a prison sentence.

**Article 26 – Reservations**

1  Any Contracting Party may, when signing this Convention or when depositing its instrument of ratification or accession, make a reservation in respect of any provision or provisions of the Convention.

2  Any Contracting Party which has made a reservation shall withdraw it as soon as circumstances permit. Such withdrawal shall be made by notification to the Secretary General of the Council of Europe.

3  A Contracting Party which has made a reservation in respect of a provision of the Convention may not claim application of the said provision by another Party save in so far as it has itself accepted the provision.

**Article 27 – Territorial application**

1  This Convention shall apply to the metropolitan territories of the Contracting Parties.

2  In respect of France, it shall also apply to Algeria and to the overseas Departments and, in respect of the United Kingdom of Great Britain and Northern Ireland, to the Channel Islands and to the Isle of Man.

3  The Federal Republic of Germany may extend the application of this Convention to the *Land* of Berlin by notice addressed to the Secretary General of the Council of Europe, who shall notify the other Parties of such declaration.

4  By direct arrangement between two or more Contracting Parties, the application of this Convention may be extended, subject to the conditions laid down in the arrangement, to any territory of such Parties, other than the territories mentioned in paragraphs 1, 2 and 3 of this article, for whose international relations any such Party is responsible.

**Article 28 – Relations between this Convention and bilateral Agreements**

1  This Convention shall, in respect of those countries to which it applies, supersede the provisions of any bilateral treaties, conventions or agreements governing extradition between any two Contracting Parties.

2  The Contracting Parties may conclude between themselves bilateral or multilateral agreements only in order to supplement the provisions of this Convention or to facilitate the application of the principles contained therein.

3  Where, as between two or more Contracting Parties, extradition takes place on the basis of a uniform law, the Parties shall be free to regulate their mutual relations in respect of extradition exclusively in accordance with such a system notwithstanding the provisions of this Convention. The same principle shall apply as between two or more Contracting Parties each of which has in force a law providing for the execution in its territory of warrants of arrest issued in the territory of the other Party or Parties. Contracting Parties which exclude or may in the future exclude the application of this Convention as

between themselves in accordance with this paragraph shall notify the Secretary General of the Council of Europe accordingly. The Secretary General shall inform the other Contracting Parties of any notification received in accordance with this paragraph.

### Article 29 – Signature, ratification and entry into force

1   This Convention shall be open to signature by the members of the Council of Europe. It shall be ratified. The instruments of ratification shall be deposited with the Secretary General of the Council.

2   The Convention shall come into force 90 days after the date of deposit of the third instrument of ratification.

3   As regards any signatory ratifying subsequently the Convention shall come into force 90 days after the date of the deposit of its instrument of ratification.

### Article 30 – Accession

1   The Committee of Ministers of the Council of Europe may invite any State not a member of the Council to accede to this Convention, provided that the resolution containing such invitation receives the unanimous agreement of the members of the Council who have ratified the Convention.

2   Accession shall be by deposit with the Secretary General of the Council of an instrument of accession, which shall take effect 90 days after the date of its deposit.

### Article 31 – Denunciation

Any Contracting Party may denounce this Convention in so far as it is concerned by giving notice to the Secretary General of the Council of Europe. Denunciation shall take effect six months after the date when the Secretary General of the Council received such notification.

### Article 32 – Notifications

The Secretary General of the Council of Europe shall notify the members of the Council and the government of any State which has acceded to this Convention of:

   a   the deposit of any instrument of ratification or accession;
   b   the date of entry into force of this Convention;
   c   any declaration made in accordance with the provisions of Article 6, paragraph 1, and of Article 21, paragraph 5;
   d   any reservation made in accordance with Article 26, paragraph 1;
   e   the withdrawal of any reservation in accordance with Article 26, paragraph 2;
   f   any notification of denunciation received in accordance with the provisions of Article 31 and by the date on which such denunciation will take effect.

In witness whereof the undersigned, being duly authorised thereto, have signed this Convention.

Done at Paris, this 13th day of December 1957, in English and French, both texts being equally authentic, in a single copy which shall remain deposited in the archives of the Council of Europe. The Secretary General of the Council of Europe shall transmit certified copies to the signatory governments.

# APPENDIX 8

## Commonwealth Scheme for the Rendition of Fugitive Offenders

## As Amended in 1990

1. (1) The general provisions set out in this Scheme will govern the return of a person from one part of the Commonwealth, in which he is found, to another part thereof, in which he is accused of an offence; and in particular his return will only be precluded by law, or be subject to refusal by the competent executive authority, in the circumstances mentioned in this Scheme.

   (2) For the purpose of this Scheme a person liable to return as mentioned in paragraph (1) is described as a fugitive offender and each of the following areas is described as constituting a separate part of the Commonwealth, that is to say
   - (a) each sovereign and independent country within the Commonwealth together with any dependent territories (which expression, for the purpose aforesaid, includes protectorates and protected States) which that country designates, and
   - (b) each country within the Commonwealth, which, though not sovereign and independent, is not a territory designated for the purposes of the preceding subparagraph.

### Returnable Offences

2. (1) A fugitive will only be returned for a returnable offence.

   (2) For the purpose of this Scheme a returnable offence is an offence however described which is punishable in the part of the Commonwealth where the fugitive is located and the part of the Commonwealth to which return is requested by imprisonment for two years or a greater penalty.

   (3) Offences described in paragraph (2) are returnable offences notwithstanding that any such offences are of a purely fiscal character, where such offences are returnable under the law of the requested part of the Commonwealth.

### Warrants, Other than Provisional Warrants

3. (1) A fugitive offender will only be returned if a warrant for his arrest has been issued in that part of the Commonwealth to which his return is requested and either
   - (a) that warrant is endorsed by a competent judicial authority in the part in which he is found (in which case, the endorsed warrant will be sufficient authority for his arrest), or
   - (b) A further warrant for his arrest is issued by the competent judicial authority in the part in which he is found, not being a provisional warrant issued as mentioned in clause 4.

   (2) The endorsement or issue of a warrant as mentioned in this clause may be made conditional on the competent executive authority having previously issued an order to proceed.

### Provisional Warrants

4. (1) Where a fugitive offender is, or is suspected of being, in or on his way to any part of the Commonwealth but no warrant has been endorsed as mentioned in clause 3(1)(a) or issued as mentioned in clause 3(1)(b), the competent judicial authority in that part of the Commonwealth may issue a provisional warrant for his arrest on such information and under such circumstances as would, in the authority's opinion, justify the issue of a warrant if the returnable offence of which the fugitive

is accused had been an offence committed within the authority's jurisdiction and for the purposes of this paragraph information contained in an international notice issued by the International Criminal Police Organisation (INTERPOL) in respect of a fugitive may be considered by the authority, either alone or with other information, in deciding whether a provisional warrant should be issued for the arrest of that fugitive.

(2) A report of the issue of such a provisional warrant, together with the information in justification or a certified copy thereof, will be sent to the competent executive authority and, in a case in which that authority decides on the said information and any other information which may have become available that the fugitive should be discharged, that authority may so order.

## Committal Proceedings

5. (1) A fugitive offender arrested under a warrant endorsed or issued as mentioned in clause (1), or under a provisional warrant issued as mentioned in clause 4, will be brought, as soon as practicable, before the competent judicial authority who will hear the case in the same manner and have the same jurisdiction and powers, as nearly as may be, including power to remand and admit to bail, as if the fugitive were charged with an offence committed within that authority's jurisdiction.

(2) The competent judicial authority will receive any evidence which may be tendered to show that the return of the fugitive offender is precluded by law.

(3) Where a provisional warrant has been issued as mentioned in clause 4, but within such reasonable time as with reference to the circumstances of the case the competent judicial authority may fix,
   (a) a warrant has not been endorsed or issued as mentioned in clause 3(1), or
   (b) where such endorsement or issued of a warrant has been made conditional on the issue of an order to proceed, as mentioned in clause 3(2), no such order has been issued, the competent judicial authority will order the fugitive to be discharged.

(4) Where a warrant has been endorsed or issued as mentioned in clause 3(1) the competent judicial authority may commit the fugitive to prison to await his return if
   (a) such evidence is produced as establishes a prima facie case that he committed the offence of which he is accused, and
   (b) his return is not precluded by law but, otherwise, will order him to be discharged.

(5) Where a fugitive offender is committed to prison to await his return as mentioned in the preceding paragraph, notice of the fact will forthwith be given to the competent executive authority in that part of the Commonwealth in which he is committed.

## Consent Order for Return

6. (1) A fugitive offender may waive committal proceedings, and if satisfied that the fugitive offender has voluntarily and with an understanding of its significance requested such waiver, the competent judicial authority may make an order by consent for the committal of the fugitive offender to prison, or for his admission to bail, to await return.

(2) The competent executive authority may thereafter order return at any time, notwithstanding the provisions of clause 7.

(3) The provisions of clause 15 shall apply in relation to a fugitive offender returned under this Clause unless waived by him.

## Return or Discharge by Executive Authority

7. After the expiry of 15 days from the date of the committal of a fugitive offender to prison to await his return, as mentioned in clause 5, or, if a writ of habeas corpus or other like process is issued with reference to him, from the date of the final decision thereon of the competent judicial authority (whichever date is the later), the competent executive authority will order his return unless it appears to that authority that, in accordance with the provisions set out in this Scheme, his return is precluded by law or should be refused, in which case that authority will order his discharge.

**Discharge by Judicial Authority**

8. (1) Where after the expiry of the period mentioned in paragraph (2) a fugitive offender has not been returned, an application to the competent judicial authority may be made by or on behalf of the fugitive for his discharge and if

    (a) reasonable notice of the application has been given to the competent executive authority, and

    (b) sufficient cause for the delay is not shown, the competent judicial authority will order his discharge.

  (2) The period referred to in paragraph (1) will be prescribed by law and will be one expiring either

    (a) not later than two months from the fugitive's committal to prison as mentioned in clause 5, or

    (b) not later than one month from the date of the order for his return made as mentioned in clause 7.

**Habeas Corpus and Review**

9. (1) It will be provided that an application may be made by or on behalf of a fugitive offender for a writ of habeas corpus or other like process.

  (2) It will be provided that an application may be made by or on behalf of the government of the requesting part of the Commonwealth for review of the decision of the competent judicial authority in committal proceedings.

**Circumstances Precluding Return**

10. (1) (a) The return of a fugitive offender will be precluded by law if the competent judicial or executive authority is satisfied that the offence is of a political character.

    (b) Paragraph (a) shall not apply in relation to offences established under any multilateral international convention to which both the requesting and the requested parts of the Commonwealth are parties and which are declared thereby not to be regarded as political offences for the purposes of extradition.

    (c) Any part of the Commonwealth may adopt the provisions set out in Annex 1.

  (2) The return of a fugitive offender will be precluded by law if it appears to the competent judicial or executive authority

    (a) that the request for his surrender although purporting to be made for a returnable offence was in fact made for the purpose of prosecuting or punishing the person on account of his race, religion, nationality or political opinions, or

    (b) that he may be prejudiced at his trial or punished, detained or restricted in his personal liberty by reason of his race, religion, nationality or political opinions.

  (3) The return of a fugitive offender, or his return before the expiry of a specified period, will be precluded by law if the competent judicial or executive authority is satisfied that by reason of

    (a) the trivial nature of the case, or

    (b) the accusation against the fugitive not having been made in good faith or in the interests of justice, or

    (c) the passage of time since the commission of the offence, or

    (d) any other sufficient cause,

    it would, having regard to all the circumstances be unjust or oppressive or too severe a punishment to return the fugitive or, as the case may be, to return him before the expiry of a period specified by that authority.

  (4) The return of a fugitive offender will be precluded by law if the competent judicial or executive authority is satisfied that he has been convicted (and is neither unlawfully at large nor at large in breach of a condition of a licence to be at large), or has been acquitted, whether within or outside the Commonwealth, of the offence of which he is accused.

(5) The competent authorities for the purposes of this and the next following clause will include
   (a) any judicial authority which hears or is competent to hear such an application as is mentioned in clause 9, and
   (b) the executive authority by whom any order for the fugitives return would fall to be made.

(6) It will be sufficient compliance with any one of the paragraphs (1), (2), (3), (4) and (5) if a country decides that the competent authority for the purposes of that paragraph is exclusively the judicial authority or the executive authority.

(7) If the competent executive authority -
   (a) is empowered by law to certify that the offence of which a fugitive offender is accused is an offence of a political character, and
   (b) in the case of a particular fugitive offender, so certifies,
   the certificate will be conclusive in the matter and binding upon the competent judicial authority for the purposes mentioned in this clause.

## Offences Under Military Law

11. The return of a fugitive offender will either be precluded by law, or be subject to refusal by the competent authority if the competent authority is satisfied that the offence is an offence only under military law or a law relating to military obligations.

## Double-Criminality Rule

12. The return of a fugitive offender will whether be precluded by law or be subject to refusal by the competent executive authority if the facts on which the request for his return is grounded do not constitute an offence under the law of the country or territory in which he is found.

## Postponement of Return of Fugitive and Temporary Transfer of Prisoners to Stand Trial

13. (1) Subject to the following provisions of this clause, where a fugitive offender
   (a) has been charged with an offence triable by a court in that part of the Commonwealth in which he is found, or
   (b) is serving a sentence imposed by a court in that part of the Commonwealth, then until such a time as he has been discharged (whether by acquittal, the expiration or remission of his sentence, or otherwise) his return will either be precluded by law or be subject to refusal by the competent executive authority as the law of the country or territory concerned may provide.

   (2) Subject to the provisions of this Scheme, a prisoner serving such a sentence who is also a fugitive offender may, at the discretion of the competent executive authority of that part of the Commonwealth in which the prisoner is held, be returned temporarily to another part of the Commonwealth in which he is accused of a returnable offence to enable proceedings to be brought against the prisoner in relation to that offence on such conditions as are agreed between the respective parts of the Commonwealth.

## Priority Where Two or More Requests Made

14. Where requests for the return of a fugitive offender or two or more parts of the Commonwealth fall to be dealt with at the same time, the competent executive authority will determine to which part he should be returned and, accordingly, may refuse the other requests; and in determining the matter that authority will consider all the circumstances of the case and in particular -
   (a) the relative seriousness of the offences,
   (b) the relative dates on which the requests were made, and
   (c) the citizenship or other national status of the fugitive and his ordinary residence.

## Speciality Rule

15. (1) This clause relates to a fugitive offender who has been returned from one part of the Commonwealth to another part thereof, so long as he has not had a reasonable opportunity of leaving the second mentioned part.

(2) In the case of a fugitive offender to whom this clause relates, his detention or trial in the part of the Commonwealth to which he has been returned for any offence committed prior to his return (other than the one for which he was returned or any lesser offence proved by the facts on which that return was grounded, or, with the consent of the requested country or territory, any returnable offence) will be precluded by law.

(3) When considering a request for consent under paragraph (2) the executive authority of the requested part of the Commonwealth may call for such particulars as it may require in order that it may be satisfied that such request is otherwise consistent with the principles or this Scheme, and shall not unreasonably withhold consent; but where in the opinion of the requested part of the Commonwealth it appears that, on the facts known to the requesting part of the Commonwealth at the time of the original application for return of the fugitive offender, application should have been made in respect or such offences at that time, that fact may constitute a ground for refusal.

(4) The requesting part of the Commonwealth shall not, without the consent of the requested part, return or surrender to another country or territory a fugitive offender returned to the requesting part and sought by such other country or territory in respect of any offence committed prior to his return; and in considering a request under this paragraph the requested part of the Commonwealth may call for the particulars referred to in paragraph (3) and shall not unreasonably withhold consent.

(5) Nothing in this clause shall prevent a court in the requesting part of the Commonwealth from taking into account at the request of the fugitive any other offence, whether returnable or not under this Scheme, for the purpose of passing sentence on a fugitive convicted of an offence for which he has been returned under this Scheme, where the fugitive desires that such other offence shall be taken into account.

## Return of Escaped Prisoners

16. (1) In the case of a person who –
    (a) has been convicted of a returnable offence by a court in any part of the Commonwealth and is unlawfully at large before the expiry of his sentence for that offence, and
    (b) is found in some other part of the Commonwealth, the provisions set out in this Scheme, as applied for the purposes of this clause by paragraph (2), will govern his return to the part of the Commonwealth in which he was convicted.

    (2) For the purposes of this clause this Scheme shall be construed, subject to any necessary adaptations or modifications, as though the person unlawfully at large were accused of the offence of which he was convicted and, in particular
    (a) any reference to a fugitive offender shall be construed as including a reference to such a person as is mentioned in paragraph (1), and
    (b) the reference in clause 5(4) to such evidence as establishes a prima facie case that he committed the offence of which he is accused shall be construed as a reference to such evidence as establishes that he has been convicted.

    (3) The references in this clause to a person unlawfully at large shall be construed as including reference to a person at large in breach of a condition of a licence to be at large.

## Ancillary Provisions

17. Each Commonwealth country or territory will take, subject to its constitution, any legislative and other steps which may be necessary or expedient in the circumstances to facilitate and effectuate
    (a) the return of a fugitive offender who is in transit in its territory for that purpose,
    (b) the delivery of property found in the possession of a fugitive offender at the time of his arrest which may be material evidence of the offence at which he is accused, and
    (c) the proof of warrants, certificates of conviction, depositions and other documents.

**Alternative Arrangements and Modifications**

18. Nothing in this Scheme shall prevent
    (a) the making of arrangements between two or more parts of the Commonwealth for further or alternative provision for the return of offenders, or
    (b) the application of the Scheme with modifications by an part of the Commonwealth in relation to any other part which has not brought clauses 1 to 17 fully into effect.

**Supplementary Provisions**

19. (1) Any part of the Commonwealth may or may not adopt either or both of the supplementary provisions set out in Annex 1 but, where such a provision is adopted, any other part of the Commonwealth may in relation to the first part reserve its position as to whether it will give effect to clauses 1 to 17 or will give effect to them subject to such exceptions and modifications as appear to it to be necessary or expedient or give effect to any arrangement made under clause 18(a).

    (2) Two or more parts of the Commonwealth may make arrangements under which in matters of rendition between them clause 5(4) will be replaced either by Annex 3 or by other provisions agreed by the Governments of those parts.

## ANNEX 1

## Discretion as to Definition of Political Offences

1. It may be provided by a law in any part of the Commonwealth that certain acts shall not be held to be offences of a political character including
   (a) an offence against the life or person of a Head of State or a member of his immediate family or any related offence (i.e. aiding and abetting, or counselling or procuring the commission of, or being an accessory before or after the fact to, or attempting or conspiring to commit such an offence),
   (b) an offence against the life or person of a Head of Government, or of a Minister of a Government, or any related offence as aforesaid,
   (c) murder, or any related offence as aforesaid
   (d) an act declared to constitute an offence under a multilateral international convention whose purpose is to prevent or repress a specific category of offences and which imposes on the parties thereto an obligation either to extradite or to prosecute the person sought.

2. Any part of the Commonwealth may restrict the application of any of the provisions made under paragraph 1 to a request from a part of the Commonwealth which has made similar provisions in its laws.

ANNEX 2

## Supplementary Provisions
## Discretion as Respects Return for Offences
## Punishable by Death

1. (1) The return of a fugitive offender may be refused by the competent executive authority where it appears to that authority that, by reason that -
   (a) if he was returned he would be likely to suffer the death penalty for the offence for which his return is requested, and
   (b) in the country or territory in which he is found or in any part thereof that offence is not punishable by death,
   it would, having regard to all the circumstances of the case and to any likelihood that if not returned he would be immune from punishment, be unjust or oppressive or too severe a punishment to return him.

   (2) In determining whether a fugitive would be likely to suffer the death penalty, the executive authority shall take into account any representations which the authorities of the requesting part of the Commonwealth may make with regard to the possibility that the death penalty, if imposed, will not be carried out.

## Discretion as Respects Return of Citizens Etc.

2. (1) The return of a fugitive offender who is a national or permanent resident of the part of the Commonwealth in which he is found -
   (a) may be precluded by law, or
   (b) may be refused by the competent executive authority:
   provided that return will not be so refused if the fugitive is also national of that part of the Commonwealth to which his return is requested.

   (2) For the purposes of this paragraph a fugitive shall be treated as a national of a part of the Commonwealth if that part consists of, or includes -
   (a) a Commonwealth country of which he is a citizen, or
   (b) a country or territory his connection with which determines his national status,
   in either case at the date of the request.

# ANNEX 3

# Alternative Provisions as to Committal Proceedings

1. Where a warrant has been endorsed or issued as mentioned In clause 3(1) the competent judicial authority may commit the fugitive to prison to await his return if -

   (a) the contents of the record of the case received under this Annex whether or not admissible in evidence, under the law of the requested part, and any other evidence admissible under the law of the requested part, are sufficient to warrant a trial of the charges for which rendition has been requested; and

   (b) the fugitive's return Is not precluded by law, but otherwise will order the fugitive to be discharged.

2. The competent judicial authority will receive a record of the case prepared by an Investigating authority in the requesting part if it is accompanied by

   (a) an affidavit of an officer of the investigating authority stating that the record of the case was prepared by or under the direction of that officer, and that the evidence has been preserved for use in court; and

   (b) a certificate of the Attorney General of the requesting part that in his opinion the record of the case discloses the existence of evidence under the law of the requesting part sufficient to justify a prosecution.

3. The record of the case will contain –

   (a) particulars of the description, identity, nationality and, to the extent available, whereabouts of the person sought;

   (b) particulars of each offence or conduct in respect of which rendition is requested, specifying the date and place of commission, the legal definition of the offence and the relevant provisions in the law of the requesting part, including a certified copy of any such definition in the written law of that part;

   (c) the original or a certified copy of any document of process issued in the requesting part against the person whom it seeks to have committed for rendition;

   (d) a recital of the evidence acquired to support the request for rendition of the person sought; and

   (e) a certified copy, reproduction or photograph of exhibits or documents evidence.

## APPENDIX II

# Note of Legal Costs Arising out of Extradition and Fugitive Offenders Proceedings

Particulars of legislation, case-law or State-practice regarding the legal costs of extradition and fugitive offenders proceedings in certain Commonwealth countries.

### Australia

The Australian practice is to offer the services of the Director of Public Prosecutions to represent requesting countries in extradition proceedings, including any proceedings by way of appeal or review. In consequence, costs and disbursements incurred are borne by the Australian Government. Normally an officer of the Office of the Director of Public Prosecutions in the State or Territory in which the application is made appears for the requesting country. Alternatively, the Director of Public Prosecutions may brief counsel if that course appears desirable. This practice is largely based on reciprocity of treatment and is liable to be varied in the event of a particular country being unwilling to make similar arrangements for, or to meet the costs of, legal representations when Australia makes a request.

### Barbados

Although legislative provisions regarding extradition make no mention of legal costs, State-practice in extradition proceedings is described as follows:

> "The fugitive offender is brought to trial on a magistrate's warrant for which no fee is required. But expenses are required for briefing and obtaining the services of an Attorney-at-law in connection with the trial. Current practice requires the requesting State to meet these expenses. In an effort to ensure payment, the requesting State is required to give an undertaking at the time of requisition.

> In the event that there are habeas corpus proceedings the requesting State may also be required to pay the necessary court fees in accordance with Order 54 Rule 2 of the Supreme Court Rules. But if there is any existing treaty arrangement providing for exemption of fees in these matters, this will be facilitated by Order 54, Rule 3.

> There are no concrete cases arising out of the definition."

### Lesotho

Since the Act of 1967, Lesotho entertained one extradition request made by Swaziland in 1972. A problem arose after surrender and trial - the fugitive was found guilty in Swaziland but was given a suspended sentence and permitted to return to Lesotho - as to who should bear the costs of repatriation. The problem was solved through the good offices of the British High Commission and the bail money standing in the name of the fugitive in Lesotho.

Another question is whether any procedure exists to enforce the suspended sentence if the condition of release should be breached?

### New Zealand

According to New Zealand the Extradition Act makes no mention of legal costs, therefore the question of costs would be disposed of in accordance with the terms of the relevant treaty. The only treaty concluded by New Zealand in this respect is with the USA. Concluded in 1970 the Treaty provides that expenses relating to transportation of the person sought shall be paid by the requesting Party and that appropriate legal officers of the county in which extradition proceedings take place shall, by all legal means within their power, assist the officers of the requesting Party before the respective judges and magistrates.

**Tonga**

As regards legal costs, Tonga expressed its inability to comment until bilateral treaties were concluded between Tonga and other countries. However, attention has been drawn to the procedure for arrest and committal in the Extradition Act being similar to criminal prosecutions in which the costs involved are borne by the Government of Tonga with exception of costs for the repatriation of the offender which is expected to be borne by the requesting State.

**United Kingdom**

Provision has been made in extradition treaties or separate administrative arrangements, concluded by the United Kingdom with other Western European countries and the United States, for the requested Party to make all necessary arrangements for, and meet the cost of, the legal representation of the requesting Party in any proceedings arising out of a request for extradition.

Arrangements have been made between England and Wales and a number of Commonwealth countries (Australia, Barbados, Canada Cyprus, Ghana, Gibraltar, Hong Kong, Kenya, Malta, Nauru, New Zealand and Swaziland) for the requested State to arrange and meet the costs of legal representation on behalf of the requesting State. Similar arrangements have not been necessary for Scotland where the requesting State is represented without charge by the Lord Advocate (the Chief Public Prosecutor) or on his behalf by his local prosecutors, the Procurators Fiscal.

Since 1969 non-statutory arrangements have existed with the Republic of Ireland whereby the Attorney-General of the Republic of Ireland represents United Kingdom interests in any extradition proceedings in the Republic and the Director of Public Prosecutions undertakes a reciprocal service in any habeas corpus proceedings in England and Wales under the Backing of Warrants (Republic or Ireland) Act, 1965. Similar reciprocal services in Scotland are offered and undertaken by the Lord Advocate.

United States No. 1 (2003)

# Extradition Treaty

between the Government of the United Kingdom of
Great Britain and Northern Ireland and the Government of the
United States of America

Washington, 31 March 2003

[Instruments of ratification have not been exchanged]

*Presented to Parliament*
*by the Secretary of State for Foreign and Commonwealth Affairs*
*by Command of Her Majesty*
*May 2003*

# EXTRADITION TREATY BETWEEN THE GOVERNMENT OF THE UNITED KINGDOM OF GREAT BRITAIN AND NORTHERN IRELAND AND THE GOVERNMENT OF THE UNITED STATES OF AMERICA

The Government of the United Kingdom of Great Britain and Northern Ireland and the Government of the United States of America,

Recalling the Extradition Treaty between the Government of the United States of America and the Government of the United Kingdom of Great Britain and Northern Ireland signed at London, June 8, 1972[1], as amended by the Supplementary Treaty between the two States, signed at Washington, June 25, 1985[2]; and

Desiring to provide for more effective cooperation between the two States in the suppression of crime, and, for that purpose, to conclude a new treaty for the extradition of offenders;

Have agreed as follows:

## ARTICLE 1

## Obligation to Extradite

The Parties agree to extradite to each other, pursuant to the provisions of this Treaty, persons sought by the authorities in the Requesting State for trial or punishment for extraditable offenses.

## ARTICLE 2

## Extraditable Offenses

1. An offense shall be an extraditable offense if the conduct on which the offense is based is punishable under the laws in both States by deprivation of liberty for a period of one year or more or by a more severe penalty.

2. An offense shall also be an extraditable offense if it consists of an attempt or a conspiracy to commit, participation in the commission of, aiding or abetting, counselling or procuring the commission of, or being an accessory before or after the fact to any offense described in paragraph 1 of this Article.

3. For the purposes of this Article, an offense shall be an extraditable offense:

   (a) whether or not the laws in the Requesting and Requested States place the offense within the same category of offenses or describe the offense by the same terminology; or

   (b) whether or not the offense is one for which United States federal law requires the showing of such matters as interstate transportation, or use of the mails or of other facilities affecting interstate or foreign commerce, such matters being jurisdictional only.

---

1 Treaty Series No. 16 (1977) Cmnd 6723
2 Treaty Series No. 6 (1988) Cm 294

4. If the offense has been committed outside the territory of the Requesting State, extradition shall be granted in accordance with the provisions of the Treaty if the laws in the Requested State provide for the punishment of such conduct committed outside its territory in similar circumstances. If the laws in the Requested State do not provide for the punishment of such conduct committed outside of its territory in similar circumstances, the executive authority of the Requested State, in its discretion, may grant extradition provided that all other requirements of this Treaty are met.

5. If extradition has been granted for an extraditable offense, it may also be granted for any other offense specified in the request if the latter offense is punishable by less than one year's deprivation of liberty, provided that all other requirements for extradition are met.

## ARTICLE 3

## Nationality

Extradition shall not be refused based on the nationality of the person sought.

## ARTICLE 4

## Political and Military Offenses

1. Extradition shall not be granted if the offense for which extradition is requested is a political offense.

2. For the purposes of this Treaty, the following offenses shall not be considered political offenses:
   (a) an offense for which both Parties have the obligation pursuant to a multilateral international agreement to extradite the person sought or to submit the case to their competent authorities for decision as to prosecution;
   (b) a murder or other violent crime against the person of a Head of State of one of the Parties, or of a member of the Head of State's family;
   (c) murder, manslaughter, malicious wounding, or inflicting grievous bodily harm;
   (d) an offense involving kidnaping, abduction, or any form of unlawful detention, including the taking of a hostage;
   (e) placing or using, or threatening the placement or use of, an explosive, incendiary, or destructive device or firearm capable of endangering life, of causing grievous bodily harm, or of causing substantial property damage;
   (f) possession of an explosive, incendiary, or destructive device capable of endangering life, of causing grievous bodily harm, or of causing substantial property damage;
   (g) an attempt or a conspiracy to commit, participation in the commission of, aiding or abetting, counseling or procuring the commission of, or being an accessory before or after the fact to any of the foregoing offenses.

3. Notwithstanding the terms of paragraph 2 of this Article, extradition shall not be granted if the competent authority of the Requested State determines that the request was politically motivated. In the United States, the executive branch is the competent authority for the purposes of this Article.

4. The competent authority of the Requested State may refuse extradition for offenses under military law that are not offenses under ordinary criminal law. In the United States, the executive branch is the competent authority for the purposes of this Article.

# ARTICLE 5

## Prior Prosecution

1.  Extradition shall not be granted when the person sought has been convicted or acquitted in the Requested State for the offense for which extradition is requested.
2.  The Requested State may refuse extradition when the person sought has been convicted or acquitted in a third state in respect of the conduct for which extradition is requested.
3.  Extradition shall not be precluded by the fact that the competent authorities of the Requested State:
    (a) have decided not to prosecute the person sought for the acts for which extradition is requested;
    (b) have decided to discontinue any criminal proceedings which have been instituted against the person sought for those acts; or
    (c) are still investigating the person sought for the same acts for which extradition is sought.

# ARTICLE 6

## Statute of Limitations

The decision by the Requested State whether to grant the request for extradition shall be made without regard to any statute of limitations in either State.

# ARTICLE 7

## Capital Punishment

When the offense for which extradition is sought is punishable by death under the laws in the Requesting State and is not punishable by death under the laws in the Requested State, the executive authority in the Requested State may refuse extradition unless the Requesting State provides an assurance that the death penalty will not be imposed or, if imposed, will not be carried out.

# ARTICLE 8

## Extradition Procedures and Required Documents

1.  All requests for extradition shall be submitted through the diplomatic channel.
2.  All requests for extradition shall be supported by:
    (a) as accurate a description as possible of the person sought, together with any other information that would help to establish identity and probable location;
    (b) a statement of the facts of the offense(s);
    (c) the relevant text of the law(s) describing the essential elements of the offense for which extradition is requested;

(d) the relevant text of the law(s) prescribing punishment for the offense for which extradition is requested; and

(e) documents, statements, or other types of information specified in paragraphs 3 or 4 of this Article, as applicable.

3.  In addition to the requirements in paragraph 2 of this Article, a request for extradition of a person who is sought for prosecution shall be supported by:

(a) a copy of the warrant or order of arrest issued by a judge or other competent authority;

(b) a copy of the charging document, if any; and

(c) for requests to the United States, such information as would provide a reasonable basis to believe that the person sought committed the offense for which extradition is requested.

4.  In addition to the requirements in paragraph 2 of this Article, a request for extradition relating to a person who has been convicted of the offense for which extradition is sought shall be supported by:

(a) information that the person sought is the person to whom the finding of guilt refers;

(b) a copy of the judgment or memorandum of conviction or, if a copy is not available, a statement by a judicial authority that the person has been convicted;

(c) a copy of the sentence imposed, if the person sought has been sentenced, and a statement establishing to what extent the sentence has been carried out; and

(d) in the case of a person who has been convicted *in absentia*, information regarding the circumstances under which the person was voluntarily absent from the proceedings.

## ARTICLE 9

## Authentication of Documents

The documents that support an extradition request shall be deemed to be authentic and shall be received in evidence in extradition proceedings without further proof if:

(a) regarding a request from the United States
   (i) they are authenticated by the oath of a witness, or
   (ii) they purport to be signed by a judge, magistrate, or officer of the United States and they purport to be certified by being sealed with the official seal of the Secretary of State of the United States;

(b) regarding a request from the United Kingdom, they are certified by the principal diplomatic or principal consular officer of the United States resident in the United Kingdom, as provided by the extradition laws of the United States;

(c) regarding a request from a territory of the United Kingdom, they are certified either by the principal diplomatic or principal consular officer of the United States responsible for that territory; or

(d) regarding a request from either Party, they are certified or authenticated in any other manner acceptable under the law in the Requested State.

## ARTICLE 10

## Additional Information

If the Requested State requires additional information to enable a decision to be taken on the request for extradition, the Requesting State shall respond to the request within such time as the Requested State requires.

## ARTICLE 11

## Translation

All documents submitted under this Treaty by the Requesting State shall be in English or accompanied by a translation into English.

## ARTICLE 12

## Provisional Arrest

1. In an urgent situation, the Requesting State may request the provisional arrest of the person sought pending presentation of the request for extradition. A request for provisional arrest may be transmitted through the diplomatic channel or directly between the United States Department of Justice and such competent authority as the United Kingdom may designate for the purposes of this Article.

2. The application for provisional arrest shall contain:
   (a) a description of the person sought;
   (b) the location of the person sought, if known;
   (c) a brief statement of the facts of the case including, if possible, the date and location of the offense(s);
   (d) a description of the law(s) violated;
   (e) a statement of the existence of a warrant or order of arrest or a finding of guilt or judgment of conviction against the person sought; and
   (f) a statement that the supporting documents for the person sought will follow within the time specified in this Treaty.

3. The Requesting State shall be notified without delay of the disposition of its request for provisional arrest and the reasons for any inability to proceed with the request.

4. A person who is provisionally arrested may be discharged from custody upon the expiration of sixty (60) days from the date of provisional arrest pursuant to this Treaty if the executive authority of the Requested State has not received the formal request for extradition and the documents supporting the extradition request as required in Article 8. For this purpose, receipt of the formal request for extradition and supporting documents by the Embassy of the Requested State in the Requesting State shall constitute receipt by the executive authority of the Requested State.

5. The fact that the person sought has been discharged from custody pursuant to paragraph 4 of this Article shall not prejudice the subsequent re-arrest and extradition of that person if the extradition request and supporting documents are delivered at a later date.

## ARTICLE 13

## Decision and Surrender

1. The Requested State shall promptly notify the Requesting State of its decision on the request for extradition. Such notification should be transmitted directly to the competent authority designated by the Requesting State to receive such notification and through the diplomatic channel.

2. If the request is denied in whole or in part, the Requested State shall provide reasons for the denial. The Requested State shall provide copies of pertinent judicial decisions upon request.

3. If the request for extradition is granted, the authorities of the Requesting and Requested States shall agree on the time and place for the surrender of the person sought.

4.  If the person sought is not removed from the territory of the Requested State within the time period prescribed by the law of that State, that person may be discharged from custody, and the Requested State, in its discretion, may subsequently refuse extradition for the same offense(s).

## ARTICLE 14

## Temporary and Deferred Surrender

1.  If the extradition request is granted for a person who is being proceeded against or is serving a sentence in the Requested State, the Requested State may temporarily surrender the person sought to the Requesting State for the purpose of prosecution. If the Requested State requests, the Requesting State shall keep the person so surrendered in custody and shall return that person to the Requested State after the conclusion of the proceedings against that person, in accordance with conditions to be determined by mutual agreement of the States.

2.  The Requested State may postpone the extradition proceedings against a person who is being prosecuted or who is serving a sentence in that State. The postponement may continue until the prosecution of the person sought has been concluded or until such person has served any sentence imposed.

## ARTICLE 15

## Requests for Extradition Made by Several States

If the Requested State receives requests from two or more States for the extradition of the same person, either for the same offense or for different offenses, the executive authority of the Requested State shall determine to which State, if any, it will surrender the person. In making its decision, the Requested State shall consider all relevant factors, including but not limited to:

(a) whether the requests were made pursuant to a treaty;

(b) the place where each offense was committed;

(c) the gravity of the offenses;

(d) the possibility of any subsequent extradition between the respective Requesting States; and

(e) the chronological order in which the requests were received from the respective Requesting States.

## ARTICLE 16

## Seizure and Surrender of Property

1.  To the extent permitted under its law, the Requested State may seize and surrender to the Requesting State all items in whatever form, and assets, including proceeds, that are connected with the offense in respect of which extradition is granted. The items and assets mentioned in this Article may be surrendered even when the extradition cannot be effected due to the death, disappearance, or escape of the person sought.

2.  The Requested State may condition the surrender of the items upon satisfactory assurances from the Requesting State that the property will be returned to the Requested State as soon as practicable. The Requested State may also defer the surrender of such items if they are needed as evidence in the Requested State.

## ARTICLE 17

## Waiver of Extradition

If the person sought waives extradition and agrees to be surrendered to the Requesting State, the Requested State may surrender the person as expeditiously as possible without further proceedings.

## ARTICLE 18

## Rule of Specialty

1. A person extradited under this Treaty may not be detained, tried, or punished in the Requesting State except for:
   (a) any offense for which extradition was granted, or a differently denominated offense based on the same facts as the offense on which extradition was granted, provided such offense is extraditable, or is a lesser included offense;
   (b) any offense committed after the extradition of the person; or
   (c) any offense for which the executive authority of the Requested State waives the rule of specialty and thereby consents to the person's detention, trial, or punishment. For the purpose of this subparagraph:
      (i) the executive authority of the Requested State may require the submission of the documentation called for in Article 8; and
      (ii) the person extradited may be detained by the Requesting State for 90 days, or for such longer period of time as the Requested State may authorize, while the request for consent is being processed.
2. A person extradited under this Treaty may not be the subject of onward extradition or surrender for any offense committed prior to extradition to the Requesting State unless the Requested State consents.
3. Paragraphs 1 and 2 of this Article shall not prevent the detention, trial, or punishment of an extradited person, or the extradition of the person to a third State, if the person:
   (a) leaves the territory of the Requesting State after extradition and voluntarily returns to it; or
   (b) does not leave the territory of the Requesting State within 20 days of the day on which that person is free to leave.
4. If the person sought waives extradition pursuant to Article 17, the specialty provisions in this Article shall not apply.

## ARTICLE 19

## Transit

1. Either State may authorize transportation through its territory of a person surrendered to the other State by a third State or from the other State to a third State. A request for transit shall contain a description of the person being transported and a brief statement of the facts of the case. A person in transit shall be detained in custody during the period of transit.
2. Authorization is not required when air transportation is used by one State and no landing is scheduled on the territory of the other State. If an unscheduled landing does occur, the State in which the

unscheduled landing occurs may require a request for transit pursuant to paragraph 1 of this Article, and it may detain the person until the request for transit is received and the transit is effected, as long as the request is received within 96 hours of the unscheduled landing.

# ARTICLE 20

# Representation and Expenses

1. The Requested State shall advise, assist, and appear on behalf of, the Requesting State in any proceedings in the courts of the Requested State arising out of a request for extradition or make all necessary arrangements for the same.
2. The Requesting State shall pay all the expenses related to the translation of extradition documents and the transportation of the person surrendered. The Requested State shall pay all other expenses incurred in that State in connection with the extradition proceedings.
3. Neither State shall make any pecuniary claim against the other State arising out of the arrest, detention, examination, or surrender of persons under this Treaty.

# ARTICLE 21

# Consultation

The Parties may consult with each other in connection with the processing of individual cases and in furtherance of efficient implementation of this Treaty.

# ARTICLE 22

# Application

1. This Treaty shall apply to offenses committed before as well as after the date it enters into force.
2. This Treaty shall apply:
   (a) in relation to the United Kingdom: to Great Britain and Northern Ireland, the Channel Islands, the Isle of Man; and to any territory for whose international relations the United Kingdom is responsible and to which this agreement has been extended by agreement of the Parties; and
   (b) to the United States of America.
3. The application of this Treaty to any territory in respect of which extension has been made in accordance with paragraph 2 of this Article may be terminated by either State giving six months' written notice to the other through the diplomatic channel.
4. A request by the United States for the extradition of an offender who is found in any of the territories to which this Treaty applies in accordance with paragraph 2 of this Article may be made to the Governor or other competent authority of that territory, who may take the decision himself or refer the matter to the Government of the United Kingdom for its decision. A request on the part of any of the territories to which this Treaty applies in accordance with paragraph 2 of this Article for the extradition of an offender who is found in the United States of America may be made to the Government of the United States by the Governor or other competent authority of that territory.

## ARTICLE 23

## Ratification and Entry into Force

1.  This Treaty shall be subject to ratification; the instruments of ratification shall be exchanged as soon as possible.
2.  This Treaty shall enter into force upon the exchange of the instruments of ratification.
3.  Upon the entry into force of this Treaty, the Extradition Treaty signed at London on June 8, 1972, and the Supplementary Treaty signed at Washington on June 25, 1985, (together, "the prior Treaty") shall cease to have any effect as between the United States and the United Kingdom, except as otherwise provided below. The prior Treaty shall apply to any extradition proceedings in which the extradition documents have already been submitted to the courts of the Requested State at the time this Treaty enters into force, except that Article 18 of this Treaty shall apply to persons found extraditable under the prior Treaty.
4.  The prior Treaty shall also apply to any territory to which it has been extended in accordance with Article II of that Treaty, until such time as the provisions of this Treaty have been extended to such a territory under Article 22(2).

## ARTICLE 24

## Termination

Either State may terminate this Treaty at any time by giving written notice to the other State through the diplomatic channel, and the termination shall be effective six months after the date of receipt of such notice.

IN WITNESS WHEREOF, the undersigned, being duly authorized by their respective Governments, have signed this Treaty.

DONE at Washington, in duplicate, this 31st day of March, 2003.

FOR THE GOVERNMENT OF THE
UNITED KINGDOM OF GREAT
BRITAIN AND NORTHERN IRELAND:

FOR THE GOVERNMENT OF THE
UNITED STATES OF AMERICA:

DAVID BLUNKETT

JOHN ASHCROFT

# Crime (International Co-operation) Act 2003 (as amended)

The Act is printed as amended by subsequent legislation.

## 2003 CHAPTER 32

An Act to make provision for furthering co-operation with other countries in respect of criminal proceedings and investigations; to extend jurisdiction to deal with terrorist acts or threats outside the United Kingdom; to amend section 5 of the Forgery and Counterfeiting Act 1981 and make corresponding provision in relation to Scotland; and for connected purposes.

[30th October 2003]

BE IT ENACTED by the Queen's most Excellent Majesty, by and with the advice and consent of the Lords Spiritual and Temporal, and Commons, in this present Parliament assembled, and by the authority of the same, as follows:–

## PART 1

### MUTUAL ASSISTANCE IN CRIMINAL MATTERS

#### CHAPTER 1

##### MUTUAL SERVICE OF PROCESS ETC.

*Service of overseas process in the UK*

**1 Service of overseas process**

(1) The power conferred by subsection (3) is exercisable where the Secretary of State receives any process or other document to which this section applies from the government of, or other authority in, a country outside the United Kingdom, together with a request for the process or document to be served on a person in the United Kingdom.

(2) This section applies–
   (a) to any process issued or made in that country for the purposes of criminal proceedings,
   (b) to any document issued or made by an administrative authority in that country in administrative proceedings,
   (c) to any process issued or made for the purposes of any proceedings on an appeal before a court in that country against a decision in administrative proceedings,
   (d) to any document issued or made by an authority in that country for the purposes of clemency proceedings.

(3) The Secretary of State may cause the process or document to be served by post or, if the request is for personal service, direct the chief officer of police for the area in which that person appears to be to cause it to be personally served on him.

(4) In relation to any process or document to be served in Scotland, references in this section to the Secretary of State are to be read as references to the Lord Advocate.

**2 Service of overseas process: supplementary**

(1) Subsections (2) and (3) apply to any process served in a part of the United Kingdom by virtue of section 1 requiring a person to appear as a party or attend as a witness.

(2) No obligation under the law of that part to comply with the process is imposed by virtue of its service.

(3) The process must be accompanied by a notice–
   (a) stating the effect of subsection (2),
   (b) indicating that the person on whom it is served may wish to seek advice as to the possible consequences of his failing to comply with the process under the law of the country where it was issued or made, and
   (c) indicating that under that law he may not be accorded the same rights and privileges as a party or as a witness as would be accorded to him in proceedings in the part of the United Kingdom in which the process is served.

(4) Where a chief officer of police causes any process or document to be served under section 1, he must at once–
   (a) tell the Secretary of State (or, as the case may be, the Lord Advocate) when and how it was served, and
   (b) (if possible) provide him with a receipt signed by the person on whom it was served.

(5) Where the chief officer of police is unable to cause any process or document to be served as directed, he must at once inform the Secretary of State (or, as the case may be, the Lord Advocate) of that fact and of the reason.

*Service of UK process abroad*

**3 General requirements for service of process**

(1) This section applies to any process issued or made for the purposes of criminal proceedings by a court in England and Wales or Northern Ireland.

(2) The process may be issued or made in spite of the fact that the person on whom it is to be served is outside the United Kingdom.

(3) Where the process is to be served outside the United Kingdom and the person at whose request it is issued or made believes that the person on whom it is to be served does not understand English, he must–
   (a) inform the court of that fact, and
   (b) provide the court with a copy of the process, or of so much of it as is material, translated into an appropriate language.

(4) Process served outside the United Kingdom requiring a person to appear as a party or attend as a witness–
   (a) must not include notice of a penalty,
   (b) must be accompanied by a notice giving any information required to be given by rules of court.

(5) If process requiring a person to appear as a party or attend as a witness is served outside the United Kingdom, no obligation to comply with the process under the law of the part of the United Kingdom in which the process is issued or made is imposed by virtue of the service.

(6) Accordingly, failure to comply with the process does not constitute contempt of court and is not a ground for issuing a warrant to secure the attendance of the person in question.

(7) But the process may subsequently be served on the person in question in the United Kingdom (with the usual consequences for non-compliance).

**4 Service of process otherwise than by post**

(1) Process to which section 3 applies may, instead of being served by post, be served on a person outside the United Kingdom in accordance with arrangements made by the Secretary of State.

(2) But where the person is in a participating country, the process may be served in accordance with those arrangements only if one of the following conditions is met.

(3) The conditions are–
    (a) that the correct address of the person is unknown,
    (b) that it has not been possible to serve the process by post,
    (c) that there are good reasons for thinking that service by post will not be effective or is inappropriate.

## 5 General requirements for effecting Scottish citation etc.

(1) This section applies to any citation for the purposes of criminal proceedings in Scotland and to any document issued there for such purposes by the prosecutor or by the court.

(2) The citation may proceed or document be issued in spite of the fact that the person against whom it is to be effected or on whom it is to be served is outside the United Kingdom.

(3) Where–
    (a) citation or issue is by the prosecutor,
    (b) the citation is to be effected or the document issued is to be served outside the United Kingdom, and
    (c) the prosecutor believes that the person against whom it is to be effected or on whom it is to be served does not understand English,
the citation or document must be accompanied by a translation of it (or, in the case of a document, by a translation of so much of it as is material) in an appropriate language.

(4) Where–
    (a) citation or issue is by the court,
    (b) the citation is to be effected or the document issued is to be served outside the United Kingdom, and
    (c) the person at whose request that is to happen believes that the person against whom it is to be effected or on whom it is to be served does not understand English,
he must inform the court of that fact, and provide the court with a copy of the citation or document (or, in the case of a document, so much of it as is material) translated into an appropriate language.

(5) A citation effected outside the United Kingdom–
    (a) must not include notice of a penalty,
    (b) must be accompanied by a notice giving any information required to be given by rules of court.

(6) If a citation is effected outside the United Kingdom, no obligation under the law of Scotland to comply with the citation is imposed by virtue of its being so effected.

(7) Accordingly, failure to comply with the citation does not constitute contempt of court and is not a ground for issuing a warrant to secure the attendance of the person in question or for imposing any penalty.

(8) But the citation may subsequently be effected against the person in question in the United Kingdom (with the usual consequences for non-compliance).

## 6 Effecting Scottish citation etc. otherwise than by post

(1) A citation or document to which section 5 applies may, instead of being effected or served by post, be effected against or served on a person outside the United Kingdom in accordance with arrangements made by the Lord Advocate.

(2) But where the person is in a participating country, the citation may be effected or document served in accordance with those arrangements only if one of the following conditions is met.

(3) The conditions are–
    (a) that the correct address of the person is unknown,
    (b) that it has not been possible to effect the citation or serve the document by post,
    (c) that there are good reasons for thinking that citation or (as the case may be) service by post will not be effective or is inappropriate.

## CHAPTER 2

### MUTUAL PROVISION OF EVIDENCE

*Assistance in obtaining evidence abroad*

**7 Requests for assistance in obtaining evidence abroad**

(1) If it appears to a judicial authority in the United Kingdom on an application made by a person mentioned in subsection (3)–

    (a) that an offence has been committed or that there are reasonable grounds for suspecting that an offence has been committed, and

    (b) that proceedings in respect of the offence have been instituted or that the offence is being investigated,

the judicial authority may request assistance under this section.

(2) The assistance that may be requested under this section is assistance in obtaining outside the United Kingdom any evidence specified in the request for use in the proceedings or investigation.

(3) The application may be made–

    (a) in relation to England and Wales and Northern Ireland, by a prosecuting authority,

    (b) in relation to Scotland, by the Lord Advocate or a procurator fiscal,

    (c) where proceedings have been instituted, by the person charged in those proceedings.

(4) The judicial authorities are–

    (a) in relation to England and Wales, any judge or justice of the peace,

    (b) in relation to Scotland, any judge of the High Court or sheriff,

    (c) in relation to Northern Ireland, any judge or resident magistrate.

(5) In relation to England and Wales or Northern Ireland, a designated prosecuting authority may itself request assistance under this section if–

    (a) it appears to the authority that an offence has been committed or that there are reasonable grounds for suspecting that an offence has been committed, and

    (b) the authority has instituted proceedings in respect of the offence in question or it is being investigated.

"Designated" means designated by an order made by the Secretary of State.

(6) In relation to Scotland, the Lord Advocate or a procurator fiscal may himself request assistance under this section if it appears to him–

    (a) that an offence has been committed or that there are reasonable grounds for suspecting that an offence has been committed, and

    (b) that proceedings in respect of the offence have been instituted or that the offence is being investigated.

(7) If a request for assistance under this section is made in reliance on Article 2 of the 2001 Protocol (requests for information on banking transactions) in connection with the investigation of an offence, the request must state the grounds on which the person making the request considers the evidence specified in it to be relevant for the purposes of the investigation.

**8 Sending requests for assistance**

(1) A request for assistance under section 7 may be sent–

    (a) to a court exercising jurisdiction in the place where the evidence is situated, or

    (b) to any authority recognised by the government of the country in question as the appropriate authority for receiving requests of that kind.

(2) Alternatively, if it is a request by a judicial authority or a designated prosecuting authority it may be sent to the Secretary of State (in Scotland, the Lord Advocate) for forwarding to a court or authority mentioned in subsection (1).

(3) In cases of urgency, a request for assistance may be sent to–

    (a) the International Criminal Police Organisation, or

(b) any body or person competent to receive it under any provisions adopted under the Treaty on European Union,

for forwarding to any court or authority mentioned in subsection (1).

**9 Use of evidence obtained**

(1) This section applies to evidence obtained pursuant to a request for assistance under section 7.

(2) The evidence may not without the consent of the appropriate overseas authority be used for any purpose other than that specified in the request.

(3) When the evidence is no longer required for that purpose (or for any other purpose for which such consent has been obtained), it must be returned to the appropriate overseas authority, unless that authority indicates that it need not be returned.

(4) In exercising the discretion conferred by [...] Article 5 of the Criminal Justice (Evidence, Etc.) (Northern Ireland) Order 1988 (S.I. 1988/ 1847 (N.I. 17)) (exclusion of evidence otherwise admissible) in relation to a statement contained in the evidence, the court must have regard–
   (a) to whether it was possible to challenge the statement by questioning the person who made it, and
   (b) if proceedings have been instituted, to whether the local law allowed the parties to the proceedings to be legally represented when the evidence was being obtained.

(5) In Scotland, the evidence may be received in evidence without being sworn to by witnesses, so far as that may be done without unfairness to either party.

(6) In this section, the appropriate overseas authority means the authority recognised by the government of the country in question as the appropriate authority for receiving requests of the kind in question.

**10 Domestic freezing orders**

(1) If it appears to a judicial authority in the United Kingdom, on an application made by a person mentioned in subsection (4)–
   (a) that proceedings in respect of a listed offence have been instituted or such an offence is being investigated,
   (b) that there are reasonable grounds to believe that there is evidence in a participating country which satisfies the requirements of subsection (3), and
   (c) that a request has been made, or will be made, under section 7 for the evidence to be sent to the authority making the request,
the judicial authority may make a domestic freezing order in respect of the evidence.

(2) A domestic freezing order is an order for protecting evidence which is in the participating country pending its transfer to the United Kingdom.

(3) The requirements are that the evidence–
   (a) is on premises specified in the application in the participating country,
   (b) is likely to be of substantial value (whether by itself or together with other evidence) to the proceedings or investigation,
   (c) is likely to be admissible in evidence at a trial for the offence, and
   (d) does not consist of or include items subject to legal privilege.

(4) The application may be made–
   (a) in relation to England and Wales and Northern Ireland, by a constable,
   (b) in relation to Scotland, by the Lord Advocate or a procurator fiscal.

(5) The judicial authorities are–
   (a) in relation to England and Wales, any judge or justice of the peace,
   (b) in relation to Scotland, any judge of the High Court or sheriff,
   (c) in relation to Northern Ireland, any judge or resident magistrate.

(6) This section does not prejudice the generality of the power to make a request for assistance under section 7.

**11 Sending freezing orders**

(1) A domestic freezing order made in England and Wales or Northern Ireland is to be sent to the Secretary of State for forwarding to–
    (a) a court exercising jurisdiction in the place where the evidence is situated, or
    (b) any authority recognised by the government of the country in question as the appropriate authority for receiving orders of that kind.

(2) A domestic freezing order made in Scotland is to be sent to the Lord Advocate for forwarding to such a court or authority.

(3) The judicial authority is to send the order to the Secretary of State or the Lord Advocate before the end of the period of 14 days beginning with its being made.

(4) The order must be accompanied by a certificate giving the specified information and, unless the certificate indicates when the judicial authority expects such a request to be made, by a request under section 7 for the evidence to be sent to the authority making the request.

(5) The certificate must include a translation of it into an appropriate language of the participating country (if that language is not English).

(6) The certificate must be signed by or on behalf of the judicial authority who made the order and must include a statement as to the accuracy of the information given in it.

The signature may be an electronic signature.

**12 Variation or revocation of freezing orders**

(1) The judicial authority that made a domestic freezing order may vary or revoke it on an application by a person mentioned below.

(2) The persons are–
    (a) the person who applied for the order,
    (b) in relation to England and Wales and Northern Ireland, a prosecuting authority,
    (c) in relation to Scotland, the Lord Advocate,
    (d) any other person affected by the order.

Assisting overseas authorities to obtain evidence in the UK

**13 Requests for assistance from overseas authorities**

(1) Where a request for assistance in obtaining evidence in a part of the United Kingdom is received by the territorial authority for that part, the authority may–
    (a) if the conditions in section 14 are met, arrange for the evidence to be obtained under section 15, or
    (b) direct that a search warrant be applied for under or by virtue of section 16 or 17 or, in relation to evidence in Scotland, 18.

(2) The request for assistance may be made only by–
    (a) a court exercising criminal jurisdiction, or a prosecuting authority, in a country outside the United Kingdom,
    (b) any other authority in such a country which appears to the territorial authority to have the function of making such requests for assistance,
    (c) any international authority mentioned in subsection (3).

(3) The international authorities are–
    (a) the International Criminal Police Organisation,
    (b) any other body or person competent to make a request of the kind to which this section applies under any provisions adopted under the Treaty on European Union.

**14 Powers to arrange for evidence to be obtained**

(1) The territorial authority may arrange for evidence to be obtained under section 15 if the request for assistance in obtaining the evidence is made in connection with–
    (a) criminal proceedings or a criminal investigation, being carried on outside the United Kingdom,
    (b) administrative proceedings, or an investigation into an act punishable in such proceedings, being carried on there,

(c) clemency proceedings, or proceedings on an appeal before a court against a decision in administrative proceedings, being carried on, or intended to be carried on, there.

(2) In a case within subsection (1)(a) or (b), the authority may arrange for the evidence to be so obtained only if the authority is satisfied–
   (a) that an offence under the law of the country in question has been committed or that there are reasonable grounds for suspecting that such an offence has been committed, and
   (b) that proceedings in respect of the offence have been instituted in that country or that an investigation into the offence is being carried on there.
   An offence includes an act punishable in administrative proceedings.

(3) The territorial authority is to regard as conclusive a certificate as to the matters mentioned in subsection (2)(a) and (b) issued by any authority in the country in question which appears to him to be the appropriate authority to do so.

(4) If it appears to the territorial authority that the request for assistance relates to a fiscal offence in respect of which proceedings have not yet been instituted, the authority may not arrange for the evidence to be so obtained unless–
   (a) the request is from a country which is a member of the Commonwealth or is made pursuant to a treaty to which the United Kingdom is a party, or
   (b) the authority is satisfied that if the conduct constituting the offence were to occur in a part of the United Kingdom, it would constitute an offence in that part.

**15 Nominating a court etc. to receive evidence**

(1) Where the evidence is in England and Wales or Northern Ireland, the Secretary of State may by a notice nominate a court to receive any evidence to which the request relates which appears to the court to be appropriate for the purpose of giving effect to the request.

(2) But if it appears to the Secretary of State that the request relates to an offence involving serious or complex fraud, he may refer the request (or any part of it) to the Director of the Serious Fraud Office for the Director to obtain any evidence to which the request or part relates which appears to him to be appropriate for the purpose of giving effect to the request or part.

(3) Where the evidence is in Scotland, the Lord Advocate may by a notice nominate a court to receive any evidence to which the request relates which appears to the court to be appropriate for the purpose of giving effect to the request.

(4) But if it appears to the Lord Advocate that the request relates to an offence involving serious or complex fraud, he may give a direction under section 27 of the Criminal Law (Consolidation) (Scotland) Act 1995 (c. 39) (directions applying investigatory provisions).

(5) Schedule 1 is to have effect in relation to proceedings before a court nominated under this section.

**16 Extension of statutory search powers in England and Wales and Northern Ireland**

(1) Part 2 of the Police and Criminal Evidence Act 1984 (c. 60) (powers of entry, search and seizure) is to have effect as if references to [indictable offences] in section 8 of, and Schedule 1 to, that Act included any conduct which–
   (a) constitutes an offence under the law of a country outside the United Kingdom, and
   (b) would, if it occurred in England and Wales, constitute [an indictable offence].

(2) But an application for a warrant or order by virtue of subsection (1) may be made only–
   (a) in pursuance of a direction given under section 13, or
   (b) if it is an application for a warrant or order under section 8 of, or Schedule 1 to, that Act by a constable for the purposes of an investigation by an international joint investigation team of which he is a member.

(3) Part 3 of the Police and Criminal Evidence (Northern Ireland) Order 1989 (S.I. 1989/1341 (N.I.12)) (powers of entry, search and seizure) is to have effect as if references to serious arrestable offences in Article 10 of, and Schedule 1 to, that Order included any conduct which–
   (a) constitutes an offence under the law of a country outside the United Kingdom, and
   (b) would, if it occurred in Northern Ireland, constitute a serious arrestable offence.

(4) But an application for a warrant or order by virtue of subsection (3) may be made only–
    (a) in pursuance of a direction given under section 13, or
    (b) if it is an application for a warrant or order under Article 10 of, or Schedule 1 to, that Order, by a constable for the purposes of an investigation by an international joint investigation team of which he is a member.

(5) In this section, "international joint investigation team" has the meaning given by section 88(7) of the Police Act 1996 (c. 16).

## 17 Warrants in England and Wales or Northern Ireland

(1) A justice of the peace may issue a warrant under this section if he is satisfied, on an application made by a constable, that the following conditions are met.

(2) But an application for a warrant under subsection (1) may be made only in pursuance of a direction given under section 13.

(3) The conditions are that–
    (a) criminal proceedings have been instituted against a person in a country outside the United Kingdom or a person has been arrested in the course of a criminal investigation carried on there,
    [(b) the conduct constituting the offence which is the subject of the proceedings or investigation would (if it occurred in England and Wales) constitute an indictable offence, or (if it occurred in Northern Ireland) constitute an arrestable offence, and]
    (c) there are reasonable grounds for suspecting that there is on premises in England and Wales or (as the case may be) Northern Ireland occupied or controlled by that person evidence relating to the offence.
    "Arrestable offence" has the same meaning as in […] the Police and Criminal Evidence (Northern Ireland) Order 1989 (S.I. 1989/ 1341 (N.I.12)).

(4) A warrant under this section may authorise a constable–
    (a) to enter the premises in question and search the premises to the extent reasonably required for the purpose of discovering any evidence relating to the offence,
    (b) to seize and retain any evidence for which he is authorised to search.

## 18 Warrants in Scotland

(1) If, on an application made by the procurator fiscal, it appears to the sheriff–
    (a) that there are reasonable grounds for suspecting that an offence under the law of a country outside the United Kingdom has been committed, and
    (b) that the conduct constituting the offence would, if it occurred in Scotland, constitute an offence punishable by imprisonment,
    the sheriff has the like power to grant warrant authorising entry, search and seizure by any constable or customs officer as he has under section 134 of the Criminal Procedure (Scotland) Act 1995 (c. 46) in respect of any offence punishable at common law in Scotland.

(2) But an application for a warrant by virtue of subsection (1) may be made only–
    (a) in pursuance of a direction given under section 13, or
    (b) if it is an application made at the request of an international joint investigation team for the purposes of their investigation.
    "International joint investigation team" has the meaning given by section 39(6) of the Police (Scotland) Act 1967 (c. 77).

## 19 Seized evidence

(1) Any evidence seized by a constable under or by virtue of section 16, 17 or 18 is to be sent to the court or authority which made the request for assistance or to the territorial authority for forwarding to that court or authority.

(2) So far as may be necessary in order to comply with the request for assistance–
    (a) where the evidence consists of a document, the original or a copy is to be sent, and
    (b) where the evidence consists of any other article, the article itself or a description, photograph or other representation of it is to be sent.

(3) This section does not apply to evidence seized under or by virtue of section 16(2)(b) or (4)(b) or 18(2)(b).

## *Overseas freezing orders*

### 20 Overseas freezing orders

(1) Section 21 applies where an overseas freezing order made by a court or authority in a participating country is received from the court or authority which made or confirmed the order by the territorial authority for the part of the United Kingdom in which the evidence to which the order relates is situated.

(2) An overseas freezing order is an order–
  (a) for protecting, pending its transfer to the participating country, evidence which is in the United Kingdom and may be used in any proceedings or investigation in the participating country, and
  (b) in respect of which the following requirements of this section are met.

(3) The order must have been made by–
  (a) a court exercising criminal jurisdiction in the country,
  (b) a prosecuting authority in the country,
  (c) any other authority in the country which appears to the territorial authority to have the function of making such orders.

(4) The order must relate to–
  (a) criminal proceedings instituted in the participating country in respect of a listed offence, or
  (b) a criminal investigation being carried on there into such an offence.

(5) The order must be accompanied by a certificate which gives the specified information; but a certificate may be treated as giving any specified information which is not given in it if the territorial authority has the information in question.

(6) The certificate must–
  (a) be signed by or on behalf of the court or authority which made or confirmed the order,
  (b) include a statement as to the accuracy of the information given in it,
  (c) if it is not in English, include a translation of it into English (or, if appropriate, Welsh).
  The signature may be an electronic signature.

(7) The order must be accompanied by a request for the evidence to be sent to a court or authority mentioned in section 13(2), unless the certificate indicates when such a request is expected to be made.

(8) References below in this Chapter to an overseas freezing order include its accompanying certificate.

### 21 Considering the order

(1) In relation to England and Wales and Northern Ireland, where this section applies the Secretary of State must–
  (a) by a notice nominate a court in England and Wales or (as the case may be) Northern Ireland to give effect to the overseas freezing order,
  (b) send a copy of the overseas freezing order to the nominated court and to the chief officer of police for the area in which the evidence is situated,
  (c) tell the chief officer which court has been nominated.

(2) In relation to Scotland, where this section applies the Lord Advocate must–
  (a) by a notice nominate a sheriff to give effect to the overseas freezing order,
  (b) send a copy of the overseas freezing order to the sheriff and to the procurator fiscal.
  In relation to Scotland, references below in this section and in sections 22 to 25 to the nominated court are to be read as references to the nominated sheriff.

(3) The nominated court is to consider the overseas freezing order on its own initiative within a period prescribed by rules of court.

(4) Before giving effect to the overseas freezing order, the nominated court must give the chief officer of police or (as the case may be) the procurator fiscal an opportunity to be heard.

(5) The court may decide not to give effect to the overseas freezing order only if, in its opinion, one of the following conditions is met.

(6) The first condition is that, if the person whose conduct is in question were charged in the participating country with the offence to which the overseas freezing order relates or in the United Kingdom with a corresponding offence, he would be entitled to be discharged under any rule of law relating to previous acquittal or conviction.

(7) The second condition is that giving effect to the overseas freezing order would be incompatible with any of the Convention rights (within the meaning of the Human Rights Act 1998 (c. 42)).

## 22 Giving effect to the order

(1) The nominated court is to give effect to the overseas freezing order by issuing a warrant authorising a constable–
   (a) to enter the premises to which the overseas freezing order relates and search the premises to the extent reasonably required for the purpose of discovering any evidence to which the order relates, and
   (b) to seize and retain any evidence for which he is authorised to search.

(2) But, in relation to England and Wales and Northern Ireland, so far as the overseas freezing order relates to excluded material or special procedure material the court is to give effect to the order by making a production order.

(3) A production order is an order for the person who appears to the court to be in possession of the material to produce it to a constable before the end of the period of seven days beginning with the date of the production order or such longer period as the production order may specify.

(4) The constable may take away any material produced to him under a production order; and the material is to be treated for the purposes of section 21 of the Police and Criminal Evidence Act 1984 (c. 60) or (as the case may be) Article 23 of the Police and Criminal Evidence (Northern Ireland) Order 1989 (S.I. 1989/ 1341 (N.I.12)) (access and copying) as if it had been seized by the constable.

(5) If a person fails to comply with a production order, the court may (whether or not it deals with the matter as a contempt of court) issue a warrant under subsection (1) in respect of the material to which the production order relates.

(6) Section 409 of the Proceeds of Crime Act 2002 (c. 29) (jurisdiction of sheriff) has effect for the purposes of subsection (1) as if that subsection were included in Chapter 3 of Part 8 of that Act.

## 23 Postponed effect

The nominated court may postpone giving effect to an overseas freezing order in respect of any evidence–
   (a) in order to avoid prejudicing a criminal investigation which is taking place in the United Kingdom, or
   (b) if, under an order made by a court in criminal proceedings in the United Kingdom, the evidence may not be removed from the United Kingdom.

## 24 Evidence seized under the order

(1) Any evidence seized by or produced to the constable under section 22 is to be retained by him until he is given a notice under subsection (2) or authorised to release it under section 25.

(2) If–
   (a) the overseas freezing order was accompanied by a request for the evidence to be sent to a court or authority mentioned in section 13(2), or
   (b) the territorial authority subsequently receives such a request,
   the territorial authority may by notice require the constable to send the evidence to the court or authority that made the request.

## 25 Release of evidence held under the order

(1) On an application made by a person mentioned below, the nominated court may authorise the release of any evidence retained by a constable under section 24 if, in its opinion–
   (a) the condition in section 21(6) or (7) is met, or
   (b) the overseas freezing order has ceased to have effect in the participating country.

(2) In relation to England and Wales and Northern Ireland, the persons are–
   (a) the chief officer of police to whom a copy of the order was sent,
   (b) the constable,
   (c) any other person affected by the order.

(3) In relation to Scotland, the persons are–
   (a) the procurator fiscal to whom a copy of the order was sent,
   (b) any other person affected by the order.

(4) If the territorial authority decides not to give a notice under section 24(2) in respect of any evidence retained by a constable under that section, the authority must give the constable a notice authorising him to release the evidence.

## *General*

### 26 Powers under warrants

(1) A court in England and Wales or Northern Ireland, or a justice of the peace, may not issue a warrant under section 17 or 22 in respect of any evidence unless the court or justice has reasonable grounds for believing that it does not consist of or include items subject to legal privilege, excluded material or special procedure material.

(2) Subsection (1) does not prevent a warrant being issued by virtue of section 22(5) in respect of excluded material or special procedure material.

(3) In Schedule 1 to the Criminal Justice and Police Act 2001 (c. 16) (powers of seizure), in Part 1 (powers to which the additional powers in section 50 apply)–
   (a) paragraph 49 is omitted,
   (b) after paragraph 73B there is inserted–
      "**73C Crime (International Co-operation) Act 2003**
      The power of seizure conferred by sections 17 and 22 of the Crime (International Co-operation) Act 2003 (seizure of evidence relevant to overseas investigation or offence)."

(4) References in this Chapter to evidence seized by a person by virtue of or under any provision of this Chapter include evidence seized by a person by virtue of section 50 of the Criminal Justice and Police Act 2001 (additional powers of seizure), if it is seized in the course of a search authorised by a warrant issued by virtue of or under the provision in question.

(5) Subsection (4) does not require any evidence to be sent to the territorial authority or to any court or authority–
   (a) before it has been found, on the completion of any examination required to be made by arrangements under section 53(2) of the Criminal Justice and Police Act 2001, to be property within subsection (3) of that section (property which may be retained after examination), or
   (b) at a time when it constitutes property in respect of which a person is required to ensure that arrangements such as are mentioned in section 61(1) of that Act (duty to secure) are in force.

### 27 Exercise of powers by others

(1) The Treasury may by order provide, in relation to England and Wales or Northern Ireland–
   (a) for any function conferred on the Secretary of State (whether or not in terms) under sections 10, 11 and 13 to 26 to be exercisable instead in prescribed circumstances by the [Commissioners for Revenue and Customs],
   (b) for any function conferred on a constable under those sections to be exercisable instead in prescribed circumstances by [an officer of Revenue and Customs] or a person acting under the direction of such an officer.
   "Prescribed" means prescribed by the order.

(2) The Secretary of State may by order provide, in relation to England and Wales or Northern Ireland–
   (a) for any function conferred on him under sections 13 to 26 to be exercisable instead in prescribed circumstances by a prescribed person,
   (b) for any function conferred on a constable under those sections to be exercisable instead in prescribed circumstances by a prescribed person.
   "Prescribed" means prescribed by the order.

(3) Subsection (2)(b) does not apply to any powers exercisable by virtue of section 16(2)(b) or (4)(b).

## 28 Interpretation of Chapter 2

(1) In this Chapter–

"domestic freezing order" has the meaning given by section 10(2),

"notice" means a notice in writing,

"overseas freezing order" has the meaning given by section 20,

"premises" has the same meaning as in the Police and Criminal Evidence Act 1984 (c. 60), Chapter 3 of Part 8 of the Proceeds of Crime Act 2002 (c. 29) or the Police and Criminal Evidence (Northern Ireland) Order 1989 (S.I. 1989/1341 (N.I.12)) (as the case may be),

"the relevant Framework Decision" means the Framework Decision on the execution in the European Union of orders freezing property or evidence adopted by the Council of the European Union on 22nd July 2003.

(2) The following provisions have effect for the purposes of this Chapter.

(3) In relation to England and Wales and Northern Ireland, "items subject to legal privilege" , "excluded material" and "special procedure material" have the same meaning as in the Police and Criminal Evidence Act 1984 or (as the case may be) the Police and Criminal Evidence (Northern Ireland) Order 1989.

(4) In relation to Scotland, "items subject to legal privilege" has the same meaning as in Chapter 3 of Part 8 of the Proceeds of Crime Act 2002.

(5) A listed offence means–

(a) an offence described in Article 3(2) of the relevant Framework Decision, or

(b) an offence prescribed or of a description prescribed by an order made by the Secretary of State.

(6) An order prescribing an offence or a description of offences under subsection (5)(b) may require, in the case of an overseas freezing order, that the conduct which constitutes the offence or offences would, if it occurred in a part of the United Kingdom, constitute an offence in that part.

(7) Specified information, in relation to a certificate required by section 11(4) or 20(5), means–

(a) any information required to be given by the form of certificate annexed to the relevant Framework Decision, or

(b) any information prescribed by an order made by the Secretary of State.

(8) In relation to Scotland, references above in this section to the Secretary of State are to be read as references to the Scottish Ministers.

(9) The territorial authority–

(a) in relation to evidence in England and Wales or Northern Ireland, is the Secretary of State,

(b) in relation to evidence in Scotland, is the Lord Advocate.

## CHAPTER 3

### HEARING EVIDENCE THROUGH TELEVISION LINKS OR BY TELEPHONE

## 29 Hearing witnesses abroad through television links

(1) The Secretary of State may by order provide for section 32(1A) of the Criminal Justice Act 1988 (c. 33) or Article 81(1A) of the Police and Criminal Evidence (Northern Ireland) Order 1989 (S.I. 1989/1341 (N.I.12)) (proceedings in which evidence may be given through television link) to apply to any further description of criminal proceedings, or to all criminal proceedings.

(2) The Scottish Ministers may by order provide for section 273(1) of the Criminal Procedure (Scotland) Act 1995 (c. 46) (proceedings in which evidence may be given through television link) to apply to any further description of criminal proceedings, or to all criminal proceedings.

## 30 Hearing witnesses in the UK through television links

(1) This section applies where the Secretary of State receives a request, from an authority mentioned in subsection (2) ("the external authority"), for a person in the United Kingdom to give evidence

through a live television link in criminal proceedings before a court in a country outside the United Kingdom.

Criminal proceedings include any proceedings on an appeal before a court against a decision in administrative proceedings.

(2) The authority referred to in subsection (1) is the authority in that country which appears to the Secretary of State to have the function of making requests of the kind to which this section applies.

(3) Unless he considers it inappropriate to do so, the Secretary of State must by notice in writing nominate a court in the United Kingdom where the witness may be heard in the proceedings in question through a live television link.

(4) Anything done by the witness in the presence of the nominated court which, if it were done in proceedings before the court, would constitute contempt of court is to be treated for that purpose as done in proceedings before the court.

(5) Any statement made on oath by a witness giving evidence in pursuance of this section is to be treated for the purposes of–
(a) section 1 of the Perjury Act 1911 (c. 6),
(b) Article 3 of the Perjury (Northern Ireland) Order 1979 (S.I. 1979/ 1714 (N.I. 19)),
(c) sections 44 to 46 of the Criminal Law (Consolidation) (Scotland) Act 1995 (c. 39) or, in relation to Scotland, any matter pertaining to the common law crime of perjury,
as made in proceedings before the nominated court.

(6) Part 1 of Schedule 2 (evidence given by television link) is to have effect.

(7) Subject to subsections (4) and (5) and the provisions of that Schedule, evidence given pursuant to this section is not to be treated for any purpose as evidence given in proceedings in the United Kingdom.

(8) In relation to Scotland, references in this section and Part 1 of Schedule 2 to the Secretary of State are to be read as references to the Lord Advocate.

### 31 Hearing witnesses in the UK by telephone

(1) This section applies where the Secretary of State receives a request, from an authority mentioned in subsection (2) ("the external authority") in a participating country, for a person in the United Kingdom to give evidence by telephone in criminal proceedings before a court in that country.

Criminal proceedings include any proceedings on an appeal before a court against a decision in administrative proceedings.

(2) The authority referred to in subsection (1) is the authority in that country which appears to the Secretary of State to have the function of making requests of the kind to which this section applies.

(3) A request under subsection (1) must–
(a) specify the court in the participating country,
(b) give the name and address of the witness,
(c) state that the witness is willing to give evidence by telephone in the proceedings before that court.

(4) Unless he considers it inappropriate to do so, the Secretary of State must by notice in writing nominate a court in the United Kingdom where the witness may be heard in the proceedings in question by telephone.

(5) Anything done by the witness in the presence of the nominated court which, if it were done in proceedings before the court, would constitute contempt of court is to be treated for that purpose as done in proceedings before the court.

(6) Any statement made on oath by a witness giving evidence in pursuance of this section is to be treated for the purposes of–
(a) section 1 of the Perjury Act 1911 (c. 6),
(b) Article 3 of the Perjury (Northern Ireland) Order 1979 (S.I. 1979/ 1714 (N.I. 19)),
(c) sections 44 to 46 of the Criminal Law (Consolidation) (Scotland) Act 1995 (c. 39) or, in relation to Scotland, any matter pertaining to the common law crime of perjury,
as made in proceedings before the nominated court.

(7) Part 2 of Schedule 2 (evidence given by telephone link) is to have effect.

(8) Subject to subsections (5) and (6) and the provisions of that Schedule, evidence given in pursuance of this section is not to be treated for any purpose as evidence given in proceedings in the United Kingdom.

(9) In relation to Scotland, references in this section to the Secretary of State are to be read as references to the Lord Advocate.

CHAPTER 4

INFORMATION ABOUT BANKING TRANSACTIONS

*Requests for information about banking transactions in england and wales and northern ireland for use abroad*

**32 Customer information**

(1) This section applies where the Secretary of State receives a request from an authority mentioned in subsection (2) for customer information to be obtained in relation to a person who appears to him to be subject to an investigation in a participating country into serious criminal conduct.

(2) The authority referred to in subsection (1) is the authority in that country which appears to the Secretary of State to have the function of making requests of the kind to which this section applies.

(3) The Secretary of State may–
   (a) direct a senior police officer to apply, or arrange for a constable to apply, for a customer information order,
   (b) direct a senior customs officer to apply, or arrange for a customs officer to apply, for such an order.

(4) A customer information order is an order made by a judge that a financial institution specified in the application for the order must, on being required to do so by notice in writing given by the applicant for the order, provide any such customer information as it has relating to the person specified in the application.

(5) A financial institution which is required to provide information under a customer information order must provide the information to the applicant for the order in such manner, and at or by such time, as the applicant requires.

(6) Section 364 of the Proceeds of Crime Act 2002 (c. 29) (meaning of customer information), except subsections (2)(f) and (3)(i), has effect for the purposes of this section as if this section were included in Chapter 2 of Part 8 of that Act.

(7) A customer information order has effect in spite of any restriction on the disclosure of information (however imposed).

(8) Customer information obtained in pursuance of a customer information order is to be given to the Secretary of State and sent by him to the authority which made the request.

**33 Making, varying or discharging customer information orders**

(1) A judge may make a customer information order, on an application made to him pursuant to a direction under section 32(3), if he is satisfied that–
   (a) the person specified in the application is subject to an investigation in the country in question,
   (b) the investigation concerns conduct which is serious criminal conduct,
   (c) the conduct constitutes an offence in England and Wales or (as the case may be) Northern Ireland, or would do were it to occur there, and
   (d) the order is sought for the purposes of the investigation.

(2) The application may be made ex parte to a judge in chambers.

(3) The application may specify–
   (a) all financial institutions,

(b) a particular description, or particular descriptions, of financial institutions, or

(c) a particular financial institution or particular financial institutions.

(4) The court may discharge or vary a customer information order on an application made by–

(a) the person who applied for the order,

(b) a senior police officer,

(c) a constable authorised by a senior police officer to make the application,

(d) a senior customs officer,

(e) a customs officer authorised by a senior customs officer to make the application.

## 34 Offences

(1) A financial institution is guilty of an offence if without reasonable excuse it fails to comply with a requirement imposed on it under a customer information order.

(2) A financial institution guilty of an offence under subsection (1) is liable on summary conviction to a fine not exceeding level 5 on the standard scale.

(3) A financial institution is guilty of an offence if, in purported compliance with a customer information order, it–

(a) makes a statement which it knows to be false or misleading in a material particular, or

(b) recklessly makes a statement which is false or misleading in a material particular.

(4) A financial institution guilty of an offence under subsection (3) is liable–

(a) on summary conviction, to a fine not exceeding the statutory maximum, or

(b) on conviction on indictment, to a fine.

## 35 Account information

(1) This section applies where the Secretary of State receives a request from an authority mentioned in subsection (2) for account information to be obtained in relation to an investigation in a participating country into criminal conduct.

(2) The authority referred to in subsection (1) is the authority in that country which appears to the Secretary of State to have the function of making requests of the kind to which this section applies.

(3) The Secretary of State may–

(a) direct a senior police officer to apply, or arrange for a constable to apply, for an account monitoring order,

(b) direct a senior customs officer to apply, or arrange for a customs officer to apply, for such an order.

(4) An account monitoring order is an order made by a judge that a financial institution specified in the application for the order must, for the period stated in the order, provide account information of the description specified in the order to the applicant in the manner, and at or by the time or times, stated in the order.

(5) Account information is information relating to an account or accounts held at the financial institution specified in the application by the person so specified (whether solely or jointly with another).

(6) An account monitoring order has effect in spite of any restriction on the disclosure of information (however imposed).

(7) Account information obtained in pursuance of an account monitoring order is to be given to the Secretary of State and sent by him to the authority which made the request.

## 36 Making, varying or discharging account monitoring orders

(1) A judge may make an account monitoring order, on an application made to him in pursuance of a direction under section 35(3), if he is satisfied that–

(a) there is an investigation in the country in question into criminal conduct, and

(b) the order is sought for the purposes of the investigation.

(2) The application may be made ex parte to a judge in chambers.

(3) The application may specify information relating to–
    (a) all accounts held by the person specified in the application for the order at the financial institution so specified,
    (b) a particular description, or particular descriptions, of accounts so held, or
    (c) a particular account, or particular accounts, so held.

(4) The court may discharge or vary an account monitoring order on an application made by–
    (a) the person who applied for the order,
    (b) a senior police officer,
    (c) a constable authorised by a senior police officer to make the application,
    (d) a senior customs officer,
    (e) a customs officer authorised by a senior customs officer to make the application.

(5) Account monitoring orders have effect as if they were orders of the court.

*Requests for information about banking transactions in Scotland*
*for use abroad*

### 37 Customer information

(1) This section applies where the Lord Advocate receives a request from an authority mentioned in subsection (2) for customer information to be obtained in relation to a person who appears to him to be subject to an investigation in a participating country into serious criminal conduct.

(2) The authority referred to in subsection (1) is the authority in that country which appears to the Lord Advocate to have the function of making requests of the kind to which this section applies.

(3) The Lord Advocate may direct a procurator fiscal to apply for a customer information order.

(4) A customer information order is an order made by a sheriff that a financial institution specified in the application for the order must, on being required to do so by notice in writing given by the applicant for the order, provide any such customer information as it has relating to the person specified in the application.

(5) A financial institution which is required to provide information under a customer information order must provide the information to the applicant for the order in such manner, and at or by such time, as the applicant requires.

(6) Section 398 of the Proceeds of Crime Act 2002 (c. 29) (meaning of customer information), except subsections (2)(f) and (3)(i), has effect for the purposes of this section as if this section were included in Chapter 3 of Part 8 of that Act.

(7) A customer information order has effect in spite of any restriction on the disclosure of information (however imposed).

(8) Customer information obtained in pursuance of a customer information order is to be given to the Lord Advocate and sent by him to the authority which made the request.

### 38 Making, varying or discharging customer information orders

(1) A sheriff may make a customer information order, on an application made to him pursuant to a direction under section 37(3), if he is satisfied that–
    (a) the person specified in the application is subject to an investigation in the country in question,
    (b) the investigation concerns conduct which is serious criminal conduct,
    (c) the conduct constitutes an offence in Scotland, or would do were it to occur in Scotland, and
    (d) the order is sought for the purposes of the investigation.

(2) The application may be made ex parte to a sheriff in chambers.

(3) The application may specify–
    (a) all financial institutions,
    (b) a particular description, or particular descriptions, of financial institutions, or
    (c) a particular financial institution or particular financial institutions.

(4) The court may discharge or vary a customer information order on an application made by the procurator fiscal.

(5) Section 409 of the Proceeds of Crime Act 2002 (jurisdiction of sheriff) has effect for the purposes of this section as if this section were included in Chapter 3 of Part 8 of that Act.

## 39 Offences

(1) A financial institution is guilty of an offence if without reasonable excuse it fails to comply with a requirement imposed on it under a customer information order.

(2) A financial institution guilty of an offence under subsection (1) is liable on summary conviction to a fine not exceeding level 5 on the standard scale.

(3) A financial institution is guilty of an offence if, in purported compliance with a customer information order, it–
  (a) makes a statement which it knows to be false or misleading in a material particular, or
  (b) recklessly makes a statement which is false or misleading in a material particular.

(4) A financial institution guilty of an offence under subsection (3) is liable–
  (a) on summary conviction, to a fine not exceeding the statutory maximum, or
  (b) on conviction on indictment, to a fine.

## 40 Account information

(1) This section applies where the Lord Advocate receives a request from an authority mentioned in subsection (2) for account information to be obtained in relation to an investigation in a participating country into criminal conduct.

(2) The authority referred to in subsection (1) is the authority in that country which appears to the Lord Advocate to have the function of making requests of the kind to which this section applies.

(3) The Lord Advocate may direct a procurator fiscal to apply for an account monitoring order.

(4) An account monitoring order is an order made by a sheriff that a financial institution specified in the application for the order must, for the period stated in the order, provide account information of the description specified in the order to the applicant in the manner, and at or by the time or times, stated in the order.

(5) Account information is information relating to an account or accounts held at the financial institution specified in the application by the person so specified (whether solely or jointly with another).

(6) An account monitoring order has effect in spite of any restriction on the disclosure of information (however imposed).

(7) Account information obtained in pursuance of an account monitoring order is to be given to the Lord Advocate and sent by him to the authority which made the request.

## 41 Making, varying or discharging account monitoring orders

(1) A sheriff may make an account monitoring order, on an application made to him in pursuance of a direction under section 40(3), if he is satisfied that–
  (a) there is an investigation in the country in question into criminal conduct, and
  (b) the order is sought for the purposes of the investigation.

(2) The application may be made ex parte to a sheriff in chambers.

(3) The application may specify information relating to–
  (a) all accounts held by the person specified in the application for the order at the financial institution so specified,
  (b) a particular description, or particular descriptions, of accounts so held, or
  (c) a particular account, or particular accounts, so held.

(4) The court may discharge or vary an account monitoring order on an application made by the procurator fiscal.

(5) Section 409 of the Proceeds of Crime Act 2002 (c. 29) (jurisdiction of sheriff) has effect for the purposes of this section as if this section were included in Chapter 3 of Part 8 of that Act.

*Disclosure of information*

### 42 Offence of disclosure

(1) This section applies where–
   - (a) a financial institution is specified in a customer information order or account monitoring order made in any part of the United Kingdom, or
   - (b) the Secretary of State or the Lord Advocate receives a request under section 13 for evidence to be obtained from a financial institution in connection with the investigation of an offence in reliance on Article 2 (requests for information on banking transactions) of the 2001 Protocol.

(2) If the institution, or an employee of the institution, discloses any of the following information, the institution or (as the case may be) the employee is guilty of an offence.

(3) That information is–
   - (a) that the request to obtain customer information or account information, or the request mentioned in subsection (1)(b), has been received,
   - (b) that the investigation to which the request relates is being carried out, or
   - (c) that, in pursuance of the request, information has been given to the authority which made the request.

(4) An institution guilty of an offence under this section is liable–
   - (a) on summary conviction, to a fine not exceeding the statutory maximum,
   - (b) on conviction on indictment, to a fine.

(5) Any other person guilty of an offence under this section is liable–
   - (a) on summary conviction, to imprisonment for a term not exceeding six months or to a fine not exceeding the statutory maximum, or to both,
   - (b) on conviction on indictment, to imprisonment for a term not exceeding five years or to a fine, or to both.

*Requests for information about banking transactions for use in UK*

### 43 Information about a person's bank account

(1) If it appears to a judicial authority in the United Kingdom, on an application made by a prosecuting authority, that–
   - (a) a person is subject to an investigation in the United Kingdom into serious criminal conduct,
   - (b) the person holds, or may hold, an account at a bank which is situated in a participating country, and
   - (c) the information which the applicant seeks to obtain is likely to be of substantial value for the purposes of the investigation,
   the judicial authority may request assistance under this section.

(2) The judicial authorities are–
   - (a) in relation to England and Wales, any judge or justice of the peace,
   - (b) in relation to Scotland, any sheriff,
   - (c) in relation to Northern Ireland, any judge or resident magistrate.

(3) If it appears to a prosecuting authority mentioned in subsection (4) that paragraphs (a) to (c) of subsection (1) are met, the authority may itself request assistance under this section.

(4) The prosecuting authorities are–
   - (a) in relation to England and Wales and Northern Ireland, a prosecuting authority designated by an order made by the Secretary of State,
   - (b) in relation to Scotland, the Lord Advocate or a procurator fiscal.

(5) The assistance that may be requested under this section is any assistance in obtaining from a participating country one or more of the following–
   - (a) information as to whether the person in question holds any accounts at any banks situated in the participating country,
   - (b) details of any such accounts,
   - (c) details of transactions carried out in any period specified in the request in respect of any such accounts.

(6) A request for assistance under this section must–
  (a) state the grounds on which the authority making the request thinks that the person in question may hold any account at a bank which is situated in a participating country and (if possible) specify the bank or banks in question,
  (b) state the grounds on which the authority making the request considers that the information sought to be obtained is likely to be of substantial value for the purposes of the investigation, and
  (c) include any information which may facilitate compliance with the request.

(7) For the purposes of this section, a person holds an account if–
  (a) the account is in his name or is held for his benefit, or
  (b) he has a power of attorney in respect of the account.
  In relation to Scotland, a power of attorney includes a factory and commission.

## 44 Monitoring banking transactions

(1) If it appears to a judicial authority in the United Kingdom, on an application made by a prosecuting authority, that the information which the applicant seeks to obtain is relevant to an investigation in the United Kingdom into criminal conduct, the judicial authority may request assistance under this section.

(2) The judicial authorities are–
  (a) in relation to England and Wales, any judge or justice of the peace,
  (b) in relation to Scotland, any sheriff,
  (c) in relation to Northern Ireland, any judge or resident magistrate.

(3) If it appears to a prosecuting authority mentioned in subsection (4) that the information which it seeks to obtain is relevant to an investigation into criminal conduct, the authority may itself request assistance under this section.

(4) The prosecuting authorities are–
  (a) in relation to England and Wales and Northern Ireland, a prosecuting authority designated by an order made by the Secretary of State,
  (b) in relation to Scotland, the Lord Advocate or a procurator fiscal.

(5) The assistance that may be requested under this section is any assistance in obtaining from a participating country details of transactions to be carried out in any period specified in the request in respect of any accounts at banks situated in that country.

## 45 Sending requests for assistance

(1) A request for assistance under section 43 or 44, other than one to which subsection (3) or (4) applies, is to be sent to the Secretary of State for forwarding–
  (a) to a court specified in the request and exercising jurisdiction in the place where the information is to be obtained, or
  (b) to any authority recognised by the participating country in question as the appropriate authority for receiving requests for assistance of the kind to which this section applies.

(2) But in cases of urgency the request may be sent to a court referred to in subsection (1)(a).

(3) Such a request for assistance by the Lord Advocate is to be sent to a court or authority mentioned in subsection (1)(a) or (b).

(4) Such a request for assistance by a sheriff or a procurator fiscal is to be sent to such a court or authority, or to the Lord Advocate for forwarding to such a court or authority.

*General*

## 46 Interpretation of Chapter 4

(1) In this Chapter–
  "the court" means the Crown Court or, in Scotland, the sheriff,
  "senior police officer" means a police officer who is not below the rank of superintendent
  and "senior customs officer" means a customs officer who is not below the grade designated by the Commissioners of Customs and Excise as equivalent to that rank.

(2) The following provisions apply for the purposes of this Chapter.

(3) Serious criminal conduct means conduct which constitutes–
    (a) an offence to which paragraph 3 of Article 1 (request for information on bank accounts) of the 2001 Protocol applies, or
    (b) an offence specified in an order made by the Secretary of State or, in relation to Scotland, the Scottish Ministers for the purpose of giving effect to any decision of the Council of the European Union under paragraph 6 of that Article.

(4) A financial institution–
    (a) means a person who is carrying on business in the regulated sector, and
    (b) in relation to a customer information order or an account monitoring order, includes a person who was carrying on business in the regulated sector at a time which is the time to which any requirement for him to provide information under the order is to relate.
"Business in the regulated sector" is to be interpreted in accordance with Schedule 9 to the Proceeds of Crime Act 2002 (c. 29).

(5) A judge means–
    (a) in relation to England and Wales, a judge entitled to exercise the jurisdiction of the Crown Court,
    (b) in relation to Northern Ireland, a Crown Court judge.

## Chapter 5

### Transfer of Prisoners

**47 Transfer of UK prisoner to assist investigation abroad**

(1) The Secretary of State may pursuant to an agreement with the competent authority of a participating country issue a warrant providing for any person to whom this section applies ("a prisoner") to be transferred to that country for the purpose of assisting there in the investigation of an offence.

The offence must be one which was or may have been committed in the United Kingdom.

(2) This section applies to a person–
    (a) serving a sentence in a prison,
    (b) in custody awaiting trial or sentence, or
    (c) committed to prison for default in paying a fine.

(3) But, in relation to transfer from Scotland–
    (a) this section applies to any person detained in custody,
    (b) references in this section to the Secretary of State are to be read as references to the Scottish Ministers.

(4) A warrant may be issued in respect of a prisoner under subsection (1) only if–
    (a) the prisoner, or
    (b) in the circumstances mentioned in subsection (5), a person appearing to the Secretary of State to be an appropriate person to act on the prisoner's behalf,
has made a written statement consenting to his being transferred for the purpose mentioned in subsection (1).

(5) The circumstances are those in which it appears to the Secretary of State to be inappropriate for the prisoner to act for himself, by reason of his physical or mental condition or his youth.

(6) Such consent cannot be withdrawn after the issue of the warrant.

(7) A warrant under this section authorises–
    (a) the taking of the prisoner to a place in the United Kingdom and his delivery at a place of departure from the United Kingdom into the custody of a person representing the appropriate authority of the participating country to which the prisoner is to be transferred, and
    (b) the bringing of the prisoner back to the United Kingdom and his transfer in custody to the place where he is liable to be detained under the sentence or order to which he is subject.

(8) References to a prison in this section include any other institution to which the Prison Act 1952 (c. 52), the Prison Act (Northern Ireland) 1953 (c. 18 (N.I.)) or Article 45(1) of the Criminal Justice (Children) (Northern Ireland) Order 1998 (S.I. 1998/ 1504 (N.I.9)) applies.

(9) [Subsections (4) to (8) of section 5] of the 1990 Act (transfer of UK prisoner to give evidence or assist investigation overseas) have effect in relation to a warrant issued under this section as they have effect in relation to a warrant issued under that section.

## 48 Transfer of EU etc. prisoner to assist UK investigation

(1) The Secretary of State may pursuant to an agreement with the competent authority of a participating country issue a warrant providing for any person to whom this section applies ("the overseas prisoner") to be transferred to the United Kingdom for the purpose of assisting in the investigation of an offence.

The offence must be one which was or may have been committed in the participating country.

(2) This section applies to a person who is detained in custody in a participating country–
(a) by virtue of a sentence or order of a court exercising criminal jurisdiction there, or
[(b) in consequence of—
(a) having been transferred there, or responsibility for his detention and release having been transferred there, from the United Kingdom under the Repatriation of Prisoners Act 1984;
(b) having been transferred there, or responsibility for his detention and release having been transferred there, under any similar provision or arrangement from any other country or territory.]

(3) But, in relation to transfer to Scotland–
(a) this section applies to any person who is detained in custody in a participating country,
(b) the reference in subsection (1) to the Secretary of State is to be read as a reference to the Scottish Ministers.

(4) A warrant may be issued in respect of an overseas prisoner under subsection (1) only if the competent authority provides a written statement made by the prisoner consenting to his being transferred for the purpose mentioned in that subsection.

(5) Such consent cannot be withdrawn after the issue of the warrant.

(6) A warrant under this section authorises–
(a) the bringing of the prisoner to the United Kingdom,
(b) the taking of the prisoner to, and his detention in custody at, any place or places in the United Kingdom specified in the warrant,
(c) the returning of the prisoner to the country from which he has come.

(7) Subsections (4) to (8) of section 5 of the 1990 Act have effect in relation to a warrant issued under this section as they have effect in relation to a warrant issued under that section.

(8) A person is not subject to the Immigration Act 1971 (c. 77) in respect of his entry into or presence in the United Kingdom pursuant to a warrant under this section; but if the warrant ceases to have effect while he is still in the United Kingdom–
(a) he is to be treated for the purposes of that Act as if he has then illegally entered the United Kingdom, and
(b) the provisions of Schedule 2 to that Act have effect accordingly except that paragraph 20(1) (liability of carrier for expenses of custody etc. of illegal entrant) does not have effect in relation to directions for his removal given by virtue of this subsection.

CHAPTER 6

SUPPLEMENTARY

## 49 Rules of court[1]

(1) Provision may be made by rules of court as to the practice and procedure to be followed in connection with proceedings under this Part.

---

[1] Not yet in force.

(2) Rules of court made under this section by the High Court in Scotland are to be made by Act of Adjournal.

(3) The power to make rules of court under this section does not prejudice any existing power to make rules.

## 50 Subordinate legislation[2]

(1) Any power to make an order conferred by this Part on the Secretary of State, the Treasury or the Scottish Ministers is exercisable by statutory instrument.

(2) Such an order may make different provision for different purposes.

(3) A statutory instrument (other than an instrument to which subsection (5) applies) containing an order made by the Secretary of State or the Treasury is to be subject to annulment in pursuance of a resolution of either House of Parliament.

(4) A statutory instrument (other than an instrument to which subsection (5) applies) containing an order made by the Scottish Ministers is to be subject to annulment in pursuance of a resolution of the Scottish Parliament.

(5) A statutory instrument containing an order under section 51(2)(b) designating a country other than a member State is not to be made unless–

    (a) in the case of an order to be made by the Secretary of State, a draft of the instrument has been laid before, and approved by resolution of, each House of Parliament,

    (b) in the case of an order to be made by the Scottish Ministers, a draft of the instrument has been laid before, and approved by resolution of, the Scottish Parliament.

## 51 General interpretation[3]

(1) In this Part–

"the 1990 Act" means the Criminal Justice (International Co-operation) Act 1990 (c. 5),

"the 2001 Protocol" means the Protocol to the Mutual Legal Assistance Convention, established by Council Act of 16th October 2001 (2001/C326/01),

"administrative proceedings" means proceedings outside the United Kingdom to which Article 3(1) of the Mutual Legal Assistance Convention applies (proceedings brought by administrative authorities in respect of administrative offences where a decision in the proceedings may be the subject of an appeal before a court),

"chief officer of police"–

    (a) in relation to any area in Scotland, means the chief constable for the police force maintained for that area,

    (b) in relation to any area in Northern Ireland, means the Chief Constable of the Police Service of Northern Ireland,

"clemency proceedings" means proceedings in a country outside the United Kingdom, not being proceedings before a court exercising criminal jurisdiction, for the removal or reduction of a penalty imposed on conviction of an offence,

"country" includes territory,

"court" includes a tribunal,

"criminal proceedings" include criminal proceedings outside the United Kingdom in which a civil order may be made,

"customs officer" means an officer commissioned by the Commissioners of Customs and Excise under section 6(3) of the Customs and Excise Management Act 1979 (c. 2),

"evidence" includes information in any form and articles, and giving evidence includes answering a question or producing any information or article,

"the Mutual Legal Assistance Convention" means the Convention on Mutual Assistance in Criminal Matters established by Council Act of 29th May 2000 (2000/C197/01),

"the Schengen Convention" means the Convention implementing the Schengen Agreement of 14th June 1985.

---

[2] Not yet in force.
[3] Not yet in force.

(2) A participating country, in relation to any provision of this Part, means–
  (a) a country other than the United Kingdom which is a member State on a day appointed for the commencement of that provision, and
  (b) any other country designated by an order made by the Secretary of State or, in relation to Scotland, the Scottish Ministers.

(3) In this Part, "process", in relation to England and Wales and Northern Ireland, means any summons or order issued or made by a court and includes–
  (a) any other document issued or made by a court for service on parties or witnesses,
  (b) any document issued by a prosecuting authority outside the United Kingdom for the purposes of criminal proceedings.

(4) In this Part, "process", in relation to service in Scotland, means a citation by a court or by a prosecuting authority, or an order made by a court, and includes any other document issued or made as mentioned in subsection (3)(a) or (b).

## PART 2

### TERRORIST ACTS AND THREATS: JURISDICTION

#### 52 Jurisdiction for terrorist offences

After section 63 of the Terrorism Act 2000 (c. 11) there is inserted–

  "Extra-territorial jurisdiction for other terrorist offences etc.

#### 63A Other terrorist offences under this Act: jurisdiction

(1) If–
  (a) a United Kingdom national or a United Kingdom resident does anything outside the United Kingdom, and
  (b) his action, if done in any part of the United Kingdom, would have constituted an offence under section 54 or any of sections 56 to 61,
  he shall be guilty in that part of the United Kingdom of the offence.

(2) For the purposes of this section and sections 63B and 63C a "United Kingdom national" means an individual who is–
  (a) a British citizen, a British overseas territories citizen, a British National (Overseas) or a British Overseas citizen,
  (b) a person who under the British Nationality Act 1981 is a British subject, or
  (c) a British protected person within the meaning of that Act.

(3) For the purposes of this section and sections 63B and 63C a "United Kingdom resident" means an individual who is resident in the United Kingdom.

#### 63B Terrorist attacks abroad by UK nationals or residents: jurisdiction

(1) If–
  (a) a United Kingdom national or a United Kingdom resident does anything outside the United Kingdom as an act of terrorism or for the purposes of terrorism, and
  (b) his action, if done in any part of the United Kingdom, would have constituted an offence listed in subsection (2),
  he shall be guilty in that part of the United Kingdom of the offence.

(2) These are the offences–
  (a) murder, manslaughter, culpable homicide, rape, assault causing injury, assault to injury, kidnapping, abduction or false imprisonment,
  (b) an offence under section 4, 16, 18, 20, 21, 22, 23, 24, 28, 29, 30 or 64 of the Offences against the Person Act 1861,
  (c) an offence under any of sections 1 to 5 of the Forgery and Counterfeiting Act 1981,
  (d) the uttering of a forged document or an offence under section 46A of the Criminal Law (Consolidation) (Scotland) Act 1995,
  (e) an offence under section 1 or 2 of the Criminal Damage Act 1971,

(f)  an offence under Article 3 or 4 of the Criminal Damage (Northern Ireland) Order 1977,

(g)  malicious mischief,

(h)  wilful fire-raising.

**63C Terrorist attacks abroad on UK nationals, residents and diplomatic staff etc: jurisdiction**

(1)  If–

(a)  a person does anything outside the United Kingdom as an act of terrorism or for the purposes of terrorism,

(b)  his action is done to, or in relation to, a United Kingdom national, a United Kingdom resident or a protected person, and

(c)  his action, if done in any part of the United Kingdom, would have constituted an offence listed in subsection (2),

he shall be guilty in that part of the United Kingdom of the offence.

(2)  These are the offences–

(a)  murder, manslaughter, culpable homicide, rape, assault causing injury, assault to injury, kidnapping, abduction or false imprisonment,

(b)  an offence under section 4, 16, 18, 20, 21, 22, 23, 24, 28, 29, 30 or 64 of the Offences against the Person Act 1861,

(c)  an offence under section 1, 2, 3, 4 or 5(1) or (3) of the Forgery and Counterfeiting Act 1981,

(d)  the uttering of a forged document or an offence under section 46A(1) of the Criminal Law (Consolidation) (Scotland) Act 1995.

(3)  For the purposes of this section and section 63D a person is a protected person if–

(a)  he is a member of a United Kingdom diplomatic mission within the meaning of Article 1(b) of the Vienna Convention on Diplomatic Relations signed in 1961 (as that Article has effect in the United Kingdom by virtue of section 2 of and Schedule 1 to the Diplomatic Privileges Act 1964),

(b)  he is a member of a United Kingdom consular post within the meaning of Article 1(g) of  the Vienna Convention on Consular Relations signed in 1963 (as that Article has effect in the United Kingdom by virtue of section 1 of and Schedule 1 to the Consular Relations Act 1968),

(c)  he carries out any functions for the purposes of the European Agency for the Evaluation of Medicinal Products, or

(d)  he carries out any functions for the purposes of a body specified in an order made by the Secretary of State.

(4)  The Secretary of State may specify a body under subsection (3)(d) only if–

(a)  it is established by or under the Treaty establishing the European Community or the Treaty on European Union, and

(b)  the principal place in which its functions are carried out is a place in the United Kingdom.

(5)  If in any proceedings a question arises as to whether a person is or was a protected person, a certificate–

(a)  issued by or under the authority of the Secretary of State, and

(b)  stating any fact relating to the question,

is to be conclusive evidence of that fact.

**63D Terrorist attacks or threats abroad in connection with UK diplomatic premises etc: jurisdiction**

(1)  If–

(a)  a person does anything outside the United Kingdom as an act of terrorism or for the purposes of terrorism,

(b)  his action is done in connection with an attack on relevant premises or on a vehicle ordinarily used by a protected person,

(c)  the attack is made when a protected person is on or in the premises or vehicle, and

(d)  his action, if done in any part of the United Kingdom, would have constituted an offence listed in subsection (2),

he shall be guilty in that part of the United Kingdom of the offence.

(2)  These are the offences–

(a)  an offence under section 1 of the Criminal Damage Act 1971,

(b)  an offence under Article 3 of the Criminal Damage (Northern Ireland) Order 1977,

    (c) malicious mischief,

    (d) wilful fire-raising.

(3) If–

    (a) a person does anything outside the United Kingdom as an act of terrorism or for the purposes of terrorism,

    (b) his action consists of a threat of an attack on relevant premises or on a vehicle ordinarily used by a protected person,

    (c) the attack is threatened to be made when a protected person is, or is likely to be, on or in the premises or vehicle, and

    (d) his action, if done in any part of the United Kingdom, would have constituted an offence listed in subsection (4),

he shall be guilty in that part of the United Kingdom of the offence.

(4) These are the offences–

    (a) an offence under section 2 of the Criminal Damage Act 1971,

    (b) an offence under Article 4 of the Criminal Damage (Northern Ireland) Order 1977,

    (c) breach of the peace (in relation to Scotland only).

(5) "Relevant premises" means–

    (a) premises at which a protected person resides or is staying, or

    (b) premises which a protected person uses for the purpose of carrying out his functions as such a person.

### 63E Sections 63B to 63D: supplementary

(1) Proceedings for an offence which (disregarding the Acts listed in subsection (2)) would not be an offence apart from section 63B, 63C or 63D are not to be started–

    (a) in England and Wales, except by or with the consent of the Attorney General,

    (b) in Northern Ireland, except by or with the consent of the Advocate General for Northern Ireland.

(2) These are the Acts–

    (a) the Internationally Protected Persons Act 1978,

    (b) the Suppression of Terrorism Act 1978,

    (c) the Nuclear Material (Offences) Act 1983,

    (d) the United Nations Personnel Act 1997.

(3) For the purposes of sections 63C and 63D it is immaterial whether a person knows that another person is a United Kingdom national, a United Kingdom resident or a protected person.

(4) In relation to any time before the coming into force of section 27(1) of the Justice (Northern Ireland) Act 2002, the reference in subsection (1)(b) to the Advocate General for Northern Ireland is to be read as a reference to the Attorney General for Northern Ireland."

### 53 Jurisdiction for offence under section 113 of the Anti-terrorism, Crime and Security Act 2001

After section 113 of the Anti-terrorism, Crime and Security Act 2001 (c. 24) (use of noxious substances or things to cause harm and intimidate) there is inserted–

### "113A Application of section 113

(1) Section 113 applies to conduct done–

    (a) in the United Kingdom; or

    (b) outside the United Kingdom which satisfies the following two conditions.

(2) The first condition is that the conduct is done for the purpose of advancing a political, religious or ideological cause.

(3) The second condition is that the conduct is–

    (a) by a United Kingdom national or a United Kingdom resident;

    (b) by any person done to, or in relation to, a United Kingdom national, a United Kingdom resident or a protected person; or

    (c) by any person done in circumstances which fall within section 63D(1)(b) and (c) or (3)(b) and (c) of the Terrorism Act 2000.

(4) The following expressions have the same meaning as they have for the purposes of sections 63C and 63D of that Act–
   (a) "United Kingdom national";
   (b) "United Kingdom resident";
   (c) "protected person".

(5) For the purposes of this section it is immaterial whether a person knows that another is a United Kingdom national, a United Kingdom resident or a protected person.

**113B Consent to prosecution for offence under section 113**

(1) Proceedings for an offence committed under section 113 outside the United Kingdom are not to be started–
   (a) in England and Wales, except by or with the consent of the Attorney General;
   (b) in Northern Ireland, except by or with the consent of the Advocate General for Northern Ireland.

(2) Proceedings for an offence committed under section 113 outside the United Kingdom may be taken, and the offence may for incidental purposes be treated as having been committed, in any part of the United Kingdom.

(3) In relation to any time before the coming into force of section 27(1) of the Justice (Northern Ireland) Act 2002, the reference in subsection (1)(b) to the Advocate General for Northern Ireland is to be read as a reference to the Attorney General for Northern Ireland."

PART 3

ROAD TRAFFIC

CHAPTER 1

CONVENTION ON DRIVING DISQUALIFICATIONS

*Road traffic offences in UK*

**54 Application of section 55[4]**

(1) Section 55 applies where–
   (a) an individual ("the offender") who is normally resident in a member State other than the United Kingdom is convicted of an offence mentioned in Schedule 3,
   (b) no appeal is outstanding in relation to the offence, and
   (c) the driving disqualification condition is met in relation to the offence.

(2) The driving disqualification condition is met–
   (a) in relation to an offence mentioned in Part 1 of Schedule 3, if an order of disqualification is made in respect of the offence,
   (b) in relation to an offence mentioned in Part 2 of that Schedule, if an order of disqualification for a period not less than the minimum period is made in respect of the offence.

(3) The minimum period is–
   (a) a period of six months, or
   (b) where the State in which the offender normally resides is a prescribed State, a shorter period equal to the period prescribed in relation to the State.

(4) Section 55 does not apply in prescribed circumstances.

(5) For the purposes of this section no appeal is outstanding in relation to an offence if–
   (a) no appeal is brought against an offender's conviction of the offence, or any order made on his conviction, within the time allowed for making such appeals, or
   (b) such an appeal is brought and the proceedings on appeal are finally concluded.

---

[4] Not yet in force.

## 55 Duty to give notice to foreign authorities of driving disqualification of a non UK resident[5]

(1) Where this section applies, the appropriate Minister must give the central authority of the State in which the offender is normally resident a notice under this section.

(2) A notice under this section must–
   (a) give the name, address and date of birth of the offender,
   (b) give particulars of the offence,
   (c) state that no appeal is outstanding in relation to it,
   (d) give particulars of the disqualification,
   (e) state whether or not the offender took part in the proceedings in which the disqualification was imposed,
   (f) state that the offender has been informed that any decision made for the purposes of the convention on driving disqualifications will have no effect on the disqualification.

(3) A notice under this section may contain such other information as the appropriate Minister considers appropriate.

(4) A notice under this section must be accompanied by the original or a certified copy of the order of disqualification.

(5) Where the offender did not take part in the proceedings mentioned in subsection (2)(e), a notice under this section must also be accompanied by evidence that the offender was duly notified of those proceedings.

(6) Where the offender is the holder of a Community licence, a notice under this section must also be accompanied by the licence unless it has been returned to the driver–
   (a) under section 91A(7)(b)(ii) of the Road Traffic Offenders Act 1988 (c. 53), or
   (b) under Article 92A(7)(b)(ii) of the Road Traffic Offenders (Northern Ireland) Order 1996 (S.I. 1996/ 1320 (N.I.10)).

(7) Where the period of disqualification is reduced by virtue of section 34A of that Act or Article 36 of that Order, the appropriate Minister must give the central authority particulars of the reduction.

(8) Where the disqualification is removed by an order under section 42 of that Act or Article 47 of that Order, the appropriate Minister must give the central authority particulars of the removal.

(9) The appropriate Minister must provide–
   (a) the central authority, or
   (b) the competent authority of the State mentioned in subsection (1),
   with any further information which it requires for the purposes of the convention on driving disqualifications.

*Disqualification in respect of road traffic offences outside UK*

## 56 Application of section 57[6]

(1) Section 57 applies where–
   (a) an individual ("the offender") who is normally resident in the United Kingdom is convicted in another member State of an offence falling within subsection (5),
   (b) no appeal is outstanding in relation to the offence,
   (c) the driving disqualification condition is met in relation to the offence, and
   (d) the offender was duly notified of the proceedings ("the relevant proceedings") in which the disqualification was imposed and was entitled to take part in them.

(2) The driving disqualification condition is met–
   (a) in relation to an offence falling within subsection (5)(a), if, as a result of the offence, the offender is disqualified in the State in which the conviction is made,
   (b) in relation to an offence falling within subsection (5)(b), if, as a result of the offence, the offender is disqualified in that State for a period not less than the minimum period.

---

[5] Not yet in force.
[6] Not yet in force.

(3) For the purposes of this section an offender is disqualified in a State if he is disqualified in that State for holding or obtaining a licence to drive a motor vehicle granted under the law of that State (however the disqualification is described under that law).

(4) The minimum period is–
   (a) a period of six months, or
   (b) where the State in which the conviction is made is a prescribed State, a shorter period equal to the period prescribed in relation to that State.

(5) An offence falls within this subsection if it is constituted by–
   (a) conduct falling within any of paragraphs 1 to 5 of the Annex to the convention on driving disqualifications, or
   (b) other conduct which constitutes a road traffic offence for the purposes of that convention.

(6) Section 57 does not apply if the relevant proceedings were brought later than the time at which summary proceedings for any corresponding offence under the law of the part of the United Kingdom in which the offender is normally resident could have been brought.

(7) An offence is a corresponding offence if–
   (a) the conduct constituting the offence outside the United Kingdom took place in any part of the United Kingdom, and
   (b) that conduct is, or corresponds to, conduct which would constitute an offence under the law of that part.

(8) The appropriate Minister may make regulations treating offences under the law of a part of the United Kingdom as corresponding to offences under the law of a member State other than the United Kingdom.

(9) For the purposes of this section no appeal is outstanding in relation to an offence if–
   (a) no appeal is brought against an offender's conviction of the offence, or any decision made as a result of his conviction, within the time allowed for making such appeals, or
   (b) such an appeal is brought and the proceedings on appeal are finally concluded.

**57 Recognition in United Kingdom of foreign driving disqualification[7]**

(1) Where this section applies, the appropriate Minister–
   (a) must give the offender a notice under this section if the unexpired period of the foreign disqualification is not less than one month, and
   (b) may give him a notice under this section if that period is less than one month.

(2) The unexpired period of the foreign disqualification is–
   (a) the period of the foreign disqualification, less
   (b) any period of that disqualification which is treated by regulations made by the appropriate Minister as having been served in the State in which the offender was convicted.

(3) The provision which may be made by regulations under subsection (2)(b) includes provision for treating any period during which a central authority or competent authority of a State has seized a licence without returning it as a period which has been served in that State.

(4) If the appropriate Minister gives the offender a notice under this section, the offender is disqualified in each part of the United Kingdom–
   (a) for the relevant period, and
   (b) if the foreign disqualification is also effective until a condition is satisfied, until the condition or a corresponding prescribed condition is satisfied.

(5) The relevant period is the period which–
   (a) begins at the end of the period of 21 days beginning with the day on which the notice is given, and
   (b) is equal to the unexpired period of the foreign disqualification.

(6) But if the foreign disqualification is at any time removed otherwise than in prescribed circumstances, the offender ceases to be disqualified in each part of the United Kingdom from that time.

---

[7] Not yet in force.

(7) The appropriate Minister may make regulations substituting a longer period for the period for the time being mentioned in subsection (5)(a).

(8) Where the foreign disqualification is for life–
  (a) the condition in subsection (1)(a) is to be treated as satisfied, and
  (b) the other references in this section and section 58 to the unexpired period of the foreign disquali-fication are to be read as references to a disqualification for life.

## 58 Notice under section 57[8]

(1) A notice under section 57 must–
  (a) give particulars of the offence in respect of which the foreign disqualification was imposed and the period of that disqualification,
  (b) state that the offender is disqualified in each part of the United Kingdom for a period equal to the unexpired period of the foreign disqualification,
  (c) state the date from which, and period for which, he is disqualified,
  (d) give particulars of any relevant condition mentioned in section 57(4)(b),
  (e) give details of his right to appeal under section 59.

(2) A notice under section 57 must be in writing.

(3) A notice under section 57 may contain such other information as the appropriate Minister considers appropriate.

## *Appeals*

## 59 Appeal against disqualification[9]

(1) A person who is disqualified by virtue of section 57 may, after giving notice to the appropriate Minister of his intention to do so, appeal to the appropriate court against the disqualification.

(2) The appropriate court is–
  (a) in relation to England and Wales, a magistrates' court […],
  (b) in relation to Scotland, the sheriff within whose jurisdiction the applicant resides,
  (c) in relation to Northern Ireland, a court of summary jurisdiction acting for the petty sessions district in which the applicant resides.

(3) The appeal must be made before the end of the period of 21 days beginning with the day on which the notice under section 57 is given to the applicant.

(4) But the appropriate Minister may make regulations substituting a longer period for the period for the time being mentioned in subsection (3).

(5) If the appropriate court is satisfied that section 57 does not apply to the applicant's case, it must allow the appeal.

(6) Otherwise it must dismiss the appeal.

(7) Where on an appeal against the disqualification the appeal is allowed, the court by which the appeal is allowed must send notice of that fact to the appropriate Minister.

(8) The notice must–
  (a) be sent in such manner and to such address, and
  (b) contain such particulars,
  as the appropriate Minister may determine.

## 60 Power of appellate courts in England and Wales to suspend disqualification[10]

(1) This section applies where a person is disqualified by virtue of section 57.

(2) Where the person appeals to a magistrates' court against the disqualification, the court may, if it thinks fit, suspend the disqualification.

---

[8] Not yet in force.
[9] Not yet in force.
[10] Not yet in force.

(3) Where the person makes an application in respect of the decision of the court under section 111 of the Magistrates' Courts Act 1980 (c. 43) (statement of case), the High Court may, if it thinks fit, suspend the disqualification.

(4) Where the person has appealed, or applied for leave to appeal, to the [Supreme Court] under section 1 of the Administration of Justice Act 1960 (c. 65) from any decision of the High Court which is material to the disqualification, the High Court may, if it thinks fit, suspend the disqualification.

(5) Any power of a court under this section to suspend the disqualification is a power to do so on such terms as the court thinks fit.

(6) Where, by virtue of this section, a court suspends the disqualification, it must send notice of the suspension to the Secretary of State.

(7) The notice must–
   (a) be sent in such manner and to such address, and
   (b) contain such particulars,
   as the Secretary of State may determine.

### 61 Power of appellate courts in Scotland to suspend disqualification[11]

(1) This section applies where a person is disqualified by virtue of section 57.

(2) Where the person appeals to the sheriff against the disqualification, the sheriff may, if he thinks fit, suspend the disqualification on such terms as he thinks fit.

(3) Where the person appeals to the High Court of Justiciary from any decision of the sheriff, the court may, if it thinks fit, suspend the disqualification on such terms as it thinks fit.

   The power conferred by this subsection may be exercised by a single judge of the court.

(4) Where, by virtue of this section, a court suspends the disqualification, it must send notice of the suspension to the Secretary of State.

(5) The notice must–
   (a) be sent in such manner and to such address, and
   (b) contain such particulars,
   as the Secretary of State may determine.

### 62 Power of appellate courts in Northern Ireland to suspend disqualification[12]

(1) This section applies where a person is disqualified by virtue of section 57.

(2) Where the person appeals to a court of summary jurisdiction against the disqualification, the court may, if it thinks fit, suspend the disqualification.

(3) Where the person makes an application in respect of the decision of the court under Article 146 of the Magistrates' Courts (Northern Ireland) Order 1981 (S.I. 1981/ 1675 (N.I. 26)) (statement of case), the Court of Appeal may, if it thinks fit, suspend the disqualification.

(4) Where the person has appealed, or applied for leave to appeal, to the [Supreme Court] under section 41 of the Judicature (Northern Ireland) Act 1978 (c. 23) from any decision of the Court of Appeal which is material to the disqualification, the Court of Appeal may, if it thinks fit, suspend the disqualification.

(5) Any power of a court under this section to suspend the disqualification is a power to do so on such terms as the court thinks fit.

(6) Where, by virtue of this section, a court suspends the disqualification, it must send notice of the suspension to the Department.

(7) The notice must–
   (a) be sent in such manner and to such address, and
   (b) contain such particulars,
   as the Department may determine.

---

[11] Not yet in force.
[12] Not yet in force.

*Production of licence*

### 63 Production of licence: Great Britain[13]

(1) A person who–
    (a) is given a notice under section 57 by the Secretary of State, and
    (b) is the holder of a licence,
must deliver his licence and its counterpart to the Secretary of State before the end of the period of 21 days beginning with the day on which the notice is given.

(2) The Secretary of State may make regulations substituting a longer period for the period for the time being mentioned in subsection (1).

(3) If–
    (a) a person delivers a current receipt for his licence and its counterpart to the Secretary of State within the period for the time being mentioned in subsection (1), and
    (b) on the return of his licence and its counterpart immediately delivers them to the Secretary of State,
the duty under subsection (1) is to be taken as satisfied.
"Receipt" means a receipt issued under section 56 of the Road Traffic Offenders Act 1988 (c. 53).

(4) Subsection (1) does not apply if the competent authority of the relevant State–
    (a) has the licence and its counterpart, or
    (b) has delivered them to the Secretary of State.

(5) The relevant State is the State in which the offence in relation to which the notice was given was committed.

(6) If the holder of a licence does not deliver his licence and its counterpart to the Secretary of State as required by subsection (1), he is guilty of an offence.

(7) A person is not guilty of an offence under subsection (6) if he satisfies the court that he has applied for a new licence and has not received it.

In relation to the holder of a Northern Ireland licence or Community licence, a new licence includes the counterpart of such a licence.

(8) A person guilty of an offence under subsection (6) is liable on summary conviction to a fine not exceeding level 3 on the standard scale.

(9) "Licence" means a Great Britain licence, a Northern Ireland licence or a Community licence.

### 64 Production of licence: Northern Ireland[14]

(1) A person who–
    (a) is given a notice under section 57 by the Department, and
    (b) is the holder of a licence,
must deliver his licence and its counterpart to the Department before the end of the period of 21 days beginning with the day on which the notice is given.

(2) The Department may make regulations substituting a longer period for the period for the time being mentioned in subsection (1).

(3) If–
    (a) a person delivers a current receipt for his licence and its counterpart to the Department within the period for the time being mentioned in subsection (1), and
    (b) on the return of his licence and its counterpart immediately delivers them to the Department,
the duty under subsection (1) is to be taken as satisfied.
"Receipt" means a receipt issued under Article 62 of the Road Traffic Offenders (Northern Ireland) Order 1996 (S.I. 1996/ 1320 (N.I.10)).

(4) Subsection (1) does not apply if the competent authority of the relevant State–
    (a) has the licence and its counterpart, or
    (b) has delivered them to the Department.

---

[13] Not yet in force.
[14] Not yet in force.

(5) The relevant State is the State in which the offence in relation to which the notice was given was committed.

(6) If the holder of a licence does not deliver his licence and its counterpart to the Department as required by subsection (1), he is guilty of an offence.

(7) A person is not guilty of an offence under subsection (6) if he satisfies the court that he has applied for a new licence and has not received it.

In relation to the holder of a Great Britain licence or Community licence, a new licence includes the counterpart of such a licence.

(8) A person guilty of an offence under subsection (6) is liable on summary conviction to a fine not exceeding level 3 on the standard scale.

(9) "Licence" means a Northern Ireland licence, a Great Britain licence or a Community licence.

### 65 Production of licence: Community licence holders[15]

(1) This section applies where–
  (a) the holder of a Community licence is disqualified by virtue of section 57, and
  (b) the licence is sent to the Secretary of State or the Department under section 63 or 64.

(2) The Secretary of State or (as the case may be) the Department must send–
  (a) the holder's name and address, and
  (b) particulars of the disqualification,
  to the licensing authority in the EEA State in respect of which the licence was issued.

(3) But subsection (2) does not apply if the EEA State is the same as the State in which the offence in relation to which the holder is disqualified was committed.

(4) The Secretary of State or (as the case may be) the Department must return the licence to the holder–
  (a) on the expiry of the relevant period of the disqualification (within the meaning of section 57), or
  (b) if earlier, on being satisfied that the holder has left Great Britain or (as the case may be) Northern Ireland and is no longer normally resident there.

(5) But subsection (4) does not apply at any time where–
  (a) the Secretary of State or the Department would otherwise be under a duty under paragraph (a) of that subsection to return the licence, and
  (b) the holder would not at that time be authorised by virtue of section 99A(1) of the Road Traffic Act 1988 (c. 52) or Article 15A(1) of the Road Traffic (Northern Ireland) Order 1981 (S.I. 1981/154 (N.I.1)) to drive in Great Britain or Northern Ireland a motor vehicle of any class.

(6) In that case the Secretary of State or (as the case may be) the Department must–
  (a) send the licence to the licensing authority in the EEA State in respect of which it was issued, and
  (b) explain to that authority the reasons for so doing.

(7) "EEA State" has the same meaning as in Part 3 of the Road Traffic Act 1988.

### *Disqualification*

### 66 Effect of disqualification by virtue of section 57[16]

Where the holder of a Great Britain licence or Northern Ireland licence is disqualified by virtue of section 57, the licence is to be treated as revoked with effect from the beginning of the period of disqualification.

[15] Not yet in force.
[16] Not yet in force.

### 67 Rule for determining end of period of disqualification[17]

In determining the expiration of the period for which a person is disqualified by virtue of section 57, any time during which–

   (a)  the disqualification is suspended, or
   (b)  he is not disqualified,
        is to be disregarded.

*Endorsement*

### 68 Endorsement of licence: Great Britain[18]

(1) This section applies where a person who is normally resident in Great Britain is disqualified by virtue of section 57.

(2) The Secretary of State must secure that particulars of the disqualification are endorsed on the counterpart of any Great Britain licence or of any Northern Ireland licence or Community licence which the person–
   (a)  may then hold, or
   (b)  may subsequently obtain,
   until he becomes entitled under subsection (4) or (5) to have a Great Britain licence and its counterpart, or a counterpart of his Northern Ireland licence or Community licence, issued to him free from those particulars.

(3) On the issue to the person of–
   (a)  a new Great Britain licence, or
   (b)  a new counterpart of a Northern Ireland licence or Community licence,
   those particulars must be entered on the counterpart of the new licence or the new counterpart unless he has become so entitled.

(4) The person is entitled to have issued to him with effect from the end of the period for which the endorsement remains effective a new Great Britain licence with a counterpart free from the endorsement if he–
   (a)  applies for a new licence under section 97(1) of the Road Traffic Act 1988 (c. 52),
   (b)  surrenders any subsisting licence and its counterpart,
   (c)  pays the fee prescribed by regulations under Part 3 of that Act, and
   (d)  satisfies the other requirements of section 97(1).

(5) The person is entitled to have issued to him with effect from the end of that period a new counterpart of any Northern Ireland licence or Community licence then held by him free from the endorsement if he makes an application to the Secretary of State for that purpose in such manner as the Secretary of State may determine.

(6) The endorsement remains effective until four years have elapsed since he was convicted of the offence in relation to which he is disqualified by virtue of section 57.

(7) Where the person ceases to be disqualified by virtue of section 57(6), the Secretary of State must secure that the relevant particulars are endorsed on the counterpart of the Great Britain licence or of any Northern Ireland licence or Community licence previously held by him.

### 69 Endorsement of licence: Northern Ireland[19]

(1) This section applies where a person who is normally resident in Northern Ireland is disqualified by virtue of section 57.

(2) The Department must secure that particulars of the disqualification are endorsed on the counterpart of any Northern Ireland licence or the counterpart of any Great Britain licence or Community licence which the person–
   (a)  may then hold, or

---

[17]  Not yet in force.
[18]  Not yet in force.
[19]  Not yet in force.

(b) may subsequently obtain,

until he becomes entitled under subsection (4) or (5) to have a Northern Ireland licence and its counterpart, or a counterpart of his Great Britain licence or Community licence, issued to him free from those particulars.

(3) On the issue to the person of–
(a) a new Northern Ireland licence, or
(b) a new counterpart of a Great Britain licence or Community licence,
those particulars must be entered on the counterpart of the new licence or the new counterpart unless he has become so entitled.

(4) The person is entitled to have issued to him with effect from the end of the period for which the endorsement remains effective a new Northern Ireland licence with a counterpart free from the endorsement if he–
(a) applies for a new licence under Article 13(1) of the Road Traffic (Northern Ireland) Order 1981 (S.I. 1981/ 154 (N.I.1)),
(b) surrenders any subsisting licence and its counterpart,
(c) pays the fee prescribed by regulations under Part 2 of that Order, and
(d) satisfies the other requirements of Article 13(1).

(5) The person is entitled to have issued to him with effect from the end of that period a new counterpart of any Great Britain licence or Community licence then held by him free from the endorsement if he makes an application to the Department for that purpose in such manner as it may determine.

(6) The endorsement remains effective until four years have elapsed since he was convicted of the offence in relation to which he is disqualified by virtue of section 57.

(7) Where the person ceases to be disqualified by virtue of section 57(6), the Department must secure that the relevant particulars are endorsed on the counterpart of the Northern Ireland licence or the counterpart of any Great Britain licence or Community licence previously held by him.

*General*

## 70 Duty of appropriate Minister to inform competent authority[20]

(1) This section applies where a competent authority of any State gives the appropriate Minister a notice under the convention on driving disqualifications in respect of any person.

(2) If the appropriate Minister gives a notice under section 57 to that person, he must give the competent authority particulars of the disqualification which arises by virtue of that section.

(3) If the appropriate Minister does not give such a notice, he must give his reasons to the competent authority.

## 71 Notices[21]

(1) A notice authorised or required under this Chapter to be given by the appropriate Minister to an individual, or a Community licence required to be returned to its holder by section 65, may be given or returned to him by–
(a) delivering it to him,
(b) leaving it at his proper address, or
(c) sending it to him by post.

(2) For the purposes of–
(a) subsection (1), and
(b) section 7 of the Interpretation Act 1978 (c. 30) in its application to that subsection,
the proper address of any individual is his latest address as known to the appropriate Minister.

---

[20] Not yet in force.
[21] Not yet in force.

### 72 Regulations: Great Britain[22]

(1) Any power to make regulations conferred by this Chapter on the Secretary of State is exercisable by statutory instrument.

(2) A statutory instrument containing any such regulations is subject to annulment in pursuance of a resolution of either House of Parliament.

(3) The regulations may make different provision for different purposes.

### 73 Regulations: Northern Ireland[23]

(1) Any power to make regulations conferred by this Chapter on the Department is exercisable by statutory rule for the purposes of the Statutory Rules (Northern Ireland) Order 1979 (S.I. 1979/ 1573 (N.I. 12)).

(2) Any such regulations are subject to negative resolution (within the meaning of the Interpretation Act (Northern Ireland) 1954 (c. 33 (N.I.)).

(3) The regulations may make different provision for different purposes.

### 74 Interpretation[24]

(1) In this Chapter–
"appropriate Minister" means–
    (a) in relation to Great Britain, the Secretary of State,
    (b) in relation to Northern Ireland, the Department,

"central authority", in relation to a State, means an authority designated by the State as a central authority for the purposes of the convention on driving disqualifications,
"Community licence"–
    (a) in relation to Great Britain, has the same meaning as in Part 3 of the Road Traffic Act 1988 (c. 52),
    (b) in relation to Northern Ireland, has the same meaning as in Part 2 of the Road Traffic (Northern Ireland) Order 1981 (S.I. 1981/ 154 (N.I.1)),

"competent authority", in relation to a State, means an authority which is a competent authority in relation to the State for the purposes of the convention on driving disqualifications,
"the convention on driving disqualifications" means the Convention drawn up on the basis of Article K.3 of the Treaty on European Union on Driving Disqualifications signed on 17th June 1998,
"counterpart"–
    (a) in relation to Great Britain, has the same meaning as in Part 3 of the Road Traffic Act 1988 (c. 52),
    (b) in relation to Northern Ireland, has the same meaning as in Part 2 of the Road Traffic (Northern Ireland) Order 1981 (S.I. 1981/ 154 (N.I.1)),

"the Department" means the Department of the Environment,
"disqualified" , except in section 56, means–
    (a) in relation to Great Britain, disqualified for holding or obtaining a Great Britain licence,
    (b) in relation to Northern Ireland, disqualified for holding or obtaining a Northern Ireland licence,

and "disqualification" is to be interpreted accordingly,
"foreign disqualification" means the disqualification mentioned in section 56,
"Great Britain licence" means a licence to drive a motor vehicle granted under Part 3 of the Road Traffic Act 1988,
"motor vehicle"–
    (a) in relation to Great Britain, has the same meaning as in the Road Traffic Act 1988,
    (b) in relation to Northern Ireland, has the same meaning as in the Road Traffic (Northern Ireland) Order 1995 (S.I. 1995/ 2994 (N.I.18)),

---

[22] Not yet in force.
[23] Not yet in force.
[24] Not yet in force.

"Northern Ireland licence" means a licence to drive a motor vehicle granted under Part 2 of the Road Traffic (Northern Ireland) Order 1981,

"prescribed" means prescribed by regulations made by the appropriate Minister.

(2) In this Chapter a disqualification, or foreign disqualification, for life is to be treated as being for a period of not less than six months.

### 75 Application to Crown[25]

This Chapter applies to vehicles and persons in the public service of the Crown.

## CHAPTER 2

### MUTUAL RECOGNITION WITHIN THE UNITED KINGDOM ETC.

### 76 Recognition in Great Britain of disqualifications in Northern Ireland etc.

After section 102 of the Road Traffic Act 1988 there is inserted–

"Disqualification if disqualified in Northern Ireland etc.

### 102A Disqualification while disqualified in Northern Ireland, Isle of Man, Channel Islands or Gibraltar

(1) A person is disqualified for holding or obtaining a licence to drive a motor vehicle of any class so long as he is subject to a relevant disqualification imposed outside Great Britain.

(2) For the purposes of this section a person is subject to a relevant disqualification imposed outside Great Britain if, in respect of any offence–

  (a) a court in Northern Ireland disqualifies him for holding or obtaining a Northern Ireland licence,

  (b) a court in the Isle of Man or any of the Channel Islands disqualifies him for holding or obtaining a British external licence, or

  (c) a court in Gibraltar disqualifies him for holding or obtaining a licence to drive a motor vehicle granted under the law of Gibraltar.

(3) A certificate signed by the Secretary of State which states, in respect of a person, any matter relating to the question whether he is subject to a relevant disqualification imposed outside Great Britain shall be evidence (in Scotland, sufficient evidence) of the matter so stated.

(4) A certificate stating that matter and purporting to be so signed shall be deemed to be so signed unless the contrary is proved."

### 77 Endorsement of counterparts issued to Northern Ireland licence holders

(1) After section 109 of the Road Traffic Act 1988 (c. 52) there is inserted–

### "109A Counterparts issued to Northern Ireland licence holders

(1) The Secretary of State may issue to any Northern Ireland licence holder who–

  (a) has delivered his Northern Ireland licence to the Secretary of State, and

  (b) has provided him with the information specified in, or required under, subsection (3) below (whether or not in pursuance of this section),

  a document (referred to in this Part of this Act in relation to a Northern Ireland licence as a "counterpart").

(2) The counterpart must–

  (a) be in such form, and

  (b) contain such information,

  designed for the endorsement of particulars relating to the Northern Ireland licence as the Secretary of State may determine.

---

[25] Not yet in force.

(3) The information referred to in subsection (1) above is–

    (a) the name and address (whether in Great Britain or Northern Ireland) of the Northern Ireland licence holder;

    (b) his date of birth;

    (c) the classes of vehicle which he is authorised by his Northern Ireland licence to drive;

    (d) the period of validity of the licence;

    (e) whether it was granted in exchange for a licence issued by a state other than an EEA State; and

    (f) such other information as the Secretary of State may require for the purposes of the proper exercise of any of his functions under this Part or Part 4 of this Act.

(4) The Secretary of State–

    (a) may endorse a Northern Ireland licence delivered to him (whether or not in pursuance of this section) in such manner as he may determine–

        (i) with any part of the information specified in, or required under, subsection (3) above; or

        (ii) with information providing a means of ascertaining that information or any part of it; and

    (b) must return the Northern Ireland licence to the holder.

(5) Subsections (6) to (9), (11) (with the omission of paragraph (a)) and (12) of section 99B of this Act apply for the purposes of this section as if the references to a Community licence were references to a Northern Ireland licence."

(2) After section 91 of the Road Traffic Offenders Act 1988 (c. 53) there is inserted–

**"91ZA Application to Northern Ireland licence holders**

(1) The references to a licence in the following provisions of this Act include references to a Northern Ireland licence–

    (a) section 7,

    (b) section 26(7) and (8) and (9)(b),

    (c) section 27,

    (d) section 29(1),

    (e) section 30,

    (f) section 31(1),

    (g) section 32,

    (h) section 42(5),

    (i) section 44(1),

    (j) section 46(2),

    (k) section 47(2) and (3),

    (l) section 48(1) and (2).

(2) Accordingly, the reference in section 27(3)(b) of this Act to the suspension of a licence is to be construed in relation to a Northern Ireland licence holder as a reference to his ceasing to be authorised by virtue of section 109(1) of the Road Traffic Act 1988 to drive in Great Britain a motor vehicle of any class.

(3) The references in sections 26(9)(a) and 27(3) of this Act to a new licence include references to a counterpart of a Northern Ireland licence.

(4) In relation to a Northern Ireland licence holder to whom a counterpart is issued under section 109A of the Road Traffic Act 1988, the references in Part 3 of this Act (except sections 75(12), 76(8) and 77(9)) to a licence include references to a Northern Ireland licence.

(5) Where a court orders the endorsement of the counterpart of any Northern Ireland licence held by a person, it must send notice of the endorsement to the Secretary of State.

(6) The notice must–

    (a) be sent in such manner and to such address, and

    (b) contain such particulars,

as the Secretary of State may determine.

(7) Where a court orders the holder of a Northern Ireland licence to be disqualified, it must send the Northern Ireland licence and its counterpart (if any), on their being produced to the court, to the Secretary of State.

(8) The licence and its counterpart must be sent to such address as the Secretary of State may determine.

(9) Where–
    (a) a notice is sent to the Secretary of State under subsection (5) above, and
    (b) the particulars contained in the notice include–
        (i) particulars of an offence in respect of which the holder of a Northern Ireland licence is disqualified by an order of a court, and
        (ii) particulars of the disqualification,
        the Secretary of State must send a notice containing the particulars mentioned in paragraph (b)(i) and (ii) to the licensing authority in Northern Ireland.

**91ZB Effect of endorsement on Northern Ireland licence holders**

Section 91B applies in relation to Northern Ireland licences as it applies in relation to Community licences."

## 78 Prohibition on holding or obtaining Great Britain and Northern Ireland licences

(1) The Road Traffic Act 1988 (c. 52) is amended as follows.

(2) In section 97 (grant of licences)–
    (a) in subsection (1)(c), after sub-paragraph (i) there is inserted–
    "(ia) any Northern Ireland licence held by him together with its Northern Ireland counterpart and its counterpart (if any) issued to him under this Part of this Act,",
    (b) after subsection (1A) there is inserted–
"(1AA) Where a licence under this Part of this Act is granted to a person who surrenders under sub-paragraph (ia) of subsection (1)(c) above his Northern Ireland licence together with the counterparts mentioned in that sub-paragraph to the Secretary of State–
    (a) that person ceases to be authorised by virtue of section 109(1) of this Act to drive in Great Britain a motor vehicle of any class, and
    (b) the Secretary of State must send the Northern Ireland licence and its Northern Ireland counterpart to the licensing authority in Northern Ireland together with particulars of the class of motor vehicles to which the licence granted under this Part of this Act relates."

(3) In section 99 (duration of licences), after subsection (3) there is inserted–
"(3A) Where–
    (a) the Secretary of State is sent under a provision of Northern Ireland law corresponding to section 97(1AA) of this Act a licence granted under this Part of this Act to a person to drive a motor vehicle of any class, and
    (b) the Secretary of State is satisfied that a Northern Ireland licence to drive a motor vehicle of that or a corresponding class has been granted to that person,
    the Secretary of State must serve notice in writing on that person revoking the licence granted under this Part of this Act."

(4) In section 102 (disqualification to prevent duplication of licences), at the end there is inserted–
"(2) A person is also disqualified for holding or obtaining a licence authorising him to drive a motor vehicle of any class so long as he is authorised by virtue of section 109(1) of this Act to drive a motor vehicle of that or a corresponding class."

## 79 Disability and prospective disability

(1) The Road Traffic Act 1988 (c. 52) is amended as follows.

(2) After section 109A (as inserted by section 77 of this Act) there is inserted–

**"109B Revocation of authorisation conferred by Northern Ireland licence because of disability or prospective disability**

(1) If the Secretary of State is at any time satisfied on inquiry–
    (a) that a Northern Ireland licence holder is suffering from a relevant disability, and
    (b) that he would be required by virtue of section 92(3) of this Act to refuse an application made by the holder at that time for a licence authorising him to drive a vehicle of the class in respect of which his Northern Ireland licence was issued or a class corresponding to that class,

he may serve notice in writing requiring the licence holder to deliver immediately to the Secretary of State his Northern Ireland licence together with its Northern Ireland counterpart and its counterpart (if any) issued to him under this Part of this Act ("the relevant counterparts").

(2) If the Secretary of State is satisfied on inquiry that a Northern Ireland licence holder is suffering from a prospective disability, he may–

   (a) serve notice in writing on the Northern Ireland licence holder requiring him to deliver immediately to the Secretary of State his Northern Ireland licence together with the relevant counterparts, and

   (b) on receipt of the Northern Ireland licence and those counterparts and of an application made for the purposes of this subsection, grant to the Northern Ireland licence holder, free of charge, a licence for a period determined by the Secretary of State under section 99(1)(b) of this Act.

(3) The Secretary of State may require a person to provide–

   (a) evidence of his name, address, sex and date and place of birth, and

   (b) a photograph which is a current likeness of him,

   before granting a licence to him on an application for the purposes of subsection (2) above.

(4) A person who–

   (a) is required under, or by virtue of, this section to deliver to the Secretary of State his Northern Ireland licence and the relevant counterparts, but

   (b) without reasonable excuse, fails to do so,

   is guilty of an offence.

(5) Where a Northern Ireland licence holder to whom a counterpart is issued under section 109A of this Act–

   (a) is required under, or by virtue of, this section to deliver his Northern Ireland licence and that counterpart to the Secretary of State, and

   (b) is not in possession of them in consequence of the fact that he has surrendered them to a constable or authorised person (within the meaning of Part 3 of the Road Traffic Offenders Act 1988) on receiving a fixed penalty notice given to him under section 54 of that Act,

   he does not fail to comply with any such requirement if he delivers them to the Secretary of State immediately on their return.

(6) Where a Northern Ireland licence holder is served with a notice in pursuance of this section, he shall cease to be authorised by virtue of section 109(1) of this Act to drive in Great Britain a motor vehicle of any class from such date as may be specified in the notice, not being earlier than the date of service of the notice.

(7) Where a Northern Ireland licence is delivered to the Secretary of State in pursuance of this section, he must–

   (a) send the licence and its Northern Ireland counterpart to the licensing authority in Northern Ireland, and

   (b) explain to them his reasons for so doing.

**109C Information relating to disabilities etc**

Section 94 of this Act shall apply to a Northern Ireland licence holder who is normally resident in Great Britain as if–

(a) in subsection (1), for the words from the beginning to "aware" there were substituted "If a Northern Ireland licence holder who is authorised by virtue of section 109(1) of this Act to drive in Great Britain a motor vehicle of any class, is aware immediately before the relevant date, or becomes aware on or after that date",

(b) after that subsection there were inserted–

   "(1A) For the purposes of subsection (1)"relevant date" means–

      (a) in the case where the licence holder first became normally resident in Great Britain on or before the date on which section 79 of the Crime (International Co-operation) Act 2003 comes into force, that date; and

      (b) in any other case, the date on which he first became so resident.",

(c) for subsection (3A) there were substituted–

"(3A) A person who–
    (a) is authorised by virtue of section 109(1) of this Act to drive in Great Britain a motor vehicle of any class, and
    (b) drives on a road a motor vehicle of that class,
    is guilty of an offence if at any earlier time while he was so authorised he was required by subsection (1) above to notify the Secretary of State but has failed without reasonable excuse to do so.",

    (d) in subsection (4), the words "an applicant for, or" (in both places) were omitted,
    (e) in subsection (5), the words "applicant or" and the words from the beginning of paragraph (c) to "provisional licence" were omitted,
    (f) in subsection (6)(b), the words "applicant or" (in both places) were omitted,
    (g) in subsection (7), the words "applicant or" were omitted, and
    (h) in subsection (8)–
        (i) for "93" there were substituted "109B", and
        (ii) the words "applicant or" (in both places) were omitted."

(3) In section 93 (revocation of licence because of disability or prospective disability)–
    (a) in subsection (2A), at the end there is inserted "or subsection (6) below",
    (b) at the end there is inserted–

"(5) Where the Secretary of State–
    (a) is at any time sent by the licensing authority in Northern Ireland a licence under a provision of Northern Ireland law corresponding to section 109B of this Act, and
    (b) by virtue of the reasons given by that authority for sending the licence is at that time satisfied as mentioned in subsection (1)(a) and (b) above or that the licence holder is suffering from a prospective disability,
the Secretary of State may serve notice in writing on the licence holder revoking the licence with effect from such date as may be specified in the notice, not being earlier than the date of service of the notice.

(6) Where the reasons given by the licensing authority in Northern Ireland for sending the licence relate to a prospective disability of the holder, the Secretary of State may, on an application made for the purposes of this subsection, grant to the holder, free of charge, a new licence for a period determined by the Secretary of State under section 99(1)(b) of this Act."

PART 4

MISCELLANEOUS

*Information*

## 80 Disclosure of information by SFO

In section 3 of the Criminal Justice Act 1987 (c. 38) (disclosure of information)–
    (a) in subsection (5), for paragraph (c) there is substituted–
    "(c) for the purposes of any criminal investigation or criminal proceedings, whether in the United Kingdom or elsewhere",
    (b) at the end of subsection (6) there is inserted–
    "(n) any person or body having, under the Treaty on European Union or any other treaty to which the United Kingdom is a party, the function of receiving information of the kind in question,
    (o) any person or body having, under the law of any country or territory outside the United Kingdom, the function of receiving information relating to the proceeds of crime",
    and the "and" preceding paragraph (m) is omitted.

## 81 Inspection of overseas information systems

After section 54 of the Data Protection Act 1998 (c. 29) there is inserted–

### "54A Inspection of overseas information systems

(1) The Commissioner may inspect any personal data recorded in–
    (a) the Schengen information system,

    (b)  the Europol information system,

    (c)  the Customs information system.

(2)  The power conferred by subsection (1) is exercisable only for the purpose of assessing whether or not any processing of the data has been or is being carried out in compliance with this Act.

(3)  The power includes power to inspect, operate and test equipment which is used for the processing of personal data.

(4)  Before exercising the power, the Commissioner must give notice in writing of his intention to do so to the data controller.

(5)  But subsection (4) does not apply if the Commissioner considers that the case is one of urgency.

(6)  Any person who–

    (a)  intentionally obstructs a person exercising the power conferred by subsection (1), or

    (b)  fails without reasonable excuse to give any person exercising the power any assistance he may reasonably require,

is guilty of an offence.

(7)  In this section–

"the Customs information system" means the information system established under Chapter II of the Convention on the Use of Information Technology for Customs Purposes,

"the Europol information system" means the information system established under Title II of the Convention on the Establishment of a European Police Office,

"the Schengen information system" means the information system established under Title IV of the Convention implementing the Schengen Agreement of 14th June 1985, or any system established in its place in pursuance of any Community obligation."

### 82 Driver licensing information

Information held in any form–

    (a)  by the Secretary of State under Part 3 of the Road Traffic Act 1988 (c. 52), or

    (b)  by the Department of the Environment under Part 2 of the Road Traffic (Northern Ireland) Order 1981 (S.I. 1981/154 (N.I.1)),

(licensing of drivers of vehicles) may be disclosed for the purposes of the Schengen information system (within the meaning of section 81).

## *Cross-border surveillance*

### 83 Foreign surveillance operations

After section 76 of the Regulation of Investigatory Powers Act 2000 (c. 23) there is inserted–

"76A Foreign surveillance operations

(1)  This section applies where–

    (a)  a foreign police or customs officer is carrying out relevant surveillance outside the United Kingdom which is lawful under the law of the country or territory in which it is being carried out;

    (b)  circumstances arise by virtue of which the surveillance can for the time being be carried out only in the United Kingdom; and

    (c)  it is not reasonably practicable in those circumstances for a United Kingdom officer to carry out the surveillance in the United Kingdom in accordance with an authorisation under Part 2 or the Regulation of Investigatory Powers (Scotland) Act 2000.

(2)  "Relevant surveillance" means surveillance which–

    (a)  is carried out in relation to a person who is suspected of having committed a relevant crime; and

    (b)  is, for the purposes of Part 2, directed surveillance or intrusive surveillance.

(3)  "Relevant crime" means crime which–

    (a)  falls within Article 40(7) of the Schengen Convention; or

    (b)  is crime for the purposes of any other international agreement to which the United Kingdom is a party and which is specified for the purposes of this section in an order made by the Secretary of State with the consent of the Scottish Ministers.

(4) Relevant surveillance carried out by the foreign police or customs officer in the United Kingdom during the permitted period is to be lawful for all purposes if–

(a) the condition mentioned in subsection (6) is satisfied;

(b) the officer carries out the surveillance only in places to which members of the public have or are permitted to have access, whether on payment or otherwise; and

(c) conditions specified in any order made by the Secretary of State with the consent of the Scottish Ministers are satisfied in relation to its carrying out;

but no surveillance is lawful by virtue of this subsection if the officer subsequently seeks to stop and question the person in the United Kingdom in relation to the relevant crime.

(5) The officer is not to be subject to any civil liability in respect of any conduct of his which is incidental to any surveillance that is lawful by virtue of subsection (4).

(6) The condition in this subsection is satisfied if, immediately after the officer enters the United Kingdom–

(a) he notifies a person designated by the Director General of the National Criminal Intelligence Service of that fact; and

(b) (if the officer has not done so before) he requests an application to be made for an authorisation under Part 2, or the Regulation of Investigatory Powers (Scotland) Act 2000, for the carrying out of the surveillance.

(7) "The permitted period" means the period of five hours beginning with the time when the officer enters the United Kingdom.

(8) But a person designated by an order made by the Secretary of State may notify the officer that the surveillance is to cease being lawful by virtue of subsection (4) when he gives the notification.

(9) The Secretary of State is not to make an order under subsection (4) unless a draft of the order has been laid before Parliament and approved by a resolution of each House.

(10) In this section references to a foreign police or customs officer are to a police or customs officer who, in relation to a country or territory other than the United Kingdom, is an officer for the purposes of–

(a) Article 40 of the Schengen Convention; or

(b) any other international agreement to which the United Kingdom is a party and which is specified for the purposes of this section in an order made by the Secretary of State with the consent of the Scottish Ministers.

(11) In this section–

"the Schengen Convention" means the Convention implementing the Schengen Agreement of 14th June 1985;

"United Kingdom officer" means–

(a) a member of a police force;

(b) a member of the National Criminal Intelligence Service;

(c) a member of the National Crime Squad or of the Scottish Crime Squad (within the meaning of the Regulation of Investigatory Powers (Scotland) Act 2000);

(d) a customs officer."

### 84 Assaults on foreign officers

(1) For the purposes of section 89 of the Police Act 1996 (c. 16) (assaults on constables) any person who is carrying out surveillance in England and Wales under section 76A of the Regulation of Investigatory Powers Act 2000 (c. 23) is to be treated as if he were acting as a constable in the execution of his duty.

(2) For the purposes of section 41 of the Police (Scotland) Act 1967 (c. 77) (assaults on constables) any person who is carrying out surveillance in Scotland under section 76A of that Act of 2000 is to be so treated.

(3) For the purposes of section 66 of the Police (Northern Ireland) Act 1998 (c. 32) (assaults on constables) any person who is carrying out surveillance in Northern Ireland under section 76A of that Act of 2000 is to be so treated.

### 85 [...]

*Extradition*

86 […]

87 […]

*False monetary instruments*

### 88 False monetary instruments: England and Wales and Northern Ireland

(1) Section 5 of the Forgery and Counterfeiting Act 1981 (c. 45) (offences relating to money orders, share certificates, passports, etc.) is amended as follows.

(2) In subsection (5)–
    (a) in paragraph (g), at the end there is inserted "and other bills of exchange",
    (b) after paragraph (h) there is inserted–
        "(ha) bankers' drafts;
        (hb) promissory notes;",
    (c) after paragraph (j) there is inserted–
        "(ja) debit cards;".

(3) After subsection (6) there is inserted–

    "(7) An instrument is also an instrument to which this section applies if it is a monetary instrument specified for the purposes of this section by an order made by the Secretary of State.

    (8) The power under subsection (7) above is exercisable by statutory instrument subject to annulment in pursuance of a resolution of either House of Parliament."

### 89 False monetary instruments: Scotland

After section 46 of the Criminal Law (Consolidation) (Scotland) Act 1995 (c. 39) there is inserted–
"False monetary instruments

#### 46A False monetary instruments

(1) A person who counterfeits or falsifies a specified monetary instrument with the intention that it be uttered as genuine is guilty of an offence.

(2) A person who has in his custody or under his control, without lawful authority or excuse–
    (a) anything which is, and which he knows or believes to be, a counterfeited or falsified specified monetary instrument; or
    (b) any machine, implement or computer programme, or any paper or other material, which to his knowledge is specially designed or adapted for the making of a specified monetary instrument,
is guilty of an offence.

(3) For the purposes of subsections (1) and (2)(a) above, it is immaterial that the specified monetary instrument (or purported specified monetary instrument) is not in a fit state to be uttered or that the counterfeiting or falsifying of it has not been finished or perfected.

(4) A person guilty of an offence under this section is liable on summary conviction–
    (a) to a fine not exceeding the statutory maximum;
    (b) to imprisonment for a term not exceeding six months; or
    (c) both to a fine and to such imprisonment.

(5) A person guilty of an offence–
    (a) under subsection (1) above is liable on conviction on indictment–
        (i) to a fine;
        (ii) to imprisonment for a term not exceeding ten years; or
        (iii) both to a fine and to such imprisonment;
    (b) under subsection (2) above is liable on conviction on indictment–
        (i) to a fine;
        (ii) if it is proved that the offence was committed with the intention that the specified monetary instrument in question be uttered (or as the case may be that a specified monetary instrument be uttered), to imprisonment for a term not exceeding ten years and if it is not so proved, to imprisonment for a term not exceeding two years; or

(iii) both to a fine and to imprisonment for a term not exceeding ten years, if it is proved as mentioned in sub-paragraph (ii) above, or both to a fine and to imprisonment for a term not exceeding two years if it is not so proved.

(6) Where an offence under this section which has been committed–
    (a) by a body corporate is proved to have been committed with the consent or connivance of, or to be attributable to any neglect on the part of, a director, manager, secretary or other similar officer of that body; or
    (b) by a Scottish partnership is proved to have been committed with the consent or connivance of, or to be attributable to any neglect on the part of, a member of that partnership,
or by any person who was purporting to act in any such capacity, he as well as the body corporate, or as the case may be the partnership, is guilty of that offence and is liable to be proceeded against and punished accordingly.

(7) Where the affairs of a body corporate are managed by its members, subsection (6) above applies in relation to the actings and defaults of a member in connection with his functions of management as if he were a director of the body corporate.

(8) In subsections (1) to (5) above, "specified" means for the time being specified for the purposes of this section, by order made by the Scottish Ministers.

(9) The power to make an order under subsection (8) above–
    (a) includes power to make such incidental, supplemental, transitional or transitory provision as the Scottish Ministers think necessary or expedient; and
    (b) is exercisable by statutory instrument.

(10) A statutory instrument containing such an order is subject to annulment in pursuance of a resolution of the Scottish Parliament."

*Freezing of terrorist property*

### 90 Freezing of terrorist property[26]

Schedule 4 is to have effect.

## Part 5

## Final Provisions

## Chapter 1

## Amendments and Repeals

### 91 Amendments and repeals

(1) Schedule 5 (minor and consequential amendments) is to have effect.

(2) The enactments set out in Schedule 6 are repealed to the extent specified.

## Chapter 2

## Miscellaneous

### 92 Northern Ireland

An Order in Council under paragraph 1(1) of the Schedule to the Northern Ireland Act 2000 (c. 1) (legislation for Northern Ireland during suspension of devolved government) which contains a statement that it is made only for purposes corresponding to those of Chapter 2 of Part 3 of this Act–
    (a) is not to be subject to paragraph 2 of that Schedule (affirmative resolution of both Houses of Parliament), but
    (b) is to be subject to annulment in pursuance of a resolution of either House of Parliament.

---

[26] Not yet in force.

**93 Supplementary and consequential provision**

(1) The appropriate Minister may by order made by statutory instrument make–
  (a) any supplementary, incidental or consequential provision,
  (b) any transitory, transitional or saving provision,
    which he considers necessary or expedient for the purposes of, in consequence of or for giving full effect to any provision of this Act.

(2) The appropriate Minister means–
  (a) in relation to any provision that would, if included in an Act of the Scottish Parliament, be within the legislative competence of that Parliament, the Scottish Ministers,
  (b) in relation to any other provision, the Secretary of State.

(3) The provision which may be made under subsection (1) includes provision amending or repealing any enactment or instrument.

(4) An order under this section may make different provision for different purposes.

(5) A statutory instrument (other than an instrument to which subsection (6) applies) containing an order under this section made by the Secretary of State is subject to annulment in pursuance of a resolution of either House of Parliament.

(6) A statutory instrument containing such an order which adds to, replaces or omits any part of the text of an Act is not to be made unless a draft of the instrument has been laid before, and approved by a resolution of, each House of Parliament.

(7) A statutory instrument (other than an instrument to which subsection (8) applies) containing an order under this section made by the Scottish Ministers is subject to annulment in pursuance of a resolution of the Scottish Parliament.

(8) A statutory instrument containing such an order which adds to, replaces or omits any part of the text of an Act or of an Act of the Scottish Parliament is not to be made unless a draft of the instrument has been laid before, and approved by a resolution of, the Scottish Parliament.

**94 Commencement**

(1) This Act (except this Chapter and the provisions mentioned in subsection (3)) is to come into force on such day as the Secretary of State may by order made by statutory instrument appoint.

(2) Any day appointed for the purposes of Part 1 (other than sections 32 to 41), and the related amendments and repeals, is to be one decided by the Secretary of State and the Scottish Ministers.

(3) The following are to come into force on such day as the Scottish Ministers may by order made by statutory instrument appoint–
  (a) sections 37 to 41,
  (b) section 89.

(4) An order under this section may make different provision for different purposes.

**95 Extent**

(1) Sections 32 to 36 extend only to England and Wales and Northern Ireland.

(2) Sections 37 to 41 extend only to Scotland.

**96 Short title**

This Act may be cited as the Crime (International Co-operation) Act 2003.

SCHEDULE 1

PROCEEDINGS OF A NOMINATED COURT UNDER SECTION 15

Section 15

*Securing attendance of witnesses*

1  The court has the like powers for securing the attendance of a witness as it has for the purposes of other proceedings before the court.

2  In Scotland the court has power to issue a warrant to officers of law to cite witnesses, and section 156 of the Criminal Procedure (Scotland) Act 1995 (c. 46) applies in relation to a witness so cited.

### Power to administer oaths

3  The court may take evidence on oath.

### Proceedings

4  Rules of court under section 49 may, in particular, make provision in respect of the persons entitled to appear or take part in the proceedings and for excluding the public from the proceedings.

### Privilege of witnesses

5  (1) A person cannot be compelled to give any evidence which he could not be compelled to give–
   (a) in criminal proceedings in the part of the United Kingdom in which the nominated court exercises jurisdiction, or
   (b) subject to sub-paragraph (2), in criminal proceedings in the country from which the request for the evidence has come.

   (2) Sub-paragraph (1)(b) does not apply unless the claim of the person questioned to be exempt from giving the evidence is conceded by the court or authority which made the request.

   (3) Where the person's claim is not conceded, he may be required to give the evidence to which the claim relates (subject to the other provisions of this paragraph); but the evidence may not be forwarded to the court or authority which requested it if a court in the country in question, on the matter being referred to it, upholds the claim.

   (4) A person cannot be compelled to give any evidence if his doing so would be prejudicial to the security of the United Kingdom.

   (5) A certificate signed by or on behalf of the Secretary of State or, where the court is in Scotland, the Lord Advocate to the effect that it would be so prejudicial for that person to do so is conclusive evidence of that fact.

   (6) A person cannot be compelled to give any evidence in his capacity as an officer or servant of the Crown.

   (7) Sub-paragraphs (4) and (6) are without prejudice to the generality of sub paragraph (1).

### Forwarding evidence

6  (1) The evidence received by the court is to be given to the court or authority that made the request or to the territorial authority for forwarding to the court or authority that made the request.

   (2) So far as may be necessary in order to comply with the request–
   (a) where the evidence consists of a document, the original or a copy is to be provided,
   (b) where it consists of any other article, the article itself, or a description, photograph or other representation of it, is to be provided.

### Supplementary

7  The Bankers' Books Evidence Act 1879 (c. 11) applies to the proceedings as it applies to other proceedings before the court.

8  No order for costs may be made.

## SCHEDULE 2

### EVIDENCE GIVEN BY TELEVISION LINK OR TELEPHONE

*Sections 30 and 31*

### PART 1

### EVIDENCE GIVEN BY TELEVISION LINK

#### *Securing attendance of witnesses*

1 The nominated court has the like powers for securing the attendance of the witness to give evidence through the link as it has for the purpose of proceedings before the

2 In Scotland the nominated court has power to issue a warrant to officers of law to cite the witness for the purpose of securing his attendance to give evidence through the link, and section 156 of the Criminal Procedure (Scotland) Act 1995 (c. 46) applies in relation to the witness if so cited.

#### *Conduct of hearing*

3 The witness is to give evidence in the presence of the nominated court.

4 The nominated court is to establish the identity of the witness.

5 The nominated court is to intervene where it considers it necessary to do so to safeguard the rights of the witness.

6 The evidence is to be given under the supervision of the court of the country concerned.

7 The evidence is to be given in accordance with the laws of that country and with any measures for the protection of the witness agreed between the Secretary of State and the authority in that country which appears to him to have the function of entering into agreements of that kind.

8 Rules of court under section 49 must make provision for the use of interpreters.

#### *Privilege of witness*

9 (1) The witness cannot be compelled to give any evidence which he could not be compelled to give in criminal proceedings in the part of the United Kingdom in which the nominated court exercises jurisdiction.

   (2) The witness cannot be compelled to give any evidence if his doing so would be prejudicial to the security of the United Kingdom.

   (3) A certificate signed by or on behalf of the Secretary of State or, where the court is in Scotland, the Lord Advocate to the effect that it would be so prejudicial for that person to do so is to be conclusive evidence of that fact.

   (4) The witness cannot be compelled to give any evidence in his capacity as an officer or servant of the Crown.

   (5) Sub-paragraphs (2) and (4) are without prejudice to the generality of sub paragraph (1).

#### *Record of hearing*

10 Rules of court under section 49 must make provision–
   (a) for the drawing up of a record of the hearing,
   (b) for sending the record to the external authority.

PART 2

EVIDENCE GIVEN BY TELEPHONE

*Notification of witness*

11  The nominated court must notify the witness of the time when and the place at which he is to give evidence by telephone.

*Conduct of hearing*

12  The nominated court must be satisfied that the witness is willingly giving evidence by telephone.

13  The witness is to give evidence in the presence of the nominated court.

14  The nominated court is to establish the identity of the witness.

15  The evidence is to be given under the supervision of the court of the participating country.

16  The evidence is to be given in accordance with the laws of that country.

17  Rules of court under section 49 must make provision for the use of interpreters.

SCHEDULE 3

OFFENCES FOR THE PURPOSES OF SECTION 54

Section 54

PART 1

OFFENCES WHERE ORDER OF DISQUALIFICATION FOR
A MINIMUM PERIOD UNNECESSARY

1[27]  (1) Manslaughter or culpable homicide by the driver of a motor vehicle.

(2) "Driver"–
   (a) in relation to Great Britain, has the same meaning as in the Road Traffic Act 1988 (c. 52),
   (b) in relation to Northern Ireland, has the same meaning as in Article 2(2) of the Road Traffic (Northern Ireland) Order 1995 (S.I. 1995/ 2994 (N.I.18)).

2[28]  An offence under section 89(1) of the Road Traffic Regulation Act 1984 (c. 27) or Article 43(1) of the Road Traffic Regulation (Northern Ireland) Order 1997 (S.I. 1997/ 276 (N.I.2)) (exceeding speed limit).

3[29]  An offence under any of the following sections of the Road Traffic Act 1988 or Articles of the Road Traffic (Northern Ireland) Order 1995–
   (a) section 1 or Article 9 (causing death by dangerous driving),
   (b) section 2 or Article 10 (dangerous driving),
   [(ba) section 2B (causing death by careless, or inconsiderate, driving), ]
   (c) section 3 or Article 12 (careless, and inconsiderate, driving),
   [(ca) section 3ZB (causing death by driving: unlicensed, disqualified or uninsured drivers),]
   (d) section 3A or Article 14 (causing death by careless driving when under influence of drink or drugs),
   (e) section 4 or Article 15 (driving, or being in charge, when under influence of drink or drugs),
   (f) section 5 or Article 16 (driving, or being in charge, of a motor vehicle with alcohol concentration above prescribed limit),
   (g) section 6 or Article 17 (failing to provide a specimen of breath for a breath test),
   (h) section 7 or Article 18 (failing to provide specimen for analysis or laboratory test).

---

[27]  Not yet in force.
[28]  Not yet in force.
[29]  Not yet in force.

4[30] An offence under section 12 of the Road Traffic Act 1988 (motor racing and speed trials on public ways).

5[31] An offence under section 103(1)(b) of the Road Traffic Act 1988 or Article 167(1) of the Road Traffic (Northern Ireland) Order 1981 (S.I. 1981/ 154 (N.I.1)) (driving while disqualified).

6[32] An offence under section 170(4) of the Road Traffic Act 1988 or Article 175(2) of the Road Traffic (Northern Ireland) Order 1981 (failing to stop after accident and give particulars or report of accident).

## PART 2

### OFFENCES WHERE ORDER OF DISQUALIFICATION FOR MINIMUM PERIOD NECESSARY

7[33] An offence which–

(a) is mentioned in Part 1 of Schedule 2 to the Road Traffic Offenders Act 1988 (c. 53) or Part 1 of Schedule 1 to the Road Traffic Offenders (Northern Ireland) Order 1996 (S.I. 1996/ 1320 (N.I.10)), but

(b) is not an offence mentioned in Part 1 of this Schedule.

## SCHEDULE 4

### TERRORIST PROPERTY: FREEZING ORDERS

Section 90

1[34] The Terrorism Act 2000 (c. 11) is amended as follows.

2[35] In section 123 (orders and regulations), in subsection (2)(i), for "paragraph" there is substituted "paragraphs 11A, 25A, 41A and".

3[36] In Part 1 of Schedule 4 (forfeiture orders: England and Wales), after paragraph 11 there is inserted–

"Domestic and overseas freezing orders

**11A** (1) This paragraph has effect for the purposes of paragraphs 11B to 11G.

(2) The relevant Framework Decision means the Framework Decision on the execution in the European Union of orders freezing property or evidence adopted by the Council of the European Union on 22nd July 2003.

(3) A listed offence means–

(a) an offence described in Article 3(2) of the relevant Framework Decision, or

(b) a prescribed offence or an offence of a prescribed description.

(4) An order under sub-paragraph (3)(b) which, for the purposes of paragraph 11D, prescribes an offence or a description of offences may require that the conduct which constitutes the offence or offences would, if it occurred in a part of the United Kingdom, constitute an offence in that part.

(5) Specified information, in relation to a certificate under paragraph 11B or 11D, means–

(a) any information required to be given by the form of certificate annexed to the relevant Framework Decision, or

(b) any prescribed information.

---

[30] Not yet in force.
[31] Not yet in force.
[32] Not yet in force.
[33] Not yet in force.
[34] Not yet in force.
[35] Not yet in force.
[36] Not yet in force.

(6) In this paragraph, "prescribed" means prescribed by an order made by the Secretary of State.

(7) A participating country means–
(a) a country other than the United Kingdom which is a member State on a day appointed for the commencement of Schedule 4 to the Crime (International Co-operation) Act 2003, and
(b) any other member State designated by an order made by the Secretary of State.

(8) "Country" includes territory.

(9) Section 14(2)(a) applies for the purposes of determining what are the proceeds of the commission of an offence.

### Domestic freezing orders: certification

**11B** (1) If any of the property to which an application for a restraint order relates is property in a participating country, the applicant may ask the High Court to make a certificate under this paragraph.

(2) The High Court may make a certificate under this paragraph if–
(a) it makes a restraint order in relation to property in the participating country, and
(b) it is satisfied that there is a good arguable case that the property is likely to be used for the purposes of a listed offence or is the proceeds of the commission of a listed offence.

(3) A certificate under this paragraph is a certificate which–
(a) is made for the purposes of the relevant Framework Decision, and
(b) gives the specified information.

(4) If the High Court makes a certificate under this paragraph–
(a) the restraint order must provide for notice of the certificate to be given to the person affected by it, and
(b) paragraph 6(2) to (4) applies to the certificate as it applies to the restraint order.

### Sending domestic freezing orders

**11C** (1) If a certificate is made under paragraph 11B, the restraint order and the certificate are to be sent to the Secretary of State for forwarding to–
(a) a court exercising jurisdiction in the place where the property is situated, or
(b) any authority recognised by the government of the participating country as the appropriate authority for receiving orders of that kind.

(2) The restraint order and the certificate must be accompanied by a forfeiture order, unless the certificate indicates when the court expects a forfeiture order to be sent.

(3) The certificate must include a translation of it into an appropriate language of the participating country (if that language is not English).

(4) The certificate must be signed by or on behalf of the court and must include a statement as to the accuracy of the information given in it.

The signature may be an electronic signature.

(5) If the restraint order and the certificate are not accompanied by a forfeiture order, but a forfeiture order is subsequently made, it is to be sent to the Secretary of State for forwarding as mentioned in sub-paragraph (1).

### Overseas freezing orders

**11D** (1) Paragraph 11E applies where an overseas freezing order made by an appropriate court or authority in a participating country is received by the Secretary of State from the court or authority which made or confirmed the order.

(2) An overseas freezing order is an order prohibiting dealing with property–
(a) which is in the United Kingdom,
(b) which the appropriate court or authority considers is likely to be used for the purposes of a listed offence or is the proceeds of the commission of such an offence, and

    (c) in respect of which an order has been or may be made by a court exercising criminal jurisdiction in the participating country for the forfeiture of the property, and in respect of which the following requirements of this paragraph are met.

(3) The action which the appropriate court or authority considered would constitute or, as the case may be, constituted the listed offence is action done as an act of terrorism or for the purposes of terrorism.

(4) The order must relate to–
    (a) criminal proceedings instituted in the participating country, or
    (b) a criminal investigation being carried on there.

(5) The order must be accompanied by a certificate which gives the specified information; but a certificate may be treated as giving any specified information which is not given in it if the Secretary of State has the information in question.

(6) The certificate must–
    (a) be signed by or on behalf of the court or authority which made or confirmed the order,
    (b) include a statement as to the accuracy of the information given in it,
    (c) if it is not in English, include a translation of it into English (or, if appropriate, Welsh).

The signature may be an electronic signature.

(7) The order must be accompanied by an order made by a court exercising criminal jurisdiction in that country for the forfeiture of the property, unless the certificate indicates when such an order is expected to be sent.

(8) An appropriate court or authority in a participating country in relation to an overseas freezing order is–
    (a) a court exercising criminal jurisdiction in the country,
    (b) a prosecuting authority in the country,
    (c) any other authority in the country which appears to the Secretary of State to have the function of making such orders.

(9) References in paragraphs 11E to 11G to an overseas freezing order include its accompanying certificate.

### Enforcement of overseas freezing orders

**11E** (1) Where this paragraph applies the Secretary of State must send a copy of the overseas freezing order to the High Court and to the Director of Public Prosecutions.

(2) The court is to consider the overseas freezing order on its own initiative within a period prescribed by rules of court.

(3) Before giving effect to the overseas freezing order, the court must give the Director an opportunity to be heard.

(4) The court may decide not to give effect to the overseas freezing order only if, in its opinion, giving effect to it would be incompatible with any of the Convention rights (within the meaning of the Human Rights Act 1998).

**11F** The High Court may postpone giving effect to an overseas freezing order in respect of any property–
    (a) in order to avoid prejudicing a criminal investigation which is taking place in the United Kingdom, or
    (b) if, under an order made by a court in criminal proceedings in the United Kingdom, the property may not be dealt with.

**11G** (1) Where the High Court decides to give effect to an overseas freezing order, it must–
    (a) register the order in that court,
    (b) provide for notice of the registration to be given to any person affected by it.

(2) For the purpose of enforcing an overseas freezing order registered in the High Court, the order is to have effect as if it were an order made by that court.

(3) Paragraph 7 applies to an overseas freezing order registered in the High Court as it applies to a restraint order under paragraph 5.

(4) The High Court may cancel the registration of the order, or vary the property to which the order applies, on an application by the Director of Public Prosecutions or any other person affected by it, if or to the extent that–
   (a) the court is of the opinion mentioned in paragraph 11E(4), or
   (b) the court is of the opinion that the order has ceased to have effect in the participating country.

(5) Her Majesty may by Order in Council make further provision for the enforcement in England and Wales of registered overseas freezing orders.

(6) An Order in Council under this paragraph–
   (a) may make different provision for different cases,
   (b) is not to be made unless a draft of it has been laid before and approved by resolution of each House of Parliament."

**4**[37] In paragraph 14 of that Schedule (enforcement of orders made in designated countries), in sub-paragraph (2), after the second "order" there is inserted "(other than an overseas freezing order within the meaning of paragraph 11D)".

**5**[38] In Part 2 of that Schedule (forfeiture orders: Scotland), after paragraph 25 there is inserted–

### "Domestic and overseas freezing orders

**25A** (1) This paragraph has effect for the purposes of paragraphs 25B to 25G.

(2) The relevant Framework Decision means the Framework Decision on the execution in the European Union of orders freezing property or evidence adopted by the Council of the European Union on 22nd July 2003.

(3) A listed offence means–
   (a) an offence described in Article 3(2) of the relevant Framework Decision, or
   (b) a prescribed offence or an offence of a prescribed description.

(4) An order under sub-paragraph (3)(b) which, for the purposes of paragraph 25D, prescribes an offence or a description of offences may require that the conduct which constitutes the offence or offences would, if it occurred in a part of the United Kingdom, constitute an offence in that part.

(5) Specified information, in relation to a certificate under paragraph 25B or 25D, means–
   (a) any information required to be given by the form of certificate annexed to the relevant Framework Decision, or
   (b) any prescribed information.

(6) In this paragraph, "prescribed" means prescribed by an order made by the Secretary of State.

(7) A participating country means–
   (a) a country other than the United Kingdom which is a member State on a day appointed for the commencement of Schedule 4 to the Crime (International Co-operation) Act 2003, and
   (b) any other member State designated by an order made by the Secretary of State.

(8) "Country" includes territory.

(9) Section 14(2)(a) applies for the purposes of determining what are the proceeds of the commission of an offence.

---

[37] Not yet in force.
[38] Not yet in force.

### Domestic freezing orders: certification

**25B** (1) If any of the property to which an application for a restraint order relates is property in a participating country, the applicant may ask the Court of Session to make a certificate under this paragraph.

(2) The Court of Session may make a certificate under this paragraph if–
   (a) it makes a restraint order in relation to property in the participating country, and
   (b) it is satisfied that there is a good arguable case that the property is likely to be used for the purposes of a listed offence or is the proceeds of the commission of a listed offence.

(3) A certificate under this paragraph is a certificate which–
   (a) is made for the purposes of the relevant Framework Decision, and
   (b) gives the specified information.

(4) If the Court of Session makes a certificate under this paragraph–
   (a) the restraint order must provide for notice of the certificate to be given to the person affected by it, and
   (b) paragraph 19(2) to (4) applies to the certificate as it applies to the restraint order.

### Sending domestic freezing orders

**25C** (1) If a certificate is made under paragraph 25B, the restraint order and the certificate are to be sent to the Lord Advocate for forwarding to–
   (a) a court exercising jurisdiction in the place where the property is situated, or
   (b) any authority recognised by the government of the participating country as the appropriate authority for receiving orders of that kind.

(2) The restraint order and the certificate must be accompanied by a forfeiture order, unless the certificate indicates when the court expects a forfeiture order to be sent.

(3) The certificate must include a translation of it into an appropriate language of the participating country (if that language is not English).

(4) The certificate must be signed by or on behalf of the court and must include a statement as to the accuracy of the information given in it.

   The signature may be an electronic signature.

(5) If the restraint order and the certificate are not accompanied by a forfeiture order, but a forfeiture order is subsequently made, it is to be sent to the Lord Advocate for forwarding as mentioned in sub-paragraph (1).

### Overseas freezing orders

**25D** (1) Paragraph 25E applies where an overseas freezing order made by an appropriate court or authority in a participating country is received by the Secretary of State from the court or authority which made or confirmed the order.

(2) An overseas freezing order is an order prohibiting dealing with property–
   (a) which is in the United Kingdom,
   (b) which the appropriate court or authority considers is likely to be used for the purposes of a listed offence or is the proceeds of the commission of such an offence, and
   (c) in respect of which an order has been or may be made by a court exercising criminal jurisdiction in the participating country for the forfeiture of the property,
   and in respect of which the following requirements of this paragraph are met.

(3) The action which the appropriate court or authority considered would constitute or, as the case may be, constituted the listed offence is action done as an act of terrorism or for the purposes of terrorism.

(4) The order must relate to–
   (a) criminal proceedings instituted in the participating country, or
   (b) a criminal investigation being carried on there.

(5) The order must be accompanied by a certificate which gives the specified information; but a certificate may be treated as giving any specified information which is not given in it if the Secretary of State has the information in question.

(6) The certificate must–
   (a) be signed by or on behalf of the court or authority which made or confirmed the order,
   (b) include a statement as to the accuracy of the information given in it,
   (c) if it is not in English, include a translation of it into English.

The signature may be an electronic signature.

(7) The order must be accompanied by an order made by a court exercising criminal jurisdiction in that country for the forfeiture of the property, unless the certificate indicates when such an order is expected to be sent.

(8) An appropriate court or authority in a participating country in relation to an overseas freezing order is–
   (a) a court exercising criminal jurisdiction in the country,
   (b) a prosecuting authority in the country,
   (c) any other authority in the country which appears to the Secretary of State to have the function of making such orders.

(9) References in paragraphs 25E to 25G to an overseas freezing order include its accompanying certificate.

### Enforcement of overseas freezing orders

**25E** (1) Where this paragraph applies the Secretary of State must send a copy of the overseas freezing order to the Court of Session and to the Lord Advocate.

(2) The court is to consider the overseas freezing order on its own initiative within a period prescribed by rules of court.

(3) Before giving effect to the overseas freezing order, the court must give the Lord Advocate an opportunity to be heard.

(4) The court may decide not to give effect to the overseas freezing order only if, in its opinion, giving effect to it would be incompatible with any of the Convention rights (within the meaning of the Human Rights Act 1998).

**25F** The Court of Session may postpone giving effect to an overseas freezing order in respect of any property–
(a) in order to avoid prejudicing a criminal investigation which is taking place in the United Kingdom, or
(b) if, under an order made by a court in criminal proceedings in the United Kingdom, the property may not be dealt with.

**25G** (1) Where the Court of Session decides to give effect to an overseas freezing order, the Deputy Principal Clerk of Session must–
   (a) register the order in the Books of Council and Session,
   (b) provide for notice of the registration to be given to any person affected by it.

(2) For the purpose of enforcing an overseas freezing order registered in the Books of Council and Session, the order is to have effect as if it were an order made by the Court of Session.

(3) Paragraphs 20 and 21 apply to an overseas freezing order registered in the Books of Council and Session as they apply to a restraint order under paragraph 18.

(4) The Court of Session may cancel the registration of the order, or vary the property to which the order applies, on an application by the Lord Advocate or any other person affected by it, if or to the extent that–
   (a) the court is of the opinion mentioned in paragraph 25E(4), or
   (b) the court is of the opinion that the order has ceased to have effect in the participating country.

(5) Her Majesty may by Order in Council make further provision for the enforcement in Scotland of registered overseas freezing orders.

(6) An Order in Council under this paragraph–
  (a) may make different provision for different cases,
  (b) is not to be made unless a draft of it has been laid before and approved by resolution of each House of Parliament."

6[39] In paragraph 28 of that Schedule (enforcement of orders made in designated countries), in sub-paragraph (2), after the second "order" there is inserted "(other than an overseas freezing order within the meaning of paragraph 25D)".

7[40] In Part 3 of that Schedule (forfeiture orders: Northern Ireland), after paragraph 41 there is inserted–

### "Domestic and overseas freezing orders

**41A** (1) This paragraph has effect for the purposes of paragraphs 41B to 41G.

(2) The relevant Framework Decision means the Framework Decision on the execution in the European Union of orders freezing property or evidence adopted by the Council of the European Union on 22nd July 2003.

(3) A listed offence means–
  (a) an offence described in Article 3(2) of the relevant Framework Decision, or
  (b) a prescribed offence or an offence of a prescribed description.

(4) An order under sub-paragraph (3)(b) which, for the purposes of paragraph 41D, prescribes an offence or a description of offences may require that the conduct which constitutes the offence or offences would, if it occurred in a part of the United Kingdom, constitute an offence in that part.

(5) Specified information, in relation to a certificate under paragraph 41B or 41D, means–
  (a) any information required to be given by the form of certificate annexed to the relevant Framework Decision, or
  (b) any prescribed information.

(6) In this paragraph, "prescribed" means prescribed by an order made by the Secretary of State.

(7) A participating country means–
  (a) a country other than the United Kingdom which is a member State on a day appointed for the commencement of Schedule 4 to the Crime (International Co-operation) Act 2003, and
  (b) any other member State designated by an order made by the Secretary of State.

(8) "Country" includes territory.

(9) Section 14(2)(a) applies for the purposes of determining what are the proceeds of the commission of an offence.

### Domestic freezing orders: certification

**41B** (1) If any of the property to which an application for a restraint order relates is property in a participating country, the applicant may ask the High Court to make a certificate under this paragraph.

(2) The High Court may make a certificate under this paragraph if–
  (a) it makes a restraint order in relation to property in the participating country, and
  (b) it is satisfied that there is a good arguable case that the property is likely to be used for the purposes of a listed offence or is the proceeds of the commission of a listed offence.

(3) A certificate under this paragraph is a certificate which–
  (a) is made for the purposes of the relevant Framework Decision, and
  (b) gives the specified information.

---

[39] Not yet in force.
[40] Not yet in force.

(4) If the High Court makes a certificate under this paragraph–
  (a) the restraint order must provide for notice of the certificate to be given to the person affected by it, and
  (b) paragraph 34(2) to (4) applies to the certificate as it applies to the restraint order.

### Sending domestic freezing orders

**41C** (1) If a certificate is made under paragraph 41B, the restraint order and the certificate are to be sent to the Secretary of State for forwarding to–
  (a) a court exercising jurisdiction in the place where the property is situated, or
  (b) any authority recognised by the government of the participating country as the appropriate authority for receiving orders of that kind.

(2) The restraint order and the certificate must be accompanied by a forfeiture order, unless the certificate indicates when the court expects a forfeiture order to be sent.

(3) The certificate must include a translation of it into an appropriate language of the participating country (if that language is not English).

(4) The certificate must be signed by or on behalf of the court and must include a statement as to the accuracy of the information given in it.

The signature may be an electronic signature.

(5) If the restraint order and the certificate are not accompanied by a forfeiture order, but a forfeiture order is subsequently made, it is to be sent to the Secretary of State for forwarding as mentioned in sub-paragraph (1).

### Overseas freezing orders

**41D** (1) Paragraph 41E applies where an overseas freezing order made by an appropriate court or authority in a participating country is received by the Secretary of State from the court or authority which made or confirmed the order.

(2) An overseas freezing order is an order prohibiting dealing with property–
  (a) which is in the United Kingdom,
  (b) which the appropriate court or authority considers is likely to be used for the purposes of a listed offence or is the proceeds of the commission of such an offence, and
  (c) in respect of which an order has been or may be made by a court exercising criminal jurisdiction in the participating country for the forfeiture of the property,
  and in respect of which the following requirements of this paragraph are met.

(3) The action which the appropriate court or authority considered would constitute or, as the case may be, constituted the listed offence is action done as an act of terrorism or for the purposes of terrorism.

(4) The order must relate to–
  (a) criminal proceedings instituted in the participating country, or
  (b) a criminal investigation being carried on there.

(5) The order must be accompanied by a certificate which gives the specified information; but a certificate may be treated as giving any specified information which is not given in it if the Secretary of State has the information in question.

(6) The certificate must–
  (a) be signed by or on behalf of the court or authority which made or confirmed the order,
  (b) include a statement as to the accuracy of the information given in it,
  (c) if it is not in English, include a translation of it into English.

The signature may be an electronic signature.

(7) The order must be accompanied by an order made by a court exercising criminal jurisdiction in that country for the forfeiture of the property, unless the certificate indicates when such an order is expected to be sent.

(8) An appropriate court or authority in a participating country in relation to an overseas freezing order is–

    (a) a court exercising criminal jurisdiction in the country,

    (b) a prosecuting authority in the country,

    (c) any other authority in the country which appears to the Secretary of State to have the function of making such orders.

(9) References in paragraphs 41E to 41G to an overseas freezing order include its accompanying certificate.

Enforcement of overseas freezing orders

**41E** (1) Where this paragraph applies the Secretary of State must send a copy of the overseas freezing order to the High Court and to the Director of Public Prosecutions for Northern Ireland.

(2) The court is to consider the overseas freezing order on its own initiative within a period prescribed by rules of court.

(3) Before giving effect to the overseas freezing order, the court must give the Director an opportunity to be heard.

(4) The court may decide not to give effect to the overseas freezing order only if, in its opinion, giving effect to it would be incompatible with any of the Convention rights (within the meaning of the Human Rights Act 1998).

**41F** The High Court may postpone giving effect to an overseas freezing order in respect of any property–

    (a) in order to avoid prejudicing a criminal investigation which is taking place in the United Kingdom, or

    (b) if, under an order made by a court in criminal proceedings in the United Kingdom, the property may not be dealt with.

**41G**

(1) Where the High Court decides to give effect to an overseas freezing order, it must–

    (a) register the order in that court,

    (b) provide for notice of the registration to be given to any person affected by it.

(2) For the purpose of enforcing an overseas freezing order registered in the High Court, the order is to have effect as if it were an order made by that court.

(3) Paragraph 35 applies to an overseas freezing order registered in the High Court as it applies to a restraint order under paragraph 33.

(4) The High Court may cancel the registration of the order, or vary the property to which the order applies, on an application by the Director of Public Prosecutions for Northern Ireland or any other person affected by it, if or to the extent that–

    (a) the court is of the opinion mentioned in paragraph 41E(4), or

    (b) the court is of the opinion that the order has ceased to have effect in the participating country.

(5) Her Majesty may by Order in Council make further provision for the enforcement in Northern Ireland of registered overseas freezing orders.

(6) An Order in Council under this paragraph–

    (a) may make different provision for different cases,

    (b) is not to be made unless a draft of it has been laid before and approved by resolution of each House of Parliament."

**8**[41] In paragraph 44 of that Schedule (enforcement of orders made in designated countries), in subparagraph (2), after the second "order" there is inserted "(other than an overseas freezing order within the meaning of paragraph 41D)".

---

[41]  Not yet in force.

**9**[42]  In Part 4 of that Schedule (insolvency), in paragraph 45, at the end of paragraph (c) of the definition of "restraint order" there is inserted "or an order which is enforceable in England and Wales, Scotland or Northern Ireland by virtue of paragraph 11G, 25G or 41G".

SCHEDULE 5

MINOR AND CONSEQUENTIAL AMENDMENTS

SECTION 91

### *The internationally protected persons act 1978 (c. 17)*

**1**  The Internationally Protected Persons Act 1978 is amended as follows.

**2**  In section 2 (supplementary provisions), in subsections (1) and (2), for "and the United Nations Personnel Act 1997" there is substituted ", the United Nations Personnel Act 1997 and the Terrorism Act 2000".

### *The Suppression of Terrorism Act 1978 (c. 26)*

**3**  The Suppression of Terrorism Act 1978 is amended as follows.

**4**  In section 4 (jurisdiction in respect of offences committed outside United Kingdom), in subsections (4) and (5), for "and the United Nations Personnel Act 1997" there is substituted ", the United Nations Personnel Act 1997 and the Terrorism Act 2000".

### *The Road Traffic (Northern Ireland) Order 1981 (S.I. 1981/ 154 (N.I. 1))*

**5**[43]  The Road Traffic (Northern Ireland) Order 1981 is amended as follows.

**6**[44]  In Article 4 (exceptions to offence under Article 3), in paragraph (3)(a), after "Road Traffic Orders" there is inserted "or Chapter 1 of Part 3 of the Crime (International Co-operation) Act 2003".

### *The Nuclear Material (Offences) Act 1983 (c. 18)*

**7**  The Nuclear Material (Offences) Act 1983 is amended as follows.

**8**  In section 3 (supplemental), in subsections (1) and (2), for "and the United Nations Personnel Act 1997" there is substituted ", the United Nations Personnel Act 1997 and the Terrorism Act 2000".

### *The Child Abduction Act 1984 (c. 37)*

**9**  The Child Abduction Act 1984 is amended as follows.

**10**  In section 11 (consequential amendments and repeals), in subsection (3), after "the Internationally Protected Persons Act 1978" there is inserted "and sections 63B(2) and 63C(2) of the Terrorism Act 2000".

### *The Criminal Justice Act 1987 (c. 38)*

**11**  The Criminal Justice Act 1987 is amended as follows.

**12**  In section 2 (investigation powers of Director of Serious Fraud Office)–

(a)  in subsection (1A), for paragraph (b) there is substituted–
   "(b) the Secretary of State acting under section 15(2) of the Crime
       (International Co-operation) Act 2003, in response to a request received by him from a
       person mentioned in section 13(2) of that Act (an "overseas authority").",
(b)  in subsection (8A), for the words from "furnished" to the end there is substituted "given to the overseas authority which requested it or given to the Secretary of State for forwarding to that overseas authority)",

---

[42]  Not yet in force.
[43]  Not yet in force.
[44]  Not yet in force.

   (c)  subsection (8B) is omitted,

   (d)  in subsection (8C), for "transmitted" (in both places) there is substituted "forwarded",

   (e)  in subsection (18), "(8B)" is omitted.

## The Criminal Justice Act 1988 (c. 33)

**13** The Criminal Justice Act 1988 is amended as follows.

**14** In section 24 (business etc. documents), in subsection (4), for "section 3 of the Criminal Justice (International Co-operation) Act 1990" there is substituted "section 7 of the Crime (International Co-operation) Act 2003".

**15** In section 26 (statements in documents that appear to have been prepared for the purposes of criminal proceedings or investigations), for "section 3 of the Criminal Justice (International Co-operation) Act 1990" there is substituted "section 7 of the Crime (International Co-operation) Act 2003".

**16** In paragraph 6 of Schedule 13 (evidence before courts-martial etc.)–

   (a)  in sub-paragraph (1)–

     (i)  for "section 3 of the Criminal Justice (International Co-operation) Act 1990" there is substituted "section 7 of the Crime (International Co-operation) Act 2003", and

     (ii)  for "letters of request or corresponding documents" there is substituted "requests for assistance in obtaining outside the United Kingdom evidence", and

   (b)  in sub-paragraph (4), for "letters of request or corresponding documents" there is substituted "requests for assistance in obtaining evidence".

## The Road Traffic Act 1988 (c. 52)

**17** The Road Traffic Act 1988 is amended as follows.

**18**[45] In section 88 (exceptions to offence under section 87)–

   (a)  in subsection (1A)(b)(ii), for "section 4(1) of or paragraph 6(1) or 9(1)" there is substituted "section 4 of or paragraph 6 or 9",

   (b)  in subsection (1B)(a), after "Road Traffic Acts" there is inserted "or Chapter 1 of Part 3 of the Crime (International Co-operation) Act 2003".

**19** In section 92 (requirements as to physical fitness of drivers), in subsection (7D), after "99D" there is inserted "or 109C".

**20** In section 94A (driving after refusal or revocation of licence), in subsection (1)–

   (a)  in paragraph (a)(ii), for "section 93(1) or (2)" there is substituted "section 93",

   (b)  in paragraph (a)(iii)–

     (i) after "section 99C(1) or (2)" there is inserted "or 109B",

     (ii) after "Community licence" there is inserted "or Northern Ireland licence",

   (c)  in paragraph (b)(ii), at the end there is inserted "or Northern Ireland licence".

**21** In section 97 (grant of licences), in subsection (1)(d), for "section 4(1) of or paragraph 6(1) or 9(1)" there is substituted "section 4 of or paragraph 6 or 9".

**22** In section 100 (appeals relating to licences), in subsection (1)–

   (a)  in paragraph (c), after "99(3)" there is inserted "or (3A)",

   (b)  for "or 99C" there is substituted ", 99C or 109B".

**23** In section 105 (regulations)–

   (a)  in subsection (2)–

     (i)  in paragraph (a), after "this Act," there is inserted "Northern Ireland licences,",

     (ii)  in paragraph (b)(iii), after "this Act" there is inserted ", of Northern Ireland licences",

     (iii) in paragraph (ea), after "counterparts" (in the first place) there is inserted "of Northern Ireland licences or" and after "counterparts" (in the second place) there is inserted "of Northern Ireland licences or (as the case may be)",

---

[45]  Partially in force.

(iv) in paragraph (f), before "Community licences" there is inserted "Northern Ireland licences or",

(b) in subsection (5), for ", 91A and" there is substituted "and 91ZA to".

24  In section 107 (service of notices), for "99B or 99E" there is substituted "99B, 99E or 109A".

25  In section 108 (interpretation), in subsection (1)–
(a) in the definition of "counterpart", the "and" at the end of paragraph (a) is omitted and after that paragraph there is inserted–
"(aa) in relation to a Northern Ireland licence, has the meaning given by section 109A of this Act (except in the definition of "Northern Ireland counterpart" below), and",
(b) in the definition of "Northern Ireland driving licence" and "Northern Ireland licence", at the end there is inserted "and "Northern Ireland counterpart" means the document issued with the Northern Ireland licence as a counterpart under the law of Northern Ireland".

26  In section 109 (provisions as to Northern Ireland drivers' licences)–
(a) in subsection (1), after "Great Britain," there is inserted "in accordance with that licence",
(b) in subsection (2), paragraph (b) and the "and" preceding it are omitted,
(c) subsections (3) to (5) are omitted.

27[46] In section 164 (power of constables to require production of driving licence etc.)–
(a) in subsection (3)–
(i) in paragraph (a), before "the Secretary of State" there is inserted "a person is required to deliver his licence and its counterpart to the Secretary of State under section 63 of the Crime (International Co-operation) Act 2003 or",
(ii) in paragraph (a)(iii), after "99C" there is inserted ", 109B",
(iii) in paragraph (b), after "99C" there is inserted ", 109B" and after "or 118" there is inserted "or section 63 of the Crime (International Co-operation) Act 2003",
(b) in subsection (11)–
(i) in the definition of "licence", after "this Act" there is inserted ", a Northern Ireland licence",
(ii) after ""counterpart"," there is inserted ""Northern Ireland licence".

28  In section 167 (power of arrest for constable in Scotland), before "Community licence" there is inserted "Northern Ireland licence or".

29  In section 173 (forgery of documents, etc.)–
(a) in subsection (2)(aa), after "counterpart of a" there is inserted "Northern Ireland licence or",
(b) in subsection (4), for "and "Community licence"" there is substituted ", "Community licence" and "Northern Ireland licence" ".

30  In section 176 (power to seize certain articles)–
(a) in subsection (1A), before "Community licence" (in both places) there is inserted "Northern Ireland licence or",
(b) in subsection (3A), after "such licence or" there is inserted "of a Northern Ireland licence or",
(c) in subsection (8), for "and "Community licence"" there is substituted ", "Community licence" and "Northern Ireland licence"".

31  In section 193A (tramcars and trolley vehicles), in subsection (2)(b), for "91A," there is substituted "91ZA to".

## The Road Traffic Offenders Act 1988 (c. 53)

32  The Road Traffic Offenders Act 1988 is amended as follows.

33  In section 3 (restriction on institution of proceedings for certain offences), in subsection (2A), after "99D" there is inserted "or 109C".

34  In section 26 (interim disqualification), in subsection (10), for the words from "and 91A(5)" to "licences)" there is substituted ", 91ZA(7) and 91A(5) of this Act".

---

[46]  Partially in force.

**35** In section 98 (general interpretation), in subsection (1)–
  (a) in the definition of "the provisions connected with the licensing of drivers", for "91A," there is substituted "91ZA to",
  (b) for "and "EEA State" " there is substituted ", "EEA State" and "Northern Ireland licence"".

**36** In Schedule 1 (offences to which sections 1, 6, 11 and 12(1) of the Act apply)–
  (a) in the entry for section 94(3) of the Road Traffic Act 1988, in column 1, at the end there is inserted "or 109C",
  (b) in the entry for section 94(3A) of that Act, in column 1, at the end there is inserted "or 109C(c)",
  (c) in the entry for section 94A of that Act, in column 2, at the end there is inserted "or 109B",
  (d) in the entry for section 99B(11) of that Act–
    (i) in column 1, at the end there is inserted "and that subsection as applied by RTA section 109A(5)",
    (ii) in column 2, at the end there is inserted "or a requirement under section 99B(6) or (7) as applied by section 109A(5)".

**37** In Schedule 2 (prosecution and punishment of offences)–
  (a) in the entry for section 94(3) of the Road Traffic Act 1988, in column 2, at the end there is inserted "or 109C",
  (b) in the entry for section 94(3A) of that Act, in column 2, at the end there is inserted "or 109C(c)",
  (c) in the entry for section 94A of that Act, in column 2, at the end there is inserted "or 109B",
  (d) in the entry for section 99B(11) of that Act–
    (i) in column 1, at the end there is inserted "and that subsection as applied by RTA section 109A(5)",
    (ii) in column 2, at the end there is inserted "or a requirement under section 99B(6) or (7) as applied by section 109A(5)",
  (e) the entry for section 109 of that Act is omitted,
  (f) before the entry for section 114 of that Act there is inserted–

| "RTA section 109B(4) | Failure to deliver Northern Ireland licence to Secretary of State when required by notice under section 109B. | Summarily | Level 3 on the standard scale. | | | " |
|---|---|---|---|---|---|---|

### *The Criminal Justice (Evidence, Etc.) (Northern Ireland) Order 1988 (S.I. 1988/1847 (N.I. 17))*

**38** The Criminal Justice (Evidence, Etc.) (Northern Ireland) Order 1988 is amended as follows.

**39** In Article 4 (business etc. documents), in paragraph (4), for "section 3 of the Criminal Justice (International Co-operation) Act 1990" there is substituted "section 7 of the Crime (International Co-operation) Act 2003".

**40** In Article 6 (statements in documents that appear to have been prepared for the purposes of criminal proceedings or investigations), for "section 3 of the Criminal Justice (International Co-operation) Act 1990" there is substituted "section 7 of the Crime (International Co-operation) Act 2003".

### *The Criminal Justice (International Co-operation) Act 1990 (c. 5)*

**41** The Criminal Justice (International Co-operation) Act 1990 is amended as follows.

**42** Sections 1 to 4, 7, 8 and 11 (mutual service of process and provision of evidence) are omitted.

**43** In section 5 (transfer of UK prisoner to give evidence or assist investigation overseas), after subsection (3) there is inserted–
  "(3A) A warrant under this section has effect in spite of section 127(1) of the Army Act 1955, section 127(1) of the Air Force Act 1955 or section 82A(1) of the Naval Discipline Act 1957

(restriction on removing persons out of the United Kingdom who are serving military sentences)."

**44** Schedule 1 (proceedings of nominated court) is omitted.

*The Road Traffic (New Drivers) Act 1995 (c. 13)*

**45** The Road Traffic (New Drivers) Act 1995 is amended as follows.

**46** In section 2 (surrender of licences), at the end there is inserted–
"(6) In this section and section 3"licence" includes a Northern Ireland licence."

**47** In section 3 (revocation of licences)–
(a) after subsection (1) there is inserted–
"(1A) Where the Secretary of State serves on the holder of a Northern Ireland licence a notice under subsection (1), the Secretary of State must send to the licensing authority in Northern Ireland–
(a) particulars of the notice; and
(b) the Northern Ireland licence.
(1B) Where the Secretary of State is sent by that licensing authority particulars of a notice served on the holder of a licence under a provision of Northern Ireland law corresponding to subsection (1), he must by notice served on the holder revoke the licence.",
(b) [...]
(c) at the end, there is inserted–
"(3) In this section references to the revocation of a person's Northern Ireland licence are references to its revocation as respects Great Britain; and, accordingly, the person ceases to be authorised by virtue of section 109(1) of the Road Traffic Act 1988 to drive in Great Britain a motor vehicle of any class."

**48** In section 4 (re-testing)–
(a) in subsection (1)–
(i) for "section 3(1)" there is substituted "section 3",
(ii) after "full licence" (in the second place it occurs) there is inserted "or (as the case may be) full Northern Ireland licence",
(b) after subsection (1) there is inserted–
"(1A) Subject to subsection (5), the Secretary of State may not under that Part grant a person whose Northern Ireland licence has been revoked under a provision of Northern Ireland law corresponding to section 3(1) a full licence to drive any class of vehicles in relation to which the revoked licence was issued as a full Northern Ireland licence unless he satisfies the Secretary of State as mentioned in subsection (1).",
(c) in subsections (2) and (3), at the end there is inserted "or (as the case may be) full Northern Ireland licence",
(d) in subsection (5)–
(i) for "Subsection (1) does" there is substituted "Subsections (1) and (1A) do", and
(ii) for "section 3(1)" there is substituted "section 3 or whose Northern Ireland licence has been revoked under a provision of Northern Ireland law corresponding to section 3(1)".

**49** In section 5 (restoration of licence without re-testing in certain cases)–
(a) in subsections (1), (4) and (6), for "section 3(1)" there is substituted "section 3",
(b) in subsections (3)(a) and (4)(c), after "section 2" there is inserted "or (as the case may be) the provision of Northern Ireland law corresponding to that section",
(c) at the end there is inserted–
"(11) Nothing in this section applies in relation to a person whose Northern Ireland licence has been revoked under section 3(1)."

**50** In section 7 (early termination of probationary period)–
(a) in paragraph (b), for "section 3(1)" there is substituted "section 3",
(b) in paragraph (c)–
(i) for "paragraph 5(1)" there is substituted "paragraph 5",
(ii) for "paragraph 8(1)" there is substituted "paragraph 8".

**51** In section 9 (interpretation), after subsection (2) there is inserted–
"(2A) In this Act–
"full Northern Ireland licence" means a Northern Ireland licence other than a Northern Ireland provisional licence,
"Northern Ireland provisional licence" means a Northern Ireland licence which corresponds to a provisional licence.";

**52** Schedule 1 (newly qualified drivers holding test certificates) is amended as follows.

**53** In paragraph 1, at the end there is inserted–
"(3) In this Schedule "licence" includes a Northern Ireland licence, "full licence" includes a full Northern Ireland licence and "provisional licence" includes a Northern Ireland provisional licence.
(4) In relation to the holder of a Northern Ireland licence, the following sub-paragraphs have effect for the purposes of this Schedule.
(5) References to a test certificate are references to a certificate or other document (in this Schedule referred to as a "Northern Ireland test certificate") which is evidence that he has not more than two years previously passed a Northern Ireland test of competence to drive corresponding to the test mentioned in sub-paragraph (1).
(6) References to prescribed conditions are references to conditions subject to which the Northern Ireland provisional licence was granted."

**54** In paragraph 2, after sub-paragraph (4) there is inserted–
"(4A) In relation to the holder of a Northern Ireland licence, the reference in sub-paragraph (4)(b) to section 98(2) of the Road Traffic Act 1988 is a reference to the corresponding provision under the law of Northern Ireland."

**55** In paragraph 5–
(a) after sub-paragraph (1) there is inserted–
"(1A) Where the Secretary of State serves on the holder of a Northern Ireland licence a notice under sub-paragraph (1), the Secretary of State must send to the licensing authority in Northern Ireland particulars of the notice together with the Northern Ireland test certificate.
(1B) Where the Secretary of State is sent by that licensing authority particulars of a notice served on the holder of a licence under a provision of Northern Ireland law corresponding to sub-paragraph (1), he must by notice served on that person revoke his test certificate.",
(b) [...]
(c) at the end there is inserted–
"(4) In this paragraph and paragraph 8 references to the revocation of a person's Northern Ireland test certificate are references to its revocation as respects Great Britain.
(5) The effect of the revocation of a person's Northern Ireland test certificate as respects Great Britain is that any prescribed conditions to which his Northern Ireland provisional licence ceased to be subject when he became a qualified driver shall again apply for the purposes of section 109(1) of the Road Traffic Act 1988."

**56** In paragraph 6, in sub-paragraph (1), for "paragraph 5(1)" there is substituted "paragraph 5, or whose Northern Ireland test certificate has been revoked under a provision of Northern Ireland law corresponding to paragraph 5(1),".

**57** In paragraph 8–
(a) after sub-paragraph (1) there is inserted–
"(1A) Where the Secretary of State serves on the holder of a Northern Ireland licence a notice under sub-paragraph (1), the Secretary of State must send to the licensing authority in Northern Ireland particulars of the notice together with the Northern Ireland licence and the Northern Ireland test certificate.
(1B) Where the Secretary of State is sent by that licensing authority particulars of a notice served on the holder of a licence under a provision of Northern Ireland law corresponding

to sub-paragraph (1), he must by notice served on that person revoke his licence and test certificate.",

(b) [...]

(c) at the end there is inserted–

"(3) In this paragraph references to the revocation of a person's Northern Ireland licence are references to its revocation as respects Great Britain; and, accordingly, the person ceases to be authorised by virtue of section 109(1) of the Road Traffic Act 1988 to drive in Great Britain a motor vehicle of any class."

**58** In paragraph 9–

(a) in sub-paragraph (1), for "paragraph 8(1)" there is substituted "paragraph 8, or whose Northern Ireland licence and Northern Ireland test certificate have been revoked under a provision of Northern Ireland law corresponding to paragraph 8(1),",

(b) in sub-paragraph (4)(b)(i), after "1988" there is inserted ", or under a provision of Northern Ireland law corresponding to that section,".

**59** In paragraph 10(a)–

(a) for "paragraph 5(1)" there is substituted "paragraph 5 (or a person's Northern Ireland test certificate has been revoked under a provision of Northern Ireland law corresponding to paragraph 5(1))",

(b) for "paragraph 8(1)" there is substituted "paragraph 8 (or a person's Northern Ireland licence and Northern Ireland test certificate have been revoked under a provision of Northern Ireland law corresponding to paragraph 8(1))".

**60** In paragraph 11–

(a) in sub-paragraphs (1) and (2)(c), for "paragraph 5(1)" and "paragraph 8(1)" there is substituted "paragraph 5" and "paragraph 8" respectively,

(b) in sub-paragraph (1)(d), after "section 2" there is inserted "or (as the case may be) the provision of Northern Ireland law corresponding to that section".

### The Criminal Law (Consolidation) (Scotland) Act 1995 (c. 39)

**61** The Criminal Law (Consolidation) (Scotland) Act 1995 is amended as follows.

**62** In section 27 (Lord Advocate's direction), in subsection (2), for "section 4(2B) of the Criminal Justice (International Co-operation) Act 1990" there is substituted "section 15(4) of the Crime (International Co-operation) Act 2003".

**63**

In section 28 (powers of investigation)–

(a) in subsection (8), for the words from "by the" to the end there is substituted "by virtue of section 27(2) of this Act shall be given to the overseas authority which requested it or to the Lord Advocate for forwarding to that authority",

(b) subsection (9) is omitted,

(c) in subsection (10), for "transmitted" (in both places) there is substituted "forwarded".

### The Criminal Procedure (Scotland) Act 1995 (c. 46)

**64** The Criminal Procedure (Scotland) Act 1995 is amended as follows.

**65** In section 210(1)(c) (consideration, in passing sentence of imprisonment or detention, of time spent in custody), at the end there is inserted "so however that a period of time spent both in custody on remand and, by virtue of section 47(1) of the Crime (International Co-operation) Act 2003, abroad is not for any reason to be discounted in a determination under paragraph (a) above or specification under paragraph (b) above".

### The United Nations Personnel Act 1997 (c. 13)

**66** The United Nations Personnel Act 1997 is amended as follows.

**67** In section 5 (supplementary provisions), in subsections (1) and (2), for "and the Nuclear Material (Offences) Act 1983" there is substituted ", the Nuclear Material (Offences) Act 1983 and the Terrorism Act 2000".

### *The Data Protection Act 1998 (c. 29)*

68  The Data Protection Act 1998 is amended as follows.

69  In section 28(1) (national security), for "section" there is substituted "sections 54A and".

70  In section 60(2) and (3) (prosecutions and penalties), before "paragraph 12" there is inserted "section 54A and".

71  In section 63(5) (application to the Crown), for "section" there is substituted "sections 54A and".

### *The Powers of Criminal Courts (Sentencing) Act 2000 (c. 6)*

72  The Powers of Criminal Courts (Sentencing) Act 2000 is amended as follows.

73  In section 146 (driving disqualification for any offence)–
   (a)  in subsection (4), the "or" at the end of paragraph (a) is omitted and after that paragraph there is inserted–
      "(aa)  in the case where he holds a Northern Ireland licence (within the meaning of Part 3 of the Road Traffic Act 1988), his Northern Ireland licence and its counterpart (if any); or",
   (b)  in subsection (5), in the definition of "counterpart", the "and" at the end of paragraph (a) is omitted and after that paragraph there is inserted–
      "(aa)  in relation to a Northern Ireland licence, has the meaning given by section 109A of that Act; and".

74  In section 147 (driving disqualification where vehicle used for purposes of crime), in subsection (5), the "or" at the end of paragraph (a) is omitted and after that paragraph there is inserted–
   "(aa)  in the case where he holds a Northern Ireland licence (within the meaning of Part 3 of the Road Traffic Act 1988), his Northern Ireland licence and its counterpart (if any); or".

### *The Terrorism Act 2000 (c. 11)*

75  The Terrorism Act 2000 is amended as follows.

76  In section 121 (interpretation), in the definition of "premises", before "includes" (in the first place) there is inserted ", except in section 63D,".

77  In section 123 (orders and regulations), in subsection (2), after paragraph (b) there is inserted–
   "(ba)  section 63C(3)(d);".

### *The Regulation of Investigatory Powers Act 2000 (c. 23)*

78  The Regulation of Investigatory Powers Act 2000 is amended as follows.

79  In section 65 (investigatory powers tribunal)–
   (a)  in subsection (5)–
      (i)  after paragraph (c) there is inserted–
         "(ca)  the carrying out of surveillance by a foreign police or customs officer (within the meaning of section 76A);",
      (ii)  in paragraph (d), at the beginning there is inserted "other",
   (b)  after subsection (7), there is inserted–
      "(7A)  For the purposes of this section conduct also takes place in challengeable circumstances if it takes place, or purports to take place, under section 76A."

80  In section 78 (orders, regulations and rules), in subsection (3)(a), for "or 71(9)" there is substituted ", 71(9) or 76A(9)".

### *The Armed Forces Act 2001 (c. 19)*

81  In section 31 of the Armed Forces Act 2001 (power to make provision in consequence of enactments relating to criminal justice), in subsection (7)–
   (a)  after "section" there is inserted "section 5 of the Criminal Justice (International Co-operation) Act 1990 and",
   (b)  for "is" there is substituted "are".

*The Proceeds of Crime Act 2002 (c. 29)*

82 [...]
83 [...]

## SCHEDULE 6

### REPEALS

Section 91

| Short title and chapter | Extent of repeal |
|---|---|
| Criminal Justice Act 1987 (c. 38) | In section 2– |
| | subsection (8B), |
| | in subsection (18), the word "(8B)". |
| | In section 3(6), the "and" preceding paragraph (m). |
| Road Traffic Act 1988 (c. 52) | In section 108(1), in the definition of "counterpart", the "and" at the end of paragraph (a). |
| | In section 109– |
| | in subsection (2), paragraph (b) and the "and" preceding it, subsections (3) to (5). |
| Road Traffic Offenders Act 1988 (c. 53) | In Schedule 2, the entry for section 109 of the Road Traffic Act 1988. |
| Criminal Justice (International Co-operation) Act 1990 (c. 5) | Sections 1 to 4, 7, 8 and 11. |
| | Schedule 1. |
| | In Schedule 4, paragraphs 6(2) and 8. |
| Criminal Justice and Public Order Act 1994 (c. 33) | Section 164(1). |
| Criminal Law (Consolidation) (Scotland) Act 1995 (c. 39) | Section 28(9). |
| Powers of Criminal Courts (Sentencing) Act 2000 (c. 6) | In section 146– |
| | in subsection (4), the "or" at the end of paragraph (a), |
| | in subsection (5), in the definition of "counterpart", the "and" at the end of paragraph (a). |
| | In section 147(5), the "or" at the end of paragraph (a). |
| Criminal Justice and Police Act 2001 (c. 16) | In Schedule 1, paragraph 49. |
| Proceeds of Crime Act 2002 (c. 29) | Section 376(5). |

# APPENDIX 11

# The Proceeds of Crime Act 2002 (External Requests and Orders) Order 2005 (as amended)

### 2005 No. 3181

### PROCEEDS OF CRIME

The Order is printed as amended by subsequent legislation.

| | |
|---|---|
| *Made* | *15th November 2005* |
| *Laid before Parliament* | *25th November 2005* |
| *Coming into force* | *1st January 2006* |

At the Court at Buckingham Palace, the 15th day of November 2005

Present,

The Queen's Most Excellent Majesty in Council

Her Majesty, in pursuance of sections 444 and 459(2) of the Proceeds of Crime Act 2002, is pleased, by and with the advice of Her Privy Council, to order, and it is ordered, as follows:—

## Part 1
### General Provisions

**1. Title and commencement**

This Order may be cited as the Proceeds of Crime Act 2002 (External Requests and Orders) Order 2005 and shall come into force on 1st January 2006.

**2. Interpretation**

In this Order—

"the Act" means the Proceeds of Crime Act 2002;

[…]

"country" includes territory;

"external order" has the meaning set out in section 447(2) of the Act;

"external request" has the meaning set out in section 447(1) of the Act;

"a relevant officer of Revenue and Customs" means such an officer exercising functions by virtue of section 6 of the Commissioners for Revenue and Customs Act 2005.

**3.— Insolvency practitioners**

(1) Paragraphs (2) and (3) apply if a person acting as an insolvency practitioner seizes or disposes of any property in relation to which his functions are not exercisable because—

(a) it is for the time being subject to a restraint order made under article 8, 58 or 95; or

(b) it is for the time being subject to a property freezing order made under article 147, an interim receiving order made under article 151, a prohibitory property order made under article 161 or an interim administration order made under article 167,

and at the time of the seizure or disposal he believes on reasonable grounds that he is entitled (whether in pursuance of an order of a court or otherwise) to seize or dispose of the property.

(2) He is not liable to any person in respect of any loss or damage resulting from the seizure or disposal, except so far as the loss or damage is caused by his negligence.

(3) He has a lien on the property or the proceeds of its sale—

    (a) for such of his expenses as were incurred in connection with the liquidation, bankruptcy, sequestration or other proceedings in relation to which he purported to make the seizure or disposal, and

    (b) for so much of his remuneration as may reasonably be assigned to his acting in connection with those proceedings.

(4) Paragraph (2) does not prejudice the generality of any provision of the 1985 Act, the 1986 Act, the 1989 Order or any Act or Order which confers a protection from liability on him.

(5) Paragraph (7) applies if—

    (a) property is subject to a restraint order made under article 8, 58 or 95,

    (b) a person acting as an insolvency practitioner incurs expenses in respect of property subject to the restraint order, and

    (c) he does not know (and has no reasonable grounds to believe) that theproperty is subject to the restraint order.

(6) Paragraph (7) also applies if—

    (a) property is subject to a restraint order made under article 8, 58 or 95,

    (b) a person acting as an insolvency practitioner incurs expenses which are not ones in respect of property subject to the restraint order, and

    (c) the expenses are ones which (but for the effect of the restraint order) might have been met by taking possession of and realising property subject to it.

(7) Whether or not he has seized or disposed of any property, he is entitled to payment of the expenses under—

    (a) [article 33(2) or 34(3)] if the restraint order was made under article 7,

    (b) article 77(2) or 78(3) if the restraint order was made under article 58,

    (c) [article 119(2) or 120(3)] if the restraint order was made under article 95.

(8) Paragraph (10) applies if—

    (a) property is subject to a property freezing order made under article 147, an interim receiving order made under article 151, a prohibitory property order made under article 161 or an interim administration order made under article 167,

    (b) a person acting as an insolvency practitioner incurs expenses in respect of property subject to the order, and

    (c) he does not know (and has no reasonable grounds to believe) that the property is subject to the order.

(9) Paragraph (10) also applies if—

    (a) property is subject to a property freezing order made under article 147, an interim receiving order made under article 151, a prohibitory property order made under article 161 or an interim administration order made under article 167,

    (b) a person acting as an insolvency practitioner incurs expenses which are not ones in respect of property subject to the order, and

    (c) the expenses are ones which (but for the effect of the order) might have been met by taking possession of and realising property subject to it.

(10) Whether or not he has seized or disposed of any property, he is entitled to payment of the expenses under article 191.

### 4.— Insolvency practitioners: interpretation

(1) This article applies for the purposes of article 3.

(2) A person acts as an insolvency practitioner if he so acts within the meaning given by section 388 of the 1986 Act or Article 3 of the 1989 Order; but this is subject to paragraphs (3) to (5).

(3) The expression "person acting as an insolvency practitioner" includes the official receiver acting as receiver or manager of the property concerned.

(4) In applying section 388 of the 1986 Act under paragraph (2) above—

    (a) the reference in section 388(2)(a) to a permanent or interim trustee in sequestration must be taken to include a reference to a trustee in sequestration;

(b) section 388(5) (which includes provision that nothing in the section applies to anything done by the official receiver or the Accountant in Bankruptcy) must be ignored.

(5) In applying Article 3 of the 1989 Order under paragraph (2) above, paragraph (5) (which includes provision that nothing in the Article applies to anything done by the official receiver) must be ignored.

(6) The following sub-paragraphs apply to references to Acts or Orders—

(a) the 1913 Act is the Bankruptcy (Scotland) Act 1913;
(b) the 1914 Act is the Bankruptcy Act 1914;
(c) the 1985 Act is the Bankruptcy (Scotland) Act 1985;
(d) the 1986 Act is the Insolvency Act 1986;
(e) the 1989 Order is the Insolvency (Northern Ireland) Order 1989.

(7) An award of sequestration is made on the date of sequestration within the meaning of section 12(4) of the 1985 Act.

### 5.— Orders and regulations

(1) References in this article to subordinate legislation are to—
(a) any order under this Order (other than one falling to be made by a court);
(b) any regulations under this Order.

(2) Subordinate legislation—
(a) may make different provision for different purposes;
(b) may include supplementary, incidental, saving or transitional provisions.

(3) Any power to make subordinate legislation is exercisable by statutory instrument and, subject to paragraph (4), is subject to annulment in pursuance of a resolution of either House of Parliament.

(4) A statutory instrument containing regulations made under paragraph 6(2) of Schedule 1 is subject to annulment in pursuance of a resolution of the Scottish Parliament.

## PART 2
### GIVING EFFECT IN ENGLAND AND WALES TO EXTERNAL REQUESTS IN CONNECTION WITH CRIMINAL INVESTIGATIONS OR PROCEEDINGS AND TO EXTERNAL ORDERS ARISING FROM SUCH PROCEEDINGS

## Chapter 1
### External Requests

#### 6.— Action on receipt of external request in connection with criminal investigations or proceedings

(1) Except where paragraph (2) applies, the Secretary of State may refer an external request in connection with criminal investigations or proceedings in the country from which the request was made and concerning relevant property in England or Wales to—
(a) […]
(b) the Director of Public Prosecutions;
(c) the Director of Revenue and Customs Prosecutions,
to process it.

(2) This paragraph applies where it appears to the Secretary of State that the request—
(a) is made in connection with criminal investigations or proceedings which relate to an offence involving serious or complex fraud, and
(b) concerns relevant property in England or Wales.

(3) Where paragraph (2) applies, the Secretary of State may refer the request to the Director of the Serious Fraud Office to process it.

(4) In this Chapter "the relevant Director" means the Director to whom an external request is referred under paragraph (1) or (3).

(5) The relevant Director may ask the overseas authority which made the request for such further information as may be necessary to determine whether the request is likely to satisfy either of the conditions in article 7.

(6) A request under paragraph (5) may include a request for statements which may be used as evidence.

(7) Where a request concerns relevant property which is in Scotland or Northern Ireland as well as England or Wales, so much of the request as concerns such property shall be dealt with under Part 3 or 4, respectively.

### 7.— Conditions for Crown Court to give effect to external request

(1) The Crown Court may exercise the powers conferred by article 8 if either of the following conditions is satisfied.

(2) The first condition is that—
   (a) relevant property in England and Wales is identified in the external request;
   (b) a criminal investigation has been started in the country from which the external request was made with regard to an offence, and
   (c) there is reasonable cause to believe that the alleged offender named in the request has benefited from his criminal conduct.

(3) The second condition is that—
   (a) relevant property in England and Wales is identified in the external request;
   (b) proceedings for an offence have been started in the country from which the external request was made and not concluded, and
   (c) there is reasonable cause to believe that the defendant named in the request has benefited from his criminal conduct.

(4) In determining whether the conditions are satisfied and whether the request is an external request within the meaning of the Act, the Court must have regard to the definitions in subsections (1), (4) to (8) and (11) of section 447 of the Act.

(5) If the first condition is satisfied, references in this Chapter to the defendant are to the alleged offender.

### 8.— Restraint orders

(1) If either condition set out in article 7 is satisfied, the Crown Court may make an order ("a restraint order") prohibiting any specified person from dealing with relevant property which is identified in the external request and specified in the order.

(2) A restraint order may be made subject to exceptions, and an exception may in particular—
   (a) make provision for reasonable living expenses and reasonable legal expenses in connection with the proceedings seeking a restraint order or the registration of an external order;
   (b) make provision for the purpose of enabling any person to carry on any trade, business, profession or occupation;
   (c) be made subject to conditions.

(3) Paragraph (4) applies if—
   (a) a court makes a restraint order, and
   (b) the applicant for the order applies to the court to proceed under paragraph (4) (whether as part of the application for the restraint order or at any time afterwards).

(4) The court may make such order as it believes is appropriate for the purpose of ensuring that the restraint order is effective.

(5) A restraint order does not affect property for the time being subject to a charge under any of these provisions—
   (a) section 9 of the Drug Trafficking Offences Act 1986;
   (b) section 78 of the Criminal Justice Act 1988;
   (c) Article 14 of the Criminal Justice (Confiscation) (Northern Ireland) Order 1990;
   (d) section 27 of the Drug Trafficking Act 1994;
   (e) Article 32 of the Proceeds of Crime (Northern Ireland) Order 1996.

(6) Dealing with property includes removing it from England and Wales.

**9.— Application, discharge and variation of restraint orders**

(1) A restraint order—
  (a) may be made only on an application by the relevant Director;
  (b) may be made on an ex parte application to a judge in chambers.

(2) An application to discharge or vary a restraint order or an order under article 8(4) may be made to the Crown Court by—
  (a) the relevant Director;
  (b) any person affected by the order.

(3) Paragraphs (4) to (7) apply to an application under paragraph (2).

(4) The court—
  (a) may discharge the order;
  (b) may vary the order.

(5) If the condition in article 7 which was satisfied was that proceedings were started, the court must discharge the order if, at the conclusion of the proceedings, no external order has been made.

(6) If the condition in article 7 which was satisfied was that proceedings were started, the court must discharge the order if within a reasonable time an external order has not been registered under Chapter 2 of this Part.

(7) If the condition in article 7 which was satisfied was that an investigation was started, the court must discharge the order if within a reasonable time proceedings for the offence are not started.

**10.— Appeal to Court of Appeal about restraint orders**

(1) If on an application for a restraint order the Crown Court decides not to make one, the relevant Director may appeal to the Court of Appeal against the decision.

(2) If an application is made under article 9(2) in relation to a restraint order or an order under article 8(4), the following persons may appeal to the Court of Appeal in respect of the Crown Court's decision on the application—
  (a) the relevant Director;
  (b) any person affected by the order.

(3) On an appeal under paragraph (1) or (2) the Court of Appeal may—
  (a) confirm the decision, or
  (b) make such order as it believes is appropriate.

**11.— Appeal to House of Lords about restraint orders**

(1) An appeal lies to the House of Lords from a decision of the Court of Appeal on an appeal under article 10.

(2) An appeal under this article lies at the instance of any person who was a party to the proceedings before the Court of Appeal.

(3) On an appeal under this article the House of Lords may—
  (a) confirm the decision of the Court of Appeal, or
  (b) make such order as it believes is appropriate.

**12.— Seizure in pursuance of restraint order**

(1) If a restraint order is in force a constable or a relevant officer of Revenue and Customs may seize any property which is specified in it to prevent its removal from England and Wales.

(2) Property seized under paragraph (1) must be dealt with in accordance with the directions of the court which made the order.

**13.— Hearsay evidence in restraint proceedings**

(1) Evidence must not be excluded in restraint proceedings on the ground that it is hearsay (of whatever degree).

(2) Sections 2 to 4 of the Civil Evidence Act 1995 apply in relation to restraint proceedings as those sections apply in relation to civil proceedings.

(3) Restraint proceedings are proceedings—
  (a) for a restraint order;

      (b)  for the discharge or variation of a restraint order;

      (c)  on an appeal under article 10 or 11.

(4)  Hearsay is a statement which is made otherwise than by a person while giving oral evidence in the proceedings and which is rendered as evidence of the matters stated

(5)  Nothing in this article affects the admissibility of evidence which is admissible apart from this article.

### 14.— Supplementary (restraint orders)

(1)  The registration Acts—

      (a)  apply in relation to restraint orders as they apply in relation to orders which affect land and are made by the court for the purpose of enforcing judgments or recognisances;

      (b)  apply in relation to applications for restraint orders as they apply in relation to other pending land actions.

(2)  The registration Acts are—

      (a)  the Land Charges Act 1972;

      (b)  the Land Registration Act 2002.

(3)  But no notice may be entered in the register of title under the Land Registration Act 2002 in respect of a restraint order.

### 15.— Appointment of management receivers

(1)  Paragraph (2) applies if—

      (a)  the Crown Court makes a restraint order, and

      (b)  the relevant Director applies to the court to proceed under paragraph (2) (whether as part of the application for the restraint order or at any time afterwards).

(2)  The Crown Court may by order appoint a receiver in respect of any property which is specified in the restraint order.

### 16.— Powers of management receivers

(1)  If the court appoints a receiver under article 15 it may act under this article on the application of the relevant Director.

(2)  The court may by order confer on the receiver the following powers in relation to any property which is specified in the restraint order—

      (a)  power to take possession of the property;

      (b)  power to manage or otherwise deal with the property;

      (c)  power to start, carry on or defend any legal proceedings in respect of the property;

      (d)  power to realise so much of the property as is necessary to meet the receiver's remuneration and expenses.

(3)  The court may by order confer on the receiver power to enter any premises in England and Wales and to do any of the following—

      (a)  search for or inspect anything authorised by the court;

      (b)  make or obtain a copy, photograph or other record of anything so authorised;

      (c)  remove anything which the receiver is required or authorised to take possession of in pursuance of an order of the court.

(4)  The court may by order authorise the receiver to do any of the following for the purpose of the exercise of his functions—

      (a)  hold property;

      (b)  enter into contracts;

      (c)  sue and be sued;

      (d)  employ agents;

      (e)  execute powers of attorney, deeds or other instruments;

      (f)  take any other steps the court thinks appropriate.

(5)  The court may order any person who has possession of property which is specified in the restraint order to give possession of it to the receiver.

(6) The court—
    (a) may order a person holding an interest in property which is specified in the restraint order to make to the receiver such payment as the court specifies in respect of a beneficial interest held by the defendant or the recipient of a tainted gift;
    (b) may (on the payment being made) by order transfer, grant or extinguish any interest in the property.

(7) Paragraphs (2), (5) and (6) do not apply to property for the time being subject to a charge under any of these provisions—
    (a) section 9 of the Drug Trafficking Offences Act 1986;
    (b) section 78 of the Criminal Justice Act 1988;
    (c) Article 14 of the Criminal Justice (Confiscation) (Northern Ireland) Order 1990;
    (d) section 27 of the Drug Trafficking Act 1994;
    (e) Article 32 of the Proceeds of Crime (Northern Ireland) Order 1996.

(8) The court must not—
    (a) confer the power mentioned in paragraph (2)(b) or (d) in respect of property, or
    (b) exercise the power conferred on it by paragraph (6) in respect of property,
unless it gives persons holding interests in the property a reasonable opportunity to make representations to it.

[(8A) Paragraph (8), so far as relating to the power mentioned in paragraph (2)(b), does not apply to property which—
    (a) is perishable; or
    (b) ought to be disposed of before its value diminishes.]

(9) The court may order that a power conferred by an order under this article is subject to such conditions and exceptions as it specifies.

(10) Managing or otherwise dealing with property includes—
    (a) selling the property or any part of it or interest in it;
    (b) carrying on or arranging for another person to carry on any trade or business the assets of which are or are part of the property;
    (c) incurring capital expenditure in respect of the property.

### 17.— Restrictions relating to restraint orders

(1) Paragraphs (2) to (4) apply if a court makes a restraint order.

(2) No distress may be levied against any property which is specified in the order except with the leave of the Crown Court and subject to any terms the Crown Court may impose.

(3) If the order applies to a tenancy of any premises, no landlord or other person to whom rent is payable may exercise a right within paragraph (4) except with the leave of the Crown Court and subject to any terms the Crown Court may impose.

(4) A right is within this paragraph if it is a right of forfeiture by peaceable re-entry in relation to the premises in respect of any failure by the tenant to comply with any term or condition of the tenancy.

(5) If a court in which proceedings are pending in respect of any property is satisfied that a restraint order has been applied for or made in respect of the property, the court may either stay the proceedings or allow them to continue on any terms it thinks fit.

(6) Before exercising any power conferred by paragraph (5), the court must give an opportunity to be heard to—
    (a) the relevant Director, and
    (b) any receiver appointed in respect of the property under [article 15 or 27].

# Chapter 2
## External Orders

### 18.— Action on receipt of external order in connection with criminal convictions

(1) Except where paragraph (2) applies, the Secretary of State may refer an external order arising from a criminal conviction in the country from which the order was sent and concerning relevant property in England or Wales to—

    (a) [...]

    (b) the Director of Public Prosecutions;

    (c) the Director of Revenue and Customs Prosecutions,

to process it.

(2) This paragraph applies where it appears to the Secretary of State that—

    (a) the property or sum of money specified in the order was found, or was believed, to have been obtained as a result of, or in connection with, criminal conduct involving serious or complex fraud, and

    (b) the order concerns relevant property in England or Wales.

(3) Where paragraph (2) applies, the Secretary of State may refer the order to the Director of the Serious Fraud Office to process it.

(4) In this Chapter "the relevant Director" means the Director to whom an external order is referred under paragraph (1) or (3).

(5) Where an order concerns relevant property which is in Scotland or Northern Ireland as well as England or Wales, so much of the request as concerns such property shall be dealt with under Part 3 or 4, respectively.

### 19.— Authentication by the overseas court

(1) Paragraph (2) applies where an overseas court has authenticated its involvement in—

    (a) any judgment,

    (b) any order,

    (c) any other document concerned with such a judgment or order or proceedings relating to it.

(2) Where this paragraph applies, any statement in the judgment, order or document is admissible in evidence in proceedings under this Chapter.

### 20.— Applications to give effect to external orders

(1) An application may be made by the relevant Director to the Crown Court to give effect to an external order.

(2) No application to give effect to such an order may be made otherwise than under paragraph (1).

(3) An application under paragraph (1)—

    (a) shall include a request to appoint the relevant Director as the enforcement authority for the order;

    (b) may be made on an ex parte application to a judge in chambers.

### 21.— Conditions for Crown Court to give effect to external orders

(1) The Crown Court must decide to give effect to an external order by registering it where all of the following conditions are satisfied.

(2) The first condition is that the external order was made consequent on the conviction of the person named in the order and no appeal is outstanding in respect of that conviction.

(3) The second condition is that the external order is in force and no appeal is outstanding in respect of it.

(4) The third condition is that giving effect to the external order would not be incompatible with any of the Convention rights (within the meaning of the Human Rights Act 1998) of any person affected by it.

(5) The fourth condition applies only in respect of an external order which authorises the confiscation of property other than money that is specified in the order.

(6) That condition is that the specified property must not be subject to a charge under any of the following provisions—

(a) section 9 of the Drug Trafficking Offences Act 1986;

(b) section 78 of the Criminal Justice Act 1988;

(c) Article 14 of the Criminal Justice (Confiscation) (Northern Ireland) Order 1990;

(d) section 27 of the Drug Trafficking Act 1994;

(e) Article 32 of the Proceeds of Crime (Northern Ireland) Order 1996.

(7) In determining whether the order is an external order within the meaning of the Act, the Court must have regard to the definitions in subsections (2), (4), (5), (6), (8) and (10) of section 447 of the Act.

(8) In paragraph (3) "appeal" includes—

(a) any proceedings by way of discharging or setting aside the order; and

(b) an application for a new trial or stay of execution.

### 22.— Registration of external orders

(1) Where the Crown Court decides to give effect to an external order, it must—

(a) register the order in that court;

(b) provide for notice of the registration to be given to any person affected by it; and

(c) appoint the relevant Director as the enforcement authority for the order.

(2) Only an external order registered by the Crown Court may be implemented under this Chapter.

(3) The Crown Court may cancel the registration of the external order, or vary the property to which it applies, on an application by the relevant Director or any person affected by it if, or to the extent that, the court is of the opinion that any of the conditions in article 21 is not satisfied.

(4) The Crown Court must cancel the registration of the external order, on an application by the relevant Director or any person affected by it, if it appears to the court that the order has been satisfied—

(a) in the case of an order for the recovery of a sum of money specified in it, by payment of the amount due under it, or

(b) in the case of an order for the recovery of specified property, by the surrender of the property, or

(c) by any other means.

(5) Where the registration of an external order is cancelled or varied under paragraph (3) or (4), the Crown Court must provide for notice of this to be given to the relevant Director and any person affected by it.

### 23.— Appeal to Court of Appeal about external orders

(1) If on an application for the Crown Court to give effect to an external order by registering it, the court decides not to do so, the relevant Director may appeal to the Court of Appeal against the decision.

(2) If an application is made under article 22(3) or (4) in relation to the registration of an external order, the following persons may appeal to the Court of Appeal in respect of the Crown Court's decision on the application—

(a) the relevant Director;

(b) any person affected by the registration.

(3) On an appeal under paragraph (1) or (2) the Court of Appeal may—

(a) confirm or set aside the decision to register; or

(b) direct the Crown Court to register the external order (or so much of it as relates to property other than to which article 21(6) applies).

### 24.— Appeal to House of Lords about external orders

(1) An appeal lies to the House of Lords from a decision of the Court of Appeal on an appeal under article 23.

(2) An appeal under this article lies at the instance of any person who was a party to the proceedings before the Court of Appeal.

(3) On an appeal under this article the House of Lords may—

(a) confirm or set aside the decision of the Court of Appeal, or

(b) direct the Crown Court to register the external order (or so much of it as relates to property other than property to which article 21(6) applies).

## 25.— Sums in currency other than sterling

(1) This article applies where the external order which is registered under article 22 specifies a sum of money.

(2) If the sum of money which is specified is expressed in a currency other than sterling, the sum of money to be recovered is to be taken to be the sterling equivalent calculated in accordance with the rate of exchange prevailing at the end of the working day immediately preceding the day when the Crown Court registered the external order under article 22.

(3) The sterling equivalent must be calculated by the relevant Director.

(4) The notice referred to in article 22(1)(b) and (5) must set out the amount in sterling which is to be paid.

(5) In this article "working day" means any day other than—

(a) a Saturday or Sunday;

(b) Christmas Day;

(c) Good Friday;

(d) any day that is a bank holiday in England and Wales under the Banking and Financial Dealings Act 1971.

## 26.— Time for payment

(1) This article applies where the external order is for the recovery of a specified sum of money.

(2) Subject to paragraphs (3) to (6), the amount ordered to be paid under—

(a) an external order that has been registered under article 22, or

(b) where article 25(2) applies, the notice under article 22(1)(b),

must be paid on the date on which the notice under article 22(1)(b) is delivered to the person affected by it.

(3) Where there is an appeal under article 23 or 24 and a sum falls to be paid when the appeal has been determined or withdrawn, the duty to pay is delayed until the day on which the appeal is determined or withdrawn.

(4) If the person affected by an external order which has been registered shows that he needs time to pay the amount ordered to be paid, the Crown Court which registered the order may make an order allowing payment to be made in a specified period.

(5) The specified period—

(a) must start with the day on which the notice under article 22(1)(b) was delivered to the person affected by the order or the day referred to in paragraph (3), as the case may be, and

(b) must not exceed six months.

(6) If within the specified period the person affected by an external order applies to the Crown Court which registered the order for the period to be extended and the court believes that there are exceptional circumstances, it may make an order extending the period.

(7) The extended period—

(a) must start with the day on which the notice under article 22(1)(b) was delivered to the person affected by it or the day referred to in paragraph (3), as the case may be, and

(b) must not exceed 12 months.

(8) An order under paragraph (6)—

(a) may be made after the end of the specified period, but

(b) must not be made after the end of the extended period.

(9) The court must not make an order under paragraph (4) or (6) unless it gives the relevant Director an opportunity to make representations.

## 27.— Appointment of enforcement receivers

(1) This article applies if—

(a) an external order is registered,

(b) it is not satisfied, and

(c) in the case of an external order for the recovery of a specified sum of money, any period specified by order under article 26 has expired.

(2) On the application of the relevant Director […] the Crown Court may by order appoint a receiver in respect of—
(a) where the external order is for the recovery of a specified sum of money, realisable property;
(b) where the external order is for the recovery of specified property, that property.

**28.— Powers of enforcement receivers in respect of monetary external orders**

(1) If the court appoints a receiver under article 27 , it may act under this article on the application of the relevant Director […] where the external order is for the recovery of a specified sum of money.
(2) The court may by order confer on the receiver the following powers in relation to any realisable property—
(a) power to take possession of the property;
(b) power to manage or otherwise deal with the property;
(c) power to realise the property, in such manner as the court may specify;
(d) power to start, carry on or defend any legal proceedings in respect of the property.
(3) The court may by order confer on the receiver power to enter any premises in England and Wales and to do any of the following—
(a) search for or inspect anything authorised by the court;
(b) make or obtain a copy, photograph or other record, of anything so authorised;
(c) remove anything which the receiver is required or authorised to take possession of in pursuance of an order of the court.
(4) The court may by order authorise the receiver to do any of the following for the purposes of the exercise of his functions—
(a) hold property;
(b) enter into contracts;
(c) sue and be sued;
(d) employ agents;
(e) execute powers of attorney, deeds or other instruments;
(f) take any other steps the court thinks appropriate.
(5) The court may order any person who has possession of realisable property to give possession of it to the receiver.
(6) The court—
(a) may order a person holding an interest in realisable property to make to the receiver such payment as the court specifies in respect of a beneficial interest held by the defendant or the recipient of a tainted gift;
(b) may (on payment being made) by order transfer, grant or extinguish any interest in the property.
(7) Paragraphs (2), (5) and (6) do not apply to property for the time being subject to a charge under any of these provisions—
(a) section 9 of the Drug Trafficking Offences Act 1986;
(b) section 78 of the Criminal Justice Act 1988;
(c) Article 14 of the Criminal Justice (Confiscation) (Northern Ireland) Order 1990;
(d) section 27 of the Drug Trafficking Act 1994;
(e) Article 32 of the Proceeds of Crime (Northern Ireland) Order 1996.
(8) The court must not—
(a) confer the power mentioned in paragraph (2)(b) or (c) in respect of property, or
(b) exercise the power conferred on it by paragraph (6) in respect of property,
unless it gives persons holding interests in the property a reasonable opportunity to make representations to it.
[(8A) Paragraph (8), so far as relating to the power mentioned in paragraph (2)(b), does not apply to property which—
(a) is perishable; or
(b) ought to be disposed of before its value diminishes.]

(9) The court may order that a power conferred by an order under this article is subject to such conditions and exceptions as it specifies.

(10) Managing or otherwise dealing with property includes—

    (a) selling the property or any part of it or interest in it;

    (b) carrying on or arranging for another person to carry on any trade or business the assets of which are or are part of the property;

    (c) incurring capital expenditure in respect of the property.

**29.— Powers of enforcement receivers in respect of external orders for the recovery of specified property**

(1) If the court appoints a receiver under article 27 , it may act under this article on the application of the relevant Director […] where the external order is for the recovery of property specified in the order ("the specified property").

(2) The court may by order confer on the receiver the following powers in relation to the specified property—

    (a) power to take possession of the property;

    (b) power to manage or otherwise deal with the property;

    (c) power to realise the property, in such manner as the court may specify;

    (d) power to start, carry on or defend any legal proceedings in respect of the property.

(3) The court may by order confer on the receiver power to enter any premises in England and Wales and to do any of the following—

    (a) search for or inspect anything authorised by the court;

    (b) make or obtain a copy, photograph or other record of anything so authorised;

    (c) remove anything which the receiver is required or authorised to take possession of in pursuance of an order of the court.

(4) The court may by order authorise the receiver to do any of the following for the purposes of the exercise of his functions—

    (a) hold property;

    (b) enter into contracts;

    (c) sue and be sued;

    (d) employ agents;

    (e) execute powers of attorney, deeds or other instruments;

    (f) take any other steps the court thinks appropriate.

(5) The court may order any person who has possession of the specified property to give possession of it to the receiver.

(6) The court—

    (a) may order a person holding an interest in the specified property to make to the receiver such payment as the court specifies in respect of a beneficial interest held by the defendant or the recipient of a tainted gift;

    (b) may (on the payment being made) by order transfer, grant or extinguish any interest in the property.

(7) The court must not—

    (a) confer the power mentioned in paragraph (2)(b) or (c) in respect of property, or

    (b) exercise the power conferred on it by paragraph (6) in respect of property,

unless it gives persons holding interests in the property a reasonable opportunity to make representations to it.

[(7A) Paragraph (7), so far as relating to the power mentioned in paragraph (2)(b), does not apply to property which—

    (a) is perishable; or

    (b) ought to be disposed of before its value diminishes.]

(8) The court may order that a power conferred by an order under this article is subject to such conditions and exceptions as it specifies.

(9) Managing or otherwise dealing with property includes—

    (a) selling the property or any part of it or interest in it;

(b) carrying on or arranging for another person to carry on any trade or business the assets of which are or are part of the property;
(c) incurring capital expenditure in respect of the property.

30.— [...]

31.— [...]

32.— [...]

### 33.— Application of sums by enforcement receivers

(1) This article applies to sums which are in the hands of a receiver appointed under article 27 if they are—
(a) the proceeds of the realisation of property under article 28 or 29;
(b) where article 28 applies, sums (other than those mentioned in sub-paragraph (a)) in which the defendant holds an interest.

(2) The sums must be applied as follows—
(a) first, they must be applied in payment of such expenses incurred by a person acting as an insolvency practitioner as are payable under this paragraph by virtue of article 3;
(b) second, they must be applied in making any payments directed by the Crown Court;
(c) third, they must be applied on the defendant's behalf towards satisfaction of the external order.

(3) If the amount payable under the external order has been fully paid and any sums remain in the receiver's hands he must distribute them—
(a) among such persons who held (or hold) interests in the property concerned as the Crown Court directs; and
(b) in such proportions as it directs.

(4) Before making a direction under paragraph (3) the court must give persons who held (or hold) interests in the property concerned a reasonable opportunity to make representations to it.

(5) For the purposes of paragraphs (3) and (4) the property concerned is—
(a) the property represented by the proceeds mentioned in paragraph (1)(a);
(b) the sums mentioned in paragraph (1)(b).

(6) The receiver applies sums as mentioned in paragraph (2)(c) by paying them to the relevant Director on account of the amount payable under the order.

### 34.— Sums received by relevant Director

(1) This article applies if a relevant Director receives sums on account of the amount payable under a registered external order or the value of the property specified in the order.

(2) The relevant Director's receipt of the sums reduces the amount payable under the order, but he must apply the sums received as follows.

(3) First he must apply them in payment of such expenses incurred by a person acting as an insolvency practitioner as—
(a) are payable under this paragraph by virtue of article 3, but
(b) are not already paid under article 33(2)(a).

(4) He must next apply them—
(a) first, in payment of the remuneration and expenses of a receiver appointed under article 15 to the extent that they have not been met by virtue of the exercise by that receiver of a power conferred under article 16(2)(d);
(b) second, in payment of the remuneration and expenses of the receiver appointed under article 27.

(5) Any sums which remain after the relevant Director has made any payments required by the preceding provisions of this article must be paid into the Consolidated Fund.

(6) Paragraph (4) does not apply if the receiver is a member of the staff of the Crown Prosecution Service, the Serious Fraud Office or the Revenue and Customs Prosecution Office; and it is immaterial whether he is a permanent or temporary member or he is on secondment from elsewhere.

**35.—** [...]

**36.—** [...]

**37.— Satisfaction of external order**

(1) A registered external order is satisfied when no amount is due under it.
(2) Where such an order authorises the recovery of property specified in it, no further amount is due under the order when all of the specified property has been sold.

**38.— Restrictions relating to enforcement receivers**

(1) Paragraphs (2) to (4) apply if a court makes an order under article 27 appointing a receiver in respect of any realisable property or specified property.
(2) No distress may be levied against the property except with the leave of the Crown Court and subject to any terms the Crown Court may impose.
(3) If the receiver is appointed in respect of a tenancy of any premises, no landlord or other person to whom rent is payable may exercise a right within paragraph (4) except with the leave of the Crown Court and subject to any terms the Crown Court may impose.
(4) A right is within this paragraph if it is a right of forfeiture by peaceable re-entry in relation to the premises in respect of any failure by the tenant to comply with any term or condition of the tenancy.
(5) If a court in which proceedings are pending in respect of any property is satisfied that an order under article 27 appointing a receiver in respect of the property has been applied for or made, the court may either stay the proceedings or allow them to continue on any terms it thinks fit.
(6) Before exercising any power conferred by paragraph (5), the court must give an opportunity to be heard to—
   (a) the relevant Director [...] , and
   (b) the receiver (if the order under article 27 has been made).

**39.—** [...]

# Chapter 3
## Receivers and Procedure

**40. Protection of receiver appointed under articles 15, 27 and 30**

If a receiver appointed under [article 15 or 27] —
   (a) takes action in relation to property which is not realisable property or, as the case may be, the specified property,
   (b) would be entitled to take the action if it were realisable property or, as the case may be, the specified property, and
   (c) believes on reasonable grounds that he is entitled to take the action,
he is not liable to any person in respect of any loss or damage resulting from the action, except so far as the loss or damage is caused by his negligence.

**41.— Further applications by receivers**

(1) This article applies to a receiver appointed under [article 15 or 27].
(2) The receiver may apply to the Crown Court for an order giving directions as to the exercise of his powers.
(3) The following persons may apply to the Crown Court—
   (a) any person affected by action taken by the receiver;
   (b) any person who may be affected by action the receiver proposes to take.
(4) On an application under this article the court may make such order as it believes is appropriate.

**42.— Discharge and variation of receiver orders**

(1) The following persons may apply to the Crown Court to vary or discharge an order made under [article 15, 16 or 27 to 29]—
   (a) the receiver;

(b) the relevant Director;

(c) any person affected by the order.

(2) On an application under this article the court—

(a) may discharge the order;

(b) may vary the order.

(3) But in the case of an order under article 15 or 16—

(a) if the condition in article 7 which was satisfied was that proceedings were started, the court must discharge the order if at the conclusion of the proceedings no external order has been made;

(b) if the condition which was satisfied was that proceedings were started, the court must discharge the order if within a reasonable time an external order has not been registered under Chapter 2 of this Part;

(c) if the condition which was satisfied was that an investigation was started, the court must discharge the order if within a reasonable time proceedings for the offence are not started.

### 43.— Management receivers: discharge

(1) This article applies if—

(a) a receiver stands appointed under article 15 in respect of property which is identified in the restraint order (the management receiver), and

(b) the court appoints a receiver under article 27 [...] 24 .

(2) The court must order the management receiver to transfer to the other receiver all property held by the management receiver by virtue of the powers conferred on him by article 16.

(3) [...]

(4) Paragraph (2) does not apply to property which the management receiver holds by virtue of the exercise by him of his power under article 16(2)(d).

(5) If the management receiver complies with an order under paragraph (2) he is discharged—

(a) from his appointment under article 15;

(b) from any obligation under this Order arising from his appointment.

(6) If this article applies the court may make such a consequential or incidental order as it believes is appropriate.

### 44.— Appeal to Court of Appeal about receivers

(1) If on an application for an order under any of [articles 15, 16 or 27 to 29] the court decides not to make one, the person who applied for the order may appeal to the Court of Appeal against the decision.

(2) If the court makes an order under any of articles 15, 16, 27 to 29, 31 or 32, the following persons may appeal to the Court of Appeal in respect of the court's decision—

(a) the person who applied for the order;

(b) any person affected by the order.

(3) If on an application for an order under article 41 the court decides not to make one, the person who applied for the order may appeal to the Court of Appeal against the decision.

(4) If the court makes an order under article 41 the following persons may appeal to the Court of Appeal in respect of the court's decision—

(a) the person who applied for the order;

(b) any person affected by the order;

(c) the receiver.

(5) The following persons may appeal to the Court of Appeal against a decision of the court on an application under article 42—

(a) the person who applied for the order in respect of which the application was made [...] ;

(b) any person affected by the court's decision;

(c) the receiver.

(6) On an appeal under this article the Court of Appeal may—

(a) confirm the decision, or

(b) make such order as it believes is appropriate.

### 45.— Appeal to the House of Lords about receivers

(1) An appeal lies to the House of Lords from a decision of the Court of Appeal on an appeal under article 44.

(2) An appeal under this article lies at the instance of any person who was a party to the proceedings before the Court of Appeal.

(3) On an appeal under this article the House of Lords may—
   (a) confirm the decision of the Court Appeal, or
   (b) make such order as it believes is appropriate.

### 46.— Powers of court and receiver

(1) This article applies to—
   (a) the powers conferred on a court by this Part;
   (b) the powers of a receiver appointed under [article 15 or 27].

(2) The powers—
   (a) must be exercised with a view to the value for the time being of realisable property or specified property being made available (by the property's realisation) for satisfying an external order that has been or may be made against the defendant;
   (b) must be exercised, in a case where an external order has not been made, with a view to securing that there is no diminution in the value of the property identified in the external request;
   (c) must be exercised without taking account of any obligation of a defendant or a recipient of a tainted gift if the obligation conflicts with the object of satisfying any external order against the defendant that has been or may be registered under article 22;
   (d) may be exercised in respect of a debt owed by the Crown.

(3) Paragraph (2) has effect subject to the following rules—
   (a) the powers must be exercised with a view to allowing a person other than the defendant or a recipient of a tainted gift to retain or recover the value of any interest held by him;
   (b) in the case of realisable property or specified property held by a recipient of a tainted gift, the powers must be exercised with a view to realising no more than the value for the time being of the gift;
   (c) in a case where an external order has not been made against the defendant, property must not be sold if the court so orders under paragraph (4).

(4) If on an application by the defendant or the recipient of a tainted gift, the court decides that property cannot be replaced it may order that it must not be sold.

(5) An order under paragraph (4) may be revoked or varied.

### 47.— Procedure on appeal to Court of Appeal under Part 2

(1) An appeal to the Court of Appeal under this Part lies only with the leave of that Court.

(2) Subject to rules of court made under section 53(1) of the Supreme Court Act 1981 (distribution of business between civil and criminal divisions) the criminal division of the Court of Appeal is the division—
   (a) to which an appeal to that Court under this Part is to lie, and
   (b) which is to exercise that Court's jurisdiction under this Part.

(3) In relation to appeals to the Court of Appeal under this Part, the Secretary of State may make an order containing provision corresponding to any provision in the Criminal Appeal Act 1968, subject to any specified modifications.

(4) Subject to any rules of court, the costs of and incidental to all proceedings on an appeal to the criminal division of the Court of Appeal under article 10, 23 or 44 are in the discretion of the court.

(5) The court shall have full power to determine by whom and to what extent the costs are to be paid.

(6) In any proceedings mentioned in paragraph (4), the court may—
   (a) disallow, or
   (b) (as the case may be) order the legal or other representative concerned to meet,
   the whole of any wasted costs or such part of them as may be determined in accordance with rules of court.

(7) In paragraph (6) "wasted costs" means any costs incurred by a party—
   (a) as a result of any improper, unreasonable or negligent act or omission on the part of any legal or other representative or any employee of such a representative, or
   (b) which, in the light of any such act or omission occurring after they were incurred, the court considers it unreasonable to expect that party to pay.
(8) "Legal or other representative", in relation to a party to proceedings, means any person exercising a right of audience or right to conduct litigation on his behalf.

### 48.— Procedure on appeal to House of Lords under Part 2

(1) Section 33(3) of the Criminal Appeal Act 1968 (limitation on appeal from criminal division of the Court of Appeal) does not prevent an appeal to the House of Lords under this Part.
(2) In relation to appeals to the House of Lords under this Part, the Secretary of State may make an order containing provision corresponding to any provision in the Criminal Appeal Act 1968, subject to any specified modifications.

## Chapter 4
## Interpretation

### 49.— Property

(1) In this Part, "realisable property" means in a case where the external order specifies a sum of money, any free property held by the defendant or by the recipient of a tainted gift.
(2) "Free property" has the same meaning as in section 82 of the Act (free property).
(3) The rules in paragraphs (a) and (c) to (g) of section 84(2) of the Act (property: general provisions) apply in relation to property under this Order (in addition to section 447(4) to (6) of the Act (interpretation)) as they apply in relation to property under Part 2 of the Act.

### 50.— Tainted gifts

(1) In this Part, a gift is tainted if it was made by the defendant at any time after—
   (a) the date on which the offence to which the external order or external request relates was committed, or
   (b) if his criminal conduct consists of two or more such offences and they were committed on different dates, the date of the earliest.
(2) For the purposes of paragraph (1), an offence which is a continuing offence is committed on the first occasion when it is committed.
(3) A gift may be a tainted gift whether it was made before or after the coming into force of this Order.

### 51.— Gifts and their recipients

(1) In this Part, a defendant is to be treated as making a gift if he transfers property to another person for a consideration whose value is significantly less than the value of the property at the time of the transfer.
(2) If paragraph (1) applies, the property given is to be treated as such share in the property transferred as is represented by the fraction—
   (a) whose numerator is the difference between the two values mentioned in paragraph (1), and
   (b) whose denominator is the value of the property at the time of the transfer.
(3) In this Part references to a recipient of a tainted gift are to a person to whom the defendant has made the gift.

### 52.— Value: the basic rule

(1) Subject to article 53, this article applies where it is necessary under this Part to decide the value at any time of property then held by a person.
(2) Its value is the market value of the property at that time.
(3) But if at that time another person holds an interest in the property its value, in relation to the person mentioned in paragraph (1), is the market value of his interest at that time, ignoring any charging order under a provision listed in paragraph (4).

(4) Those provisions are—
    (a) section 9 of the Drug Trafficking Offences Act 1986;
    (b) section 78 of the Criminal Justice Act 1988;
    (c) Article 14 of the Criminal Justice (Confiscation) (Northern Ireland) Order 1990;
    (d) section 27 of the Drug Trafficking Act 1994;
    (e) Article 32 of the Proceeds of Crime (Northern Ireland) Order 1996.

### 53.— Value of tainted gifts

(1) The value at any time (the material time) of a tainted gift is the greater of the following—
    (a) the value (at time of the gift) of the property given, adjusted to take account of later changes in the value of money;
    (b) the value (at the material time) of the property found under paragraph (2).

(2) The property found under this paragraph is as follows—
    (a) if the recipient holds the property given, the property found under this paragraph is that property;
    (b) if the recipient holds no part of the property given, the property found under this paragraph is any property which directly or indirectly represents it in his hands;
    (c) if the recipient holds part of the property given, the property found under this paragraph is that part and any property which directly or indirectly represents the other part in his hands.

(3) The references in paragraph (1)(a) and (b) to the value are to the value found in accordance with article 52.

### 54. Meaning of "defendant"

In this Part "defendant"—
    (a) in relation to a restraint order means—
        (i) in a case in which the first condition in article 7 is satisfied, the alleged offender;
        (ii) in a case in which the second condition in article 7 is satisfied, the person against whom proceedings for an offence have been started in a country outside the United Kingdom (whether or not he has been convicted);
    (b) in relation to an external order, the person convicted of criminal conduct.

### 55. Other interpretation

In this Part—
    "relevant Director" has the meaning—
        (a) in the context of an external request, set out in article 6(4);
        (b) in the context of an external order, set out in article 18(4);

    "relevant property" means property which satisfies the test in section 447(7) of the Act;
    "specified property" means property specified in an external order (other than an order that specifies a sum of money).

PART 3

GIVING EFFECT IN SCOTLAND TO EXTERNAL REQUESTS IN CONNECTION
WITH CRIMINAL INVESTIGATIONS OR PROCEEDINGS AND TO EXTERNAL
ORDERS ARISING FROM SUCH PROCEEDINGS

## Chapter 1
## External Requests

### 56.— Action on receipt of external request in connection with criminal investigations or proceedings

(1) The Lord Advocate may make an application under article 59 where—
    (a) he receives an external request in relation to relevant property in Scotland; and
    (b) he considers that the request is likely to satisfy either of the conditions in article 57.

(2) The Lord Advocate may ask the overseas authority which made the request for such further information as may be necessary to determine whether the request is likely to satisfy either of the conditions in article 57.

(3) Where a request concerns relevant property which is in England and Wales or Northern Ireland as well as Scotland, so much of the request as concerns such property shall be dealt with under Part 2 or 4 respectively.

### 57.— Conditions for court to give effect to external request

(1) The court may exercise the powers conferred by article 58 if either of the following conditions is satisfied.

(2) The first condition is that—
  (a) relevant property within Scotland is identified in the external request;
  (b) a criminal investigation has been instituted in the country from which the external request was made with regard to an offence; and
  (c) there is reasonable cause to believe that the alleged offender named in the request has benefited from his criminal conduct.

(3) The second condition is that—
  (a) relevant property within Scotland is identified in the external request;
  (b) proceedings for an offence have been instituted in the country from which the external request was made and not concluded, and
  (c) there is reasonable cause to believe that the accused named in the request has benefited from his criminal conduct.

(4) In determining whether the conditions are satisfied and whether the request is an external request within the meaning of the Act, the court must have regard to the definitions in subsections (1), (4) to (8) and (11) of section 447 of the Act.

(5) If the first condition is satisfied references in this Chapter to the accused are to the alleged offender.

### 58.— Restraint orders

(1) If either condition set out in article 57 is satisfied, the court may make an order ("a restraint order") interdicting any specified person from dealing with relevant property which is identified in the external request and specified in the order.

(2) A restraint order may be made subject to exceptions, and an exception may in particular—
  (a) make provision for reasonable living expenses and reasonable legal expenses in connection with the proceedings seeking a restraint order or the registration of an external order;
  (b) make provision for the purpose of enabling any person to carry on any trade, business, profession or occupation;
  (c) be made subject to conditions.

(3) But an exception to a restraint order must not make provision for any legal expenses which—
  (a) relate to the criminal conduct mentioned in article 57(2), if the first condition is satisfied, or article 57(3), if the second condition is satisfied; and
  (b) are incurred by a person against whom proceedings for the offence have been instituted or by a recipient of a tainted gift.

(4) The court may make such order as it believes is appropriate for the purpose of ensuring that the restraint order is effective.

(5) A restraint order does not affect property for the time being subject to a charge under—
  (a) section 9 of the Drug Trafficking Offences Act 1986;
  (b) section 78 of the Criminal Justice Act 1988;
  (c) Article 14 of the Criminal Justice (Confiscation) (Northern Ireland) Order 1990;
  (d) section 27 of the Drug Trafficking Act 1994;
  (e) Article 32 of the Proceeds of Crime (Northern Ireland) Order 1996.

(6) Dealing with property includes removing the property from Scotland.

### 59.— Application, recall and variation

(1) A restraint order may be made on an ex parte application by the Lord Advocate, which may be heard in chambers.
(2) The Lord Advocate must intimate an order to every person affected by it.
(3) Paragraph (2) does not affect the time when the order becomes effective.
(4) The Lord Advocate and any person affected by the order may apply to the court to recall the order or to vary it and paragraphs (5) to (7) apply in such a case.
(5) If an application under paragraph (4) in relation to an order has been made but not determined, realisable property to which the order applies must not be realised.
(6) The court may—
  (a) recall the order;
  (b) vary the order.
(7) If the condition in article 57 which was satisfied was that proceedings were instituted, the court must recall the order if, at the conclusion of the proceedings, no external order has been made.
(8) If the condition in article 57 which was satisfied was that proceedings were instituted, the court must recall the order if within a reasonable time an external order has not been registered under Chapter 2 of this Part.
(9) If the condition in article 57 which was satisfied was that an investigation was instituted, the court must recall the order if within a reasonable time proceedings for the offence are not instituted.

### 60.— Appeals

(1) If on an application for a restraint order the court decides not to make one, the Lord Advocate may reclaim against the decision.
(2) The Lord Advocate and any person affected by the order may reclaim against the decision of the court on an application under article 59(4).

### 61.— Inhibition of property affected by order

(1) On the application of the Lord Advocate, the court may, in relation to the property mentioned in paragraph (2), grant warrant for inhibition against any person specified in a restraint order.
(2) That property is the heritable realisable property to which the restraint order applies (whether generally or such of it as is specified in the application).
(3) The warrant for inhibition—
  (a) has effect as if granted on the dependence of an action for debt by the Lord Advocate against the person and may be executed, recalled, loosed or restricted accordingly, and
  (b) has the effect of letters of inhibition and must forthwith be registered by the Lord Advocate in the Register of Inhibitions and Adjudications.
(4) Section 155 of the Titles to Land Consolidation (Scotland) Act 1868 (effective date of inhibition) applies in relation to an inhibition for which warrant is granted under paragraph (1) as it applies to an inhibition by separate letters or contained in a summons.
(5) The execution of an inhibition under this article in respect of property does not prejudice the exercise of an administrator's powers under or for the purposes of this Part in respect of that property.
(6) An inhibition executed under this article ceases to have effect when, or in so far as, the restraint order ceases to apply in respect of the property in relation to which the warrant for inhibition was granted.
(7) If an inhibition ceases to have effect to any extent by virtue of paragraph (6) the Lord Advocate must—
  (a) apply for the recall or, as the case may be, the restriction of the inhibition, and
  (b) ensure that the recall or restriction is reflected in the Register of Inhibitions and Adjudications.

### 62.— Arrestment of property affected by order

(1) On the application of the Lord Advocate the court may, in relation to moveable realisable property to which a restraint order applies (whether generally or such of it as is specified in the application), grant warrant for arrestment.
(2) Such a warrant for arrestment may be granted only if the property would be arrestable if the person entitled to it were a debtor.

(3) A warrant under paragraph (1) has effect as if granted on the dependence of an action for debt at the instance of the Lord Advocate against the person and may be executed, recalled, loosed or restricted accordingly.

(4) The execution of an arrestment under this article in respect of property does not prejudice the exercise of an administrator's powers under or for the purposes of this Part in respect of that property.

(5) An arrestment executed under this article ceases to have effect when, or in so far as, the restraint order ceases to apply in respect of the property in relation to which the warrant for arrestment was granted.

(6) If an arrestment ceases to have effect to any extent by virtue of paragraph (5) the Lord Advocate must apply to the court for an order recalling, or as the case may be, restricting the arrestment.

### 63.— Management administrators

(1) If the court makes a restraint order it may at any time, on the application of the Lord Advocate—
   (a) appoint an administrator to take possession of any realisable property to which the order applies and (in accordance with the court's directions) to manage or otherwise deal with the property;
   (b) order a person who has possession of property in respect of which an administrator is appointed to give him possession of it.

(2) An appointment of an administrator may be made subject to conditions or exceptions.

(3) Where the court makes an order under paragraph (1)(b), the clerk of court must notify the accused and any person subject to the order of the making of the order.

(4) Any dealing of the accused or any such person in relation to property to which the order applies is of no effect in a question with the administrator unless the accused or, as the case may be, that person had no knowledge of the administrator's appointment.

(5) The court—
   (a) may order a person holding an interest in realisable property to which the restraint order applies to make to the administrator such payment as the court specifies in respect of a beneficial interest held by the accused or the recipient of a tainted gift;
   (b) may (on the payment being made) by order transfer, grant or extinguish any interest in the property.

(6) The court must not—
   (a) confer the power mentioned in paragraph (1) to manage or otherwise deal with the property, or
   (b) exercise the power conferred on it by paragraph (5),
   unless it gives persons holding interests in the property a reasonable opportunity to make representations to it.

(7) The court may order that a power conferred by an order under this article is subject to such conditions and exceptions as it specifies.

(8) Managing or otherwise dealing with property includes—
   (a) selling the property or any part of it or interest in it;
   (b) carrying on or arranging for another person to carry on any trade or business the assets of which are or are part of the property;
   (c) incurring capital expenditure in respect of the property.

(9) Paragraphs (1)(b) and (5) do not apply to property for the time being subject to a charge under—
   (a) section 9 of the Drug Trafficking Offences Act 1986;
   (b) section 78 of the Criminal Justice Act 1988;
   (c) Article 14 of the Criminal Justice (Confiscation) (Northern Ireland) Order 1990;
   (d) section 27 of the Drug Trafficking Act 1994;
   (e) Article 32 of the Proceeds of Crime (Northern Ireland) Order 1996.

### 64.— Seizure in pursuance of restraint order

(1) If a restraint order is in force a constable or a relevant officer of Revenue and Customs may seize any realisable property to which it applies to prevent its removal from Scotland.

(2) Property seized under paragraph (1) must be dealt with in accordance with the directions of the court which made the order.

**65.— Restraint orders: restrictions on proceedings and remedies**

(1) While a restraint order has effect, the court may sist any action, execution or any legal process in respect of the property to which the order applies.

(2) If the court in which proceedings are pending in respect of any property is satisfied that a restraint order has been applied for or made in respect of the property, the court may either sist the proceedings or allow them to continue on any terms it thinks fit.

(3) Before exercising any power conferred by paragraph (2), the court must give an opportunity to be heard to—

(a) the Lord Advocate, and

(b) any administrator appointed in respect of the property under article 63.

## Chapter 2
## External Orders

**66.— Application to give effect to external orders**

(1) Where the Lord Advocate receives an external order arising from a criminal conviction and concerning relevant property in Scotland, he may make an ex parte application to the court to give effect to the order.

(2) No application to give effect to such an order may be made otherwise than under paragraph (1).

(3) An application under paragraph (1) may be heard in chambers.

(4) Where an order concerns relevant property which is in England and Wales or Northern Ireland as well as Scotland, so much of the request as concerns such property shall be dealt with under Part 2 or 4 respectively.

**67.— Authentication by an overseas court**

(1) Paragraph (2) applies where an overseas court has authenticated its involvement in—

(a) any judgement;

(b) any order;

(c) any other document concerned with such a judgement or order or proceedings relating to it.

(2) Where this paragraph applies, any statement in the judgement, order or document is admissible in evidence in proceedings under this Chapter.

**68.— Conditions for the court to give effect to external orders**

(1) The court must decide to give effect to an external order by registering it where all of the following conditions are satisfied.

(2) The first condition is that the external order was made consequent on the conviction of the person named in the order and no appeal is outstanding in respect of that conviction.

(3) The second condition is that the order is in force and no appeal is outstanding in respect of it.

(4) The third condition is that giving effect to the order would not be incompatible with any of the Convention rights (within the meaning of the Human Rights Act 1998 of any person affected by it.

(5) The fourth condition applies only in respect of an external order which authorises the confiscation of property other than money that is specified in the order.

(6) That condition is that the specified property must not be subject to a charge under—

(a) section 9 of the Drug Trafficking Offences Act 1986;

(b) section 78 of the Criminal Justice Act 1988;

(c) Article 14 of the Criminal Justice (Confiscation) (Northern Ireland) Order 1990;

(d) section 27 of the Drug Trafficking Act 1994; or

(e) Article 32 of the Proceeds of Crime (Northern Ireland) Order 1996.

(7) In determining whether the order is an external order within the meaning of the Act the court must have regard to the definitions in subsections (2), (4), (5), (6), (8) and (10) of section 447 of the Act.

(8) In paragraph (3) "appeal" includes—

(a) any proceedings by way of discharging or setting aside the order; and

(b) an application for a new trial or suspension or delay in execution of any penalty or sentence.

**69.— Registration of external orders**

(1) Where the court decides to give effect to an external order, it must—
   (a) register the order;
   (b) provide for notice of the registration to be given to any person affected by it; and
   (c) appoint a sheriff clerk for the purposes of the receipt of payment under articles 72(2) and 77(6).

(2) Only an external order registered by the court may be implemented under this Chapter.

(3) The court may cancel the registration of the external order, or vary the property to which it applies, on an application by the Lord Advocate or any person affected by it if, or to the extent that, the court is of the opinion that any of the conditions in article 68 is not satisfied.

(4) Notice of an application under paragraph (3) must be given—
   (a) in the case of an application by the Lord Advocate, to any person affected by the registration of the external order; and
   (b) in any other case, to the Lord Advocate and any other person affected by the registration of the external order.

(5) The court shall not cancel the registration of the external order or vary the property to which it applies under paragraph (3) unless it gives the Lord Advocate and any person affected by it the opportunity to make representations to it.

(6) The court must cancel the registration of the external order on an application by the Lord Advocate or any person affected by it, if it appears to the court that the order has been satisfied—
   (a) in the case of an order for the recovery of a sum of money specified in it, by payment of the amount due under it, or
   (b) in the case of an order for the recovery of specified property, by the surrender of the property, or
   (c) by any other means.

(7) Where the registration of an external order is cancelled or varied under paragraph (3) or (6), the court must provide for notice of this to be given to the Lord Advocate and any person affected by it.

**70.— Appeal about external orders**

(1) If on an application for the court to give effect to an external order by registering it, the court decides not to do so, the Lord Advocate may reclaim against the decision.

(2) If an application is made under article 69(3) or (6) in relation to the registration of an external order, the following persons may reclaim against the court's decision on the application—
   (a) the Lord Advocate;
   (b) any person affected by the registration.

(3) On a reclaiming motion under paragraph (1) or (2) the court may—
   (a) confirm or set aside the decision to register; or
   (b) direct the court to register the external order (or so much of it as relates to property other than that to which article 68(6) applies).

**71.— Sums in currency other than sterling**

(1) This article applies where the external order which is registered under article 69 specifies a sum of money.

(2) If the sum of money which is specified is expressed in a currency other than sterling, the sum of money to be recovered is to be taken to be the sterling equivalent calculated in accordance with the rate of exchange prevailing at the end of the working day immediately preceding the day when the court registered the external order under article 69.

(3) The sterling equivalent must be calculated by the Lord Advocate.

(4) The notice referred to in article 69(1)(b) and (7) must set out the amount in sterling which is to be paid.

(5) In this article "working day" means any day other than—
   (a) a Saturday or Sunday;
   (b) Christmas Day; or
   (c) Good Friday;
   (d) any day that is a bank holiday in Scotland under the Banking and Financial Dealings Act 1971.

**72.— Time for payment**

(1) This article applies where the external order is for the recovery of a specified sum of money.

(2) Subject to paragraphs (3) to (6), the amount ordered to be paid under—

    (a) an external order that has been registered under article 69; or

    (b) where article 71 applies, the notice under article 69(1)(b),

    must be paid to the appropriate clerk of court on the date on which the notice under article 69(1)(b) is delivered to the person affected by it.

(3) Where there is a reclaiming motion under article 70 the duty to pay is delayed until the day on which the reclaiming motion is determined or withdrawn.

(4) If the person affected by an external order which has been registered shows that he needs time to pay the amount ordered to be paid, the court may make an order allowing payment to be made within a specified period.

(5) The specified period—

    (a) must start with the day on which the notice under article 69(1)(b) was delivered to the person affected by the order or the day referred to in paragraph (3) as the case may be; and

    (b) must not exceed six months.

(6) If within the specified period the person affected by an external order applies to the court for the period to be extended and the court believes that there are exceptional circumstances, it may make an order extending the period.

(7) The extended period—

    (a) must start with the day on which the notice under article 69(1)(b) was delivered to the person affected by it; and

    (b) must not exceed 12 months.

(8) An order under paragraph (6)—

    (a) may be made after the end of the specified period; but

    (b) must not be made after the end of the extended period.

(9) The court must not make an order under paragraph (4) or (6) unless it gives the Lord Advocate an opportunity to make representations.

(10) The appropriate clerk of court is the sheriff clerk appointed under article 69(1).

**73.— Appointment of enforcement administrators**

(1) This article applies if—

    (a) an external order is registered;

    (b) it is not satisfied; and

    (c) in the case of an external order for the recovery of a specified sum of money, any period specified by order under article 72 has expired.

(2) On the application of the Lord Advocate the court may appoint an administrator in respect of—

    (a) where the external order is for the recovery of a specified sum of money, realisable property;

    (b) where the external order is for the recovery of specified property, that property.

**74.— Powers of enforcement administrators in respect of monetary external orders**

(1) If the court appoints an administrator under article 73, it may act under this article on the application of the Lord Advocate where the external order is for the recovery of a specified sum of money.

(2) The court may confer on the administrator the following powers in relation to any realisable property—

    (a) power to take possession of the property;

    (b) power to manage or otherwise deal with the property;

    (c) power to realise the property in such manner as the court may specify.

(3) The court may order any person who has possession of realisable property to give possession of it to the administrator.

(4) The clerk of court must notify the offender and any person subject to an order under paragraph (3) of the making of that order.

(5) Any dealing of the offender or any such persons in relation to property to which the order applies is of no effect in a question with the administrator unless the offender or, as the case may be, that person had no knowledge of the administrator's appointment.

(6) The court—

    (a) may order a person holding an interest in realisable property to make to the administrator such payment as the court specifies in respect of a beneficial interest held by the offender or the recipient of a tainted gift;

    (b) may (on payment being made) by order transfer, grant or extinguish any interest in the property.

(7) The court must not—

    (a) confer the power mentioned in paragraph (2)(b) or (c) in respect of the property, or

    (b) exer cise the power conferred on it by paragraph (6) in respect of the property,

unless it gives persons holding interests in the property a reasonable opportunity to make representations to it.

(8) Managing or otherwise dealing with property includes—

    (a) selling the property or any part of it or interest in it;

    (b) carrying on or arranging for another person to carry on any trade or business the assets of which are part of the property;

    (c) incurring capital expenditure in respect of the property.

(9) The court may order that a power conferred by an order under this article is subject to such conditions and exceptions as it specifies.

(10) Paragraph (2) does not apply to property for the time being subject to a charge under—

    (a) section 9 of the Drug Trafficking Offences Act 1986;

    (b) section 78 of the Criminal Justice Act 1988;

    (c) Article 14 of the Criminal Justice (Confiscation) (Northern Ireland) Order 1990;

    (d) section 27 of the Drug Trafficking Act 1994;

    (e) Article 32 of the Proceeds of Crime (Northern Ireland) Order 1996.

**75.— Powers of enforcement administrators in respect of external orders for the recovery of specified property**

(1) If the court appoints an administrator under article 73, it may act under this article on the application of the Lord Advocate where the external order is for the recovery of property specified in the order ("the specified property").

(2) The court may confer on the administrator the following powers in relation to the specified property—

    (a) power to take possession of the property;

    (b) power to manage or otherwise deal with the property;

    (c) power to realise the property in such manner as the court may specify.

(3) The court may order any person who has possession of the specified property to give possession of it to the administrator.

(4) The clerk of court must notify the offender and any person subject to an order under paragraph (3) of the making of that order.

(5) Any dealing of the offender or any such person in relation to property to which the order applies is of no effect in a question with the administrator unless the person had no knowledge of the administrator's appointment.

(6) The court—

    (a) may order a person holding an interest in the specified property to make to the administrator such payment as the court specifies in respect of a beneficial interest held by the offender or the recipient of a tainted gift;

    (b) may (on the payment being made) by order transfer, grant or extinguish any interest in the property.

(7) The court must not—

    (a) confer the power mentioned in paragraph (2)(b) or (c) in respect of the property; or

    (b) exercise the power conferred on it by paragraph (6) in respect of property,

unless it gives persons holding interests in the property a reasonable opportunity to make representations about it.

(8) The court may order that a power conferred by an order under this article is subject to such conditions and exceptions as it specifies.

(9) Managing or otherwise dealing with property includes—
   (a) selling the property or any part of it or interest in it;
   (b) carrying on or arranging for another person to carry on any trade or business the assets of which are or are part of the property;
   (c) incurring capital expenditure in respect of the property.

### 76.— Disposal of family home

(1) This article applies where the court confers power on the administrator under article 74(2) in respect of the offender's family home.

(2) Where this article applies, then, before the administrator disposes of any right or interest in the offender's family home he shall—
   (a) obtain the relevant consent; or
   (b) where he is unable to do so, apply to the court for authority to carry out the disposal.

(3) On an application being made to it under paragraph (2)(b), the court, after having regard to all the circumstances of the case including—
   (a) the needs and financial resources of the spouse of the offender;
   (b) the needs and financial resources of any child of the family;
   (c) the length of the period during which the family home has been used as a residence by any of the persons referred to in sub-paragraph (a) or (b),
   may refuse to grant the application or may postpone the granting of the application for such period (not exceeding 12 months) as it may consider reasonable in the circumstances or may grant the application subject to such conditions as it may prescribe.

(4) Paragraph (3) shall apply—
   (a) to an action for division and sale of the family home of the person concerned; or
   (b) to an action for the purpose of obtaining vacant possession of that home,
   brought by an administrator as it applies to an application under paragraph (2)(b) and, for the purposes of this paragraph, any reference in paragraph (3) to the granting of the application shall be construed as a reference to the granting of decree in the action.

(5) In this article—
   "family home", in relation to any offender means any property in which the offender has or had (whether alone or in common with any other person) a right or interest, being property which is occupied as a residence by the offender and his or her spouse or by the offender's spouse or former spouse (in any case with or without a child of the family) or by the offender with a child of the family;
   "child of the family" includes any child or grandchild of either the offender or his or her spouse or former spouse, and any person who has been treated by either the offender or his or her spouse or former spouse, whatever the age of such a child, grandchild or person may be; and
   "relevant consent" means in relation to the disposal of any right or interest in a family home—
      (a) in a case where the family home is occupied by the spouse or former spouse of the offender, the consent of the spouse or, as the case may be, of the former spouse, whether or not the family home is also occupied by the offender;
      (b) where sub-paragraph (a) does not apply, in a case where the family home is occupied by the offender with a child of the family, the consent of the offender.

### 77.— Application of sums by enforcement administrator

(1) This article applies to sums which are in the hands of an administrator appointed under article 73 if they are—
   (a) the proceeds of the realisation of property under article 74 or 75;
   (b) where article 74 applies, sums (other than those mentioned in sub-paragraph (a)) in which the offender holds an interest.

(2) The sums must be applied as follows—
  (a) first, they must be applied in payment of such expenses incurred by a person acting as an insolvency practitioner as are payable under this paragraph by virtue of article 3;
  (b) second, they must be applied in making any payments as directed by the court;
  (c) third, they must be applied on the offender's behalf towards satisfaction of the external order.

(3) If the amount payable under the external order has been fully paid and any sums remain in the administrator's hands he must distribute them—
  (a) among such persons who held (or hold) interests in the property concerned as the court directs; and
  (b) in such proportions as it directs.

(4) Before making a direction under paragraph (3) the court must give persons who held (or hold) interests in the property concerned a reasonable opportunity to make representations to it.

(5) For the purposes mentioned in paragraphs (3) and (4) the property concerned is—
  (a) the property represented by the proceeds mentioned in paragraph (1)(a);
  (b) the sums mentioned in paragraph (1)(b).

(6) The administrator applies sums as mentioned in paragraph (2)(c) by paying them to the appropriate clerk of court on account of the amount payable under the order.

(7) The appropriate clerk of court is the sheriff clerk appointed article 69(1).

### 78.— Sums received by clerk of court

(1) This section applies if a clerk of court receives sums on account of the amount payable under a registered external order or the value of the property specified in the order.

(2) The clerk of court's receipt of the sums reduces the amount payable under the order, but he must apply the sums received as follows.

(3) First he must apply them in payment of such expenses incurred by a person acting as an insolvency practitioner as—
  (a) are payable under this paragraph by virtue of article 3; but
  (b) are not already paid under article 77(2)(a).

(4) If the Lord Advocate has reimbursed the administrator in respect of remuneration or expenses under article 80 the clerk of court must next apply the sums in reimbursing the Lord Advocate.

(5) If the clerk of court received the sums under article 77 he must next apply them in payment of the administrator's remuneration and expenses.

(6) If any amount remains after the clerk of court makes any payments required by the preceding paragraphs of this article, the amount must be disposed of in accordance with section 211(5) of the Criminal Procedure (Scotland) Act 1995 as if it were a fine imposed in the High Court.

### 79.— Satisfaction of external order

(1) A registered external order is satisfied when no amount is due under it.

(2) Where such an order authorises the recovery of property specified in it, no amount is due under the order when all of the specified property has been sold.

## Chapter 3
## Administrators and Procedure

### 80.— Protection of administrator appointed under article 63 or 73

(1) If an administrator appointed under article 63 or 73—
  (a) takes action in relation to property which is not realisable property, or as the case may be, the specified property;
  (b) would be entitled to take the action if it were realisable property or, as the case may be, the specified property; and
  (c) believes on reasonable grounds that he is entitled to take action,
  he is not liable to any person in respect of any loss or damage resulting from the action, except so far as the loss or damage is caused by his negligence.

(2) Paragraph (3) applies if an administrator incurs expenses in the exercise of his functions at a time when—
  (a) an external order has not been registered; and
  (b) an external order has been registered but the administrator has recovered no money.

(3) As soon as practicable after they have been incurred the expenses must be reimbursed by the Lord Advocate.

(4) Paragraph (5) applies if—
  (a) an amount is due in respect of the administrator's remuneration and expenses; but
  (b) nothing (or not enough) is available to be applied in payment of them under article 78(4).

(5) The remuneration and expenses must be paid (to the extent of the shortfall) by the Lord Advocate.

### 81.— Protection of persons affected

(1) This paragraph applies where an administrator is appointed under article 63 or 73.

(2) The following persons may apply to the court—
  (a) any person affected by action taken by the administrator;
  (b) any person who may be affected by action the administrator proposes to take.

(3) On an application under this article the court may make such order as it thinks appropriate.

### 82.— Recall and variation of order

(1) The Lord Advocate, an administrator and any other person affected by an order made under article 63 or articles 73 to 75 may apply to the court to vary or recall the order.

(2) On an application under this article the court—
  (a) may vary the order;
  (b) may recall the order.

(3) But in the case of an order under article 63—
  (a) if the condition in article 57 which was satisfied was that proceedings were instituted, the court must recall the order if at the conclusion of the proceedings no external order (within the meaning of section 447(2) of the Act) has now been made;
  (b) if the condition which was satisfied was that an investigation was instituted the court must recall the order if within a reasonable period proceedings for the offence are not instituted.

### 83.— Management administrators: discharge

(1) This article applies if—
  (a) an administrator stands appointed under article 63 in respect of property which is identified in the restraint order (the management administrator); and
  (b) the court appoints an administrator under article 73.

(2) The Court must order the management administrator to transfer to the other administrator all property held by the management administrator by virtue of the powers conferred on him by article 63.

(3) If the management administrator complies with an order under paragraph (2) he is discharged—
  (a) from his appointment under article 63;
  (b) from any obligation under this Order arising from his appointment.

### 84.— Appeals

(1) If on an application for an order under article 63 or articles 73 to 75 the court decides not to make one, the Lord Advocate may reclaim in respect of the decision.

(2) If the court makes an order under article 63 or articles 73 to 75 the following persons may reclaim in respect of the court's decision—
  (a) the Lord Advocate;
  (b) any person affected by the Order.

(3) If on an application for an order under article 81 the court decides not to make one, the person who applied for the order may reclaim in respect of the decision.

(4) If the court makes an order under article 81, the following persons may reclaim in respect of the court's decision—
   (a) the person who applied for the order in respect of which the application was made;
   (b) any person affected by the court's decision;
   (c) the administrator.

(5) The following persons may reclaim in respect of a decision of the court on an application under article 82—
   (a) the person who applied for the order in respect of which the application was made;
   (b) any person affected by the court's decision;
   (c) the administrator.

(6) On a reclaiming motion under this article the court may—
   (a) confirm the decision;
   (b) make such order as it believes is appropriate.

### 85. Administrators: further provision

Schedule 1 which makes further provision about administrators appointed under articles 63 and 73 has effect.

### 86.— Administrators: restrictions on proceedings and remedies

(1) Where an administrator is appointed under article 73, the court may sist any action, execution or other legal process in respect of the property to which the order appointing the administrator relates.

(2) If a court (whether the Court of Session or any other court) in which proceedings are pending, in respect of any property is satisfied that an application has been made for the appointment of an administrator or that an administrator has been appointed in relation to that property, the court may either sist the proceedings or allow them to continue on any terms it thinks fit.

(3) Before exercising any power conferred by paragraph (2) the court must give an opportunity to be heard to—
   (a) the Lord Advocate;
   (b) if appointed, the administrator.

## Chapter 4
## Interpretation

### 87.— Property

(1) In this Part, "realisable property" means in a case where an external order specifies a sum of money, any free property held by the accused or offender, as the case may be, or the recipient of a tainted gift.

(2) The rules in paragraphs (a) and (c) to (g) of section 150(2) of the Act (property: general provisions) apply in relation to property under this Order (in addition to section 447(4) to (6)) of the Act (interpretation) as they apply in relation to property under Part 3 of the Act.

### 88.— Tainted gifts and their recipients

(1) In this Part, a gift is tainted if it was made by the accused or offender, as the case may be, at any time after—
   (a) the date on which the offence to which the external order or external request relates was committed, or
   (b) if his criminal conduct consists of two or more such offences and they were committed on different dates, the date of the earliest.

(2) For the purposes of paragraph (1), an offence which is a continuing offence is committed on the first occasion when it is committed.

(3) A gift may be a tainted gift whether it was made before or after the coming into force of this Order.

(4) In this Part, an accused or offender, as the case may be, is to be treated as making a gift if he transfers property to another person for a consideration whose value is significantly less than the value of the property at the time of the transfer.

(5) If paragraph (4) applies, the property given is to be treated as such share in the property transferred as is represented by the fraction—
    (a) whose numerator is the difference between the two values mentioned in paragraph (4), and
    (b) whose denominator is the value of the property at the time of the transfer.

(6) In this Part, references to a recipient of a tainted gift are to a person to whom the accused or offender, as the case may be, has (whether directly or indirectly) made the gift.

### 89.— Value: the basic rule

(1) Subject to article 90, this article applies where it is necessary under this Part to decide the value at any time of property then held by that person.
(2) Its value is the market value of the property at that time.
(3) But if at that time another person holds an interest in the property its value, in relation to the person mentioned in paragraph (1) is the market value of his interest at that time ignoring any charging order under a provision listed in paragraph (4).
(4) Those provisions are—
    (a) section 9 of the Drug Trafficking Offences Act 1986;
    (b) section 78 of the Criminal Justice Act 1988;
    (c) Article 14 of the Criminal Justice (Confiscation) (Northern Ireland) Order 1990;
    (d) Section 27 of the Drug Trafficking Act 1994
    (e) Article 32 of the Proceeds of Crime (Northern Ireland) Order 1996.

### 90.— Value of tainted gifts

(1) The value at any time (the material time) of a tainted gift is the greater of the following—
    (a) the value (at the time of the gift) of the property gives, adjusted to take account of later changes in the value of money;
    (b) the value (at the material time) of the property found under paragraph (2).

(2) The property found under this paragraph is as follows—
    (a) if the recipient holds the property given, that property;
    (b) if the recipient holds no part of the property given, any property which directly or indirectly represents it in his hands;
    (c) if the recipient holds part of the property given, that part and any property which directly or indirectly represents the other part in his hands.

(3) The references in paragraph (1)(a) and (b) to the value are to the value found in accordance with article 89.

### 91. Meaning of "accused" and "offender"

In this Part—
    "accused", in relation to a restraint order means—
    (a) in a case in which the first condition in article 57 is satisfied, the alleged offender;
    (b) in a case in which the second condition in article 57 is satisfied, the person against whom proceedings for an offence have been instituted in a country outside the United Kingdom (whether or not he has been convicted);
    "offender", in relation to an external order means the person convicted of criminal conduct.

### 92. Other interpretation

In this Part—
    "court" means the Court of Session;
    "relevant property" means property which satisfies the test set out in section 447(7) of the Act;
    "specified property" means that property specified in the external request (other than a request that specifies a sum of money).

PART 4

GIVING EFFECT IN NORTHERN IRELAND TO EXTERNAL REQUESTS
IN CONNECTION WITH CRIMINAL INVESTIGATIONS OR PROCEEDINGS
AND TO EXTERNAL ORDERS ARISING FROM SUCH PROCEEDINGS

## Chapter 5
## External Requests

**93.— Action on receipt of external request in connection with criminal investigations or proceedings**

(1) Except where paragraph (2) applies, the Secretary of State may refer an external request in connection with criminal investigations or proceedings in the country from which the request was made and concerning relevant property in Northern Ireland to—
   (a) [...]
   (b) the Director of Public Prosecutions for Northern Ireland;
   to process it.

(2) This paragraph applies where it appears to the Secretary of State that the request—
   (a) is made in connection with criminal investigations or proceedings which relate to an offence involving serious or complex fraud, and
   (b) concerns relevant property in Northern Ireland.

(3) Where paragraph (2) applies, the Secretary of State may refer the request to the Director of the Serious Fraud Office to process it.

(4) In this Chapter "the relevant Director" means the Director to whom an external request is referred under paragraph (1) or (3).

(5) The relevant Director may ask the overseas authority which made the request for such further information as may be necessary to determine whether the request is likely to satisfy either of the conditions in article 94.

(6) A request under paragraph (5) may include a request for statements which may be used as evidence.

(7) Where a request concerns relevant property which is in England, Wales or Scotland as well as Northern Ireland, so much of the request as concerns such property shall be dealt with under Part 2 or 3 respectively.

**94.— Conditions for High Court to give effect to external request**

(1) The High Court may exercise the powers conferred by article 95 if either of the following conditions is satisfied.

(2) The first condition is that—
   (a) relevant property in Northern Ireland is identified in the external request;
   (b) a criminal investigation has been started in the country from which the external request was made with regard to an offence, and
   (c) there is reasonable cause to believe that the alleged offender named in the request has benefited from his criminal conduct.

(3) The second condition is that—
   (a) relevant property in Northern Ireland is identified in the external request;
   (b) proceedings for an offence have been started in the country from which the external request was made and not concluded, and
   (c) there is reasonable cause to believe that the defendant named in the request has benefited from his criminal conduct.

(4) In determining whether the conditions are satisfied and whether the request is an external request within the meaning of the Act, the court must have regard to the definitions in subsections (1), (4) to (8) and (11) of section 447 of the Act.

(5) If the first condition is satisfied, references in this Chapter to the defendant are to the alleged offender.

### 95.— Restraint orders

(1) If either condition set out in article 94 is satisfied, the High Court may make an order ("a restraint order") prohibiting any specified person from dealing with relevant property which is identified in the external request and specified in the order.

(2) A restraint order may be made subject to exceptions, and an exception may in particular—
  (a) make provision for reasonable living expenses and reasonable legal expenses in connection with the proceedings seeking a restraint order or the registration of an external order;
  (b) make provision for the purpose of enabling any person to carry on any trade, business, profession or occupation;
  (c) be made subject to conditions.

(3) Paragraph (4) applies if—
  (a) a court makes a restraint order, and
  (b) the applicant for the order applies to the court to proceed under paragraph (4) (whether as part of the application for the restraint order or at any time afterwards).

(4) The court may make such order as it believes is appropriate for the purpose of ensuring that the restraint order is effective.

(5) A restraint order does not affect property for the time being subject to a charge under any of these provisions—
  (a) section 9 of the Drug Trafficking Offences Act 1986;
  (b) section 78 of the Criminal Justice Act 1988;
  (c) Article 14 of the Criminal Justice (Confiscation) (Northern Ireland) Order 1990;
  (d) section 27 of the Drug Trafficking Act 1994;
  (e) Article 32 of the Proceeds of Crime (Northern Ireland) Order 1996.

(6) Dealing with property includes removing it from Northern Ireland.

### 96.— Application, discharge and variation of restraint orders

(1) A restraint order—
  (a) may be made only on an application by the relevant Director;
  (b) may be made on an ex parte application to a judge in chambers.

(2) An application to discharge or vary a restraint order or an order under article 95(4) may be made to the High Court by—
  (a) the relevant Director;
  (b) any person affected by the order.

(3) Paragraphs (4) to (7) apply to an application under paragraph (2).

(4) The court—
  (a) may discharge the order;
  (b) may vary the order.

(5) If the condition in article 94 which was satisfied was that proceedings were started, the court must discharge the order if, at the conclusion of the proceedings, no external order has been made.

(6) If the condition in article 94 which was satisfied was that proceedings were started, the court must discharge the order if within a reasonable time an external order has not been registered under Chapter 2 of this Part.

(7) If the condition in article 94 which was satisfied was that an investigation was started, the court must discharge the order if within a reasonable time proceedings for the offence are not started.

### 97.— Appeal to Court of Appeal about restraint orders

(1) If on an application for a restraint order the High Court decides not to make one, the relevant Director may appeal to the Court of Appeal against the decision.

(2) If an application is made under article 96(2) in relation to a restraint order or an order under article 95(4), the following persons may appeal to the Court of Appeal in respect of the High Court's decision on the application—
  (a) the relevant Director;
  (b) any person affected by the order.

(3) On an appeal under paragraph (1) or (2) the Court of Appeal may—
   (a) confirm the decision, or
   (b) make such order as it believes is appropriate.

### 98.— Appeal to House of Lords about restraint orders

(1) An appeal lies to the House of Lords from a decision of the Court of Appeal on an appeal under article 97.
(2) An appeal under this article lies at the instance of any person who was a party to the proceedings before the Court of Appeal.
(3) On an appeal under this article the House of Lords may—
   (a) confirm the decision of the Court of Appeal, or
   (b) make such order as it believes is appropriate.

### 99.— Seizure in pursuance of restraint order

(1) If a restraint order is in force a constable may seize any property which is specified in it to prevent its removal from Northern Ireland.
(2) Property seized under paragraph (1) must be dealt with in accordance with the directions of the court which made the order.

### 100.— Supplementary (restraint orders)

(1) The person applying for a restraint order must be treated for the purposes of section 66 of the Land Registration Act (Northern Ireland) 1970 (cautions) as a person interested in relation to any registered land to which—
   (a) the application relates, or
   (b) a restraint order made in pursuance of the application relates.
(2) Upon being served with a copy of a restraint order, the Registrar shall, in respect of any registered land to which a restraint order or an application for a restraint order relates, make an entry inhibiting any dealing with the land without the consent of the High Court.
(3) Subsections (2) and (4) of section 67 of the Land Registration Act (Northern Ireland) 1970 (inhibitions) shall apply to an entry made under subsection (2) as they apply to an entry made on the application of any person interested in the registered land under subsection (1) of that section.
(4) Where a restraint order has been protected by an entry registered under the Land Registration Act (Northern Ireland) 1970 or the Registration of Deeds Acts, an order discharging the restraint order may require that the entry be vacated.
(5) In this article—
"Registrar" and "entry" have the same meanings as in the Land Registration Act (Northern Ireland) 1970; and
"Registration Deeds Acts" has the meaning given by section 46(2) of the Interpretation Act (Northern Ireland) 1954.

### 101.— Appointment of management receivers

(1) Paragraph (2) applies if—
   (a) the High Court makes a restraint order, and
   (b) the relevant Director applies to the court to proceed under paragraph (2) (whether as part of the application for the restraint order or at any time afterwards).
(2) The High Court may by order appoint a receiver in respect of any property which is specified in the restraint order.

### 102.— Powers of management receivers

(1) If the court appoints a receiver under article 101 it may act under this article on the application of the relevant Director.
(2) The court may by order confer on the receiver the following powers in relation to any property which is specified in the restraint order—
   (a) power to take possession of the property;
   (b) power to manage or otherwise deal with the property;

    (c) power to start, carry on or defend any legal proceedings in respect of the property;

    (d) power to realise so much of the property as is necessary to meet the receiver's remuneration and expenses.

(3) The court may by order confer on the receiver power to enter any premises in Northern Ireland and to do any of the following—

    (a) search for or inspect anything authorised by the court;

    (b) make or obtain a copy, photograph or other record of anything so authorised;

    (c) remove anything which the receiver is required or authorised to take possession of in pursuance of an order of the court.

(4) The court may by order authorise the receiver to do any of the following for the purpose of the exercise of his functions—

    (a) hold property;

    (b) enter into contracts;

    (c) sue and be sued;

    (d) employ agents;

    (e) execute powers of attorney, deeds or other instruments;

    (f) take any other steps the court thinks appropriate.

(5) The court may order any person who has possession of property which is specified in the restraint order to give possession of it to the receiver.

(6) The court—

    (a) may order a person holding an interest in property which is specified in the restraint order to make to the receiver such payment as the court specifies in respect of a beneficial interest held by the defendant or the recipient of a tainted gift;

    (b) may (on the payment being made) by order transfer, grant or extinguish any interest in the property.

(7) Paragraphs (2), (5) and (6) do not apply to property for the time being subject to a charge under any of these provisions—

    (a) section 9 of the Drug Trafficking Offences Act 1986;

    (b) section 78 of the Criminal Justice Act 1988;

    (c) Article 14 of the Criminal Justice (Confiscation) (Northern Ireland) Order 1990;

    (d) section 27 of the Drug Trafficking Act 1994;

    (e) Article 32 of the Proceeds of Crime (Northern Ireland) Order 1996.

(8) The court must not—

    (a) confer the power mentioned in paragraph (2)(b) or (d) in respect of property, or

    (b) exercise the power conferred on it by paragraph (6) in respect of property,

    unless it gives persons holding interests in the property a reasonable opportunity to make representations to it.

[(8A) Paragraph (8), so far as relating to the power mentioned in paragraph (2)(b), does not apply to property which—

    (a) is perishable; or

    (b) ought to be disposed of before its value diminishes.]

(9) The court may order that a power conferred by an order under this article is subject to such conditions and exceptions as it specifies.

(10) Managing or otherwise dealing with property includes—

    (a) selling the property or any part of it or interest in it;

    (b) carrying on or arranging for another person to carry on any trade or business the assets of which are or are part of the property;

    (c) incurring capital expenditure in respect of the property.

### 103.— Restrictions relating to restraint orders

(1) Paragraphs (2) and (3) apply if a court makes a restraint order.

(2) If the order applies to a tenancy of any premises, no landlord or other person to whom rent is payable may exercise a right within paragraph (3) except with the leave of the High Court and subject to any terms the High Court may impose.

(3) A right is within this paragraph if it is a right of forfeiture by peaceable re-entry in relation to the premises in respect of any failure by the tenant to comply with any term or condition of the tenancy.

(4) If a court in which proceedings are pending in respect of any property is satisfied that a restraint order has been applied for or made in respect of the property, the court may either stay the proceedings or allow them to continue on any terms it thinks fit.

(5) Before exercising any power conferred by paragraph (4), the court must give an opportunity to be heard to—
    (a) the relevant Director, and
    (b) any receiver appointed in respect of the property under [article 101 or 113].

## Chapter 2
## External Orders

### 104.— Action on receipt of external order in connection with criminal convictions

(1) Except where paragraph (2) applies, the Secretary of State may refer an external order arising from a criminal conviction in the country from which the order was sent and concerning relevant property in Northern Ireland to—
    (a) [...]
    (b) the Director of Public Prosecutions for Northern Ireland;
to process it.

(2) This paragraph applies where it appears to the Secretary of State that—
    (a) the property or sum of money specified in the order was found, or was believed, to have been obtained as a result of, or in connection with, criminal conduct involving serious or complex fraud, and
    (b) the order concerns relevant property in Northern Ireland.

(3) Where paragraph (2) applies, the Secretary of State may refer the order to the Director of the Serious Fraud Office to process it.

(4) In this Chapter "the relevant Director" means the Director to whom an external order is referred under paragraph (1) or (3).

(5) Where an order concerns relevant property which is in England, Wales or Scotland as well as Northern Ireland, so much of the request as concerns such property shall be dealt with under Part 2 or 3, respectively.

### 105.— Authentication by the overseas court

(1) Paragraph (2) applies where an overseas court has authenticated its involvement in—
    (a) any judgment,
    (b) any order,
    (c) any other document concerned with such a judgment or order or proceedings relating to it.

(2) Where this paragraph applies, any statement in the judgment, order or document is admissible in evidence in proceedings under this Chapter.

### 106.— Applications to give effect to external orders

(1) An application may be made by the relevant Director to the Crown Court to give effect to an external order.

(2) No application to give effect to such an order may be made otherwise than under paragraph (1).

(3) An application under paragraph (1)—
    (a) shall include a request to appoint the relevant Director as the enforcement authority for the order;
    (b) may be made on an ex parte application to a judge in chambers.

**107.— Conditions for Crown Court to give effect to external orders**

(1) The Crown Court must decide to give effect to an external order by registering it where all of the following conditions are satisfied.

(2) The first condition is that the external order was made consequent on the conviction of the person named in the order and no appeal is outstanding in respect of that conviction.

(3) The second condition is that the external order is in force and no appeal is outstanding in respect of it.

(4) The third condition is that giving effect to the external order would not be incompatible with any of the Convention rights (within the meaning of the Human Rights Act 1998) of any person affected by it.

(5) The fourth condition applies only in respect of an external order which authorises the confiscation of property other than money that is specified in the order.

(6) That condition is that the specified property must not be subject to a charge under any of the following provisions—
   (a) section 9 of the Drug Trafficking Offences Act 1986;
   (b) section 78 of the Criminal Justice Act 1988;
   (c) Article 14 of the Criminal Justice (Confiscation) (Northern Ireland) Order 1990;
   (d) section 27 of the Drug Trafficking Act 1994;
   (e) Article 32 of the Proceeds of Crime (Northern Ireland) Order 1996.

(7) In determining whether the order is an external order within the meaning of the Act, the Court must have regard to the definitions in subsections (2), (4), (5), (6), (8) and (10) of section 447 of the Act.

(8) In paragraph (3) "appeal" includes—
   (a) any proceedings by way of discharging or setting aside the order; and
   (b) an application for a new trial or stay of execution.

**108.— Registration of external orders**

(1) Where the Crown Court decides to give effect to an external order, it must—
   (a) register the order in that court;
   (b) provide for notice of the registration to be given to any person affected by it; and
   (c) appoint the relevant Director as the enforcement authority for the order.

(2) Only an external order registered by the Crown Court may be implemented under this Chapter.

(3) The Crown Court may cancel the registration of the external order, or vary the property to which it applies, on an application by the relevant Director or any person affected by it if, or to the extent that, the court is of the opinion that any of the conditions in article 107 is not satisfied.

(4) The Crown Court must cancel the registration of the external order, on an application by the relevant Director or any person affected by it, if it appears to the court that the order has been satisfied—
   (a) in the case of an order for the recovery of a sum of money specified in it, by payment of the amount due under it, or
   (b) in the case of an order for the recovery of specified property, by the surrender of the property, or
   (c) by any other means.

(5) Where the registration of an external order is cancelled or varied under paragraph (3) or (4), the Crown Court must provide for notice of this to be given to the relevant Director and any person affected by it.

**109.— Appeal to Court of Appeal about external orders**

(1) If on an application for the Crown Court to give effect to an external order by registering it, the court decides not to do so, the relevant Director may appeal to the Court of Appeal against the decision.

(2) If an application is made under article 108(3) in relation to the registration of an external order, the following persons may appeal to the Court of Appeal in respect of the Crown Court's decision on the application—
   (a) the relevant Director;
   (b) any person affected by the registration.

(3) On an appeal under paragraph (1) or (2) the Court of Appeal may—
   (a) confirm the decision or set aside the decision to register; or

(b) direct the Crown Court to register the external order (or so much of it as relates to property other than that to which article 107(6) applies).

## 110.— Appeal to House of Lords about external orders

(1) An appeal lies to the House of Lords from a decision of the Court of Appeal on an appeal under article 109.
(2) An appeal under this article lies at the instance of any person who was a party to the proceedings before the Court of Appeal.
(3) On an appeal under this article the House of Lords may—
　(a) confirm or set aside the decision of the Court of Appeal, or
　(b) direct the Crown Court to register the external order (or so much of it as relates to property other than that to which article 107(6) applies).

## 111.— Sums in currency other than sterling

(1) This article applies where the external order which is registered under article 108 specifies a sum of money.
(2) If the sum of money which is specified is expressed in a currency other than sterling, the sum of money to be recovered is to be taken to be the sterling equivalent calculated in accordance with the rate of exchange prevailing at the end of the working day immediately preceding the day when the Crown Court registered the external order under article 108.
(3) The sterling equivalent must be calculated by the relevant Director.
(4) The notice referred to in article 108(1)(b) and (5) must set out the amount in sterling which is to be paid.
(5) In this article "working day" means any day other than—
　(a) a Saturday or Sunday;
　(b) Christmas Day;
　(c) Good Friday;
　(d) any day that is a bank holiday in Northern Ireland under the Banking and Financial Dealings Act 1971.

## 112.— Time for payment

(1) This article applies where the external order is for the recovery of a specified sum of money.
(2) Subject to paragraphs (3) to (6), the amount ordered to be paid under—
　(a) an external order that has been registered under article 108, or
　(b) where article 111(2) applies, the notice under article 108(1)(b),
　must be paid on the date on which the notice under article 108(1)(b) is delivered to the person affected by it.
(3) Where there is an appeal under article 109 or 110 and a sum falls to be paid when the appeal has been determined or withdrawn, the duty to pay is delayed until the day on which the appeal is determined or withdrawn.
(4) If the person affected by an external order which has been registered shows that he needs time to pay the amount ordered to be paid, the Crown Court which registered the order may make an order allowing payment to be made in a specified period.
(5) The specified period—
　(a) must start with the day on which the notice under 108(1)(b) was delivered to the person affected by the order or the day referred to in paragraph (3), as the case may be, and
　(b) must not exceed six months.
(6) If within the specified period the person affected by an external order applies to the Crown Court which registered the order for the period to be extended and the court believes that there are exceptional circumstances, it may make an order extending the period.
(7) The extended period—
　(a) must start with the day on which the notice under article 108(1)(b) was delivered to the person affected by it or the day referred to in paragraph (3), as the case may be, and
　(b) must not exceed 12 months.

(8) An order under paragraph (6)—
    (a) may be made after the end of the specified period, but
    (b) must not be made after the end of the extended period.

(9) The court must not make an order under paragraph (4) or (6) unless it gives the relevant Director an opportunity to make representations.

### 113.— Appointment of enforcement receivers

(1) This article applies if—
    (a) an external order is registered,
    (b) it is not satisfied, and
    (c) in the case of an external order for the recovery of a specified sum of money, any period specified by order under article 112 has expired.

(2) On the application of the relevant Director […] the Crown Court may by order appoint a receiver in respect of—
    (a) where the external order is for the recovery of a specified sum of money, realisable property;
    (b) where the external order is for the recovery of specified property, that property.

### 114.— Powers of enforcement receivers in respect of monetary external orders

(1) If the court appoints a receiver under article 113 , it may act under this article on the application of the relevant Director […] where the external order is for the recovery of a specified sum of money.

(2) The court may by order confer on the receiver the following powers in relation to any realisable property—
    (a) power to take possession of the property;
    (b) power to manage or otherwise deal with the property;
    (c) power to realise the property, in such manner as the court may specify;
    (d) power to start, carry on or defend any legal proceedings in respect of the property.

(3) The court may by order confer on the receiver power to enter any premises in Northern Ireland and to do any of the following—
    (a) search for or inspect anything authorised by the court;
    (b) make or obtain a copy, photograph or other record, of anything so authorised;
    (c) remove anything which the receiver is required or authorised to take possession of in pursuance of an order of the court.

(4) The court may by order authorise the receiver to do any of the following for the purposes of the exercise of his functions—
    (a) hold property;
    (b) enter into contracts;
    (c) sue and be sued;
    (d) employ agents;
    (e) execute powers of attorney, deeds or other instruments;
    (f) take any other steps the court thinks appropriate.

(5) The court may order any person who has possession of realisable property to give possession of it to the receiver.

(6) The court—
    (a) may order a person holding an interest in realisable property to make to the receiver such payment as the court specifies in respect of a beneficial interest held by the defendant or the recipient of a tainted gift;
    (b) may (on payment being made) by order transfer, grant or extinguish any interest in the property.

(7) Paragraphs (2), (5) and (6) do not apply to property for the time being subject to a charge under any of these provisions—
    (a) section 9 of the Drug Trafficking Offences Act 1986;
    (b) section 78 of the Criminal Justice Act 1988;
    (c) Article 14 of the Criminal Justice (Confiscation) (Northern Ireland) Order 1990;

    (d)  section 27 of the Drug Trafficking Act 1994;

    (e)  Article 32 of the Proceeds of Crime (Northern Ireland) Order 1996.

(8)  The court must not—

    (a)  confer the power mentioned in paragraph (2)(b) or (c) in respect of property, or

    (b)  exercise the power conferred on it by paragraph (6) in respect of property,

unless it gives persons holding interests in the property a reasonable opportunity to make representations to it.

[(8A)  Paragraph (8), so far as relating to the power mentioned in paragraph (2)(b), does not apply to property which—

    (a)  is perishable; or

    (b)  ought to be disposed of before its value diminishes.]

(9)  The court may order that a power conferred by an order under this article is subject to such conditions and exceptions as it specifies.

(10)  Managing or otherwise dealing with property includes—

    (a)  selling the property or any part of it or interest in it;

    (b)  carrying on or arranging for another person to carry on any trade or business the assets of which are or are part of the property;

    (c)  incurring capital expenditure in respect of the property.

**115.— Powers of enforcement receivers in respect of external orders for the recovery of**

**specified property**

(1)  If the court appoints a receiver under article 113 , it may act under this article on the application of the relevant Director […] where the external order is for the recovery of property specified in the order ("the specified property").

(2)  The court may by order confer on the receiver the following powers in relation to the specified property—

    (a)  power to take possession of the property;

    (b)  power to manage or otherwise deal with the property;

    (c)  power to realise the property, in such manner as the court may specify;

    (d)  power to start, carry on or defend any legal proceedings in respect of the property.

(3)  The court may by order confer on the receiver power to enter any premises in Northern Ireland and to do any of the following—

    (a)  search for or inspect anything authorised by the court;

    (b)  make or obtain a copy, photograph or other record of anything so authorised;

    (c)  remove anything which the receiver is required or authorised to take possession of in pursuance of an order of the court.

(4)  The court may by order authorise the receiver to do any of the following for the purposes of the exercise of his functions—

    (a)  hold property;

    (b)  enter into contracts;

    (c)  sue and be sued;

    (d)  employ agents;

    (e)  execute powers of attorney, deeds or other instruments;

    (f)  take any other steps the court thinks appropriate.

(5)  The court may order any person who has possession of the specified property to give possession of it to the receiver.

(6)  The court—

    (a)  may order a person holding an interest in the specified property to make to the receiver such payment as the court specifies in respect of a beneficial interest held by the defendant or the recipient of a tainted gift;

    (b)  may (on the payment being made) by order transfer, grant or extinguish any interest in the property.

(7) The court must not—
    (a) confer the power mentioned in paragraph (2)(b) or (c) in respect of property, or
    (b) exercise the power conferred on it by paragraph (6) in respect of property,
unless it gives persons holding interests in the property a reasonable opportunity to make representations to it.

[(7A) Paragraph (7), so far as relating to the power mentioned in paragraph (2)(b), does not apply to property which—
    (a) is perishable; or
    (b) ought to be disposed of before its value diminishes.]

(8) The court may order that a power conferred by an order under this article is subject to such conditions and exceptions as it specifies.

(9) Managing or otherwise dealing with property includes—
    (a) selling the property or any part of it or interest in it;
    (b) carrying on or arranging for another person to carry on any trade or business the assets of which are or are part of the property;
    (c) incurring capital expenditure in respect of the property.

**116.—** [...]

**117.—** [...]

**118.—** [...]

### 119.— Application of sums by enforcement receivers

(1) This article applies to sums which are in the hands of a receiver appointed under article 113 if they are—
    (a) the proceeds of the realisation of property under article 114 or 115;
    (b) where article 114 applies, sums (other than those mentioned in sub-paragraph (a)) in which the defendant holds an interest.

(2) The sums must be applied as follows—
    (a) first, they must be applied in payment of such expenses incurred by a person acting as an insolvency practitioner as are payable under this paragraph by virtue of article 3;
    (b) second, they must be applied in making any payments directed by the Crown Court;
    (c) third, they must be applied on the defendant's behalf towards satisfaction of the external order.

(3) If the amount payable under the external order has been fully paid and any sums remain in the receiver's hands he must distribute them—
    (a) among such persons who held (or hold) interests in the property concerned as the Crown Court directs; and
    (b) in such proportions as it directs.

(4) Before making a direction under paragraph (3) the court must give persons who held (or hold) interests in the property concerned a reasonable opportunity to make representations to it.

(5) For the purposes of paragraphs (3) and (4) the property concerned is—
    (a) the property represented by the proceeds mentioned in paragraph (1)(a);
    (b) the sums mentioned in paragraph (1)(b).

(6) The receiver applies sums as mentioned in paragraph (2)(c) by paying them to the appropriate chief clerk on account of the amount payable under the order.

(7) The appropriate chief clerk is the chief clerk of the court at the place where the external order was registered.

### 120.— Sums received by appropriate chief clerk

(1) This article applies if the appropriate chief clerk receives sums on account of the amount payable under a registered external order or the value of the property specified in the order.

(2) The appropriate chief clerk's receipt of the sums reduces the amount payable under the order, but he must apply the sums received as follows.

(3) First he must apply them in payment of such expenses incurred by a person acting as an insolvency practitioner as—

(a)  are payable under this paragraph by virtue of article 3, but

(b)  are not already paid under article 119(2)(a).

(4) He must next apply them—

(a)  first, in payment of the remuneration and expenses of a receiver appointed under article 101 to the extent that they have not been met by virtue of the exercise by that receiver of a power conferred under article 102(2)(d);

(b)  second, in payment of the remuneration and expenses of the receiver appointed under article 113.

(5) If any amount remains after the appropriate chief clerk makes any payments required by the preceding provisions of this article, the amount must be treated for the purposes of section 20 of the Administration of Justice Act (Northern Ireland) 1954 (application of fines) as if it were a fine.

(6) Paragraph (4) does not apply if the receiver is a member of the staff of the Public Prosecution Service for Northern Ireland, or the Serious Fraud Office; and it is immaterial whether he is a permanent or temporary member or he is on secondment from elsewhere.

121.— [...]

122.— [...]

### 123.— Satisfaction of external order

(1) A registered external order is satisfied when no amount is due under it.

(2) Where such an order authorises the recovery of property specified in it, no further amount is due under the order when all of the specified property has been sold.

### 124.— Restrictions relating to enforcement receivers

(1) Paragraphs (2) and (3) apply if a court makes an order under article 113 appointing a receiver in respect of any realisable property or specified property.

(2) If the receiver is appointed in respect of a tenancy of any premises, no landlord or other person to whom rent is payable may exercise a right within paragraph (3) except with the leave of the Crown Court and subject to any terms the Crown Court may impose.

(3) A right is within this paragraph if it is a right of forfeiture by peaceable re-entry in relation to the premises in respect of any failure by the tenant to comply with any term or condition of the tenancy.

(4) If a court in which proceedings are pending in respect of any property is satisfied that an order under article 113 appointing a receiver in respect of the property has been applied for or made, the court may either stay the proceedings or allow them to continue on any terms it thinks fit.

(5) Before exercising any power conferred by paragraph (4), the court must give an opportunity to be heard to—

(a)  the relevant Director [...], and

(b)  the receiver (if the order under article 113 has been made).

125.— [...]

## Chapter 3
## Receivers and Procedure

### 126. Protection of receiver appointed under articles 101, 113 and 116

If a receiver appointed under [article 101 or 113] —

(a)  takes action in relation to property which is not realisable property or, as the case may be, the specified property,

(b) would be entitled to take the action if it were realisable property or, as the case may be, the specified property, and

(c) believes on reasonable grounds that he is entitled to take the action,

he is not liable to any person in respect of any loss or damage resulting from the action, except so far as the loss or damage is caused by his negligence.

### 127.— Further applications by receivers

(1) This article applies to a receiver appointed under [article 101 or 113].

(2) The receiver may apply to—

(a) the High Court if he is appointed under article 101;

(b) the Crown Court if he is appointed under [article 113],

for an order giving directions as to the exercise of his powers.

(3) The following persons may apply to the High Court if the receiver is appointed under article 101 or to the Crown Court if the receiver is appointed under [article 113]—

(a) any person affected by action taken by the receiver;

(b) any person who may be affected by action the receiver proposes to take.

(4) On an application under this article the court may make such order as it believes is appropriate.

### 128.— Discharge and variation of receiver orders

(1) The following persons may apply to the High Court to vary or discharge an order made under article 101 or 102 or to the Crown Court to vary or discharge an order made under any of [articles 113 to 115]—

(a) the receiver;

(b) the relevant Director;

(c) any person affected by the order.

(2) On an application under this article the court—

(a) may discharge the order;

(b) may vary the order.

(3) But in the case of an order under article 101 or 102—

(a) if the condition in article 94 which was satisfied was that proceedings were started, the court must discharge the order if at the conclusion of the proceedings no external order has been made;

(b) if the condition which was satisfied was that proceedings were started, the court must discharge the order if within a reasonable time an external order has not been registered under Chapter 2 of this Part;

(c) if the condition which was satisfied was that an investigation was started, the court must discharge the order if within a reasonable time proceedings for the offence are not started.

### 129.— Management receivers: discharge

(1) This article applies if—

(a) a receiver stands appointed under article 101 in respect of property which is identified in the restraint order (the management receiver), and

(b) the court appoints a receiver under article 113 […].

(2) The court must order the management receiver to transfer to the other receiver all property held by the management receiver by virtue of the powers conferred on him by article 102.

(3) […]

(4) Paragraph (2) does not apply to property which the management receiver holds by virtue of the exercise by him of his power under article 102(2)(d).

(5) If the management receiver complies with an order under paragraph (2) he is discharged—

(a) from his appointment under article 101;

(b) from any obligation under this Order arising from his appointment.

(6) If this article applies the court may make such a consequential or incidental order as it believes is appropriate.

### 130.— Appeal to Court of Appeal about receivers

(1) If on an application for an order under any of [articles 101, 102 or 113 to 115 ], the court decides not to make one, the person who applies for the order may appeal to the Court of Appeal against the decision.

(2) If the court makes an order under any of [articles 101, 102 or 113 to 115 ], the following persons may appeal to the Court of Appeal in respect of the court's decision—
   (a) the person who applied for the order;
   (b) any person affected by the order.

(3) If on an application for an order under article 127 the court decides not to make one, the person who applied for the order may appeal to the Court of Appeal against the decision.

(4) If the court makes an order under article 127 the following persons may appeal to the Court of Appeal in respect of the court's decision—
   (a) the person who applied for the order;
   (b) any person affected by the order;
   (c) the receiver.

(5) The following persons may appeal to the Court of Appeal against a decision of the court on an application under article 128—
   (a) the person who applied for the order in respect of which the application was made [...];
   (b) any person affected by the court's decision;
   (c) the receiver.

(6) On an appeal under this article the Court of Appeal may—
   (a) confirm the decision, or
   (b) make such order as it believes is appropriate.

### 131.— Appeal to the House of Lords about receivers

(1) An appeal lies to the House of Lords from a decision of the Court of Appeal on an appeal under article 130.

(2) An appeal under this article lies at the instance of any person who was a party to the proceedings before the Court of Appeal.

(3) On an appeal under this article the House of Lords may—
   (a) confirm the decision of the Court Appeal, or
   (b) make such order as it believes is appropriate.

### 132.— Powers of court and receiver

(1) This article applies to—
   (a) the powers conferred on a court by this Part;
   (b) the powers of a receiver appointed under [article 101 or 113].

(2) The powers—
   (a) must be exercised with a view to the value for the time being of realisable property or specified property being made available (by the property's realisation) for satisfying an external order that has been or may be made against the defendant;
   (b) must be exercised, in a case where an external order has not been made, with a view to securing that there is no diminution in the value of the property identified in the external request;
   (c) must be exercised without taking account of any obligation of a defendant or a recipient of a tainted gift if the obligation conflicts with the object of satisfying any external order against the defendant that has been or may be registered under article 108;
   (d) may be exercised in respect of a debt owed by the Crown.

(3) Paragraph (2) has effect subject to the following rules—
   (a) the powers must be exercised with a view to allowing a person other than the defendant or a recipient of a tainted gift to retain or recover the value of any interest held by him;
   (b) in the case of realisable property or specified property held by a recipient of a tainted gift, the powers must be exercised with a view to realising no more than the value for the time being of the gift;
   (c) in a case where an external order has not been made against the defendant, property must not be sold if the court so orders under paragraph (4).

(4) If on an application by the defendant or the recipient of a tainted gift, the court decides that property cannot be replaced it may order that it must not be sold.

(5) An order under paragraph (4) may be revoked or varied.

### 133.— Procedure on appeal to Court of Appeal under Part 4

(1) An appeal to the Court of Appeal under this Part lies only with the leave of that Court.

(2) In relation to appeals to the Court of Appeal under this Part, the Secretary of State may make an order containing provision corresponding to any provision in the Criminal Appeal (Northern Ireland) Act 1980, subject to any specified modifications.

(3) Subject to any rules of court, the costs of and incidental to all proceedings on an appeal to the Court of Appeal under article 97, 109 or 130 are in the discretion of the court.

(4) The court shall have full power to determine by whom and to what extent the costs are to be paid.

(5) In any proceedings mentioned in paragraph (3), the court may—
    (a) disallow, or
    (b) (as the case may be) order the legal or other representative concerned to meet,
    the whole of any wasted costs or such part of them as may be determined in accordance with rules of court.

(6) In paragraph (5) "wasted costs" means any costs incurred by a party—
    (a) as a result of any improper, unreasonable or negligent act or omission on the part of any legal or other representative or any employee of such a representative, or
    (b) which, in the light of any such act or omission occurring after they were incurred, the court considers it unreasonable to expect that party to pay.

(7) "Legal or other representative", in relation to a party to proceedings, means any person exercising a right of audience or right to conduct litigation on his behalf.

### 134. Procedure on appeal to House of Lords under Part 4

In relation to appeals to the House of Lords under this Part, the Secretary of State may make an order containing provision corresponding to any provision in the Criminal Appeal (Northern Ireland) Act 1980, subject to any specified modifications.

## Chapter 4
## Interpretation

### 135.— Property

(1) In this Part, "realisable property" means in a case where the external order specifies a sum of money, any free property held by the defendant or by the recipient of a tainted gift.

(2) "Free property" has the same meaning as in section 230 of the Act (free property).

(3) The rules in paragraphs (a) and (c) to (g) of section 232(2) of the Act (property: general provisions) apply in relation to property under this Order (in addition to section 447(4) to (6) of the Act (interpretation)) as they apply in relation to property under Part 4 of the Act.

### 136.— Tainted gifts

(1) In this Part, a gift is tainted if it was made by the defendant at any time after—
    (a) the date on which the offence to which the external order or external request relates was committed, or
    (b) if his criminal conduct consists of two or more such offences and they were committed on different dates, the date of the earliest.

(2) For the purposes of paragraph (1), an offence which is a continuing offence is committed on the first occasion when it is committed.

(3) A gift may be a tainted gift whether it was made before or after the coming into force of this Order.

### 137.— Gifts and their recipients

(1) In this Part, a defendant is to be treated as making a gift if he transfers property to another person for a consideration whose value is significantly less than the value of the property at the time of the transfer.

(2) If paragraph (1) applies, the property given is to be treated as such share in the property transferred as is represented by the fraction—

  (a) whose numerator is the difference between the two values mentioned in paragraph (1), and

  (b) whose denominator is the value of the property at the time of the transfer.

(3) In this Part references to a recipient of a tainted gift are to a person to whom the defendant has made the gift.

### 138.— Value: the basic rule

(1) Subject to article 139, this article applies where it is necessary under this Part to decide the value at any time of property then held by a person.

(2) Its value is the market value of the property at that time.

(3) But if at that time another person holds an interest in the property its value, in relation to the person mentioned in paragraph (1), is the market value of his interest at that time, ignoring any charging order under a provision listed in paragraph (4).

(4) Those provisions are—

  (a) section 9 of the Drug Trafficking Offences Act 1986;

  (b) section 78 of the Criminal Justice Act 1988;

  (c) Article 14 of the Criminal Justice (Confiscation) (Northern Ireland) Order 1990;

  (d) section 27 of the Drug Trafficking Act 1994;

  (e) Article 32 of the Proceeds of Crime (Northern Ireland) Order 1996.

### 139.— Value of tainted gifts

(1) The value at any time (the material time) of a tainted gift is the greater of the following—

  (a) the value (at time of the gift) of the property given, adjusted to take account of later changes in the value of money;

  (b) the value (at the material time) of the property found under paragraph (2).

(2) The property found under this paragraph is as follows—

  (a) if the recipient holds the property given, the property found under this paragraph is that property;

  (b) if the recipient holds no part of the property given, the property found under this paragraph is any property which directly or indirectly represents it in his hands;

  (c) if the recipient holds part of the property given, the property found under this paragraph is that part and any property which directly or indirectly represents the other part in his hands.

(3) The references in paragraph (1)(a) and (b) to the value are to the value found in accordance with article 138.

### 140. Meaning of "defendant"

In this Part "defendant"—

  (a) in relation to a restraint order means—

    (i) in a case in which the first condition in article 94 is satisfied, the alleged offender;

    (ii) in a case in which the second condition in article 94 is satisfied, the person against whom proceedings for an offence have been started in a country outside the United Kingdom (whether or not he has been convicted);

  (b) in relation to an external order, the person convicted of criminal conduct.

### 141. Other interpretation

In this Part—

  "relevant Director" has the meaning—

  (a) in the context of an external request, set out in article 93(4);

  (b) in the context of an external order, set out in article 104(4);

  "relevant property" means property which satisfies the test in section 447(7) of the Act;

  "specified property" means property specified in an external order (other than an order that specifies a sum of money).

## PART 5
### GIVING EFFECT IN THE UNITED KINGDOM TO EXTERNAL ORDERS BY MEANS OF CIVIL RECOVERY

## Chapter 1
## Introduction

**142.— Action to give effect to an order**

(1) The Secretary of State may forward an external order to the enforcement authority.

(2) This Part has effect for the purpose of enabling the enforcement authority to realise recoverable property (within the meaning of article 202) in civil proceedings before the High Court or Court of Session for the purpose of giving effect to an external order.

(3) The powers conferred by this Part are exercisable in relation to any property whether or not proceedings have been brought in the country from which the external order was sent for criminal conduct (within the meaning of section 447(8) of the Act) in connection with the property.

## Chapter 2
## Civil Recovery In The High Court Or Court Of Session
*Proceedings for recovery orders*

**143.— Proceedings for recovery orders in England and Wales or Northern Ireland**

(1) Proceedings for a recovery order pursuant to the registration of an external order may be taken by the enforcement authority in the High Court against any person who the authority thinks holds recoverable property.

(2) The enforcement authority must serve the claim form—
   (a) on the respondent, and
   (b) unless the court dispenses with service, on any other person who the authority thinks holds any associated property which the authority wishes to be subject to a recovery order,
   wherever domiciled, resident or present.

(3) In the case of an external order which is for the recovery of property other than a sum of money which is specified in the external order ("the specified property"), that property must also be specified in the claim form.

(4) Paragraph (5) applies in the case of an external order which is for the recovery of a specified sum of money.

(5) If any property which the enforcement authority wishes to be subject to a recovery order is not specified in the claim form, it must be described in the form in general terms and the form must state whether it is alleged to be recoverable property or associated property.

(6) The references above to the claim form include the particulars of claim, where they are served subsequently.

**144.— Proceedings for recovery orders in Scotland**

(1) Proceedings for a recovery order pursuant to the registration of an external order may be taken by the enforcement authority in the Court of Session against any person who the authority thinks holds recoverable property.

(2) The enforcement authority must serve the application—
   (a) on the respondent, and
   (b) unless the court dispenses with service, on any other person who the authority thinks holds any associated property which the authority wishes to be subject to a recovery order,
   wherever domiciled, resident or present.

(3) In the case of an external order which is for the recovery of property other than a sum of money which is specified in the external order ("the specified property"), the property must also be specified in the application.

(4) Paragraph (5) applies in the case of an external order which is for the recovery of a specified sum of money.

(5) If any property which the enforcement authority wishes to be subject to a recovery order is not specified in the application it must be described in the application in general terms; and the application must state whether it is alleged to be recoverable property or associated property.

### 145.— Sums in a currency other than sterling

(1) This article applies where the external order in respect of which proceedings for a recovery order are taken specifies a sum of money.

(2) If the sum of money which is specified in an external order is expressed in a currency other than sterling, the sum of money to be recovered is to be taken to be the sterling equivalent calculated in accordance with the rate of exchange prevailing at the end of day on which the external order was made.

(3) This amount must be specified—
   (a) in England and Wales or Northern Ireland, in the claim form or the particulars of claim where they are served subsequently, or
   (b) in Scotland, in the application.

### 146.— "Associated property"

(1) "Associated property" means property of any of the following descriptions (including property held by the respondent) which is not itself the recoverable property—
   (a) any interest in the recoverable property,
   (b) any other interest in the property in which the recoverable property subsists,
   (c) if the recoverable property is a tenancy in common, the tenancy of the other tenant,
   (d) if (in Scotland) the recoverable property is owned in common, the interest of the other owner,
   (e) if the recoverable property is part of a larger property, but not a separate part, the remainder of that property.

(2) References to property being associated with recoverable property are to be read accordingly.

(3) No property is to be treated as associated with recoverable property consisting of rights under a pension scheme (within the meaning of articles 184 to 186).

*Property freezing orders (England and Wales and Northern Ireland)*

### 147.— Application for property freezing order

(1) Where the enforcement authority may take proceedings for a recovery order pursuant to the registration of an external order in the High Court, the authority may apply to the court for a property freezing order (whether before or after starting the proceedings).

(2) A property freezing order is an order that—
   (a) specifies or describes the property to which it applies, and
   (b) subject to any exclusions (see article 149(1)(b) and (2)), prohibits any person to whose property the order applies from in any way dealing with property.

(3) An application for a property freezing order may be made without notice if the circumstances are such that notice of the application would prejudice any right of the enforcement authority to obtain a recovery order in respect of any property.

(4) The court may make a property freezing order on an application if it is satisfied that the condition in paragraph (5) is met and, where applicable, that the condition in paragraph (6) is met.

(5) The first condition is that there is a good arguable case—
   (a) that the property to which the application for the order relates is or includes recoverable property, and
   (b) that, if any of it is not recoverable property, it is associated property.

(6) The second condition is that, if—
- (a) the property to which the application for the order relates includes property alleged to be associated property, and
- (b) the enforcement authority has not established the identity of the person who holds it,

the authority has taken all reasonable steps to do so.

### 148.—Variation and setting aside of property freezing order

(1) The court may at any time vary or set aside a property freezing order.
(2) If the court makes an interim receiving order that applies to all of the property to which a property freezing order applies, it must set aside the property freezing order.
(3) If the court makes an interim receiving order that applies to some but not all of the property to which a property freezing order applies, it must vary the property freezing order so as to exclude any property to which the interim receiving order applies.
(4) If the court decides that any property to which a property freezing order applies is neither recoverable property nor associated property, it must vary the order so as to exclude the property.
(5) Before exercising the power to vary or set aside a property freezing order, the court must (as well as giving the parties to the proceedings an opportunity to be heard) give such an opportunity to any person who may be affected by its decision.
(6) Paragraph (5) does not apply where the court is acting as required by paragraph (2) or (3).

### 149.— Property freezing orders: exclusions

(1) The power to vary a property freezing order includes (in particular) power to make exclusions as follows—
- (a) power to exclude property from the order, and
- (b) power, otherwise than by excluding property from the order, to make exclusions from the prohibition on dealing with the property to which the order applies.

(2) Exclusions from the prohibition on dealing with the property to which the order applies (other than exclusions of property from the order) may also be made when the order is made.
(3) An exclusion may, in particular, make provision for the purpose of enabling any person—
- (a) to meet his reasonable living expenses. or
- (b) to carry on any trade, business, profession or occupation.

(4) An exclusion may be made subject to conditions.
(5) Where the court exercises the power to make an exclusion for the purpose of enabling a person to meet legal expenses that he has incurred, or may incur, in respect of proceedings under this Part, it must ensure that the exclusion—
- (a) is limited to reasonable legal expenses that the person has reasonably incurred or that he reasonably incurs,
- (b) specifies the total amount that may be released for legal expenses in pursuance of the exclusion, and
- (c) is made subject to the required conditions (see article 198) in addition to any conditions imposed under paragraph (4).

(6) The court, in deciding whether to make an exclusion for the purpose of enabling a person to meet legal expenses of his in respect of proceedings under this Part—
- (a) must have regard (in particular) to the desirability of the person being represented in any proceedings under this Part in which he is a participant, and
- (b) must, where the person is the respondent, disregard the possibility that legal representation of the person in any such proceedings might, were an exclusion not made, be funded by the Legal Services Commission or the Northern Ireland Legal Services Commission.

(7) If excluded property is not specified in the order it must be described in the order in general terms.
(8) The power to make exclusions must, subject to paragraph (6), be exercised with a view to ensuring, so far as practicable, that the satisfaction of any right of the enforcement authority to recover the property which satisfies the tests in article 202(1) and (2) is not unduly prejudiced.
(9) Paragraph (8) does not apply where the court is acting as required by article 148(3) or (4).

**150.— Property freezing orders: restrictions on proceedings and remedies**

(1) While a property freezing order has effect—
  (a) the court may stay any action, execution or other legal process in respect of the property to which the order applies, and
  (b) no distress may be levied against the property to which the order applies except with the leave of the court and subject to any terms the court may impose.

(2) If a court (whether the High Court or any other court) in which proceedings are pending in respect of any property is satisfied that a property freezing order has been applied for or made in respect of the property, it may either stay the proceedings or allow them to continue on any terms it thinks fit.

(3) If a property freezing order applies to a tenancy of any premises, no landlord or other person to whom rent is payable may exercise the right of forfeiture by peaceable re-entry in relation to the premises in respect of any failure by the tenant to comply with any term or condition of the tenancy, except with the leave of the court and subject to any terms the court may impose.

(4) Before exercising any power conferred by this article, the court must (as well as giving the parties to any of the proceedings concerned an opportunity to be heard) give such an opportunity to any person who may be affected by the court's decision.

**[150A.— Receivers in connection with property freezing orders**

(1) Paragraph (2) applies if—
  (a) the High Court makes a property freezing order on an application by an enforcement authority, and
  (b) the authority applies to the court to proceed under paragraph (2) (whether as part of the application for the property freezing order or at any time afterwards).

(2) The High Court may by order appoint a receiver in respect of any property to which the property freezing order applies.

(3) An application for an order under this article may be made without notice if the circumstances are such that notice of the application would prejudice any right of the enforcement authority to obtain a recovery order in respect of any property.

(4) In its application for an order under this article, the enforcement authority must nominate a suitably qualified person for appointment as a receiver.

(5) Such a person may be a member of staff of the enforcement authority.

(6) The enforcement authority may apply a sum received by it under article 191(2) in making payment of the remuneration and expenses of a receiver appointed under this article.

(7) Paragraph (6) does not apply in relation to the remuneration of the receiver if he is a member of the staff of the enforcement authority (but it does apply in relation to such remuneration if the receiver is a person providing services under arrangements made by the enforcement authority).]

**[150B.— Powers of receivers appointed under article 150A**

(1) If the High Court appoints a receiver under article 150A on an application by an enforcement authority, the court may act under this article on the application of the authority.

(2) The court may by order authorise or require the receiver—
  (a) to exercise any of the powers mentioned in paragraph 5 of Schedule 2 (management powers) in relation to any property in respect of which the receiver is appointed,
  (b) to take any other steps the court thinks appropriate in connection with the management of any such property (including securing the detention, custody or preservation of the property in order to manage it).

(3) The court may by order require any person in respect of whose property the receiver is appointed—
  (a) to bring the property to a place (in England and Wales, or as the case may be, Northern Ireland) specified by the receiver or to place it in the custody of the receiver (if, in either case, he is able to do so),
  (b) to do anything he is reasonably required to do by the receiver for the preservation of the property.

(4) The court may by order require any person in respect of whose property the receiver is appointed to bring any documents relating to the property which are in his possession or control to a place (in England and Wales or, as the case may be, Northern Ireland) specified by the receiver or to place them in the custody of the receiver.

(5) In paragraph (4), "document" means anything in which information of any description is recorded.

(6) Any prohibition on dealing with property imposed by a property freezing order does not prevent a person from complying with any requirements imposed by virtue of this article.

(7) If—

    (a) the receiver deals with any property which is not property in respect of which he is appointed under article 150A, and

    (b) at the time he deals with the property he believes on reasonable grounds that he is entitled to do so by virtue of his appointment,

the receiver is not liable to any person in respect of any loss or damage resulting from his dealing with the property except so far as the loss or damage is caused by his negligence.]

## [150C.— Supervision of article 150A receiver and variations

(1) Any of the following persons may at any time apply to the High Court for directions as to the exercise of the functions of a receiver appointed under article 150A–

    (a) the receiver,

    (b) any party to the proceedings for the appointment of the receiver or the property freezing order concerned,

    (c) any person affected by any action taken by the receiver,

    (d) any person who may be affected by any action proposed to be taken by the receiver.

(2) Before giving any directions under paragraph (1), the court must give an opportunity to be heard to—

    (a) the receiver,

    (b) the parties to the proceedings for the appointment of the receiver and for the property freezing order concerned,

    (c) any person who may be interested in the application under paragraph (1).

(3) The court may at any time vary or set aside the appointment of a receiver under article 150A, any order under article 150B or any directions under this article.

(4) Before exercising any power under paragraph (3), the court must give an opportunity to be heard to—

    (a) the receiver,

    (b) the parties to the proceedings for the appointment of the receiver, for the order under article 150B or, as the case may be, for the directions under this article,

    (c) the parties to the proceedings for the property freezing order concerned,

    (d) any person who may be affected by the court's decision.]

### *Interim receiving orders (England and Wales and Northern Ireland)*

## 151.— Application for interim receiving order

(1) Where the enforcement authority may take proceedings for a recovery order pursuant to the registration of an external order in the High Court, the authority may apply to the court for an interim receiving order (whether before or after starting the proceedings).

(2) An interim receiving order is an order for—

    (a) the detention, custody or preservation of property, and

    (b) the appointment of an interim receiver.

(3) An application for an interim receiving order may be made without notice if the circumstances are such that notice of the application would prejudice any right of the enforcement authority to obtain a recovery order in respect of any property.

(4) The court may make an interim receiving order on the application if it is satisfied that the conditions in paragraphs (5) and, where applicable, (6) are met.

(5) The first condition is that there is a good arguable case—
   (a) that the property to which the application for the order relates is or includes recoverable property, and
   (b) that, if any of it is not recoverable property, it is associated property.

(6) The second condition is that, if—
   (a) the property to which the application for the order relates includes property alleged to be associated property, and
   (b) the enforcement authority has not established the identity of the person who holds it,
   the authority has taken all reasonable steps to do so.

(7) In its application for an interim receiving order, the enforcement authority must nominate a suitably qualified person for appointment as interim receiver, but the nominee may not be a member of the staff of the [enforcement authority].

(8) The extent of the power to make an interim receiving order is not limited by articles 152 to 160.

### 152.— Functions of interim receiver

(1) An interim receiving order may authorise or require the interim receiver—
   (a) to exercise any of the powers mentioned in Schedule 2,
   (b) to take any other steps the court thinks appropriate,
   for the purpose of securing the detention, custody or preservation of the property to which the order applies or of taking any steps under paragraph (2).

(2) An interim receiving order—
   (a) must require the interim receiver to take any steps which the court thinks necessary to establish whether or not the property to which the order applies is recoverable property or associated property, and
   (b) may require him to take any steps which the court thinks necessary to establish whether or not any other property is recoverable property (which satisfies the tests in article 202(1) and (2) or 203) and, if it is, who holds it.

(3) If—
   (a) the interim receiver deals with any property which is not property to which the order applies, and
   (b) at the time he deals with the property he believes on reasonable grounds that he is entitled to do so in pursuance of the order,
   the interim receiver is not liable to any person in respect of any loss or damage resulting from his dealing with the property except so far as the loss or damage is caused by negligence.

*Property freezing orders and interim receiving orders: registration*

### 153.— Registration of property freezing orders and interim receiving orders

(1) The registration Acts—
   (a) apply in relation to property freezing orders, and in relation to interim receiving orders as they apply in relation to orders which affect land and are made by the court for the purpose of enforcing judgments or recognisances,
   (b) apply in relation to applications for property freezing orders and in relation to applications for interim receiving orders as they apply in relation to other pending land actions.

(2) The registration Acts are—
   (a) the Land Charges Act 1972, and
   (b) the Land Registration Act 2002.

(3) But no notice may be entered in the register of title under the Land Registration Act 2002 in respect of a property freezing order or an interim receiving order.

### 154.— Registration (Northern Ireland) of such orders

(1) A person applying for a property freezing order or an interim receiving order must be treated for the purposes of section 66 of the Land Registration Act (Northern Ireland) 1970 (cautions) as a person interested in relation to any registered land to which—
   (a) the application relates, or

    (b) a property freezing order or an interim receiving order made in pursuance of the application relates.

(2) Upon being served with a copy of a property freezing order, the Registrar must, in respect of any registered land to which a property freezing order or an application for a property freezing order relates, make an entry inhibiting any dealing with the land without the consent of the High Court.

(3) Upon being served with a copy of an interim receiving order, the Registrar must, in respect of any registered land to which an interim receiving order or an application for an interim receiving order relates, make an entry inhibiting any dealing with the land without the consent of the High Court.

(4) Subsections (2) and (4) of section 67 of the Land Registration Act (Northern Ireland) 1970 (inhibitions) apply to an entry made under paragraph (2) or (3) as they apply to an entry made on the application of any person interested in the registered land under subsection (1) of that section.

(5) Where a property freezing order or an interim receiving order has been protected by an entry registered under the Land Registration Act (Northern Ireland) 1970 or the Registration of Deeds Acts, an order setting aside the property freezing order or interim receiving order may require that entry to be vacated.

(6) In this article—

"Registrar" and "entry" have the same meanings as in the Land Registration Act (Northern Ireland) 1970; and

"Registration of Deeds Acts" has the meaning given by section 46(2) of the Interpretation Act (Northern Ireland) 1954.

### *Interim receiving orders: further provisions*

**155.— Interim receiving orders: duties of respondent etc.**

(1) An interim receiving order may require any person to whose property the order applies—
    (a) to bring the property to a place (in England and Wales or, as the case may be, Northern Ireland) specified by the interim receiver or place it in the custody of the interim receiver (if, in either case, he is able to do so),
    (b) to do anything he is reasonably required to do by the interim receiver for the preservation of the property.

(2) An interim receiving order may require any person to whose property the order applies to bring any documents relating to the property which are in his possession or control to a place (in England and Wales, or, as the case may be, Northern Ireland) specified by the interim receiver or to place them in the custody of the interim receiver.

"Document" means anything in which information of any description is recorded.

**156.— Supervision of interim receiver and variation of order**

(1) The interim receiver, any party to the proceedings and any person affected by any action taken by the interim receiver, or who may be affected by any action proposed to be taken by him, may at any time apply to the court for directions as to the exercise of the interim receiver's functions.

(2) Before giving any directions under paragraph (1), the court must (as well as giving the parties to the proceedings an opportunity to be heard) give such an opportunity to the interim receiver and to any person who may be interested in the application.

(3) The court may at any time vary or set aside an interim receiving order.

(4) Before exercising any power to vary or set aside an interim receiving order, the court must (as well as giving the parties to the proceedings an opportunity to be heard) give such an opportunity to the interim receiver and to any person who may be affected by the court's decision.

**157.— Interim receiving orders: restrictions on dealing etc. with property**

(1) An interim receiving order must, subject to any exclusions made in accordance with this article, prohibit any person to whose property the order applies from dealing with the property.

(2) Exclusions may be made when the interim receiving order is made or on an application to vary the order.

(3) An exclusion may, in particular, make provision for the purpose of enabling any person—
   (a) to meet his reasonable living expenses, or
   (b) to carry on any trade, business, profession or occupation,
   (c) and may be made subject to conditions.

(4) Where the court exercises the power to make an exclusion for the purpose of enabling a person to meet legal expenses that he has incurred, or may incur, in respect of proceedings under this Part, it must ensure that the exclusion—
   (a) is limited to reasonable legal expenses that the person has reasonably incurred or that he reasonably incurs,
   (b) specifies the total amount that may be released for legal expenses in pursuance of the exclusion, and
   (c) is made subject to the required conditions (see article 198) in addition to any conditions imposed under paragraph (3).

(5) The court, in deciding whether to make an exclusion for the purposes of enabling a person to meet legal expenses of his in respect of proceedings under this Part—
   (a) must have regard (in particular) to the desirability of the person being represented in any proceedings under this Part in which he is a participant, and
   (b) must, where the person is the respondent, disregard the possibility that legal representation of the person in any such proceedings might, were an exclusion not made, be funded by the Legal Services Commission or the Northern Ireland Legal Services Commission.

(6) If the excluded property is not specified in the order it must be described in the order in general terms.

(7) The power to make exclusions must, subject to paragraph (5), be exercised with a view to ensuring so far as practicable, that the satisfaction of any right of the enforcement authority to recover the property obtained through conduct which satisfies the test in article 202(2) is not unduly prejudiced.

**158.— Interim receiving orders: restriction on proceedings and remedies**

(1) While an interim receiving order has effect—
   (a) the court may stay any action, execution or other legal process in respect of the property to which the order applies,
   (b) no distress may be levied against the property to which the order applies except with the leave of the court and subject to any terms the court may impose.

(2) If a court (whether the High Court or any other court) in which proceedings are pending in respect of any property is satisfied that an interim receiving order has been applied for or made in respect of the property, the court may either stay the proceedings or allow them to continue on any terms it thinks fit.

(3) If the interim receiving order applies to a tenancy of any premises, no landlord or other person to whom rent is payable may exercise any right of forfeiture by peaceable re-entry in relation to the premises in respect of any failure by the tenant to comply with any term or condition of the tenancy, except with the leave of the court and subject to any terms the court may impose.

(4) Before exercising any power conferred by this article, the court must (as well as giving the parties to any of the proceedings in question an opportunity to be heard) give such an opportunity to the interim receiver (if appointed) and any person who may be affected by the court's decision.

**159.— Exclusion of property which is not recoverable etc. under interim receiving order**

(1) If the court decides that any property to which an interim receiving order applies is neither recoverable property nor associated property, it must vary the order so as to exclude it.

(2) The court may vary an interim receiving order so as to exclude from the property to which the order applies any property which is alleged to be associated property if the court thinks that the satisfaction of any right of the enforcement authority to recover the property which satisfies the tests in article 202(1) and (2) will not be prejudiced.

(3) The court may exclude any property within paragraph (2) on any terms or conditions, applying while the interim receiving order has effect, which the court thinks necessary or expedient.

### 160.— Reporting under interim receiving order

(1) An interim receiving order must require the interim receiver to inform the enforcement authority and the court as soon as reasonably practicable if he thinks that—
   (a) any property to which the order applies by virtue of a claim that it is recoverable property is not recoverable property,
   (b) any property to which the order applies by virtue of a claim that it is associated property is not associated property,
   (c) any property to which the order does not apply is recoverable property (which satisfies the tests in article 202(1) and (2)) or associated property, or
   (d) any property to which the order applies is held by a person who is different from the person it is claimed holds it,
   or if he thinks that there has been any other material change of circumstances.

(2) An interim receiving order must require the interim receiver—
   (a) to report his findings to the court,
   (b) to serve copies of his report on the enforcement authority and on any person who holds any property to which the order applies or who may otherwise be affected by the report.

*Prohibitory property orders (Scotland)*

### 161.— Application for prohibitory property order

(1) Where the enforcement authority may take proceedings for a recovery order pursuant to the registration of an external order in the Court of Session, the authority may apply to the court for a prohibitory property order (whether before or after starting the proceedings).

(2) A prohibitory property order is an order that—
   (a) specifies or describes the property to which it applies, and
   (b) subject to any exclusions (see article 163(1)(b) and (2)), prohibits any person to whose property the order applies from in any way dealing with the property.

(3) An application for a prohibitory property order may be made without notice if the circumstances are such that notice of the application would prejudice any right of the enforcement authority to obtain a recovery order in respect of any property.

(4) The court may make a prohibitory property order on an application if it is satisfied that the condition in paragraph (5) is met and, where applicable, that the condition in paragraph (6) is met.

(5) The first condition is that there is a good arguable case—
   (a) that the property to which the application for the order relates is or includes recoverable property, and
   (b) that, if any of it is not recoverable property, it is associated property.

(6) The second condition is that, if—
   (a) the property to which the application for the order relates includes property alleged to be associated property, and
   (b) the enforcement authority has not established the identity of the person who holds it,
   the authority has taken all reasonable steps to so.

### 162.— Variation and recall of prohibitory property order

(1) The court may at any time vary or recall a prohibitory property order.

(2) If the court makes an interim administration order that applies to all of the property to which a prohibitory property order applies, it must recall the prohibitory property order.

(3) If the court makes an interim administration order that applies to some but not all of the property to which a prohibitory property order applies, it must vary the prohibitory property order so as to exclude any property to which the interim administration order applies.

(4) If the court decides that any property to which a prohibitory property order applies is neither recoverable property nor associated property, it must vary the order so as to exclude the property.

(5) Before exercising power under this Chapter to vary or recall a prohibitory property order, the court must (as well as giving the parties to the proceedings an opportunity to be heard) give such an opportunity to any person who may be affected by its decision.

(6) Paragraph (5) does not apply where the court is acting as required by paragraph (2) or (3).

### 163.— Prohibitory property orders: exclusions

(1) The power to vary a prohibitory property order includes (in particular) power to make exclusion as follows—
   (a) power to exclude property from the order, and
   (b) power, otherwise than by excluding property from the order, to make exclusions from the prohibition on dealing with the property to which the order applies.

(2) Exclusions from the prohibition on dealing with the property to which the order applies (other than exclusions of property from the order) may also be made when the order is made.

(3) An exclusion may, in particular, make provision for the purpose of enabling any person—
   (a) to meet his reasonable living expenses, or
   (b) to carry on any trade, business, profession or occupation.

(4) An exclusion may be made subject to conditions.

(5) An exclusion may not be made for the purpose of enabling any person to meet any legal expenses in respect of proceedings under this Part.

(6) If excluded property is not specified in the order it must be described in the order in general terms.

(7) The power to make exclusions must be exercised with a view to ensuring, so far as practicable, that the satisfaction of any right of the enforcement authority to recover the property which satisfies the tests in article 202(1) and (2) is not unduly prejudiced.

(8) Paragraph (7) does not apply where the court is acting as required by article 162(3) or (4).

### 164.— Prohibitory property orders: restriction on proceedings and remedies

(1) While a prohibitory property order has effect the court may sist any action, execution or other legal process in respect of the property to which the order applies.

(2) If a court (whether the Court of Session or any other court) in which proceedings are pending in respect of any property is satisfied that a prohibitory property order has been applied for or made in respect of the property, it may either sist the proceedings or allow them to continue on any terms it thinks fit.

(3) Before exercising any power conferred by this article, the court must (as well as giving the parties to any of the proceedings concerned an opportunity to be heard) give such an opportunity to any person who may be affected by the court's decision.

### 165.— Arrestment of property affected by prohibitory property order

(1) On the application of the enforcement authority the Court of Session may, in relation to moveable recoverable property to which a prohibitory property order applies (whether generally or to such of it as is specified in the application), grant warrant for arrestment.

(2) An application under paragraph (1) may be made at the same time as the application for the prohibitory property order or at any time thereafter.

(3) Such a warrant for arrestment may be granted only if the property would be arrestable if the person entitled to it were a debtor.

(4) A warrant under paragraph (1) has effect as if granted on the dependence of an action for debt at the instance of the enforcement authority against the person and may be executed, recalled, loosed or restricted accordingly.

(5) An arrestment executed under this article ceases to have effect when, or in so far as, the prohibitory property order ceases to apply in respect of the property to which the warrant for arrestment was granted.

(6) If an arrestment ceases to have effect to any extent by virtue of paragraph (5) the enforcement authority must apply to the Court of Session for an order recalling or, as the case may be, restricting the arrestment.

**166.— Inhibition of property affected by prohibitory property order**

(1) On the application of the enforcement authority, the Court of Session may, in relation to the property mentioned in paragraph (2), grant warrant for inhibition against any person specified in a prohibitory property order.

(2) That property is heritable property situated in Scotland to which the prohibitory property order applies (whether generally or to such of it as is specified in the application).

(3) The warrant for inhibition—

    (a) has effect as if granted on the dependence of an action for debt by the enforcement authority against the person and may be executed, recalled, loosed or restricted accordingly, and

    (b) has the effect of letters of inhibition and must forthwith be registered by the enforcement authority in the register of inhibition and adjudications.

(4) Section 155 of the Titles to Land Consolidation (Scotland) Act 1868 (effective date of inhibition) applies in relation to an inhibition for which warrant is granted under paragraph (1) as it applies to an inhibition by separate letters or contained in a summons.

(5) An inhibition executed under this article ceases to have effect when, or in so far as, the prohibitory property order ceases to apply in respect of the property in relation to which the warrant for inhibition was granted.

(6) If an inhibition ceases to have effect to any extent by virtue of paragraph (5) the enforcement authority must—

    (a) apply for the recall or, as the case may be, the restriction of the inhibition, and

    (b) ensure that the recall or restriction is reflected in the register of inhibitions and adjudications.

### *Interim administration orders (Scotland)*

**167.— Application for interim administration order**

(1) Where the enforcement authority may take proceedings for a recovery order pursuant to the registration of an external order in the Court of Session, the authority may apply to the court for an interim administration order (whether before or after starting the proceedings).

(2) An interim administration order is an order for—

    (a) the detention, custody or preservation of property, and

    (b) the appointment of an interim administrator.

(3) An application for an interim administration order may be made without notice if the circumstances are such that notice of the application would prejudice any right of the enforcement authority to obtain a recovery order in respect of any property.

(4) The court may make an interim administration order on the application if it is satisfied that the conditions in paragraphs (5) and, where applicable, (6) are met.

(5) The first condition is that there is a probabilis causa litigandi—

    (a) that the property to which the application for the order relates is or includes recoverable property, and

    (b) that, if any of it is not recoverable property, it is associated property.

(6) The second condition is that, if—

    (a) the property to which the application for the order relates includes property alleged to be associated property, and

    (b) the enforcement authority has not established the identity of the person who holds it,

    the authority has taken all reasonable steps to do so.

(7) In its application for an interim administration order, the enforcement authority must nominate a suitably qualified person for appointment as interim administrator, but the nominee may not be a member of the staff of the Scottish Administration.

(8) The extent of the power to make an interim administration order is not limited by articles 168 to 175.

**168.— Functions of interim administrator**

(1) An interim administrator order may authorise or require the interim administrator—

    (a) to exercise any of the powers mentioned in Schedule 2,

(b)  to take any other steps the court thinks appropriate,

for the purpose of securing the detention, custody or preservation of the property to which the order applies or of taking any steps under paragraph (2).

(2)  An interim administration order must require the interim administrator to take any steps which the court thinks necessary to establish—

(a)  whether or not the property to which the order applies is recoverable property or associated property,

(b)  whether or not any other property is recoverable property (which satisfies the tests in article 202(1) and (2) or 203), and, if it is, who holds it.

(3)  If—

(a)  the interim administrator deals with any property which is not property to which the order applies, and

(b)  at the time he deals with the property he believes on reasonable grounds that he is entitled to do so in pursuance of the order,

the interim administrator is not liable to any person in respect of any loss or damage resulting from his dealing with the property except so far as the loss or damage is caused by his negligence.

### 169.— Inhibition of property affected by order

(1)  On the application of the enforcement authority, the Court of Session may, in relation to the property mentioned in paragraph (2), grant warrant for inhibition against any person specified in an interim administration order.

(2)  That property is heritable property situated in Scotland to which the interim administration order applies (whether generally or such of it as is specified in the application).

(3)  The warrant for inhibition—

(a)  has effect as if granted on the dependence of an action for debt by the enforcement authority against the person and may be executed, recalled, loosed or restricted accordingly, and

(b)  has the effect of letters of inhibition and must forthwith be registered by the enforcement authority in the register of inhibitions and adjudications.

(4)  Section 155 of the Titles to Land Consolidation (Scotland) Act 1868 (effective date of inhibition) applies in relation to an inhibition for which warrant is granted under paragraph (1) as it applies to an inhibition by separate letters or contained in a summons.

(5)  The execution of an inhibition under this article in respect of property does not prejudice the exercise of an interim administrator's powers under or for the purposes of this Part in respect of that property.

(6)  An inhibition under this article ceases to have effect when, or in so far as, the interim administration order ceases to apply in respect of the property in relation to which the warrant for inhibition was granted.

(7)  If an inhibition ceases to have effect to any extent by virtue of paragraph (6) the enforcement authority must—

(a)  apply for the recall or, as the case may be, the restriction of the inhibition, and

(b)  ensure that the recall or restriction is reflected in the register of inhibitions and adjudications.

### 170.— Interim administration orders: duties of respondent etc.

(1)  An interim administration order may require any person to whose property the order applies—

(a)  to bring the property to a place (in Scotland) specified by the interim administrator or place it in the custody of the interim administrator (if, in either case, he is able to do so),

(b)  to do anything he is reasonably required to do by the interim administrator for the preservation of the property.

(2)  An interim administration order may require any person to whose property the order applies to bring any documents relating to the property which are in his possession or control to a place (in Scotland) specified by the interim administrator or to place them in the custody of the interim administrator.

"Document" means anything in which information of any description is recorded.

**171.— Supervision of interim administrator and variation of order**

(1) The interim administrator, any party to the proceedings and any person affected by an action taken by the interim administrator, or who may be affected by any action proposed to be taken by him, may at any time apply to the court for directions as to the exercise of the interim administrator's functions.

(2) Before giving any directions under paragraph (1), the court must (as well as giving the parties to the proceedings an opportunity to be heard) give such an opportunity to the interim administrator and to any person who may be interested in the application.

(3) The court may at any time vary or recall an interim administration order.

(4) Before exercising any power to vary or set aside an interim administration order, the court must (as well as giving the parties to the proceedings an opportunity to be heard) give such an opportunity to the interim administrator and to any person who may be affected by the court's decision.

**172.— Interim administration orders: restrictions on dealing etc. with property**

(1) An interim administration order must, subject to any exclusions made in accordance with this article, prohibit any person to whose property the order applies from dealing with the property.

(2) Exclusions may be made when the interim administration order is made or on an application to vary the order.

(3) An exclusion may, in particular, make provision for the purpose of enabling any person—
    (a) to meet his reasonable living expenses, or
    (b) to carry on any trade, business, profession or occupation,
    and may be made subject to conditions.

(4) But an exclusion may not be made for the purpose of enabling any person to meet any legal expenses in respect of proceedings under this Part.

(5) If the excluded property is not specified in the order it must be described in the order in general terms.

(6) The power to make exclusions must be exercised with a view to ensuring, so far as practicable, that the satisfaction of any right of the enforcement authority to recover the property obtained through conduct which satisfies the test in article 202(2) is not unduly prejudiced.

**173.— Interim administration orders: restrictions on proceedings and remedies**

(1) While an interim administration order has effect, the court may sist any action, execution or other legal process in respect of the property to which the order applies.

(2) If a court (whether the Court of Session or any other court) in which proceedings are pending in respect of any property is satisfied that an interim administration order has been applied for or made in respect of the property, the court may either sist the proceedings or allow them to continue on any terms it thinks fit.

(3) Before exercising any power conferred by this article, the court must (as well as giving the parties to any of the proceedings in question an opportunity to be heard) give such an opportunity to the interim administrator (if appointed) and any person who may be affected by the court's decision.

**174.— Exclusion of property which is not recoverable etc. under interim administration order**

(1) If the court decides that any property to which an interim administration order applies is neither recoverable property nor associated property, it must vary the order so as to exclude it.

(2) The court may vary an interim administration order so as to exclude from the property to which the order applies any property which is alleged to be associated property if the court thinks that the satisfaction of any right of the enforcement authority to recover the property which satisfies the tests in article 202(1) and (2) will not be prejudiced.

(3) The court may exclude any property within paragraph (2) on any terms or conditions, applying while the interim administration order has effect, which the court thinks necessary or expedient.

**175.— Reporting under interim administration order**

(1) An interim administration order must require the interim administrator to inform the enforcement authority and the court as soon as reasonably practicable if he thinks that—
    (a) any property to which the order applies by virtue of a claim that it is recoverable property is not recoverable property,

(b) any property to which the order applies by virtue of a claim that it is associated property is not associated property,

(c) any property to which the order does not apply is recoverable property (which satisfies the tests in article 202(1) and (2)) or associated property, or

(d) any property to which the order applies is held by a person who is different from the person it is claimed holds it,

or if he thinks that there has been any other material change of circumstances.

(2) An interim administration order must require the interim administrator—

(a) to report his findings to the court,

(b) to serve copies of his report on the enforcement authority and on any person who holds any property to which the order applies or who may otherwise be affected by the report.

### 176.— Arrestment of property affected by interim administration order

(1) On the application of the enforcement authority or the interim administrator the Court of Session may, in relation to moveable recoverable property to which an interim administration order applies (whether generally or such of it as is specified in the application), grant warrant for arrestment.

(2) An application by the enforcement authority under paragraph (1) may be made at the same time as the application for the interim administration order or at any time thereafter.

(3) Such a warrant for arrestment may be granted only if the property would be arrestable if the person entitled to it were a debtor.

(4) A warrant under paragraph (1) has effect as if granted on the dependence of an action for debt at the instance of the enforcement authority or, as the case may be, the interim administrator against the person and may be executed, recalled, loosed or restricted accordingly.

(5) The execution of an arrestment under this article in respect of property does not prejudice the exercise of an interim administrator's powers under or for the purposes of this Part in respect of that property.

(6) An arrestment executed under this article ceases to have effect when, or in so far as, the interim administration order ceases to apply in respect of the property in relation to which the warrant for arrestment was granted.

(7) If an arrestment ceases to have effect to any extent by virtue of paragraph (6) the enforcement authority or, as the case may be, the interim administrator must apply to the Court of Session for an order recalling or, as the case may be, restrict the arrestment.

### *Vesting and realisation of recoverable property*

### 177.— Recovery orders

(1) The court must decide to give effect to an external order which falls within the meaning of section 447(2) of the Act by registering it and making a recovery order if it determines that any property or sum of money which is specified in it is recoverable property.

(2) In making such a determination the court must have regard to—

(a) the definitions in subsections (2), (4), (5), (6), (8) and (10) of section 447 of the Act, and

(b) articles 202 to 207.

(3) The recovery order must vest the recoverable property in the trustee for civil recovery.

(4) But the court may not make in a recovery order—

(a) any provision in respect of any recoverable property if each of the conditions in paragraph (5) or (as the case may be) (6) is met and it would not be just and equitable to do so, or

(b) any provision which is incompatible with any of the Convention rights (within the meaning of the Human Rights Act 1998).

(5) In relation to a court in England and Wales or Northern Ireland, the conditions referred to in paragraph (4)(a) are that—

(a) the respondent obtained the recoverable property in good faith,

(b) he took steps after obtaining the property which he would not have taken if he had not obtained it or he took steps before obtaining the property which he would not have taken if he had not believed he was going to obtain it,

    (c) when he took the steps, he had no notice that the property was recoverable,

    (d) if a recovery order were made in respect of the property, it would, by reason of the steps, be detrimental to him.

(6) In relation to a court in Scotland, the conditions referred to in paragraph (4)(a) are that—

    (a) the respondent obtained the recoverable property in good faith,

    (b) he took steps after obtaining the property which he would not have taken if he had not obtained it or he took steps before obtaining the property which he would not have taken if he had not believed he was going to obtain it,

    (c) when he took steps, he had no reasonable grounds for believing that the property was recoverable,

    (d) if a recovery order were made in respect of the property, it would, by reason of the steps, be detrimental to him.

(7) In deciding whether it would be just and equitable to make the provision in the recovery order where the conditions in paragraph (5) or (as the case may be) (6) are met, the court must have regard to—

    (a) the degree of detriment that would be suffered by the respondent if the provision were made,

    (b) the enforcement authority's interest in receiving the realised proceeds of the recoverable property.

(8) A recovery order may sever any property.

(9) A recovery order may impose conditions as to the manner in which the trustee for civil recovery may deal with any property vested by the order for the purpose of realising it.

(10) A recovery order made by a court in England and Wales or Northern Ireland may provide for payment under article 191 of reasonable legal expenses that a person has reasonably incurred, or may reasonably incur, in respect of—

    (a) the proceedings under this Part in which the order is made, or

    (b) any related proceedings under this Part.

(11) If regulations under article 199 apply to an item of expenditure, a sum in respect of the item is not payable under article 199 in pursuance of provision under paragraph (10) unless—

    (a) the enforcement authority agrees to its payment, or

    (b) the court has assessed the amount allowed by the regulations in respect of that item and the sum is paid in respect of the assessed amount.

(12) This article is subject to articles 181 to 189.

### 178.— Functions of the trustee for civil recovery

(1) The trustee for civil recovery is a person appointed by the court to give effect to a recovery order.

(2) The enforcement authority must nominate a suitably qualified person for appointment as the trustee.

(3) The functions of the trustee are—

    (a) to secure the detention, custody or preservation of any property vested in him by the recovery order,

    (b) in the case of property other than money, to realise the value of the property for the benefit of the enforcement authority, and

    (c) to perform any other functions conferred on him by virtue of this Chapter.

(4) In performing his functions, the trustee acts on behalf of the enforcement authority and must comply with any directions given by the authority.

(5) The trustee is to realise the value of property vested in him by the recovery order, so far as practicable, in the manner best calculated to maximise the amount payable to the enforcement authority.

(6) The trustee has the powers mentioned in Schedule 3.

(7) References in this article to a recovery order include an order under article E46 and references to property vested in the trustee by a recovery order include property vested in him in pursuance of an order under article 187.

### 179.— Recording of recovery order (Scotland)

(1) The clerk of the court must immediately after the making of a recovery order which relates to heritable property situated in Scotland send a certified copy of it to the keeper of the register of inhibitions and adjudications for recording in that register.

(2) Recording under paragraph (1) is to have the effect as from the date of the recovery order, of an inhibition at the instance of the trustee for civil recovery against the person in whom the heritable property was vest prior to that date.

### 180.— Rights of pre-emption etc.

(1) A recovery order is to have effect in relation to any property despite any provision (of whatever nature) which would otherwise prevent, penalise or restrict the vesting of the property.

(2) A right of pre-emption, right of irritancy, right of return or other similar right does not operate or become exercisable as a result of the vesting of any property under a recovery order.
A right of return means any right under a provision for the return or reversion of property in specified circumstances.

(3) Where property is vested under a recovery order, any such right is to have effect as if the person in whom the property is vested were the same person in law as the person who held the property and as if no transfer of the property had taken place.

(4) References to rights in paragraphs (2) and (3) do not include any rights in respect of which the recovery order was made.

(5) This article applies in relation to the creation of interests, or the doing of anything else, by a recovery order as it applies in relation to the vesting of property.

### 181.— Associated and joint property

(1) Articles 182 and 183 apply if the court makes a recovery order in respect of any recoverable property in a case within paragraph (2) or (3).

(2) A case is within this paragraph if—
  (a) the property to which the proceedings relate includes property which is associated with the recoverable property and is specified or described in the claim form or (in Scotland) application, and
  (b) if the associated property is not the respondent's property, the claim form or application has been served on the person whose property it is or the court has dispensed with service.

(3) A case is within this paragraph if—
  (a) the recoverable property belongs to joint tenants, and
  (b) one of the tenants is an excepted joint owner.

(4) An excepted joint owner is a person who obtained the property in circumstances in which it would not be recoverable as against him; and references to the excepted joint owner's share of the recoverable property are to so much of the recoverable property as would have been his if the joint tenancy had been severed.

(5) Paragraphs (3) and (4) do not extend to Scotland.

### 182.— Agreements about associated and joint property

(1) Where—
  (a) this article applies, and
  (b) the enforcement authority (on the one hand) and the person who holds the associated property or who is the excepted joint owner (on the other) agree,
the recovery order may, instead of vesting the recoverable property in the trustee for civil recovery, require the person who holds the associated property or who is the excepted joint owner to make a payment to the trustee.

(2) A recovery order which makes any requirement under paragraph (1) may, so far as required for giving effect to the agreement, include provision for vesting, creating, or extinguishing any interest in property.

(3) The amount of the payment is to be the amount which the enforcement authority and that person agree represents—
  (a) in a case within article 181(2), the value of the recoverable property,
  (b) in a case within article 181(3), the value of the recoverable property less the value of the excepted joint owner's share.

(4) But if—
  (a) a property freezing order, an interim receiving order, a prohibitory property order or an interim administration order applied at any time to the associated property or joint tenancy, and
  (b) the enforcement authority agrees that the person has suffered loss as a result of the order mentioned in sub-paragraph (a),
  the amount of the payment may be reduced by any amount the enforcement authority and that person agree is reasonable, having regard to that loss and to any other relevant circumstances.

(5) If there is more than one such item of associated property or excepted joint owner, the total amount to be paid to the trustee, and the part of that amount which is to be provided by each person who holds any such associated property or who is an excepted joint owner, is to be agreed between both (or all) of them and the enforcement authority.

(6) A recovery order which makes any requirement under paragraph (1) must make provision for any recoverable property to cease to be recoverable.

### 183.— Associated and joint property: default of agreement

(1) Where this article applies, the court may make the following provision if—
  (a) there is no agreement under article 182, and
  (b) the court thinks it just and equitable to do so.

(2) The recovery order may provide—
  (a) for the associated property to vest in the trustee for civil recovery or (as the case may be) for the excepted joint owner's interest to be extinguished, or
  (b) in the case of an excepted joint owner, for the severance of his interest.

(3) A recovery order making any provision by virtue of paragraph (2)(a) may provide—
  (a) for the trustee to pay an amount to the person who holds the associated property or who is an excepted joint owner, or
  (b) for the creation of interests in favour of that person, or the imposition of liabilities or conditions, in relation to the property vested in the trustee,
  or for both.

(4) In making any provision in a recovery order by virtue of paragraph (2) or (3), the court must have regard to—
  (a) the rights of any person who holds the associated property or who is an excepted joint owner and the value to him of that property or, as the case may be, of his share (including any value which cannot be assessed in terms of money),
  (b) the enforcement authority's interest in receiving the realised proceeds of the recoverable property.

(5) If—
  (a) a property freezing order, an interim receiving order, a prohibitory property order or an interim administration order applied at any time to the associated property or joint tenancy, and
  (b) the court is satisfied that the person who holds the associated property or who is an excepted joint owner has suffered loss as a result of the order mentioned in sub-paragraph (a), a recovery order making any provision by virtue of paragraph (2) or (3) may require the enforcement authority to pay compensation to that person.

(6) The amount of compensation to be paid under paragraph (5) is the amount the court thinks reasonable, having regard to the person's loss and to any other relevant circumstances.

[(7) In subsection (5) the reference to the enforcement authority is, in the case of an enforcement authority in relation to England and Wales or Northern Ireland, a reference to the enforcement authority which obtained the property freezing order or interim receiving order concerned.]

### 184.— Payments in respect of rights under pension schemes

(1) This article applies to recoverable property consisting of rights under a pension scheme.

(2) A recovery order in respect of the property must, instead of vesting the property in the trustee for civil recovery, require the trustees or managers of the pension scheme—

    (a) to pay to the trustee for civil recovery within the period determined in accordance with paragraph 5 of Schedule 4 ("the prescribed period") the amount determined by the trustees or managers to be equal to the value of the rights, and

    (b) to give effect to any other provision made by virtue of this article and the two following articles in respect of the scheme.

    This paragraph is subject to articles 187 to 189.

(3) A recovery order made by virtue of paragraph (2) overrides the provisions of the pension scheme to the extent that they conflict with the provisions of the order.

(4) A recovery order made by virtue of paragraph (2) may provide for the recovery by the trustees or managers of the scheme (whether by deduction from any amount which they are required to pay to the trustee for civil recovery or otherwise) of costs incurred by them in—

    (a) complying with the recovery order, or

    (b) providing information, before the order was made, to the enforcement authority, [receiver appointed under article 150A,] interim receiver or interim administrator.

(5) None of the following provisions applies to a court making a recovery order by virtue of paragraph (2)—

    (a) any provision of section 159 of the Pension Schemes Act 1993, section 155 of the Pension Schemes (Northern Ireland) Act 1993, section 91 of the Pensions Act 1995 or Article 89 of the Pensions (Northern Ireland) Order 1995 (which prevent assignment and the making of orders that restrain a person from receiving anything which he is prevented from assigning),

    (b) any provision of any enactment (whenever passed or made) corresponding to any of the provisions mentioned in sub-paragraph (a),

    (c) any provision of the pension scheme in question corresponding to any to those provisions.

### 185.— Consequential adjustment of liabilities under pension schemes

(1) A recovery order made by virtue of article 184(2) must require the trustees or managers of the pension scheme to make such reduction in the liabilities of the scheme as they think necessary in consequence of the payment made in pursuance of that paragraph.

(2) Accordingly, the order must require the trustees or managers to provide for the liabilities of the pension scheme in respect of the respondent's recoverable property to which article 184 applies to cease.

(3) So far as the trustees or managers are required by the recovery order to provide for the liabilities of the pension scheme in respect of the respondent's recoverable property to which article 184 applies to cease, their powers include (in particular) power to reduce the amount of—

    (a) any benefit or future benefit to which the respondent may be entitled under the scheme,

    (b) any future benefit to which any other person may be entitled under the scheme in respect of that property.

### 186.— Pension schemes: supplementary

(1) Schedule 4 has effect for the purposes of the exercise by trustees or managers of their powers under articles 184 and 185, including provision about the calculation and verification of the value at any time of rights and liabilities.

(2) A pension scheme means an occupational pension scheme or a personal pension scheme; and those expressions have the same meaning as in the Pension Schemes Act 1993 or, in relation to Northern Ireland, the Pension Schemes (Northern Ireland) Act 1993.

(3) In relation to an occupational pension scheme or a personal pension scheme, the trustees or managers means—

    (a) in the case of a scheme established under a trust, the trustees,

    (b) in any other case, the managers.

(4) References to a pension scheme include—

    (a) a retirement annuity contract (within the meaning of Part 3 of the Welfare Reform and Pensions Act 1999 or, in relation to Northern Ireland, Part 4 of the Welfare Reform and Pensions (Northern Ireland) Order 1999),

   (b)  an annuity or insurance policy purchased, or transferred, for the purpose of giving effect to rights under an occupational pension scheme or a personal scheme,

   (c)  an annuity purchased, or entered into, for the purpose of discharging any liability in respect of a pension credit under section 29(1)(b) of the Welfare Reform and Pensions Act 1999 or, in relation to Northern Ireland, Article 26(1)(b) of the Welfare Reform and Pensions (Northern Ireland) Order 1999.

(5)  References to the trustees or managers—

   (a)  in relation to a retirement annuity contract or other annuity, are to the provider of the annuity,

   (b)  in relation to an insurance policy, are to the insurer.

(6)  Paragraphs (2) to (5) have effect for the purposes of this group of articles (that is, articles 184, 185 and this article).

### 187.— Consent orders

(1)  The court may make an order staying (in Scotland, sisting) any proceedings for a recovery order on terms agreed by the parties for the disposal of the proceedings if each person to whose property the proceedings, or the agreement, relates is a party both to the proceedings and the agreement.

(2)  An order under paragraph (1) may, as well as staying (or sisting) the proceedings on terms—

   (a)  make provision for any property which may be recoverable property to cease to be recoverable,

   (b)  make any further provision which the court thinks appropriate.

(3)  Article 191 applies to property vested in the trustee for civil recovery, or money paid to him, in pursuance of the agreement as it applies to property vested in him by a recovery order or money paid under article 182.

### 188.— Consent orders: pensions

(1)  This article applies where recoverable property to which proceedings under this Chapter relate includes rights under a pension scheme.

(2)  An order made under article 187—

   (a)  may not stay (in Scotland, sist) the proceedings on terms that the rights are vested in any other person, but

   (b)  may include provision imposing the following requirement, if the trustees or managers of the scheme are parties to the agreement by virtue of which the order is made.

(3)  The requirement is that the trustees or managers of the pension scheme—

   (a)  make a payment in accordance with the agreement, and

   (b)  give effect to any other provision made by virtue of this article in respect of the scheme.

(4)  The trustees or managers of the pension scheme have power to enter into an agreement in respect of the proceedings on any terms on which an order made under article 187 may stay (in Scotland, sist) the proceedings.

(5)  The following provisions apply in respect of an order under article 187, so far as it includes the requirement mentioned in paragraph (3).

(6)  The order overrides the provisions of the pension scheme to the extent that they conflict with the requirement.

(7)  The order may provide for the recovery by the trustees or managers of the scheme (whether by deduction from any amount which they are required to pay in pursuance of the agreement or otherwise) of costs incurred by them in—

   (a)  complying with the order, or

   (b)  providing information, before the order was made, to the enforcement authority, [receiver appointed under article 150A,] interim receiver or interim administrator.

(8)  Articles 184(5) and 185 (read with article 186) apply as if the requirement were included in an order made by virtue of article 184(2).

(9)  Paragraphs (4) to (7) of article 186 have effect for the purposes of this article.

**189.— Limit on recovery**

(1) This article applies if the enforcement authority seeks a recovery order—
- (a) in respect of both property which is or represents property which satisfies the tests in article 202(1) or (2) and related property, or
- (b) in respect of property which is or represents property which satisfies those tests where such an order, or an order under article 187, has previously been made in respect of related property.

(2) For the purposes of this article—
- (a) the original property means the property specified in the external order or a sum of money so specified,
- (b) the original property, and any items of property which represent the original property, are to be treated as related to each other.

(3) The court is not to make a recovery order if it thinks that the enforcement authority's right to recover the original property has been satisfied by a previous recovery order or order under article 187.

(4) Subject to paragraph (3), the court may act under paragraph (5) if it thinks that—
- (a) a recovery order may be made in respect of two or more related items of recoverable property, but
- (b) the making of a recovery order in respect of both or all of them is not required in order to satisfy the enforcement authority's right to recover the original property.

(5) The court may in order to satisfy that right to the extent required make a recovery order in respect of—
- (a) only some of the related items of property, or
- (b) only a part of any of the related items of property,

or both.

(6) Where the court may make a recovery order in respect of any property, this article does not prevent the recovery of any profits which have accrued in respect of the property.

(7) If—
- (a) an order is made under section 298 of the Act for the forfeiture of recoverable property, and
- (b) the enforcement authority subsequently seeks a recovery order in respect of related property,

the order under section 298 is to be treated, for the purposes of this article as if it were a recovery order obtained by the enforcement authority in respect of the forfeited property.

(8) If—
- (a) in pursuance of a judgment in civil proceedings (whether in the United Kingdom or elsewhere), the claimant has obtained property from the defendant ("the judgment property"),
- (b) the claim was based on the defendant's having obtained the judgment property or related property through unlawful conduct within the meaning of section 242 of the Act, and
- (c) the enforcement authority subsequently seeks a recovery order in respect of property which is related to the judgment property,

the judgment is to be treated for the purposes of this article as if it were a recovery order obtained by the enforcement authority in respect of the judgment property.

In relation to Scotland, "claimant" and "defendant" are to be read as "pursuer" and "defender".

(9) If—
- (a) property has been taken into account in deciding the amount of a person's benefit from criminal conduct for the purpose of making a confiscation order, and
- (b) the enforcement authority subsequently seeks a recovery order in respect of related property,

the confiscation order is to be treated for the purposes of this article as it were a recovery order obtained by the enforcement authority in respect of the property referred to in sub-paragraph (a).

(10) In paragraph (9), a confiscation order means—
- (a) an order under section 6, 92 or 156 of the Act or an external order registered under Parts 2, 3 or 4 of this Order,
- (b) an order under a corresponding provision of an enactment mentioned in section 8(7)(a) to (g) of the Act,

and, in relation to an order mentioned in sub-paragraph (b), the reference to the amount of a person's benefit from criminal conduct is to be read as a reference to the corresponding amount under the enactment in question.

**190.— Article 189: supplementary**

(1) Paragraphs (2) and (3) give examples of the satisfaction of the enforcement authority's right to recover the original property.

(2) If—
    (a) there is a disposal, other than a part disposal, of the original property, and
    (b) other property (the representative property) is obtained in its place,
the enforcement authority's right to recover the original property is satisfied by the making of a recovery order in respect of either the original property or the representative property.

(3) If—
    (a) there is a part disposal of the original property, and
    (b) other property (the representative property) is obtained in place of the property disposed of,
the enforcement authority's right to recover the original property is satisfied by the making of a recovery order in respect of the remainder of the original property together with either the representative property or the property disposed of.

(4) In this article—
    (a) a part disposal means a disposal to which article 211(1) applies,
    (b) the original property has the same meaning as in article 189.

**191.— Applying realised proceeds**

(1) This article applies to—
    (a) sums which represent the realised proceeds of property which was vested in the trustee for civil recovery by a recovery order or which he obtained in pursuance of a recovery order,
    (b) sums vested in the trustee by a recovery order or obtained by him in pursuance of a recovery order.

(2) The trustee is to make out of the sums—
    (a) first, any payment required to be made by him by virtue of article 183,
    (b) next, any payment of legal expenses which, after giving effect to article 177(11), are payable under this paragraph in pursuance of provision under article 177(10) contained in the recovery order,
    (c) next, any payment of expenses incurred by a person acting as an insolvency practitioner which are payable under this paragraph by virtue of article 3(10),
and any sum which remains is to be paid to the enforcement authority.

(3) The [enforcement authority (unless it is the Scottish Ministers)] may apply a sum received by [it] under paragraph (2) in making payment of the remuneration and expenses of—
    (a) the trustee, or
    (b) any interim receiver appointed in, or in anticipation of, the proceedings for the recovery order.

(4) Paragraph (3)(a) does not apply in relation to the remuneration of the trustee if the trustee is a member of the staff of the [enforcement authority concerned].

*Exemptions etc.*

**192.— Victims of theft etc.**

(1) In proceedings for a recovery order, a person who claims that any property alleged to be recoverable property, or any part of the property, belongs to him may apply for a declaration under this article.

(2) If the applicant appears to the court to meet the following condition, the court may make a declaration to that effect.

(3) The condition is that—
    (a) the person was deprived of the property he claims, or of property which it represents, by unlawful conduct within the meaning of section 241 of the Act,
    (b) the property he was deprived of was not recoverable property immediately before he was deprived of it, and
    (c) the property he claims belongs to him.

(4) Property to which a declaration under this article applies is not recoverable property.

**193.— Other exemptions**

(1) Proceedings for a recovery order may not be taken against the Financial Services Authority in respect of any recoverable property held by the authority.

(2) Proceedings for a recovery order may not be taken in respect of any property which is subject to any of the following charges—
  (a) a collateral security charge, within the meaning of the Financial Markets and Insolvency (Settlement Finality) Regulations 1999,
  (b) a market charge, within the meaning of Part 7 of the Companies Act 1989,
  (c) a money market charge, within the meaning of the Financial Markets and Insolvency (Money Market) Regulations 1995,
  (d) a system charge, within the meaning of the Financial Markets and Insolvency Regulations 1996 or the Financial Markets and Insolvency Regulations (Northern Ireland) 1996.

(3) Proceedings for a recovery order may not be taken against any person in respect of any recoverable property which he holds by reason of his acting or having acted, as an insolvency practitioner. Acting as an insolvency practitioner has the same meaning as in article 4.

*Miscellaneous*

**194.— Compensation**

(1) If, in the case of any property to which a property freezing order, an interim receiving order, a prohibitory property order or an interim administration order has at any time applied, the court does not in the course of the proceedings, decide that the property is recoverable property or associated property, the person whose property it is may make an application to the court for compensation.

(2) Paragraph (1) does not apply if the court—
  (a) has made a declaration in respect of the property by virtue of article 192, or
  (b) makes an order under article 187.

(3) If the court has made a decision by reason of which no recovery order could be made in respect of the property, the application for compensation must be made within the period of three months beginning—
  (a) in relation to a decision of the High Court in England and Wales, with the date of the decision or, if any application is made for leave to appeal, with the date on which the application is withdrawn or refused or (if the application is granted) on which any proceedings on appeal are finally concluded,
  (b) in relation to a decision of the Court of Session or of the High Court in Northern Ireland, with the date of the decision or, if there an appeal against the decision, with the date on which any proceedings on appeal are finally concluded.

(4) If, in England and Wales or Northern Ireland, the proceedings in respect of the property have been discontinued, the application for compensation must be made within the period of three months beginning with the discontinuance.

(5) If the court is satisfied that the applicant has suffered loss as a result of the order mentioned in paragraph (1), it may require the enforcement authority to pay compensation to him.

(6) If, but for article 180(2), any right mentioned there would have operated in favour of, or become exercisable by, any person, he may make an application to the court for compensation.

(7) The application for compensation under paragraph (6) must be made within the period of three months beginning with the vesting referred to in article 180(2).

(8) If the court is satisfied that, in consequence of the operation of article 180, the right in question cannot subsequently operate in favour of the applicant or (as the case may be) become exercisable by him, it may require the enforcement authority to pay compensation to him.

(9) The amount of compensation to be paid under this article is the amount the court thinks reasonable, having regard to the loss suffered and any other relevant circumstances.

[(10) In the case of an enforcement authority in relation to England and Wales or Northern Ireland—
  (a) the reference in paragraph (5) to the enforcement authority is a reference to the enforcement authority which obtained the property freezing order or interim receiving order concerned, and
  (b) the reference in paragraph (8) to the enforcement authority is a reference to the enforcement authority which obtained the recovery order concerned.]

### 195.— Payment of interim administrator or trustee (Scotland)

(1) Any fees or expenses incurred by an interim administrator, or a trustee for civil recovery appointed by the Court of Session, in the exercise of his functions are to be reimbursed by the Scottish Ministers as soon as is practicable after they have been incurred.

(2) The Scottish Ministers may apply a sum received by them under article 191(2) in making payment of such fees or expenses.

(3) Paragraph (2) does not apply in relation to the fees of a trustee for civil recovery if the trustee is a member of their staff.

### 196.— Effect on diligence of recovery order (Scotland)

(1) An arrestment or poinding of any recoverable property executed on or after the appointment of the trustee for civil recovery is ineffectual in a question with the trustee.

(2) Any recoverable property so arrested or poinded, or (if the property has been sold) the proceeds of sale, must be handed over to the trustee for civil recovery.

(3) A poinding of the ground in respect of recoverable property on or after such an appointment is ineffectual in a question with the trustee for civil recovery except for the interest mentioned in paragraph (4).

(4) That interest is—

    (a) interest on the debt of a secured creditor for the current half yearly term, and

    (b) arrears of interest on that debt for one year immediately before the commencement of that term.

(5) On and after such appointment no other person may raise or insist in an adjudication against recoverable property or be confirmed as an executor-creditor on that property.

(6) An inhibition on recoverable property shall cease to have effect in relation to any heritable property comprised in the recoverable property on such appointment.

(7) The provision of this article apply in relation to—

    (a) an action of maills and duties, and

    (b) an action for sequestration of rent,

as they apply in relation to an arrestment or poinding.

### 197.— Scope of powers (Scotland)

(1) Orders under this Chapter may be made by the Court of Session in respect of a person wherever domiciled, resident or present.

(2) But such an order in respect of a person's moveable property may not be made by the Court of Session where—

    (a) the person is not domiciled, resident or present in Scotland, and

    (b) the property is not situated in Scotland,

unless the conduct which satisfies the test in article 202(2) took place in Scotland.

### 198.— Legal expenses excluded from freezing: required conditions

(1) The Lord Chancellor may by regulations specify the required conditions for the purposes of article 149(5) or 157(4).

(2) A required condition may (in particular)—

    (a) restrict who may receive sums released in pursuance of the exclusion (by, for example, requiring released sums to be paid to professional legal advisers), or

    (b) be made for the purpose of controlling the amount of any sum released in pursuance of the exclusion in respect of an item of expenditure.

(3) A required condition made for the purpose mentioned in paragraph (2)(b) may (for example)—

    (a) provide for sums to be released only with the agreement of the enforcement authority;

    (b) provide for a sum to be released in respect of an item of expenditure only if the court has assessed the amount allowed by regulations under article 199 in respect of that item and the sum is released for payment of the assessed amount;

    (c) provide for a sum to be released in respect of an item of expenditure only if—

        (i) the enforcement authority agrees to its release, or

        (ii) the court has assessed the amount allowed by regulations under article 199 in respect of that item and the sum is released for payment of the assessed amount.

(4) Before making regulations under this article, the Lord Chancellor must consult such persons as he considers appropriate.

### 199.— Legal expenses: regulations for purposes of article 177(11) or 198(3)

(1) The Lord Chancellor may by regulations—
  (a) make provision for the purposes of article 177(11);
  (b) make provision for the purposes of required conditions that make provision of the kind mentioned in article 198(3)(b) or (c).

(2) Regulations under this article may (in particular)—
  (a) limit the amount of remuneration allowable to representatives for a unit of time worked;
  (b) limit the total amount of remuneration allowable to representatives for work done in connection with proceedings or a step in proceedings;
  (c) limit the amount allowable in respect of an item of expense incurred by a representative or incurred, otherwise than in respect of the remuneration of a representative, by a party to proceedings.

(3) Before making regulations under this article, the Lord Chancellor must consult such persons as he considers appropriate.

### 200.— Financial threshold

(1) The enforcement authority may not start proceedings for a recovery order unless the authority reasonably believes that the aggregate value of the recoverable property which the authority wishes to be subject to a recovery order is not less than £10,000.

(2) If the authority applies for a property freezing order, an interim receiving order, a prohibitory property order or an interim administration order before starting the proceedings, paragraph (1) applies to the application instead of to the start of the proceedings.

(3) This article does not affect the continuation of proceedings for a recovery order which have been properly started or the making or continuing effect of a property freezing order, an interim receiving order, a prohibitory property order or an interim administration order which has been properly applied for.

### 201.— Limitation

(1) After section 27A of the Limitation Act 1980 there is inserted—

#### "27B Actions for recovery of property for purposes of an external order

(1) None of the time limits given in the preceding provisions of this Act applies to any proceedings under Chapter 2 of Part 5 of the Proceeds of Crime Act 2002 (External Requests and Orders) Order 2005 (civil proceedings for the realisation of property to give effect to an external order).

(2) Proceedings under that Chapter for a recovery order in respect of any recoverable property shall not be brought after the expiration of the period of twelve years from the date on which the Director's cause of action accrued.

(3) Proceedings under that Chapter are brought when—
  (a) a claim form is issued, or
  (b) an application is made for a property freezing order, or
  (c) an application is made for an interim receiving order,
  whichever is earliest.

(4) The Director's cause of action accrues in respect of any recoverable property—
  (a) in the case of proceedings for a recovery order in respect of property obtained, or believed to have been obtained, as a result of or in connection with criminal lconduct, when the property is so obtained,
  (b) in the case of proceedings for a recovery order in respect of any other recoverable property, when the property obtained, or believed to have been obtained, as a result of or in connection with criminal conduct which it represents is so obtained.

(5) If—
  (a) a person would (but for the preceding provisions of this Act) have a cause of action in respect of the conversion of a chattel, and

(b)  proceedings are started under that Chapter for a recovery order in respect of the chattel,

section 3(2) of this Act does not prevent his asserting on an application under article 192 of that Order that the property belongs to him, or the court making a declaration in his favour under that article.

(6)  If the court makes such a declaration, his title to the chattel is to be treated as not having been extinguished by section 3(2) of this Act.

(7)  In this section—

(a)  "criminal conduct" is to be construed in accordance with section 447(8) of the Proceeds of Crime Act 2002, and

(b)  expressions used in this section which are also used in Part 5 of the Proceeds of Crime Act 2002 (External Requests and Orders) Order 2005 have the same meaning in this section as in that Part.".

(2)  After section 19B of the Prescription and Limitation (Scotland) Act 1973 there is inserted—

### "19C Actions for recovery of property for the purposes of an external order

(1)  None of the time limits given in the preceding provisions of this Act applies to any proceedings under Chapter 2 of Part 5 of the Proceeds of Crime Act 2002 (External Requests and Orders) Order 2005 (civil proceedings for the realisation of property to give effect to an external order).

(2)  Proceedings under that Chapter for a recovery order in respect of any recoverable property shall not be commenced after the expiration of the period of twelve years from the date on which the Scottish Ministers' right of action accrued.

(3)  Proceedings under that Chapter are commenced when—

(a)  the proceedings are served,

(b)  an application is made for a prohibitory property order, or

(c)  an application is made for an interim administration order, whichever is the earliest.

(4)  The Scottish Ministers' right of action accrues in respect of any recoverable property—

(a)  in the case of proceedings for a recovery order in respect of property obtained, or believed to have been obtained, as a result of or in connection with criminal conduct, when the property is so obtained,

(b)  in the case of proceedings for a recovery order in respect of any other recoverable property, when the property obtained, or believed to have been obtained, as a result of or in connection with criminal conduct which it represents is so obtained.

(5)  In this section—

(a)  "criminal conduct" is to be construed in accordance with section 447(8) of the Proceeds of Crime Act 2002, and

(b)  expressions used in this section which are also used in Part 5 of the Proceeds of Crime Act 2002 (External Requests and Orders) Order 2005 have the same meaning in this section as in that Part.".

(3)  After Article 72A of the Limitation (Northern Ireland) Order 1989 there is inserted—

### "72B Actions for recovery of property for purposes of an external order

(1)  None of the time limits fixed by Parts 2 and 3 of this Order applies to any proceedings under Chapter 2 of Part 5 of the Proceeds of Crime Act 2002 (External Requests and Orders) Order 2005 (civil proceedings for the realisation of property to give effect to an external order).

(2)  Proceedings under that Chapter for a recovery order in respect of any recoverable property shall not be brought after the expiration of the period of twelve years from the date on which the Director's cause of action accrued.

(3)  Proceedings under that Chapter are brought when—

(a)  a claim form is issued, or

(b)  an application is made for a property freezing order, or

(c)  an application is made for an interim receiving order,

whichever is earliest.

(4)  The Director's cause of action accrues in respect of any recoverable property—

(a)  in the case of proceedings for a recovery order in respect of property obtained, or believed to have been obtained, as a result of or in connection with criminal conduct, when the property is so obtained,

(b) in the case of proceedings for a recovery order in respect of any other recoverable property, when the property obtained, or believed to have been obtained, as a result of or in connection with criminal conduct which it represents is so obtained.

(5) If—

    (a) a person would (but for a time limit fixed by this Order) have a cause of action in respect of the conversion of a chattel, and

    (b) proceedings are started under that Chapter for a recovery order in respect of the chattel,

article 17(2) of this Order does not prevent his asserting on an application under article 192 of that Order that the property belongs to him, or the court making a declaration in his favour under that article.

(6) If the court makes such a declaration, his title to the chattel is to be treated as not having been extinguished by article 17(2) of this Order.

(7) In this article—

    (a) "criminal conduct" is to be construed in accordance with section 447(8) of the Proceeds of Crime Act 2002, and

    (b) expressions used in this article which are also used in Part 5 of the Proceeds of Crime Act 2002 (External Requests and Orders) Order 2005 have the same meaning in this article as in that Part."

## Chapter 3
## General
### *Recoverable property*

**202.— Recoverable property: property or sum of money specified in the external order**

(1) Property or a sum of money is recoverable property if it is specified in an external order (within the meaning of section 447(2) of the Act).

(2) Accordingly, the property (including money) must have been found to have been obtained as a result of or in connection with criminal conduct (within the meaning of section 447(8) of the Act) or must have been believed to have been so obtained.

(3) But if property (including money) which is specified in the external order has been disposed of (since it was so obtained), it is recoverable property only if it is held by a person into whose hands it may be followed.

(4) Recoverable property specified in an external order may be followed into the hands of a person obtaining it on a disposal by—

    (a) the person who through the conduct obtained the property, or

    (b) a person into whose hands it may (by virtue of this paragraph) be followed.

(5) Where an external order specifies property other than a sum of money, only that property is recoverable property.

**203.— Tracing property, etc.**

(1) This article applies only where an external order specifies a sum of money.

(2) Where property which satisfies the tests in article 202(1) and (2) ("the original property") is or has been recoverable, property which represents the original property is also recoverable property.

(3) If a person enters into a transaction by which—

    (a) he disposes of recoverable property, whether the original property or property which (by virtue of this Chapter) represents the original property, and

    (b) he obtains other property in place of it,

the other property represents the original property.

(4) If a person disposes of recoverable property which represents the original property, the property may be followed into the hands of the person who obtains it (and it continues to represent the original property).

**204.— Mixing property**

(1) This article applies only where an external order specifies a sum of money.

(2) Paragraph (3) applies if a person's recoverable property is mixed with other property (whether his property or another's).

(3) The portion of the mixed property which is attributable to the recoverable property represents the property which satisfies the tests in article 202(1) and (2).

(4) Recoverable property is mixed with other property if (for example) it is used—

    (a) to increase funds held in a bank account,

    (b) in part payment for the acquisition of an asset,

    (c) for the restoration or improvement of land,

    (d) by a person holding a leasehold interest in the property to acquire the freehold.

**205.— Recoverable property: general exceptions**

(1) If—

    (a) a person disposes of recoverable property, and

    (b) the person who obtains it on the disposal does so in good faith, for value and without notice that it was recoverable property,

the property may not be followed into that person's hands and, accordingly, it ceases to be recoverable.

(2) If recoverable property is vested, forfeited or otherwise disposed of in pursuance of powers conferred by virtue of this Part, it ceases to be recoverable.

(3) If—

    (a) in pursuance of a judgment in civil proceedings (whether in the United Kingdom or elsewhere), the defendant makes a payment to the claimant or the claimant otherwise obtains property from the defendant,

    (b) the claimant's claim is based on any conduct by the defendant which satisfies the test in article 202(2), and

    (c) apart from this paragraph, the sum received, or the property obtained, by the claimant would be recoverable property,

the property ceases to be recoverable.

In relation to Scotland, "claimant" and "defendant" are to be read as "pursuer" and "defender".

(4) If—

    (a) a payment is made to a person in pursuance of a compensation order under Article 14 of the Criminal Justice (Northern Ireland) Order 1994, section 249 of the Criminal Procedure (Scotland) Act 1995 or section 130 of the Powers of Criminal Court (Sentencing) Act 2000, and

    (b) apart from this paragraph, the sum received would be recoverable property,

the property ceases to be recoverable.

(5) If—

    (a) a payment is made to a person in pursuance of a restitution order under section 27 of the Theft Act (Northern Ireland) 1969 or section 148(2) of the Powers of Criminal Courts (Sentencing) Act 2000 or a person otherwise obtains any property in pursuance of such an order, and

    (b) apart from this paragraph, the sum received, or the property obtained, would be recoverable property,

the property ceases to be recoverable.

(6) If—

    (a) in pursuance of an order made by the court under section 382(3) or 383(5) of the Financial Services and Markets Act 2000 (restitution orders), an amount is paid to or distributed among any persons in accordance with the court's directions, and

    (b) apart from this paragraph, the sum received by them would be recoverable property,

the property ceases to be recoverable.

(7) If—

    (a) in pursuance of a requirement of the Financial Services Authority under section 384(5) of the Financial Services and Markets Act 2000 (power of authority to pursue restitution), an amount is paid to or distributed among any persons and

(b) apart from this paragraph, the sum received by them would be recoverable property,

the property ceases to be recoverable.

(8) Property is not recoverable while a restraint order applies to it, that is—

   (a) an order under section 41, 120 or 190 of the Act or article 8, 58 or 95 of this Order, or

   (b) an order under any corresponding provision of an enactment mentioned in section 8(7)(a) to (g) of the Act.

(9) Property is not recoverable if it has been taken into account in deciding the amount of a person's benefit from criminal conduct for the purpose of making a confiscation order, that is—

   (a) an order under section 6, 92 or 156 of the Act or an external order registered under Part 2, 3 or 4 of this Order, or

   (b) an order under a corresponding provision of an enactment mentioned in section 8(7)(a) to (g) of the Act,

and, in relation to an order mentioned in sub paragraph (b), the reference to the amount of a person's benefit from criminal conduct is to be read as a reference to the corresponding amount under the enactment in question.

(10) Where—

   (a) a person enters into a transaction to which article 203(3) applies, and

   (b) the disposal is one to which paragraph (1) or (2) applies,

this article does not affect the recoverability (by virtue of article 203(3)) of any property obtained on the transaction in place of the property disposed of.

## 206.— Other exemptions

(1) Property, which apart from this article, would be recoverable property and is—

   (a) forfeited in pursuance of powers conferred by the customs and excise Acts, as defined by section 1(1) of the Customs and Excise Management Act 1979, or

   (b) disposed of in pursuance of an enactment prescribed in Schedule 5,

is not recoverable or (as the case may be) associated property.

(2) But where particular circumstances are prescribed in Schedule 5 in relation to an enactment, paragraph (1)(b) applies only in those circumstances.

## 207.— Granting interests

(1) If a person grants an interest in his recoverable property, the question whether the interest is also recoverable is to be determined in the same manner as it is on any other disposal of recoverable property.

(2) Accordingly, on his granting an interest in the property ("the property in question")—

   (a) where the property in question is property which satisfies the tests in article 202(1) and (2), the interest is also to be treated as satisfying those tests,

   (b) where the property in question represents in his hands property which satisfies the tests in article 202(1) and (2), the interest is also to be treated as representing in his hands property which satisfies those tests.

*Insolvency*

## 208.— Insolvency

(1) Proceedings for a recovery order may not be taken or continued in respect of property to which paragraph (2) applies unless the appropriate court gives leave and the proceedings are taken or (as the case may be) continued in accordance with any terms imposed by that court.

(2) This paragraph applies to recoverable property, or property associated with it, if—

   (a) it is an asset of a company being wound up in pursuance of a resolution for voluntary winding up,

   (b) it is an asset of a company and a voluntary arrangement under Part 1 of the 1986 Act or Part 2 of the 1989 Order, has effect in relation to the company,

   (c) an order under section 2 of the 1985 Act, section 286 of the 1986 Act or Article 259 of the 1989 Order (appointment of interim trustee or interim receiver) has effect in relation to the property,

(d) it is an asset comprised in the estate of an individual who has been adjudged bankrupt or, in relation to Scotland, of a person whose estate has been sequestrated,

(e) it is an asset of an individual and a voluntary arrangement under Part 8 of the 1986 Act, or Part 8 of the 1989 Order, has effect in relation to him, or

(f) in relation to Scotland, it is property comprised in the estate of a person who has granted a trust deed within the meaning of the 1985 Act.

(3) An application under this article, or under any provision of the 1986 Act or the 1989 Order, for leave to take proceedings for a recovery order may be made without notice to any person.

(4) Paragraph (3) does not affect any requirement for notice of an application to given to any person acting as an insolvency practitioner or to the official receiver (whether or not acting as an insolvency practitioner).

(5) References to the provisions of the 1986 Act in sections 420 and 421 of that Act, or to the provisions of the 1989 Order in Articles 364 or 365 of that Order, (insolvent partnerships and estates of deceased persons) include paragraphs (1) and (2) above.

(6) In this article—

(a) the 1985 Act means the Bankruptcy (Scotland) Act 1985,

(b) the 1986 Act means the Insolvency Act 1986,

(c) the 1989 Order means the Insolvency (Northern Ireland) Order 1989,

and in paragraph (7) "the applicable enactment" means whichever enactment mentioned in sub-paragraphs (a) to (c) is relevant to the resolution, arrangement, order or trust deed mentioned in paragraph (2).

(7) In this article—

(a) an asset means any property within the meaning of the applicable enactment or, where the 1985 Act is the applicable enactment, any property comprised in an estate to which the 1985 Act applies,

(b) the appropriate court means the court which, in relation to the resolution, arrangement, order or trust deed mentioned in paragraph (2), is the court for the purposes of the applicable enactment or, in relation to Northern Ireland, the High Court,

(c) acting as an insolvency practitioner has the same meaning as in article 4,

(d) other expressions used in this article and in the applicable enactment have the same meaning as in that enactment.

### *Delegation of enforcement functions*

### 209.— Performance of functions of Scottish Ministers by constables in Scotland

(1) In Scotland, a constable engaged in temporary service with the Scottish Ministers in connection with their functions under this Part may perform functions, other than those specified in subsection (2), on behalf of the Scottish Ministers.

(2) The specified functions are the functions conferred on the Scottish Ministers by—

(a) articles 144(1) and (2) and 167(1) and (7) (proceedings in the Court of Session),

(b) article 178(2) (trustee for civil recovery),

(c) articles 182(3) and (4) and 183(5) (agreements about associated and joint property),

(d) article 186(3) (pension schemes),

(e) article 193(1) (exemptions),

(f) article 194(5) and (8) (compensation),

(g) article 200(2) (financial threshold).

210.— [...]

### *Interpretation*

### 211. Obtaining and disposing of property

References to a person disposing of his property include a reference—

(a) to his disposing of a part of it, or

(b) to his granting an interest in it,

(or to both), and references to the property disposed of are to any property obtained on the disposal.

(2) A person who makes a payment to another is to be treated as making a disposal of his property to the other, whatever form the payment takes.

(3) Where a person's property passes to another under a will or intestacy or by operation of law, it is to be treated as disposed of by him to the other.

(4) A person is only to be treated as having obtained his property for value in a case where he gave unexecuted consideration if the consideration has become executed consideration.

### 212. Northern Ireland courts

In relation to the practice and procedure of courts in Northern Ireland, expressions used in this Part are to be read in accordance with rules of court.

### 213.— General interpretation

(1) In this Part—
"associated property" has the meaning given by article 146,
"constable", in relation to Northern Ireland, means a police officer within the meaning of the Police (Northern Ireland) Act 2000,
"the court" except in articles 158(2) and (3) and 173(2) and (3) means the High Court or (in relation to proceedings in Scotland) the Court of Session,
"dealing" with property includes disposing of it, taking possession of it or removing it from the United Kingdom,
[...]
"enforcement authority"—
  [(a)  in relation to England and Wales, means SOCA, the Director of Public Prosecutions, the Director of Revenue and Customs Prosecutions or the Director of the Serious Fraud Office,]
   (b)  in relation to Scotland, means the Scottish Ministers,
  [(c)  in relation to Northern Ireland, means SOCA, the Director of the Serious Fraud Office or the Director of Public Prosecutions for Northern Ireland,]
"excepted joint owner" has the meaning given by article 181(4),
"interest", in relation to land—
  (a)  in the case of land in England and Wales or Northern Ireland, means any legal estate and any equitable interest or power,
  (b)  in the case of land in Scotland, means any estate, interest, servitude or other heritable right in or over land, including a heritable security,
"interest", in relation to property other than land, includes any right (including a right to possession of the property),
"interim administration order" has the meaning given by article 167(2),
"interim receiving order" has the meaning given by article 151(2),
"part", in relation to property, includes a portion,
"premises" has the same meaning as in the Police and Criminal Evidence Act 1984,
"prohibitory property order" has the meaning given in article 171(2),
"property freezing order" has the meaning given in article 147(2),
"recoverable property" is to be read in accordance with articles 202 to 207,
"recovery order" means an order made under article 177,
"respondent" means—
  (a)  where proceedings are brought by the enforcement authority, the person against whom the proceedings are brought,
  (b)  where no such proceedings have been brought but the enforcement authority has applied for a property freezing order, an interim receiving order, a prohibitory property order or an interim administration order, the person against whom he intends to bring such proceedings,
"share", in relation to an excepted joint owner, has the meaning given by article 181(4),
"specified property" means property other than a sum of money that is specified in an external order,
"value" means market value.

(2) The following provisions apply for the purposes of this Part.

(3) For the purpose of deciding whether or not property was recoverable at any time (including times before commencement), it is to be assumed that this Part was in force at that and any other relevant time.

(4) Property is all property wherever situated and includes—
    (a) money,
    (b) all forms of property, real or personal, heritable or moveable,
    (c) things in action and other intangible or incorporeal property.

(5) Any reference to a person's property (whether expressed as a reference to the property he holds or otherwise) is to be read as follows.

(6) In relation to land, it is a reference to any interest which he holds in the land.

(7) In relation to property other than land, it is a reference—
    (a) to the property (if it belongs to him), or
    (b) to any other interest which he holds in the property.

(8) References to the satisfaction of the enforcement authority's right to recover any property which satisfies the tests in article 202(1) and (2) are to read in accordance with article 189.

[(8A) In relation to an order in England and Wales or Northern Ireland which is a recovery order, a property freezing order, an interim receiving order or an order under article 187, references to the enforcement authority are, unless the context otherwise requires, references to the enforcement authority which is seeking, or (as the case may be) has obtained, the order.]

*A.K. Galloway*
Clerk of the Privy Council

SCHEDULE 1

ADMINISTRATORS (SCOTLAND): FURTHER PROVISION

Article 85

**1. General**

In this Schedule, unless otherwise expressly provided—
    (a) references to an administrator are to an administrator appointed under article 63 or 73(2);
    (b) references to realisable property are to the realisable property in respect of which the administrator is appointed; and
    (c) references to specified property are to the specified property in respect of which the administrator is appointed.

**2.— Appointment etc.**

(1) If the office of administrator is vacant, for whatever reason, the court must appoint a new administrator.

(2) Any property vested in the previous administrator by virtue of paragraph 5(4) vests in the new administrator.

(3) Any order under article 63, 74(3) or 75(3) in relation to the previous administrator applies in relation to the new administrator when he gives written notice of his appointment to the person subject to the order.

(4) The administration of property by an administrator must be treated as continuous despite any temporary vacancy in that office.

(5) The appointment of an administrator is subject to such conditions as to caution as the accountant of court may impose.

(6) The premium of any bond of caution or other security required by such conditions must be treated as part of the administrator's expenses in the exercise of his functions.

**3.— Functions**

(1) An administrator—
    (a) may, if appointed under article 63; and

   (b)  must, if appointed under article 73(2), as soon as practicable take possession of the realisable property or specified property, as the case may be, and of the documents mentioned in sub-paragraph (2).

(2)  Those documents are any document which—
   (a)  is in the possession or control of the person ("A") in whom the property is vested (or would be vested but for an order made under paragraph 5(4)); and
   (b)  relates to the property or to A's assets, business or financial affairs.

(3)  An administrator is entitled to have access to, and to copy, any document relating to the property or to A's assets, business or financial affairs ad not falling within sub-paragraph (2)(a).

(4)  An administrator may bring, defend or continue any legal proceedings relating to the property.

(5)  An administrator may borrow money so far as it is necessary to do so to safeguard the property and may for the purposes of such borrowing create a security over any part of the property.

(6)  An administrator may, if he considers that it would be beneficial for the management or realisation of the property—
   (a)  carry on any business of A;
   (b)  exercise any right of A as holder of securities in a company;
   (c)  grant a lease of the property or take on lease any other property;
   (d)  enter into any contract, or execute any deed, as regards the property or as regards A's business.

(7)  An administrator may, where any right, option or other power forms part of A's estate, make payments or incur liabilities with a view to—
   (a)  obtaining property which is the subject of; or
   (b)  maintaining,
the right, option or power.

(8)  An administrator may effect or maintain insurance policies as regards the property on A's business.

(9)  An administrator may, if appointed under article 73(2), complete any uncompleted title which A has to any heritable estate; but completion of title in A's name does not validate by accretion any unperfected right in favour of any person other than the administrator.

(10)  An administrator may sell, purchase or exchange property or discharge any security for an obligation due to A; but it is incompetent for the administrator or an associate of his (within the meaning of section 74 of the Bankruptcy (Scotland) Act 1985 to purchase any of A's property in pursuance of this sub-paragraph.

(11)  An administrator may claim, vote and draw dividends in the sequestration of the estate for bankruptcy or liquidation) of a debtor of A and may accede to a voluntary trust deed for creditors of such a debtor.

(12)  An administrator may discharge any of his functions through agents or employees, but is personally liable to meet the fees and expenses of any such agent or employee out of which remuneration as is payable to the administrator on a determination by the accountant of court.

(13)  An administrator may take such professional advice as he considers necessary in connection with the exercise of his functions.

(14)  An administrator may at any time apply to the court for directions as regards the exercise of his functions.

(15)  An administrator may exercise any power specifically conferred on him by the court, whether conferred on his appointment or subsequently.

(16)  An administrator may—
   (a)  enter any premises;
   (b)  search for or inspect anything authorised by the court;
   (c)  make or obtain a copy, photograph or other record of anything so authorised;
   (d)  remove anything which the administrator is required or administered to take possession of in pursuance of an order of the court.

(17)  An administrator may do anything incidental to the powers and duties listed in the previous provisions of this paragraph.

### 4. Consent of accountant of court

An administrator proposing to exercise any power conferred by paragraph 3(4) to (7) must first obtain the consent of the accountant of court.

### 5.— Dealings in good faith with administrator

(1) A person dealing with an administrator in good faith and for value is not concerned to enquire whether the administrator is acting within the powers mentioned in paragraph 3.

(2) Sub-paragraph (1) does not apply where the administrator or an associate purchases property in contravention of paragraph 3(10).

(3) The validity of any title is not challengeable by reason only of the administrator having acted out with the powers mentioned in paragraph 3.

(4) The exercise of a power mentioned in paragraph 3(4) to (11) must be in A's name except where and in so far as an order made by the court under this sub-paragraph vests the property in the administrator (or in a previous administrator).

(5) The court may make an order under sub-paragraph (4) on the application of the administrator or on its own motion.

### 6.— Money received by administrator

(1) All money received by an administrator in the exercise of his functions must be deposited by him, in the name (unless vested in the administrator by virtue of paragraph 5(4)) of the holder of the property realised, in an appropriate bank or institution.

(2) But the administrator may at any time retain in his hands a sum not exceeding £200 or such other sum as may be prescribed by the Scottish Ministers by regulations.

(3) In sub-paragraph (1), "appropriate bank or institution" means a bank or institution mentioned in section 3(1) of the Banking Act 1987 or for the time being specified in Schedule 2 to that Act.

### 7.— Effect of appointment of administrator on diligence

(1) An arrestment or poinding of realisable property or specified property, as the case may be, executed on or after the appointment of an administrator does not create a preference for the arrester or poinder.

(2) Any realisable property or specified property so arrested or poinded, or (if the property has been sold) the proceeds of sale, must be handed over to the administrator.

(3) A poinding of the ground in respect of realisable property or specified property on or after such appointment is ineffectual in a question with the administrator except for the interest mentioned in sub-paragraph (4).

(4) That interest is—

  (a) interest on the debt of a secured creditor for the current half-yearly term; and

  (b) arrears of interest on that debt for one year immediately before the commencement of that term.

(5) On and after such appointment no other person may raise or insist in an adjudication against realisable property or specified property or be confirmed as executor — creditor on that property.

(6) An inhibition on realisable property or specified property which takes effect on or after such appointment does not create a preference for the inhibitor in a question with the administrator.

(7) This paragraph is without prejudice to articles 61 and 62.

(8) In this paragraph, the reference to an administrator is to an administrator appointed under article 73(2).

### 8. Supervision

If the accountant of court reports to the court that an administrator has failed to perform any duty imposed on him, the court may, after giving the administrator an opportunity to be heard as regards the matter—

  (a) remove him from office;

  (b) censure him; or

  (c) make such order as it thinks fit.

(2) Section 6 of the Judicial Factors (Scotland) Act 1889 does not apply in relation to an administrator.

#### 9.— Accounts and remuneration

(1) Not later than two weeks after the issuing of any determination by the accountant of court as to the remuneration and expenses payable to the administrator, the administrator or the Lord Advocate may appeal against it to the court.

(2) The amount of remuneration payable to the administrator must be determined on the basis of the value of the work reasonably undertaken by him, regard being had to the extent of the responsibilities involved.

(3) The accountant of court may authorise the administrator to pay without taxation an account in respect of legal services incurred by the administrator.

#### 10.— Discharge of administrator

(1) After an administrator has lodged his final accounts under paragraph 9(1), he may apply to the accountant of court to be discharged from office.

(2) A discharge, if granted, frees the administrator from all liability (other than liability arising from fraud) in respect of any act or omission of his in exercising his functions as administrator.

## Schedule 2
### Powers Of Interim Receiver Or Administrator

Articles 152 and 168

#### 1. Seizure

Power to seize property to which the order applies.

#### 2.— Information

(1) Power to obtain information or to require a person to answer any question.

(2) A requirement imposed in the exercise of the power has effect in spite of any restriction on the disclosure of information (however imposed).

(3) An answer given by a person in pursuance of such a requirement may not be used in evidence against him in criminal proceedings.

(4) Sub-paragraph (3) does not apply—

(a) on a prosecution for an offence under section 5 of the Perjury Act 1911, section 44(2) of the Criminal Law (Consolidation) (Scotland) Act 1995 or Article 10 of the Perjury (Northern Ireland) Order 1979 (false statements), or

(b) on a prosecution for some other offence where, in giving evidence, he makes a statement inconsistent with it.

(5) But an answer may not be used by virtue of sub-paragraph (4)(b) against a person unless—

(a) evidence relating to it is adduced, or

(b) a question relating to it is asked,

by him or on his behalf in the proceedings arising out of the prosecution.

#### 3.— Entry, search, etc.

(1) Power to—

(a) enter any premises in the United Kingdom to which the interim receiving order applies, and

(b) take any of the following steps.

(2) Those steps are—

(a) to carry out a search for or inspection of anything described in the order,

(b) to make or obtain a copy, photograph or other record of anything so described,

(c) to remove anything which he is required to take possession of in pursuance of the order or which may be required as evidence in the proceedings under Chapter 2 of Part 5.

(3) The order may describe anything generally, whether by reference to a class or otherwise.

### 4.— Supplementary

(1) An order making any provision under paragraph 2 or 3 must make provision in respect of legal professional privilege (in Scotland, legal privilege within the meaning of Chapter 3 of Part 8 of the Act).

(2) An order making any provision under paragraph 3 may require any person—

    (a) to give the interim receiver or administrator access to any premises which he may enter in pursuance of paragraph 3,

    (b) to give the interim receiver or administrator any assistance he may require for taking the steps mentioned in that paragraph.

### 5.— Management

(1) Power to manage any property to which the order applies.

(2) Managing property includes—

    (a) selling or otherwise disposing of assets comprised in the property which are perishable or which ought to be disposed of before their value diminishes,

    (b) where the property comprises assets of a trade or business, carrying on, or arranging for another to carry on, the trade or business,

    (c) incurring capital expenditure in respect of the property.


## SCHEDULE 3
## POWERS OF TRUSTEE FOR CIVIL RECOVERY

Article 178

### 1. Sale

Power to sell the property or any part of it or interest in it.

### 2. Expenditure

Power to incur expenditure for the purpose of—

    (a) acquiring any part of the property, or any interest in it, which is not vested in him,

    (b) discharging any liabilities, or extinguishing any rights, to which the property is subject.

### 3.— Management

(1) Power to manage property.

(2) Managing property includes doing anything mentioned in paragraph 5(2) of Schedule 1.

### 4. Legal proceedings

Power to start, carry on or defend any legal proceedings in respect of the property.

### 5. Compromise

Power to make any compromise or other arrangement in connection with any claim relating to the property.

### 6.— Supplementary

(1) For the purpose of, or in connection with, the exercise of any of his powers—

    (a) power by his official name to do any of the things mentioned in sub-paragraph (2),

    (b) power to do any other act which is necessary or expedient.

(2) Those things are—

    (a) holding property,

    (b) entering into contracts,

    (c) suing and being sued,

    (d) employing agents,

    (e) executing a power of attorney, deed or other instrument.

SCHEDULE 4

RECOVERY FROM PENSION SCHEMES

Articles 184 and 186

**1. Interpretation**

In this Schedule—

"destination arrangement" means a pension arrangement under which some or all of the rights are derived, directly or indirectly, from a pension sharing transaction;

"pension recovery order" means a recovery order made by virtue of article 184(2);

"pension sharing transaction" means an order or provision falling within section 28(1) of the Welfare Reform and Pensions Act 1999 (activation of pension sharing) or article 25(1) of the Welfare Reform and Pensions (Northern Ireland) Order 1999 (activation of pension sharing);

"relevant person" means the person whose rights under a pension scheme are the subject of a pension recovery order; and

"valuation date" means a date within the period prescribed by paragraph 5 in respect of which the trustees or managers of the pension scheme decide to value the relevant person's pension rights in accordance with paragraph 2 or 3.

**2.— Calculation and verification of the value of rights under pension schemes**

(1) This paragraph applies where the High Court or the Court of Session makes a pension recovery order, other than in respect of rights derived from a pension sharing transaction under a destination arrangement in a pension scheme.

(2) The trustees or managers of the pension scheme in respect of which the pension recovery order has been made must calculate and verify the cash equivalent of the value at the valuation date of the rights which are the subject of the pension recovery order and must pay to the trustee for civil recovery a sum equal to that cash equivalent.

(3) In relation to the calculation and verification by the trustees or managers of the cash equivalent referred to in sub-paragraph (2)—

(a) in the case of a pension scheme wholly or mainly administered in England and Wales, regulation 3 of the Pensions on Divorce etc. (Provision of Information) Regulations 2000 (information about pensions and divorce: valuation of pension benefits), except paragraph (2) thereof, shall have effect as it has effect for the valuation of benefits in connection with the supply of information in connection with domestic and overseas divorce etc. in England and Wales, with the modification that for "the date on which the request for valuation was received" in each place where it appears in that regulation, there shall be substituted "the valuation date for the purposes of Schedule 4 to the Proceeds of Crime Act 2002 (External Requests and Orders) Order 2005";

(b) in the case of a pension scheme wholly or mainly administered in Scotland, regulation 3 of the Divorce etc. (Pensions) (Scotland) Regulations 2000 (valuation), except paragraph (11) thereof, shall have effect as it has effect for the valuation of benefits in connection with the supply of information in connection with divorce in Scotland, with the modification that for "the relevant date" in each place where it appears in that regulation, there shall be substituted "the valuation date for the purposes of Schedule 4 to the Proceeds of Crime Act 2002 (External Requests and Orders) Order 2005"; and

(c) in the case of a pension scheme wholly or mainly administered in Northern Ireland, regulation 3 of the Pensions on Divorce etc. (Provision of Information) Regulations (Northern Ireland) 2000 (information about pensions on divorce: valuation of pension benefits), except paragraph (2) thereof, shall have effect as it has effect for the valuation of benefits in connection with the supply of information in connection with domestic and overseas divorce etc. in Northern Ireland, with the modification that, for "the date on which the request for the valuation was received" in each place where it appears in that regulation, there shall be substituted "the valuation date for the purposes of Schedule 4 to the Proceeds of Crime Act 2002 (External Requests and Orders) Order 2005."

**3.— Calculation and verification of the value of rights under destination arrangements**

(1) This paragraph applies where the High Court or the Court of Session makes a pension recovery order in respect of rights derived from a pension sharing transaction under a destination arrangement in a pension scheme.

(2) The trustees or managers of the pension scheme in respect of which the pension recovery order has been made must calculate and verify the cash equivalent of the value at the valuation date of the rights which are the subject of the pension recovery order and must pay to the trustee for civil recovery a sum equal to that cash equivalent.

(3) In relation to the calculation and verification by the trustees or managers of the cash equivalent referred to in sub-paragraph (2)—

   (a) in the case of a pension arrangement in a scheme that is wholly or mainly administered in either England and Wales or Scotland, regulation 24 of the Pension Sharing (Pension Credit Benefit) Regulations 2000 (manner of calculation and verification of cash equivalents) shall have effect as it has effect for the calculation and verification of pension credit for the purposes of those Regulations; and

   (b) in the case of a pension arrangement in a scheme that is wholly or mainly administered in Northern Ireland, regulation 24 of the Pension Sharing (Pension Credit and Benefit) Regulations (Northern Ireland) 2000 (manner of calculation and verification of cash equivalents) shall have effect as it has effect for the calculation and verification of pension credit for the purposes of those Regulations.

**4.— Approval of manner of calculation and verification of the value of rights**

(1) This paragraph applies where the relevant person is also a trustee or manager of the pension scheme in respect of which the pension recovery order has been made.

(2) When the trustees or managers of the pension scheme have, under paragraph 2 or 3, calculated and verified the value of the rights which are the subject of a pension recovery order, the manner in which the trustees or managers have calculated and verified the value of the rights must be approved by—

   (a) a Fellow of the Institute of Actuaries; or

   (b) a Fellow of the Faculty of Actuaries.

(3) Where the person referred to in sub-paragraph (2) is not able to approve the manner in which the trustees or managers have calculated and verified the value of the rights which are the subject of a pension recovery order, he must give notice in writing of that fact to the trustee for civil recovery and the trustees or managers of the scheme.

(4) Where the trustees or managers of the scheme have been given notice under sub-paragraph (3), they must re-calculate and re-verify the value of the rights which are the subject of a pension recovery order for the purposes of paragraph 2 or 3.

**5.— Time for compliance with a pension recovery order**

(1) In this paragraph, "the prescribed period" means the period prescribed for the purposes of article 184(2)(a).

(2) Subject to sub-paragraphs (3) and (4), the prescribed period is the period of 60 days beginning on the day on which the pension recovery order is made.

(3) Where an application for permission to appeal the pension recovery order is made within the period referred to in sub-paragraph (2), the prescribed period is the period of 60 days beginning on—

   (a) the day on which permission to appeal is finally refused;

   (b) the day on which the appeal is withdrawn; or

   (c) the day on which the appeal is dismissed,

   as the case may be.

(4) Where the person referred to in paragraph 4(2) gives notice, in accordance with paragraph 4(3) and within the period referred to in sub-paragraph (2), to the trustee for civil recovery and trustees or managers of the scheme that he is unable to approve the manner in which the trustees or managers have calculated the value of the rights which are the subject of the pension recovery order, the prescribed period is the period of 60 days beginning on the day on which such notice is given.

SCHEDULE 5

PRESCRIBED ENACTMENTS — PROPERTY WHICH IS NOT
RECOVERABLE PROPERTY

Article 206

Section 31 of the Salmon Fisheries (Scotland) Act 1868 (forfeiture of articles found in possession of any offender).

Section 8 of the Diseases of Fish Act 1937 (penalties and legal proceedings).

Sections 19 and 20 of the Salmon and Freshwater Fisheries (Protection) (Scotland) Act 1951.

Section 138 of the Army Act 1955 (restitution or compensation for theft etc.) (including where it has effect by virtue of paragraph 17 of Schedule 3 to the Armed Forces Act 1976), in circumstances other than where the disposal is of money which is paid as or towards compensation under section 138(5) of that Act or the disposal is the restitution of property given in exchange under section 138(6) of that Act.

Section 138 of the Air Force Act 1955 (restitution or compensation for theft etc.) in circumstances other than where the disposal is of money is paid as or towards compensation under section 138(5) of that Act or the disposal is the restitution of property given in exchange under section 138(6) of that Act.

Section 76 of the Naval Discipline Act 1957 (restitution or compensation on conviction of larceny etc.), in circumstances other than where the disposal is the restitution of property given in exchange under section 76(2)(a) of that Act or the disposal is of money which is paid as or towards compensation under section 76(2)(b) or (3) of that Act.

Section 3 of the Obscene Publications Act 1959 (powers of search and seizure).

Section 11(2) of the Sea Fish (Conservation) Act 1967 (penalties for offences).

Section 46(4) of the Courts-Martial (Appeals) Act 1968 (restitution of property), in circumstances where if the order had been made by the court-martial or Defence Council this Order would have provided that the property was not recoverable or (as the case may be) associated property.

Section 52 of the Firearms Act 1968 (forfeiture and disposal of firearms).

Section 27 of the Misuse of Drugs Act 1971 (forfeiture).

Sections 7 and 24 of the Forgery and Counterfeiting Act 1981 (powers of search, forfeiture etc.).

Section 4(4) of the Inshore Fishing (Scotland) Act 1984.

Section 25 of the Public Order Act 1986 (power to order forfeiture).

Section 66 of the Criminal Justice and Public Order Act 1994 (power of court to forfeit sound equipment) in the circumstances where no order is made under section 66(5) by virtue of section 66(6) of that Act for the delivery of property to a person appearing to be the owner of the property.

Section 43 of the Drug Trafficking Act 1994 (forfeiture).

Section 22 of the Proceeds of Crime (Scotland) Act 1995 (forfeiture: district court).

Section 24 of the Proceeds of Crime (Scotland) Act 1995 (forfeiture of property subject to suspended forfeiture order), in the circumstances where no order is made under section 26 of that Act in relation to the property.

Paragraph 3 of the Schedule to the Noise Act 1996 (forfeiture), in the circumstances where no order is made under paragraph 4 of that Schedule for the delivery of the equipment to a person appearing to be the owner of the equipment.

Section 6 of the Knives Act 1997 (forfeiture of knives and publications), in the circumstances where no order is made under section 7 of that Act for the delivery of property to a person appearing to be the owner of the property.

Section 143 of the Powers of Criminal Courts (Sentencing) Act 2000 (powers to deprive offender of property used etc for purposes of crime), in the circumstances where no order is made under the Police (Property) Act 1897, as applied by section 144 of the Powers of Criminal Courts (Sentencing) Act 2000, for the delivery of the property to a person appearing to be the owner of the property.

541

Section 23 of the Terrorism Act 2000 (forfeiture).

Section 6 of the Royal Parks (Trading) Act 2000 (seizure, retention, disposal and forfeiture of property).

Paragraph 6 of Schedule 1 to the Anti-terrorism, Crime and Security Act 2001 (forfeiture).

Regulations 15 (disposal of vehicles) and 17 (disposal of contents) of the Goods Vehicles (Enforcement Powers) Regulations 2001, in the circumstances where the proceeds of sale have not been applied in meeting a claim to the proceeds of sale established under regulation 18(2) of those Regulations[. Regulations made under Section 94 of the Armed Forces Act 2006 (property in possession of service police or CO).]

# APPENDIX 12

*(Acts adopted pursuant to Title VI of the Treaty on European Union)*

## COUNCIL ACT
### of 29 May 2000

establishing in accordance with Article 34 of the Treaty on European Union
the Convention on Mutual Assistance in Criminal Matters between the Member States
of the European Union

(2000/C 197/01)

THE COUNCIL OF THE EUROPEAN UNION,

Having regard to the Treaty on European Union, and in particular Articles 31(a) and 34(2)(d) thereof,

Having regard to the initiative of the Member States,

Having regard to the opinion of the European Parliament[1],

Whereas:

(1) For the purposes of achieving the objectives of the Union the rules on mutual assistance in criminal matters between the Member States of the European Union should be improved and a Convention, as set out in the Annex hereto, should be established to that end.

(2) Some of the provisions of the Convention fall within the scope of Article 1 of Council Decision 1999/437/EC of 17 May 1999 on certain arrangements for the application of the Agreement concluded by the Council of the European Union and the Republic of Iceland and the Kingdom of Norway concerning the association of those two States with the implementation, application and development of the Schengen *acquis*[2].

(3) This is the case with Articles 3, 5, 6, 7, 12 and 23, and, to the extent relevant to Article 12, with Articles 15 and 16, and, to the extent relevant to the Articles referred to, with Article 1.

(4) The procedures set out in the Agreement concluded by the Council of the European Union with the Republic of Iceland and the Kingdom of Norway concerning the latters' association with the implementation, application and development of the Schengen *acquis*[3] have been observed in respect of these provisions.

(5) When the adoption of this Act is notified to the Republic of Iceland and the Kingdom of Norway in accordance with Article 8(2)(a) of the aforementioned Agreement, those two States will be informed in particular of the contents of Article 29 on entry into force for Iceland and Norway and will be invited to submit, at the time they inform the Council and the Commission of the fulfilment of their constitutional requirements, the relevant statements under Article 24 of the Convention.

HAS DECIDED that the Convention, the text of which is given in the Annex and which has been signed today by the Representatives of the Governments of the Member States of the Union, is hereby established,

---

[1] Opinion delivered on 17 February 2000 (not yet published in the Official Journal).
[2] OJ L 176, 10.7.1999, p.31.
[3] OJ L 176, 10.7.1999, p.36.

RECOMMENDS that it be adopted by the Member States in accordance with their respective constitutional requirements,

INVITES the Member States to begin the procedures applicable for that purpose before 1 January 2001.

Done at Brussels, 29 May 2000.

*For the Council*
*The President*
A. COSTA

## ANNEX

## CONVENTION

**Established by the Council in accordance with Article 34 of the Treaty on European Union, on Mutual Assistance in Criminal Matters between the Member States of the European Union**

THE HIGH CONTRACTING PARTIES to this Convention, Member States of the European Union,

REFERRING to the Council Act establishing the Convention on Mutual Assistance in Criminal Matters between the Member States of the European Union,

WISHING to improve judicial cooperation in criminal matters between the Member States of the Union, without prejudice to the rules protecting individual freedom,

POINTING OUT the Member States' common interest in ensuring that mutual assistance between the Member States is provided in a fast and efficient manner compatible with the basic principles of their national law, and in compliance with the individual rights and principles of the European Convention for the Protection of Human Rights and Fundamental Freedoms, signed in Rome on 4 November 1950,

EXPRESSING their confidence in the structure and functioning of their legal systems and in the ability of all Member States to guarantee a fair trial,

RESOLVED to supplement the European Convention on Mutual Assistance in Criminal Matters of 20 April 1959 and other Conventions in force in this area, by a Convention of the European Union,

RECOGNISING that the provisions of those Conventions remain applicable for all matters not covered by this Convention,

CONSIDERING that the Member States attach importance to strengthening judicial cooperation, while continuing to apply the principle of proportionality,

RECALLING that this Convention regulates mutual assistance in criminal matters, based on the principles of the Convention of 20 April 1959,

WHEREAS, however, Article 20 of this Convention covers certain specific situations concerning interception of telecommunications, without having any implications with regard to other such situations outside the scope of the Convention,

WHEREAS the general principles of international law apply in situations which are not covered by this Convention,

RECOGNISING that this Convention does not affect the exercise of the responsibilities incumbent upon Member States with regard do the maintenance of law and order and the safeguarding of internal security, and that it is a matter for each Member State to determine, in accordance with Article 33 of the Treaty on European Union, under which conditions it will maintain law and order and safeguard internal security,

## HAVE AGREED ON THE FOLLOWING PROVISIONS:

# TITLE I

## GENERAL PROVISIONS

### *Article 1*

### Relationship to other conventions on mutual assistance

1.  The purpose of this Convention is to supplement the provisions and facilitate the application between the Member States of the European Union, of:
    (a) the European Convention on Mutual Assistance in Criminal Matters of 20 April 1959, hereinafter referred to as the 'European Mutual Assistance Convention';
    (b) the Additional Protocol of 17 March 1978 to the European Mutual Assistance Convention;
    (c) the provisions on mutual assistance in criminal matters of the Convention of 19 June 1990 implementing the Schengen Agreement of 14 June 1985 on the gradual abolition of checks at common borders (hereinafter referred to as the 'Schengen Implementation Convention') which are not repealed pursuant to Article 2(2);
    (d) Chapter 2 of the Treaty on Extradition and Mutual Assistance in Criminal Matters between the Kingdom of Belgium, the Grand Duchy of Luxembourg and the Kingdom of the Netherlands of 27 June 1962, as amended by the Protocol of 11 May 1974, (hereinafter referred to as the 'Benelux Treaty'), in the context of relations between the Member States of the Benelux Economic Union.

2.  This Convention shall not affect the application of more favourable provisions in bilateral or multilateral agreements between Member States or, as provided for in Article 26(4) of the European Mutual Assistance Convention, arrangements in the field of mutual assistance in criminal matters agreed on the basis of uniform legislation or of a special system providing for the reciprocal application of measures of mutual assistance in their respective territories.

### *Article 2*

### Provisions relating to the Schengen acquis

1.  The provisions of Articles 3, 5, 6, 7, 12 and 23 and, to the extent relevant to Article 12, of Articles 15 and 16, to the extent relevant to the Articles referred to, of Article 1 constitute measures amending or building upon the provisions referred to in Annex A to the Agreement concluded by the Council of the European Union and the Republic of Iceland and the Kingdom of Norway concerning the latters' association with the implementation, application and development of the Schengen *acquis*[4].
2.  The provisions of Articles 49(a), 52, 53 and 73 of the Schengen Implementation Convention are hereby repealed.

### *Article 3*

### Proceedings in connection with which mutual assistance is also to be afforded

1.  Mutual assistance shall also be afforded in proceedings brought by the administrative authorities in respect of acts which are punishable under the national law of the requesting or the requested Member State, or both, by virtue of being infringements of the rules of law, and where the decision may give rise to proceedings before a court having jurisdiction in particular in criminal matters.
2.  Mutual assistance shall also be afforded in connection with criminal proceedings and proceedings as referred to in paragraph 1 which relate to offences or infringements for which a legal person may be held liable in the requesting Member State.

---

[4] OJ L 176, 10.7.1999, p. 36.

*Article 4*

**Formalities and procedures in the execution of requests for mutual assistance**

1. Where mutual assistance is afforded, the requested Member State shall comply with the formalities and procedures expressly indicated by the requesting Member State, unless otherwise provided in this Convention and provided that such formalities and procedures are not contrary to the fundamental principles of law in the requested Member State.

2. The requested Member State shall execute the request for assistance as soon as possible, taking as full account as possible of the procedural deadlines and other deadlines indicated by the requesting Member State. The requesting Member State shall explain the reasons for the deadline.

3. If the request cannot, or cannot fully, be executed in accordance with the requirements set by the requesting Member State, the authorities of the requested Member State shall promptly inform the authorities of the requesting Member State and indicate the conditions under which it might be possible to execute the request. The authorities of the requesting and the requested Member State may subsequently agree on further action to be taken concerning the request, where necessary by making such action subject to the fulfilment of those conditions.

4. If it is foreseeable that the deadline set by the requesting Member State for executing its request cannot be met, and if the reasons referred to in paragraph 2, second sentence, indicate explicitly that any delay will lead to substantial impairment of the proceedings being conducted in the requesting Member State, the authorities of the requested Member State shall promptly indicate the estimated time needed for execution of the request. The authorities of the requesting Member State shall promptly indicate whether the request is to be upheld nonetheless. The authorities of the requesting and requested Member States may subsequently agree on further action to be taken concerning the request.

*Article 5*

**Sending and service of procedural documents**

1. Each Member State shall send procedural documents intended for persons who are in the territory of another Member State to them directly by post.

2. Procedural documents may be sent via the competent authorities of the requested Member State only if:
   (a) the address of the person for whom the document is intended is unknown or uncertain; or
   (b) the relevant procedural law of the requesting Member State requires proof of service of the document on the addressee, other than proof that can be obtained by post; or
   (c) it has not been possible to serve the document by post; or
   (d) the requesting Member State has justified reasons for considering that dispatch by post will be ineffective or is inappropriate.

3. Where there is reason to believe that the addressee does not understand the language in which the document is drawn up, the document, or at least the important passages thereof, must be translated into (one of) the language(s) of the Member State in the territory of which the addressee is staying. If the authority by which the procedural document was issued knows that the addressee understands only some other language, the document, or at least the important passages thereof, must be translated into that other language.

4. All procedural documents shall be accompanied by a report stating that the addressee may obtain information from the authority by which the document was issued or from other authorities in that Member State regarding his or her rights and obligations concerning the document. Paragraph 3 shall also apply to that report.

5. This Article shall not affect the application of Articles 8, 9 and 12 of the European Mutual Assistance Convention and Articles 32, 34 and 35 of the Benelux Treaty.

*Article 6*

**Transmission of requests for mutual assistance**

1. Requests for mutual assistance and spontaneous exchanges of information referred to in Article 7 shall be made in writing, or by any means capable of producing a written record under conditions

allowing the receiving Member State to establish authenticity. Such requests shall be made directly between judicial authorities with territorial competence for initiating and executing them, and shall be returned through the same channels unless otherwise specified in this Article. Any information laid by a Member State with a view to proceedings before the courts of another Member State within the meaning of Article 21 of the European Mutual Assistance Convention and Article 42 of the Benelux Treaty may be the subject of direct communications between the competent judicial authorities.

2.  Paragraph 1 shall not prejudice the possibility of requests being sent or returned in specific cases:
    (a) between a central authority of a Member State and a central authority of another Member State; or
    (b) between a judicial authority of one Member State and a central authority of another Member State.

3.  Notwithstanding paragraph 1, the United Kingdom and Ireland, respectively, may, when giving the notification provided for in Article 27(2), declare that requests and communications to it, as specified in the declaration, must be sent via its central authority. These Member States may at any time by a further declaration limit the scope of such a declaration for the purpose of giving greater effect to paragraph 1. They shall do so when the provisions on mutual assistance of the Schengen Implementation Convention are put into effect for them. Any Member State may apply the principle of reciprocity in relation to the declarations referred to above.

4.  Any request for mutual assistance may, in case of urgency, be made via the International Criminal Police Organisation (Interpol) or any body competent under provisions adopted pursuant to the Treaty on European Union.

5.  Where, in respect of requests pursuant to Articles 12, 13 or 14, the competent authority is a judicial authority or a central authority in one Member State and a police or customs authority in the other Member State, requests may be made and answered directly between these authorities. Paragraph 4 shall apply to these contacts.

6.  Where, in respect of requests for mutual assistance in relation to proceedings as envisaged in Article 3(1), the competent authority is a judicial authority or a central authority in one Member State and an administrative authority in the other Member State, requests may be made and answered directly between these authorities.

7.  Any Member State may declare, when giving the notification provided for in Article 27(2), that it is not bound by the first sentence of paragraph 5 or by paragraph 6 of this Article, or both or that it will apply those provisions only under certain conditions which it shall specify. Such a declaration may be withdrawn or amended at any time.

8.  The following requests or communications shall be made through the central authorities of the Member States:
    (a) requests for temporary transfer or transit of persons held in custody as referred to in Article 9 of this Convention, in Article 11 of the European Mutual Assistance Convention and in Article 33 of the Benelux Treaty;
    (b) notices of information from judicial records as referred to in Article 22 of the European Mutual Assistance Convention and Article 43 of the Benelux Treaty. However, requests for copies of convictions and measures as referred to in Article 4 of the Additional Protocol to the European Mutual Assistance Convention may be made directly to the competent authorities.

## Article 7

### Spontaneous exchange of information

1.  Within the limits of their national law, the competent authorities of the Member States may exchange information, without a request to that effect, relating to criminal offences and the infringements of rules of law referred to in Article 3(1), the punishment or handling of which falls within the competence of the receiving authority at the time the information is provided.

2.  The providing authority may, pursuant to its national law, impose conditions on the use of such information by the receiving authority.

3.  The receiving authority shall be bound by those conditions.

# TITLE II

## REQUEST FOR CERTAIN SPECIFIC FORMS OF MUTUAL ASSISTANCE

*Article 8*

### Restitution

1. At the request of the requesting Member State and without prejudice to the rights of *bona fide* third parties, the requested Member State may place articles obtained by criminal means at the disposal of the requesting State with a view to their return to their rightful owners.
2. In applying Articles 3 and 6 of the European Mutual Assistance Convention and Articles 24(2) and 29 of the Benelux Treaty, the requested Member State may waive the return of articles either before or after handling them over to the requesting Member State if the restitution of such articles to the rightful owner may be facilitated thereby. The rights of *bona fide* third parties shall not be affected.
3. In the event of a waiver before handing over the articles to the requesting Member State, the requested Member State shall exercise no security right or other right of recourse under tax or customs legislation in respect of these articles. A waiver as referred to in paragraph 2 shall be without prejudice to the right of the requested Member State to collect taxes or duties from the rightful owner.

*Article 9*

### Temporary transfer of persons held in custody for purpose of investigation

1. Where there is agreement between the competent authorities of the Member States concerned, a Member State which has requested an investigation for which the presence of the person held in custody on its own territory is required may temporarily transfer that person to the territory of the Member State in which the investigation is to take place.
2. The agreement shall cover the arrangements for the temporary transfer of the person and the date by which he or she must be returned to the territory of the requesting Member State.
3. Where consent to the transfer is required from the person concerned, a statement of consent or a copy thereof shall be provided promptly to the requested Member State.
4. The period of custody in the territory of the requested Member State shall be deducted from the period of detention which the person concerned is or will be obliged to undergo in the territory of the requesting Member State.
5. The provisions of Articles 11(2) and (3), 12 and 20 of the European Mutual Assistance Convention shall apply *mutatis mutandis* to this Article.
6. When giving the notification provided for in Article 27(2), each Member State may declare that, before an agreement is reached under paragraph 1 of this Article, the consent referred to in paragraph 3 of this Article will be required or will be required under certain conditions indicated in the declaration.

*Article 10*

### Hearing by videoconference

1. If a person is in one Member State's territory and has to be heard as a witness or expert by the judicial authorities of another Member State, the latter may, where it is not desirable or possible for the person to be heard to appear in its territory in person, request that the hearing take place by videoconference, as provided for in paragraphs 2 to 8.
2. The requested Member State shall agree to the hearing by videoconference provided that the use of the videoconference is not contrary to fundamental principles of its law and on condition that it has the technical means to carry out the hearing. If the requested Member State has no access to the technical means for videoconferencing, such means may be made available to it by the requesting Member State by mutual agreement.
3. Requests for a hearing by videoconference shall contain, in addition to the information referred to in Article 14 of the European Mutual Assistance Convention and Article 37 of the Benelux Treaty, the

reason why it is not desirable or possible for the witness or expert to attend in person, the name of the judicial authority and of the persons who will be conducting the hearing.

4. The judicial authority of the requested Member State shall summon the person concerned to appear in accordance with the forms laid down by its law.

5. With reference to hearing by videoconference, the following rules shall apply:

   (a) a judicial authority of the requested Member State shall be present during the hearing, where necessary assisted by an interpreter, and shall also be responsible for ensuring both the identification of the person to be heard and respect for the fundamental principles of the law of the requested Member State. If the judicial authority of the requested Member State is of the view that during the hearing the fundamental principles of the law of the requested Member State are being infringed, it shall immediately take the necessary measures to ensure that the hearing continues in accordance with the said principles;

   (b) measures for the protection of the person to be heard shall be agreed, where necessary, between the competent authorities of the requesting and the requested Member States;

   (c) the hearing shall be conducted directly by, or under the direction of, the judicial authority of the requesting Member State in accordance with its own laws;

   (d) at the request of the requesting Member State or the person to be heard the requested Member State shall ensure that the person to be heard is assisted by an interpreter, if necessary;

   (e) the person to be heard may claim the right not to testify which would accrue to him or her under the law of either the requested or the requesting Member State.

6. Without prejudice to any measures agreed for the protection of the persons, the judicial authority of the requested Member State shall on the conclusion of the hearing draw up minutes indicating the date and place of the hearing, the identity of the person heard, the identities and functions of all other persons in the requested Member State participating in the hearing, any oaths taken and the technical conditions under which the hearing took place. The document shall be forwarded by the competent authority of the requested Member State to the competent authority of the requesting Member State.

7. The cost of establishing the video link, costs related to the servicing of the video link in the requested Member State, the remuneration of interpreters provided by it and allowances to witnesses and experts and their travelling expenses in the requested Member State shall be refunded by the requesting Member State to the requested Member State, unless the latter waives the refunding of all or some of these expenses.

8. Each Member State shall take the necessary measures to ensure that, where witnesses or experts are being heard within its territory in accordance with this Article and refuse to testify when under an obligation to testify or do not testify according to the truth, its national law applies in the same way as if the hearing took place in a national procedure.

9. Member States may at their discretion also apply the provisions of this Article, where appropriate and with the agreement of their competent judicial authorities, to hearings by videoconference involving an accused person. In this case, the decision to hold the videoconference, and the manner in which the videoconference shall be carried out, shall be subject to agreement between the Member States concerned, in accordance with their national law and relevant international instruments, including the 1950 European Convention for the Protection of Human Rights and Fundamental Freedoms.

   Any Member State may, when giving its notification pursuant to Article 27(2), declare that it will not apply the first subparagraph. Such a declaration may be withdrawn at any time.

   Hearings shall only be carried out with the consent of the accused person. Such rules as may prove to be necessary, with a view to the protection of the rights of accused persons, shall be adopted by the Council in a legally binding instrument.

### Article 11

#### Hearing of witnesses and experts by telephone conference

1. If a person is one Member State's territory and has to be heard as a witness or expert by judicial authorities of another Member State, the latter may, where its national law so provides, request

assistance of the former Member State to enable the hearing to take place by telephone conference, as provided for in paragraphs 2 to 5.

2. A hearing may be conducted by telephone conference only if the witness or expert agrees that the hearing take place by that method.

3. The requested Member State shall agree to the hearing by telephone conference where this is not contrary to fundamental principles of its law.

4. A request for a hearing by telephone conference shall contain, in addition to the information referred to in Article 14 of the European Mutual Assistance Convention and Article 37 of the Benelux Treaty, the name of the judicial authority and of the persons who will be conducting the hearing and an indication that the witness or expert is willing to take part in a hearing by telephone conference.

5. The practical arrangements regarding the hearing shall be agreed between the Member States concerned. When agreeing such arrangements, the requested Member State shall undertake to:
   (a) notify the witness or expert concerned of the time and the venue of the hearing;
   (b) ensure the identification of the witness or expert;
   (c) verify that the witness or expert agrees to the hearing by telephone conference.

The requested Member State may make its agreement subject, fully or in part, to the relevant provisions of Article 10(5) and (8). Unless otherwise agreed, the provisions of Article 10(7) shall apply *mutatis mutandis.*

## Article 12

### Controlled deliveries

1. Each Member State shall undertake to ensure that, at the request of another Member State, controlled deliveries may be permitted on its territory in the framework of criminal investigations into extraditable offences.

2. The decision to carry out controlled deliveries shall be taken in each individual case by the competent authorities of the requested Member State, with due regard for the national law of that Member State.

3. Controlled deliveries shall take place in accordance with the procedures of the requested Member State. The right to act and to direct and control operations shall lie with the competent authorities of that Member State.

## Article 13

### Joint investigation teams

1. By mutual agreement, the competent authorities of two or more Member States may set up a joint investigation team for a specific purpose and a limited period, which may be extended by mutual consent, to carry out criminal investigations in one or more of the Member States setting up the team. The composition of the team shall be set out in the agreement.

   A joint investigation team may, in particular, be set up where:
   (a) a Member State's investigations into criminal offences require difficult and demanding investigations having links with other Member States;
   (b) a number of Member States are conducting investigations into criminal offences in which the circumstances of the case necessitate coordinated, concerted action in the Member States involved.

   A request for the setting up of a joint investigation team may be made by any of the Member States concerned. The team shall be set up in one of the Member States in which the investigations are expected to be carried out.

2. In addition to the information referred to in the relevant provisions of Article 14 of the European Mutual Assistance Convention and Article 37 of the Benelux Treaty, requests for the setting up of a joint investigation team shall include proposals for the composition of the team.

3. A joint investigation team shall operate in the territory of the Member States setting up the team under the following general conditions:
   (a) the leader of the team shall be a representative of the competent authority participating in criminal investigations from the Member State in which the team operates. The leader of the team shall act within the limits of his or her competence under national law;

(b) the team shall carry out its operations in accordance with the law of the Member State in which it operates. The members of the team shall carry out their tasks under the leadership of the person referred to in subparagraph (a), taking into account the conditions set by their own authorities in the agreement on setting up the team;

(c) the Member State in which the team operates shall make the necessary organisational arrangements for it to do so.

4. In this Article, members of the joint investigation team from Member States other than the Member State in which the team operates are referred to as being 'seconded' to the team.

5. Seconded members of the joint investigation team shall be entitled to be present when investigative measures are taken in the Member State of operation. However, the leader of the team may, for particular reasons, in accordance with the law of the Member State where the team operates, decide otherwise.

6. Seconded members of the joint investigation team may, in accordance with the law of the Member State where the team operates, be entrusted by the leader of the team with the task of taking certain investigative measures where this has been approved by the competent authorities of the Member State of operation and the seconding Member State.

7. Where the joint investigation team needs investigative measures to be taken in one of the Member States setting up the team, members seconded to the team by that Member State may request their own competent authorities to take those measures. Those measures shall be considered in that Member State under the conditions which would apply if they were requested in a national investigation.

8. Where the joint investigation team needs assistance from a Member State other than those which have set up the team, or from a third State, the request for assistance may be made by the competent authorities of the State of operations to the competent authorities of the other State concerned in accordance with the relevant instruments or arrangements.

9. A member of the joint investigation team may, in accordance with his or her national law and within the limits of his or her competence, provide the team with information available in the Member State which has seconded him or her for the purpose of the criminal investigations conducted by the team.

10. Information lawfully obtained by a member or seconded member while part of a joint investigation team which is not otherwise available to the competent authorities of the Member States concerned may be used for the following purposes:

(a) for the purposes for which the team has been set up;

(b) subject to the prior consent of the Member State where the information became available, for detecting, investigation and prosecuting other criminal offences. Such consent may be withheld only in cases where such use would endanger criminal investigations in the Member State concerned or in respect of which that Member State could refuse mutual assistance;

(c) for preventing an immediate and serious threat to public security, and without prejudice to subparagraph (b) if subsequently a criminal investigation is opened;

(d) for other purposes to the extent that this is agreed between Member States setting up the team.

11. This Article shall be without prejudice to any other existing provisions or arrangements on the setting up or operation of joint investigation teams.

12. To the extent that the laws of the Member States concerned or the provisions of any legal instrument applicable between them permit, arrangements may be agreed for persons other than representatives of the competent authorities of the Member States setting up the joint investigation team to take part in the activities of the team. Such persons may, for example, include officials of bodies set up pursuant to the Treaty on European Union. The rights conferred upon the members or seconded members of the team by virtue of this Article shall not apply to these persons unless the agreement expressly states otherwise.

## Article 14

### Covert investigations

1. The requesting and the requested Member State may agree to assist one another in the conduct of investigations into crime by officers acting under covert or false identity (covert investigations).

2. The decision on the request is taken in each individual case by the competent authorities of the requested Member State with due regard to its national law and procedures. The duration of the

covert investigation, the detailed conditions, and the legal status of the officers concerned during covert investigations shall be agreed between the Member States with due regard to their national law and procedures.

3. Covert investigations shall take place in accordance with the national law and procedures of the Member States on the territory of which the covert investigation takes place. The Member States involved shall cooperate to ensure that the covert investigation is prepared and supervised and to make arrangements for the security of the officers acting under covert or false identity.

4. When giving the notification provided for in Article 27(2), any Member State may declare that it is not bound by this Article. Such a declaration may be withdrawn at any time.

### Article 15

#### Criminal liability regarding officials

During the operations referred to in Articles 12, 13 and 14, officials from a Member State other than the Member State of operation shall be regarded as officials of the Member State of operation with respect of offences committed against them or by them.

### Article 16

#### Civil liability regarding officials

1. Where, in accordance with Articles 12, 13 and 14, officials of a Member State are operating in another Member State, the first Member State shall be liable for any damage caused by them during their operations, in accordance with the law of the Member State in whose territory they are operating.

2. The Member State in whose territory the damage referred to in paragraph 1 was caused shall make good such damage under the conditions applicable to damage caused by its own officials.

3. The Member State whose officials have caused damage to any person in the territory of another Member State shall reimburse the latter in full any sums it has paid to the victims or persons entitled on their behalf.

4. Without prejudice to the exercise of its rights vis-à-vis third parties and with the exception of paragraph 3, each Member State shall refrain in the case provided for in paragraph 1 from requesting reimbursement of damages it has sustained from another Member State.

## TITLE III

## INTERCEPTION OF TELECOMMUNICATIONS

### Article 17

#### Authorities competent to order interception of telecommunications

For the purpose of the application of the provisions of Articles 18, 19 and 20, 'competent authority' shall mean a judicial authority, or, where judicial authorities have no competence in the area covered by those provisions, an equivalent competent authority, specified pursuant to Article 24(1)(e) and acting for the purpose of a criminal investigation.

### Article 18

#### Requests for interception of telecommunications

1. For the purpose of a criminal investigation, a competent authority in the requesting Member State may, in accordance with the requirements of its national law, make a request to a competent authority in the requested Member State for:
   (a) the interception and immediate transmission to the requesting Member State of telecommunications; or

    (b) the interception, recording and subsequent transmission to the requesting Member State of the recording of telecommunications.

2. Requests under paragraph 1 may be made in relation to the use of means of telecommunications by the subject of the interception, if this subject is present in:

    (a) the requesting Member State and the requesting Member State needs the technical assistance of the requested Member State to intercept his or her communications;

    (b) the requesting Member State and his or her communications can be intercepted in that Member State;

    (c) a third Member State which has been informed pursuant to Article 20(2)(a) and the requesting Member State needs the technical assistance of the requested Member State to intercept his or her communications.

3. By way of derogation from Article 14 of the European Mutual Assistance Convention and Article 37 of the Benelux Treaty, requests under this Article shall include the following:

    (a) an indication of the authority making the request;

    (b) confirmation that a lawful interception order or warrant has been issued in connection with a criminal investigation;

    (c) information for the purpose of identifying the subject of this interception;

    (d) an indication of the criminal conduct under investigation;

    (e) the desired duration of the interception; and

    (f) if possible, the provision of sufficient technical data, in particular the relevant network connection number, to ensure that the request can be met.

4. In the case of a request pursuant to paragraph 2(b), a request shall also include a summary of the facts. The requested Member State may require any further information to enable it to decide whether the requested measure would be taken by it in a similar national case.

5. The requested Member State shall undertake to comply with requests under paragraph 1(a):

    (a) in the case of a request pursuant to paragraph 2(a) and 2(c), on being provided with the information in paragraph 3. The requested Member State may allow the interception to proceed without further formality;

    (b) in the case of a request pursuant to paragraph 2(b), on being provided with the information in paragraphs 3 and 4 and where the requested measure would be taken by it in a similar national case. The requested Member State may make its consent subject to any conditions which would have to be observed in a similar national case.

6. Where immediate transmission is not possible, the requested Member State shall undertake to comply with requests under paragraph 1(b) on being provided with the information in paragraphs 3 and 4 and where the requested measure would be taken by it in a similar national case. The requested Member State may make its consent subject to any condition which would have to be observed in a similar national case.

7. When giving the notification provided for in Article 27(2), any Member State may declare that it is bound by paragraph 6 only when it is unable to provide immediate transmission. In this case the other Member State may apply the principle of reciprocity.

8. When making a request under paragraph 1(b), the requesting Member State may, where it has a particular reason to do so, also request a transcription of the recording. The requested Member State shall consider such requests in accordance with its national law and procedures.

9. The Member State receiving the information provided under paragraphs 3 and 4 shall keep that information confidential in accordance with its national law.

### Article 19

### Interceptions of telecommunications on national territory by the use of service providers

1. Member States shall ensure that systems of telecommunications services operated via a gateway on their territory, which for the lawful interception of the communications of a subject present in another Member State are not directly accessible on the territory of the latter, may be made directly accessible for the lawful interception by that Member State through the intermediary of a designated service provider present on its territory.

2. In the case referred to in paragraph 1, the competent authorities of a Member State shall be entitled, for the purposes of a criminal investigation and in accordance with applicable national law and provided that the subject of the interception is present in that Member State, to carry out the interception through the intermediary of a designated service provider present on its territory without involving the Member State on whose territory the gateway is located.

3. Paragraph 2 shall also apply where the interception is carried out upon a request made pursuant to Article 18(2)(b).

4. Nothing in this Article shall prevent a Member State from making a request to the Member State on whose territory the gateway is located for the lawful interception of telecommunications in accordance with Article 18, in particular where there is no intermediary in the requesting Member State.

*Article 20*

**Interception of telecommunications without the technical assistance of another Member State**

1. Without prejudice to the general principles of international law as well as to the provisions of Article 18(2)(c), the obligations under this Article shall apply to interception orders made or authorised by the competent authority of one Member State in the course of criminal investigations which present the characteristics of being an investigation following the commission of a specific criminal offence, including attempts in so far as they are criminalised under national law, in order to identify and arrest, charge, prosecute or deliver judgment on those responsible.

2. Where for the purpose of a criminal investigation, the interception of telecommunications is authorised by the competent authority of one Member State (the 'intercepting Member State'), and the telecommunication address of the subject specified in the interception order is being used on the territory of another Member State (the 'notified Member State') from which no technical assistance is needed to carry out the interception, the intercepting Member State shall inform the notified Member State of the interception:
   (a) prior to the interception in cases where it knows when ordering the interception that the subject is on the territory of the notified Member State;
   (b) in other cases, immediately after it becomes aware that the subject of the interception is on the territory of the notified Member State.

3. The information to be notified by the intercepting Member State shall include:
   (a) an indication of the authority ordering the interception;
   (b) confirmation that a lawful interception order has been issued in connection with a criminal investigation;
   (c) information for the purpose of identifying the subject of the interception;
   (d) an indication of the criminal conduct under investigation; and
   (e) the expected duration of the interception.

4. The following shall apply where a Member State is notified pursuant to paragraphs 2 and 3:
   (a) Upon receipt of the information provided under paragraph 3 the competent authority of the notified Member State shall, without delay, and at the latest within 96 hours, reply to the intercepting Member State, with a view to:
      (i) allowing the interception to be carried out or to be continued. The notified Member State may make its consent subject to any conditions which would have to be observed in a similar national case;
      (ii) requiring the interception not to be carried out or to be terminated where the interception would not be permissible pursuant to the national law of the notified Member State, or for the reasons specified in Article 2 of the European Mutual Assistance Convention. Where the notified Member State imposes such a requirement, it shall give reasons for its decision in writing;
      (iii) in cases referred to in point (ii), requiring that any material already intercepted while the subject was on its territory may not be used, or may only be used under conditions which it shall specify. The notified Member State shall inform the intercepting Member State of the reasons justifying the said conditions;

    (iv) requiring a short extension, of up to a maximum period of eight days, to the original 96-hour deadline, to be agreed with the intercepting Member State, in order to carry out internal procedures under its national law. The notified Member State shall communicate, in writing, to the intercepting Member State, the conditions which, pursuant to its national law, justify the requested extension of the deadline.

(b) Until a decision has been taken by the notified Member State pursuant to points (i) or (ii) of subparagraph (a), the intercepting Member State:
  (i) may continue the interception; and
  (ii) may not use the material already intercepted, except:
     — if otherwise agreed between the Member States concerned; or
     — for taking urgent measures to prevent an immediate and serious threat to public security. The notified Member State shall be informed of any such use and the reasons justifying it.

(c) The notified Member State may request a summary of the facts of the case and any further information necessary to enable it to decide whether interception would be authorised in a similar national case. Such a request does not affect the application of subparagraph (b), unless otherwise agreed between the notified Member State and the intercepting Member State.

(d) The Member States shall take the necessary measures to ensure that a reply can be given within the 96-hour period. To this end they shall designate contact points, on duty twenty-four hours a day, and include them in their statements under Article 24(1)(e).

5. The notified Member State shall keep the information provided under paragraph 3 confidential in accordance with its national law.

6. Where the intercepting Member State is of the opinion that the information to be provided under paragraph 3 is of a particularly sensitive nature, it may be transmitted to the competent authority through a specific authority where that has been agreed on a bilateral basis between the Member States concerned.

7. When giving its notification under Article 27(2), or at any time thereafter, any Member State may declare that it will not be necessary to provide it with information on interceptions as envisaged in this Article.

*Article 21*

**Responsibility for charges made by telecommunications operators**

Costs which are incurred by telecommunications operators or service providers in executing requests pursuant to Article 18 shall be borne by the requesting Member State.

*Article 22*

**Bilateral arrangements**

Nothing in this Title shall preclude any bilateral or multilateral arrangements between Member States for the purpose of facilitating the exploitation of present and future technical possibilities regarding the lawful interception of telecommunications.

TITLE IV

*Article 23*

**Personal data protection**

1. Personal data communicated under this Convention may be used by the Member State to which they have been transferred:
   (a) for the purpose of proceedings to which this Convention applies;
   (b) for other judicial and administrative proceedings directly related to proceedings referred to under point (a);

    (c)  for preventing an immediate and serious threat to public security;

    (d)  for any other purpose, only with the prior consent of the communicating Member State, unless the Member State concerned has obtained the consent of the data subject.

2.  This Article shall also apply to personal data not communicated but obtained otherwise under this Convention.

3.  In the circumstances of the particular case, the communicating Member State may require the Member State to which the personal data have been transferred to give information on the use made of the data.

4.  Where conditions on the use of personal data have been imposed pursuant to Articles 7(2), 18(5)(b), 18(6) or 20(4), these conditions shall prevail. Where no such conditions have been imposed, this Article shall apply.

5.  The provisions of Article 13(10) shall take precedence over this Article regarding information obtained under Article 13.

6.  This Article does not apply to personal data obtained by a Member State under this Convention and originating from that Member State.

7.  Luxembourg may, when signing the Convention, declare that where personal data are communicated by Luxembourg under this Convention to another Member State, the following applies:

Luxembourg may, subject to paragraph 1(c), in the circumstances of a particular case require that unless that Member State concerned has obtained the consent of the data subject, the personal data may only be used for the purposes referred to in paragraph 1(a) and (b) with the prior consent of Luxembourg in respect of proceedings for which Luxembourg could have refused or limited the transmission or use of the personal data in accordance with the provisions of this Convention or the instruments referred to in Article 1.

If, in a particular case, Luxembourg refuses to give its consent to a request from a Member State pursuant to the provisions of paragraph 1, it must give reasons for its decision in writing.

## TITLE V

## FINAL PROVISIONS

### Article 24

#### Statements

1.  When giving the notification referred to in Article 27(2), each Member State shall make a statement naming the authorities which, in addition to those already indicated in the European Mutual Assistance Convention and the Benelux Treaty, are competent for the application of this Convention and the application between the Member States of the provisions on mutual assistance in criminal matters of the instruments referred to in Article 1(1), including in particular:

    (a)  the competent administrative authorities within the meaning of Article 3(1), if any;

    (b)  one or more central authorities for the purposes of applying Article 6 as well as the authorities competent to deal with the requests referred to in Article 6(8);

    (c)  the police or customs authorities competent for the purpose of Article 6(5), if any;

    (d)  the administrative authorities competent for the purposes of Article 6(6), if any; and

    (e)  the authority or authorities competent for the purposes of the application of Articles 18 and 19 and Article 20(1) to (5).

2.  Statements made in accordance with paragraph 1 may be amended in whole or in part at any time by the same procedure.

### Article 25

#### Reservations

No reservations may be entered in respect of this Convention, other than those for which it makes express provision.

*Article 26*

**Territorial application**

The application of this Convention to Gibraltar will take effect upon extension of the European Mutual Assistance Convention to Gibraltar.

The United Kingdom shall notify in writing the President of the Council when it wishes to apply the Convention to the Channel Islands and the Isle of Man following extension of the European Mutual Assistance Convention to those territories. A decision on this request shall be taken by the Council acting with the unanimity of its members.

*Article 27*

**Entry into force**

1. This Convention shall be subject to adoption by the Member States in accordance with their respective constitutional requirements.
2. Member States shall notify the Secretary-General of the Council of the European Union of the completion of the constitutional procedures for the adoption of this Convention.
3. This Convention shall, 90 days after the notification referred to in paragraph 2 by the State, member of the European Union at the time of adoption by the Council of the Act establishing this Convention, which is the eighth to complete this formality, enter into force for the eight Member States concerned.
4. Any notification by a Member State subsequent to the receipt of the eighth notification referred to in paragraph 2 shall have the effect that, 90 days after the subsequent notification, this Convention shall enter into force as between this Member State and those Member States for which the Convention has already entered into force.
5. Before the Convention has entered into force pursuant to paragraph 3, any Member State may, when giving the notification referred to in paragraph 2 or at any time thereafter, declare that it will apply this Convention in its relations with Member States which have made the same declaration. Such declarations shall take effect 90 days after the date of deposit thereof.
6. This Convention shall apply to mutual assistance initiated after the date on which it has entered into force, or is applied pursuant to paragraph 5, between the Member States concerned.

*Article 28*

**Accession of new Member States**

1. This Convention shall be open to accession by any State which becomes a member of the European Union.
2. The text of this Convention in the language of the acceding State, drawn up by the Council of the European Union, shall be authentic.
3. The instruments of accession shall be deposited with the depositary.
4. This Convention shall enter into force with respect to any State which accedes to it 90 days after the deposit of its instrument of accession or on the date of entry into force of this Convention if it has not already entered into force at the time of expiry of the said period of 90 days.
5. Where this Convention is not yet in force at the time of the deposit of their instrument of accession, Article 27(5) shall apply to acceding Member States.

*Article 29*

**Entry into force for Iceland and Norway**

1. Without prejudice to Article 8 of the Agreement concluded by the Council of the European Union and the Republic of Iceland and the Kingdom of Norway concerning the latters' association with the implementation, application and development of the Schengen *acquis* (the 'Association Agreement'), the provisions referred to in Article 2(1) shall enter into force for Iceland and Norway 90 days after the receipt by the Council and the Commission of the information pursuant to

Article 8(2) of the Association Agreement upon fulfilment of their constitutional requirements, in their mutual relations with any Member State for which this Convention has already entered into force pursuant to Article 27(3) or (4).

2. Any entry into force of this Convention for a Member State after the date of entry into force of the provisions referred to in Article 2(1) for Iceland and Norway, shall render these provisions also applicable in the mutual relations between that Member State and Iceland and Norway.

3. The provisions referred to in Article 2(1) shall in any event not become binding on Iceland and Norway before the date to be fixed pursuant to Article 15(4) of the Association Agreement.

4. Without prejudice to paragraphs 1, 2 and 3 above, the provisions referred to in Article 2(1) shall enter into force for Iceland and Norway not later than on the date of entry into force of this Convention for the fifteenth State, being a member of the European Union at the time of the adoption by the Council of the Act establishing this Convention.

*Article 30*

### Depositary

1. The Secretary-General of the Council of the European Union shall act as depositary of this Convention.
2. The depositary shall publish in the *Official Journal of the European Communities* information on the progress of adoptions and accessions, statements and reservations and also any other notification concerning this Convention.

### Council Declaration on Article 10(9)

When considering the adoption of an instrument as referred to in Article 10(9), the Council shall respect Member States' obligations under the European Convention on Human Rights.

### Declaration by the United Kingdom on Article 20

This Declaration shall form an agreed, integral part of the Convention

In the United Kingdom, Article 20 will apply in respect of interception warrants issued by the Secretary of State to the police service or HM Customs & Excise where, in accordance with national law on the interception of communications, the stated purpose of the warrant is the detection of serious crime. It will also apply to such warrants issued to the Security Service where, in accordance with national law, it is acting in support of an investigation presenting the characteristics described in Article 20(1).

# APPENDIX 13

## SCHEME RELATING TO MUTUAL ASSISTANCE
## IN CRIMINAL MATTERS WITHIN THE COMMONWEALTH
### including amendments made by Law Ministers in April 1990,
### November 2002 and October 2005

### PURPOSE AND SCOPE

1. (1) The purpose of this Scheme is to increase the level and scope of assistance rendered between Commonwealth Governments in criminal matters. It augments, and in no way derogates from existing forms of co-operation, both formal and informal; nor does it preclude the development of enhanced arrangements in other fora.

    (2) This Scheme provides for the giving of assistance by the competent authorities of one country (the requested country) in respect of criminal matters arising in another country (the requesting country).

    (3) Assistance in criminal matters under this Scheme includes assistance in
    a) identifying and locating persons;
    b) serving documents;
    c) examining witnesses;
    d) search and seizure;
    e) obtaining evidence;
    f) facilitating the personal appearance of witnesses;
    g) effecting a temporary transfer of persons in custody to appear as a witness;
    h) obtaining production of judicial or official records;
    i) tracing, seizing and confiscating the proceeds or instrumentalities of crime; and
    j) preserving computer data.

### MEANING OF COUNTRY

2. For the purposes of this Scheme, each of the following is a separate country, that is to say
    (a) each sovereign and independent country within the Commonwealth together with any dependent territories which that country designates; and
    (b) each country within the Commonwealth which, though not sovereign and independent, is not designated for the purposes of the preceding sub-paragraph.

### CRIMINAL MATTER

3. (1) For the purposes of this Scheme, a criminal matter arises in a country if the Central Authority of that country certifies that criminal or forfeiture proceedings have been instituted in a court exercising jurisdiction in that country or that there is reasonable cause to believe that an offence has been committed in respect of which such criminal proceedings could be so instituted.

    (2) "Offence", in the case of a federal country or a country having more than one legal system, includes an offence under the law of the country or any part thereof.

    (3) "Forfeiture proceedings" means proceedings, whether civil or criminal, for an order
    (a) restraining dealings with any property in respect of which there is reasonable cause to believe that it has been
        (i) derived or obtained, whether directly or indirectly, from; or
        (ii) used in, or in connection with,
            the commission of an offence;
    (b) confiscating any property derived or obtained as provided in paragraph (a)(i) or used as provided in paragraph (a)(ii); or

    (c)  imposing a pecuniary penalty calculated by reference to the value of any property derived or obtained as provided in paragraph (a)(i) or used as provided in paragraph (a)(ii).

## REQUESTS FOR COMPUTER DATA – DEFINITIONS

4. For the purposes of this Scheme
   (1) "subscriber information" means any information contained in the form of computer data or any other form that is held by a service provider, relating to subscribers of its services other than traffic or content data and by which can be established:
       a.  the type of communication service used and the period of service;
       b.  the subscriber's identity, postal or geographic address, telephone and other access number, billing and payment information, available on the basis of the service agreement or arrangement;
       c.  any other information on the site of the installation of communication equipment, available on the basis of the service agreement or arrangement.
   (2) "computer system" means a device or a group of interconnected or related devices, including the Internet, one or more of which, pursuant to a program, performs automatic processing of data;
   (3) "computer data" means any representation of facts, information or concepts in a form suitable for processing in a computer system, including a program suitable to cause a computer system to perform a function;
   (4) "service provider" means:
       a.  a public or private entity that provides to users of its services the ability to communicate by means of a computer system, and
       b.  any other entity that processes or stores computer data on behalf of that entity or those users.
   (5) "traffic data" means any computer data:
       a.  that relates to a communication by means of a computer system; and
       b.  is generated by a computer system that formed a part in the chain of communication; and
       c.  shows the communication's origin, destination, route, time, date, size, duration, or type of underlying service.
   (6) "Content data" means the content of the communication; that is, the meaning or purpose of the communication, or the message or information being conveyed by the communication. It is everything transmitted as part of the communication that is not traffic data.
   (7) "Preservation of computer data" means the protection of computer data which already exists in a stored form from modification or deletion, or from anything that would cause its current quality or condition to change or deteriorate. Computer data that is stored on a highly transitory basis as an integral function of the technology used in its transmission is not computer data which already exists in a stored form for the purposes of this definition.

## CENTRAL AUTHORITIES

5. Each country shall designate a Central Authority to transmit and to receive requests for assistance under this Scheme.

## ACTION IN THE REQUESTING COUNTRY

6. (1) A request for assistance under this Scheme may be initiated by any law enforcement agency or public prosecution or judicial authority competent under the law of the requesting country.
   (2) The Central Authority of the requesting country shall, if it is satisfied that the request can properly be made under this Scheme, transmit the request to the central Authority of the requested country and shall ensure that the request contains all the information required by the provisions of this Scheme.
   (3) The Central Authority of the requesting country shall provide as far as practicable additional information sought by the Central Authority of the requested country.

## ACTION IN THE REQUESTED COUNTRY

7. (1) Subject to the provisions of this Scheme, the requested country shall grant the assistance requested as expeditiously as practicable.

   (2) The Central Authority of the requested country shall, subject to the following provisions of this paragraph, take the necessary steps to ensure that the competent authorities of that country comply with the request.

   (3) If the Central Authority of the requested country considers
      (a) that the request does not comply with the provisions of this Scheme, or
      (b) that in accordance with the provisions of this Scheme the request for assistance is to be refused in whole or in part, or
      (c) that the request cannot be complied with, in whole or in part, or
      (d) that there are circumstances which are likely to cause a significant delay in complying with the request,
      it shall promptly inform the Central Authority of the requesting country, giving reasons.

   (4) The requested country may make the granting of assistance subject to the requesting country giving an undertaking that:
      (a) the evidence provided will not be used directly or indirectly in relation to the investigation or prosecution of a specified person; or
      (b) a court in the requesting country will determine whether or not the material is subject to privilege.

   (5) If the requesting country refuses to give the undertaking under sub-paragraph (4), the requested country may refuse to grant the assistance sought in whole or in part.

## REFUSAL OF ASSISTANCE

8. (1) The requested country may refuse to comply in whole or in part with a request for assistance under this Scheme if the criminal matter appears to the Central Authority of that country to concern
      (a) conduct which would not constitute an offence under the law of that country; or
      (b) an offence or proceedings of a political character; or
      (c) conduct which in the requesting country is an offence only under military law or a law relating to military obligations; or
      (d) conduct in relation to which the person accused or suspected of having committed an offence has been acquitted or convicted by a court in the requested country.

   (2) The requested country may refuse to comply in whole or in part with a request for assistance under this Scheme
      (a) to the extent that it appears to the Central Authority of that country that compliance would be contrary to the Constitution of that country, or would prejudice the security, international relations or other essential public interests of that country; or
      (b) where there are substantial grounds leading the Central Authority of that country to believe that compliance would facilitate the prosecution or punishment of any person on account of his race, religion, nationality or political opinions or would cause prejudice for any of these reasons to any person affected by the request.

   (3) The requested country may refuse to comply in whole or in part with a request for assistance to the extent that the steps required to be taken in order to comply with the request cannot under the law of that country be taken in respect of criminal matters arising in that country.

   (4) An offence shall not be an offence of a political character for the purposes of this paragraph if it is an offence within the scope of any international convention to which both the requesting and requested countries are parties and which imposes on the parties thereto an obligation either to extradite or prosecute a person accused of the commission of the offence.

## MEASURES OF COMPULSION

9. (1) The competent authorities of the requested country shall in complying with a request under this Scheme use only such measures of compulsion as are available under the law of that country in respect of criminal matters arising in that country.

(2) Where under the law of the requested country measures of compulsion cannot be applied to any person to take the steps necessary to secure compliance with a request under this Scheme but the person concerned is willing to act voluntarily in compliance or partial compliance with the terms of the request, the competent authorities of the requested country shall make available the necessary facilities.

## SCHEME NOT TO COVER ARREST OR EXTRADITION

10. Nothing in this Scheme is to be construed as authorising the extradition, or the arrest or detention with a view to extradition, of any person.

## CONFIDENTIALITY

11. The Central Authorities and the competent authorities of the requesting and requested countries shall use their best efforts to keep confidential a request and its contents and the information and materials supplied in compliance with a request except for disclosure in criminal proceedings and where otherwise authorised by the Central Authority of the other country.

## LIMITATION OF USE OF INFORMATION OR EVIDENCE

12. The requesting country shall not use any information or evidence obtained in response to a request for assistance under this Scheme in connection with any matter other than the criminal matter specified in the request without the prior consent of the Central Authority of the requested country

## EXPENSES OF COMPLIANCE

13. (1) Except as provided in the following provisions of this paragraph, compliance with a request under this Scheme shall not give rise to any claim against the requesting country for expenses incurred by the Central Authority or other competent authorities of the requested country.

(2) The requesting country shall be responsible for the travel and incidental expenses of witnesses travelling to the requesting country, including those of accompanying officials, for fees of experts, and for the costs of any translation required by the requesting country.

(3) If in the opinion of the requested country, the expenses required in order to comply with the request are of an extraordinary nature, the Central Authority of the requested country shall consult with the Central Authority of the requesting country as to the terms and conditions under which compliance with the request may continue, and in the absence of agreement the requested country may refuse to comply further with the request.

## CONTENTS REQUEST FOR ASSISTANCE

14. (1) Except in the case of a request for the preservation of computer data under Article 1 (3) (j) of this Scheme, a request under the Scheme shall:

    (a) specify the nature of the assistance requested;

    (b) contain the information appropriate to the assistance sought as specified in the following provisions of this Scheme;

    (c) indicate any time-limit within which compliance with the request is desired, stating reasons;

    (d) contain the following information:

        (i) the identity of the agency or authority initiating the request;

        (ii) the nature of the criminal matter; and

        (iii) whether or not criminal proceedings have been instituted.

    (e) where criminal proceedings have been instituted, contain the following information:

        (i) the court exercising jurisdiction in the proceedings;

        (ii) the identity of the accused person;

        (iii) the offences of which he stands accused, and a summary of the facts;

        (iv) the stage reached in the proceedings; and

        (v) any date fixed for further stages in the proceedings.

(f) where criminal proceedings have not been instituted, state the offence which the Central Authority of the requesting country has reasonable cause to believe to have been committed, with a summary of known facts.

(2) A request shall normally be in writing, and if made orally in the case of urgency, shall be confirmed in writing forthwith.

## REQUESTS FOR THE PRESERVATION OF COMPUTER DATA

15. (1) A request for the preservation of computer data under this Article made by an agency or authority competent to make such a request under the laws of the requesting country can be directly transmitted to an agency or authority competent to receive such a request under the laws of the requested country.

(2) A request for the preservation of computer data shall
   (a) specify the identity of the agency or authority making the request;
   (b) contain a brief description of the conduct under investigation;
   (c) contain a description of the computer data to be preserved and its relationship to the investigation or prosecution, and in particular identifying whether the computer data to be preserved includes:
      (i) subscriber information
      (ii) traffic data
      (iii) content data.
   (d) contain a statement that the requesting country intends to submit a request for mutual assistance to obtain the computer data within the period permitted under this Article.

(3) The preservation of computer data pursuant to a request made under this Article shall be for a period of 120 (one hundred and twenty) days, pending submission by the requesting country of a request for assistance to obtain the preserved computer data. Following the receipt of such a request, the data shall continue to be preserved pending the determination of that request and, if the request is granted, until the data is obtained pursuant to the request for assistance.

(4) If the requested country considers that the preservation of computer data pursuant to a request made under this Article will not ensure the future availability of the computer data, or will threaten the confidentiality of, or otherwise prejudice the investigation in the requesting country, it shall promptly inform the requesting country, which shall then determine whether the request should nevertheless be executed.

(5) Notwithstanding the general grounds for refusal contained in Article 8, a request for the preservation of computer data under this Article may be refused only to the extent that it appears to the requested country that compliance would be contrary to the laws and/or constitution of that country, or would prejudice the security, international relations, or other essential public interests of that country.

## IDENTIFYING AND LOCATING PERSONS

16. (1) A request under this Scheme may seek assistance in identifying or locating persons believed to be within the requested country.

(2) The request shall indicate the purpose for which the information is requested and shall contain such information as is available to the Central Authority of the requesting country as to the whereabouts of the person concerned and such other information as it possesses as may facilitate the identification of that person.

## SERVICE OF DOCUMENTS

17. (1) A request under this Scheme may seek assistance in the service of documents relevant to a criminal matter arising in the requesting country.

(2) The request shall be accompanied by the documents to be served and, where those documents relate to attendance in the requesting country, such notice as the Central Authority of that country is reasonably able to provide of outstanding warrants or other judicial orders in criminal matters against the person to be served.

    (3) The Central Authority of the requested country shall endeavour to have the documents served:

        (a) by any particular method stated in the request, unless such method is incompatible with the law of that country; or

        (b) by any method prescribed by the law of that country for the service of documents in criminal proceedings.

    (4) The requested country shall transmit to the Central Authority of the requesting country a certificate as to the service of the documents or, if they have not been served, as to the reasons which have prevented service.

    (5) A person served in compliance with a request with a summons to appear as a witness in the requesting country and who fails to comply with the summons shall not by reason thereof be liable to any penalty or measure of compulsion in either the requesting or the requested country notwithstanding any contrary statement in the summons.

## EXAMINATION OF WITNESSES

18. (1) A request under this Scheme may seek assistance in the examination of witnesses in the requested country.

    (2) The request shall specify, as appropriate and so far as the circumstances of the case permit:

        (a) the names and addresses or the official designations of the witnesses to be examined;

        (b) the questions to be put to the witnesses or the subject matter about which they are to be examined;

        (c) whether it is desired that the witnesses be examined orally or in writing;

        (d) whether it is desired that the oath be administered to the witnesses (or, as the law of the requested country allows, that they be required to make their solemn affirmation);

        (e) any provisions of the law of the requesting country as to privilege or exemption from giving evidence which appear especially relevant to the request; and

        (f) any special requirements of the law of the requesting country as to the manner of taking evidence relevant to its admissibility in that country.

    (3) The request may ask that, so far as the law of the requested country permits, the accused person or his legal representative may attend the examination of the witness and ask questions of the witness.

## SEARCH AND SEIZURE

19. (1) A request under this Scheme may seek assistance in the search for, and seizure of property or computer data in the requested country.

    (2) The request shall specify the property or computer data to be searched for and seized and shall contain, so far as reasonably practicable, all information available to the Central Authority of the requesting country which may be required to be adduced in an application under the law of the requested country for any necessary warrant or authorization to effect the search and seizure.

    (3) The requested country shall provide such certification as may be required by the requesting country concerning the result of any search, the place and circumstances of seizure, and the subsequent custody of the property or computer data seized.

## OTHER ASSISTANCE IN OBTAINING EVIDENCE

20. (1) A request under this Scheme may seek other assistance in obtaining evidence.

    (2) The request shall specify, as appropriate and so far as the circumstance of the case permit:

        (a) the documents, records, property or computer data to be inspected, preserved, photographed, copied or transmitted;

        (b) the samples of any property or computer data to be taken, examined or transmitted; and

        (c) the site to be viewed or photographed.

## PRIVILEGE

21. (1) No person shall be compelled in response to a request under this Scheme to give any evidence in the requested country which he could not be compelled to give:

        (a) in criminal proceedings in that country; or

(b) in criminal proceedings in the requesting country.

(2) For the purposes of this paragraph any reference to giving evidence includes references to answering any question and to producing any document.

## PRODUCTION OF JUDICIAL OR OFFICIAL RECORDS

22. (1) A request under this Scheme may seek the production of judicial or official records relevant to a criminal matter arising in the requesting country.

(2) For the purposes of this paragraph "judicial records" means judgements, orders and decisions of courts and other documents held by judicial authorities and "official records" means documents held by government departments or agencies or prosecution authorities.

(3) The requested country shall provide copies of judicial or official records which are publicly available.

(4) The requested country may provide copies of judicial or official records not publicly available, to the same extent and under the same conditions as apply to the provision of such records to its own law enforcement agencies or prosecution or judicial authorities.

## TRANSMISSION AND RETURN OF MATERIAL

23. (1) Where compliance with a request under this Scheme would involve the transmission to the requesting country of any document, record or property, the requested country

(a) may postpone the transmission of the material if it is required in connection with proceedings in that country, and in such a case shall provide certified copies of a document or record pending transmission of the original;

(b) may require the requesting country to agree to terms and conditions to protect third party interests in the material to be transmitted and may refuse to effect such transmission pending such agreement.

(2) Where any document, record or property is transmitted to the requesting country in compliance with a request under this Scheme, it shall be returned to the requested country when it is no longer required in connection with the criminal matter specified in the request unless that country has indicated that its return is not desired.

(3) The requested country shall authenticate material that is to be transmitted by that country.

## AUTHENTICATION

24. A document or other material transmitted for the purposes of or in response to a request under this Scheme shall be deemed to be duly authenticated if it:

(a) purports to be signed or certified by a judge or Magistrate, or to bear in the stamp or seal of a Minister, government department or Central Authority; or

(b) is verified by the oath of a witness or of a public officer of the Commonwealth country from which the document or material emanates.

## PERSONAL APPEARANCE OF WITNESSES IN THE REQUESTING COUNTRY

25. (1) A request under this Scheme may seek assistance in facilitating the personal appearance of the witnesses before a court exercising jurisdiction in the requesting country.

(2) The request shall specify

(a) the subject matter upon which it is desired to examine the witnesses;

(b) the reasons for which the personal appearance of the witnesses is required; and

(c) details of the travelling, subsistence and other expenses payable by the requesting country in respect of the personal appearance of the witnesses.

(3) The competent authorities of the requested country shall invite persons whose appearance as witnesses in the requesting country is desired; and

(a) ask whether they agree to appear;

(b) inform the Central Authority of the requesting country of their answer; and

(c) if they are willing to appear, make appropriate arrangements to facilitate the personal appearance of the witnesses.

(4) A person whose appearance as a witness is the subject of a request and who does not agree to appear shall not by reason thereof be liable to any penalty or measure of compulsion in either the requesting or requested country.

## PERSONAL APPEARANCE OF PERSONS IN CUSTODY

26. (1) A request under this Scheme may seek the temporary transfer of persons in custody in the requested country to appear as witnesses before a court exercising jurisdiction in the requesting country.
   (2) The request shall specify:
      (a) the subject matter upon which it is desired to examine the witnesses;
      (b) the reasons for which the personal appearance of the witnesses is required.
   (3) The requested country shall refuse to comply with a request for the transfer of persons in custody if the persons concerned do not consent to the transfer.
   (4) The requested country may refuse to comply with a request for the transfer of persons in custody and shall be under no obligation to inform the requesting country of the reasons for such refusal.
   (5) A person in custody whose transfer is the subject of a request and who does not consent to the transfer shall not by reason thereof be liable to any penalty or measure of compulsion in either the requesting or requested country.
   (6) Where persons in custody are transferred, the requested country shall notify the requesting country of:
      (a) the dates upon which the persons are due under the law of the requested country to be released from custody; and
      (b) the dates by which the requested country requires the return of the persons
      and shall notify any variations in such dates.
   (7) The requesting country shall keep the persons transferred in custody, and shall return the persons to the requested country when their presence as witnesses in the requesting country is no longer required, and in any case by the earlier of the dates notified under sub-paragraph (6).
   (8) The obligation to return the persons transferred shall subsist notwithstanding the fact that they are nationals of the requesting country.
   (9) The period during which the persons transferred are in custody in the requesting country shall be deemed to be service in the requested country of an equivalent period of custody in that country for all purposes.
   (10) Nothing in this paragraph shall preclude the release in the requesting country without return to the requested country of any person transferred where the two countries and the person concerned agreed.

## IMMUNITY OF PERSONS APPEARING

27. (1) Subject to the provisions of paragraph 24, witnesses appearing in the requesting country in response to a request under paragraph 23 or persons transferred to that country in response to a request under paragraph 24 shall be immune in that country from prosecution, detention or any other restriction of personal liberty in respect of criminal acts, omissions or convictions before the time of their departure from the requested country.
   (2) The immunity provided for in that paragraph shall cease:
      (a) in the case of witnesses appearing in response to a request under paragraph 23, when the witnesses having had, for a period of 15 consecutive days from the dates when they were notified by the competent authority of the requesting country that their presence was no longer required by the court exercising jurisdiction in the criminal matter, an opportunity of leaving have nevertheless remained in the requesting country, or having left that country have returned to it;
      (b) in the case of persons transferred in response to a request under paragraph 24 and remaining in custody when they have been returned to the requested country.

## TRACING THE PROCEEDS OR INSTRUMENTALITIES OF CRIME

28. (1) A request under this Scheme may seek assistance in identifying, locating and assessing the value of property believed to have been derived or obtained, directly or indirectly, from, or to have been used in, or in connection with, the commission of an offence and believed to be within the requested country.

    (2) The request shall contain such information as is available to the Central Authority of the requesting country as to the nature and location of the property and as to any person in whose possession or control the property is believed to be.

## SEIZING AND CONFISCATING THE PROCEEDS OF INSTRUMENTALITIES OF CRIME

29. (1) A request under this Scheme may seek assistance in securing:
    (a) the making in the requested country of an order relating to the proceeds of instrumentalities of crime; or
    (b) the recognition or enforcement in that country of such an order made in the requesting country.

    (2) For the purpose of this paragraph, "an order relating to the proceeds of instrumentalities of crime" means:
    (a) an order restraining dealings with any property in respect of which there is reasonable cause to believe that it has been derived or obtained, directly or indirectly, from, or used in, or in connection with, the commission of an offence;
    (b) an order confiscating property derived or obtained, directly or indirectly, from, or used in or in connection with, the commission of an offence; and
    (c) an order imposing a pecuniary penalty calculated by reference to the value of any property so derived, obtained or used.

    (3) Where the requested country cannot enforce an order made in the requesting country, the requesting country may request the making of any similar order available under the law of the requested country.

    (4) The request shall be accompanied by a copy of any order made in the requesting country and shall contain so far as reasonably practicable, all information available to the Central Authority of the requesting country which may be required in connection with the procedures to be followed in the requested country.

    (5) The law of the requested country shall apply to determine the circumstances and manner in which an order may be made, recognised or enforced in response to the request.

    (6) The law of the requested country may provide for the protection of the interests of bona fide third parties in property restrained or confiscated as a result of a request made pursuant to this Scheme, by providing:
    (a) for the giving of notice of the making of orders restraining or confiscating property; and
    (b) that any third party claiming an interest in property so restrained or confiscated may make an application to a court of competent jurisdiction for an order
      (i) declaring that the interest of the applicant in the property or part thereof was acquired bona fide; and
      (ii) restoring such property or the value of the interest therein to the applicant.

## DISPOSAL OR RELEASE OF PROPERTY

30. (1) The law of the requested country shall apply to determine the disposal of any property
    (a) forfeited; or
    (b) obtained as a result of the enforcement of a pecuniary penalty order
    as a result of a request under this Scheme.

    (2) The law of the requested country shall apply to determine the circumstances in which property made the subject of interim seizure as a result of a request under this Scheme may be released from the effects of such seizure.

(3) The law of the requested country may provide that the proceeds of an order of the type referred to in sub-paragraphs 27(2)(b) and (c), or the value thereof, may be

(a) returned to the requesting country; or

(b) shared with the requesting country in such proportion as the requested country in its discretion deems appropriate in all the circumstances.

## CONSULTATION

31. The Central Authorities of the requested and requesting countries shall consult promptly, at the request of either, concerning matters arising under this Scheme.

## OTHER ASSISTANCE

32. After consultation between the requesting and the requested countries assistance not within the scope of this Scheme may be given in respect of a criminal matter on such terms and conditions as may be agreed by those countries.

## NOTIFICATION OF DESIGNATIONS

33. Designations of dependent territories under paragraph 2 and of Central Authorities under paragraph 4 shall be notified to the Commonwealth Secretary-General.

# APPENDIX 14

## European Convention on Mutual Assistance in Criminal Matters
## Strasbourg, 20.IV.1959

**Preamble**

The governments signatory hereto, being members of the Council of Europe,

Considering that the aim of the Council of Europe is to achieve greater unity among its members;

Believing that the adoption of common rules in the field of mutual assistance in criminal matters will contribute to the attainment of this aim;

Considering that such mutual assistance is related to the question of extradition, which has already formed the subject of a Convention signed on 13th December 1957,

Have agreed as follows:

**Chapter I – General provisions**

**Article 1**

1. The Contracting Parties undertake to afford each other, in accordance with the provisions of this Convention, the widest measure of mutual assistance in proceedings in respect of offences the punishment of which, at the time of the request for assistance, falls within the jurisdiction of the judicial authorities of the requesting Party.
2. This Convention does not apply to arrests, the enforcement of verdicts or offences under military law which are not offences under ordinary criminal law.

**Article 2**

Assistance may be refused:

a. if the request concerns an offence which the requested Party considers a political offence, an offence connected with a political offence, or a fiscal offence;
b. if the requested Party considers that execution of the request is likely to prejudice the sovereignty, security, *ordre public* or other essential interests of its country.

**Chapter II – Letters rogatory**

**Article 3**

1. The requested Party shall execute in the manner provided for by its law any letters rogatory relating to a criminal matter and addressed to it by the judicial authorities of the requesting Party for the purpose of procuring evidence or transmitting articles to be produced in evidence, records or documents.
2. If the requesting Party desires witnesses or experts to give evidence on oath, it shall expressly so request, and the requested Party shall comply with the request if the law of its country does not prohibit it.
3. The requested Party may transmit certified copies or certified photostat copies of records or documents requested, unless the requesting Party expressly requests the transmission of originals, in which case the requested Party shall make every effort to comply with the request.

**Article 4**

On the express request of the requesting Party the requested Party shall state the date and place of execution of the letters rogatory. Officials and interested persons may be present if the requested Party consents.

### Article 5

1.  Any Contracting Party may, by a declaration addressed to the Secretary General of the Council of Europe, when signing this Convention or depositing its instrument of ratification or accession, reserve the right to make the execution of letters rogatory for search or seizure of property dependent on one or more of the following conditions:
    a.  that the offence motivating the letters rogatory is punishable under both the law of the requesting Party and the law of the requested Party;
    b.  that the offence motivating the letters rogatory is an extraditable offence in the requested country;
    c.  that execution of the letters rogatory is consistent with the law of the requested Party.
2.  Where a Contracting Party makes a declaration in accordance with paragraph 1 of this article, any other Party may apply reciprocity.

### Article 6

1.  The requested Party may delay the handing over of any property, records or documents requested, if it requires the said property, records or documents in connection with pending criminal proceedings.
2.  Any property, as well as original records or documents, handed over in execution of letters rogatory shall be returned by the requesting Party to the requested Party as soon as possible unless the latter Party waives the return thereof.

### Chapter III – Service of writs and records of judicial verdicts – Appearance of witnesses, experts and prosecuted persons

### Article 7

1.  The requested Party shall effect service of writs and records of judicial verdicts which are transmitted to it for this purpose by the requesting Party. Service may be effected by simple transmission of the writ or record to the person to be served. If the requesting Party expressly so requests, service shall be effected by the requested Party in the manner provided for the service of analogous documents under its own law or in a special manner consistent with such law.
2.  Proof of service shall be given by means of a receipt dated and signed by the person served or by means of a declaration made by the requested Party that service has been effected and stating the form and date of such service. One or other of these documents shall be sent immediately to the requesting Party. The requested Party shall, if the requesting Party so requests, state whether service has been effected in accordance with the law of the requested Party. If service cannot be effected, the reasons shall be communicated immediately by the requested Party to the requesting Party.
3.  Any Contracting Party may, by a declaration addressed to the Secretary General of the Council of Europe, when signing this Convention or depositing its instrument of ratification or accession, request that service of a summons on an accused person who is in its territory be transmitted to its authorities by a certain time before the date set for appearance. This time shall be specified in the aforesaid declaration and shall not exceed 50 days. This time shall be taken into account when the date of appearance is being fixed and when the summons is being transmitted.

### Article 8

A witness or expert who has failed to answer a summons to appear, service of which has been requested, shall not, even if the summons contains a notice of penalty, be subjected to any punishment or measure of restraint, unless subsequently he voluntarily enters the territory of the requesting Party and is there again duly summoned.

### Article 9

The allowances, including subsistence, to be paid and the travelling expenses to be refunded to a witness or expert by the requesting Party shall be calculated as from his place of residence and shall be at rates at least equal to those provided for in the scales and rules in force in the country where the hearing is intended to take place.

### Article 10

1. If the requesting Party considers the personal appearance of a witness or expert before its judicial authorities especially necessary, it shall so mention in its request for service of the summons and the requested Party shall invite the witness or expert to appear. The requested Party shall inform the requesting Party of the reply of the witness or expert.
2. In the case provided for under paragraph 1 of this article the request or the summons shall indicate the approximate allowances payable and the travelling and subsistence expenses refundable.
3. If a specific request is made, the requested Party may grant the witness or expert an advance. The amount of the advance shall be endorsed on the summons and shall be refunded by the requesting Party.

### Article 11

1. A person in custody whose personal appearance as a witness or for purposes of confrontation is applied for by the requesting Party shall be temporarily transferred to the territory where the hearing is intended to take place, provided that he shall be sent back within the period stipulated by the requested Party and subject to the provisions of Article 12 in so far as these are applicable.

   Transfer may be refused:
   a. if the person in custody does not consent;
   b. if his presence is necessary at criminal proceedings pending in the territory of the requested Party;
   c. if transfer is liable to prolong his detention, or
   d. if there are other overriding grounds for not transferring him to the territory of the requesting Party.
2. Subject to the provisions of Article 2, in a case coming within the immediately preceding paragraph, transit of the person in custody through the territory of a third State, Party to this Convention, shall be granted on application, accompanied by all necessary documents, addressed by the Ministry of Justice of the requesting Party to the Ministry of Justice of the Party through whose territory transit is requested. A Contracting Party may refuse to grant transit to its own nationals.
3. The transferred person shall remain in custody in the territory of the requesting Party and, where applicable, in the territory of the Party through which transit is requested, unless the Party from whom transfer is requested applies for his release.

### Article 12

1. A witness or expert, whatever his nationality, appearing on a summons before the judicial authorities of the requesting Party shall not be prosecuted or detained or subjected to any other restriction of his personal liberty in the territory of that Party in respect of acts or convictions anterior to his departure from the territory of the requested Party.
2. A person, whatever his nationality, summoned before the judicial authorities of the requesting Party to answer for acts forming the subject of proceedings against him, shall not be prosecuted or detained or subjected to any other restriction of his personal liberty for acts or convictions anterior to his departure from the territory of the requested Party and not specified in the summons.
3. The immunity provided for in this article shall cease when the witness or expert or prosecuted person, having had for a period of fifteen consecutive days from the date when his presence is no longer required by the judicial authorities an opportunity of leaving, has nevertheless remained in the territory, or having left it, has returned.

### Chapter IV – Judicial records

### Article 13

1. A requested Party shall communicate extracts from and information relating to judicial records, requested from it by the judicial authorities of a Contracting Party and needed in a criminal matter, to the same extent that these may be made available to its own judicial authorities in like case.
2. In any case other than that provided for in paragraph 1 of this article the request shall be complied with in accordance with the conditions provided for by the law, regulations or practice of the requested Party.

**Chapter V – Procedure**

**Article 14**

1.  Requests for mutual assistance shall indicate as follows:
    a.  the authority making the request,
    b.  the object of and the reason for the request,
    c.  where possible, the identity and the nationality of the person concerned, and
    d.  where necessary, the name and address of the person to be served.
2.  Letters rogatory referred to in Articles 3, 4 and 5 shall, in addition, state the offence and contain a summary of the facts.

**Article 15**

1.  Letters rogatory referred to in Articles 3, 4 and 5 as well as the applications referred to in Article 11 shall be addressed by the Ministry of Justice of the requesting Party to the Ministry of Justice of the requested Party and shall be returned through the same channels.
2.  In case of urgency, letters rogatory may be addressed directly by the judicial authorities of the requesting Party to the judicial authorities of the requested Party. They shall be returned together with the relevant documents through the channels stipulated in paragraph 1 of this article.
3.  Requests provided for in paragraph 1 of Article 13 may be addressed directly by the judicial authorities concerned to the appropriate authorities of the requested Party, and the replies may be returned directly by those authorities. Requests provided for in paragraph 2 of Article 13 shall be addressed by the Ministry of Justice of the requesting Party to the Ministry of Justice of the requested Party.
4.  Requests for mutual assistance, other than those provided for in paragraphs 1 and 3 of this article and, in particular, requests for investigation preliminary to prosecution, may be communicated directly between the judicial authorities.
5.  In cases where direct transmission is permitted under this Convention, it may take place through the International Criminal Police Organisation (Interpol).
6.  A Contracting Party may, when signing this Convention or depositing its instrument of ratification or accession, by a declaration addressed to the Secretary General of the Council of Europe, give notice that some or all requests for assistance shall be sent to it through channels other than those provided for in this article, or require that, in a case provided for in paragraph 2 of this article, a copy of the letters rogatory shall be transmitted at the same time to its Ministry of Justice.
7.  The provisions of this article are without prejudice to those of bilateral agreements or arrangements in force between Contracting Parties which provide for the direct transmission of requests for assistance between their respective authorities.

**Article 16**

1.  Subject to paragraph 2 of this article, translations of requests and annexed documents shall not be required.
2.  Each Contracting Party may, when signing or depositing its instrument of ratification or accession, by means of a declaration addressed to the Secretary General of the Council of Europe, reserve the right to stipulate that requests and annexed documents shall be addressed to it accompanied by a translation into its own language or into either of the official languages of the Council of Europe or into one of the latter languages, specified by it. The other Contracting Parties may apply reciprocity.
3.  This article is without prejudice to the provisions concerning the translation of requests or annexed documents contained in the agreements or arrangements in force or to be made between two or more Contracting Parties.

**Article 17**

Evidence or documents transmitted pursuant to this Convention shall not require any form of authentication.

## Article 18

Where the authority which receives a request for mutual assistance has no jurisdiction to comply therewith, it shall, *ex officio,* transmit the request to the competent authority of its country and shall so inform the requesting Party through the direct channels, if the request has been addressed through such channels.

## Article 19

Reasons shall be given for any refusal of mutual assistance.

## Article 20

Subject to the provisions of Article 10, paragraph 3, execution of requests for mutual assistance shall not entail refunding of expenses except those incurred by the attendance of experts in the territory of the requested Party or the transfer of a person in custody carried out under Article 11.

### Chapter VI – Laying of information in connection with proceedings

### Article 21

1. Information laid by one Contracting Party with a view to proceedings in the courts of another Party shall be transmitted between the Ministries of Justice concerned unless a Contracting Party avails itself of the option provided for in paragraph 6 of Article 15.
2. The requested Party shall notify the requesting Party of any action taken on such information and shall forward a copy of the record of any verdict pronounced.
3. The provisions of Article 16 shall apply to information laid under paragraph 1 of this article.

### Chapter VII – Exchange of information from judicial records

### Article 22

Each Contracting Party shall inform any other Party of all criminal convictions and subsequent measures in respect of nationals of the latter Party, entered in the judicial records. Ministries of Justice shall communicate such information to one another at least once a year. Where the person concerned is considered a national of two or more other Contracting Parties, the information shall be given to each of these Parties, unless the person is a national of the Party in the territory of which he was convicted.

### Chapter VIII – Final provisions

### Article 23

1. Any Contracting Party may, when signing this Convention or when depositing its instrument of ratification or accession, make a reservation in respect of any provision or provisions of the Convention.
2. Any Contracting Party which has made a reservation shall withdraw it as soon as circumstances permit. Such withdrawal shall be made by notification to the Secretary General of the Council of Europe.
3. A Contracting Party which has made a reservation in respect of a provision of the Convention may not claim application of the said provision by another Party save in so far as it has itself accepted the provision.

### Article 24

A Contracting Party may, when signing the Convention or depositing its instrument of ratification or accession, by a declaration addressed to the Secretary General of the Council of Europe, define what authorities it will, for the purpose of the Convention, deem judicial authorities.

### Article 25

1. This Convention shall apply to the metropolitan territories of the Contracting Parties.
2. In respect of France, it shall also apply to Algeria and to the overseas Departments, and, in respect of Italy, it shall also apply to the territory of Somaliland under Italian administration.

3. The Federal Republic of Germany may extend the application of this Convention to the *Land* of Berlin by notice addressed to the Secretary General of the Council of Europe.
4. In respect of the Kingdom of the Netherlands, the Convention shall apply to its European territory. The Netherlands may extend the application of this Convention to the Netherlands Antilles, Surinam and Netherlands New Guinea by notice addressed to the Secretary General of the Council of Europe.
5. By direct arrangement between two or more Contracting Parties and subject to the conditions laid down in the arrangement, the application of this Convention may be extended to any territory, other than the territories mentioned in paragraphs 1, 2, 3 and 4 of this article, of one of these Parties, for the international relations of which any such Party is responsible.

### Article 26

1. Subject to the provisions of Article 15, paragraph 7, and Article 16, paragraph 3, this Convention shall, in respect of those countries to which it applies, supersede the provisions of any treaties, conventions or bilateral agreements governing mutual assistance in criminal matters between any two Contracting Parties.
2. This Convention shall not affect obligations incurred under the terms of any other bilateral or multilateral international convention which contains or may contain clauses governing specific aspects of mutual assistance in a given field.
3. The Contracting Parties may conclude between themselves bilateral or multilateral agreements on mutual assistance in criminal matters only in order to supplement the provisions of this Convention or to facilitate the application of the principles contained therein.
4. Where, as between two or more Contracting Parties, mutual assistance in criminal matters is practised on the basis of uniform legislation or of a special system providing for the reciprocal application in their respective territories of measures of mutual assistance, these Parties shall, notwithstanding the provisions of this Convention, be free to regulate their mutual relations in this field exclusively in accordance with such legislation or system. Contracting Parties which, in accordance with this paragraph, exclude as between themselves the application of this Convention shall notify the Secretary General of the Council of Europe accordingly.

### Article 27

1. This Convention shall be open to signature by the members of the Council of Europe. It shall be ratified. The instruments of ratification shall be deposited with the Secretary General of the Council.
2. The Convention shall come into force 90 days after the date of deposit of the third instrument of ratification.
3. As regards any signatory ratifying subsequently the Convention shall come into force 90 days after the date of the deposit of its instrument of ratification.

### Article 28

1. The Committee of Ministers of the Council of Europe may invite any State not a member of the Council to accede to this Convention, provided that the resolution containing such invitation obtains the unanimous agreement of the members of the Council who have ratified the Convention.
2. Accession shall be by deposit with the Secretary General of the Council of an instrument of accession which shall take effect 90 days after the date of its deposit.

### Article 29

Any Contracting Party may denounce this Convention in so far as it is concerned by giving notice to the Secretary General of the Council of Europe. Denunciation shall take effect six months after the date when the Secretary General of the Council received such notification.

### Article 30

The Secretary General of the Council of Europe shall notify the members of the Council and the government of any State which has acceded to this Convention of:

    a. the names of the signatories and the deposit of any instrument of ratification or accession;
    b. the date of entry into force of this Convention;

c.  any notification received in accordance with the provisions of Article 5 – paragraph 1, Article 7 – paragraph 3, Article 15 – paragraph 6, Article 16 – paragraph 2, Article 24, Article 25 – paragraphs 3 and 4, Article 26 – paragraph 4;

d.  any reservation made in accordance with Article 23, paragraph 1;

e.  the withdrawal of any reservation in accordance with Article 23, paragraph 2;

f.  any notification of denunciation received in accordance with the provisions of Article 29 and the date on which such denunciation will take effect.

In witness whereof the undersigned, being duly authorised thereto, have signed this Convention.

Done at Strasbourg, this 20th day of April 1959, in English and French, both texts being equally authoritative, in a single copy which shall remain deposited in the archives of the Council of Europe. The Secretary General of the Council of Europe shall transmit certified copies to the signatory and acceding governments.

# INDEX

References are to chapter and paragraph number, e.g. 3.14, or appendix number, e.g. Appendix 1.

Printed and bound by CPI Group (UK) Ltd, Croydon, CR0 4YY